"Right-wing authoritarian populist movements, parties, and governments arise in great part from the discontents fueled by the iniquities of neoliberal capitalist globalisation. This book breaks new ground in searching for the usually neglected rural roots behind and consequences of such authoritarian populisms. The book is comparative in scope, so that its central argument about the significance of the agrarian and rural order is adequately tested and confirmed. The book is also a call for further global research and study with the aim of identifying possibilities – a 'rural politics' and agential sources – that respectively can be articulated and mobilised to combat such populisms. The remarkable upsurge of farmers and rural workers against the Hindu nationalist Modi regime in India is a powerful testimony to the truth of the very politics that this book seeks to underscore."

Achin Vanaik, *Retired Professor of International Politics and Global Studies, University of Delhi*

Critical Agrarian Studies

Series Editor: *Saturnino M. Borras Jr.*

Critical Agrarian Studies is the accompanying book series to *The Journal of Peasant Studies*. It publishes selected special issues of the journal and, occasionally, books that offer major contributions in the field of critical agrarian studies. The book series builds on the long and rich history of the journal and its former accompanying book series, the Library of Peasant Studies (1973–2008) which had published several important monographs and special-issues-as-books.

Agrarian Marxism
Edited by Michael Levien, Michael Watts and Hairong Yan

Gender and Generation in Southeast Asian Agrarian Transformations
Edited by Clara Mi Young Park and Ben White

De-centring Land Grabbing
Edited by Peter Vandergeest and Laura Schoenberger

Soy, Globalization, and Environmental Politics in South America
Edited by Gustavo de L. T. Oliveira and Susanna B. Hecht

An Endogenous Theory of Property Rights
Edited by Peter Ho

Global Land Grabbing and Political Reactions 'from Below'
Edited by Marc Edelman, Ruth Hall, Saturnino M. Borras Jr., Ian Scoones and Wendy Wolford

Critical Perspectives in Rural Development Studies
Edited by Saturnino M. Borras Jr.

The Politics of Biofuels, Land and Agrarian Change
Edited by Saturnino M. Borras Jr., Philip McMichael and Ian Scoones

New Frontiers of Land Control
Edited by Nancy Lee Peluso and Christian Lund

Outcomes of Post-2000 Fast Track Land Reform in Zimbabwe
Edited by Lionel Cliffe, Jocelyn Alexander, Ben Cousins and Rudo Gaidzanwa

Green Grabbing: A New Appropriation of Nature
Edited by James Fairhead, Melissa Leach and Ian Scoone

The New Enclosures: Critical Perspectives on Corporate Land Deals
Edited by Ben White, Saturnino M. Borras Jr., Ruth Hall, Ian Scoones and Wendy Wolford

Authoritarian Populism and the Rural World
Edited by Ian Scoones, Marc Edelman, Saturnino M. Borras Jr., Lyda Fernanda Forero, Ruth Hall, Wendy Wolford and Ben White

For more information about this series, please visit:
www.routledge.com/Critical-Agrarian-Studies/book-series/CAG.

Authoritarian Populism and the Rural World

The rise of authoritarian, nationalist forms of populism and the implications for rural actors and settings is one of the most crucial foci for critical agrarian studies today, with many consequences for political action.

Authoritarian Populism and the Rural World reflects on the rural origins and consequences of the emergence of authoritarian and populist leaders across the world, as well as on the rise of multi-class mobilisation and resistance, alongside wider counter-movements and alternative practices, which together confront authoritarianism and nationalist populism. The book includes 20 chapters written by contributors to the Emancipatory Rural Politics Initiative (ERPI), a global network of academics and activists committed to both reflective analysis and political engagement. Debates about 'populism', 'nationalism', 'authoritarianism' and more have exploded recently, but relatively little of this has focused on the rural dimensions. Yet, wherever one looks, the rural aspects are key – not just in electoral calculus, but in understanding underlying drivers of authoritarianism and populism, and potential counter-movements to these. Whether because of land grabs, voracious extractivism, infrastructural neglect or lack of services, rural peoples' disillusionment with the *status quo* has had deeply troubling consequences and occasionally hopeful ones, as the chapters in this book show.

The chapters in this book were originally published in *The Journal of Peasant Studies*.

Ian Scoones is Professorial Fellow at the Institute of Development Studies at the University of Sussex, and co-director of the ESRC STEPS Centre.

Marc Edelman is Professor of Anthropology at Hunter College and the Graduate Center of the City University of New York.

Saturnino M. Borras Jr. is Professor of Agrarian Studies at the International Institute of Social Studies (ISS) in The Hague, the Netherlands, an Adjunct Professor at China Agricultural University in Beijing, and a fellow of the Amsterdam-based Transnational Institute (TNI).

Lyda Fernanda Forero was, until April 2020, coordinator of the Agrarian and Environmental Justice (AEJ) program of the Transnational Institute. She is currently with the secretariat of the Trade Union Confederation of the Americas (TUCA).

Ruth Hall is Professor of Land and Agrarian Studies at the Institute for Poverty, Land and Agrarian Studies (PLAAS) at the University of the Western Cape, South Africa.

Wendy Wolford is Polson Professor of Global Development at Cornell University, USA.

Ben White is Emeritus Professor of Rural Sociology at the International Institute of Social Studies (ISS) in The Hague.

Authoritarian Populism and the Rural World

Edited by
Ian Scoones, Marc Edelman,
Saturnino M. Borras Jr., Lyda Fernanda Forero,
Ruth Hall, Wendy Wolford and Ben White

First published 2021
by Routledge
2 Park Square, Milton Park, Abingdon, Oxon OX14 4RN

and by Routledge
605 Third Avenue, New York, NY 10158

Routledge is an imprint of the Taylor & Francis Group, an informa business

Preface, Chapters 1–6, 8–10, 12–14, 16 and 18–20 © 2022 Taylor & Francis
Chapter 7 © 2018 Fikret Adaman, Murat Arsel and Bengi Akbulut. Originally published as Open Access.
Chapter 11 © 2019 Noémi Gonda. Originally published as Open Access.
Chapter 15 © 2019 Daniela Andrade. Originally published as Open Access.
Chapter 17 © 2020 Antonio Roman-Alcalá. Originally published as Open Access.

The Open Access version of this book, available at www.taylorfrancis.com, has been made available under a Creative Commons Attribution-Non Commercial-No Derivatives 4.0 license.

Trademark notice: Product or corporate names may be trademarks or registered trademarks, and are used only for identification and explanation without intent to infringe.

British Library Cataloguing in Publication Data
A catalogue record for this book is available from the British Library

ISBN: 978-0-367-75387-0 (hbk)
ISBN: 978-0-367-75394-8 (pbk)
ISBN: 978-1-003-16235-3 (ebk)

DOI: 10.4324/9781003162353

Typeset in Minion Pro
by Newgen Publishing UK

Publisher's Note
The publisher accepts responsibility for any inconsistencies that may have arisen during the conversion of this book from journal articles to book chapters, namely the inclusion of journal terminology.

Disclaimer
Every effort has been made to contact copyright holders for their permission to reprint material in this book. The publishers would be grateful to hear from any copyright holder who is not here acknowledged and will undertake to rectify any errors or omissions in future editions of this book.

Contents

Citation Information ... ix
Notes on Contributors ... xii
Preface ... xv

1 Emancipatory rural politics: confronting authoritarian populism ... 1
 Ian Scoones, Marc Edelman, Saturnino M. Borras Jr., Ruth Hall, Wendy Wolford and Ben White

2 Counterrevolution, the countryside and the middle classes: lessons from five countries ... 21
 Walden Bello

3 People and places left behind: work, culture and politics in the rural United States ... 59
 Jessica D. Ulrich-Schad and Cynthia M. Duncan

4 Power and powerlessness in an Appalachian Valley – revisited ... 80
 John Gaventa

5 The rural roots of the rise of the Justice and Development Party in Turkey ... 97
 Burak Gürel, Bermal Küçük and Sercan Taş

6 Rural rage: right-wing populism and Patriot movement in the United States ... 120
 Spencer Sunshine and Chip Berlet

7 Neoliberal developmentalism, authoritarian populism, and extractivism in the countryside: the Soma mining disaster in Turkey ... 154
 Fikret Adaman, Murat Arsel and Bengi Akbulut

8 The vanishing exception: republican and reactionary specters of populism in rural Spain ... 177
 Jaume Franquesa

9 Understanding the silent majority in authoritarian populism: what can we learn from popular support for Putin in rural Russia? ... 201
 Natalia Mamonova

10 Authoritarian populism in rural Belarus: distinction, commonalities, and projected finale 226
Aleh Ivanou

11 Land grabbing and the making of an authoritarian populist regime in Hungary 246
Noémi Gonda

12 Authoritarian populism and neo-extractivism in Bolivia and Ecuador: the unresolved agrarian question and the prospects for food sovereignty as counter-hegemony 266
Mark Tilzey

13 Pockets of liberal media in authoritarian regimes: what the crackdown on emancipatory spaces means for rural social movements in Cambodia 293
Alice Beban, Laura Schoenberger and Vanessa Lamb

14 Confronting agrarian authoritarianism: dynamics of resistance to PROSAVANA in Mozambique 313
Boaventura Monjane and Natacha Bruna

15 Populism from above and below: the path to regression in Brazil 338
Daniela Andrade

16 'They say they don't see color, but maybe they should!' Authoritarian populism and colorblind liberal political culture 365
Michael Carolan

17 Agrarian anarchism and authoritarian populism: towards a more (state-)critical 'critical agrarian studies' 389
Antonio Roman-Alcalá

18 'Actually existing' right-wing populism in rural Europe: insights from eastern Germany, Spain, the United Kingdom and Ukraine 420
Natalia Mamonova, Jaume Franquesa and Sally Brooks

19 Unpacking 'authoritarian populism' and rural politics: some comments on ERPI 448
Henry Bernstein

20 From 'populist moment' to authoritarian era: challenges, dangers, possibilities 465
Marc Edelman

Index 492

Citation Information

The following chapters were originally published in different issues of *The Journal of Peasant Studies*. When citing this material, please use the original citations and page numbering for each article, as follows:

Chapter 1
Emancipatory rural politics: confronting authoritarian populism
Ian Scoones, Marc Edelman, Saturnino M. Borras Jr., Ruth Hall, Wendy Wolford and Ben White
The Journal of Peasant Studies, volume 45, issue 1 (2018), pp. 1–20

Chapter 2
Counterrevolution, the countryside and the middle classes: lessons from five countries
Walden Bello
The Journal of Peasant Studies, volume 45, issue 1 (2018), pp. 21–58

Chapter 3
People and places left behind: work, culture and politics in the rural United States
Jessica D. Ulrich-Schad and Cynthia M. Duncan
The Journal of Peasant Studies, volume 45, issue 1 (2018), pp. 59–79

Chapter 4
Power and powerlessness in an Appalachian Valley – revisited
John Gaventa
The Journal of Peasant Studies, volume 46, issue 3 (2019), pp. 440–456

Chapter 5
The rural roots of the rise of the Justice and Development Party in Turkey
Burak Gürel, Bermal Küçük and Sercan Taş
The Journal of Peasant Studies, volume 46, issue 3 (2019), pp. 457–479

Chapter 6
Rural rage: the roots of right-wing populism in the United States
Chip Berlet and Spencer Sunshine
The Journal of Peasant Studies, volume 46, issue 3 (2019), pp. 480–513

Chapter 7
Neoliberal developmentalism, authoritarian populism, and extractivism in the countryside: the Soma mining disaster in Turkey
Fikret Adaman, Murat Arsel and Bengi Akbulut
The Journal of Peasant Studies, volume 46, issue 3 (2019), pp. 514–536

Chapter 8
The vanishing exception: republican and reactionary specters of populism in rural Spain
Jaume Franquesa
The Journal of Peasant Studies, volume 46, issue 3 (2019), pp. 537–560

Chapter 9
Understanding the silent majority in authoritarian populism: what can we learn from popular support for Putin in rural Russia?
Natalia Mamonova
The Journal of Peasant Studies, volume 46, issue 3 (2019), pp. 561–585

Chapter 10
Authoritarian populism in rural Belarus: distinction, commonalities, and projected finale
Aleh Ivanou
The Journal of Peasant Studies, volume 46, issue 3 (2019), pp. 586–605

Chapter 11
Land grabbing and the making of an authoritarian populist regime in Hungary
Noémi Gonda
The Journal of Peasant Studies, volume 46, issue 3 (2019), pp. 606–625

Chapter 12
Authoritarian populism and neo-extractivism in Bolivia and Ecuador: the unresolved agrarian question and the prospects for food sovereignty as counter-hegemony
Mark Tilzey
The Journal of Peasant Studies, volume 46, issue 3 (2019), pp. 626–652

Chapter 13
Pockets of liberal media in authoritarian regimes: what the crackdown on emancipatory spaces means for rural social movements in Cambodia
Alice Beban, Laura Schoenberger and Vanessa Lamb
The Journal of Peasant Studies, volume 47, issue 1 (2020), pp. 95–115

Chapter 14
Confronting agrarian authoritarianism: dynamics of resistance to PROSAVANA in Mozambique
Boaventura Monjane and Natacha Bruna
The Journal of Peasant Studies, volume 47, issue 1 (2020), pp. 69–94

Chapter 15
Populism from above and below: the path to regression in Brazil
Daniela Andrade
The Journal of Peasant Studies, volume 47, issue 7 (2020), pp. 1470–1496

Chapter 16
'They say they don't see color, but maybe they should!' Authoritarian populism and colorblind liberal political culture
Michael Carolan
The Journal of Peasant Studies, volume 47, issue 7 (2020), pp. 1445–1469

Chapter 17
Agrarian anarchism and authoritarian populism: towards a more (state-)critical 'critical agrarian studies'
Antonio Roman-Alcalá
The Journal of Peasant Studies, volume 48, issue 2 (2021), pp. 298–328

Chapter 18
'Actually existing' right-wing populism in rural Europe: insights from eastern Germany, Spain, the United Kingdom and Ukraine
Natalia Mamonova, Jaume Franquesa and Sally Brooks
The Journal of Peasant Studies, volume 47, issue 7 (2020), pp. 1497–1525

Chapter 19
Unpacking 'authoritarian populism' and rural politics: some comments on ERPI
Henry Bernstein
The Journal of Peasant Studies, volume 47, issue 7 (2020), pp. 1526–1542

Chapter 20
From 'populist moment' to authoritarian era: challenges, dangers, possibilities
Marc Edelman
The Journal of Peasant Studies, volume 47, issue 7 (2020), pp. 1418–1444

For any permission-related enquiries please visit:
www.tandfonline.com/page/help/permissions

Notes on Contributors

Fikret Adaman is Professor at the Department of Economics, Boğaziçi University. His research lies within the fields of political economy, ecological economics, development studies and history of economic thought.

Bengi Akbulut is Assistant Professor at the Department of Geography, Planning and Environment, Concordia University. Her work lies within the fields of political economy, ecological economics, development studies and feminist economics.

Daniela Andrade is PhD researcher at the International Institute of Social Studies (ISS) in The Hague. Her research interests include the political economy of agriculture and agrarian change from a macro perspective, especially in Brazil and Mozambique.

Murat Arsel is Associate Professor of Environment and Development at the International Institute of Social Studies of Erasmus University Rotterdam. His research concerns the political economy of the relationship with capitalism and nature, focusing especially on environmental conflicts and state-society dynamics.

Alice Beban is Lecturer in Sociology at Massey University in Aotearoa, New Zealand. She holds a PhD in Development Sociology from Cornell University. Her research focuses on the intersections between land rights, agricultural production, state formation and gender concerns to understand rural people's changing relationships with land.

Walden Bello is International Adjunct Professor of Sociology at the State University of New York at Binghamton. He served as a member of the House of Representatives of the Philippines from 2009 to 2015.

Chip Berlet is an investigative journalist and photographer recruited by progressive sociologists to help research right-wing movements. Active in the antiwar and civil rights movements, in 1977 he and his partner moved to Chicago and spent 10 years involved in labour and anti-racism projects, including challenging violence by neo-Nazis and Klansmen.

Henry Bernstein is Adjunct Professor at the College of Humanities and Development Studies (COHD), China Agricultural University, Beijing, and Professor Emeritus of Development Studies, School of Oriental and African Studies (SOAS), University of London, UK.

Saturnino M. Borras Jr. is Professor of Agrarian Studies at the International Institute of Social Studies (ISS) in The Hague, the Netherlands, an Adjunct Professor at China Agricultural University in Beijing and a fellow of the Amsterdam-based Transnational Institute (TNI).

Sally Brooks is Honorary Fellow in the Department of Social Policy and Social Work and a member of the Interdisciplinary Global Development Centre at the University of York. Her research centres on the critical examination of global development imaginaries, interventions, and institutions.

Natacha Bruna is PhD candidate at the International Institute of Social Studies, Erasmus University Rotterdam, in the Political Ecology research group. Her research is about the agrarian change brought up by the intersections of resource grabbing as a result of extractivism and environmental politics.

Michael Carolan is Professor of Sociology and Associate Dean of Research and Graduate Affairs for the College of Liberal Arts. He has published over 200 peer review articles and chapters. Dr. Carolan is also Associate Editor for the *Journal of Rural Studies, Society and Natural Resources* and *Sustainability*.

Cynthia M. Duncan is Senior Fellow at the Carsey School of Public Policy, USA.

Marc Edelman is Professor of Anthropology at Hunter College and the Graduate Center of the City University of New York, USA.

Lyda Fernanda Forero was, until April 2020, coordinator of the Agrarian and Environmental Justice (AEJ) programme of the Transnational Institute. She is currently with the secretariat of the Trade Union Confederation of the Americas (TUCA).

Jaume Franquesa is Associate Professor of Anthropology at the University at Buffalo, New York. His research focuses on the relationship between the commodification of resources, the making of local livelihoods and forms of political mobilisation.

John Gaventa is former Research Director and a Fellow at the Institute of Development Studies (IDS) in the UK. He worked from 1971 to 1996 as a scholar-activist in the Appalachian Region, including with the Highlander Research and Education Center.

Noémi Gonda is post-doctoral researcher at the Department of Urban and Rural Development of the Swedish University of Agricultural Sciences. She holds a PhD from the Central European University. Her PhD research (2016) was a feminist ethnography in Nicaragua focused on the politics of gender and climate change.

Burak Gürel is Assistant Professor in the Department of Sociology at Koç University. His scholarly interests include political economy, historical sociology, rural development, social movements and welfare politics, with a focus on China, India and Turkey.

Ruth Hall is Professor of Land and Agrarian Studies at the Institute for Poverty, Land and Agrarian Studies (PLAAS) at the University of the Western Cape, South Africa.

Aleh Ivanou is a Belarusian independent researcher with a PhD in Environmental Social Science from the University of Kent, UK.

Bermal Küçük is PhD student in the Department of Sociology at Koç University. Her research interests are in rural development, sociology of food and political ecology, with a focus on the labour and the knowledge of women.

Vanessa Lamb is Senior Lecturer in the School of Geography at the University of Melbourne. In research and teaching, she focuses on human-environment geographies and political ecology of Southeast Asia.

Natalia Mamonova is research fellow in the Russia and Eurasia Programme of the Swedish Institute of International Affairs (UI) in Stockholm and an affiliated researcher at the Institute for Russian and Eurasian Studies (IRES) of Uppsala University, Sweden. Her research interests primarily focus on contemporary rural politics in Russia and Ukraine.

Boaventura Monjane is a postdoctoral researcher at the Institute for Poverty, Land and Agrarian Studies (PLAAS), University of the Western Cape (South Africa), fellow of the International Research Group on Authoritarianism and Counter-Strategies of the Rosa Luxemburg Foundation (RLS), and associate fellow at the Centro de Estudos Africanos (CEA) at Eduardo Mondlane University, Mozambique.

Antonio Roman-Alcalá is an educator, researcher and organiser based in California. He has been involved in US food movements primarily through urban farming and participatory democratic network organising, and his research focuses on collaborative efforts to improve movement effectiveness.

Laura Schoenberger is Banting Postdoctoral Fellow at the School of International Development and Global Studies, University of Ottawa. Her research interests are in political ecology, state power, land and property relations and feminist epistemology.

Ian Scoones is Professorial Fellow at the Institute of Development Studies at the University of Sussex and co-director of the ESRC STEPS Centre.

Spencer Sunshine has a PhD in sociology and studies organised racist, fascist and antisemitic movements and organisations. He is the author of the guide *40 Ways to Fight Nazis: Forty Community-Based Actions You Can Take to Resist White Nationalist Organizing* published by Showing Up for Racial Justice (SURJ).

Sercan Taş is a PhD student in the Department of Sociology at Koç University. His research interests include rural development, urbanisation, and environmental governance, with a focus on Turkey.

Mark Tilzey is Associate Professor in the Governance of Food Systems for Resilience, Centre for Agroecology, Water and Resilience, Coventry University, UK. His research interests lie in political ecology, food regimes, agrarian change and agroecology, agri-environmental politics and governance and the international political economy of agri-food systems.

Jessica D. Ulrich-Schad is Assistant Professor of Sociology and Rural Studies at South Dakota State, USA.

Ben White is Emeritus Professor of Rural Sociology at the International Institute of Social Studies (ISS) in The Hague.

Wendy Wolford is Polson Professor of Global Development at Cornell University, USA.

Preface
Authoritarian populism and the rural world

The rise of authoritarian, nationalist forms of populism and the implications for rural settings is perhaps one of the most crucial foci for critical agrarian studies today, with many consequences for political action. Responding to this, the Emancipatory Rural Politics Initiative (ERPI)[1] was launched in early 2017, and this book is a compilation of 20 articles published in the 'Authoritarian populism and the rural world' Forum in *The Journal of Peasant Studies* (*JPS*) as part of the Initiative.

The ERPI emerged through a series of conversations amongst the founding group – and authors of this preface – in late 2016/early 2017. This was in the wake of Donald Trump's election to the White House, the Brexit referendum in the UK and the emergence of a number of authoritarian and populist leaders across the world – whether Narendra Modi in India, Recep Tayip Erdoğan in Turkey, Viktor Orbán in Hungary, Rodrigo Duterte in the Philippines or Jacob Zuma in South Africa. Our conversations also centred on the rise of multi-class mobilisation and resistance alongside wider counter-movements and alternative practices that together confronted authoritarianism and nationalist populism. In different ways, we were all questioning why all this had happened and what should we do about it? In short, in the narrow corridor between rage and hope, we wanted to pursue a research initiative and political conversation that responded to the political conjuncture, linking rigorous academic research with political engagement.

The first chapter of this book, which came out in *JPS* online in mid-2017, provided an initial framing for our work, fleshing out our questions in more detail and offering a starting point for a wider debate.[2] In this framing piece, we highlight the emergence of what we call 'authoritarian populism', and particularly its rural roots and consequences. We draw in particular on the arguments of Stuart Hall and others made in the context of Thatcherism in the UK.[3] In Gramscian terms, authoritarian populisms can emerge when the 'balance of forces' changes, creating a new 'political-ideological conjuncture'. Drawing on populist discontents a transformist, authoritarian movement, often with a strong figurehead leader, gains ground, mobilising around 'moral panics' and 'authoritarian closure', and generating, in Hall's words, 'the gloss of populist consent'. In 2017 – and still today – this sounded very familiar.

The term 'authoritarian populism' has caused much debate in relation to the current conjuncture; some of it helpful, some of it distracting. Others prefer alternative terminologies, focusing on axes of left and right politics, the dimensions of nationalism and nativism and so

---

[1] www.iss.nl/en/research/research-networks/emancipatory-rural-politics-initiative
[2] www.tandfonline.com/doi/abs/10.1080/03066150.2017.1339693?journalCode=fjps20
[3] See Hall (1980, 1985, 1986).

on. Of course, across the world authoritarian populisms take many forms in different places and at different moments, with contrasting consequences for class dynamics, gender relations and economic and environmental outcomes. Despite the diversity, some core features are clear. This has provided a concrete political focus for the ERPI, and has guided the contributions to this book in chapters that equally reflect the array of contexts and interpretations of an emergent phenomenon.

Debates about 'populism', 'nationalism', 'authoritarianism' and more have exploded in the last few years, but relatively little of this has focused on the rural dimensions. Yet wherever you look, the rural aspects are key – not just in electoral calculus, but in understanding underlying drivers of authoritarianism and populism, and potential counter-movements to these. Whether it is because of land grabs, voracious extractivism, infrastructural neglect or lack of services, people's disillusionment with the *status quo*, across often disconnected rural areas and small towns, is tangible across settings, as the chapters in this book show.

Too often, this leads to the fragmenting of communities and loss of security and identity. Lack of jobs and livelihoods is blamed on outsiders – often immigrant populations working in agricultural industries in marginalised areas. Declining rural and small town livelihoods are often, in turn, linked to drug abuse and physical and mental ill-health and increasing despair. Across cases explored in the chapters of this book, the disenchantment and disenfranchisement felt in such areas is seen to be firmly the result of state neglect over decades, thanks to neoliberal policies that brought austerity, extraction and exploitation. The COVID-19 pandemic has only exacerbated these fractures, exposing inequalities and the failures of mainstream neoliberal capitalism, and reinforcing patterns of authoritarianism in some settings.[4]

Populist right-wing parties, despite the dissonance in values and messages, have appealed to many with promises of jobs, investment and renewal, combined with a nationalist anti-immigrant rhetoric that resonates with those who feel under threat. Meanwhile, the cosmopolitan, mostly urban, educated 'left' elite has too often failed to engage with these real concerns and traumas in the rural areas, while organised labour has defended remaining formal jobs to the exclusion of others who are unemployed or surviving on the margins.

Yet amongst much despair, disenfranchisement and deepening inequalities, more positively, there are emancipatory alternatives being created at the same time in rural areas and small towns that offer the opportunity for prefiguring a new politics. As chapters in this book, from very diverse settings, indicate these are rooted in communities, linked to rural skills, trades and cultures and encourage collectivity and solidarity, often around forms of 'commoning'. Very often they make use of modern technology to encourage connectivity, sharing and building solidarities. Movements, such as around food sovereignty, for example, help mobilise around and extend such alternatives. As many cases documented in this book show, such initiatives can help to build a new economy, which is sustainable and addresses the threats of climate chaos. These efforts also serve as platforms for broader political conversations that concern matters far beyond self-help projects and their local communities, to discussing issues of system-wide transformations, class politics and political power.

As many contributors to the ERPI have argued, unless progressive politics focuses on such alternatives, and helps articulate and scale them up, the prospects for countering the rise of authoritarian populism in rural areas looks slim. This counter-movement requires new forms of organising, movement-construction and coalition-building that are necessarily multi-class

---

[4]Leach *et al.* (2021). https://doi.org/10.1016/j.worlddev.2020.105233

in character, focusing on real issues and people, and building from communities upwards and outwards. It requires different solutions for different places; not grand planning deals struck from above. And, as the basis for a politics of mobilisation and struggle, it requires attention to altered structures of rural class relations and changing dynamics in and between sites of economic production and social reproduction, as inflected by gender, generation, race, ethnicity, nationality and other differences.[5]

Widening the conversation

From our initial conversations and the writing of the framing paper in 2017, the ERPI moved to a wider engagement across different people and places. Through a small grants fund for writing up experiences – by academics, practitioners, movement activists and others – the Initiative mobilised a huge amount of comparative learning across the world. The importance of the rural dimension was confirmed, and in our major meeting at the International Institute of Social Studies (ISS) in The Hague in early 2018, around 300 people from five continents came together to discuss these experiences.[6] From land activists from South Africa, to agroecology practitioners from Germany, to democracy and human rights activists from India, to organisers who worked with the Bernie Sanders' campaign in the US, to activist Flamenco performers from Andalucía to a radical activist painter from the Philippines, a huge array of insights were shared. Emerging from the event, and in collaboration with the online platform, openDemocracy, we produced a series of videos and short articles, profiling a diversity of perspectives, summarised in a short film.[7]

During the 2018 event, it was clear that, in order to embed our on-going research in political action on the ground, the ERPI network had to be polycentric, and a series of regional working groups were formed. They have continued the research and reflection – not only diagnosing the problems, but also exploring solutions. For example, ERPI Europe[8] has been engaged in a number of events, and has published a path-breaking special issue in *Sociologia Ruralis*,[9] while ERPI North America has produced an important series of papers in a special issue of the *Journal of Rural Studies*.[10] ERPI Africa has been engaging in field-based exchange visits and writing up these experiences, feeding into activist initiatives.[11] ERPI Latin America is also collecting a set of papers in a special issue of *Latin American Perspectives*.[12] Meanwhile, ERPI South Asia met in Sri Lanka to exchange experiences from across the region, and ERPI Southeast Asia met in Thailand to foster a dialogue among academics and activists within the region. Finally, the ERPI group focusing on implications for human rights, linked to core ERPI partner the Transnational Institute (TNI), has also produced another significant piece, *A View from the Countryside*.[13]

---

[5]Borras (2020). https://onlinelibrary.wiley.com/doi/abs/10.1111/joac.12311
[6]https://steps-centre.org/authoritarian-populism-rural-world/; see also https://wakelet.com/wake/456372d5-1d29-45d4-bcba-9dc97015ffd5
[7]www.opendemocracy.net/en/authoritarian-populism-and-rural-world/ and www.facebook.com/openDemocracy/videos/rural-populism/975798742603589/
[8]https://www.arc2020.eu/right-wing-populism-emancipatory-rural-politics-initiative-europe/;seealso:https://steps-centre.org/blog/rural-resistance-and-the-far-right-news-from-erpi-europe/
[9]See Mamonova and Franquesa (2019). https://onlinelibrary.wiley.com/doi/10.1111/soru.12291
[10]See de Wit *et al.* (2019). www.sciencedirect.com/science/article/abs/pii/S0743016719305200
[11]www.pambazuka.org/land-environment/zimbabwe's-shashe-agroecology-village-inspiration-emancipatory-rural-initiative
[12]https://latinamericanperspectives.com/authoritarian-populism-and-the-rural-world/
[13]See Sandwell *et al.* (2019). www.tni.org/en/countryside

Following on from the small grants competition and the ERPI event in The Hague, a series of articles began to be published as part of a special *JPS* Forum linked to the ERPI. This book presents a compilation of these, including contributions from Belarus, Bolivia, Brazil, Cambodia, Ecuador, Hungary, Mozambique, Russia, Spain, Turkey and the US, as well as several overview pieces with comparative regional assessments. The book concludes with two chapters reflecting on the work of the ERPI as a whole. These pieces come from very diverse experiences and are rooted in quite different conceptual traditions. Some make very direct use of the concepts laid out in the framing paper; others take a different tack. There has been no attempt to enforce uniformity nor require a singular analytical perspective. Indeed quite the opposite; as the ERPI decentralised and the initiative took on regional characteristics, different concerns arose, requiring distinct analytical frames that spoke to contrasting empirical contexts. This book must be read in this light.

Beyond the ERPI, other efforts have of course engaged with these debates, increasingly with a focus on the rural dimensions. Important contributions to date include the special issue on 'Environmental Governance in a Populist/Authoritarian Era' in the *Annals of the American Association of Geographers* edited by James McCarthy;[14] a section of the *Canadian Journal of Development Studies* edited by Ben McKay, Gustavo Oliveira and Juan Liu; a special issue of *Geoforum* edited by Murat Arsel, Fikret Adaman and Alfredo Saad Filho and an anthology titled *Beyond Populism: Angry Politics and the Twilight of Neoliberalism* edited by Jeff Maskovsky and Sophie Bjork-James (2020).[15] From different standpoints and using different analytical perspectives, these all add to the growing empirical resource.

What ties all these contributions together is first and foremost a recognition that rural dimensions matter, and that the new politics of authoritarian populism (or whatever term is preferred for similar phenomena) reconfigures agrarian relations and politics in important new ways. This has major implications for how we conceive of 'peasant studies' or 'agrarian studies' at this moment in history and most significantly how we construct political alternatives that are progressive and sustainable.

Common threads: rural populism and alternatives to authoritarian politics

What emerges from this growing corpus of work and what are the implications? Reading across and beyond the contributions to this book a number of common threads emerge. They each suggest the importance of new areas of research, and new foci for action.

First, the emergence of populism with a strong rural base needs a careful analysis of the social, cultural and class dynamics of rural change, asking why it is that young people, women, peasant farmers, rural workers and others are often strongly behind reactionary populist positions. Some liberals and leftists may argue that this does not serve their interests, but we need to look beyond such rationalist arguments and think harder about the politics of identity, belonging, recognition and community, and how these intersect with class dynamics. These themes come out strongly in the chapters in this book, yet are perhaps not central enough to the classic formulations of conventional writing in agrarian political economy. Interest-based analyses (centred on class or whatever category) and conventional political economy may be insufficient for explaining complex, personal, located, subjective phenomena.

---

[14] See McCarthy (2019). www.tandfonline.com/doi/full/10.1080/24694452.2018.1554393
[15] See McKay *et al.* (2020). www.tandfonline.com/doi/full/10.1080/02255189.2020.1814707

Second, in developing a now globally comparative perspective across cases, represented in this book and beyond, it is worth exploring how different forms of populism – broadly characterised as authoritarian or progressive – emerge around the world. This depends very much on the historical, structural engagements with globalisation, as well as forms of imperialism and processes of decolonisation. Populists may mobilise either around ethno-nationalist arguments – for example when global migration flows create discontents – or around class divisions – such as when global trade has impacts on livelihoods.[16] The cases in this book begin to draw out how particular globalisation processes affect rural spaces in different ways – through forms of extractivism, land and resource grabbing, infrastructure development and so on. This contrasts with the impacts on urban metropoles – with different implications for class, gender, race or age – and so processes of political mobilisation. Critical agrarian studies needs to engage with these questions, moving beyond the singular local or national case to bring to the fore perspectives on global political economy, where the economic impacts and political consequences are taken seriously.

Third, the politics of authoritarian populism provides an impetus to the continuation of extractive exploitation of rural resources – as land, water and resource grabbing continues apace. At the same time, green and conservation policies are generating authoritarian, neoliberal dynamics in the countryside in many places. However, today there is also a nationalist tinge, with new capital-elite-state alliances being forged. These processes, which were initially a response to the 2008 global financial crisis and the desperate search for investment opportunities by global capital – extensively documented in the pages of *The Journal of Peasant Studies* and emerging from the ERPI precursor, the Land Deals Politics Initiative[17] – now have a new context in many settings. We need to ask today: how do new configurations of power, and a populist, nationalist, often anti-globalisation narrative, affect the politics of dispossession in rural spaces and so the dynamics of accumulation among local and international elites? These wider political shifts mean that research and action around resource grabbing and extractivism in rural settings require an expanded frame that takes populist politics seriously.

Fourth, as already discussed, many of the contributors to this book are interested in how alternatives are forged and resistances mobilised to authoritarian populism. This requires asking whether conventional frames for mobilisation are able to respond in the face of authoritarian populisms. For example, the food sovereignty movement has been a site for progressive discussion about agrarian alternatives over the last decade or so. Yet the notions of sovereignty, localism, autonomy and rejection of the role of the state and globalism have frequently been captured by regressive, populist positions. Why do peasant farmers support such political leaders? Partly because they claim to offer a voice and a commitment to protecting their autonomy from the ill-winds of global trade and state interference. For example, in India ideas about 'natural farming' based on agro-ecological principles have got wrapped up in exclusionary Hindutva nationalism, yet are celebrated as a food sovereignty success.[18] A new politics of the mainstream, increasingly framed by diverse forms of authoritarian populism, therefore requires a new politics of the alternative, and contributions to this book offer some pointers to such alternative framing and positioning.

---

[16]See Rodrik (2018). https://drodrik.scholar.harvard.edu/files/dani-rodrik/files/populism_and_the_economics_of_globalization.pdf
[17]www.iss.nl/en/research/research-networks/land-deal-politics-initiative
[18]See Khadse *et al.* (2018).

In sum, a new moment is emerging: a critical, historical conjuncture, when the tectonic plates of global power relations shift. Despite some positive changes, such as the election of Joe Biden in the US, we cannot pretend this is not happening. Across the world, political reconfigurations are underway, responding in different ways to a quite fundamental crisis in globalised neoliberal capitalism, with huge ramifications across rural worlds everywhere. New contexts require new questions and new analytical frames, new coalitions of social forces and new forms of mobilisation. With this moment unfolding rapidly, in alliance with others, the intellectual and political project of agrarian studies must rise to the challenge. This book, and its 20 chapters, offers a small contribution to this.[19]

Ian Scoones, Marc Edelman, Saturnino M. Borras Jr., Lyda Fernanda Forero, Ruth Hall, Wendy Wolford and Ben White
Brighton; Dingmans Ferry, Pennsylvania; The Hague; Montevideo; Cape Town, and Ithaca
May 2021

Acknowledgements

The ERPI has benefited from a wide range of support, most of it unfunded and voluntary. The initial participating institutions were the International Institute of Social Studies (ISS), Cornell University, the City University of New York (CUNY), the ESRC STEPS Centre at the Institute of Development Studies at the University of Sussex, PLAAS at the University of the Western Cape and the Transnational Institute (TNI). For financial support, we would like to thank the Ford Foundation, the UK Economic and Social Research Council (via the STEPS Centre's 'transformations' theme), the Rosa Luxemburg Foundation and the Open Society Foundations, as well as the RRUSHES-5 research project at ISS that has received funding from the European Research Council (ERC) under the European Union's Horizon 2020 research and innovation programme (grant agreement No. 834006). We would like to thank the many reviewers for *JPS* who contributed to the final versions of the papers that appear as chapters here.

References

Borras Jr, Saturnino M. 2020. Agrarian social movements: The absurdly difficult but not impossible agenda of defeating right-wing populism and exploring a socialist future. *Journal of Agrarian Change* 20, no. 1: 3–36.
de Wit, Maywa Montenegro, Antonio Roman-Alcalá, Alex Liebman and Siena Chrisman. 2019. Agrarian origins of authoritarian populism in the United States: What can we learn from 20th-century struggles in California and the Midwest? *Journal of Rural Studies* 82: 518–530.
Hall, Stuart. 1980. Popular-democratic versus authoritarian populism. In *Marxism and democracy*, ed. A. Hunt, 157–87. London: Laurence and Wishart.
Hall, Stuart. 1985. Authoritarian populism: A reply to Jessop *et al*. *New Left Review* 151: 115–24.
Hall, Stuart. 1986. Gramsci's relevance for the study of race and ethnicity. *Journal of Communication Inquiry* 10, no. 5: 4–27.
Khadse, Ashlesha, Peter Michael Rosset, Helda Morales and Bruce G. Ferguson. 2018. Taking agroecology to scale: The zero budget natural farming peasant movement in Karnataka, India. *Journal of Peasant Studies* 45, no. 1: 192–219.
Leach, Melissa, Hayley MacGregor, Ian Scoones and Annie Wilkinson. 2021. Post-pandemic transformations: How and why COVID-19 requires us to rethink development. *World Development* 138, 105233. https://doi.org/10.1016/j.worlddev.2020.105233.

---

[19]This preface draws on several blogs published by the ESRC STEPS Centre, including: https://steps-centre.org/blog/rural-support-for-authoritarian-populism-is-strong-but-another-way-is-possible/ and https://steps-centre.org/blog/agrarian-studies-confront-rise-authoritarian-populist-movements/.

Mamonova, Natalia, and Jaume Franquesa. 2020. Populism, neoliberalism and agrarian movements in Europe. Understanding rural support for right-wing politics and looking for progressive solutions. *Sociologia Ruralis* 60, no. 4: 702–209.

Maskovsky, Jeff, and Sophie Bjork-James, eds. 2020. *Beyond Populism: Angry Politics and the Twilight of Neoliberalism*. Morgantown: West Virginia University Press.

McCarthy, James. 2019. Authoritarianism, Populism, and the Environment: Comparative Experiences, Insights, and Perspectives. *Annals of the American Association of Geographers*, 109, no. 2: 301–313.

McKay, Ben, Gustavo de L.T. Oliveira and Juan Liu. 2020. Authoritarianism, populism, nationalism and resistance in the agrarian South. *Canadian Journal of Development Studies / Revue Canadienne d'Études du Développement*, 41, no. 3: 347–362.

Rodrik, Dani. 2018. Populism and the economics of globalization. *Journal of International Business Policy*; https://doi.org/10.1057/s42214-018-0001-4

Sandwell, Katie, Angélica Castañeda Flores, Lyda Fernanda Forero, Jennifer Franco, Sofia Monsalve Suárez, Andrea Nuila and Philip Seufert. 2019. *A View from the Countryside: Contesting and Constructing Human Rights in an Age of Converging Crises*. Amsterdam: Transnational Institute (TNI).

Scoones, Ian, Marc Edelman, Saturnino M. Borras Jr., Ruth Hall, Wendy Wolford and Ben White. 2018. Emancipatory rural politics: confronting authoritarian populism. *The Journal of Peasant Studies*, 45, no. 1: 1–20.

Emancipatory rural politics: confronting authoritarian populism

Ian Scoones, Marc Edelman, Saturnino M. Borras Jr., Ruth Hall, Wendy Wolford and Ben White

> A new political moment is underway. Although there are significant differences in how this is constituted in different places, one manifestation of the new moment is the rise of distinct forms of authoritarian populism. In this opening paper of the *JPS* Forum series on 'Authoritarian Populism and the Rural World', we explore the relationship between these new forms of politics and rural areas around the world. We ask how rural transformations have contributed to deepening regressive national politics, and how rural areas shape and are shaped by these politics. We propose a global agenda for research, debate and action, which we call the Emancipatory Rural Politics Initiative (ERPI, www.iss.nl/erpi). This centres on understanding the contemporary conjuncture, working to confront authoritarian populism through the analysis of and support for alternatives.

Introduction

If a new political moment can be said to be underway, what are its features? At a time of increasing inequality between rich and poor, rural and urban, labour and capital, the following seem particularly relevant: the rise of protectionist politics and the embrace of nationalism over regional or global integration, whether in trade blocs or international agreements; highly contested national elections, resonant with broad-brush appeals to 'the people', in which candidates are rewarded for 'strong man' talk that pits insiders against outsiders of different colours, religions and origins; growing concern over the 'mobile poor', including refugees and migrants whose presence seems to threaten a shrinking resource base; appeals for security at the expense of civil liberties; a concerted push to increase extractive capitalism at all costs; and, finally, a radical undermining of the state's ability to support the full range of citizens, while utilising state powers to increase surplus for a minority.

These elements are not evident everywhere, nor are they necessarily evident in their entirety anywhere. At the same time, many are actively working to counter these elements and nowhere is any single political approach absolute. What we see, however, is the rise of politicians, movements and spaces where these political-economic dynamics are playing out, with connections between them; we name these dynamics and these features authoritarian populism.[1]

Our concern in this contribution is not to provide an overarching theorisation of authoritarian populism, but rather to ask: how are these aspects of the contemporary moment playing out in rural areas? How are they shaped by prior transformations in rural society and economy and how do they portend even more dramatic – and usually negative – changes for rural areas?

Authoritarian populism was probably best defined by Hall (1985, 1980), who in the 1980s revived this 'contradictory term' to signify 'a movement towards a dominative and "authoritarian" form of democratic class politics – paradoxically, apparently rooted in the "transformism" (Gramsci's term) of populist discontents' (Hall 1985, 118). Mobilising around 'moral panics', 'authoritarian closure' was given 'the gloss of populist consent' (Hall 1985, 116). As Hall (1985, 119) describes, authoritarian populism characterises 'certain strategic shifts in the political/ideological conjuncture. Essentially, it refers to changes in the "balance of forces". It refers directly to the modalities of political and ideological relationships between the ruling bloc, the state and the dominated classes'.

Authoritarian populism, as we understand it, is a subset of populism, a capacious and at times problematic category. The political right has often employed 'populism' as a synonym for demagoguery, while the left, notably in Latin America, has used it to attack even progressive or anti-imperialist governments with a multi-class base that claimed to defend 'popular' or national, rather than solely working-class, interests. Populist projects usually involve personal ties between a leader and the masses, sections of which are incorporated into the state through clientelist mechanisms, rather than via apolitical and durable institutions or bureaucracies, as might occur in a social democracy (Sandbrook et al. 2007). Clientelism or corporatist forms of mobilisation and incorporation typically substitute for genuinely autonomous labour unions or other class- or interest-based organisations.

A crucial element in analysing populism is determining who is incorporated and to what extent, and who is excluded, and under what conditions. It is important to emphasise, following Jacques Rancière, that:

> The term 'populism' does not serve to characterize a defined political force. On the contrary, it benefits from the amalgams that it allows between political forces that range from the extreme right to the radical left. It does not designate an ideology or even a coherent political style. It serves simply to draw the image of a certain people. (Rancière 2016, 102)

Rancière goes on to state that those 'figures of the people' are

> constructed by privileging certain modes of assembling, certain distinctive traits, certain capacities or incapacities; an ethnic people defined by the community of land or blood. ... [R]acism is essential for this construction. (Rancière 2016, 102)

Authoritarian populism – our main concern here – typically depicts politics as a struggle between 'the people' and some combination of malevolent, racialised and/or unfairly advantaged 'Others', at home or abroad or both. It justifies interventions in the name of 'taking back control' in favour of 'the people', returning the nation to 'greatness' or

---

[1] As Gusterson (2017) explains, a range of terms are used for the same broad phenomenon, including nationalist populism, authoritarian populism, right-wing populism, cultural nationalism, nostalgic nationalism and neo-nationalism.

'health' after real or imagined degeneration attributed to those Others. Conflating a diverse and democratic people with images of dangerous and threatening crowds – 'a brutal and ignorant mass' (Rancière 2013) – allows for the putting of one ideology and position 'first', while excluding others and generating tensions across society. Authoritarian populism frequently circumvents, eviscerates or captures democratic institutions, even as it uses them to legitimate its dominance, centralise power and crush or severely limit dissent. Charismatic leaders, personality cults and nepotistic, familial or kleptocratic rule combined with impunity are common, though not essential, features of authoritarian populism.

Different authoritarian populisms range from 'competitive' regimes that allow some political space for opponents to 'non-competitive' ones that in extreme cases border on full-blown dictatorships (Levitsky and Way 2010). Dictatorships are often abetted by populist appeals, as Arendt (1951) argued in *The origins of totalitarianism*: tyrannical regimes frequently manipulate populations by creating isolation, separating people from each other, crushing their capacity for critical thinking, and reducing their power to resist, something typically achieved through divisive narratives of 'us against them'.

Appeals to sectarian religious forces further exacerbate tensions, whether these involve evangelical Christians in the US, parts of Europe and Africa; diverse forms of radical Islam in the Middle East, North Africa, Turkey or Indonesia; Hindu nationalists in India or Buddhists in Sri Lanka or Burma. Such political-religious movements – all with strong rural bases – must be seen as symptoms rather than the causes of current crises, both feeding on and feeding into ordinary people's longstanding resentments, sense of isolation and narratives of 'heroic confrontation with the Other' (Hasan 2016, 212). In many regions, rural areas have long been the centre of right-wing electoral support, as well as nationalist political support (Sinha 2016; Edelman 2003; Berlet and Lyons 2000). In exploring rural politics, we therefore must understand, but not judge, the social base, and its class, gender, ethnic and cultural-religious dimensions, which gives rise to regressive and exclusionary, sometimes violent, political movements.

Contemporary populist politics are far from uniform and are often contradictory: for example shoring up exclusionary and even violent political power, while selectively offering progressive policies, whether free tertiary education in the Philippines, land reform in South Africa or Zimbabwe, or targeted investment in rural communities in the US, Europe or India. In South Africa, for example, political discourses embracing equity and land redistribution sit alongside deeply conservative practices favouring elites' claims to land and land uses and the intransigent refusal by officials to subdivide commercial farmland (Hall and Kepe 2017). The consolidation of alliances between patriarchal traditional authorities and state authorities has even led to people being charged rent to remain on their ancestral land (Claassens 2011). In Ethiopia, the reassertion of central state control over land and the allocation of land as commercial concessions have prompted the revival of popular opposition to authoritarian state clamp-downs, even though this does not always take the form of overt and collective resistance (Moreda 2015).

Not all populism is right-wing and authoritarian. As Badiou (2016) explains, arguments in favour of 'the people' can be a positive, mobilising force of solidarity and emancipation. In Latin America, for example, the so-called 'pink tide' swept in several left-leaning neo-populist governments that achieved impressive gains in poverty reduction and expanded political recognition and government support for previously marginalised groups. These advances nonetheless depended on rents from oil and mineral extraction and environmentally destructive export agriculture, and frequently also involved restricting political space, especially for protests against extractivism, concentrating power in executive branches and sometimes in the person of charismatic leaders (Malamud 2017; Svampa 2015, 2017; Gudynas 2009). In

Brazil, the populist appeal of the Workers' Party arguably created a stunning backlash that saw one president impeached and a decade of distributive reforms undone. Meanwhile, in Myanmar, Aung San Suu Kyi's populist rhetoric has not brought deeper social reforms, such as land redistribution and restitution, in a country where many poor rural villagers were displaced in land grabs by companies linked to the military (Franco 2016; TNI 2015).

Having outlined our understanding of authoritarian populism, in the remainder of the paper, we explore three themes: (1) understanding current contexts, the emergence of authoritarian populism and its rural roots and consequences; (2) conceptualising an emancipatory rural politics, posing questions and raising debates; and (3) exploring forms of resistance and mobilisation, and the generation of emancipatory alternatives. The paper concludes by outlining a set of challenges for critical, engaged scholar-activists, including the methodological approaches required.

Understanding current contexts

Rural transformations of course have occurred over centuries; many contemporary processes of deagrarianisation, migration and rural disenfranchisement are not new. We cannot understand them without understanding rural areas historically, both in recent years and over the longue durée. Central is the political economy of resource extraction (human, financial, natural) in and from 'the rural' and the persistent, grinding poverty of many rural people, sometimes in the midst of growing general abundance. Through processes of financialisation particular to contemporary neoliberal capitalism, commodification, appropriation and extraction of rural resources are intensifying through increasingly aggressive enclosures (Clapp 2014; Fairbairn 2014; Haiven 2014; White et al. 2012). Land, energy, mineral, green or water 'grabs' aim at capturing resources in the hope that future scarcities will generate super-profits (Hall, Scoones, and Tsikata 2015; Edelman, Oya, and Borras 2013; Wolford et al. 2013; Fairhead, Leach, and Scoones 2012; Mehta, Veldwisch, and Franco 2012; Borras et al. 2011). Massive exclusions and dispossessions have swelled the 'relative surplus population' scattered throughout rural, peri-urban and urban areas (Li 2010). State-led programmes, often supported by international 'aid' flows, are reconfiguring rural areas, using discourses of food security in support of agribusiness, as epitomised by the New Alliance for Food Security and Nutrition in Africa (Crankshaw 2016). In South Africa, the African National Congress's recent proposals to ban foreign purchases of agricultural land won popular support, but were profoundly undermined by provisions to exempt 'institutional funds' (i.e. hedge and pension funds), exposing the contradictions between populist nationalist appeals and efforts to appease national and global capital. In Brazil, high-profile efforts to limit foreign ownership of land did little to stop increasing investment and concentration in land ownership and agricultural production (ActionAid et al. 2017; Rede Social et al. 2015; Sauer and Leite 2012). In these instances, supposedly popular and left-wing appeals to the interests of the poor actually advanced narrow interests of foreign and domestic capital.

Dominant models of economic growth have failed to provide for the majority, instead facilitating accumulation by the 'one percent' (Oxfam 2017). Inequality, social mobility and future prospects for the majority are worsening (ISSC et al. 2016). Forms of 'progressive neoliberalism' – peddled inaccurately as social democracy – have failed to stem disillusionment, disenfranchisement and marginalisation (Fraser 2017). Aiming for the poor to capture an equal share of future growth is not enough; reversing inequality requires a redistribution of wealth and income (ISSC et al. 2016). Austerity economics, imposed on the heels of capitalism's latest convulsions, has squeezed both the middle class and the working poor (Piketty 2014; Pollin 2013). As with earlier waves of austerity, some of the worst impacts of the withdrawal of public services and support have been felt in rural areas (Murphy and Scott 2014; Deere and Royce 2009). In the United States, for example, rural and urban 'sacrifice zones' have suffered interrelated waves of home foreclosures from the 2008 bursting of the mortgage derivatives bubble and rising drug addiction related to the physical and emotional pain resulting from lack of work, housing and adequate medical care (Lopez and Frostenson 2017; Economist 2017; Hedges 2014). These assaults, and the deep alienation that they bring, have wrought havoc and destroyed the social fabric in many rural communities.

For rural areas, the flow of people and finance to the cities, and the generation of poor, disenfranchised 'left-behind' populations who are elderly or children, is well documented, for example in China (Ye et al. 2016; Ye and Lu 2011), Mexico (Durand and Massey 2006) and the Philippines (Cortes 2015). Changing rural demographics and labour relations, including the aging of the farm population and the role of youth and migrants, have been affected by and in turn have affected the politics of the countryside. Young people in particular need a special place in our understanding of both current regressive political trends, and the possibilities for progressive change (Ansell 2016). Youth have been historically at the forefront of movements of progressive renewal, and of new ways of doing politics, challenging authority as the 'vanguard of change' (Herrera 2006, 1433). The new regimes that they have helped to install also then see them as a political vehicle that should no longer challenge, but legitimise and defend, the new order, and whose criticism is no longer welcome (Comaroff and Comaroff 2005; Ryter 2002). In many countries, state-sponsored youth organisations aim to 'tame' and channel youth aspirations in ways that suppress autonomous political mobilisation.

For example, the paramilitary National Rural Youth Service Corps in South Africa provides modest stipends to young people in rural areas, including those evicted or facing eviction (RSA 2017). The absence of strong, independent youth movements promoting young people's priorities and agendas has led frustrated and marginalised youth into apathy and demobilisation or into reactionary populist organisations, sometimes with a religious frame, such as Indonesia's *Pemuda Pancasila* and the Muslim Defenders' Front (Hasan 2016). In short, the contradictions between young people's expanding, digitalised global horizons and their shrinking material possibilities may propel them in different directions, including towards disengagement, reactionary and violent populism or towards movements of progressive renewal. As a political generation, youth are both 'makers and breakers' (Honwana and De Boeck 2005). The mobility and improved access to education of young rural men and women everywhere – again, not new, but now extending to all classes and sexes, and including mass migration to cities and also (and much less studied) return migration to rural places of origin – give them a key role in forging links between rural and urban political movements.

Unlike in the recent past, in many countries industrial economies do not provide the employment opportunities they once did. This has resulted in the 'fracturing' of classes of labour, who resort to diversified livelihood and survival strategies (Bernstein 2010). Such changes present particular challenges for women (Razavi 2002). Downward mobility, deepening poverty and insecurity, inequality and despair in rural areas are the result, as the agrarian and industrial transformation takes new forms, dominated by low-employment and mechanised business models (Monnat 2016). We need to explore the consequences of such rural transformations in diverse settings, asking, for example, how patterns of migration – including both an exodus of young people from rural areas and an in-migration of both short-term agricultural workers or herders and formerly urban elites – are affecting rural politics, across generations and classes.

The consequences for rural livelihoods, identity, self-esteem and recognition are profound. Forms of dislocation, prolonged and widespread neglect, challenges to identity and the undermining of rural communities and livelihoods have been documented widely, from the US (Duncan and Blackwell 2014; Hedges 2014; Berry 1977) to Thailand (Nishizaki 2014), Russia (Mamonova 2016) and Europe (Silverstone, Chrisafis, and Tait 2017). As Gaventa (1982) described for rural Appalachia, powerlessness emerges through the exertion of elite power, resulting often in 'quiescence' in the face of extreme inequality and injustice. Longstanding rural 'moral economies' (Scott 1977; Thompson 1971) erode, and older patterns of social cohesion weaken, influenced by wider shifts in political economy (Sayer 2000).

In the US, for example, deindustrialisation, a product of both automation and robotics and of companies moving abroad, famously hit rural areas hard, leading to the near disappearance of jobs that paid adequate wages. Moreover, small town Main Streets, historically populated with family-owned businesses that provided both off-farm income and employment for farm households and sites of human contact and thick social networks, withered as malls and big chain stores were located in nearby areas. More recently, the minimum-wage retail and service jobs that the malls provided began to vanish too with the rapid expansion of e-commerce (Lutz 2016). US households are frequently heavily indebted from college tuition, mortgages, medical expenses, credit card purchases and the automobiles that are essential transportation in most of the country (Kirk 2016). In this situation of precariousness and diminished income, even small unanticipated expenses – a medical emergency or an expensive repair to a car – can produce a desperate downward spiral into poverty and homelessness (Lutz 2014). Indeed, in recent years the rural US has seen a dramatic rise in midlife mortality among non-college educated non-Hispanic whites, with cancer and heart disease overtaken by the 'deaths of despair': drug overdoses, suicides and alcohol-related liver mortality (Case and Deaton 2017; Quiñones 2015).

At the same time, a global economy based on a voracious, unsustainable use of natural resources has devastated many rural areas. Almost half of the world's population makes a living from the land, and yet this resource base is being depleted through various forms of extractivism (Conde and Le Billon 2017; Veltmeyer and Petras 2014). Are there new discourses and practices of sustainability and environmental care emerging that are generative of a new politics and economy? Perspectives from political ecology, feminist political ecology or green Marxism, for example, can help us to think about the exercise of power and labour in the appropriation of resources, about the rise and discursive influence of metaphors of resilience, adaptation, transformation, sustainable development, ecosystem services and about the intimate co-construction of politics and ecology, where power always shapes access and control, as well as underlying sources of vulnerability (e.g. Scoones 2016; Perreault, Bridge, and McCarthy 2015; Harcourt and Nelson 2015; Watts and Peluso 2013). Through perspectives on critical governance and power, both in and beyond the state, we can ask how micro-politics of control and the 'power to exclude' influence access to and use of natural resources, such as land, forests, water and minerals (Beban, So, and Un 2017; Ribot 2014; Peluso and Lund 2011; Hall, Hirsch, and Li 2011; Swyngedouw 2009).

What is an emancipatory rural politics?

While the current conjuncture has given rise to forms of authoritarian populism, what alternative politics might emerge? An emancipatory politics requires an understanding of the current regressive trends – the things to be 'resisted' – and a vision of a better society and ways to move towards it. What then do we mean by emancipatory politics, and the struggles that these entail? We can potentially draw on many inspirations and traditions. In the following paragraphs we highlight some possibilities, with different conceptual starting points. There are inevitable tensions between these, and a singular, precise, *a priori* definition is impossible; instead, a range of approaches, each contextualised, each drawing on different perspectives, is necessary.

For those in the Marxist tradition, questions arise around the emergence of revolutionary moments, and the constellation of class-based alliances resisting particular forms of feudalism or capitalism. An 'epoch of social revolution' – or emancipation – thus emerges when social relations become unstable, as relations of production become less compatible with productive forces (Marx 1968 [1859], 161–62). Marxist scholars of agrarian change have identified diverse agrarian 'paths' (Bernstein 2010; Bernstein and Byres 2001), emerging from different contexts, including the role of and place for the rural in the midst of revolutionary upheavals. More narrowly, Marxists often view 'peasants' as an inherently vacillating political category, with potential for both revolutionary and reactionary politics. Much research on peasant politics during the past century drew from Marx's *Eighteenth Brumaire* and Engels' mid-1890s formulation of the peasant question, focused on how to win the votes of the peasantry (Hobsbawm 1973; Marx 1978 [1852]; Engels 1950). The question 'How do peasants become revolutionary?' was not just a question posed by Mao, but also a central debate in agrarian studies (Huizer 1975). Classic texts highlighted debates among radical scholars of agrarian politics,[2] as well as scholars with a neoclassical conception of peasant politics (e.g. Popkin 1979). Much orthodox Marxist scholarship has focused on class politics, informing debates about which peasants are most likely to be reactionary, as in Lenin's (1964) observation of late nineteenth-century Russia, and which have the greatest revolutionary promise, as in the contrasting 'rural proletarian' and 'middle peasant' perspectives of Paige (1978) and Wolf (1969), respectively.

Early agrarian Marxist scholarship examined the ways in which identity politics (linked to kinship, for example) intersected with class politics in peasant societies (Alavi 1973). Subsequent work has explored the range of peasant politics, from quiescence to everyday politics and all-out revolution, enquiring, for example, into how peasants struggle against neoliberal globalisation (Edelman 1999) or land grabbing (Hall et al. 2015). The links of contemporary agrarian politics to broader politics have been addressed in Brazil (Wolford 2016, 2010) and many other settings (e.g. Moyo, Jha, and Yeros 2013; Moyo and Yeros 2005). Then and now, relationships between peasants and the agrarian sector, revolutionary parties and the state are often critical to emancipatory political transformations (Vergara-Camus and Kay 2017; White 2016; Putzel 1995).

For those coming more from a libertarian socialist-anarchist tradition, such as Murray Bookchin, the fostering of autonomous, local, decentralised, participatory democracies, based on inspirations from 'social ecology', are the best route to emancipation (Biehl and Bookchin 1998; Bookchin 1982). Inspired by Bookchin, the jailed Kurdish leader Abdullah Öcalan has encouraged experiments in democratic confederalism in war-torn Rojava in northern Syria, based on libertarian municipalism and face-to-face assembly democracy (Biehl 2012). These innovative experiments offer insights into how emancipatory politics and economies can be organised, even under wartime conditions (Cemgil and Hoffmann 2016). They also raise questions about the role of violence in the struggle for

---

[2]For example: Brass (1991), Paige (1978), Scott (1977) and Wolf (1969).

emancipation, and the very real difficulties of organising a decentralised economy for more than survival (Üstündağ 2016).

For Ernesto Laclau, a broad notion of populism can unite diverse groups beyond conventional class formations by deploying shared meanings and symbols among otherwise fragmented sectors. Reclaiming populism, and its performative dimensions and 'dangerous logics', can thus be central to the creation of 'radical democracy' and the struggle against the normalisation of authoritarianism (Laclau 2005). This approach, adopted by political movements such as Podemos in Spain or Syriza in Greece, provides the basis for a new style of politics, which is necessarily antagonistic, unruly and dissenting. Such politics must, it is argued, challenge power in ways that are not limited by cosmopolitan idealism or simplistic appeals to community participation and deliberative democracy (Mouffe 2005, 1999; Butler, Laclau, and Žižek 2000).

Another radical position is offered by Jacques Rancière (1998), for whom true politics emerges through 'disagreement', through popular uprising, which disrupts the *status quo*, declaring an unruly 'radical equality'. This requires the reclaiming of the unheard voices and histories of the people, and accepting the radical, progressive role of the oppressed. Similarly, Alain Badiou (2016, 2005) explores the many ways 'the people' can be symbolically and practically deployed, and emphasises the radical, activist interruption of 'the event', where political subjects and emancipatory potentials emerge. Yet such subject-centred, activist perspectives on politics, with a narrow conception of 'democracy', offer little insight into how such change is sustained, and how it becomes embedded (Hewlett 2010).

Others, by contrast, emphasise the structural, institutional and political conditions for emancipatory transformations, and whether dictatorship or liberal forms of democracy result, as Moore (1966) argued half a century ago. Beginning in the 1980s there was a surge of studies on transitions from authoritarian-military regimes to 'democracy' (O'Donnell and Schmitter 2013), although many have questioned the assumption that authoritarian regimes always are moving in one direction (Levitsky and Way 2010). Fox, for example, analysed 'rural democratization', looking at Latin American and Philippine cases, arguing that 'the distribution of rural power in developing countries both shapes and is shaped by national politics' (Fox 1990: 1; see also Franco 2001 for the Philippines and Ntsebeza 2006 for South Africa). Emancipation may emerge through what Fox (2007) terms 'accountability politics', whereby, even in authoritarian settings, accountabilities are enhanced through the deepening of civil society engagements, acting to transform state structures and embedding accountabilities. While always uneven, partial and contested, and involving on-going cycles of action, such processes can build the possibilities of emancipation, but in relation to the institutional infrastructure of states and through a politics of representation (Ribot 2013).

For Polanyi (1944), the 'great transformation' of the twentieth century resulted from a mobilisation by diverse sectors of society, then supported by the state, to defend 'social protections' against 'disembedded' market capitalism. This 'double movement' was particularly pronounced in rural areas, where the commodification of land and life broke with traditional norms of land use and labour sharing (Li 2014; McMichael 2006). Today, faced with new kinds of authoritarian populism, rural–urban divides are increasingly framed in racial or ethnic terms. Thus, critical race studies – including studies of white, elite privilege (Pulido 2000) – as well as intersectional perspectives from cultural studies and critical feminism (Crenshaw 1991; Hall 1986), are all necessary to understand the present context, as well as the radical politics of emerging alternatives (Cairns 2013). At the same time, as state protections weaken and financialised, neoliberal capital assumes new forms, other movements – around, for example, women's rights, race or environmental justice – may combine, according to Fraser (2013), to generate a 'triple movement', centred on new forms of emancipatory politics (see also Ribot 2014).

In this view, a new emancipatory politics must therefore address many challenges together, rather than in piecemeal fashion. Deep inequalities, marginalisation and exclusion, persistent poverty, fractured identities and loss of esteem are all features of rural areas today, giving rise to a regressive politics. Following Fraser and Honneth (2003), a new politics therefore must combine concerns with redistribution (and so concerns with class, social difference and inequality), recognition (and so identity and identification) and representation (and so democracy, community, belonging and citizenship). Emancipation thus must encompass representation, linked to a strong state and active public sphere, as well as material distribution and recognition of diverse identities. Such a politics, Fraser argues, potentially offers new routes for and forms of mobilisation in the face of systematic marginalisation of those left behind by globalised capitalism. This must go substantially beyond the 'progressive neoliberalisms' that have unmistakably failed (Fraser 2017). Critiques of contemporary capitalism that promote a 'third way', 'inclusive growth' (Giddens 2001), and even measures of 'social protection', whether *Bolsa Família* in Brazil, social grants in South Africa, or employment-guarantee schemes in India, are insufficient (De Haan 2014). In Latin America, left-leaning governments failed to confront the power of agribusiness and dominant rural classes, and have systematically co-opted or disarticulated autonomous rural social movements, facilitating deepening differentiation and undermining resistance in the countryside (Vergara-Camus and Kay 2017). Instead, a more radical transformation needs to be imagined, rooted in mutualist, embedded forms of organisation of life and economy, ones that are simultaneously local and transnational, yet attuned to class difference and identity. Any alternatives must reclaim the 'public sphere' (Fraser 1990), reinventing citizenship, drawing on new forms of communalism and solidarity, and linking to a broad front of resistance.

In addition to exploring the contours of the 'emancipatory' through such perspectives, we also have to understand the elite, the reactionary and the non-emancipatory, and how regressive practice so often becomes hegemonic 'common sense'. We have to understand how this emerges through media representations, through the undermining of political voice and capabilities, through various forms of violence, and through the psychological appeal of authoritarian power. How was a vote for Trump or Brexit seen as a triumphant act of resistance? How do we understand the side-by-side pro- and anti-Dilma protests in Brazil or the simultaneous (and connected) rise of progressive rural movements and the entrenched politics of a minority agrarian elite (Sauer and Mészáros 2017)? The structures of oppression need to be revealed, in order to be resisted and overcome. We must ask: How are new alliances built between progressive urban and rural movements, within and outside mainstream political formations? How do informal, unruly styles of politics intersect with more formal organised movements and electoral and institutional politics? How have conflict and violence both closed down and opened up new spaces for politics?

The perspectives on emancipatory politics discussed above (along with many others) entail very different positions on core themes such as power, class, mobilisation, citizenship, institutions and democracy. By offering here a variety of perspectives, often in tension with each other, we want to encourage debate about emancipatory possibilities, and also about what is being resisted. There will never be a one-size-fits-all version of emancipatory rural politics, and locating our debate about alternatives in different contexts will hopefully generate a more nuanced and variegated view. Emancipatory politics must necessarily emerge in context, through longer histories of struggle that condition pathways of transformation. Analysing such politics requires tacking back and forth between broad theorisation and located, empirical enquiry. What we can do now is pose the questions, engage with wider theorisation and explore unfolding dynamics in particular places, both to understand the current conjuncture and to elaborate alternatives.

Resisting, organising and building alternatives

Where is resistance happening, against what, for what reasons and how? Rural and urban movements across the world are showing inspiring examples of resistance. The power of transnational coordination and organising was illustrated by the historic Women's March in Washington, DC, and around the world on 21 January 2017. People also struggle in small, often isolated ways, but how do they come to understand a particular situation and engage in collective action? How can an emancipatory politics emerge that is not just bottom-up, but also horizontal, connecting across class, gender, racial, generational and ideological divides and transcending geographic boundaries? What redistributed material base is required to generate the freedoms to engage with existing authority structures? And what democratic institutions can facilitate and enable such connections to emerge and become robust?

In different places and times, a new politics may emerge in distinct ways, combining 'everyday' with 'official' and 'advocacy' politics, frequently throwing up contradictions and new challenges (Kerkvliet 2009). For example, resistance to 'land grabs' and extractive industries has highlighted profound questions about what precisely is being defended and what constitutes a defence (Conde and Le Billon 2017; Hall et al. 2015). Confronting investments by global capital may be seen as progressive, yet defending existing informal and customary tenure can be exclusionary, patriarchal and in other ways oppressive (Ribot 2013; Ribot and Peluso 2003). In many rural areas, protagonists have struggled to unite around critiques of corporate takeovers of rural land and resources, but have also faced challenges in generating alternative visions. In exploring resistance and the promotion of alternatives, we must not assume emancipation, but interrogate its construction.

There has been increasing convergence of issues and problems, rural and urban, across sectors and across the Global South and North (Borras 2016). A broad conception of the land and agrarian question helps us link between social justice movements, whether agrarian, food sovereignty, environmental justice or climate justice movements (Claeys and Delgado Pugley 2017; Tramel 2016; Edelman and Borras 2016; Brent, Schiavoni, and Alonso-Fradejas 2015; Holt Giménez and Shattuck 2011). Alternatives are increasingly framed as inherently relational, multi-class and multi-sectoral, historical and global. Across the world, movements around environment/food/energy and sustainability/justice are building alternatives based on distributive networks and the collaborative commons. In exploring alternatives to authoritarian populism, we must ask: What experiments in rural solidarity economies are emerging that offer rural employment and new livelihoods, providing the base for a new politics?

For example, a recognition of the importance of local control and 'sovereignty' (of land, food, energy) underlies multiple critical initiatives, such as 'food sovereignty' (Schiavoni 2017; Alonso-Fradejas et al. 2015; Borras, Franco, and Monsalve 2015; Wittman, Desmarais, and Wiebe 2010; Patel 2009) and 'agroecology' or environmental justice (Martínez-Alier et al. 2016; Altieri and Toledo 2011; Rosset et al. 2011), with significant rural–urban/local–national (Robbins 2015) and urban dimensions (White 2011). Equally, some view the sharing, solidarity economy as allowing for the regeneration of livelihoods (Avelino et al. 2016; Utting 2015) and reclaiming the 'commons' as offering new forms of economic and political imagination (Bollier 2014). Others argue that new technologies allow for open-source innovation and the support of community-based grassroots initiatives (Smith et al. 2016; Kloppenburg 2014). New forms of community organisation are generating alternative ways of delivering energy, food, water and other services in rural settings (Smith and Seyfang 2013; Seyfang 2011). And perspectives on 'de-growth' and the indigenous Andean *buen vivir* or 'living well' are refashioning the ways in which we think of consumption, economy, nature and society (D'Alisa, Demaria, and Kallis 2014; Kallis 2011; Fatheuer 2011; Hamilton 2004).

These appear to be isolated cases, but do they together add up to a substantial new wave of innovation and political energy? Comparatively, across cases, we can ask: what alternatives are emerging based on collaborative commons, distributed networks, mutualism, reciprocity and moral economy, sovereignty and solidarity? And around what forms of production, service and provisioning in rural areas (such as agriculture, food, energy, water or housing services)? How are such alternatives being organised in rural areas, and by whom? What are the class, gender and identity politics involved? What relationships exist with the state and capital (and with which fractions of capital)? In surveying experiences comparatively, we must ask: what new forms of democratic organisation are emerging, with what political implications? How are rural movements connecting with each other locally, regionally and globally, and with other movements linked to urban areas?

When rethinking economies in a 'post-capitalist' age, some see non-hierarchical, distributed networks making use of open-source technology as offering potential for challenging the neoliberal order (Mason 2016). Beyond the hype, we need to ask what new forms of open science and technology might support decentralised, locally led alternatives; can, for example, information and communication technologies or blockchain registers open up space for democratic innovation? Or, as with other socio-technical transitions, can such spaces be closed down and captured with new forms of control? Whether in relation to small-scale agriculture in Africa or networked 'fab labs' in rural industrial clusters in Europe, linking new pathways of socio-technical change to social, cultural and political considerations is vital if new styles of innovation and democracy are to emerge (Smith and Stirling 2016; Scoones, Leach, and Newell 2015).

Many initiatives that challenge capitalist relations also improve livelihoods and enhance sustainability in rural spaces. In various guises, whether as community food or energy projects, or new approaches to building and settlement, they can be seen as part of diverse mobilisations against financialised capitalism's assault on rural landscapes and livelihoods. However, many such alternatives do not explicitly articulate a wider, emancipatory political vision, and sometimes their discourses and practices can be quite conservative, exclusionary and technocratic. A populist localism, framed in terms of 'community', for example, will remain isolated, perhaps the preserve of the relatively privileged and organised, or potentially captured by narrow, regressive forces if it does not confront basic questions of class, race, gender and identity that are at the heart of any emancipatory politics (Tsikata 2009). For example, in India the Natural Farming movement, centred on low-cost agroecological production, has been open to co-optation by regressive Hindu nationalists, who deploy cultural symbols and arguments about local sovereignty (Khadse et al. 2017). The radical potential of these local, rooted alternatives therefore may only be realised when they are connected to a wider debate about political transformation, in rural spaces and beyond. This in turn requires situating practical, grounded 'alternatives' in a broader historical, social and political context, where deepening, linking and scaling up become essential.

This means thinking about forms of mobilisation from above and below, and how they can connect, through both informal, unruly politics as well as more organised forms. It involves rethinking the politics of mobilisation, drawing on classic 'social movement theory' (Tilly and Tarrow 2006), as well as, for example, crowd psychology (Nye 1975) and life-cycle theory, and extending these to the challenges of 'big organising' in the digital age, connecting communities through lateral, voluntary organising, both inside and outside the state and transnationally (Bond and Exley 2016; Edelman and Borras 2016). Change needs to be understood less in terms of managed transitions, guided by policy and technocratic elites, and more in terms of unruly, relational, horizontal transformations and new forms of innovation and democratic practice (Smith and Stirling 2016; Stirling 2015).

There are plenty of experiments with alternatives – around long-term challenges, sectoral interests and society-wide visions – but they will be more profound and long-lasting if they are better understood and connected. We can take inspiration from existing spaces of resistance and galvanise new thinking about how, in rural spaces in the North and South, emancipatory alternatives are emerging to authoritarian populist politics. On-the-ground experiences of alternative practices and mobilisations that are transforming rural economies and creating new forms of democracy in practice can help us (re)theorise emancipatory politics for a new era. However, we must go beyond the documentation of multiple, particular cases to a wider synthesis that allows us to reimagine rural spaces and democracy, underpinned by an emancipatory politics.

A challenge for scholar-activists

Imagining a new politics in and linked to rural areas is an essential political and research task. Emancipatory politics has to be generated through styles of research that are open, inclusive and collaborative, although always informed by theory and disciplined by empirical data. A commitment to emancipatory research of the rural should be situated in a deep historical perspective and attentive to hinterlands, margins and frontiers. It should be interdisciplinary, comparative and integrative, articulate the local and the global, attend to class, gender and generational dynamics, and utilise multiple approaches and methods to corroborate findings and to highlight the many different meanings and perspectives at play.

What combinations of approaches and methods from critical social science can help us understand changing rural contexts and focus attention on critical conjunctures, diverse standpoints and patterns of everyday life, and point to important trends, meanings, relationships and processes? No single approach will do; each must engage in conversation with others, and respond to contextually defined questions. For example, ethnographies of elites and those excluded can be juxtaposed, exposing both the exceptional and the mundane, across different social groups and ages and between time periods (e.g. Moreira and Bruno 2015; Bobrow-Strain 2007). Sustained engagement in and across places is essential, generating 'deep histories' of change, ones that do not reify a mystical former golden age, but in which all possible paths are illuminated, as well as the decisions and detours taken (e.g. Quiñones 2015; Li 2014). Spatial perspectives, drawing on critical cartography, can help us understand how boundaries, landscapes and rural spaces are being recast, providing insights into the mapping of rural life and encouraging us to draw out new spatial relationships (e.g. Dwyer 2015). Visual methods – video, photography, art, performance or installation – may speak to how diverse actors perceive and understand rural settings (e.g. Kashi and Watts 2010). And, finally, wider understanding of patterns over time and across large populations may be enhanced by large-N surveys, both within and across sites and countries, as well as analyses of financial and demographic flows, voting preferences, and land and housing markets (e.g. Monnat 2016).

Such research and action have multiple implications in terms of timing and pace, research team-building and participation, publication format and outlets, and the requirement for widespread and accessible platforms for broader conversation around research processes and outputs. The Emancipatory Rural Politics Initiative (ERPI), in close collaboration with the Transnational Institute (TNI), will be coordinated by a network of scholar-activists/activist-scholars largely working in academic and independent research institutions, in both the Global North and the Global South. It brings to our analysis of and political action around the current conjuncture longstanding work with a rural perspective, most notably around 'land grabbing' through the Land Deals Politics Initiative.[3]

In this new initiative, we retain our focus on rural areas as sites of struggle and innovation, but of course recognise that rural and urban sites are connected. We aim for a global outlook, drawing lessons from everywhere, both North and South. We want to connect people and ideas, so that new conversations, collaborations and actions may arise. The challenge is to hear, to collect information, to turn analysis into a collective activity and to build bridges to other communities, and in so doing to construct a space where alternatives – in conception and practice – might be deepened and shared. We hope that we can help inspire more people to join in citizens' movements, community debates and local innovations and experiments, wherever these may be.

Acknowledgements

The authors would like to thank the two anonymous reviewers for helpful comments and suggestions. Any errors and omissions are our own.

Disclosure statement

No potential conflict of interest was reported by the authors.

References

ActionAid, Friends of the Earth, Inclusive Development International, and Rede Social de Justiça e Direitos Humanos. 2017. *Invested in exploitation? TIAA's links to land grabbing and deforestation*. Washington, DC: ActionAid USA.
Alavi, H. 1973. Peasant classes and primordial loyalties. *The Journal of Peasant Studies* 1, no. 1: 23–62.
Alonso-Fradejas, A., S.M. Borras Jr., T. Holmes, E. Holt-Giménez, and M. Robbins. 2015. Food sovereignty: Convergence and contradictions, conditions and challenges. *Third World Quarterly* 36, no. 3: 431–48.
Altieri, M.A., and V.M. Toledo. 2011. The agroecological revolution in Latin America: Rescuing nature, ensuring food sovereignty and empowering peasants. *The Journal of Peasant Studies* 38, no. 3: 587–612.
Ansell, N. 2016. Age and generation in the service of development? In *Generationing development: A relational approach to children, youth and development*, ed. R. Huijsmans, 315–330. London: Palgrave Macmillan.
Arendt, H. 1973 [1951]. *The origins of totalitarianism*. New York: Harcourt Brace Jovanovich.
Avelino, F., J. Grin, B. Pel, and S. Jhagroe. 2016. The politics of sustainability transitions. *Journal of Environmental Policy and Planning* 18, no. 5: 557–67.

---

[3]www.iss.nl/ldpi

Badiou, A. 2005. *Being and event*. London: Continuum.
Badiou, A. 2016. Twenty-four notes on the uses of the word "people". In *What is a people?*, eds. A. Badiou, P. Bourdieu, J. Butler, G. Didi-Huberman, S. Khiari, and J. Rancière, 21–31. New York: Columbia University Press.
Beban, A., S. So, and K. Un. 2017. From force to legitimation: Rethinking land grabs in Cambodia. *Development and Change* 48, no. 2: 590–612.
Berlet, C., and M. Lyons. 2000. *Right-wing populism in America: Too close for comfort*. New York: Guilford Press.
Bernstein, H. 2010. *Class dynamics of agrarian change*. Bloomfield, CT: Kumarian Press.
Bernstein, H., and T.J. Byres. 2001. From peasant studies to agrarian change. *Journal of Agrarian Change* 1, no. 1: 1–56.
Berry, W. 1977. *The unsettling of America: Culture and agriculture*. Washington, DC: Counterpoint.
Biehl, J. 2012. *Bookchin, Öcalan, and the dialectics of democracy*. Paper presented at Challenging Capitalist Modernity: Alternative Concepts and the Kurdish Question, February 3-5 2012, Hamburg.
Biehl, J., and M. Bookchin. 1998. *The politics of social ecology: Libertarian municipalism*. Montreal: Black Rose Books.
Bobrow-Strain, A. 2007. *Intimate enemies: Landowners, power and violence in Chiapas*. Durham, NC: Duke University Press.
Bollier, D. 2014. *Think like a commoner: A short introduction to the life of the commons*. Gabriola Island: New Society Publishers.
Bond, B., and Z. Exley. 2016. *Rules for revolutionaries: How big organizing can change everything*. White River Junction, VT: Chelsea Green.
Bookchin, M. 1982. *The ecology of freedom: The emergence and dissolution of hierarchy*. Palo Alto, CA: Cheshire Books.
Borras, S.M. 2016. *Land politics, agrarian movements and scholar-activism. Inaugural lecture*. The Hague: ISS.
Borras, S.M., J.C. Franco, and S. Monsalve. 2015. Land and food sovereignty. *Third World Quarterly* 36, no. 3: 600–17.
Borras Jr., S.M., R. Hall, I. Scoones, B. White, and W. Wolford. 2011. Towards a better understanding of global land grabbing: An editorial introduction. *The Journal of Peasant Studies* 38, no. 2: 209–16.
Brass, T. 1991. Moral economists, subalterns, new social movements, and the (re-) emergence of a (post-) modernized (middle) peasant. *The Journal of Peasant Studies* 18, no. 2: 173–205.
Brent, Z.W., C.M. Schiavoni, and A. Alonso-Fradejas. 2015. Contextualising food sovereignty: The politics of convergence among movements in the USA. *Third World Quarterly* 36, no. 3: 618–35.
Butler, J., E. Laclau, and S. Žižek. 2000. *Contingency, hegemony, universality: Contemporary dialogues on the left*. London: Verso.
Cairns, K. 2013. Youth, dirt, and the spatialization of subjectivity: An intersectional approach to white rural imaginaries. *The Canadian Journal of Sociology/Cahiers Canadiens de Sociologie* 38, no. 4: 623–46.
Case, A., and A. Deaton. 2017. *Mortality and morbidity in the 21st century*. Washington, DC: Brookings Institution. https://www.brookings.edu/wp-content/uploads/2017/03/case-deaton-postconference-april-10-2017-with-appendix-figs.pdf.
Cemgil, C., and C. Hoffmann. 2016. The 'Rojava revolution' in Syrian Kurdistan: A model of development for the Middle East? *IDS Bulletin* 47, no. 3: 53–76.
Claassens, A. 2011. The resurgence of tribal taxes in the context of recent traditional leadership laws in South Africa. *South African Journal on Human Rights* 27, no. 3: 522–45.
Claeys, P., and D. Delgado Pugley. forthcoming 2017. Peasant and indigenous transnational social movements engaging with climate justice. *Canadian Journal of Development Studies/Revue Canadienne D'Etudes du Développement* 1–16.
Clapp, J. 2014. Financialization, distance and global food politics. *The Journal of Peasant Studies* 41, no. 5: 797–814.
Comaroff, J., and J. Comaroff. 2005. Reflections on youth: From the past to the postcolony. In *Makers and breakers: Children and youth in postcolonial Africa*, eds. A. Honwana and F.de Boeck, 19–30. Oxford: James Currey.

Conde, M., and P. Le Billon. 2017. Why do some communities resist mining projects while others do not? *The Extractive Industries and Society*. http://linkinghub.elsevier.com/retrieve/pii/S2214790X17300035 (accessed May 30, 2017).
Cortes, P. 2015. The feminization of international migration and its effects on the children left behind: Evidence from the Philippines. *World Development* 65: 62–78.
Crankshaw, A. 2016. A food sovereignty critique of the G8 New Alliance on food security and nutrition. *MA thesis.*, University of the Witwatersrand.
Crenshaw, K.W. 1991. Mapping the margins: Intersectionality, identity politics and violence against women of color. *Stanford Law Review* 43: 1241–99.
D'Alisa, G., F. Demaria, and G. Kallis. 2014. *Degrowth: A vocabulary for a new era*. London: Routledge.
De Haan, A. 2014. The rise of social protection in development: progress, pitfalls and politics. *The European Journal of Development Research* 26, no. 3: 311–21.
Deere, C., and F. Royce. 2009. *Social movements in Latin America: Organizing for sustainable livelihoods*. Gainesville, FL: University of Florida Press.
Duncan, C.M., and A. Blackwell. 2014. *Worlds apart: Poverty and politics in rural America*. 2nd ed. New Haven: Yale University Press.
Durand, J., and D.S. Massey, eds. 2006. *Crossing the border: Research from the Mexican migration project*. New York: Russell Sage Foundation.
Dwyer, M. 2015. The formalization fix? Land titling, land concessions and the politics of spatial transparency in Cambodia. *The Journal of Peasant Studies* 42, no. 5: 903–28.
Economist. 2017. America's opioid epidemic is worsening. *The Economist*. http://www.economist.com/blogs/graphicdetail/2017/03/daily-chart-3 (accessed April 28, 2017).
Edelman, M. 1999. *Peasants against globalization: rural social movements in Costa Rica*. Stanford: Stanford University Press.
Edelman, M. 2003. Transnational peasant and farmer movements and networks. In *Global civil society 2003*, eds. M. Kaldor, H. Anheier, and M. Glasius, 185–200. London: Oxford University Press.
Edelman, M., and S.M. Borras Jr. 2016. *Political dynamics of transnational agrarian movements*. Halifax: Fernwood Publishing.
Edelman M., C. Oya, and S.M. Borras Jr. 2013. Global land grabs: historical processes, theoretical and methodological implications and current trajectories. *Third World Quarterly* 34, no. 9: 1517–31.
Engels, F. 1950 [1894]. The peasant question in France and Germany. In *Selected works, volume 2*, eds. K. Marx and F. Engels, 420–440. London: Lawrence and Wishart.
Fairbairn, M. 2014. 'Like gold with yield': Evolving intersections between farmland and finance. *The Journal of Peasant Studies* 41, no. 5: 777–95.
Fairhead, J., M. Leach, and I. Scoones. 2012. Green grabbing: A new appropriation of nature? *The Journal of Peasant Studies* 39, no. 2: 237–61.
Fatheuer, T. 2011. *Buen Vivir: A brief introduction to Latin America's new concepts for the good life and the rights of nature*. Berlin: Heinrich Böll Foundation, Publication Series on Ecology No. 17.
Fox, J., ed. 1990. The challenge of rural democratisation: Perspectives from Latin America and the Philippines. *Journal of Development Studies* (special issue) 26, no. 4: 79–96.
Fox, J. 2007. *Accountability politics: Power and voice in rural Mexico*. Oxford: Oxford University Press.
Franco, J.C. 2001. *Elections and democratization in the Philippines*. New York: Routledge.
Franco, J.C. 2016. *The right to land at crossroads in Myanmar*. Amsterdam: Transnational Institute. https://www.tni.org/en/article/the-right-to-land-at-crossroads-in-myanmar (accessed April 11, 2017).
Fraser, N. 1990. Rethinking the public sphere: A contribution to the critique of actually existing democracy. *Social Text* 25/26: 56–80.
Fraser, N. 2013. A triple movement? Parsing the politics of crisis after Polanyi. *New Left Review* 81: 119–32.
Fraser, N. 2017. The end of progressive neoliberalism. *Dissent* 64, no. 2: 130–4.
Fraser, N., and A. Honneth. 2003. *Redistribution or recognition? A political-philosophical exchange*. London: Verso.
Gaventa, J. 1982. *Power and powerlessness: Quiescence and rebellion in an Appalachian valley*. Chicago: University of Illinois Press.

Giddens, A., ed. 2001. *The global third way debate*. Cambridge: Polity Press.
Gudynas, E. 2009. Diez tesis urgentes sobre el nuevo extractivismo: Contextos y demandas bajo el progresismo sudamericano actual. In *Extractivismo, política y sociedad*, eds. J. Schuldt, A. Acosta, A. Barandiará, A. Bebbington, M. Folchi, A. Alayza, and E. Gudynas, 187–225. Quito: CAAP/CLAES.
Gusterson, H. 2017. From Brexit to Trump: Anthropology and the rise of nationalist populism. *American Ethnologist* 44, no. 2: 209–14.
Haiven, M. 2014. *Cultures of financialization: Fictitious capital in popular culture and everyday life*. Basingstoke: Palgrave Macmillan.
Hall, S. 1980. Popular-democratic versus authoritarian populism. In *Marxism and democracy*, ed. A. Hunt, 157–87. London: Laurence and Wishart.
Hall, S. 1985. Authoritarian populism: A reply to Jessop et al. *New Left Review* 151: 115–24.
Hall, S. 1986. Gramsci's relevance for the study of race and ethnicity. *Journal of Communication Inquiry* 10, no. 5: 4–27.
Hall, R., M. Edelman, S.M. Borras Jr, I. Scoones, B. White, and W. Wolford. 2015. Resistance, acquiescence or incorporation? An introduction to land grabbing and political reactions 'from below'. *The Journal of Peasant Studies* 42, no. 3-4: 467–88.
Hall, D., P. Hirsch, and T. Li. 2011. *Powers of exclusion: Land dilemmas in Southeast Asia*. Honolulu: University of Hawaii Press.
Hall, R., and T. Kepe. 2017. Elite capture and state neglect: New evidence on South Africa's land reform. *Review of African Political Economy* 44: 122–30.
Hall, R., I. Scoones, and D. Tsikata, eds. 2015a. *Africa's land rush: Rural livelihoods and agrarian change*. Oxford: James Currey.
Hamilton, C. 2004. *Growth fetish*. London: Pluto Press.
Harcourt, W., and I. Nelson, eds. 2015. *Practising feminist political ecologies: Moving beyond the 'green economy'*. London: Zed Books.
Hasan, N. 2016. Violent activism, Islamist ideology, and the conquest of public space among youth in Indonesia. In *Youth identities and social transformations in modern Indonesia*, ed. K. Robinson, 200–213. Leiden: Brill.
Hedges, C. 2014. *Days of destruction, days of revolt*. New York: Nation Books.
Herrera, L. 2006. What's new about youth? *Development and Change* 37: 1425–34.
Hewlett, N. 2010. *Badiou, Balibar, Rancière: Re-thinking emancipation*. London: Continuum.
Hobsbawm, E.J. 1973. Peasants and politics. *The Journal of Peasant Studies* 1, no. 1: 3–22.
Holt Giménez, E., and A. Shattuck. 2011. Food crises, food regimes and food movements: Rumblings of reform or tides of transformation? *The Journal of Peasant Studies* 38, no. 1: 109–44.
Honwana, A., and F. De Boeck 2005. *Makers and breakers: Children and youth in postcolonial Africa*. Oxford: James Currey.
Huizer, G. 1975. How peasants become revolutionaries: some cases from Latin America and Southeast Asia. *Development and Change* 6, no. 3: 27–56.
ISSC, IDS and UNESCO. 2016. *World social science report 2016. Challenging inequalities: Pathways to a just world*. Paris: UNESCO Publishing.
Kallis, G. 2011. In defence of degrowth. *Ecological Economics* 70, no. 5: 873–80.
Kashi, E., and M. Watts. 2010. *Curse of the black gold: 50 years of oil in the Niger Delta*. http://edkashi.com/project/curse-of-the-black-gold/ (accessed May 5, 2017).
Kerkvliet, B. 2009. Everyday politics in peasant societies (and ours). *The Journal of Peasant Studies* 36, no. 1: 227–43.
Khadse, A., P.M. Rosset, H. Morales, and B.G. Ferguson. 2017. Taking agroecology to scale: The zero budget natural farming peasant movement in Karnataka, India. *The Journal of Peasant Studies* 4: 1–28.
Kirk, C. 2016. Five charts that show Americans families' debt crisis. *Slate*. http://www.slate.com/articles/business/the_united_states_of_debt/2016/05/the_rise_of_household_debt_in_the_u_s_in_five_charts.html (accessed April 29, 2017).
Kloppenburg, J. 2014. Re-purposing the master's tools: The open source seed initiative and the struggle for seed sovereignty. *The Journal of Peasant Studies* 41, no. 6: 1225–46.
Laclau, E. 2005. *On populist reason*. London: Verso.
Lenin, V.I. 1964. *The development of capitalism in Russia*. 4th ed. Moscow: Progress Publishers.
Levitsky, S., and L. Way. 2010. *Competitive authoritarianism: Hybrid regimes after the Cold War*. New York: Cambridge University Press.

Li, T.M. 2010. To make live or let die? Rural dispossession and the protection of surplus populations. *Antipode* 41, no. 1: 66–93.

Li, T.M. 2014. *Land's end: Capitalist relations on an indigenous frontier*. Durham, NC: Duke University Press.

Lopez, G., and S. Frostenson. 2017. How the opioid epidemic became America's worst drug crisis ever, in 15 maps and charts. *Vox*. http://www.vox.com/science-and-health/2017/3/23/14987892/opioid-heroin-epidemic-charts (accessed April 28, 2017).

Lutz, C. 2014. The U.S. car colossus and the production of inequality. *American Ethnologist* 41, no. 2: 232–45.

Lutz, A. 2016. There's a terrifying mall 'blight' threatening communities across America. *Business Insider*. http://www.businessinsider.com/what-will-happen-when-malls-shut-down-in-america-2016-9 (accessed April 29, 2017).

Malamud, A. 2017. Qué cosa fuera la patria sin Correa. *Nueva Sociedad*. http://nuso.org/articulo/que-cosa-fuera-la-patria-sin-correa/ (accessed March 20, 2017).

Mamonova, N. 2016. Naive monarchism and rural resistance in contemporary Russia. *Rural Sociology* 81(3): 316–42.

Martínez-Alier, J., L. Temper, D. Del Bene, and A. Scheidel. 2016. Is there a global environmental justice movement? *The Journal of Peasant Studies* 43, no. 3: 731–55.

Marx, K. [1859]1968. Preface to a contribution to the critique of political economy. In *Selected works*, eds. K. Marx and F. Engels, 180–4. London: Lawrence and Wishart.

Marx, K. [1852]1978. The eighteenth brumaire of Louis Bonaparte. In *The Marx-Engels Reader*, ed. R.C. Tucker, 594–617, 2nd ed. New York: Norton.

Mason, P. 2016. *Postcapitalism: A guide to our future*. London: Macmillan.

McMichael, P. 2006. Peasant prospects in the neoliberal age. *New Political Economy* 11, no. 3: 407–18.

Mehta, L., G. Veldwisch, and J. Franco. 2012. Water grabbing? Focus on the (re)appropriation of finite water resources. *Water Alternatives* 5, no. 2: 193–207.

Monnat, S. 2016. Deaths of despair and support for Trump in the 2016 presidential election. The Pennsylvania State University Department of Agricultural Economics, Sociology, and Education Research Brief – 12/04/16, http://aese.psu.edu/directory/smm67/Election16.pdf (accessed May 30, 2017).

Moore, B. Jr. 1966. *Social origins of dictatorship and democracy: Lord and peasant in the making of the modern world*. Boston: Beacon Press.

Moreda, T.S. 2015. Listening to their silence? The political reaction of affected communities to large-scale land acquisitions: Insights from Ethiopia. *The Journal of Peasant Studies* 42, no. 3-4: 517–39.

Moreira, R.J., and R. Bruno, eds. 2015. *Dimensões rurais de políticas Brasileiras*. Rio de Janeiro: Mauad Editora Ltda.

Mouffe, C. 1999. Deliberative democracy or agonistic pluralism? *Social Research* 66, no. 3: 745–58.

Mouffe, C. 2005. *On the political*. London: Routledge.

Moyo, S., and P. Yeros. 2005. *Reclaiming the land: The resurgence of rural movements in Africa, Asia and Latin America*. London: Zed Books.

Moyo, S., P. Jha, and P. Yeros. 2013. The classical agrarian question: Myth, reality and relevance today. *Agrarian South: Journal of Political Economy* 2, no. 1: 93–119.

Murphy, E., and M. Scott. 2014. Household vulnerability in rural areas: Results of an index applied during a housing crash, economic crisis and under austerity conditions. *Geoforum* 51: 75–86.

Nishizaki, Y. 2014. Peasants and the redshirt movement in Thailand: Some dissenting voices. *The Journal of Peasant Studies* 41, no. 1: 1–28.

Ntsebeza, L. 2006. *Democracy compromised: Chiefs and the politics of the land in South Africa*. Leiden: Brill.

Nye, R.A. 1975. *The origins of crowd psychology: Gustave LeBon and the crisis of mass democracy in the third republic*. London: Sage.

O'Donnell, G., and P. Schmitter. 2013. *Transitions from authoritarian rule: Tentative conclusions about uncertain democracies*. Baltimore: JHU Press.

Paige, J.M. 1978. *Agrarian revolution*. New York: The Free Press.

Patel, R. 2009. Food sovereignty. *The Journal of Peasant Studies* 36, no. 3: 663–706.

Peluso, N.L., and C. Lund. 2011. New frontiers of land control: Introduction. *The Journal of Peasant Studies* 38, no. 4: 667–81.

Perreault, T., G. Bridge, and J. McCarthy, eds. 2015. *The Routledge handbook of political ecology*. Abingdon, UK: Routledge.
Picketty, T. 2014. *Capital in the 21st century*. Cambridge, MA: Harvard University Press.
Polanyi, K. 1944. *The great transformation: The political and economic origins of our time*. Boston, MA: Beacon Press.
Pollin, R. 2013. Austerity economics and the struggle for the soul of US capitalism. *Social Research* 80, no. 3: 749–80.
Popkin, S.L. 1979. *The rational peasant: The political economy of rural society in Vietnam*. Berkeley, CA: University of California Press.
Pulido, L. 2000. Rethinking environmental racism: White privilege and urban development in Southern California. *Annals of the Association of American Geographers* 90, no. 1: 12–40.
Putzel, J. 1995. Managing the 'main force': The communist party and the peasantry in the Philippines. *The Journal of Peasant Studies* 22, no. 4: 645–71.
Quiñones, S. 2015. *Dreamland: The true tale of America's opiate epidemic*. New York: Bloomsbury Press.
Rancière, J. 1998. *Disagreement. Politics and philosophy*. London: University of Minneapolis Press.
Rancière, J. 2013. The people are not a brutal and ignorant mass. *Verso Books blog*. http://www.versobooks.com/blogs/1226-the-people-are-not-a-brutal-and-ignorant-mass-jacques-ranciere-on-populism (accessed May 5, 2017).
Rancière, J. 2016. The populism that is not to be found. In *What is a people?*, ed. A. Badiou, 100–6. New York: Columbia University Press.
Razavi, S., ed. 2002. *Shifting burdens: Gender and agrarian change under neoliberalism*. West Hartford, CT: Kumarian Press.
Rede Social, GRAIN, Inter Pares, and Solidarity Sweden-Latin America. 2015. *Foreign pension funds and land grabbing in Brazil*. Barcelona: GRAIN.
Ribot, J. 2013. Choice, recognition and the democracy effects of decentralization. In *The imperative of good local governance: Challenges for the next decade of decentralization*, eds. J. Öjendal and A. Dellnäs, 93–120. Tokyo: UNU Press.
Ribot, J. 2014. Cause and response: vulnerability and climate in the Anthropocene. *The Journal of Peasant Studies* 41, no. 5: 667–705.
Ribot, J., and N.L. Peluso. 2003. A theory of access. *Rural Sociology* 68, no. 2: 153–81.
Robbins, M.J. 2015. Exploring the 'localisation' dimension of food sovereignty. *Third World Quarterly* 36, no. 3: 449–68.
Rosset, P., B. Machín Sosa, A. Roque Jaime, and D. Ávila Lozano. 2011. The Campesino-to-Campesino agroecology movement of ANAP in Cuba: Social process methodology in the construction of sustainable peasant agriculture and food sovereignty. *The Journal of Peasant Studies* 38, no. 1: 161–91.
RSA (Republic of South Africa). 2017. *National rural youth service programme*. Department of Rural Development and Land Reform. http://www.gov.za/about-government/government-programmes/national-rural-youth-service-corps-programme (accessed May 2, 2017).
Ryter, L. 2002. Youth, gangs and the state in Indonesia. PhD diss., University of Washington.
Sandbrook, R., M. Edelman, P. Heller, and J. Teichman. 2007. *Social democracy in the global periphery: Origins, challenges, prospects*. Cambridge: Cambridge University Press.
Sauer, S., and S. Leite. 2012. Agrarian structure, foreign investment in land, and land prices in Brazil. *The Journal of Peasant Studies* 39, no. 3-4: 873–98.
Sauer, S., and G. Mészáros. 2017. The political economy of land struggle in Brazil under Workers' Party governments. *Journal of Agrarian Change* 17, no. 2: 397–414.
Sayer, A. 2000. Moral economy and political economy. *Studies in Political Economy* 61, no. 1: 79–103.
Schiavoni, C.M. 2017. The contested terrain of food sovereignty construction: Toward a historical, relational and interactive approach. *The Journal of Peasant Studies* 44, no. 1: 1–32.
Scoones, I. 2016. The politics of sustainability and development. *Annual Review of Environment and Resources* 41: 293–319.
Scoones, I., M. Leach, and P. Newell, eds. 2015. *The politics of green transformations*. London: Routledge.
Scott, J.C. 1977. *The moral economy of the peasant: Rebellion and subsistence in Southeast Asia*. New Haven and London: Yale University Press.

Seyfang, G. 2011. *The new economics of sustainable consumption: Seeds of change*. Basingstoke: Palgrave Macmillan.
Silverstone, T., A. Chrisafis, and M. Tait. 2017. Marine Le Pen's Rise in 'forgotten France' – Video. https://www.theguardian.com/world/video/2017/apr/20/marine-le-pens-rise-in-forgotten-france-video-front-national-burgundy?CMP=Share_iOSApp_Other (accessed May 1, 2017).
Sinha, A. 2016. Why has "development" become a political issue in Indian politics? *Brown Journal of World Affairs* 23, no. 1: 189–203.
Smith, A., M. Fressoli, D. Abrol, E. Arond, and A. Ely. 2016. *Grassroots innovation movements*. London: Routledge.
Smith, A., and G. Seyfang. 2013. Constructing grassroots innovations for sustainability. *Global Environmental Change* 23, no. 5: 827–29.
Smith, A., and A. Stirling. 2016. *Grassroots innovations and democracy*. Brighton: STEPS Centre.
Stirling, A. 2015. From controlling 'the transition' to culturing plural radical progress. In *The politics of green transformations*, eds. I. Scoones, M. Leach, and P. Newell, 54–67. London: Routledge.
Svampa, M. 2015. Commodities consensus: Neo-extractivism and enclosure of the commons in Latin America. *South Atlantic Quarterly* 114, no. 1: 65–82.
Svampa, M. 2017. Populismos latinoamericanos en el fin del ciclo progresista. *Público GT*. http://publicogt.com/2017/04/16/populismos-latinoamericanos-en-el-fin-del-ciclo-progresista/ (accessed April 17, 2017).
Swyngedouw, E. 2009. The antinomies of the postpolitical city: In search of a democratic politics of environmental production. *International Journal of Urban and Regional Research* 33, no. 3: 601–20.
Thompson, E.P. 1971. The moral economy of the English crowd in the eighteenth century. *Past and Present* 50: 76–136.
Tilly, C., and S. Tarrow. 2006. *Contentious politics*. Oxford: Oxford University Press.
TNI (Transnational Institute). 2015. *Assessment of 6th draft of the National Land Use Policy (NLUP)*. Amsterdam: TNI. https://www.tni.org/en/publication/assessment-of-6th-draft-of-the-national-land-use-policy-nlup (accessed April 18, 2017).
Tramel, S. 2016. The road through Paris: Climate change, carbon, and the political dynamics of convergence. *Globalizations* 13, no. 6: 960–69.
Tsikata, D. 2009. Gender, land and labour relations and livelihoods in sub-Saharan Africa in the era of economic liberalisation: Towards a research agenda. *Feminist Africa* 12: 11–30.
Üstündağ, N. 2016. Self-Defense as a revolutionary practice in rojava, or how to unmake the state. *South Atlantic Quarterly* 115, no. 1: 197–210.
Utting, P., ed. 2015. *Social and solidarity economy: Beyond the fringe*. London: Zed Books.
Veltmeyer, H., and J. Petras. 2014. *The new extractivism: A post-neoliberal development model or imperialism of the 21st century?* London: Zed Books.
Vergara-Camus, L., and C. Kay. 2017. Agribusiness, peasants, left-wing governments, and the state in Latin America: An overview and theoretical reflections. *Journal of Agrarian Change* 17, no. 2: 239–57.
Watts, M., and N. Peluso. 2013. Resource violence. In *Critical environmental politics*, ed. C. Death, 184–198. London: Routledge.
White, M. 2011. Sisters of the soil: Urban gardening as resistance in Detroit. *Race/Ethnicity: Multidisciplinary Global Contexts* 5, no. 1: 13–28.
White, B. 2016. Remembering the Indonesian peasants' front and plantation workers' union (1945–1966). *The Journal of Peasant Studies* 43, no. 1: 1–16.
White, B., S.M. Borras Jr., R. Hall, I. Scoones, and W. Wolford. 2012. The new enclosures: Critical perspectives on corporate land deals. *The Journal of Peasant Studies* 39, no. 3-4: 619–47.
Wittman, H., A. Desmarais, and N. Wiebe. 2010. *Food sovereignty: Reconnecting food, nature and community*. Halifax: Fernwood.
Wolf, E.R. 1969. *Peasant wars of the twentieth century*. Oklahoma: University of Oklahoma Press.
Wolford, W. 2010. Participatory democracy by default: Land reform, social movements and the state in Brazil. *The Journal of Peasant Studies* 37, no. 1: 91–109.
Wolford, W. 2016. State-society dynamics in contemporary Brazilian land reform. *Latin American Perspectives* 43, no. 2: 77–95.
Wolford, W., S.M. Borras Jr., R. Hall, I. Scoones, and B. White. 2013. Governing global land deals: The role of the state in the rush for land. *Development and Change* 44, no. 2: 189–210.

Ye, J., and P. Lu. 2011. Differentiated childhoods: impacts of rural labor migration on left-behind children in China. *The Journal of Peasant Studies* 38, no. 2: 355–77.

Ye, J., C. He, J. Liu, W. Wang, and S. Chen. 2016. Left-behind elderly: shouldering a disproportionate share of production and reproduction in supporting China's industrial development. *The Journal of Peasant Studies*, 1–29. doi:10.1080/03066150.2016.1186651.

Counterrevolution, the countryside and the middle classes: lessons from five countries

Walden Bello

This contribution focuses on five societies that experienced successful counterrevolutions. It looks at how the dialectic of revolution and counterrevolution operated in Italy, Indonesia, Chile, Thailand and the Philippines. It seeks to understand the motion of different classes in periods of great political fluidity. It explores the dynamic relationship between conflict in the countryside and the overarching conflict of classes and their political representatives at the national level. Finally, it probes the relationship between domestic counterrevolution and global geopolitics.

Whether one calls them fascist, authoritarian populist or counterrevolutionary, there is no doubt that angry movements contemptuous of liberal democratic ideals and practices and espousing the use of force to resolve deep-seated social conflicts are on the rise globally. While in the North, the emergence of these forces and personalities portend to many a repeat of the 1930s, when classical fascism came to power in Italy and Germany, such counterrevolutionary developments have been recurrent phenomena in the global South over the last 50 years, where they have emerged in the course of severe class conflict and outright class war.

Much of the scholarship on counterrevolution in the North has, not surprisingly, focused on fascism, the last great counterrevolutionary movement to have successfully seized power in Europe. Some of the most insightful work has emerged in the comparative analysis of different fascist national experiences, most likely because comparative analysis calls attention to events, trends or processes that may otherwise not evoke appreciation in a work devoted solely to one national experience. Here, three authors deserve special mention: Barrington Moore, Arno Mayer and Nicos Poulantzas. Moore is associated with the idea of fascism being a wayward offspring of a 'revolution from above' undertaken by land-based elites seeking to retain their power in a society being transformed by capitalism (Moore 1966). Arno Mayer gave us a dynamic portrayal of a continent-wide counterrevolution wherein different projects clashed and complemented each other: that of 'reactionaries' seeking to restore a mythical past, 'conservatives' bent on maintaining the status quo, and 'counterrevolutionaries' who do battle with revolutionaries by adopting the latter's methods and end up with a repressive as opposed to a revolutionary transformation of society (Mayer 1971). Nicos Poulantzas provided the memorable portrait of a fascist elite that stabilizes and saves monopoly capital by creating, ironically, a state of exception that enjoys the highest degree of relative autonomy from monopoly capitalist interests (Poulantzas 1974). The three differ in some of their propositions and conclusions, but central to their methodology is the dialectic of revolution and counterrevolution in societies underdoing a rapid transition to capitalism.

There is no dearth of studies of political change in societies in the global South. However, many of them do not place the dialectic of revolution and counterrevolution at the center of their analysis. The most common paradigms have been those underpinned by modernization theory or political development theory. Moreover, there has been little comparative work on counterrevolutions. One of the few exceptions is Naomi Klein's magisterial analysis of the application of the neoliberal project in different societies (Klein 2007). However, Klein's case studies mostly begin after the dialectic of revolution and counterrevolution has been politically resolved in favor of the latter. Our interest is the analysis of the prior period, to see how and why the counterrevolution manages to get the upper hand and crushes the left politically.

The aim of this study is to look at how the dialectic of revolution and counterrevolution operated in five societies. It seeks to understand the movement of different classes in periods of great political fluidity. It explores the dynamic relationship between conflict in the countryside and the overarching conflict of classes and their political representatives at the national level. Finally, it probes the relationship between domestic counterrevolution and global geopolitics.

Four of the national experiences included here are from the global South: Indonesia, Chile, Thailand and the Philippines. The first three provide, in the author's view, the most fertile ground for the analysis of different facets of counterrevolution in the South. The Philippines has been included owing to Philippine President Rodrigo Duterte being widely seen as emblematic of the 'New Authoritarianism'. The one case from the North in our sample is Fascist Italy, and this is for two reasons: first, it provides an interesting case study of one of the major concerns of this study: the relationship between class conflict in the countryside and the national counterrevolution in the emergence of fascism; and, second, the period covered in our study, the first two decades of the twentieth century, saw Italy undergoing many of the same crises brought about by capitalist transformation that were later experienced by societies in the global South in the post-World War II period.

Our aim is not to develop a general theory of counterrevolution but to contribute toward the emergence of such a theory through a detailed comparison of five counterrevolutionary experiences that seeks to draw out the empirical convergences and divergences among these experiences, on the basis of which further theoretical work can be done.

Fascism in Italy: the decisive role of the countryside

In the class analysis of fascism in Italy, what is most often emphasized is the phenomenon of Mussolini's shock troops from the middle class serving the interests of Big Capital by crushing the working-class movement in the cities.[1] On their road to power, the fascists certainly received financial support from the big bourgeoisie, and while in power, they created the conditions for the stable reproduction of Monopoly Capital. What is less well known is the role of landed interests in promoting fascism. Fascism, Mussolini famously thought, would never succeed in the countryside. Yet it was the countryside that provided the momentum that eventually ended in the momentous March on Rome in October 1922.

---

[1] There have been many studies of fascism in Italy but few have proved as enlightening as Tasca's (1938) *The Rise of Italian Fascism*. Other important works on fascism's conquest of the countryside in Italy are Ebner (2011); Lyttleton (1982); Snowden (2004); Cardoza (1982); and Corner (1972).

Indeed, one academic authority on Italian fascism claims that 'it was the sudden expansion of rural-based fascism that in the winter of 1920–21 saved [Mussolini's] urban *fasci* from extinction' (Cardoza 1982, 3).

Fascism's mass base

Class conflict in the countryside was one of the key ingredients of fascist success. Another was the middle class.

In an Italy that shouldered tremendous costs from its participation in the First World War, there was a volatile combination of deep economic crisis, widespread worker unrest bursting out in general strikes and factory occupations, and anger and resentment among veterans returning from an unpopular war. Mussolini, who had been expelled by the Socialist Party, fished in these troubled waters, exploiting workers' discontent in competition with the Socialists, stirring up nationalist fervor in competition with the Nationalists, and making overtures to Big Capital, whose resources he coveted to expand his movement. The foot soldiers of his fledgling movement were mainly from the *déclassé* middle class. Mussolini, writes Angelo Tasca in his classic *The rise of Italian fascism*,

> appealed to the inherent anarchy of the Italian people and of the middle class in particular: disgruntled ex-officers, students fidgeting in University lecture rooms, shopkeepers struggling against taxation, declasses of every sort who wanted something new, helped to give to growing fascism its invaluable halo of lawlessness and heresy. (Tasca 1938, 32)

With old beliefs and ideas having been discredited by the war, fascism's emphasis on action struck a chord among these unstable, rootless and resentful elements, especially among the young. The psychology of fascism was subjected to insightful dissection by Tasca:

> Emphasis was laid on 'action' rather than ideas. This attracted many of the young advancing 'toward life', impatient of contradictions and eager to have a good time, to sacrifice themselves, to acquire self-confidence. Fascism drove them along the easiest way. Everything was simplified, for thoughts had no time to form themselves, connect, or conflict before they evaporated in action, exalting and melodramatic. The inner life reduced itself to the simplest reflexes, shifting from the centre of feeling and becoming externalized. Doubts and uncertainties ceased to exist. The youthful fascist in a world full of contradictions joyfully affirmed, 'I must not think; therefore I am'. (1938, 36)

One of Mussolini's chief assets was his ability to satisfy 'both the vague passions of the mob and the more precise interests of the capitalist class'. (Tasca 1938, 33). This convergence of passion and interest emerged dramatically in key areas of rural Italy, where the network of labor organizations had managed to impose strong collective discipline among agricultural laborers, enabling them to control the supply of labor and push up wages. Accompanying this control over the supply of labor by the peasant leagues were the control over prices by production cooperatives in the towns and the Socialist Party's dominant position in many local governments and parliamentary politics. These institutions were created by pressure from below within a weak bourgeois state that served as the framework of a country that had been unified politically barely 50 years before. It was these products of reform socialism that the rural elites most dreaded:

> 'The man we fear most', as a great landowner of the province of Ravenna said, 'is not the communist Bombacci but Nullo Baldini who, with his Cooperative Federation is cutting us out everywhere'. For this reason also, fascist violence was directed at such institutions set up by

reformist socialism. These institutions were spreading, and little by little were monopolizing the entire economic and political life of the district. The landed ruling classes felt they were being swept away to make room for the new social structure. (Tasca 1938, 95)

The shift in the balance of economic power was accompanied by a loss of status, and this triggered an 'outburst of accumulated hate and violence' in the classes that felt they were being displaced. Unable to use the institutions of a weak state to break the power of the unions, the landlords and agricultural capitalists found in the fascist bands the instruments that they so badly needed to restore the status quo ante. Fascism's first recruits in the countryside came from the groups that, like the landed elites, felt disadvantaged by the growing power of the peasant leagues, production cooperatives that controlled the prices of goods, and the Socialist Party's control of local governments and parliamentary politics. These were the youth of the landowning classes, university students, tradespeople and demobilized soldiers. But there were also, Barrington Moore reminds us, 'peasants who had climbed into the ranks of landowners, and even tenants who hated the monopolistic practices of the union' (Moore 2004, 268).

Capital in search of muscle

The deadly meeting of landowners needing muscle and middle-class youth seeking mindless action took place in one of the country's breadbaskets, the Po Valley, and in the province of Bologna, in 1920 and 1921. These were the most dynamic areas of Italian agriculture, mainly because of the spread of capital-intensive capitalist agriculture. Rapid economic transformation in the first few decades of the twentieth century had also provided an opportunity for organizing rural labor and poor farmers by the peasant leagues. While the more traditional landowners continued to deal with their workers and tenants with paternalistic methods, the younger commercial farmers favored 'disciplined corporate organization' (Cardoza 1982, 9). Recurrent recession and worker unrest, writes Anthony Cardoza,

> led these growers to adopt a strategy of intransigent resistance to the socialist leagues, and drew them toward coercive solutions to the problems of production, labor contracts, and interest representation on the eve of World War I. At the same time, employer militancy resulted in serious friction between agrarian interest groups and Italy's liberal political class. Mounting frustration with the difficulties of expressing their economic interests or hostility to the advance of the left within the fragmented Italian parliamentary system predisposed commercial farms in Bologna and the Po Valley toward more authoritarian movements: nationalism before 1914, fascism after the war. (1982, 9–10)

In the Po Valley and Bologna, the struggle between the landowners – in particular, the capitalist farmers–and the peasant leagues 'gave fascism an opportunity to fish in troubled waters' (Cardoza 1982, 9). Financed by the landlords and commercial capitalists, the fascist *squadristi* used force to break up the peasant leagues and other institutions of rural socialism. A good description of the 'expeditions' that sowed fear in the countryside is provided by Tasca:

> [A]n expedition would usually set out into the country from some urban centre. With arms provided by the Agrarian Association or by some regimental store, the blackshirts would ride to their destination in lorries. When they arrived they began by beating up any passerby who did not take off his hat to the colors or who was wearing a red tie, handkerchief, or shirt. If anyone protested or tried to defend himself, if a fascist was roughly treated or wounded, the punishment was intensified. They would rush to the buildings of the Chamber of Labor, the Syndicate, or the Co-operative, or to the People's House, break down the doors, hurl out the furniture, books,

or stores into the street, pour petrol on them, and in a few moments there would be a blaze. Anyone found on the premises would be severely beaten or killed, and the flags were burnt or carried off as trophies. (Tasca 1938, 103)

The fascists carried out their acts with impunity, with police and soldiers assisting them or turning a blind eye to their deeds. These agents of the state, used to safeguarding the old class hierarchy, were themselves disconcerted by the challenge posed by the subordinate classes. The fascists' peasant victims, on the other hand, were psychologically disarmed by the knowledge that if they used their pistols, they would be putting themselves outside the law and, unlike the fascists, they could expect no mercy from the police and the judges.

From the Po Valley and Bologna, the punitive expeditions were imported by fascists in Ravenna, Reggio Emilia, Julian Venetia and other regions. As fascism penetrated smaller rural communities, it became 'a mass movement without precedent in Italian history' (Ebner 2017). Force made a big difference. Provinces and districts where the networks of people's organizations had achieved hegemony after years of struggle fell in a matter of days or weeks to the fascist hordes. Tactics perfected in these punitive rural expeditions were then copied in the big urban centers to disrupt workers' strikes, destroy the unions, and overpower strongholds of the Socialist Party and its rising rival, the Communist Party. By the end of 1922, in less than two years of squad violence, Fascists or pro-Fascists controlled virtually every communal administration in Italy (2017). For the landed classes that had seen their world turned upside down in the period leading up to the so-called *biennio rosso* ('two red years'), between 1918 and 1920, when Socialists made huge electoral gains nationally and the peasant leagues and other institutions of reform socialism achieved prominence locally, the nineteenth-century order of economic, political and cultural power was restored, at the cost of much spilled blood.

While the destruction of socialist institutions and 'pacification' of working class communities was rapidly achieved, the violence continued unabated. As Michael Ebner writes,

Only by perpetuating this 'revolutionary' situation could the Fascist movement undermine the liberal state and continue its push for political power … . The power of the Ras and the bonds of squadrist camaraderie depended on Fascists sustaining a state of lawlessness and initiating new attacks. Illegal activities increased feelings of belonging and emotional interdependence among squadrists, making it more difficult for individual Blackshirts to pull out of the squads or refrain from violent acts. Any retreat, any return to normalcy, would have required dealing with potentially serious legal and psychological consequences. Violence thus became cyclical and self-sustaining. (2017)

The triumph of the counterrevolution in the Italian countryside was complete long before the fascists marched on Rome in October 1922. After its ascent to power, leaders of fascism conveyed the idea that they were 'ruralizing Italy', romanticizing the Italian peasant as the successor of the ancient Roman farmer–soldier, with Benito Mussolini as the country's 'First Farmer'. This was, as Moore notes, pure nonsense. The number of owner operators dropped by 500,000 between 1921 and 1931, while the number of share tenants rose by 400,000 (Moore 2004, 268). Fascism was propelled to power by the muscle of the rural and urban middle classes. In power it protected the interests of agrarian capital and the landed elite, even as its main service was to sweep away working-class institutions that stood in the way of the economic hegemony of Monopoly Capital.

Conclusion

A number of points might be made in conclusion.

First, the counterrevolution in Italy conquered the countryside before it was triumphant in the big urban centers.

Second, the muscle or mass base of the fascist movement was the middle strata of the towns and surrounding countryside – professionals, tradespeople, students, rich peasants, demobilized soldiers, government personnel – who were mobilized and financed by big landed interests.

Third, the propertied classes as a whole benefited from fascist violence, but it was commercial agricultural interests that played the central role in recruiting the fascists to destroy the peasant leagues and the Socialist Party, and it was they who mainly benefited.

Fourth, the fascist reaction was a response not to an insurgent, armed revolutionary movement but to the gains of reform socialism – the peasant leagues, production cooperatives, and local governments controlled by socialists – that had been achieved relatively peacefully within the bourgeois state and posed the threat of gradual political asphyxiation of the landed classes.

Fifth, while the fascist breakup of the unions and workers' institutions was carried out largely by paramilitary force, the repressive institutions of the state often lent active or passive support, or turned a blind eye to the acts of the *squadristi*.

Indonesia: rural bloodshed and national counterrevolution

The events in Indonesia in 1965–1966 have gone down as one of the most horrifying cases of counterrevolution in the last half-century. Indeed, it was counterrevolution that turned into what Daniel Goldhagen has termed 'eliminationism' (Goldhagen 2009). There continues to be great uncertainty about how many perished in this social pogrom, but the lower end of estimates is usually 500,000 and the upper end is two million. There is, in fact, greater consensus on the number of Jews murdered during the Holocaust – some six million – than on the estimate of the number killed in the Indonesian bloodbath.

The countryside and the national revolution

The countryside was the site of much of the counterrevolution – not surprising since at the time that the massacres took place, over 80 percent of the population resided in rural areas. The counterrevolution cannot, however, be understood simply as a response to rising demands for a better social deal from the peasantry and rural workers. Organizing in the countryside for higher wages among rural workers and for land reform for peasants was closely tied to a process of national mobilization for comprehensive social change led mainly by the Communist Party of Indonesia (PKI). For Max Lane, the mobilization of the left must be seen as the continuation of a national process that began with Indonesia's fight for independence from Dutch rule but had not yet been completed. Having been uneasy allies in the struggle against the Dutch, two social and political blocs competed for the direction of the newly independent country in the 1950s and early 1960s, one led by the charismatic nationalist Soekarno, the other a more conservative alliance whose mainstay was the military. What transpired, says Lane, was an 'ideological civil war over the fate of the nation':

> Just as in other great civil wars involved in the creation of nations, the two sides in this war were anchored to basic class interests. Political mobilization was more and more propelled by the energies of the proletariat and the peasantry mobilizing behind demands that they saw as reflecting their interests and behind a leadership embodied in the alliance between President Soekarno and the Indonesian Communist Party (PKI). This was reflected in the

membership of the PKI and the other main Soekarnoist organization, the Indonesian National Party (PNI), in the years before 1965. By 1965, the PKI and its mass organizations were claiming a membership of 25 million. The PNI also had several million members. This 25 million represents a massive proportion of the adult population; it was more than half of the 37 million voting population of just ten years before and was probably more than half of the 55 million voting population recorded in 1973. (Lane 2008, 30)

On the other side was 'an increasingly politically isolated alliance of parties representing the interests of landowning and business groups, and under the leadership of elements that were strong within the state apparatus, particularly the army' (Lane 2008, 33). Largely in support of these forces were the urban middle classes which 'formed a tiny and fragile social layer, squeezed economically by the hyperinflation of the final years of Soekarno's rule and threatened politically by the rising tide of communism' (Aspinall 2005, 12). As the Soekarno–PKI alliance gained ascendancy, this bloc felt increasingly threatened, but its members were not subjected to violence, arrest or arbitrary purge. The PKI had, for one, become committed to achieving power peacefully, through electoral means. 'The real terror', writes Lane, 'was that of being marginalized by opposing ideas actively supported among the population', (Lane 2008) among which were the nationalization of foreign business, land reform, worker participation in management, and cooperation with socialist states and the emerging Non-Aligned Movement.

It was within this larger national context that the struggle for land took place. The PKI front groups were in the forefront of the agrarian struggles. In North Sumatra, SARBUPRI, the union of plantation workers, launched successful campaigns, including many strikes, aimed at maintaining the living standards of plantation workers, by pushing management to include or retain in-kind provision of basic commodities like rice, cooking oil, cloth and sugar, as part of the pay package. Plantation owners tried to weaken the workers' organization by bringing in labor from elsewhere. The situation for the workers became more difficult, however, when the government nationalized the plantations in the late 1950s and early 1960s. They came into conflict with Indonesian managers, many of whom were administrators from the military, who sought to curb their militancy (White 2016).

Meanwhile, the Indonesia Peasants Union (BTI) provided the leadership for peasants pushing agrarian reform in Java, Bali and other heavily tenanted agricultural areas. Pressure from below resulted in the passage of agrarian reform legislation which regulated the conditions of share tenancy, limited the permissible size of landholdings and prohibited absentee ownership. Although the BTI and the PKI did not endorse the legislation, they later campaigned for its implementation. Landlord resistance pushed the BTI and PKI to support some forcible land seizures (*aksi sepihak*), and these actions or fear of their taking place made enemies among the landed rural elites and provoked violent responses. Caught off guard by these violent clashes with anti-land reform groups, the PKI, Ben White notes, 'urged an easing-off of *aksi sepihak*, and in late 1964 it looked as if some measure of calm was returning in the countryside' (2016).

The PKI and the electoral road

The PKI's decision to opt for taking power through electoral means was a key reason for its restraint in the struggle for land reform. Winning elections meant moderating the party's class-based politics. As Benedict Anderson observed,

> The Communists ... had discovered quite quickly that in vast, backward, heavily illiterate rural Indonesia, where the bulk of the voters resided, the most efficient way to do well electorally

was to attract to its ranks village headmen and other local notables. Once attached, these people could be counted on to bring in their villagers' votes, without the Party itself having to make substantial and expensive efforts lower down .... But since village headmen typically owned or controlled the most land in the villages, recruiting them required electoral programmes which did not threaten their interests. Furthermore, the Party's success in these elections, and the provincial elections in Java that followed in 1957, began to give Party members a personal stake in electoral offices at all levels. (Anderson 1998, 280–81)

Ironically, the party's success at the ballot box proved to be very alarming to its competitors, especially the army. Had it pursued an extra-parliamentary route to power, it would have been easier to discredit it as a legitimate force.

If the struggle for land in the countryside was greatly conditioned by national politics, so was the latter impacted on by international politics, in particular the Cold War. The United States saw Indonesia, the biggest country in Southeast Asia, as an extremely strategic asset. With the situation in Vietnam going from bad to worse for the US-supported regime there, Washington saw Indonesia as another 'domino' that was in great danger of falling to the Communists, thus upending the geopolitical balance in Southeast Asia.[2] The electoral capabilities of the PKI also worried Washington, who feared that a successful 'parliamentary road' to communist rule in Indonesia would encourage similar attempts not only in Southeast Asia but in other parts of the world.

Counterrevolution from above

When Colonel Untung and pro-Sukarno officers launched their coup on September 30, 1965, the political situation in Indonesia could be said to be 'overdetermined'. The aim of the officers was apparently to purge the high command of the right wing, then provoke mass mobilizations throughout the country for the elimination of the right wing from the officer corps as a whole (Lane 2008, 42). It is not clear whether the coup plotters intended to murder the six generals of the army that they were able to apprehend. What is certain is that their murder provided the right-wing officers with the opportunity to lance the boil of national politics, as it were, by blaming the PKI, which research has shown to have had little, if anything, to do with the coup.[3] Central to the narrative of General Suharto and the military high command were lurid, fabricated tales of women belonging to Gerwani, the women's organization affiliated to the PKI, dancing naked around the bodies of the dead generals and participating in their castration. These stories, says Saskia Wierenga, 'struck chords with the people's fear of the uncontrolled sexual powers of women, a religiously inspired apprehension that women's disobedience would endanger the entire social system, Hindu notions of all-female maniacal crowds and a male horror of castration' (Wierenga 2001).

In contrast to Italy, where the security agencies and the bureaucracy let the fascists take the leadership in wiping out the opposition, the army took the leadership in the 1965–1966 massacres in Indonesia. Most accounts agree that this was a veritable case of counterrevolution from above.

Also in Indonesia, the killing of communists was indiscriminate, targeting not only party leaders but the base, down to people whose only 'crime' was probably to vote communist. As one observer who escaped execution recounted:

---

[2] See John Roosa (2006)'s excellent study, esp. 13–16.
[3] The only one in the party leadership in touch with the coup plotters was apparently the head of the party, D.N. Aidit, who shared only vague details with the rest of the party leadership. See Wierenga's (2001) insightful essay; see also Roosa (2006).

Another was also thrown in, also headless. I couldn't count how many headless corpses passed by me. Then I heard a shout from a voice I recognized and froze; it was Pak Mataim, our bicycle repairman who I think was illiterate. He seemed very thin, and he too was dragged along like a banana stalk. He moaned, begging for mercy, for his life to be spared. They laughed, mocking him. He was terrified. The rope around his feet was taken off, leaving his hands still tied. He cried and because he couldn't keep quiet, they plugged up his mouth with a clump of earth … Rejo went into action, and like lightning, his machete cut through the neck of his victim, the one-eyed, powerless, bicycle repairman. His head went into the sack. (quoted in Goldhagen 2009, 177)

In contrast, in Italy, as Ebner notes, fascist violence was 'face-to-face violence and murder, rather than mass anonymous killing. In essence, although they could be exceeding[ly] brutal, Fascist squads practiced a selective, calibrated, and choreographed economy of violence' (Ebner 2017).

One reason for this difference in the two situations could be that in Italy the threat of the socialists taking power was not seen as an immediate one, while in Indonesia the military and its allies had convinced themselves that the communist takeover of power, as shown by the failed coup, was just around the corner, and could be thwarted only by a root-and-branch destruction of the PKI mass base instead of just its national and local leaders.

The military's leading role in the massacres and the active support to the massacre given by the landed elites have been stressed by progressive writers. But class position can only go so far in terms of explaining who was killed and who participated in the killings. The identification of executioners and victims was refracted through the prism of politics and culture. Village leaders or wealthy landlords who were identified as communist leaders could not be saved by their objective class position. At the same time, the killers included ordinary peasants, the village middle sectors, and Muslim activists from all classes who considered the PKI activists 'godless'. As Goldhagen points out, once the military decided

upon this eliminationist solution to the electorally ascendant Communist Party's political and social challenge, they easily mobilized anti-communist supporters across Indonesia, many being deeply religious, usually Islamic, or religious parties' and orders' followers, who butchered the atheistic communists among them, usually with bayonets or machetes, often leaving their bodies in rivers or caves, a potent warning to other would-be communists. (Goldhagen 2009, 355)

Indeed, throughout Bali, according to one account, 'whole villages, including children, took part in an island-wide witch-hunt for Communists, who were slashed and clubbed to death by communal consent' (John Hughes, quoted in Goldhagen 2009, 384). Hindu Balinese were encouraged to see 'the killing of people associated with the PKI as the fulfillment of a religious obligation to purify the land' (Robinson 1995, 300, quoted in Wierenga, *loc. cit.*). This phenomenon of whole villages hunting down and killing communists was also seen in East Java.[4] The ideologically motivated Islamic militias needed little encouragement from the military. As one likely participant in the massacres confessed, 'even though such events were pretty horrifying, the participants themselves felt thankful to have been given the chance to join in destroying infidels' (quoted in Goldhagen 2009, 193).

---

[4]This was the case, for instance, in the village of Pranggang in the district of Kediri in East Java. In the small Kediri district alone, 'around 10,000 people considered to be communists were killed' (Nurchayati 2017, 342).

The ideological counterrevolution continued long after the PKI was physically destroyed. Throughout Suharto's rule the PKI was associated with these two words: *penghianat* ('traitor') and *biadab* ('savage') (Wierenga, *loc cit.*). The PKI was thus excluded from the nation and even from humanity as such. Indeed, under Suharto, 'anti-communism became the state religion, complete with sacred rites, rituals, and dates', with the site of the killing of the generals turned into hallowed ground (Roosa 2006, 7–8).

If the military could count on enthusiastic Islamic militias like the Nahdatul Ulama to carry out the bloody purges in rural areas, it could also count on the support of foreign governments that had an interest in stemming the so-called Red Tide in Southeast Asia. The Central Intelligence Agency (CIA) was reported to have given the Indonesian army leadership a list of 5000 top PKI functionaries to be arrested or killed. The CIA, along with other Western intelligence agencies, also provided substantial funding and weaponry for the army after it was purged of left-leaning officers following the events of September 1965 (Cherian 2016). External support was not, however, central to the right's winning the domestic civil war.

Conclusion

In conclusion, the following features of the 1965–1966 counterrevolution in Indonesia might be emphasized.

First, the counterrevolution in the countryside must be seen within the larger context of conflict between two well-organized, bitterly opposed forces with differing visions and programs for the completion of the national revolution of Indonesia, the PKI–Soekarno alliance and the military-led social/political coalition. Though struggles over land were taking place all over the country, local dynamics were shaped much more by the broader conflict at the national level in Indonesia compared to Italy.

Second, the threat to which the right reacted with such violence was not a militant communist-led armed revolution but the prospect that the PKI could actually come to power through peaceful electoral politics in the immediate future. Feeling that this transformation could actually be brought about in the immediate future by a well-organized PKI, which had millions of members and supporters, the military decided that only the physical elimination of the left as a political force would assure its own survival and that of the conservative forces allied with it. In Italy, the landed class feared a gradual political asphyxiation, so the fascists could afford to calibrate their violence, focusing for the most part on prominent leaders and including in their arsenal beating them up, torturing then releasing them, and exiling them, in addition to murder.

Third, Indonesia's counterrevolution was directed from the highest rungs of the military and bureaucracy and implemented mainly by state agencies. This is in contrast to Italy, where the police and local bureaucracy did not lead but served as either active or passive accomplices of the Fascists.

Fourth, the security forces were supported nationwide not only by the landlords and the bureaucratic elite but also by much of the middle class. In the countryside, the killings were done with the active participation of a variety of classes and groups, acting on the basis of fear of the communists or religious righteousness, like the militias of the rural-based Nahdatul Ulama.

Fifth, external intervention in support of the counterrevolution in the form of military aid, covert action and intelligence from the West played an important role in the triumph of the counterrevolution, though not a decisive one.

One might note, in conclusion, that the annihilation, both physical and ideological, of the left was so complete that even after the ouster of Suharto 1998, no party that can be said to carry a program of the left has emerged in Indonesia, with most parties scurrying toward the center (Okamoto 2017, 436). Even current President Joko Widodo's pluralist attitude which tends to show 'some understanding of misconduct during the massacre in 1965' has triggered rumors that he is sympathetic to communists and thus to be distrusted (Okamoto 2017).

Chile: rural ferment, the middle class and the counterrevolution

In late 1972, a Chilean periodical reported that the word 'Jakarta' was seen painted on a number of walls in the capital, Santiago. I was doing research in Chile then, but I did not have the opportunity to check whether the report was accurate. But if it was, the message was chillingly clear: that the Popular Unity (UP) government and its supporters would be dealt with in a similar fashion to how the left was dealt with by the right in Indonesia.

As in Indonesia, agrarian reform was a major battleground in Chile. And, as in the former, the dynamics of rural conflict was intimately related to the agenda of political parties. When the UP came to power after its triumph in the presidential elections of September 1970, it saw its mission as leading the country on the 'peaceful, constitutional road to Socialism'. The key forces in the UP were the Communist Party, the Socialist Party and the Radical Party. Its main goals were to raise the living standards of the lower classes, nationalize the foreign-owned Kennecott and Anaconda copper mines, bring key industrial firms under state control using existing legal mechanisms, and complete land reform. Over the next three years, national politics became polarized between the UP, whose base was the working class and peasantry, and a counterrevolutionary alliance between the landed elite, the big bourgeoisie and the middle classes. Parliament was initially the main arena of struggle, but as the government and Parliament (which was controlled by an alliance between Christian Democrats and the National Party) deadlocked, the struggle shifted to the streets of the capital, Santiago, where the right and left battled for control through large demonstrations, riots, strikes and food blockades. The countryside was an important site of struggle, though it was largely in Santiago that the sharpest and most decisive clashes took place.

Radicalizing agrarian reform

Between 1964 and 1970, the centrist, middle-class-backed Christian Democratic government of President Eduardo Frei Montalva was able to pass agrarian reform legislation aimed at converting tenants in the large- and medium-sized estates into small owner operators. As in Korea and Taiwan, this US-supported enterprise aimed to create a small and medium peasant class attached to private property that would at the same time form a bulwark against the more socialist-oriented agrarian program coming from the left, which had come together in the UP coalition.

The six years of the Frei government was a time of ferment in the countryside. While attacking what they saw as the limitations of the Christian Democratic agrarian reform, the parties of the UP took advantage of the space provided by agrarian reform to expand their political influence in the cooperatives of agrarian reform beneficiaries (*asentamientos*) and other peasant organizations. Their aim was to radicalize the process by demanding the inclusion of poor peasants and rural workers among the beneficiaries, a lowering of the size of lands to be expropriated, and a speed-up in the process of reform. There was an empirical basis for this since the inroads of capitalism in the countryside had led to a decline in the numbers of *inquilinos* or tenant-farmers, and a rise in the numbers of rural workers who became the dominant work force (Steenland 1975, 51–52).[5] By the end of the Frei presidency, the countryside was marked by a five-cornered struggle among landlords, Christian Democrat-affiliated peasant groups, UP-linked peasants and workers, peasants and workers mobilized by the Movement of the Revolutionary Left (MIR), and independent groups. Owing to many glitches in land redistribution, the Christian Democratic land reform lost considerable momentum, handing over the initiative to UP organizers (see, among others, Murray 2003, 189).

When the Popular Unity government led by President Salvador Allende came to power in 1970, land reform was radicalized and speeded up. The new government decreed that all large estates over 80 basic irrigated hectares were subject to expropriation regardless of the efficiency and land-use criteria of the Frei agrarian reform. And, under pressure from an increasingly militant peasantry and indigenous groups such as the Mapuche Indians who were engaged in land seizures, the UP government in 1973 moved to expropriate inefficient farms between 40 and 80 basic irrigated hectares, with little in the way of land reserves and no compensation offered to the *patrones* or landlords (2003). Poor peasants and rural workers who had been excluded from the Frei reform were brought into the ranks of beneficiaries. Moreover, the UP went beyond the Frei reform's aim of carving up estates into smaller privately owned lands to create a stratum of small farmers from former tenants, to promoting collectivization of land as the strategic end of agrarian reform (2003).

The battle for the middle class

One of the most interesting features of rural conflict in Chile is how intense class conflict was accompanied by relatively little violence in the period from 1964 to 1971 when land reform was in full swing. Some 12 people died, though farm seizures escalated from 13 in 1965 to 1278 in 1971 (Kay 2001, 746). One researcher who studied the *tomas de fundos* during the Allende period concluded that

> the tomas themselves were not violent. There were no recorded personal attacks on the landowners or managers, such as took place in the Bolivian and Mexican revolutions. Nor was there the destruction of the fundo's property, which the new possessors wanted to preserve for their own use.

Where violence took place, it was usually where a landowner employed a paramilitary group to retake the fundo, an act called a *retoma*. But in general, 'the tomas de fundos were not violent nor did they lead to violent retomas'. (Winn 2010, 248)

The image of what was taking place, however, was very different. The conservative press sensationalized tomas as violent affairs, with photos showing peasants with crude weapons guarding the fundo. It also created the impression that the tomas were much more frequent than they actually were.

The war of images was critical because the left and the right were fighting for the allegiance of Chile's middle class, which at 30–35 percent of the population was Latin America's second biggest, after Argentina (Johnson 1961, 21). Both left and right knew that the middle class was the force on which the future of the revolution would pivot. As in other countries, there was only a rough correlation between party allegiance and social class. The

---

[5] The Frei agrarian reform beneficiaries were estimated to total only 95,000 *inquilinos* or semi-feudal resident laborers and supervisory personnel. See Aranda and Martinez (1971, 149).

Christian Democratic Party accounted for some 34 percent of the vote, and this came largely from the middle class. At the same time, a not-insignificant part of the 19 percent who voted for the right-wing National Party and the 43 percent who voted for the left-wing Popular Unity parties were also from the middle class.[6] The right wing sought to convince the middle class that socialism would mean a redistribution of poverty, their descent into the working class, and the collectivization of small farms. The strategy of the UP, in contrast, was to convince the middle-class base of the Christian Democrats that their interests were best served in a united front with the popular classes, the expression of which would be an informal UP–Christian Democratic political alliance. Whether or not the interests of the middle strata and the working class actually coincided, there was an implacable defensive rationale for placating the former. As one UP intellectual put it,

> The dominant class has many economic resources, but numerically it is insignificant. It will not be former bankers or former industrialists who will take to the streets to confront the Popular Unity Government. The task is precisely to isolate them so they cannot use small proprietors or employees and small farmers to rush out in their defense. (Garcia 1972, 116, 121)

The social security measure and wage increases of the UP were carefully calibrated to win over the urban middle class. By the end of the first year of the government, small business people had been integrated into the social security system and tax rates were lowered for small industries. And despite the risk of triggering inflation, middle-class salaried workers received bigger increases in their pay than was originally planned by the UP government, with the result that they raised their portion of the total national income from 53.7 percent in 1970 to 58.6 percent in 1971 (Lopez 1971, 21–22; ODEPLAN 1972). Indeed, the UP government was seen as too accommodating to the middle class by some sectors of the left like the MIR, which complained:

> How can one gain the middle classes if they are promised a splendid world of high consumption which cannot in practice be achieved, instead of calling on them to bear sacrifices for the construction of a more dignified, humane, and just Chile. (MIR 1972, 6)

The UP government's best year in terms of its social security and income policies toward the middle class and its management of the economy, combining high economic growth and relatively low inflation, was 1971. Yet by the end of the year, a counterrevolutionary movement based on the middle class erupted into the political scene, with the famous march of thousands of women banging pots and pans that became an icon of counterrevolutionary mobilization, complete with *grupos de choque* or paramilitary groups similar to the fascist *squadristi* that beat up and provoked violent clashes with UP supporters and construction workers.

The December 1971 clashes showed that the right had been able to 'generalize' its interests to the middle sectors, partly through the skillful employment of ideological appeals stressing the defense of individual freedom and united-front strategies that pushed the Christian Democrats to take a prima donna role while National Party and other right-wing personalities stayed in the background. So successful were the tactics of the right that the Christian Democratic base became radicalized toward the right much faster than the party leadership (*Politica y Espiritu* 1971, 78). But the tactics of the right could only

---

[6]These figures are from the results of the Senate elections in March 1973.

be effective in a situation where the latent fears of the middle sectors that stemmed from their position in the power structure had been provoked by a revolutionary process.

In the countryside, the activation of small farmers as a counterrevolutionary base was probably more rapid than that of the middle class in the cities. Small farmers were pushed to the right by conservative press reports on 'violent' *tomas*, fears that their land would also be subjected to agrarian reform, and food price controls imposed by the UP government to combat inflation. As in the cities, the strategy of the landed class was a not insignificant factor. As Jacques Chonchol, the radical Minister of Agriculture, put it, the strategy of the minor *latifundistas* or landlords

> is not directed so much at defending the *latifundio* [landed estate] , which it already knows to be condemned, but at creating the image and fear that the agrarian reform not only harms the big proprietors but also the small and medium farmers who number in the thousands in this country. To the extent that chaotic and isolated actions affect big, small, and medium proprietors, we are providing the latifundista sector with weapons to fortify its base of support and achieve that which it is trying to create: a general front … against agrarian reform. (Chonchol 1972, 153)

What Choncol feared had already come about even before the UP government moved in early 1973 to expropriate inefficient latifundio or estates between 40 to 80 basic hectares, with little reserve land and no compensation for the owners, a move that affected mainly the minor latifundistas. This was clear to me in a trip I made to Valdivia in the South of Chile around September 1972, where I stayed in the home of a middle-class farmer, an account of which I published several decades later in the *Nation:*

> I remember going to Valdivia, with an American friend, to look up a Christian Democratic farmer that had been recommended by a fellow graduate student at the Princeton sociology department. After a couple of weeks of intensive interviewing and documentary research in Santiago, I thought I would relax a bit and enjoy the famed Chilean hospitality. We were warmly received by the farmer and his family, which included a son and two teenage daughters. A goat was slaughtered for us and we sat down to a hearty dinner on our first night. Then our host started cursing Allende, calling him simply a tool for the Communist Party to 'impose its dictatorship on Chile'. The Socialist Party of Allende was no better than the Communists, and the Izquierda Cristiana, composed of former Christian Democrats that had joined the Unidad Popular, were 'traitors'. My friend and I kept our politics to ourselves and tried to guide the discussion to more innocuous topics. I wanted to interview him on his views, I said, but we could do that after dinner. He said fine, but after a few minutes, he again began on his anti-leftist tirade.
>
> The next day at breakfast, lunch, and dinner was more of the same hospitality punctuated by lengthy invectives against 'communists who will take away my property and give them to the *rotos* [broken ones]'. Finally, at dinner on our second day, I could no longer tolerate his litany of 'crimes of the left' and said I actually thought Allende was fighting for social justice and the land reform he was trying to push would actually benefit medium farmers like him and would negatively impact only the big landholders.
>
> Chileans, I had been told, could be really friendly and hospitable until they smelled your politics, after which you either became a really close friend or you became an outcast. My friend and I became outcasts, and our not being asked to breakfast the next day was a clear sign that we had overstayed our welcome. (Bello 2016)

The bitter anti-leftist stance of the Christian Democratic farmer was not surprising. Valdivia was one of the provinces of the Los Lagos region of the country, where the proportion of legally expropriable land was lowest and the economic and social importance of small and medium farmers was greater than in the rest of rural Chile. Frightened by the fundo takeovers that were magnified by the right-wing press, and attracted to the common defense of private property promoted by the big landlords, the small and medium farmers scurried to the right. The same rush to the right was evident in Cautin and the country's breadbasket, the Central Valley. That only 0.5 percent of all agricultural units nationwide experienced labor troubles or were occupied between November 1970, when Allende came to power, and May 1972, and that the vast majority of farms that were illegally seized between November 1970 and September 1971 were returned to their owners were facts that were lost on the rural middle class (Gall 1972, 8).

By early 1972, the middle class was not simply a passive actor being pulled passively to the right; it had become the mass base of the counterrevolution. This counterrevolutionary mass had gained control of the streets from a left that seemed barely aware it had lost them – a fact that Fidel Castro had pointed out during his visit to Chile in December 1971 (Castro 1971, 46). This was brought home to me when I was nearly beaten up twice by Christian Democratic youth while observing right-wing demonstrations with the Communist Party newspaper *El Siglo* tucked prominently under my arm.

In February 1972, the UP National Committee admitted that the right's 'ideological penetration' of the middle strata 'has been stronger, and it has dragged some of them – contrary to their real interests – to solidarity with the monopoly bourgeoisie and to even bring their forces into a heterogeneous National Front of the Private Sector' (*Unidad Popular* 1972, 63). But according to the UP's analysis, the reasons were mainly the deviations from the united front policy brought about by the seizures of lands and factories by the 'extreme left' and the success of the right's calculating strategy. These certainly played a role, but the main reason behind the middle's move rightward could not be grasped within the UP's 'united front' intellectual and political framework.

Underlying this view was a mechanistic and reductionist paradigm that the middle class would respond to an economic program that would not only not harm their interests but promote them. This perspective denied an independent dynamic to the middle sectors, viewing them as a mass that would passively respond to their 'real' class interest, which lay in an alliance with the working class. It was one that could not have a proper appreciation of the deep-seated fears of the middle classes that the gains of workers and the lower classes would only come at their expense. These fears stemmed from one's position in the class structure. Latent in stable times, these apprehensions rose to the surface during a revolutionary period, where they were skillfully stoked by middle-class and elite intellectuals into a powerful counterrevolutionary force that served as a concrete refutation of the left's simplistic political and economic cost–benefit calculus of middle-class behavior. In short, while departures from the left-wing united front strategy and crafty right-wing united front tactics played a role, it was the inflammation of the middle class' structural position at a time of revolutionary transformation that was the decisive factor in their counterrevolutionary trajectory.

'Matanza Masiva'

By the time I left Chile early in 1973, the right controlled the streets, mounting demonstration after demonstration and subjecting people identified with the Unidad Popular to harassment and beatings. The left still mounted demonstrations, and the streets still resounded with the happy chant '*El que no salta es momio*' ('He who does not jump is a reactionary'), but the mood of defensiveness had deepened. Increasingly, the fate of the revolution rested on the military's remaining neutral. Initially respectful of civilian rule, the military leadership ended up siding with the counterrevolutionary coalition and launched a bloody coup on 11 September 1973.

The chilling word 'Jakarta' supposedly emblazoned on some walls in Santiago in 1972 became a reality in the months following the 11 September putsch. The report of the government commission that investigated human rights violations under the Pinochet regime placed the number of people killed or disappeared at 3065 and those tortured and imprisoned at 40,018. For a country of four million people, these figures were relatively high (BBC News 2011). The terror was probably more severe in the countryside, 'where there were no embassies and no foreign journaiists', with the Mapuche, the indigenous people who had carried out numerous land occupations in the South, being especially targeted (Winn 2010, 265).

As in Indonesia, indiscriminate killings or '*matanza masiva*', as one Chilean officer described it to historian Peter Winn (2010), were designed not only to decapitate the left but to wipe it out completely. The left in Chile had not only come close to power; it had actually seized a part of the state. To the right, the situation necessitated a root-and-branch response that was so completely out of line with the country's tradition of political moderation that it shocked many Chileans who had initially supported the coup (2010).

On the question of matanza masiva, one might ask what accounts for the use of civilian auxiliaries in Indonesia and their absence in Chile. One possible explanation is simply the enormity of the task in Indonesia, which necessitated the liquidation of hundreds of thousands of people over vast stretches of an archipelago of over 80 million people. Already overstretched, the Indonesian military was simply too limited in size for such a labor-intensive task as mass killings in countless villages which had branches of the PKI and its allied party, the PNI (Indonesian National Party). Another is that overtly fascist paramilitary groups like *Patria y Libertad* (Fatherland and Liberty) in Chile were still relatively small and of recent vintage, whereas branches of the conservative Islamic organizations had been well established in many of the rural villages of Indonesia. Most likely, the most important reason is that once the Chilean military brass decided to intervene, it was determined to control the process by itself and would brook no interference from civilian auxiliaries. Pablo Rodriguez Grez, the founder of Patria y Libertad, got the message and, shortly after the coup, dissolved the fascist band, leaving its members to be recruited by the military's secret services.

As in Indonesia, geopolitical factors played an important role in the counterrevolution. The US financed right-wing efforts 'to make the economy scream', as Richard Nixon famously put it. The CIA's deputy director for planning wrote in a secret 1970 memo after Allende won the elections that '[I] t is firm and continuing policy that Allende be overthrown by a coup .... It is imperative that these actions be implemented clandestinely and securely so that the USG [United States Government] and American hand be well hidden' (Democracy Now 2013). The agency then provided the military with vital intelligence, and right-wing groups such as the fascist Patria y Libertad with funding, to destabilize the government. It is also likely to have carried out covert operations. But the contribution of foreign intervention must not be exaggerated. After the coup of 11 September, progressive analysis of the event and actions leading up to it understandably focused on the role of the United States, which was seen as directing or working intimately with Pinochet and the leadership of the National and Christian Democratic parties. That a counterrevolutionary mass base had been central in the overthrow tended to be omitted, or if it wasn't, the tendency was to regard it as largely a force manipulated by the CIA and the elites.

The reality, however, was that contrary to the prevailing explanations of the coup, which attributed Pinochet's success to US intervention and the CIA, the counterrevolution was already there prior to the US's destabilization efforts; that it was largely determined by internal class dynamics; and that the Chilean elites were able to connect with middle-class sectors terrified by the prospect of poor sectors rising up with their agenda of justice and equality.

In short, the US intervention was successful because it was inserted into an ongoing counterrevolutionary process. CIA destabilization was just one of the factors that contributed to the victory of the right, not the decisive one. This was not something that progressives wanted to hear then, since many wanted a simple black-and-white picture – that is, that the overthrow of Allende was orchestrated from the outside, by the United States. As I noted in my *Nation* piece, 'Being of the left, I could understand why politics demanded such a portrayal of events. Being a sociologist, I realized that the situation was much more nuanced' (Bello 2016).

Conclusion

In conclusion, one might advance the following observations regarding the counterrevolution in Chile:

First, the political dynamics of the countryside was inextricably linked to the national agenda of the left and the right. Compared to Indonesia, however, the left had a greater problem subordinating local struggles to its national strategy since the peasant movement, indigenous people, and revolutionary left had developed autonomous dynamics that often contradicted national policy. The land seizures, which the UP government opposed since it worried they would scare small farmers and wreck its united front policy, were a prime example of this conflict.

Second, the Chilean revolutionary process was remarkably peaceful, in both the cities and the countryside, with relatively few instances of violent deaths and property damage. The image of violent takeovers projected by the conservative media was far from the reality, but they did contribute to moving the urban and rural middle classes to the right.

Third, the middle class was the decisive battleground. Images of 'leftist' violence, land seizures and the food price controls may have contributed to the rightward movement of the middle classes, but what was probably more decisive was the activation of the latent fears of the middle class stemming from their position in the class structure by a revolutionary situation, this being the main factor making them an active counterrevolutionary force. In this fluid situation, the intellectuals and propagandists of the right were able to 'connect' with the fears of the middle class about their loss of status, falling to the ranks of the poor, society being leveled by a socialist government, and the erosion of private property. In contrast, the left operated with a united-front strategy based on a view of the middle class as a passive force and simplistic reductionist assumptions that raising social security benefits and wages for both the middle class and the lower classes and reducing inflation would bring the two together against the right. But the battle was not only ideological. It was also tactical, and here the right also had the edge, with its calculating strategy of letting the Christian Democrats take center stage and patiently working on the party's base to pull the leadership to the right. There is a great deal of truth to the observation of Armand Mattelart that in the Chilean faceoff, it was the right that proved to be more 'Leninist' than the left (see Mattelart 1973).

Fourth, the extreme violence that accompanied the coup stemmed from the right's view that political polarization into two irreconcilable camps meant the threat from the left, which had already seized part of the state through elections, could only be eliminated by physically eliminating the left itself – thus the Chilean right's adoption of matanza masiva of the Indonesian counterrevolution instead of *matanza selectiva* of Italian fascism. Again, the parallel with Indonesia is striking.

Finally, while the US role in overthrowing Allende was significant, what was decisive was the ongoing counterrevolution into which that support was injected.

Thailand: revolution and counterrevolution reloaded

When the military government of General Suchinda Krapayoon was ousted by a combination of middle class-led protests and royal intervention in May 1992, it seemed that Thailand had seen the last of its military regimes, and political analysts hailed the event as another instance of the middle class being a force for democratization. In September 2006, the Thai military ousted Prime Minister Thaksin Shinawatra, then stepped back from power over a year after elections were held to form a new civilian government. In May 2014, it entered politics again, ousting the government led by Thaksin's sister, Yingluck, and this time it apparently prepared to stay in power for a longer period. At the time of writing (2017) it remains in power, with very little overt resistance from the civilian population. The key to its rule is the support of the middle class, the same class that overthrew Suchinda a quarter of a century earlier. It was a counterrevolutionary regime, the mass base of which was a class that had turned from being insurgent to being counterrevolutionary.

In any counterrevolution, there are losers. And in Thailand the losers included the rural masses in North, Northeast and Central Thailand. These were the same areas where peasant organizing for change in production and social relations was most active in the nationwide social ferment in the 1970s. Over 30 years later these areas became the bastions of the 'Redshirts' who provided the mass support for Thaksin's populist movement. In the words of one scholar, the 1970s was a case of 'revolution interrupted' by a counterrevolution (Haberkorn 2011). The momentous events of the last 12 years might be said to be a case of 'revolution reloaded' followed by 'counterrevolution reloaded'.[7]

The revolutionary process of the 1970s, while initiated in Bangkok by students who overthrew the Thanom-Praphat military dictatorship and ushered in a parliamentary regime, was driven forward by the peasants' struggle for land. With a minimal role played by left-wing parties, this movement was spontaneous and organized by peasants themselves. The battle cry of this struggle was land reform.

Capitalism and rural crisis

In all parts of Thailand, the conditions of existence of the peasantry worsened during the decades after the Second World War. The key factor was the rapid spread of market relations or commercialization of land as Thailand was more rapidly integrated into the global capitalist economy even as an antiquated system of land tenure prevailed. Thus, the benefits from the increased production of rice that made Thailand the prime actor in the global rice market flowed unevenly, with the big landowners, middlemen and moneylenders siphoning off the greater part of the wealth created. The tenure system also ensured that most of the benefits of the increased productivity triggered by chemical-intensive Green Revolution technology would flow to the landlords.

---

[7]A big part of the analysis and data provided on the pre-Thaksin period covered in this section come from field work and research I did in the mid-1990s on the political economy of Thailand which became the basis of the book *A Siamese Tragedy: Development and Disintegration in Modern Thailand* (London: Zed Books, 1998) authored by Walden Bello, Shea Cunningham and Li Kheng Poh (1998).

In the country's rice basket, Central Thailand, symptoms of peasant distress amidst prosperity showed themselves in the rise of share-tenancy and landlessness. Before the Second World War, a great part of rice production took place in small independent landholdings. By the early 1970s, however, a study of 11 provinces in the Central Region found that 39 percent of farmers were full tenants and another 30 percent were part-tenants (Fallon 1983, 121). By 1981, over 36 percent of all landholdings were rented (Pongsapich et al. 1993, 44). Conditions were not easy for these tenants, with rents rising from over a quarter of the crop in pre-war days to half or more in the post-war period (Fallon 1983, 126).

Landless workers were also an increasing proportion of the population, reaching up to 14 or 15 percent of rural families in the central region by the mid-1970s (Pongsapich et al. 1993, 49).

As in Central Thailand, the combination of market forces and an increasingly inequitable tenure system ensured that the greater productivity made possible by the Green Revolution would be cornered by the richer strata in Northern Thailand. Tenancy became more widespread: in one survey, the percentage of tenant households rose from 18.3 percent of all households in 1967–1968 to 27 percent by 1976 (Trikat, cited in Vaddhanaputi 1984, 141). Landlessness had also shot up, with the figure of landless households in one district of Chiang Mai coming to 36 percent in 1974 (Turton 1978, 112). Landlords also had become more aggressive, in many cases taking two thirds of the harvest as rent (Bowie 1991, 10; see also Haberkorn 2011, 9).

In the Northeast, where traditionally small, owner-operated plots predominated, the booms and busts of the international market for rice and cash crops like kenaf and cassava led to widespread indebtedness, forcing farmers to sell their land and become tenant farmers or landless workers on land they formerly owned. Tenanted land rose by 56 percent between 1980 and 1991 (Pongsapich et al. 1993, 17). As in the Central Region and the North, peasant disaffection was deep and widespread in the Northeast by the late 1970s. It was, as it were, waiting to be ignited.

Peasants become political subjects

What ignited it was the fall of the Thanom-Praphat military dictatorship following massive protests by students and other urban sectors. This exposed a degree of fragility and vulnerability in the ruling system that was not lost on peasants. While peasant rebellions against the state were not new, these had been localized, spontaneous and sometimes millenarian in character, like the 'Holy Men Rebellions' in the Northeast. The peasant organizing that unfolded in the democratic interlude between 1973 and 1976 was different, being the first time the peasantry sought to organize itself autonomously as class on a national scale and on the basis of a secular program.

While communist cadres probably played some role in the formation of the key peasant organization, the Farmers' Federation of Thailand (FFT), the central role was filled by peasant grassroots leaders, and the success of the FFT was due precisely to its non-ideological style of organizing. University students provided much-needed technical and organizational support, but this was different from the approach of a vanguard party out to 'organize the masses'. The FFT served to bring together issues, concerns and demands from different regions and different sectors of the Thai peasantry, not all of whom had experienced the same problems, or had suffered from them to different degrees.

> Some were demands for immediate action, such as grants of land for the coming planting season, price regulation, reduction of farm rents, suspension of court cases involving farmers, release of those arrested for trespass, and help for flood victims. Others were longer

term demands, such as those for land reform and permanent provision of land to the landless, and a solution to the problems of indebtedness and high interest rates. Some demands were more immediately political, such as the lifting of martial law in the outlying provinces .... Over time, the demands escalated, which seems to indicate a growing political consciousness and perhaps overconfidence. (Turton 1982, 20)

The peasant support for the FFT apparently came principally from the north and the central region, where the rates of tenancy and landlessness were highest. With an estimated membership of 1.5 million farmers nationwide, the geographical scope of the Federation's organizing was unprecedented. So was the breadth of the program, which sought to speak 'for the rural poor, the landless, those with smallholdings, tenants, and in a wider sense for all those who experienced injustice and denial of democratic freedoms' (1982, 25). Most significantly, noted one observer, FFT represented a historical juncture: the peasants of Thailand 'had set up their own organization and drawn up a program of struggle to help solve the basic problems of Thai farmers' (Karunan 1984, 45).

Pressure from the peasantry was instrumental in wringing concessions from the elite reformist government that reigned, in unstable fashion, between 1973 and 1976. The two most important concessions were the Land Rent Control Act (LRCA) of 1974 and the Land Reform Act of 1975. These pieces of legislation were clumsy attempts to reduce the burden of tenancy and transform tenants into small owner-operators, and compared to the land reform measures in South Korea and Taiwan, they were generous in their treatment of landlords. But, as Tyrell Haberkorn points out, it was not so much the content of the legislation, but the way the peasants used the two laws – especially the LRCA – to alter the balance of class power that was of momentous significance:

[The] struggles for rent relief in Chiang Mai province were at once about the amount of rice to be paid as rent and about who had the right to define and enforce the terms of land rental. As farmers began to educate one another about their legal rights, and to urge landowners to follow the dictates of the new Land Rent Control Act in 1974 and 1975, landowners lost rice (in comparison to prior years), but they also lost their position as the sole determinants of *deciding* how much rice would be paid by farmers as rent. (Haberkorn 2011, 15, emphasis in original)

What made the actions of the farmers revolutionary was that they were transformed into political subjects when 'they claimed the law as a tool that they could use to secure justice and improve their lives' (Haberkorn 2011, 130). Just as the real fear of the landed elite in Italy was not a communist revolution but their gradual asphyxiation by the grassroots institutions of reformist socialism, and just as the biggest fear of the Indonesian military was the PKI's coming to power through electoral means, so was the deepest fear of the Thai landlords their tenants learning to use the law to empower themselves and disempower their social 'superiors'.

The threat of a gradual shift in the balance of class power at the local level by uppity social subordinates using the law, not the prospect of a powerful organized left taking power at the national level, shaped the landed class' response, and this was more along the lines of calibrated fascist violence abetted by the state as in Italy than the state-directed matanza masiva in Indonesia and Chile.

Counterrevolution I

As in the Po Valley in Italy, the landed elites drew on the services of already existing right-wing paramilitary groups to initiate a wave of terror against the FFT and its student supporters. These formations included the Red Gaurs, Nawaphon and the Village Scouts, who counted among their supporters people in the military, the police, and key business elites. These groups combined terror tactics with ideological appeals in the battle for the hearts and minds of the rural populace against the peasant movement and the students. The centerpiece of the right-wing ideological offensive was the slogan 'Nation-Religion-King'. In the case of the Village Scouts, one of the central organizations of the counterrevolution, there was a sophisticated effort to fuse this ideological trinity with traditional rural Thai culture to create a more secure village basis for the existing order. This effort included indoctrination programs that were clearly fascist–modernist in inspiration. Indoctrination, noted one observer, was 'emotionally stretching, from the lightheartedness of child's play to the seriousness of patriotism, humiliation to happiness, and competition to cooperation'. The purpose of the exercise was 'to make the participants feel important, and identify themselves closely with the nation, the religion, and the king' (Vaddhanaputi 1984, 556–57). Constantly cultivated by conservative forces as the symbolic lynchpin of the nation, the monarchy was a powerful ideological reserve monopolized by the right (Connors 2003, 130).

Despite the importance of ideology in the social struggle, force and repression were the principal means by which the threatened elites sought to protect their privileges. Peasant leaders were murdered systematically, with 18 FFT leaders assassinated between February and August 1975 alone. These assassinations reached their climax with the murder of a highly respected vice president of the FFT in July. As in Italy, the targeted violence severely weakened the peasant movement, which was unprepared for this kind of struggle.

Emboldened by their success in bringing the revolutionary process in the countryside to a screeching stop, conservative forces took on the weak reformist parliamentary regime in Bangkok, forcing it to put on hold the implementation of the pro-peasant land laws. This retreat, however, did not prevent the government's authority from being eroded, as the military, the bureaucracy and the ultra-conservative royalist elite worked with the country's economic elites to regain control from the bourgeois reformists via extra-parliamentary means. In a situation reminiscent of the Allende period in Chile, the authority of the legal power-holders evaporated, and the question of power came increasingly to be dominated by the battles in the streets, with the advantage gained by those who could deploy superior resources in organization, ideology and, most important, firepower. The sacking of the Prime Minister's Kukrit Pramoj residence by drunk uniformed policemen calling for respect for the law, on 20 August 1975, was a sign that real power had passed to the counterrevolutionary forces.

On 6 October 1976, the counterrevolution reached its bloody climax, when scores of students were killed, hundreds wounded and thousands arrested in an assault on Thammasat University in Bangkok by paramilitary forces instigated by state security agencies. These were militants of Nawaphon, Red Gaurs and Village Scouts, organizations which had cut their teeth suppressing the peasants. The three-year accumulation of pent-up hatred among the elites and counterrevolutionary forces was unleashed by fascist mobs that day and in the succeeding days. As in Indonesia and Chile, the level of violence was unprecedented and shocking to Thais. An interview conducted years later with a witness to the bloodletting underlined the role of the civilian paramilitary groups:

> 'The other side believed that we were armed Communists and had defamed the monarchy', Krisadang said, trying to explain the raw sadism of lynching, murder, rape and torture that seemed to have no precedent … Krisadang said he had no idea the paramilitary mob was capable of unleashing such hatred and violence. He faults political passions being whipped up to divide

people and make them turn on one another ... Krisadang said anyone who was seen as a political opponent was branded a Communist and anti-monarchist. (Rojanaphruk 2016)

These comments of the former student activist also underlined another prominent aspect of the counterrevolution. While Marxism was an influential ideological current among students, the Communist Party played a relatively minor role in the mobilizations of 1973–1976 and was active mainly in the periphery of the country, especially in the Northeast, as a guerrilla force. Anti-communism was, however, a prominent ideological aspect of the counterrevolution. The fall of Laos, Cambodia and Vietnam to indigenous communist forces in 1975 was deployed by the right in its counterrevolutionary campaign, which painted Thailand as the next domino that would fall to communism. There was, however, little foreign involvement in the right-wing campaign, probably because the organized left was never seen by the establishment as a serious threat, unlike in Indonesia, where it was seen as being on the cusp of power, and in Chile, where it had won (tenuous) control of the bureaucracy.

Interlude

The period 1976 to 1992 saw a succession of military or military-dominated regimes. The living conditions in the countryside worsened. By the late 1980s, there were about one million tenant households cultivating an area of 6 million rai or 960,000 hectares (CUSRI 1989, 114).[8] In the Northeast, where tenancy had not been as great a problem as in the North and Northeast, land under tenancy increased from one million rai in 1975 to three million at the end of the 1980s (Pongpaiboon 1991). As for the landless, a study by the Chulalongkorn University Social Research Institute (CUSRI) using the Food and Agriculture Organization definition of landless, found that they constituted some 33 percent of the agricultural population (CUSRI 1989, 1, 5–6).

With the middle-class-led ouster of the Suchinda dictatorship in May 1992, there was some hope that the new democratic regimes would bring a new deal to the countryside, only to be frustrated. The failure of reform was, however, mitigated by the country's rapid industrialization triggered by the massive entry of Japanese capital seeking cheap labor in the late 1980s and early 1990s, when Thailand joined the ranks of 'newly industrializing countries' (NICs). Much of the agricultural labor surplus from different parts of rural Thailand, especially from the Northeast, was absorbed in industries that sprang up in the Bangkok metropolitan area.

Then, in the second half of 1997, the real estate bubble in Bangkok deflated, initiating the Asian Financial Crisis. The collapse of the financial economy was followed by recession, which was deepened by International Monetary Fund (IMF)-imposed austerity measures. Many of the migrants who had found work in boom-time Bangkok were forced to return to the countryside, with an average of five migrants returning to each of the country's 60,000 villages by December, according to one estimate.[9] It was this countryside reeling in crisis, along with the rest of the country, that set the stage for the next remarkable turn of events.

Before we turn to this, it must be noted that the demise of the FFT was followed in the early 1980s by the collapse of the Communist Party of Thailand, which had provided a home to many

---

[8] A rai equals 1600 square meters (40 m × 40 m) or 0.16 hectares.
[9] Interview with Wanida Tantiwitthayapitak, spokesperson for Assembly of the Poor, 21 January 1998.

peasant leaders and student activists fleeing repression in the late 1970s. Many of these militants, however, did not give up on their ideals, and some of them reproduced the farmer–student alliance of the 1970s by hooking up with peasants in civil-society organizations around causes like the opposition to the Pak Mun Dam in the Northeast, which linked environmental degradation to poverty, inequality and the rising level of farmers' debt in the countryside. Most prominent among these groups was the Assembly of the Poor, which organized marches by the thousands of peasants to Korat, Ubon Rachatani and Bangkok in the 1990s.

Thaksin ascendant

It was, however, Thaksin Shinawatra who won the imagination of the rural masses, precipitating what we might call – though rather loosely – 'revolution reloaded'.

Thaksin will probably go down as Thailand's most controversial early twenty-first-century figure. After building up a telecommunications empire though government connections, he went into politics, rising from being a subordinate of traditional political figures to being the dominant figure in a political force, initially called the *Thai Rak Thai* (Thai Love Thai) Party, that won by a landslide the 2001 elections and the three other elections thereafter. He bent government rules to advance his business interests while he was prime minister and used his office to create opportunities for his business cronies. But he also posed as a reformer who would modernize Thailand's politics and a nationalist who freed the country from the clutches of the IMF. Most important, he set in motion a political project that drew massive support from the rural and urban masses, and from the populous North and Northeastern regions and most of Central Thailand, that threatened to upend the country's political landscape.

Thaksin was the supreme opportunist, but an extremely clever one, who saw an opening in the vacuum of leadership for the lower classes that had been created by the loss of progressive formations like the FFT and the Communist Party. Advised by former student radicals, he devised in the wake of the IMF stabilization program debacle a Keynesian strategy that pulled the country out the depths of crisis and that had a strong redistributive component. The key elements of this program were a universal health-care system that allowed people to be treated for the equivalent of a dollar, a one million baht fund for each village which villagers could invest however they wanted, and low-interest loan programs along with various kinds of food subsidies and agriculture price supports.

To the rural masses, Thaksin offered the 'New Deal' they had long been in search of, and they became a central force in the political rollercoaster that was interrupted by a military coup in 2006 against Thaksin, and by another putsch, in 2014, against a government headed by his sister Yingluck. While the rising opposition to Thaksin characterized them as 'the greedy poor' that Thaksin 'bought' with his populist politics, the reality was more complex. Naruemon Thabchumpon and Duncan McCargo claim that the characterization of the hardline Thaksin supporters known as the Redshirts as coming from the poor peasantry was simplistic. Many were, rather, 'emerging forces on the margins of the middle class' or 'urbanized villagers' who were not from the lowest class and who were motivated mainly by a demand for political justice and fair play rather than socio-economic concerns (Thabchumpon and McCargo 2011, 1018). The complex character of Thaksin's rural mass base stemmed from the fact that the spread of capitalist production relations and the commercialization of land had contradictory effects, impoverishing some while providing an opportunity for others, including people who were able to access the pro-Thaksin government support to help them build small businesses. Both losers and winners appeared to come together in support of Thaksin.

A not unfair judgment of Thaksin's impact on the rural masses is provided by political scientist Ukrist Pathamnand:

> [Thaksin's] policies were perceived to have an impact on ordinary people's lives far beyond anything experienced under previous governments. Thaksin also presented himself as a leader of ordinary people, responsive to their demands, unlike any predecessor. Many who later came to join the Red Shirts explained that they felt grateful to Thaksin for his policies and for the sense of empowerment he gave them …
>
> As a result, when Thaksin was toppled by a coup in 2006, many villages in the north, northeast, and central regions saw this as wrong and came out to join demonstrations. After the clashes at Sanam Luang, Victory Monument, and Ding Daeng junction in Bangkok in April–May 2010, many became even more opposed to state power and more sympathetic to Thaksin. (Pathamanand 2016, 153)

Many of Thaksin's supporters were not uncritical admirers. Some acknowledged he had a corrupt and authoritarian side, but also that he was a modern, capitalist force that was progressive in comparison to the reactionary military–bureaucratic–royalist elite. Others saw him as a useful symbol behind which to build a new progressive movement that would eventually develop dynamics independent of him. Indeed, the coup that overthrew Thaksin spawned the 'Redshirt' movement that became more and more independent of the self-exiled Thaksin, leading some activists to claim that 'the movement signaled a real revolution in political consciousness and organization in the countryside, reflecting a shift toward a postpeasant society' (Lertchoosakul 2016, 262). This view – that Thaksin's main contribution was to serve as a springboard to people's self-empowerment – is expounded in some detail by Ukrist:

> [Villagers'] political sophistication advanced election by election. Vote buying declined in effectiveness, as people increasingly paid attention to the policies on offer. Elections became increasingly aware of the power of the vote and their ability to use it to bring about improvement in their own lives. Loyalty to Thaksin was less and less about Thaksin himself and more and more an expression of the villagers' wish to protect their newly gained and understood power. (Pathamanand 2016, 153–54)

The middle class and counterrevolution II

Not surprisingly, Thaksin and his policies could not but come into conflict with the Thai establishment. Central to the power structure was King Bhumibol, a charismatic figure who had moved far beyond his formally designated role as constitutional monarch. In the aftermath of the counterrevolution of 1976, the monarchy had been aggressively cultivated by the establishment as a supra-political moral authority or referee of democratic competition (Connors 2003, 128–52). Behind a carefully crafted personality cult and with strategically timed political interventions, Bhumibol, writes Pavin Chachapongpun,

> built an alliance with the military, creating a 'network monarchy' which placed the royal institution at the apex of the Thai political structure. Together, the monarchy and the military designed a political system whereby elected governments would be kept weak and vulnerable. (Chachavalpongpun 2017, 429–33)

The elite knew, however, that to preserve their interests, they had to win over the country's middle class. One way to gather the support of the middle sectors was to paint the Thaksin movement as seeking to subvert the royalty, claiming that Thaksin and key advisers on the left had met in Finland in 1999 to plot the overthrow of the monarchy

(Lertchoosakul 2016, 243–44). Yet the elite did not have to resort to sensationalist claims to win the middle sectors, since the latter had themselves become alarmed at the increasing politicization and empowerment of the lower classes unleashed by Thaksin. Middle-class intellectuals themselves began to question majority rule, a core concept of democracy. A key figure was Anek Laothamatas, whose influential thinking was summed up by Pasuk and Baker:

> Anek argued that Thaksin's populism was the inevitable result of trying to make electoral democracy work in a country where most of the electorate were rural people still bound by old-style patron-client ties. In the early years of Thailand's democracy, politics was dominated by godfather politicians who translated patron–client bonds into electoral majorities. Thaksin's brilliance had been to transfer those bonds to a national leader. The rural voter used to exchange his vote for the promise of the godfather's local patronage, and now exchanged it for cheap health care and local loans. In this social setting, Anek argued, a 'pure democracy' was bound to lead to de Tocqueville's 'tyranny of the majority' and irresponsible populism. (Pasuk and Baker, 240)

Another influential figure, Thirayut Boonmee, an icon from the 1973–1976 student uprising, came out in favor of royal intervention to check democracy, saying the critics of such a move had 'to step beyond the Western frame of thinking' (Thirayut Boonmee, quoted in Lertchoosakul 2016, 237). Yet another prominent figure, a Chulalongkorn University professor, otherwise known as a liberal, confessed to me in an interview,

> For me, democracy is not the best regime. I'm in this sense an elitist. If there are people who are more capable, why not give them more weight. Why should they not come ahead of everybody else? You may call me a Nietzschean. (quoted in Bello 2014a)

This reactionary thinking emerged in the context of the rise of the anti-Thaksin 'Yellow Shirt' movement, composed mainly of the Bangkok middle class, who came out into the streets and helped trigger the coup that ousted Thaksin in September 2006. With Thaksin's electoral support remaining strong, the Yellow Shirts engaged in increasingly militant actions, such as their seizure of Bangkok's Suvarnabhumi International Airport in November 2008, to destabilize a pro-Thaksin government that had won the national elections in 2007.

When the Thaksin coalition won the parliamentary elections a fourth straight time in 2011, bringing Thaksin's sister, Yingluck, to the premiership, the elite–middle class opposition began to rapidly lose hope in a democratic reversal of what they considered a political trajectory harmful to their interests. Over the next few months, a strategy gradually evolved: use the judicial system to paralyze the government with charges of corruption and anti-constitutional moves, get the middle classes to stage massive demonstrations in Bangkok, which was largely anti-Thaksin territory, and get the military to launch a coup to resolve the political deadlock. Much like Santiago in 1972–1973, Bangkok in 2013–2014 became the site of almost daily demonstrations by the middle class led by the Democrat Party personality Suthep Thaugsuban, which were punctuated by instances of deadly violence. A last desperate effort by the government to resolve the crisis through new elections was sabotaged by demonstrators and thugs who tried to prevent people from voting, their rationale expressed in the slogan 'reform before elections', which was a sanitized code word for devising constitutional arrangements that would prevent the Redshirts from ever coming to power again.

On 22 May 2014, the military ousted the Yingluck government. In April 2017, a new constitution was promulgated, the main feature of which was a fully appointed Senate of 250 that could veto the moves of the National Assembly. Not surprisingly, this reflected the views of anti-Thaksin middle-class intellectuals like Anek, who had proposed several years earlier that to avoid the 'tyranny of the majority' that had brought Thaksin to power through thumping majorities, there had to be a 'better democracy' that was 'a balanced compromise between three elements: the representatives of the lower classes who are the majority in the country, the middle class, and the upper class' (quoted in Pasuk and Baker, 240). Laothamatas, a former communist turned counterrevolutionary thinker, was a member of the junta-appointed National Reform Council.

By the middle of 2017, the military government headed by Prime Minister Prayuth Chan-ocha, the former army chief of staff, remained in place, having gone far beyond its originally stated goal of staying in power for only 15 months. Unlike earlier military regimes, it was comfortably ensconced in power, a condition created partly by the successful intimidation of all opposition, but mainly by the solid support of a middle class that had, like Anek, turned counterrevolutionary.

A question one may ask, though, is why the overthrow of the Yingluck government was accomplished with so little violence. Part of the answer may reside in the fact that the military regarded the Redshirt movement as being still a relatively loose and inchoate network centered around a personality instead of being an organized and disciplined movement that posed a serious immediate threat to survival of the social regime. Another factor was probably a sense of the continuing strong hold of royalist sentiments among many in Thaksin's base, which the military unabashedly exploited to neutralize opposition to its seizure of power. A third reason was, unlike the 1976 counterrevolution, where fascist groups went on a rampage, the military made sure to monopolize the employment of coercion, which the leaders of the opposition were all too willing to give it since the main goal of their demonstrations – to get the military to launch a coup – had been accomplished.

Conclusion

In conclusion, the key features of the counterrevolutionary process in Thailand might be said to be the following:

First, the counterrevolution had two phases. The first developed in response to the student–peasant political ferment in the period 1973–1976, the second in response to the pro-Thaksin movement that drove the dynamics of Thai politics in the period 2001–2014.

Second, the peasant movement of the early 1970s was a largely self-organized class movement that emerged in response to the opportunities for change provided by the fluid political situation after the ouster of the military in in 1973. This movement was revolutionary in the sense that, in challenging the terms of land rent and land tenure, tenant farmers empowered themselves and became political subjects.

Third, the spread of capitalist production relations in the countryside and commercialization of land contributed to peasant distress in the period leading up to the 1973–1976 political ferment.

Fourth, the counterrevolution of 1973–1976 was clearly set in motion by the landed classes, but its development responded to the dynamics of fascist groups of a mixed-class character that were inflamed by the ideology of 'Nation-Religion-King' and received support from state security forces. This volatile mix erupted in the unprecedented violence of the counterrevolution during the right-wing invasion of Thammasat University in

October 1976. The behavior of these forces had much in common with that of the Italian fascists.

Fifth, like the peasant movement of the 1970s, the lower class mobilization of the last 15 years was set in motion not by revolutionary leadership but by the reformist agenda and populist style of Thaksin Shinawatra. The opposition's methods, however, radicalized it, and by the end of Yingluck Shinawatra's government in 2014 the so-called Red Shirt Movement appeared to have gone beyond a simple enterprise to restore Thaksin to power.

Sixth, in contrast to the base of the peasant movement of the 1970s, the Redshirt movement was composed not just of poor peasants but perhaps even more by urbanized villagers, many of whom had their feet in both agriculture and commerce, who could be classified as being on 'the margins of the middle class'. The complex character of the Redshirt movement stemmed the contradictory effects of globalization in the countryside, impoverishing some while providing an opportunity for others, including people who were able to get support from Thaksin's programs to help them build small businesses.

Seventh, the middle class formed the mass base of the counterrevolution of the Thaksin period. This middle class, however, was not simply manipulated by the traditional Thai elites. From being a force for democratization in the 1990s, its fear of the surge from below triggered by Thaksin's populist politics led it to a more and more anti-democratic position, the climax of which was its serving as the flame to provoke a military coup in 2014.

Eighth, while the ferment of the 1970s interacted with regional developments such as the fall of Vietnam, Laos and Cambodia to the communists, there was little evidence of significant foreign involvement in the Thai counterrevolution. There was also little involvement of foreign groups in the ouster of Thaksin and his sister Yingluck. In fact, relations between the military regime and the US deteriorated, owing to the US Ambassador's taking a 'hard line' against the 2014 coup (Crispin 2015).

The Philippines: emergence of a fascist original

The inclusion of the Philippines' Rodrigo Duterte in the counterrevolutionary pantheon might be regarded as premature since his administration is only slightly over a year old and its features might not have had a chance to clearly evolve into traits that could be identified as counterrevolutionary or fascist. While there might be some validity to this view, there are two powerful counter-arguments: first, Duterte is regarded globally as a prime example of the new authoritarianism; and, second, even if it is only into its second year, key features and thrusts of his regime have emerged decisively. There are, however, some limitations in discussing the Duterte case, in contrast to the first four cases studied here. Foremost among these is the fact that in the latter there already exists much historical data to enable us to do in-depth comparative work. Thus, many propositions suggested in this section will have a provisional quality, many of them having come out of the personal observations of someone who is closely engaged as an actor in national politics.[10]

Marcos as predatory ruler, Duterte as fascist

Whenever fascism or counterrevolution in Asia is discussed, the name of Ferdinand Marcos, who ruled the Philippines 50 years ago, comes up. Marcos was a dictator. But

---

[10]I was a member of the House of Representatives from 2009 to 2015. As a public figure, I have been identified as a critic of Duterte.

he was not a counterrevolutionary since, contrary to his claim, there was no immediate revolutionary threat that he was reacting to. Neither could he be said to be a fascist if in the definition of a fascist leader we mean one who is supported by a heated mass base that is engaged in acts of violence against their chosen victims. In a narrow sense, however, Marcos was a fascist, and that is because of his explicit repudiation of liberal democracy. As he himself put it,

> All that people ask is some kind of authority that can enforce the simple law of civil society .... Only an authoritarian system will be able to carry forth the mass consent and to exercise the authority necessary to implement new values, measures, and sacrifices. (Marcos 1980, 23, 25)

But perhaps the best characterization of the Marcos regime was as a project to monopolize political power for personal ends cloaked with the rhetoric of constructing some kind of developmental state – in short, a predatory state along the lines defined by Peter Evans (see Evans 1995).

Duterte is different. If we see as central to the definition of a fascist leader (1) a charismatic individual with strong inclinations toward authoritarian rule, who (2) is engaged in or supports the systematic violation of basic human, civil and political rights, (3) derives his or her strength from a heated multiclass mass base, and (4) pursues a political project that contradicts the fundamental values and aims of liberal democracy or social democracy – then Duterte fits the bill. The following sections will deal in more detail with these aspects of Duterte and his regime.[11]

Carino brutal

Duterte is charismatic, but his charisma is not the demiurgic sort like Hitler's nor does it derive so much from an emotional personal identification with the people and nation as in the case with some populists. Duterte's charisma would probably be best described as '*carino brutal*', a Filipino–Spanish term denoting a volatile mix of will to power, a commanding personality and gangster charm, that fulfills his followers' deep-seated yearning for a father figure who will finally end the national chaos.

Eliminationism

Duterte's fascist signature is his bloody war on drugs. Unlike most politicians, Duterte delivered on his main promise, which he had described as 'fattening the fish in Manila Bay' with the cadavers of criminals. Thousands of drug users have been slain either by the police or by police-controlled vigilante groups, with the police admitting that 2600 deaths were attributable to police operations while another 1400 were the work of vigilantes (Almendral 2017). Other, more reliable sources put the figure at above 7000 as of early May 2017 (Human Rights Watch 2017).

What is beyond doubt is that Duterte has brazenly encouraged the extra-judicial killings and discouraged due process. The very night of his taking his oath of office on 30 June 2016, he told an audience in one of Manila's working-class communities: 'If you know of any addicts, go ahead and kill them yourselves as getting their parents to do it would be too painful' (I-Defend 2016). In October 2016, Duterte told the country,

---

[11]Some of the points made below were originally laid out in Walden Bello, 'The Spider Spins his Web', which will appear in *Philippine Sociological Review*, vol. 65 (2017).

with characteristically sinister humor, that 20,000 to 30,000 more lives might have to be taken to cleanse the country of drugs (ABS/CBN 2016). Having learned to take Duterte seriously even when he seems to be joking, many observers expect this figure to be an underestimate. More recently, to any policemen who might be convicted of killing drug users without justification, he has offered an immediate pardon 'so you can go after the people who brought you to court' (DZRH 2017).

Duterte's matanza masiva of drug users is underpinned by an eliminationist rationale that reminds one of the pseudo-scientific basis of Nazi racial theory. A whole sector of society has been unilaterally stripped of their rights to life, due process and membership in society. This category – drug users and drug dealers – is said by Duterte to comprise some 3 to 4 million of the country's population of 104 million. Duterte has all but written off these people out of the human race. With rhetorical flourish, he told the security forces a few months ago: 'Crime against humanity? In the first place, I'd like to be frank with you: are they humans? What is your definition of a human being? (quoted in Agence France-Presse 2017)'

Drug users are consigned to outside the borders of 'humanity' since their brains have allegedly shrunk to the point that they are no longer in command of their faculties to will and think. In his speeches justifying the killings 'in self-defense' by police, Duterte said that a year or more of the use of 'shabu' – the local term for meth or metamphetamine hydrochloride – 'would shrink the brain of a person, and therefore he is no longer viable for rehabilitation'. These people are the 'living, walking dead' who are 'of no use to society anymore'. Not only do these people turn to violent crime to slake their drug habit, but they are paranoid and could resist arrest, putting the lives of policemen in danger (quoted in Villanueva 2016).

Needless to say, most neuroscientists claim that the effects of drug use on the brain are reversible and that rehabilitation, using chemical and electro-mechanical means, carried out in a supportive social context is not only possible but is actually being successfully carried out.[12]

Duterte's middle-class base

Like Mussolini and Hitler, there is no doubt that Duterte is popular, with some 82 percent of the people, according to a recent poll, registering satisfaction with his actions (Inquirer.net 2017). While he draws approval from all classes, his support is most aggressively displayed among the aspiring and downwardly mobile middle classes. Borrowing from Gramsci, one might advance the provisional observation that unlike Duterte's middle-class base, whom we might characterize as exhibiting 'active consensus' behind Duterte's authoritarian rule, the lower classes that support the president might be said to be marked by 'passive consensus'.

The Philippines provides an interesting case study of the volatility of the middle class. At times, it can be a force for democracy, as the middle classes were in the late 1980s, when they played a central role in the overthrow of Marcos and other authoritarian regimes throughout the global South. At other times, they provide the heated mass base for authoritarian rule, as they did for Mussolini in Italy and Hitler in Germany and as they do now for Duterte.

Duterte's middle-class base is not passive. Beginning with the presidential campaign in 2016, they have mobilized to dominate the social media, engaging in the worst kind of cyber-bullying of people who dare to criticize the president's policies on line. Shortly

---

[12]Interview with Dr. Yo Ying Ma, Binghamton, 5 March 2017.

after Duterte's declaration of martial law in Mindanao in May 2017, for instance, one of the most prominent pro-Duterte bloggers publicly called for the execution of two women journalists. Another Duterte fanatic registered his hope online that a woman senator, Risa Hontiveros, who had criticized Duterte's martial law declaration would be 'brutally raped'. Indeed, rational discourse is an increasingly scarce commodity among Duterte's partisans, who ape their leader's penchant for outrageous and incendiary utterances.

Duterte's political project

As for his political project, Duterte is not a reactionary seeking to restore a mythical past. He is not a conservative dedicated to defending the status quo. His project is oriented toward an authoritarian future. He is best described, using Arno Mayer's term, as a counterrevolutionary. Duterte is a counterrevolutionary and has excelled in the political improvisation characteristic of skilled counterrevolutionaries like Hitler and Mussolini.[13] Counterrevolutionaries are not always clear about what their next moves are, but they often have an instinctive sense of what would bring them closer to power. Ideological purity is not high on their agenda, with them putting a premium on the emotional power of their message rather on its intellectual coherence. But aside from seizing power, counterrevolutionaries do have an ideological agenda and ideological enemies. Mussolini and Hitler were leading a counterrevolution against the left or social revolution. In Duterte's case, the target, one can infer from his discourse and his actions, is liberal democracy, the dominant ideology and political system of our time.[14] In this sense, he is both a local expression and a pioneer of an ongoing global phenomenon: right-wing backlash against liberal democratic values and liberal democratic discourse, that Francis Fukuyama had declared as the end of history in the early 1990s (see Fukuyama 1992).

A fascist original

While Duterte fits the fascist category, it must also be pointed out that he is no simple reproduction of past actors. He is a fascist original. Interpreting his mandate as a blank check to do whatever it takes to 'defend the nation', Duterte has reversed the usual model by which fascists and authoritarian populists come to power. In the conventional model of 'creeping fascism', the fascist personality begins with violations of civil and political rights, followed by the lunge for absolute power, after which follows indiscriminate repression. Duterte reverses the process. He starts with massive, indiscriminate repression – that is, the killing with impunity of thousands of drug users – leaving the violation of civil liberties and the grab for total power as mopping-up operations in a political atmosphere where fear has largely neutralized opposition. His approach might be called 'blitzkrieg facism', in contrast to 'creeping fascism'. He is also original in the way he has incorporated the traditional left, the National Democratic Front (NDF) controlled by the Communist Party of the Phliippines, into the ruling bloc by appointing key members of the NDF to his

---

[13]Here, I find Arno Mayer's distinction among 'reactionaries', 'conservatives' and 'counterrevolutionaries' still very useful. Fascism, in Mayer's typology, falls into the counterrevolutionary category. See Mayer (1971).

[14]This is not to say that liberal democracy was not also a subject of derision on the part of Hitler and Mussolini. However, the principal targets of both leaders were the socialist project and the workers' movement, and they played on the threat of a working-class revolution to unite the right on their way to power.

cabinet. Most earlier fascist leaders, while stealing the progressive rhetoric of the left, had seen the organized left as their deadly enemy.

Moving on to the question of what accounts for Duterte's rise to power, there is no doubt that his promise to deal in a draconian fashion with the drug problem was a major factor in his being elected in a society where fear of crime is widespread among all sectors of the population. It is a testimony to his political acumen that he was able to successfully latch onto an issue that most politicians had ignored. Yet there are more profound causes for his victory and his current popularity. One cannot understand Duterte's hold on society without taking into consideration the deep disenchantment with the liberal democratic regime that came into being with the landmark 'EDSA Uprising' that overthrew the dictator Ferdinand Marcos in February 1986 (EDSA being the acronym for the north–south highway that bisects Metro-Manila where the major mass actions took place. In fact, the failure of the 'EDSA Republic' was a condition for Duterte's success).

Why EDSA's elite democracy prepared the way for Duterte

What destroyed the EDSA project and paved the way for Duterte was the deadly combination of elite monopoly of the electoral system, uncontrolled corruption, the continuing concentration of wealth, neoliberal economic policies, and the priority placed on foreign debt repayment imposed by Washington.[15]

By the time of the elections of 2016, there was a yawning gap between the EDSA Republic's promise of popular empowerment and wealth redistribution and the reality of massive poverty, scandalous inequality and pervasive corruption. The income ratio of the top 10 percent relative to the bottom 40 percent increased from 3.09 in 2003 to 3.27 in 2009 while the Gini coefficient, the best summary measure of inequality, increased from 0.438 in 1991 to 0.506 in 2009 (see Martinez et al. 2014; Remo 2013).[16] Add to this brew the widespread perception of inept governance during the preceding administration of President Benigno Aquino III, and it is not surprising that a good part of the electorate saw Duterte's tough-guy, authoritarian approach, which he had cultivated as mayor of the southern frontier city of Davao for over 30 years, as precisely what was needed.

Moreover, the EDSA Republic's discourse of democracy, human rights and rule of law had become a suffocating straitjacket for a majority of Filipinos who simply could not relate to it owing to the overpowering reality of their powerlessness. Duterte's discourse – a mixture of outright death threats, coarse street-corner language, misogynistic outbursts, and frenzied railing coupled with disdainful humor directed at the elite, whom he calls 'coños' or cunts – is a potent formula that proved exhilarating to his audience who felt themselves liberated from what they experienced as the stifling political correctness and hypocrisy of the EDSA discourse.

The decline of the peasantry as a political actor

Focusing briefly on the countryside during the EDSA period, disaffection was high owing to the EDSA Republic's very disappointing record on agrarian reform. By the end of the

---

[15] For a comprehensive analysis of the political economy of the EDSA regime, see Bello et al. (2014).
[16] According to the National Statistical Coordination Board, people from the high-income class, who account for between 15.1 and 15.9 percent of the country's population, enjoyed a 10.4-percent annual growth in income in 2011. In contrast, incomes of people in the middle-income segment grew by only 4.3 percent, and incomes of those in the low-income group by 8.2 percent. Overall inequality thus increased as the incomes of the top bracket increased faster than those of other brackets (Remo 2013).

26-year-old enterprise in 2014 that had been its centerpiece program, some 700,000 hectares of private land – 450,000 of which constituted the best agricultural land in the country – remained undistributed (Bello 2014).[17]

Frustration did not, however, translate into class mobilization in the period prior to the 2016 elections. Several factors account for this, according to a specialist on the Philippine Left and a key peasant organizer. First, during the martial law period, the Communist Party of the Philippines, which was then one of the key forces opposing Marcos, put the priority on organizing a support base for the New People's Army, not on organizing them to push for agrarian reform. Thus, when the EDSA Uprising ushered in a period of more open politics, the mass organizations of the left that pushed for agrarian reform were relatively weak. A second factor that led to peasant quiescence was the vicious internecine warfare that broke out in the 1990s between the pro-armed struggle wing of the movement and a less doctrinaire grouping that put a premium on open mass struggle and participation in elections. A third was an internal party purge in the mid-1980s that took the lives of some 2000 cadres, most of whom were working among peasants in the countryside.[18]

In any event, what pollsters in the Philippines classify as classes 'D' and 'E' – those with lower incomes – make up the vast majority of the electorate, so we can assume that in the absence of more detailed poll categories, a significant part of the 16 million voters (40 percent of the electorate) who voted for Duterte came from the rural poor.

Duterte's sozialepolitik

Turning to Duterte's *sozialepolitik*, though much of his rhetoric is populist, his approach is not a populist strategy of using the masses as a battering ram for redistributive reform. Rather, his is the classic fascist way of balancing different class forces while projecting an image of being above class conflict. His campaign promises of ending contractual labor, curbing the mining industry, and turning over to small coconut farmers the taxes collected from them by the Marcos regime have remained largely unfulfilled even as the country's key elites have positioned themselves as his allies to protect their interests. These include the landed class, big monopoly capitalist actors such as Ramon Ang and Manny Pangilinan, and Big Mining. All labor groups have rejected his labor minister's order 'banning' contractualization as a cosmetic move. No new legislation to push forward the stalled agrarian reform is entertained, which is not surprising given the fact that the so-called Visayan bloc of landowners in the Philippines' House of Representatives is one of his most solid backers.

A defining moment in the debate on whether Duterte was serious about a social agenda was the congressional confirmation hearings early in 2017 on his crusading environment minister, Gina Lopez, who had shut down, suspended or issued show-cause orders to over 100 mining operations for encroaching on watersheds and destabilizing rural and forest communities. Her campaign had captured the public imagination, but Duterte's allies in the mining industry ganged up on her, successfully pressuring the Congressional Commission on Appointments not to confirm her, with the president sitting on the sidelines, refusing to personally lobby for her retention when a simple phone call would have made the difference (Bello 2017). Duterte is not a tool of vested interests; indeed, many of the rich

---

[17]The best in-depth treatment of the failure of agrarian reform in the Philippines can be found in Borras (2007).
[18]Interview with Ricardo Reyes and Danny Carranza, Quezon City, 8 August 2017.

are scared of him and his unpredictability. But money does have its uses, and it is essential to furthering his authoritarian agenda.

But while delivering social and economic reforms is going to be central in maintaining support for his authoritarian project in the long term, it is unlikely that the lack of observable progress so far will dent Duterte's popularity with the masses in the short and medium term.

Duterte, nationalism and geopolitics

Finally, a word on Duterte and geopolitics. Like the post-coup military regime in Thailand, Duterte could not count on the support of the US government, which under the Obama administration had placed a premium on democratic competition and human rights, though this was invoked selectively. Though a novice when it comes to foreign policy, he has had an instinctive grasp of the dynamics of Philippine nationalism. His calling former US President Obama a 'son of a bitch' for criticizing his policy of extra-judicial executions and his moves toward a policy less dependent on Washington and closer to China were not expected to enjoy much popularity in the Philippines, where pro-Americanism has been regarded as deeply entrenched. Surprisingly, they met with very little protest and elicited much support on the internet. As many have observed, coexisting with admiration for the US and US institutions exhibited by ordinary Filipinos is a strong undercurrent of resentment at the colonial subjugation of the country by the US, unequal treaties that Washington has foisted on the country, and the overwhelming impact of the 'American way of life' on local culture. Here, one need not delve into the complexity of Hegel's master–servant dialectic to understand that undercurrent of the US–Philippine relationship has been the 'struggle for recognition' of the dominated party. Duterte's skill has been to tap into this emotional underside of Filipinos in a way that the left has never been able to with its anti-imperialist program. Like many of his authoritarian predecessors, Duterte has been able to splice nationalism and authoritarianism in a very effective fashion.

Duterte's much-publicized move to improve the Philippines' relations with China, to the point of placing on the back burner the resolution of the country's territorial dispute with the latter, derived not so much from a desire to spite former US President Obama, as some have claimed. It stems from a shrewd acceptance of changing power realities in Asia, of China's emerging dominant role in the region. What has often been missed, however, is another dimension: Duterte's admiration for China's authoritarian system for its ability to 'deliver results'.

With his declaration of martial law in Mindanao in May 2017, Duterte is now embarked on the next phase of his ascent to absolute power, which will most likely involve the curtailment and suppression of basic political rights. With or without the formal declaration of martial law nationwide, he is on the road to dictatorship. The US-style separation of powers has broken down, with Congress fully controlled by his allies and the Supreme Court giving him a blank check to monopolize the declaration and management of martial law. One year after his election, Duterte exercises a level of control over the political system that had not been seen since Marcos' rule in the 1970s. But he enjoyed something Marcos never achieved: popular legitimacy. As with Mussolini and Hitler, this was a far more important resource than the support he received from the military and the police. The momentum of his regime was toward dictatorship. Like Cortez, Duterte has burned his ships behind him. There is no going back. Yielding power when his six-year term ends is a vanishing option. Not least among the reasons for this is that he and many of his lieutenants would face prosecution for extra-judicial execution of thousands of people, not only locally but internationally; charges of systematic human rights violations have been filed against them in the International Criminal Court (ICC).

Conclusion

In conclusion, we might highlight the following points with respect to Duterte and his regime:

First, in contrast to the leaders, both individual and institutional, in the four other cases of counterrevolution studied here, he reincarnates the classic charismatic individual at the center of fascist movements.

Second, his fascist character is most fully displayed in his bloody war on drugs, which has taken over 7000 lives and is underpinned by an eliminationist ideology.

Third, as in the other four cases of counterrevolution, Duterte has a heated mass support which is anchored in, though not exclusively derived from, the middle class.

Fourth, his political project is essentially a counterrevolution against liberal democracy, and it is one that enjoys much popularity owing to the EDSA liberal democratic regime's crushing failure to deliver the political and economic reforms that it had promised.

Fifth, Duterte is a fascist original who follows a strategy of blitzkrieg fascism as opposed to creeping fascism.

Sixth, Duterte engages in populist rhetoric, but his intent is to project an image of being above class conflict while preserving the existing balance of class forces where the traditional elites hold sway.

Seventh, in contrast to the four other cases, the role of the countryside, as a base for either revolution or counterrevolution, is negligible in the case of the Duterte's ascent to power, except perhaps as the source of lower class voters who voted for Duterte in 2016.

Finally, Duterte has played geopolitics with skill, recognizing on the one hand the changing balance of power in the East Asian region, with power shifting from China to the United States, while also using anti-US rhetoric to burnish his nationalist credentials.

Concluding considerations

In conclusion, several points have been highlighted by this survey:

One, right-wing movements that come to power can best be understood via a paradigm in which the revolution–counterrevolution dialectic is the centerpiece. The perceived revolutionary threat may not be, however, a takeover by an armed insurgency but a progressive movement that is able to use the law and established institutions to promote social reform. This was the case in Italy, Indonesia, Chile and Thailand.

Second, the middle class has been the pivot around which politics revolves in times of great fluidity. The middle class is notoriously volatile. Under certain circumstances, such as the rule of a socially isolated dictatorship like Suchinda's military dictatorship in Thailand and the Marcos regime in the Philippines, it can play a progressive role in pushing democratization. In other circumstances, however, it may play a counterrevolutionary role, and this is especially the case in periods of great political agitation by labor and the peasantry for their rights, which the middle classes perceive as threatening not only the position of the elite but also their own position.

Third, where the state is weak or lacking in legitimacy, threatened elites resort to fascist paramilitary groups to protect their interests. This is not, however, a case of pure manipulation but one in which the middle-class elements that form the fascist bands actually see their interests as converging with those of the threatened elite. However, agencies of the state, especially the security forces like the police and the army, do not remain neutral but lend either active or passive support to the fascists. This was clearest in the case of Italy and Thailand.

On the other hand, where the state, especially the repressive agencies, is strong, it usually directs the final stage of counterrevolution – that is, the physical elimination of the leftist enemy – from above, using civilian groups mainly as junior partners, if it resorts to such formations at all.

Fourth, the local revolution–counterrevolution dialectic is often part of an international revolution–counterrevolution dialectic, so that there is sometimes significant external support for the domestic counterrevolution. However, in the cases where this was most evident – Indonesia and Chile – the role played by external intervention, while important, was not decisive. Indeed, foreign assistance only becomes effective when it is inserted into an ongoing domestic counterrevolutionary process.

Fifth, the countryside has played a key role most counterrevolutionary movements, though the dynamics of the counterrevolution in the rural areas have been intimately connected if not subordinated to the larger struggle between left and right at the national level.

In connection with this, a key question that emerges from this study is the role of the countryside in future social conflicts in the global South. Several developments seem to point in the direction of a reduced role and significance. First is the declining portion of agricultural workers and peasants in the work force as capital-intensive industrial agriculture advances. Second is the rising average age of farmers everywhere. Third is even greater differentiation of the peasantry as capitalist relations of production become dominant. Fourth is the crisis of the left, which has historically provided the leadership for militant peasant movements and often served as the political bridge between different strata of the peasantry and between the peasantry and the working class. Does the Philippines, which now has a relative quiescent peasantry, owing precisely to the impact of these factors, represent the future of the countryside in national politics in the global South?

But one might point to Thailand to argue that the rural lower classes can, despite greater differentiation and the absence of a party of the left to provide political direction, still remain an influential actor on the national scene. But was not Thaksin a unique 'event?' One cannot escape the suspicion that had Thailand's traditional elite been more accommodating, Thaksin would not have turned to mobilizing the countryside to realize his personal ambitions. This counterfactual is intriguing but will always remain a hypothesis. Perhaps the real lesson of Thailand and Thaksin, like that of Italy and Mussolini, is not so much to provide an answer to the question as to whether or not the countryside will continue to play a key role in national politics but to remind us that the politics of class continues to be capable of springing big surprises. As noted at the beginning of this essay, Mussolini himself was surprised that fascism in the countryside ended up serving as the battering ram of his drive to power.

Disclosure statement

No potential conflict of interest was reported by the author.

References

ABS/CBN News. 2016. Duterte on drug-related deaths: expect 20,000 to 30,000 more. ABS/CBN News, Oct 28, 2016. http://news.abs-cbn.com/news/10/27/16/duterte-on-drug-related-deaths-expect-20000-or-30000-more

Agence France-Presse. 2017. Criminals are not human—Aguirre. Feb 1, 2017. http://newsinfo.inquirer.net/867331/criminals-are-not-human-aguirre

Almendral, Aurora. 2017. The general running Duterte's anti-drug war. *New York Times*, June 2, 2017. https://www.nytimes.com/2017/06/02/world/asia/the-general-running-dutertes-antidrug-war.html?emc=edit_th_20170603&nl=todaysheadlines&nlid=57179294&_r=0

Anderson, Benedict. 1998. *The specter of comparisons: nationalism, Southeast Asia, and the world*. London: Verso.

Aranda, Sergio, and Alberto Martinez. 1971. Estructura economica: algunas carac- teristicas funda-mentales. In *Chile Hoy*, eds. Anibal Pinto et al., 55–172. Santiago: Editorial Universitaria.

Aspinall, Edward. 2005. *Opposing suharto: compromise, resistance, and regime change in Indonesia*. Stanford: Stanford University Press.

BBC News. 2011. Chile recognizes 9800 more victims. *BBC News*, Aug 18, 2011. http://www.bbc.com/news/world-latin-america-14584095

Bello, Walden. 2014. Agrarian Reform: Powerful Law, Ineffectual Bureaucracy. *Inquirer.net*, June 10. http://opinion.inquirer.net/75458/agrarian-reform-powerful-law-ineffectual-bureaucracy

Bello, Walden. 2014a. Military Suspends Class Conflict in Thailand. *Telesur*, August 8, http://www.telesurtv.net/english/opinion/Military-Suspends-Class-Conflict-in-Thailand-20140806-0010.html

Bello, Walden. 2016. How Middle Class Chileans Contributed to the Overthrow of Salvador Allende. *The Nation*, Oct 10, 2016. https://www.thenation.com/article/how-middle-class-chileans-contributed-to-the-overthrow-of-salvador-allende/

Bello, Walden. 2017. Burying Gina. *Rappler*, April 25. http://www.rappler.com/thought-leaders/167872-gina-lopez-mining-industry

Bello, Walden, Kenneth Cardenas, Jerome Patrick Cruz, Alinaya Fabros, Mary Ann Manahan, Clarissa Militante, Joseph Purugganan, and Jenina Joy Chavez. 2014. *State of fragmentation: The Philippines in transition*. Manila: Focus on the Global South.

Bello, Walden, Shea Cunningham, and Li Kheng Poh. 1998. *A siamese tragedy: development and disintegration in modern Thailand*. London: Zed Books.

Borras, S.M. 2007. *Pro-Poor land reform: A critique*. Ottawa: University of Ottawa Press.

Bowie, Katherine. 1991. Introduction. In *Voices from the Thai countryside*, ed. Samruan Singh, 1–41. Madison: Center for Southeast Asian Studies, University of Wisconsin.

Cardoza, Anthony. 1982. *Agrarian elites and Italian fascism: The province of Bologna, 1901-1926*. Princeton: Princeton University Press.

Castro, Fidel. 1971. Fidel analiza a fondo el proceso chileno. *Punto Final*. No. 141 (December 7): 42–58.

Chachavalpongpun, Pavin. 2017. Thai politics in the post-succession period. In *Religion and politics in Southeast Asia*, 429–433. Seoul: Korean Association of Southeast Asian Studies.

Cherian, John. 2016. Indonesia: a Forgotten Genocide. *Frontline*, Jan 10, 2016. http://www.frontline.in/world-affairs/a-forgotten-genocide/article8017859.ece

Chonchol, Jacques. 1972. La reforma agrarian y la experiencia chilena. In *Transicion al socialismo y experiencia chilena*, 149–162. Santiago: PLA.

Chulalongkorn University Social Research Institute (CUSRI). 1989. *Master plan study of the agricu-lural land reform, Vol. 2: The main report*. Bangkok: CUSRI.

Connors, Michael Kelly. 2003. *Democracy and national identity in Thailand*. Copenhagen: NIAS Press.

Corner, Paul. 1972. *Fascism in ferrara, 1915-1925*. Oxford: Oxford University Press.

Crispin, Shawn. 2015. New Ambassador Holds Key to US-Thailand Relations. *The Diplomat*, Sept 26, 2015. http://thediplomat.com/2015/09/new-ambassador-holds-key-to-us-thailand-relations/

Democracy Now. 2013. Make the economy scream: secret documents show Nixon, Kissinger Role backing 1973 Chile Coup. *Democracy Now*, Sept 10, 2013. https://www.democracynow.org/2013/9/10/40_years_after_chiles_9_11

Ebner, Michael. 2011. *Ordinary violence in mussolini's Italy*. Cambridge: Cambridge University Press.

Ebner, Michael. 2017. This is the Violence of which I approve. *Slate*, Jan 20, 2017. http://www.slate.com/articles/news_and_politics/fascism/2017/01/how_italian_fascists_succeeded_in_taking_over_italy.html

Evans, Peter. 1995. *Embedded autonomy: states and industrial transformation*. Princeton: Princeton University Press.

Fallon, Edward Bernard. 1983. The peasants of isan: social and economic transitions in northeast Thailand. *Ph.D. dissertation*, University of Washington at Madison.

Fukuyama, Francis. 1992. *The End of history and the last Man*. New York: Free Press.

Gall, Norman. 1972. The agrarian revolt in cautin, part II: land reform and the MIR. *American Universities Field Staff Reports* (West Coast South American Series) XIV, no. 5: 8.

Garcia, Norberto. 1972. Algunas aspectos de la politica de corto plazo de 1971. In *La economia chilena en 1971*, 47–270. Santiago: Instituto de Economia, Universidad de Chile.

Goldhagen, Daniel Jonah. 2009. *Worse than War*. New York: Public Affairs.

Haberkorn, Tyrell. 2011. *Revolution, Law, and violence in northern Thailand*. Chiang Mai: Silkworm Books.

Human Rights Watch. 2017. The Philippines' Drug War Death Denial Complex. *Human Rights Watch*, May 9. https://www.hrw.org/news/2017/05/09/philippines-drug-war-deaths-denial-complex

I-Defend. 2016. Statement at solidarity dinner at Del Pan Sports Complex, July 1, 2016, quoted in I-Defend. End impunity, stand up for human rights, uphold due process. Aug 12, 2016.

Inquirer.net. 2017. Pulse: duterte gets 82 per cent approval rating. *Inquirer.net*, Jul 18, 2017. http://newsinfo.inquirer.net/914730/pulse-duterte-gets-82-approval-rating

Johnson, John. 1961. The political role of the latin American middle sectors. *The Annals of the American Academy of Political and Social Science* 334: 20–29.

Karunan, Victor. 1984. *If the land could speak, It would speak for Us: Vol. 1: A history of peasant movements in Thailand and the Philippines*. Hong Kong: Plough Publications.

Kay, Cristobal. 2001. Reflections on rural violence in latin america. *Third World Quarterly* 22, no. 5: 741–775.

Klein, Naomi. 2007. *The shock doctrine and the rise of disaster capitalism*. New York: Random House.

Lane, Max. 2008. *Unfinished nation: Indonesia before and after suharto*. London: Verso.

Lertchoosakul, Kanokrat. 2016. *The rise of the octobrists in contemporary Thailand*. Chiang Mai: Silkworm Books.

Lopez, Sergio. 1971. Defensa, Critica, y dudas sobre la politica gubernativa. *Panorama Economico*, no. 261: 13–30.

Lyttleton, Adrian. 1982. Fascism and violence in post-War Italy: political strategy and social conflict. In *Social protest, violence, and terror in the nineteenth and twentieth century*, eds. W.J. Mommsen and Gerhard Hirshfield, 257–274. New York: St. Martin's Press.

Marcos, Ferdinand. 1980. *The third world alternative*. Manila: Ministry of Public Information.

Martinez, A., M. Western, M. Haynes, and W. Tomazewski. 2014. Is there income mobility in the Philippines? *Asian-Pacific Economic Literature* 28, no. 1: 96–115.

Mattelart, Armand. 1973. Notas sobre el gremialismo y la linea de masa de la burguesia chilena. *Casa de la Americas* XIV, no. 83: 69–87.

Mayer, Arno. 1971. *Dynamics of counterrevolution in Europe, 1870–1956: An analytic framework*. New York, NY: Harper and Row.

MIR. 1972. El MIR responde a los ataques del partido comunista. *El Rebelde*, no. 15: 1–6 (Feb 1-8, 1972).

Moore, Barrington. 1966. *The social origins of dictatorship and democracy: lord and peasant in the modern world*. Boston: Beacon.

Moore, Barrington. 2004. Revolution from above and fascism. In *The social dynamics of fascism*, eds. Roger Griffin and Matthew Feldman, 256–279. London: Taylor and Francis.

Murray, Warwick. 2003. From dependency to reform and back again: The Chilean peasant in the twentieth century. In *Latin American peasants*, ed. Tom Brass, 190–222. London: Frank Cass.

Nurchayati. 2017. How migration has shaped the birth and development of an east javanese village community: the case of pranggang from the 1890s to the Mid-1960s. In *Religion and politics In Southeast Asia*, 340–346. Seoul: Korean Association of Southeast Asian Studies.

ODEPLAN. 1972. *Informe economo annual de 1971*. Santiago: ODEPLAN.

Okamoto, Masasaki. 2017. Indonesian democracy in deconsolidation? populism, intolerance, and post-truth. In *Religion and politics in Southeast Asia*, 433–438. Seoul: Korean Association of Southeast Asian Studies.

Pathamanand, Ukrist. 2016. Network thaksin: structure, roles, and reaction. In *Unequal Thailand: aspects of income, wealth, and power*, eds. Pasuk Phongpaichit and Chris Baker, 136–161. Singapore: NUS Press.

Politica y Espiritu. 1971. Dos renuncias al partido democrata cristiano. *Politica y Espiritu* XXXVI, No. 323: 8–9.
Pongpaiboon, Somkiat. 1991. Powerful education through people organization: a case of movement against salt farming in the northeast of Thailand. Paper presented to ICEA sixth world conference on community education on developing the global village, July 29-August 2, Trinidad and Tobago.
Pongsapich, Amara, et al. 1993. *Sociocultural change and political development in central Thailand, 1950-1990*. Bangkok: TDRI.
Poulantzas, Nicos. 1974. *Fascism and dictatorship*. London: New Left Books.
Remo, Michelle. 2013. Rich-Poor Divide in Philippines Widening. *Philippine Daily Inquirer*, July 10. http://newsinfo.inquirer.net/441817/rich-poor-divide-in-ph-widening
Robinson, G. 1995. *The dark Side of paradise: political violence in bali*. Ithaca: Cornell University Press.
Rojanaphruk, Pravit. 2016. The Will to Remember: Survivors Recount 1976 Thammasat Massacre 40 Years Later. *Khao Sod*, Oct 6, 2016. http://www.khaosodenglish.com/politics/2016/10/05/will-remember-survivors-recount-1976-massacre-40-years-later/
Roosa, John. 2006. *Pretext for mass murder: The September 30th movement and suharto's coup d'Etat in Indonesia*. Madison: University of Wisconsin Press.
Snowden, Francis. 2004. *Fascist revolution in tuscany*. Cambridge: Cambridge University Press.
Steenland, Kyle. 1975. Notes on feudalism and capitalism in Chile and latin america. *Latin American Perspectives* 2, no. 1: 51–52.
Tasca, Angelo. 1938. *The rise of Italian fascism*. London: Methuen.
Thabchumpon, N., and D. McCargo. 2011. Urbanized villagers in the 2010 Thai redshirt protests: Not just poor farmers? *Asian Survey* 51, no. 6: 993–1018.
Turton, Andrew. 1978. The current situation in the countryside. In *Thailand: roots of conflict*, ed. Andrew Turton, 104–142. London: Spokesman Books.
Turton, Andrew. 1982. Poverty, reform, and class struggle in rural Thailand. In *Rural poverty and agrarian reform*, eds. S. Jones et al., 20–45. New Delhi: ENDA and Allied Publishers.
Unidad Popular. 1972. *Programa de gobierno de la unidad popular—declaracion de "El arrayan"*. Santiago: Unidad Popular, p. 63
Vaddhanaputi, Chayan. 1984. Cultural and ideological reproduction in rural northern Thai society. *Ph.D. dissertation*, Stanford University, Stanford.
Villanueva, Marichu. 2016. Duterte Likens Addicts to Zombies. *Philippine Star*, Aug 24, 2016. http://www.philstar.com/opinion/2016/08/24/1616655/duterte-likens-drug-addicts-zombies
White, Ben. 2016. Remembering the Indonesian peasants' front and plantation workers' union (1945–1966). *The Journal of Peasant Studies* 43, no. 1: 1–16. http://www.tandfonline.com.proxy.binghamton.edu/doi/full/10.1080/03066150.2015.1101069
Wierenga, Saskia Eleonora. 2001. Sexual slander and the 1965/66 mass killings in Indonesia: political and methodological considerations. *Journal of Contemporary Asia* 41, no. 4: 544–565. http://www.tandfonline.com/doi/full/10.1080/00472336.2011.610613
Winn, Peter. 2010. The furies of the Andes: violence and terror in the Chilean revolution and counter-revolution. In *A century of revolution: insurgent and counterinsurgent violence during latin america's long cold War*, eds. Greg Grandin and Gilbert Joseph, 239–275. Durham: Duke University Press.

People and places left behind: work, culture and politics in the rural United States

Jessica D. Ulrich-Schad and Cynthia M. Duncan

ABSTRACT

Using interview and survey data, we argue there are three types of places in the rural United States, and that their social and economic conditions help us understand emerging political trends, including the rural support for Donald Trump. More rural votes were cast for the Republican presidential candidate in 2016 than in other recent elections, yet shifts to Republican votes were greatest in places undergoing the most significant economic transitions. Work in rural communities has been a source of pride and cultural identity for people as well as places, but many feel the new economy is not working for them.

Introduction: three rural Americas

White rural residents in the United States (US) voted overwhelmingly for Donald Trump and his promise to restore an economic era in which working-class US citizens did well, and that vote brought new attention to conditions in rural places. Political leaders, journalists and the US public are asking questions about the reasons for this decisive rural vote. Rural residents of the US, traditionally committed to small government (Stock and Johnson 2001; Cramer 2016), have long backed Republican candidates overall, but the extent of Republican support in 2016 was different. While the majority of votes for Donald Trump came from suburban areas in the US (Balz 2017), rural areas did vote overwhelmingly for the Republican candidate. Donald Trump received 62 percent of the rural vote, more than any other Republican candidate in modern times (Wilson 2017). There is debate about the extent to which this strong support emerged from economic troubles versus the extent to which it is it rooted in a rural cultural identity that is seeding a new rural populism.

On the one hand, rural areas in general have been experiencing economic restructuring and decline for decades, and over that time the federal and state governments have done little to support blue-collar workers who need to make a transition to new work. Indeed, as Packer (2014) reminds us, the government pulled back on public investments in human capital just as restructuring began to change work in rural and urban rustbelt communities. Additionally, Cramer (2016) points out that some rural people harbor resentment toward urban people and places that they perceive to be getting more than their fair share in government spending.

On the other hand, some scholars and journalists argue there is growing rural–urban divide that includes not just economic differences but also 'cultural' differences, different values and attitudes about what matters and where the US is headed and should go. As we will show, rural people in the US feel important ties to place, and deeply value family and community. These qualities are among the most important reasons people stay in rural places even when jobs are disappearing. Many patch together livelihoods, sometimes relying on several jobs or informal work, or on disability payments and food stamps, and, often, help from family, so they can stay. In our interviews, many talk about their nostalgia for the lost economy, their 'heritage', as they put it, and see the loss of decent jobs as a cultural loss that has undermined their community and way of life.

While certain characteristics and changes impact all rural places in the US, our research shows there are important differences depending on local and regional economic and demographic trends, as well as the historical political economy – trends that are often tied to the character and use of the natural resources in the place. Using our own and secondary data, in this paper we argue that there are three rural Americas, and that their social and economic conditions, both now and historically, help us understand the political trends that are emerging. We describe (1) areas rich in natural amenities, (2) areas undergoing profound economic and demographic transitions, and (3) chronically poor areas. Looking at the rural US from this perspective helps provide a more nuanced framework for understanding the role of rural residents in current national politics, and especially in the last election.

Methods

We draw upon diverse, empirical data collected through surveys, interviews and focus groups, as well as secondary voting, American Community Survey, Decennial Census and Bureau of Economic Analysis data, to consider work, culture and politics in different rural US settings during a period of profound economic change. While we outline some key details about our data collection and analysis methods below, please see Hamilton et al. (2008, 2010), Ulrich-Schad, Henly, and Safford (2013) and Ulrich-Schad and Qin (2017) for additional specifics.

From 2007 to 2011, we surveyed nearly 17,000 rural residents of rural places in the US as part of the Community and Environment in Rural America (CERA) project started by the Carsey Institute at the University of New Hampshire to better understand how rural US residents think about their communities, local economies, environmental issues and the future. An economically, geographically and demographically diverse set of 38 counties in 12 states was chosen to represent some of the key differences across the rural US.[1] Participants were randomly selected at the county level to take the phone survey. Response rates ranged from 18 to 40 percent and probability weights (age, race, sex) are applied in all analyses. While respondents to our surveys are not representative of all people living in the rural US, the places they reside are illustrative of rural economies. We use this data to compare and contrast ideal types of rural places we consider amenity rich (13 counties, six states, $N = 4893$), transitioning (16 counties, seven states, $N = 7028$), and chronically poor

---

[1] Please note that we cannot disclose the locations of our survey counties or interviews, to protect the identity of the communities described in more depth in some of our other research.

(10 counties, four states, $N = 4896$) (described in more detail below).[2] We also use data from a nationally representative CERA survey ($N = 2005$) that asked comparable questions of both rural and urban respondents.

To more deeply understand what it is like to live and work in a variety of rural places, we conducted in-depth interviews in four of the places we surveyed, including with residents and community leaders in one transitioning community ($N = 35$) and two chronically poor places ($N = 85$) to update *Worlds apart: poverty and politics in rural America* in 2013 (Duncan 2015). The first author also conducted 59 interviews with residents and leaders in one amenity-rich community in 2013. While Chronically Poor Areas such as Native American reservations and the Colonias and areas in the Southwest where many Hispanic U.S. residents live are important to the story, we do not have data from these areas. The original plan for the CERA study included two high poverty predominantly Hispanic border counties as well as Native American reservations, but the logistics, legacy of exploitative research in Indian Country, and/or language differences proved too challenging given resources available.

Interviews generally lasted one to two hours; interviewees were asked to tell their life story, and to reflect on it and their community. People were often wary at first, sure that they 'had nothing to say'. But almost invariably they became caught up in their stories, seemed to feel freer to talk to someone 'from away' who both listened hard and showed some understanding of the community and its politics, challenges and strengths. We taped the interviews, and analyzed the interview transcripts for patterns. In our predominantly African American community we worked with a long-time colleague from a historically black college in Mississippi.

Introduction of the three rural Americas

The three types of rural US places we present here are ideal types. Secondary data (see Table 1) and data we collected show how they capture key trends in the rural US today. We show how economic conditions, demographic trends and civic culture converge but also clearly vary across these three rural Americas. *Amenity-rich areas* have been growing in population as their mountains, lakes or seashore, or other natural amenities make them places that are attractive to retirees, recreationists and 'laptop professionals'. There are many newcomers in these rural places, who are often college-educated professionals who have come for the natural beauty and outdoor activities – for the quality of life these places offer. These amenity-rich areas do not share the overall pattern of economic decline and out-migration that has become the dominant trend in most rural places in the US, but many have seen good blue-collar jobs disappear, and now, as an expanded

---

[2]We use two classification systems developed by the United States Department of Agriculture Economic Research Service (ERS) on economic dependence and policy-relevant themes to justify the grouping of our study counties. All counties we consider amenity rich are classified by the ERS into the policy-relevant theme of 'recreation' meaning their economies are dependent upon tourism and recreational activities and they have a high percentage of vacation homes. Along with being recreation, amenity rich counties are also considered either government, nonspecialized, or service-dependent economies. A small number of our transitioning counties are also recreation counties; however, each of these counties is also classified as manufacturing dependent by the ERS. These counties are also farming, government and nonspecialized economies. Finally, none of our chronically poor counties is recreation, and their economies are classified by the ERS as mining, manufacturing (but not also recreation), service and nonspecialized. Please note that how we have classified counties here is slightly different from other publications which grouped the counties into four types (see Hamilton et al. 2008; Ulrich 2011).

Table 1. Socioeconomic and demographic indicators for study counties and US 2015, percentage of residents.

	Amenity rich	Transitioning	Chronically poor	US
Population change, 1990–2015	19.3	10.6	−13.7	27.3
Population change, ages 25–34, 1990–2015	1.2	−18.3	−30.6	−1.3
Adults 16–64 Working (full time, year round)	41.1	42.6	36.0	47.7
Families with no workers (past 12 months)	20.0	20.6	27.8	14.8
Working age (16–64) men by disability status	16.6	15.7	22.5	10.5
No high school degree (25+)	8.9	9.4	21.5	13.3
Associate degree and above (ages 25+)	33.0	31.1	23.0	37.8
Median household income (in dollars)	45,876	51,505	30,021	53,889
Single female family households	8.4	9.7	17.3	13.0
Children (0–17) in poverty	22.2	21.0	38.4	21.7
Non-Hispanic white	83.4	83.5	62.0	62.3

Source: U.S. Census Bureau 1990, 2015.

recreation economy takes hold, they face challenges regarding affordability and year-round, well-paying jobs, as well as tensions between new and long-time residents about community identity and development going forward. Overall, the counties we studied tend to consist of mostly non-Hispanic white residents, although there are some with relatively high and growing percentages of Native Americans/Alaska Natives or Hispanic residents.

The *transitioning areas* in our study are places in the northwest, northeast, Alaska Panhandle, Midwest and Upper Peninsula of Michigan that depended on agriculture, timber and manufacturing such as paper mills or low-skill textile or technical operations. Some of these places are growing in population and some are in decline. These rural places have seen working-class jobs and Main Street businesses evaporate, and as a consequence many younger workers have moved with their families to places with greater opportunity. If desirable natural amenities are there, the future economy is or will likely be based on recreation; otherwise many transitioning places will probably continue to experience decline and outmigration. In many respects these transitioning areas are the heart of the rural US, hard hit by economic restructuring and the growing urbanization of the country. They once had a robust blue-collar middle class and a strong civic culture, but economic downturn is threatening both. Like the amenity-rich areas, these are predominantly white rural areas, including some counties that are 96 percent non-Hispanic white. Again, there are pockets with significant proportions of Native Americans/Alaska Native and Hispanic residents.

And finally, there are Chronically Poor Areas, like our study counties in Appalachia and the rural South – where educational attainment is low and economic hard times have been longstanding. Most have been steadily losing population for a long time. These places struggle with the burdensome legacy of neglect and often-ruthless exploitation by local elites, and the long-time lack of investment in essential community institutions has locked the people and the places in chronic poverty. In the rural South many are majority African American communities. When those who can have left for opportunity elsewhere, they leave behind people with fewer personal and family resources (and a few who could leave but place their commitment to their community over opportunities to find better work). Over the last decade far fewer working-age adults are working in these poor places – only about one third – and the middle class and median incomes are comparatively small. These communities are both geographically and socially isolated. Relatively few newcomers have come, and long-time residents' ties to the place go deep. Even today a few powerful families often control the economy and local politics. Education was not always available, or perhaps deemed necessary, to those from working-class families. Nearly four of every 10 children living in these places are in poverty, and one in five adults does not have a high school degree. These poor places also have a relatively high proportion of single-mother households, and higher reliance on disability and other government transfer payments than the rest of the rural US. While drug abuse and addiction plague all kinds of places across the US, here they are pervasive and affect the whole community. Conditions are very like distressed inner cities.

Demographic changes and economic restructuring in the rural US

The rural US has been losing population, in part because of outmigration, in part because of natural decrease (when 'coffins outnumber cradles', as Johnson (2011) puts it), and in part because rural areas are being absorbed by metropolitan areas. Around 60 million people lived in rural areas in 2010, 19.3 percent of the US population. Twenty years earlier, in 1990, nearly the same number lived in rural areas, yet they made up about 25 percent of the population. The US is becoming more and more metropolitan.

The demographic composition of rural places is also changing, although the changes vary considerably by geography across the nation. Rural places are becoming somewhat more racially and ethnically diverse, among children especially, although 79 percent are still non-Hispanic white (Johnson 2012). Nevertheless, in many rural places most in-migration is Hispanic (Johnson 2012). Rural places are also aging. They often lose the working- and family-age population to opportunities in urban areas (Carr and Kefalas 2010) or serve as destinations for retirees (Brown and Glasgow 2008).

Since the 1980s, globalization and neoliberal trade policies have contributed to a restructuring of the rural economy, decreasing the availability of good jobs in rural places and changing the type of work that rural people do (Falk, Schulman, and Tickamyer 2003). More specifically, in recent decades the rural US has seen the loss of manufacturing and agricultural jobs and an increase in service-sector jobs (Brown and Schafft 2011). Production jobs were central to both the economy and the identity of many rural places. In 1970, 20 percent of rural residents worked in service industries, but by 2015 41 percent did (see Figure 1). Additionally, the growing number of service-sector jobs in rural areas are often part time and low-wage, and offer few benefits (Brown and Schafft 2011), meaning service-sector workers often need to work multiple jobs to make ends meet. One interviewee in our amenity-rich area explained: 'You can't really sustain a year-long living here on rafting. When we first moved here, my husband was at [camp in area] and I had four different jobs at one time'. While the percentage of service jobs in urban areas in the US is higher, they are more often better-paid producer service jobs than those in rural places (Brown and Schafft 2011). In addition to growth in service-sector work, non-standard, on-demand work in what some refer to as the 'gig economy' is increasingly becoming the norm (De Stefano 2015). While many rural residents are accustomed to patching together different jobs in different seasons, the undermining of the core production-sector industries has left rural communities without ballast.

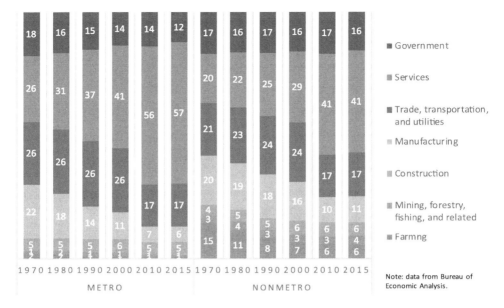

Figure 1. Industrial restructuring in the US by metro status, 1970–2015.

From 1970 to 2015 rural manufacturing jobs dropped from 20 to 11 percent of the jobs. In a community we studied in Appalachia, jobs in the coal industry decreased from 2500 in 1990 to 1200 in 2010. In 1980, 36 percent of jobs in Central Appalachia were in natural resources or manufacturing, and by 2010 only 19 percent were. In 1980 in rural Northern New England 37 percent of jobs were in those sectors, and by 2010 only 16 percent were. Jobs that do remain in some types of mining and manufacturing are among the highest paying (USDA 2016). Some local residents understand these changes are permanent, although they value the role of the industry in their community. A young man laid off from the mines told us,

> I'm a coal miner too, and I know the future is not in coal. It's sad but true. It's not easy to let go of heritages. But if this county is going to succeed, to prosper at all, it's got to go beyond coal, because coal's over. A paper mill community resident told us, the heart of [this place] was the pulp mill and the paper machine that was there. That was devastating when it closed.

Some argue that small-town industries became vulnerable to corporate raiding, mergers and acquisitions starting in the late 1970s and early 1980s, contributing to less industrial investment in rural communities and a decline of 'anchor' family-owned operations (Alexander 2017). We saw this phenomenon in some of our communities, where ownership changed from locals to national and international entities, in many cases not even in the same industry. Orejel (2017) points out that in order to attract industry, states provided tax breaks and subsidies which indebted state and local governments and ultimately undermined investment in local public institutions.

The rural–urban wage gap has also increased over time (Brown and Schafft 2011). Cramer (2016) argues that rural residents in Wisconsin reacted to these growing gaps with resentment toward urban areas and urban professionals who appeared to be doing much better and getting more of the benefits from the taxes rural residents were paying. While we did not find (or seek) evidence that our rural interviewees resented urban areas, we did find strong feelings that economic restructuring had changed rural communities for the worse, and nearly everywhere we encountered nostalgia for the lost economy of the past.[3] In fact, our survey data indicates that most residents of rural areas do not feel like they are better off financially than they were in the past – and, indeed, median income had declined in some of our study areas. Only 30 percent were optimistic about the future. As good rural jobs dry up, more and more rural workers drop out of the labor force altogether. Labor force participation rates are now about 59 percent in rural areas compared to around 64 percent in urban ones (USDA 2016), and, as we will show, are even lower in some rural areas.

While the economic changes in rural communities have been occurring for decades, the Great Recession that started in late 2007 hit rural communities hard, and they have still not fully recovered. Rural employment remains well below its pre-recession level, while urban areas have experienced a much faster recovery in employment and by 2015 had reached 4 percent above the 2007 level (USDA 2016). Data from our surveys also indicates that concern about job opportunities grew significantly from the pre-recession to the recession/post-recession years. People in rural places of the US feel these economic hardships personally and see them as they look at the closed-up storefronts on Main Street. All of this may have contributed to a sense among rural residents that rural places are shouldering the brunt of the major transformations in the US and global economy, and that government and most political leaders are not doing anything to help them transition to work in a new economy.

Data from our national CERA survey allows us to compare some perceptions that rural and urban residents have of the economic circumstances in their communities (see Table 2). For instance, while a striking 81 percent of rural residents worried about job opportunities in their communities, 73 percent of metropolitan residents did – significantly less. Rural residents were also much more concerned about population loss than urban residents were (31 and 22 percent, respectively). People living in rural places were less optimistic about their community in the future, although not to a significant degree. One indication of concern is their perception of illegal drugs in their communities: nearly 65 percent in rural areas see drug manufacturing or sales as a problem, compared to about 50 percent in urban areas. And even as our rural survey respondents overwhelmingly plan to stay in their community, a high percentage (61 percent) would advise young people to whom they are close to leave for opportunity elsewhere.

Demographic and economic indicators in the three rural Americas

Among our study counties, demographic trends over the last few decades varied considerably (refer back to Table 1). While amenity-rich and transitioning areas both grew from 1990 to 2015, population growth was much higher in amenity-rich areas (19 percent in comparison to 11 percent). Population was lost (14 percent) in chronically poor places. Amenity-rich places saw little change in their 25- to 34-year-old population from 1990 to 2015, while transitioning and chronically poor places saw this critical group shrink by

---

[3] With the notable exception of blacks in the rural South, for whom the 'old economy' was oppressive plantation labor or unpredictable factory work.

Table 2. Findings from the Community and Environment in Rural America (CERA) survey by metro status, percentage of respondents.

Variables	Metro	Nonmetro	Significant?
Job opportunities an important problem for community	73.4	80.7	*
Population loss an important problem for community	21.7	31.4	*
Believe community will be a better place to live in future	29.6	25.9	
Manufacturing/sale of illegal drugs is important problem in community	51.8	63.8	*
Plan to stay in community next 5 years	74.5	81.0	*
Would advise teen to move away	40.4	60.9	*

Notes: *Indicates a significant difference by metro/nonmetro status ($p < .05$); the Office of Management and Budget classification system of nonmetro and metropolitan counties was used.

18 and 31 percent, respectively. Worries about population loss correspond to actual loss (see Table 3). Residents of amenity-rich areas were least concerned (30 percent), while those in chronically poor places were most concerned (61 percent).

In our transitioning and amenity-rich areas, about 42 percent of working-age adults are working full time year round, and only 36 percent in the chronically poor areas have full-time work, compared to 48 percent nationally. Chronically poor areas also have more families with no workers – nearly 28 percent. High levels of disability also plague rural areas. In our chronically poor areas 23 percent of working-age men have a disability, while the same is true for about 16 percent of men in the two other rural place types, and 11 percent in the US as a whole.

Our survey data also shows some real differences in economic circumstances by rural place type (see Table 4). One in four said they have more than one job to earn extra money, with the percentage higher in amenity-rich and transitioning areas. In a period where even those with jobs cannot afford the basics they need to survive, many have also turned to the informal economy to survive. Nearly one half of our survey respondents live in households where some type of informal work for pay is done. Informal work was most common in the transitioning areas, with 56 percent saying that someone in their household had done work in the informal economy in the past year. Slightly more respondents in chronically poor areas have also lost a job in the past seven years.

Some common themes and differences also emerged about perceptions regarding economic uncertainty and challenges from our studies of rural places (see Table 3).

Table 3. Findings from the Community and Environment in Rural America (CERA) survey by county type, percentage of respondents.

	Amenity rich	Transitioning	Chronically poor	Significant?
Worries/concerns				
Population loss an important problem for community	30.3	54.3	60.8	*
Job opportunities an important problem for community	85.3	85.8	84.5	
Believe community will be a better place to live in future	30.8	26.4	26.2	*
Would advise teen to move away	65.6	61.2	67.6	*
Know someone serving in Iraq/Afghanistan	69.9	75.4	74.0	*
Feel worse off financially than 5 years prior	30.8	31.2	28.0	*
Manufacturing/sale of illegal drugs is important problem in community	60.4	60.5	79.3	*
Lack of health and social services a problem for community	38.1	35.5	51.7	*

Notes: Not all questions were asked in all iterations of the survey.
*Indicates a significant difference by county type ($p < .05$), but not which types the significant difference is between.

Table 4. Findings from the Community and Environment in Rural America (CERA) survey by county type, percentage of respondents.

	Amenity rich	Transitioning	Chronically poor	Significant?
Economic indicators				
Works full time and has extra side job (if applicable)	26.1	31.0	19.8	*
Household work in informal economy in past year	47.3	55.7	42.8	*
Lost job in past 7 years (factory closing, position abolished, etc.)	13.1	13.4	15.4	*

Notes: Not all questions were asked in all iterations of the survey.
*Indicates a significant difference by county type ($p < .05$), but not which types the significant difference is between.

Worry about job opportunities was high and similar across all types of rural places. Eighty-five percent[4] said they thought job opportunities were an important problem facing their communities. Most also did not think that their communities would be better places to live in the future, particularly those in transitioning and chronically poor places. Similarly, many would encourage their youth to leave for opportunities elsewhere, as documented by Carr and Kefalas (2010). While rural residents don't typically want young people to leave, they do understand that opportunities are more plentiful elsewhere. A teacher in Appalachia told us, 'There ain't no jobs here … for nobody. You have to get out of town to do it. My son said, "Mom, the only chance I'm going to have to make something out of my life is to just get out of [here]"'. A local elected official in the same community said, 'The kids … know, the ones who have enough intelligence, that their ticket to life is to get enough education to get a job elsewhere'. For many rural youth, serving in the military is a path to gain skills and even education. Over 70 percent of our rural survey respondents knew someone serving in Iraq or Afghanistan, with the highest percentage in transitioning and chronically poor areas where there are few other opportunities for young people.

Financially, nearly one in three feel worse than five years ago, and this feeling was greatest in transitioning areas. Tied to economic distress, and leading to what some have called 'deaths of despair' (e.g. deaths by suicide, alcohol or illegal drug use; Monnat 2016), there is real concern about illegal drugs, especially in chronically poor areas (79 percent). People also see health and social services lacking, again with chronically poor residents being the most concerned. Given what we heard in interviews about the toll of local economic change, we expect that Trump's rhetoric appeared to offer a return to the economy that had sustained rural communities, especially to those in transitioning rural places and chronically poor Appalachia, although we do not have data on why people voted the way they did.

Work, culture and politics

Numerous scholars and journalists have written about rural cultural identity in recent years. In *The politics of resentment: rural consciousness in Wisconsin*, Cramer (2016) argues that the rural groups she talked with feel a deep antipathy toward urban residents whom they perceive as working less hard and benefiting more from government policies. She believes this resentment contributed to the conservative politics that elected Governor Walker, and later President Trump. She sees how politicians can take advantage of

---

[4]Please note the percentage is different from what was reported previously because the data comes from different surveys.

rural resentment, and turn it into votes. Her research shows that economic grievances are intertwined with cultural, geographical or community, and group identities. She found 'a political culture in which political divides are rooted in our most basic understanding of ourselves, infuse our everyday relationships, and are used for electoral advantage by our political leaders' (Cramer 2016, 210).

Rural strategist Davis argues that rural support for Trump reflected a shared rural identity rather than an assessment of what policies would best serve rural people. Davis (2016) writes, 'people vote their culture, their church, their family, their neighborhood. Politics today is about creating, maintaining and expressing social identity'. The *Economist* 2017 featured a special report on 'America's urban–rural divides'. *Politico* (Evich 2016) wrote about the revenge of the rural voter:

> After years of declining electoral power, driven by hollowed-out towns, economic hardship and a sustained exodus, rural voters turned out in a big way this presidential cycle – and they voted overwhelmingly for Donald Trump, fueling the real estate mogul's upset victory.

Similarly, the *Denver Post* (Simpson 2017) recently initiated a series on the rural–urban divide entitled 'Two Colorados', and their journalists report a distinct rural identity that included resentment. To quote from their opening piece:

> Rural Coloradans exhibit strains of conservatism centered on self-reliance, independence and work ethic often colored by their relationship with the land. Many feel particularly misunderstood by urbanites when it comes to their agricultural roots. 'You know, I think there probably is a kind of disconnect', says Glen "Spike" Ausmus, a farmer and longtime Baca County commissioner. 'That being said, maybe we don't understand the lifestyle that they live. I know they all have a purpose and have jobs I'm sure are meaningful. But we sometimes feel we're not appreciated for what we do'.

Rural consciousness, rural culture, rural identity, rural lifestyle. To what extent is there a unique rural identity and culture? To what extent are we seeing working-class culture and identity? We find sociologist Swidler's (1986) way of conceptualizing culture helpful in answering these questions. She thinks of culture as a toolkit holding the symbols, stories, role models, rituals and worldviews that we draw upon when we make decisions. She regards culture as more like 'a set of skills and habits than preferences and wants'. Culture is what we know about what people like us do. It is about identity, the stories we have heard and the people we see, not just about values or customs that drive behavior. We found this view of culture helpful in understanding the behavior of the rural poor in our studies, and this perspective resonates with Davis' comments about rural identity and rural voting preferences.

In rural communities work underlies culture. People work hard, and value hard work. Of course hard work is valued everywhere, but in small rural communities where people have known each other's families over generations, families get a reputation about work. In Appalachia, rich and poor people told us there are the good families who work and the bad families who 'draw' benefits rather than work. These stigmas stick, despite evidence that they are not accurate. Even those who work with poor youth and try to improve opportunity are discouraged by and critical of those they see giving up on work and despairing about ever getting ahead. As Sherman (2009) finds in her northwestern US timber community study, the poor who work earn a moral capital that is not ascribed to those who don't. Of course, in reality there is not that clear a distinction, but it becomes part of the local lore and community culture. Vance's (2016) autobiography recounts both the structural obstacles to finding good work and people giving up on work to rely on transfer payments in the absence of good work opportunities. Recent articles on growing disability payments in the rural US by McCoy (2017a, 2017b, 2017c) in the *Washington Post* also show these complex, interconnected realities.

Although rural areas face the economic challenges we have described, rural residents still express strong ties to their communities across the board. Only one in five plan to migrate in the future (see Table 5). Intentions to migrate are higher in chronically poor areas than in amenity-rich and transitioning areas. Families, survey respondents and interviewees tell us, keep them tied to place, particularly those living in chronically poor places. 'I mean a lot of people really just stays here 'cause all their family is here', a young woman in Appalachia told us. The quality of life as well as natural beauty and outdoor recreational amenities, particularly in amenity-rich and some transitioning areas, also keep them there. In the words of a relative newcomer in an amenity-rich community, 'And I mean you just have to step out onto the street to see the mountains and it's just beautiful. I mean it is such a huge contributor to quality of life, I think'.

While the rural US is largely comprised of long-time residents, this pattern varies by rural place type. Amenity-rich areas have the most newcomers and chronically poor areas the fewest. Thus, even though residents of chronically poor areas express a greater desire to leave, in actuality there is a greater churning of the population in amenity-rich areas, which is among the reasons for a documented friction between new and seasonal residents and long-time residents over the identity and future of their communities. As a resident who was involved in local politics and planning said, 'I mean, I think the old-timers are still really suspicious of the new folks. There's been the usual political struggles over, you know, are the new people getting advantages in zoning ... and things like that'.

Rural residents value knowing and working with fellow community members to address local issues and investment in the community. A mill community resident explained, 'You get involved in a lot because you've been here so long'. These feelings and behavior were evident in our survey data. At least eight out of 10 rural residents believed that people could work together to solve local issues, that people were willing to help their neighbors,

Table 5. Findings from the Community and Environment in Rural America (CERA) survey by county type, percentage of respondents.

	Amenity rich	Transitioning	Chronically poor	Significant?
Cultural				
Plan to stay in community next 5 years	77.5	77.3	71.4	*
Stay in community to be near family	72.1	80.4	84.6	*
Stay in community for quality of life	93.7	95.1	90.4	*
Stay in community for natural amenities	90.1	88.9	82.9	*
Newcomer to area (past 10 years)	37.0	27.1	19.7	*
Think their neighbors are helpful	94.9	93.6	84.6	*
Believe their community works together	85.3	83.7	72.3	*
Believe their community gets along	89.5	88.2	77.0	*
Have no religious preference	23.9	21.6	11.3	*
Consider themselves 'born again' (of Protestants)	52.4	44.3	78.2	*
Attend religious services at least once a week	28.3	29.5	46.3	*
Belong to a local organization	52.9	49.1	41.4	*

Notes: Not all questions were asked in all iterations of the survey.
*Indicates a significant difference by county type ($p < .05$), but not which types the significant difference is between.

and that they could trust and get along with those in their communities. Another mill resident said, 'You really feel good talking to people .... There's no hidden agenda. You know the people next door and you trust the people next door'. These positive civic sentiments were significantly lower in chronically poor areas, where residents were more likely to be focused on family, and their 'belonging' was church related: they were more likely to be involved in religious activities than were residents of the other place types. About one half of rural residents are involved in local groups that meet regularly, with the percentage being lower among residents of persistently poor places. But even in poor places we found strong community ties.

Political orientation and views on political issues also varied by our rural place types (see Table 6). Our chronically poor places were more Democratic, largely driven by the counties with black majorities. Residents' belief about climate change affecting their communities was not statistically different across the rural place types. Views on regulation, however, were. Amenity-rich residents were the most supportive of rules to protect the environment (46 percent), while those in chronically poor places were the least supportive (30 percent). Views on the local government also varied, with more in chronically poor rural places seeing theirs as effective, a puzzle we have not explained.

Nationally, rural residents tend to vote Republican. From 2008 to 2016, the share of rural people voting Republican increased from 53 percent to 62 percent (Kurtzleben 2016). When examining the percentage of residents in our study counties who voted for Barack Obama in 2008 in comparison to Hillary Clinton in 2016, we also saw greater support for Republicans. The most notable shift, however, was in transitioning areas where we have seen the greatest economic uncertainty in recent years.

Our amenity-rich areas are somewhat evenly divided between support for Democrats and Republicans. For instance, in 2008 about 53 percent of voters in our amenity-rich counties voted for Obama, 44 percent voted for McCain, and two percent voted for other candidates. In 2016, however, this had flipped to 43 percent of votes for Clinton, 50 percent for Trump, and seven percent for others.

Among transitioning areas, voting patterns in our Midwest counties were distinct from those in other places. The counties we studied, as well as much of the rural Midwest, tend to lean heavily Republican, and shifted even more so from 2008 to 2016. Seventy-seven percent of voters went for McCain in 2008 and 81 percent went for Trump in 2016. In the other transitioning areas we studied, we saw a flip from the majority voting for the Democrat candidate in 2008 to a majority voting for the Republican candidate in 2016,

Table 6. Findings from the Community and Environment in Rural America (CERA) survey by county type, percentage of respondents.

	Amenity rich	Transitioning	Chronically poor	Significant?
Political				
Belong to Democrat political party	39.7	35.8	47.3	*
Believe global warming/climate change has affected their community	53.0	51.6	50.2	
Believe conservation or environmental rules good for community	46.4	40.6	29.9	*
Think their local government is effective	47.7	44.9	52.9	*

Notes: Not all questions were asked in all iterations of the survey.
*Indicates a significant difference by county type ($p < .05$), but not which types the significant difference is between.

as in amenity-rich areas. Support for Republicans went from 43 to 51 percent, and support for other candidates rose from 2 to 7 percent of the vote. Thus, overall, there was more support for Republicans in transitioning areas.

The chronically poor areas we studied in Appalachia and the Northeast were predominantly non-Hispanic white and tend to vote more Republican. Votes in these places went more strongly toward Republican (60 percent voted Republican in 2008 and 70 percent in 2016). The chronically poor places in the Mississippi Delta and the Black Belt have more black residents and tend to be more evenly split between Republican and Democratic votes. There was only a modest dip in Democratic support in these places (58 percent voted Democrat in 2008 and 57 percent in 2016). Both did shift slightly more toward voting Republican, and we saw increases in votes for other candidates; however, we did not see the shift in a majority voting Democrat to Republican as in the other rural place types.

In sum, while voting patterns differed across rural places, we did see more votes move to the Republican Party represented by Donald Trump, and we saw more votes for other candidates. While the contexts are different, we think our interview and survey data suggest why people in many of these rural place types wanted to see the economic shake-up that Trump said he would provide. The biggest shift from one party to another was in transitioning areas, where the recent economic uncertainty we have documented likely fueled feelings of discontent and need for political change. While Trump also stirred up feelings of cultural displacement and anti-immigrant sentiments, much of it was centered around the economic precariousness people were experiencing, and, importantly, were feeling was not being acknowledged by political leaders. Our findings are consistent with Cramer's (2016): many voters are looking for change, change that benefits them, and for acknowledgment of the struggles they are enduring in the new economy.

To illustrate the connections between current and historical economic conditions, community culture, local politics and recent national politics, we draw on five communities from our research – an amenity-rich community in the West; a transitioning community in the Northeast; and two chronically poor places, predominantly white Appalachia and predominantly African American Mississippi Delta, and an overview of a small section of Indian Country.

Amenity-rich River Town

An emerging rural destination, River Town, is shifting away from its mining- and agricultural-dominated past, to a place catering to recreationists, religious camps, retirees and second home owners, as well as to a dependency on the prison economy. While the population declined because of a mine closure and an economic recession in the 1980s, the town, which is rich in natural amenities yet relatively isolated from any large metropolitan area (about a two-hour drive), grew by over fifty percent from 1990 to 2016. Thus, the types of jobs people do in River Town have changed dramatically, impacting how people think about the jobs in the new economy, and community identity.

> I don't know how to say this, other than my husband said that if you worked at the mine it was respectable. But working at the prison was kind of like eh, you work with the inmates and not considered as high class as mining believe it or not. And then when [the other mine] shut down and there was no jobs there all of a sudden everybody was scurrying, some people left because they were miners and they left, but a lot of them wanted to work at the

prison, and then so the prison kind of was, like thank God we have got the prison, you know, because the town went through a really bad bust. And then the rafting started.

Once River Town began its changeover into a summer tourist community, cultural clashes over the town's identity and what type of new development belonged there ensued. While some liked the population and economic growth brought in by rafting tourists and recreational migrants, others feared the town was losing its rural character and that their quality of life would be diminished with such change.

> And we don't want to be uppity. There are those who want, I believe, the change, and then there are those who want to be able to support the kids who are graduating, they want the kids to be able to get the jobs here, they want the town to be successful, but they want River Town. We didn't move here to move to Aspen. So why did you move here if you are trying now to turn it into Aspen?

Everyone, however, expressed strong connections to the natural environment, despite differing views on how these resources should be used. Many also were concerned that development and gentrification would mean they would be unable to afford to continue to live in the community they loved.

These tensions over culture and identity, brought about by changes in the economy, are playing out in local politics. At the town level the divide seems to be less about Democrats versus Republicans and more about support for different paths for community development. On the one hand there are those who are embracing change, including new housing and business developments that look and function differently from those that many long-time rural residents are used to, and on the other hand there are those who are nostalgic for a more traditional past. Increasingly, those who embrace what are sometimes considered 'outside' lifestyles and values are gaining local political power. While more liberal newcomers who tend to vote Democrat are moving in, there remains a strong segment of the population who express conservative values and are skeptical of government interference and programs. Landowners in this area are especially wary of rising taxes and government regulations, which may be turning some away from the Democratic Party. In this county, votes for president in the recent past have not tilted strongly toward either party; however, in 2016 some former Democratic votes went to candidates outside the two mainstream parties.

Transitioning Gray Mountain

Gray Mountain, a northern New England forest community, long relied on paper and pulp mills for jobs, blue-collar jobs that sustained a blue-collar middle class and a self-consciously working-class culture. In the 1990s people talked with pride about the good working-class culture that defined the community: 'This is a very working-class town. You have the mill-town background ... the work ethic is very much alive in Gray Mountain'. Another noted, 'People who make a middle-class salary in the mill are still working-class people'. The dominant blue-collar middle class made up of millworkers and other manufacturing workers sustained a strong, inclusive civic culture. 'There is no sense of isolation, or of a separate culture. There's really no sense of class. There's a kind of a bond, a membership of the valley and the region ... '. The mutual trust in the small town was valued:

You really feel good talking to people .... There's no hidden agenda. You know the people next door and you trust the people next door. We're a small, somewhat isolated community, and therefore people tend to get along and are open with each other.

This civic culture, including trust, community-wide investment and broad participation in community affairs, supported community institutions that served everyone and contributed to equality of opportunity for young people, regardless of their parents' background. The opportunity to work in the mills after high school was taken for granted, and yet valued deeply. Work was stable; the local economy, with other small manufacturing rounding out the mill base, was relatively diverse; and community institutions had resources and leadership.

In the mid-2000s the pulp and paper mill that supported this blue-collar middle class closed for good. There had been ownership changes, shutdowns and re-openings over the years, but then it closed and did not reopen. The company that owned the plant dismantled it, to prevent competition with other struggling operations in its portfolio. But local leaders persuaded them to leave one valuable boiler: 'make sure it is the last thing you tear down. Give us a year or two'. That boiler became the focus of a wrenching debate about the community's future. Not unlike in River Town, some wanted to see Gray Mountain capitalize on its natural resources, go for high-end tourism, leave industry behind and build up the riverfront, and expand the community college to a four-year institution. Others wanted to hold on to the blue-collar character of the place and use that boiler for a biomass plant.

When the Great Recession hit, the biomass boosters won out. In the context of national economic decline, the prospects for ecotourism seemed remote and the biomass plant offered immediate tax revenue and business activity. There was local political turnover in favor of the plant, and the new mayor restored the town's logo with smoke stacks that had been removed by the tourism-focused previous mayor. 'We're proud of our heritage', he said.

The biomass plant only provides 40 some jobs directly, but other workers supply the wood chips. As is true in River Town and many other rural communities, a new state prison and new federal prison offer jobs, the former to laid-off mill workers, the latter, with age restrictions favoring younger people, to new younger workers. Local leaders have pushed outdoor recreation with snowmobile and all terrain vehicles trails. Like other transitioning areas, Gray Mountain has lost younger families and workers and is graying. Jobs in the prisons are 'middle class', people say, but not the same. 'I don't think people send their kids to college or high school and say, "I hope you are going to grow up to be a prison guard"'. As in River Town, the pride and respectability in mill work that permeated the community was not found in the prison work. The economy has changed. The vibrancy downtown has disappeared. Poor residents from elsewhere in the state moved into low-cost neglected housing, alarming long-time residents: 'Those people aren't welcome here', commented one former mill worker. Dollar stores have replaced the grocery and hardware stores. But Gray Mountain is self-consciously hanging on to its blue-collar identity, and many feel they have ridden over the most difficult period and have found a new stability, if not the vibrancy of the old economy. Still, young people are leaving and Main Street struggles. Like in other rural areas, votes shifted toward Republican candidate Trump, champion, it seemed, of the blue-collar workers and their 'heritage'.

Chronically poor Blackwell

In the 1990s Blackwell, a chronically poor Appalachian coal region, had high poverty and low educational attainment, but coal jobs were still the bedrock of the local economy. Coal jobs have long been the only good jobs available, since unionization (and mechanization) in the 1950s. But the long struggle between operators and workers created a divided community culture that persists to this day – a civic culture, in contrast to that in Gray Mountain, that is full of distrust and exclusion. People with whom we talked described a community of haves and have-nots, with no middle class. Everyone could name the handful of coal operators and merchants who 'ran things'. There was local political corruption and little trust outside the immediate family, and opportunity depended on whom you knew and your family's reputation. These patterns grew out of the turbulent coal history, the ways in which coal barons established firm control over all aspects of community life and discouraged workers' participation.

Life was family-based and church-based, and families and churches were grouped by social class. The children of the have-nots were ignored, in chaotic schools with corrupt school boards. Families struggled to make ends meet. The have-nots attended small evangelical churches with itinerant preachers focused on salvation in the next world, not family and community well-being in this world. The children of the haves, the professionals and others with good paying jobs, including coal miners from the bigger mines, attended the county seat school where standards were high and decisions were made for educational rather than politically driven patronage reasons. They went to the Presbyterian or Baptist churches. Family reputation mattered for every opportunity. 'You don't get jobs on merit, it's on who you know'. Patronage and corrupt local politics were pervasive, and the few powerful families whom everyone could name called the shots. If you crossed them or tried to bring about change, 'You will never even flip a hamburger in this place'.

But despite this broken community culture, this lack of trust and political corruption, there was pride among miners and identity as a coal mining community. 'Coal is all there is … coal mining is about the only thing around here'. Coal jobs made up 14 percent of employment but nearly a third of earned income. So even as coal employment dramatically declined, people hung on to that identity. Most experts agree that the area's coal is harder to reach now, raising costs of production, and competition from natural gas is hard to beat. An outside political group, Friends of Coal, contributed to polarization as coal production declined – you were for coal or against it. There were posters, stickers and license plates declaring Friends of Coal. They very deliberately politicized the decline, and blamed the Obama administration policies to address climate change.

As coal production and employment declined in the past two decades, out-migration, especially of younger workers and their families, increased. Between 1990 and 2013 thousands left, and those in their 20s to early 40s declined by a third.

> If you wanted to stay in Blackwell and provide for your family, you just had to go in the mines. And as the mining jobs closed out, people began to leave … and the ones that stayed behind have had to scrabble for whatever they can get.

While there are the coal boosters, there are many others who see a hard future:

> I think if the coal mines don't pick back up, it's going to be a lot of people drawing disability and don't see much of a future here. And that's hard on the men that were raised by their

family to be hard-working men. They lose their job like that, they either get on [disability] or move away; that's your options.

Losing good work takes both a financial and an emotional, psychological toll.

When we returned after 20 years, in 2013, the area had become overrun with painkiller addiction, something many relate to the loss of good mining jobs.

> 'If you're a man you have to be a coal miner ... that's the only opportunities as far as employment go. There's really nothing else, and that's why Blackwell has such bad drug problems'.

In the heyday of coal mining Blackwell voted Democratic, a strong union county. But despite evidence that competition from natural gas and harder-to-reach coal were reducing coal's market, people believed Republicans and Trump when they blamed environmental regulations for the downturn. With few options in this remote mountain region, people voted even more strongly Republican, clearly hoping that this might mean mining jobs would return. Through all this change, the broken local politics and control by local powerful families persist.

Chronically poor Dahlia

Dahlia is in many ways a classic, racially divided plantation community in the rural South. As in the coal county, social life has long been divided into haves and have-nots, and in this case the have-nots are the majority black residents. Here too everyone could name the four or five plantation-owning families who 'ran things', and as in Blackwell, you didn't want to 'cross them' or you would be blackballed from any work in the county. While the operators had discouraged worker participation to block unionization, the plantation owners made black workers vulnerable and dependent to undermine civil rights organizing and maintain low wages. But their power over opportunity extended beyond the plantation to other businesses: 'These farmers could say "well he's worth hiring" and they'll hire you ... that will be it because you get the job anywhere, even in a store'. And as in Blackwell, family reputation is inescapable: 'They say that if your parents no-good workers, you won't do no good work. They won't hire you'.

In the 1990s the farmers, catfish and sewing factories, and a handful of retailers provided low-wage, usually part-year or uncertain work. When we returned in 2013 the county had been transformed in many ways with the arrival of outside-owned casinos that drew customers from several states in the region. For 15 years the county enjoyed over USD 40 million per year in revenue from the casinos. Local taxes and infrastructure charges and fees were eliminated completely. The number of employed men and women had doubled. For the first time in its history, Dahlia saw whites and blacks hired for the same jobs. But still, as local leaders explained, the gap in skills and understanding of daily work prevented many of those who had toiled as day laborers on farms from holding down these new jobs.

Importantly, local politics had changed substantially. The five-person board of supervisors had gone from one African American to five, and these five needed to manage a growing public sector and allocate the substantial, but declining, revenue from the casinos. Whites' median income is still twice that of blacks, but the new diversification of the economy gave blacks new freedom and power to voice concerns about their well-being. 'It's not like the old time ... it has changed from when you really used to have to depend on your bossman saying certain things for you so you can get credit or whatever'.

The local black middle class is growing, and leading, but they say they must confront a mindset of dependency, vulnerability and fear among less-educated African Americans, even with all the changes. Still, the changes were enormous. The new elected black leaders are wrestling with dramatically declining casino employment and revenue, outmigration of many whites, and the ongoing legacy of poor schools. But the economic diversification did undo the whites' grip on economic, social and political life in Dahlia.

Dahlia is strongly Democrat and little changed from 2008 to 2016 in votes for either of the two major parties. Nearly three out of every four residents voted for Democratic candidates in both cycles.

Conclusion

We have described rural communities where the local blue-collar economy has largely disappeared over the last few decades, as well as areas where residents have long been struggling to make ends meet. The mines, mills and plants are laying off workers or closing operations entirely. Where new industries have emerged, the jobs are not of the same caliber as those in the past. Out-migration has increased, and younger workers especially are leaving in greater numbers. While some communities are faring better than others, rural working-class communities are in distress. With the notable exception of oppressed minorities in chronically poor areas, those who stay are nostalgic for the 'heritage' of what used to be. These are people and communities who feel left behind by a new globalizing economy. Political leaders and policymakers have failed to respond to their plight.

Our research did not explore the extent to which there is a unique rural identity or rural culture, but how rural people feel about their economic circumstances, and through our in-depth interviews we have seen the way work in rural communities has been a source of pride and identity for people as well as places. Mining, paper mills, logging and even textile operations once brought decent jobs that could sustain a working class. There was pride in the hard work these jobs required and in the community culture they sustained. As those blue-collar jobs disappeared, just as jobs in steel or auto factories in the Rust Belt disappeared, workers and their families have seen their communities unravel. Those who stay have limited options for making a living, and struggle and 'scrabble' to provide for their families. While the response to change varies by the type of rural community and its economic history, its natural amenities and its civic culture, fundamentally these rural communities are witnessing the decline of their working-class world. They long for the work and the communities the work sustained. They see a dim future for themselves and for the community they have known. If a political party, or a politician, claims they can bring back that world, it is worth a shot.

Future research might explore these questions about culture and identity in a variety of types of rural places throughout the US, considering the different trends economically, culturally and environmentally. There is also a need to better understand younger people in the rural US – their circumstances, plans and perspectives. Much of Cramer's work in Wisconsin was focused on older rural residents, and teasing out the generational differences or similarities will be important. We find rural development practitioners and rural community organizers bring deep understanding and wisdom to their work in rural communities, and more research could better document and share their valuable perspectives. Together, work like this could inform us about political currents, past, present and future, and their implications for the US as a whole in future decades.

Acknowledgements

We would like to thank the Carsey School of Public Policy, the Ford Foundation, the Annie E. Casey Foundation, the Babcock Foundation, the Rural Sociological Society and the University of New Hampshire Graduate School for their generous support of our research at various stages. We also appreciate the input provided by Lawrence C. Hamilton and Kenneth Johnson at the University of New Hampshire, and Gemma Beckley at Rust College.

Disclosure statement

No potential conflict of interest was reported by the authors.

Notes on contributors

Jessica Ulrich-Schad is an assistant professor of sociology and rural studies at South Dakota State University. She has wide-ranging interests in understanding rural people and places, particularly the vulnerable populations within them. Some of her research has focused on how amenity migration in the rural US leads to contested community identity and development; the structural and community-level factors that play a role in chronic poverty in communities the US; and how US farmers understand environmental issues associated with farming and subsequently navigate decisions to use soil- and water-conservation practices. She received her BA in social science from the University of Montana-Western, her MA in sociology from the University of Montana-Missoula, and her PhD in sociology from the University of New Hampshire. Email: Jessica.Schad@sdstate.edu

Cynthia Duncan is Professor Emerita, University of New Hampshire (UNH), and works on rural poverty and development. In addition to her work as a sociology professor and founding director of the Carsey School at UNH, she has worked on food and agriculture with the Meridian Institute's AGree initiative, and led the Community and Resource Development work at the Ford Foundation. Duncan wrote *Worlds apart: poverty and politics in rural America* (Yale University Press, 2014). She received her BA in English from Stanford University, and her MA and PhD in sociology from the University of Kentucky. Email: mil.duncan@gmail.com

References

Alexander, Brian. 2017. *Glass House: The 1% Economy and the Shattering of the All-American Town.* New York: St. Martin's Press.
Balz, Dan. 2017. "Rural America Lifted Trump to the Presidency. Support Is Strong, but Not Monolithic." The Washington Post. June 17, 2017. https://www.washingtonpost.com/politics/rural-america-lifted-trump-to-the-presidency-support-is-strong-but-not-monolithic/2017/06/16/df4f9156-4ac9-11e7-9669-250d0b15f83b_story.html?utm_term=.04a7c0130ce0
Brown, David L., and Nina Glasgow. 2008. *Rural Retirement Migration.* Dordrecht. The Netherlands: Springer.
Brown, David L., and Kai A. Schafft. 2011. *Rural People & Communities in the 21st Century: Resilience & Transformation.* Malden, MA: Polity.
Carr, P. J., and M. J. Kefalas. 2010. *Hollowing Out the Middle: The Rural Brain Drain and What It Means for America.* Boston, MA: Beacon Press.

Cramer, Katherine J. 2016. *The Politics of Resentment: Rural Consciousness in Wisconsin and the Rise of Scott Walker*. Chicago, IL: University of Chicago Press.

Davis, Dee. http://www.dailyyonder.com/analysis-giving-up-on-rural-is-not-a-winning-political-strategy/2016/12/21/16862/

De Stefano, V. 2015. The rise of the 'just-in-time workforce': On-demand work, crowd work and labour protection in the 'gig-economy'.

Duncan, Cynthia M. 2015. *Worlds Apart: Poverty and Politics in Rural America*. 2nd ed. New Haven, CT: Yale University Press.

The Economist. 2017. http://www.economist.com/news/special-report/21724129-mutual-incomprehension-between-urban-and-rural-america-can-border-malice-americas

Evich, Helena B. 2016. http://www.politico.com/story/2016/11/hillary-clinton-rural-voters-trump-231266

Falk, William W., Michael D. Schulman, and Ann R. Tickamyer, eds. 2003. *Communities of Work: Rural Restructuring in Local and Global Contexts*. Vol. 2. Athens, OH: Ohio University Press.

Hamilton, Lawrence C., Chris R. Colocousis, and Cynthia M. Duncan. 2010. "Place Effects on Environmental Views." *Rural Sociology* 75 (2): 326–347.

Hamilton, Lawrence C., Leslie R. Hamilton, Cynthia M. Duncan, and Chris R. Colocousis. 2008. "Place Matters: Challenges and Opportunities in Four Rural Americas." Reports on Rural America. Vol. 1, No. 4. Durham, NH: Carsey Institute.

Johnson, Kenneth M. 2011. *Natural Decrease in America: More Coffins than Cradles*. Issue Brief No. 30. Durham, NH: Carsey Institute.

Johnson, Kenneth M. 2012. *Rural Demographic Change in the New Century: Slower Growth, Increased Diversity*. Issue Brief No. 44. Durham, NH: Carsey Institute.

Kurtzleben, Danielle. 2016. "Rural Voters Played A Big Part In Helping Trump Defeat Clinton." *NPR*, November 14.

McCoy, Terrence. 2017a. "Disabled, or Just Desperate?" *The Washington Post*, March 30.

McCoy, Terrence. 2017b. "Generations, Disabled." *The Washington Post*, June 2.

McCoy, Terrence. 2017c. "Disabled and Disdained." *The Washington Post*, July 20.

Monnat, S. 2016. *Deaths of Despair and Support for Trump in the 2016 Presidential Election*. The Pennsylvania State University Department of Agricultural Economics, Sociology, and Education Research Brief – 12/04/16, http://aese.psu.edu/directory/smm67/Election16.pdf (accessed October 23, 2017)

Orejel, Keith. 2017. "Why Trump Won Rural America." *Dissent Magazine*. October 16, 2017. https://www.dissentmagazine.org/online_articles/rural-vote-trump-economy-manufacturing

Packer, George. 2014. *The Unwinding: An Inner History of the New America*. New York City, NY: Macmillan.

Simpson, Kevin. 2017. http://www.denverpost.com/2017/07/21/colorado-divide-rural-urban-chasm/.

Sherman, Jennifer. 2009. *Those who Work, those who don't: Poverty, Morality, and Family in Rural America*. Minneapolis, MN: University of Minnesota Press.

Stock, Catherine McNicol and Robert D. Johnson, eds. 2001. *The Countryside in the Age of the Modern State: political Histories of Rural America*. Ithaca, NY: Cornell University Press.

Swidler, Ann. 1986. "Culture in Action: Symbols and Strategies." *American Sociological Review* 51: 273–286.

Ulrich, Jessica D. 2011. *Education in Chronically Poor Rural Areas Lags across Generations*." Issue Brief No. 24. Durham, NH: The Carsey Institute University of New Hampshire.

Ulrich-Schad, Jessica D., Megan Henly, and Thomas G. Safford. 2013. "The Role of Community Assessments, Place, and the Great Recession in the Migration Intentions of Rural Americans." *Rural Sociology* 78 (3): 371–398.

Ulrich-Schad, Jessica D. and Hua Qin. 2017. "Culture Clash? Predictors of Views on Community Development in Rural Recreation Counties." *Rural Sociology*. doi:10.1111/ruso.12165.

United States Department of Agriculture (USDA). 2016. "Rural America at a Glance: 2016Edition." Economic Information Bulletin 162.

U.S. Census Bureau. 1990. "1990 U.S. Decennial Census." https://www.census.gov/main/www/cen1990.html.

U.S. Census Bureau. 2015. "2011–2015 American Community Survey 5-year estimates." https://www.census.gov/programs-surveys/acs/technical-documentation/table-and-geography-changes/2015/5-year.html.

Vance, J. D. 2016. *Hillbilly Elegy*. New York City, NY: HarperCollins.

Wilson, Reid. 2017. "How the GOP Came to Dominate, and be Dominated by, Rural Voters." *The Hill*, June 15.

Power and powerlessness in an Appalachian Valley – revisited

John Gaventa

ABSTRACT
With the rise of Trump support in rural Appalachia – the coal mining, mountainous region in the heartland of the eastern United States – media and other commentators have rushed to explain this conservative politics in 'exceptionalist' terms, largely based on cultural stereotypes. Revisiting my work on *Power and Powerlessness in an Appalachian Valley* (1980), I argue that the attention to 'Trumpism' fails to see or take into account the widespread rural resistance which exists in the region, historically and presently. A focus on the rise of place-based grassroots activism and scholarship in the region offers a more emancipatory view of rural politics.

Introduction

In 1971, almost fifty years ago, I first entered the rural Valley in the heart of the Appalachian mining region which was to become the subject of my book, *Power and Powerlessness: Quiescence and Rebellion in an Appalachian Valley* (Gaventa 1980). Freshly graduated from a university a few hours drive away, I was a volunteer on a student project examining patterns of absentee land ownership in these rural areas, and the associated failure of large corporate land and mineral owners to support local communities through the normal property tax system. While doing this project, I learned that one of the largest of these owners was a British company, ironically called the American Association.

On my way for post-graduate study in the UK, I was asked by rural residents what I naively assumed to be a simple question: 'Can you find out who owns the land in our community and tell them how bad it is?' The attempt to answer that first research question led to a several-year journey of engaged research with members of the community, which in turn formed the basis of my PhD, which became the *Power and Powerlessness* book. It was also the beginning of a career of work attempting to understand power, resistance, and the role of committed scholarship in bringing about change.

The situation I encountered in the Appalachian Valley was one of glaring inequality. This single company owned 90% of the land, through a secretive corporate empire, and at the

DOI: 10.4324/9781003162353-4

top of which (I was later to discover) sat a Lord Mayor of London, one of Britain's wealthiest men. In the Valley itself, I saw glaring poverty, poor schools, lack of health care, a degraded environment through unchecked practices of fossil-fuel extraction, a generally poor quality of life – all of these amidst enormous concentrations of wealth in the hands of a few.

Yet, my liberal political science education at the nearby university had failed to prepare me for what I saw. While the theories of American democracy would suggest that when faced with such grievances, citizens will mobilize and associate to make their voice heard, I could find little evidence of organized protest or challenge to the status quo. This led me to ask a question that is relevant and important for the broader theme of emancipatory rural politics: *Why in a situation of glaring inequality 'where one might intuitively expect upheaval, does one instead find, or appear to find, quiescence? Under what conditions and against what obstacles does rebellion begin to emerge?'* (1980, 3).

The answer, I argued, could only be found by looking at the historical construction of power relationships, which in that setting were deeply related to the corporate control of land and the exploitation of mineral resources. Over time, power served to bring certain issues and voices into the political arena, while excluding and suppressing others, and in its extreme form could, as Stephen Lukes (1974) had also posited, lead to the internalization, acceptance, and even defense of an unjust status quo. That initial encounter in Appalachia has continued to shape my thinking on power and participation to this day (Gaventa 2018). Later, I was to develop the work further in the framework now known as the 'power cube', which suggested that Lukes' three dimensions of power were, in fact, only three aspects of a single spectrum of power. How the visible, hidden, and invisible forms of power played out also varied according to the spaces (closed, invited, and claimed), and the levels (from local to global) of action. Moreover, the forms, spaces, and levels of power constantly interacted, opening and closing the possibilities for action or inaction (Gaventa 2006).

With the renewed debates on authoritarian populism and the possibilities of more emancipatory rural action emerging in many parts of the world, including in the US following the Trump election, I have found myself being drawn back to this earlier work, and to ask the questions, 'What has changed since I first entered that Appalachian Valley over almost fifty years ago? And what have we learned about the role of activist-scholarship in supporting emancipatory rural politics over these years as well?'

I offer only reflections on these questions and do so with some trepidation. Though my family roots are in this region, I was raised in the Niger Delta – another rural region shaped by extractive industry (Gaventa 2018). And while I worked intensely in the Appalachian Region some twenty-five years before shifting the focus of my work to similar issues of power and inequality internationally, I only comment now from afar, drawing from secondary sources, and not from the first-hand ethnography and action research that characterized my earlier encounter.

In this sense, building on the long tradition of 're-visits' in sociology and anthropology, this work is only an 'update', not what Burawoy (2003) would call a more comprehensive 'ethnographic re-visit', e.g. 'when an ethnographer undertakes participant observation, that is studying others in their space and time, with a view to comparing his or her site with the same one studied at an earlier point in time' (2003, 646). With Burawoy, I understand a 're-visit' inevitably is 'reflexive', in the sense that over the last fifty years, I have also changed, not only the site in which I am interested, and my observations will be shaped by both lenses, are inevitably constructivist, and engage with the 'inescapable dilemma of participating in the world we study, on the necessity of bringing theory to the field, all with a view to developing explanations of historical change' (2003, 647).

In this reflexive re-visit, several themes stand out which are especially pertinent to the wider question of emancipatory rural politics that is the focus of the broader inquiry of this special issue. These include reflections on the enduring structures of poverty and inequality despite decades of regional development; the changing political response to these inequalities; the paradox of resistance amidst consent; and the contribution of committed scholarship over several decades to creating the possibilities for imagining a different future.

Re-visiting the Appalachian Valley – the enduring persistence of inequality

Stretching along a mountain range from western New York to northern Georgia is the region of the United States known as Appalachia. Within this region is a rugged, mining sub-region known as Central Appalachia, covering parts of Kentucky, Tennessee, Virginia, and West Virginia. Historically, the images of the region are those of poverty (Duncan 1992; Catte 2018b) made especially salient in the political landscape through Michael Harrington's book, *The Other America* (Harrington 1997), and later the campaign of John Kennedy for the presidency, where he encountered conditions that helped to inspire the later War on Poverty.

And yet, as I wrote many years ago,

> Despite the images, Central Appalachia is not poor. Within its borders is tremendous wealth, in the form of natural resources, particularly the black gold of the energy era – coal. In 1964, Appalachia supplied 65% of the coal produced in the United States … Appalachia is not poor, then, but its people are … in a word, Central Appalachia is a region of poverty amidst riches, a place of glaring inequalities. (Gaventa 1980, 35)

Fast forward to the current situation, and while we can see that much has changed in the Appalachian Region, much has remained the same, and if anything, the underlying structures of poverty and inequality have deepened and spread. Today, straddling across parts of Kentucky and Tennessee, the Appalachian Valley which I studied can be seen as a microcosm of the larger political economy affecting rural communities across many parts of America, and of the debates about why poor, rural communities at the blunt edge of inequality express political preferences for Trump, or appear to engage in increasingly authoritarian politics.

Despite decades of efforts of the federal government and other government and civil society actors to promote development, the Valley, like others around it, remains poor, with poverty rates ranging from 22% to 38% in the four counties which cut across the Valley, compared to a US average of 15.5% (2011–2015). Despite some marginal gains earlier, in recent years, these counties have once again seen decline. In 2018, three of the four counties were ranked by the federal government as distressed (that is, in the bottom 10% of counties in the nation, while the Valley portion of the fourth county was also ranked the same (Kelly 2017; 2018 Distressed Communities Index: Economic Innovation Group).

But just as in earlier years, one cannot understand this poverty in isolation from larger national and global structural forces. Historically owned and controlled by external corporate land companies, the predominant ownership of the land and minerals appears to have passed from formerly British (when I did my study) to American and now to Chinese hands, though the real ownership is opaque at best due to the financial maze which surrounds it. The Chinese investments in this particular Valley are not unique, with huge influxes of Chinese capital spent on land and infrastructure in West Virginia and elsewhere in the region (Harris and McCarthy 2018), much like the Chinese rush for resources in Africa and other parts of the world.

Once a largely coal-mining region, with related jobs, mining has largely disappeared, or is done by large, environmentally destructive 'strip'-mining technologies, which destroy the land, but offer few jobs. In the town closest to the heart of the rural Valley, the largest number of jobs are found in health care and social assistance (there is a small hospital), and the motel and fast food business (it is close to a large highway). While in previous decades, mechanization in the mines led to massive outmigration, in today's economy, the costs of urban living and lack of skills offer little alternative elsewhere. Education levels are low, and while high-school graduation rates have improved, the number of college graduates is only some 40% of the national average.

In an area where health has always been an issue, compared to fifty years ago, the Valley, like much of the region, is today wracked by a contemporary public health crisis, brought on by the easy supply of opioids. The addiction rate is high, from four to six times the national average, with the entire Valley, and the areas surrounding it, to be placed on the federal Appalachia High Intensity Drug Trafficking Area Map (Kelly 2017). Meanwhile, large drug companies and investors have made millions from promoting easily available forms of addiction (Giridharadas 2018), leading one writer to coin the term 'pharmaceutical colonization' (Coombs 2018), and another to comment,

> the pharmaceutical industry has in some ways replaced the coal industry as it extracts from the social fibers of the community rather than the depleted and hard to reach coal seams once sacrificed to corporate absentee land and mineral owners. (Kelly 2017, 53)

While struggling with this new health crisis, the historical mining-related disease, 'black lung', is on the rise, with the highest rates in 25 years, largely due to the climate of de-regulation of the coal industry (Blackley, Halldin, and Laney 2018).

One could go on – but the point seems clear: patterns of desperate poverty and inequality persist in this rural area, despite decades of investment through special 'aid agencies' like the Appalachian Regional Commission, which has spent over 50 billion dollars to bring 'growth' and 'development' to the region. But, if anything has changed, it is not that this 'left behind' region has caught up with mainstream America; it is that much of rural America has also become more like this region, what I and others have called the 'Appalachianization of America' (Gaventa 1987).

While in 1980, almost all of the counties with greater than 25% non-employment rates were in Central Appalachia, by 2015 they had spread widely, with large-scale rural unemployment affecting large swathes of the American rural heartland. In 2018, The Economic Innovation Group, who publishes the Distressed Communities Index (DCI), called this the 'ruralization of distress'. Comparing the periods of 2007–2011 and 2012–2016, they found that:

While the overall population in **distressed zip codes** declined, the number of *rural* Americans in that category increased by nearly **1 million** between the two periods. Rural zip codes exhibited the most volatility and were by far the most likely to be **downwardly mobile** on the index, with 30 percent dropping into a lower quintile of prosperity—nearly twice the proportion of urban zip codes that fell into a lower quintile. (2018 Distressed Communities Index: Economic Innovation Group; emphasis in the original)

They conclude starkly: 'What was once a country of disparate places that converged towards prosperity', 'is now a country of places drifting further apart' (2018 Distressed Communities Index: Economic Innovation Group). These observations were echoed by the report of the Special Rapporteur on Poverty whose report on wealth and income inequality in America caused national controversy by comparing parts of the US to countries in the developing world, and concluded:

> The United States is one of the world's richest, most powerful and technologically innovative countries; but neither its wealth nor its power nor its technology is being harnessed to address the situation in which 40 million people continue to live in poverty. (Alston 2017)

The rise of Trump support – what has changed is the politics

While the growing deindustrialization and inequalities of America's heartland rural regions have been going on for some time, it was the elections of 2016 which brought these regions again into the national spotlight. While John F. Kennedy had campaigned in this region in 1960 with a promise to fight poverty, Trump now promised to 'Make America Great Again,' including by 'Making Coal King again.' His populist rhetoric clearly struck a chord. As the *Washington Post* pointed out in a post-election analysis:

> … in the 2,332 counties that make up small-town and rural America, he swamped his Democratic rival, winning 60 percent of the vote to Clinton's 34 percent. Trump's 26-point advantage over Clinton in rural America far exceeded the margins by which Republican nominees had won those voters in the four previous elections. (Balz 2017)[1]

Four hundred of the 420 counties in Appalachia voted for Trump (Volcovici 2017, quoted in Kelly 2017, 7).

The Appalachian Valley which I had studied was no exception. This was once a predominately Democratic area, and when I worked in the region decades ago, Presidents John Kennedy, and Franklin Roosevelt (as well as the famous mineworkers' union leader John L. Lewis), were popular heroes, with their pictures on the walls of many homes I visited. By 2016, this Democratic allegiance had overwhelmingly altered – with Trump receiving approximately 80% of the votes in the four counties in which the Valley lies.[2]

The overwhelming support for Trump by rural voters led to a rapid renewal of interest in the liberal and popular press in the politics of these areas, especially of the largely white

---

[1] At least in the Appalachian Valley, it is important to note that this shift was not sudden – in this predominately white area, there was a major shift in the 2008 and 2012 elections, when Obama also received far less than his Republican counterpart. One could argue then that Trump consolidated a growing disillusionment for these working-class voters, but this was capitalizing on a longer-term trend.

[2] It is very difficult to document the trends exactly, as the Appalachian Valley cuts across precincts, counties, and states. There has long been a historical difference between the rural non-mining-area voting, and the mining-area-voting patterns.

voters who inhabited them. In an article on rural poverty, the *New York Times* observed that

> for the last quarter century the story of these places has been one of relentless economic decline. This is, of course, not news to the people who live in rural and small-town America, who have been fighting for years to reverse the decline. But now, the nation's political class is finally noticing. The election of Donald Trump, powered in no small degree by rural voters, has brought the troubles of small-town America to national attention .... (Porter 2018)

Appalachian writer Elizabeth Catte described the onslaught of attention on the Appalachian Region more dramatically:

> During the 2016 presidential election, the national press branded Appalachia ground zero for America's "forgotten tribe" of white working-class voters ... Appalachians were often used as both the abstract and real beneficiaries of Donald Trump's promise to "make America great again", and media outlets and prestige publications – from the *New Yorker* to *Vanity Fair* – sent reporters to Appalachia to extract profiles and images of the people they assumed could demystify our fractured political moment. Their output came to form a distinct genre of writing – what I call the "Trump Country" piece – that saturated news cycles and fatigued readers with stories of complacent white woe and toxic politics. Podcaster Jayme Dale, originally from North Carolina, described 2016 as the year "the US collectively pointed a trembling finger of accusation at the Appalachian region". (Catte 2018a)

Especially perplexing to outside observers was the question of why voters on the bottom of the poverty and inequality scales seemed to vote for a man like Trump, whose policies were seen to be against their interests. Most of these focused on issues related to the culture of the region, paying little attention to the impact of the structural forces affecting poverty and inequality. The *New York Times* published a long article on 'Why Don't We Always Vote in Our Own Self-Interest?' (Edsall 2018). Summarizing his analysis, Edsall writes,

> Political analysts have talked about how ignorance, racism, sexism, nationalism, Islamophobia, economic disenfranchisement and the decline of the middle class contributed to the popularity of Mr. Trump in rural America. But this misses the deeper cultural factors that shape the thinking of the conservatives who live here.

The Atlantic also published an article on the 'Despair of Poor White Americans', arguing that:

> today, less privileged white Americans are considered to be in crisis, and the language of sociologists and pathologists predominates ... Equally jarring has been the shift in tone. A barely suppressed contempt has characterized much of the commentary about white woe, on both the left and the right ... The barely veiled implication, whichever version you consider, is that the people undergoing these travails deserve relatively little sympathy – that they maybe, kinda had this reckoning coming. Either they are layabouts drenched in self-pity or they are sad cases consumed with racial status anxiety and animus toward the nonwhites passing them on the ladder. Both interpretations are, in their own ways, strikingly ungenerous toward a huge number of fellow Americans. (MacGillis and ProPublica 2016)

Such arguments hearken back to earlier debates on Appalachia, drawing largely on a 'culture-of-poverty' explanation for political behavior. In this environment, it was perhaps not surprising that a book by J.D. Vance, *Hillbilly Elegy: A Memoir of a Family and Culture in Crisis* (2016) soared into the international bestseller list, much of it a blatant re-enforcement that with hard work and entrepreneurialism, the poor can escape their circumstances and reach the middle class in their pursuit of the American dream.

There are a number of reasons to be skeptical about this set of arguments of the political behavior of poor Appalachians. On the one handthey fail to take a more historic view, which if they did so might give another interpretation, especially by paying more attention to the structural factors affecting what Edelman has called rural 'sacrifice zones' (Edelman 2018, para. 1), which exist in other parts of the world as well. In Appalachia, for instance, Stoll provides a detailed historical account of how the settler culture of this rural area was re-shaped by its encounters with capitalism. As he prefaces,

> my purpose is to unite the experience of backcountry settlers of the southern mountains with that of agrarians elsewhere, to demonstrate that English peasants in 1650 and Malian smallholders in 2000 shared a similar fate and encountered similar sources of power as Scots-Irish farmers in 1880. (Stoll 2017, xiv)

But, there are also more contemporary explanations, based in policy and politics. In earlier eras, characterized by national attention on rural poverty, in particular the 1930s and the 1960s, rural Appalachians voted very differently, and not necessarily because their cultures had changed. Rather, in earlier eras, the popularity of key presidential figures – Roosevelt and Kennedy – can be explained by the fact that they paid attention to the difficult issues facing the region, and backed this with important sets of public policies – the New Deal in the 1930s, with a number of programs for rural jobs and rural development; and the War on Poverty in the 1960s, which also had special elements focused on the region.

Since that time, both political attention and public policies directed toward the circumstances of rural America have waned. Obama in 2012 and Clinton in 2016 scarcely visited the Central Appalachian coalfields, and Clinton famously made derogatory comments both about the white working class, as well as the future of coal. By contrast, Trump offered a vision very much in the perceived interest of the poor of this region – one based on the revival of jobs, and on 'King Coal', upon which much of identity politics rested – and he was the one national candidate to seem to be giving some voice to these concerns.

Even though the vision may have become a 'hoax' – there were fewer mining jobs at the end of 2018 than were employed by coal in the last year of the Obama administration (Patterson 2019) – by the mid-term elections of 2018, the support of rural voters in the region for Trump still remained relatively high. The lessons are clear – national policy attention, recognition of identity, and appearing to represent the voice of those ignored by others are important ways to shape political preference, even if used to conservative and demagogic ends. As Scoones et al. argue, 'forms of dislocation, prolonged and widespread neglect, challenges to identity, and the undermining of rural communities and livelihoods' can have profound consequences (2018, 6).

Rather than dwell on this analysis of voting behavior though, I would argue that the interpretations of rural politics found in the current popular debate fail for at least two other reasons. First, they overplay the role of national voting behavior as an expression of consent, while ignoring the deep resistance which exists simultaneously in the region. Secondly, they ignore the analysis of a now long history of an alternative Appalachian scholarship, deeply rooted in scholar activism from within the region, which challenges the largely externally created stereotypes of the quiescent and backward Appalachian 'other'.

Consent, quiescence or resistance?

Those who judge the political behavior and views of rural Appalachia on the basis of the participation in national elections polls miss some other fundamental realities. While rural white voters may have voted proportionately higher than other groups for Trump, usually ignored is the fact that they also had one of the highest rates of *non-participation* (e.g. voter absenteeism) compared to many other regions. A map of the predominantly white counties with low voter turnout in the 2016 elections shows their concentration in a geographic belt following the Appalachian chain, from upstate New York to Tennessee, with the greatest non-participation in the Central mining regions (Mellnik, Tierney, and Uhrmacher 2018).

While some culture-of-poverty theorists may argue that such political behavior relates to socio-economic factors, such as low levels of education, it may equally reflect a more generalized distrust, disinterest in what national politics has to offer, or indeed an opposition to it. In my earlier study, for instance, I also noted the lack of engagement in the 1972 national elections which seemed distant and removed from everyday life:

> despite the headlines in the city's television and newspapers, very few of the Valley's residents talked of the election or its issues. There were no campaign rallies held; no literature was distributed. In national politics, this community neither gives nor receives much attention. (Gaventa 1980, 142)

The key point is that non-participation can be equally important as an indicator of behavior as is participation, and one cannot presume consent for Trumpism from only a very partial sample.

More importantly, in what is seen globally as a period of disengagement from formal politics, is often accompanied by a growth of alternative forms of political expression and agency, characterized as rural populism in many parts of the world. Similarly, in rural Appalachia, simultaneous to the rise of conservative voting in white rural communities, has also been a rise of non-electoral forms of resistance and activism, that defies the stereotypical notions of either apathetic, conservative, or racist whites, challenges the underlying forces that continue to impoverish and exploit these communities, and which appears to me to be at a much higher level than in my study some five decades ago.

To approach this point, I find it useful to return to my earlier book *Power and Powerlessness* (1980). While the book has been widely used as a reference, one of the most useful critiques came from James Scott in his book *Domination and the Arts of Resistance: Hidden Transcripts* (1990, 73). In this book, building on his earlier work *Weapons of the Weak* (1985), Scott challenges certain interpretations of Gramsci's idea of hegemony as well as Marxist ideas of 'false consciousness' for failing to acknowledge more hidden forms of resistance. To him, no system of power has been created which can ensure total consent or quiescence in the face of injustice, no matter how overwhelming that power might be. Rather, he argued, we need to reverse the question:

> If there is a social phenomenon to be explained here, it is the reverse of what theories of hegemony and false consciousness purport to account for. How is it that subordinate groups such

as these have so often believed and acted as if their situations were not inevitable when a more judicious historical reading would have concluded that it was? It is not the miasma of power and thralldom that requires explanation. We require instead an understanding of a *misreading* by subordinate groups that seems to exaggerate their own power, the possibilities for emancipation, and to underestimate the power arrayed against them. If the elite-dominated public transcript tends to naturalize domination, it would seem that some countervailing influence manages often to denaturalize domination. (Scott 1990, 79, emphasis in the original)

Scott's work, as well as my increased understanding of the region over the years, have often led me to reflect on my own original study. While focusing on the question of quiescence many years ago, I had potentially ignored the extent of resistance that was also occurring, perhaps in ways hidden from researchers like me, as well as from other observers. And if we bring this argument forward to the current situation, within the Appalachian Valley I studied, alongside the story of expressed political conservatism (if not authoritarianism) sits another story. This locality, as well as others across the region, have also long been the source of strong grassroots-led organizations and mobilizations which challenge the status quo (e.g. Fisher 1993; Catte 2018b).

The key point is this: those studies which focus only on electoral behavior in presidential politics miss another narrative. Such national-level electoral behavior may disguise, or at least not reflect, subaltern patterns of organizing and resistance which are also occurring in these communities. What is at play is the difference between a form of discourse-based national politics and a more radical and potentially transformative local place-based politics, which may sit uncomfortably side by side.

There are a number of examples of such resistance, even in the small Appalachian Valley which I studied. Over the last forty years, two large community organizing groups have emerged in this area which have fought back on issues of destructive mining practices, unequal taxation, and now transitions to a new economy. These include the groups Statewide Organizing for Community eMpowerment (https://socm.org/) in Tennessee and Kentuckians for the Commonwealth (http://kftc.org/. Both of these emerged from the actions of small groups in communities highly controlled by powerful corporate mining interests, and now both have expanded across their respective states to build inter-racial grassroots organizing platforms that challenge many other issues as well. In the midst of tightly controlled communities dominated by corporate absentee ownership, other groups have worked to create alternative forms of land control including community land trusts and community housing (e.g. the Woodland Community Land Trust). Other groups such as Mountain Justice and United Mountain Defense have focused more on direct action, on such issues as 'mountain top removal' and other forms of environmental destruction, deliberately building on tactics of the 'sit-ins' or 'Freedom Rider' tactics of the civil rights movement. Many of these have been linked through alliances across the region.

These few examples in one small Valley are indicative of broader trends which defy the stereotype of 'Trump country', as a region made up of largely white and socially conservative voters, whose support for Trump may was at least in part fueled by anti-immigrant or racist behavior. In fact, the region is far more diverse racially, ethnically and culturally than is widely recognized, including a history of inter-racial organization action and resistance, found for instance in the Highlander Center, an activist training center with a long history of anti-racism work (Glen 1988). Nor far from Highlander, and not also not far from the coal valley I studied, when federal officers detained 97 illegal workers in a meatpacking plant as part of Trump's crackdown on illegal immigration, the community residents in this small town fought back, with over 300 residents marching in the streets to support the immigrant families (Jordan 2018). In a region known also for its social conservatism, a strong movement of 'Queer Appalachians' has also emerged (https://www.queerappalachia.com/). In a region whose national image is shaped by national stereotypes, other groups, such as Appalshop – have long worked to create challenge these external images through their own film, radio, theater and music productions (https://www.appalshop.org/), in the process revealing a much more diverse and nuanced understanding of the region's culture, including its history of diversity and resistance.

Another example of the challenge to the 'quiescent' image of Appalachia is found in its long history of progressive labor mobilizing, including the historic struggles of miners, textile workers and more, much of which was led by women (Wilkerson 2019). While the de-industrialization of the region could suggest that this tradition was at risk of being lost, a more recent example of collective action – one that received national attention – is found in West Virginia, the state in which 69% of voters went for Trump in 2016 (second only in level of support received in Wyoming). In 2018, the West Virginia teachers, who are amongst the lowest paid in the country, carried out a state-wide strike and won, bringing inspiration and ripple effects across the country, including teachers' strikes in Oklahoma, Arizona, California and Colorado. In an interesting expression of solidarity, the national union also devoted some of its revenues into a new project aimed at creating jobs outside of the coal industry in McDowell County, one of the poorest in the region, bringing together a unique coalition of union members, community groups, local government agencies, and others in a labor and community alliance aimed at rebuilding civic as well as economic infrastructures (Thomhave 2018). And, on the back of support for the teachers' strike, a strongly worker-oriented campaign for the local Congressional seat in the 2018 midterm saw the biggest swing vote towards Democrats in all of the 435 House elections, in an area won by Trump easily in the previous years (Karp 2018).

Not all such grassroots efforts of course are progressive. An article in *The New Republic* contrasts the direct action of a group of protestors against the pipelines and destructive strip-mine practices, with another more right-wing group, the Patriots of Appalachia, appealing to a specific form of Appalachian identity. Asking the question 'Whose Appalachia is it anyway?', the article points to the fact that the rural Appalachian electorate 'is more eclectic than it is given credit for,' and that its future can't simply 'rely on cultural stereotype' (Jones 2018). This point is strongly made in the work of Elizabeth Catte, *What You Are Getting Wrong about Appalachia*, which not only debunks the myths of 'Trump country' but offers compelling and contemporary evidence of a counter-narrative. As she summarizes, 'Far from being monolithic, helpless and degraded, this image of Appalachia is radical and diverse. This image of Appalachia does not deflect the problems of the region, but simply recognizes the voices and actions of those who have struggled against them, often sacrificing their health, comfort and even their lives' (Catte 2018b, 15).

We face two competing explanations then of political response to poverty and inequality in rural America. On the one hand, there are those who look more at voting behaviors – yet these are disconnected from a narrative of more localized place-based projects of resistance and mobilization. Side by side the formal national politics are dozens of examples of local forms of mobilization and resistance, some of which have grown in scale, often around issues of corporate control, environmental exploitation, and loss of land and place. Yet, somehow the anger and challenges to authority these represent fail to penetrate national politics and discourse.

But are these not two sides of the same coin? If we ask the question 'Why quiescence in the face of inequality?', as I did some years ago, the answer may risk under-estimating the emergence of resistance as it does occur. If, on the other hand, we ask the question that Scott suggests, 'Why does countervailing action occur in the face of enormous power differences?', then we may valorize local action, but also risk not focusing on the question of how these small-scale actions contribute to larger change. The reality is more complex – of action and inaction, authoritarianism and challenges to it – sitting together side by side simultaneously. The challenge is to understand this complexity, and to work with it to build a new kind of politics, one which bridges the local to the national and global.

Part of the answer to this challenge is found in a rich scholarship on Appalachia, one that has grown out of decades of committed scholar-activism in the region, and which offers the basis of a broader understanding of the politics of transformation. It is scholarship deeply rooted in historical analysis, a commitment to place, as well as a recognition of how this region fits in the broader global system of a development model based on exploitation of rural resources.

Building the counter-narrative: the role of scholar-activism in the region

Though there have long been studies of the Appalachian Region, these have often been led from the outside, leaving the region deeply subject to the image of the 'Other America', lacking its own knowledge, agency, and identity for social change. When I entered the Appalachian Valley as a young student and searched for books on the region, those most prominent still carried titles reflective of a culture-of-poverty view of the region, such as *Yesterday's People* (Weller 1965) or 'the Analgesic subculture of the Southern Appalachias' (Ball 1968). About this same time, a librarian in the region commented that 'more nonsense has been written about the Southern Mountains than any comparable area in the United States' and that there was 'distressingly little in the way of useful primary and secondary materials' available for research on the region (Wikipedia 2018). Despite a rich history and culture, the field of Appalachian Studies was scarcely recognized nor reflected in the curricula of the region's colleges and universities (Hay and Reichel 1997).

But I was fortunate to arrive at a time when this lack of a critical Appalachian scholarship was beginning to be challenged. Helen Lewis, a long-time sociologist in the region, was about to publish her book, *Colonialism in Modern America: The Appalachian Case* (Lewis, Johnson, and Askins 1978), which gave an alternative understanding of the region's political economy. In 1977, a number of young scholars, committed to developing a different kind of scholarship, came together to discuss the problem of knowledge in the region. In a paper written for one of these gatherings, I reflected:

> Inequalities of wealth and power translate themselves – through control of higher education, intellectuals, media, etc. – into control of information and knowledge. Struggles for economic change must involve strategies for change not only in the energy, recreation, agricultural, or manufacturing industries, but also in the 'knowledge industry'. (Gaventa 1977, 23)

Meeting again in 1978, these scholars and activists formed the Appalachian Studies Association (ASA), which has been meeting every year since that time, 'driven by our commitment to foster quality of life, democratic participation and appreciation of Appalachian experiences regionally, nationally and internationally' (see http://appalachianstudies.org/about/). Over the past forty years, this highly inter- and trans-disciplinary network has helped to transform the face of Appalachian scholarship, creating a rich field of study, and drawing largely from the research and experience of people in the region. In almost every major college and university in this area, courses on Appalachian Studies are now taught. No less than seven journals focus on the region, and countless numbers of studies, films, anthologies, and books, non-fiction and fiction, now offer a knowledge base not there before (see for instance, http://appalachianstudies.org/resources/bibliographies.php)

The growth of Appalachian Studies has also, on the whole, offered a different, more diverse, and critical interpretation of the region than the earlier culture-of-poverty scholarship, reflected again in the more recent bestselling work of J.D. Vance's *Hillbilly Elegy* (2016). This clash of narratives was powerfully seen when Vance was invited to speak on a panel on the opioid crisis in the region at the 41st meeting of the ASA. A new generation of Appalachian scholars and activists peacefully protested against his presence, arguing that he was a detrimental figure to Appalachian scholarship. As Ivy Brashear, a young activist in the Just Transition movement in the region wrote, 'the ASA and its yearly conference have existed for 41 years as a testament to standing up for the region and protecting it through scholarship, activism and organizing' (Brashear 2019). However,

> The fact that JD Vance was invited to the ASA conference in the first place is egregious. His book, *Hillbilly Elegy*, has set the work of Appalachian just economic transition back decades in the national psyche. It is a shaky defense of the ill-informed boot-strap, Culture of Poverty narrative about the region that has shaped people's understanding of us as a people not worth saving because we can't even and have no desire to save ourselves. (Brashear 2019)

Over the years, this new field of Appalachian Studies has made many contributions – so much so that Appalachian Studies itself, and its growth and success, has now become an object of study (Berry, Obermiller, and Scott 2015). One its strongest contributions is found in the now thorough documentation of how domination and control of the region's resources through absentee corporate ownership has shaped the political economy, and therefore the strategies and possibilities of change.

In particular, at about the same time as the formation of the Appalachian Studies Association, many of the same scholars and activists came together to conduct a large-scale study of 'Who Owns Appalachia?' (Appalachian Land Ownership Task Force 1983). In what still stands as one of the most extensive studies of rural land ownership in the United States, involving dozens of scholars, community residents, and students shifting by hand through the records of over 80 counties in six states, this work also became one of the early examples of large-scale participatory action research in the country. Its significance was not only its documentation of inequality, but in its lasting effects over time in shaping a new kind of scholarship.

In a revisit of the study and its impacts twenty-five years later, Scott (2008) observed that while the study did not lead to a new movement for land reform, and many of its recommendations for fundamental change were not taken up, it did have 'tangible effects on politics and social change in the Appalachian region', both through galvanizing and strengthening new organizations and networks, as well as becoming a pioneering example of participatory action research in the United States, and 'a foundational project in the interdisciplinary field of Appalachian Studies' (Scott 2008, 248). Now, forty years later, a new project, involving some of the same early participants but largely led by a new generation of scholars and activists, is working on an update of this work.

While the inequality of land ownership in Appalachia is now well known, Scoones et al. argue that a new emancipatory politics 'must combine not only concerns with redistribution (and so concern with class, social difference and inequality), but also with recognition (and so identity and identification), and representation (and so democracy, community, belonging and citizenship)' (Scoones et al. 2018, 9, quoting Fraser and Honneth 2003). Here too, we see important contributions changing the narrative of the region. Work by many (e.g. Turner and Cabbell 1985) challenges the view of a single, homogenous Appalachian culture, most often implicitly or explicitly thought to be one of 'whiteness', or of an identity given by labeling the region as 'the other', separate from broader national and global forces (Stoll 2017). Such an understanding, Catte (2018a, 2018b) argues, makes invisible the identity and agency of countless other Appalachians, ignoring for instance the rich history of many African-American or Native American communities in the region, or the fact that the most rapidly growing population group are Hispanics and Latinos, immigrating to the region in search of work.

Similarly, work by many other scholars has documented the rich history of resistance and grassroots organization in the region (e.g. Fisher and Smith 2012; Wilkerson 2019) and challenges notions of the ballot box as the sole indicator of 'representation' or agency and voice. Such a tapestry of knowledge insists on understanding the multiple identities and histories of the region, many for progressive goals, that refuse to fit neatly into the shallow, homogeneous category of the region as illiberal, regressive 'Trump country'.

There is a risk, of course, that regional and place-based studies and activism focus inward, that they see their place in history and culture as exceptional, rather than a concrete representation of larger, global connections. Yet much of the Appalachian scholarship, as well as new forms of political action, focus less on uniqueness, and more on commonality with other rural regions of the world, and place the narrative of the region in broader conversations on globalization, power, and transformation (Fisher and Smith 2012; Billings and Kingsolver 2018). As sociologist Barbara Ellen Smith writes,

> the tension between a deep sense of identity with place, especially when shared with others, and the private appropriation and even destruction of place forms a crucible of possibility that is just beginning to be realized. Organizing taking place on the ground in Appalachia today points us toward more extroverted understandings of place and from there toward a global politics of place. (Smith 2018, 60)

An example of this new politics of place was found in the 2018 climate talks in Poland. Here the only public engagement of the official Trump administration was in a panel which focused on the '"unapologetic utilization"' of coal, oil and gas, featuring 'prominent cheerleaders for fossil fuels and nuclear power' (Watts 2018). The session was interrupted by several dozen protestors. One of these was Teri Blanton, an activist from Kentucky, representing the Kentuckians for the Commonwealth, one of the grassroots organizations born out of the action scholarship of the Appalachian Land Ownership Study. 'They talk about the life cycle of coal,' he said. 'I talk about it as a death march. My father died of black lung, and I am in this struggle with others whose fathers and husbands are dying of black lung right now' (Watts 2018).

The symbolism for a new emergent politics from the region could not be more powerful. From 'Trump country' came an attack on Trumpism; from a region shaped by coal, came a demand for a post-coal future; from a local organization founded in part through activist scholarship came resistance on a global stage.

Concluding reflections

A revisit to this rural region has a number of lessons for the study of emancipatory politics. It calls for us to reject an understanding rural politics in this area as unique, and rather to locate them in global trends shaping land, jobs, migration, and futures of rural areas around the world. It insists on looking beneath surface stereotypes which focus on culture while ignoring diversity, identity, resistance, and this larger political economy. It offers some understanding of the importance of activist scholarship to contribute to change, to transform narratives, and to begin to create new possibilities for action.

To re-visit this rural region challenges my own views as well. Almost fifty years ago, my question focused on the issue of 'Why in the face of inequality, do we see quiescence and not rebellion?' Today, the question of Scott on why such resistance has emerged against overwhelming odds might be the more relevant one. As we look to the future, we need to ask both sets of questions, and their intersection: when and under what conditions does mobilization occur or not occur, and also, when and how do small-scale actions for change and resistance come together for larger-scale transformations of the dominant political landscape? How do local place-based actions add to larger national and global forces for transformative change, and how do national and global politics fuel or diminish local place-based action?

No matter how important individually, a few, or even dozens or hundreds, of local forms of mobilization may sit invisibly beneath the larger political discourse. Joined up with one another and with others around the world, at the right times and moments, we may discover that these smaller efforts have the potential to become building blocks for a new, more transformative future.

Acknowledgements

Many thanks to Michelle Mockerbee for contributing to background research on this article and to Dee Scholey for her editorial assistance. Thanks also for comments on an earlier version of the paper at the ERPI 2018 International Conference on 'Authoritarianism and the Rural World', and to the anonymous reviewers of this later version.

Disclosure statement

No potential conflict of interest was reported by the author.

ORCID

John Gaventa http://orcid.org/0000-0003-0360-3248

References

"2018 Distressed Communities Index: Economic Innovation Group." Accessed January 6, 2019. https://eig.org/dci.

Alston, Phil. 2017. "OHCHR: Statement on Visit to the USA, by Professor Philip Alston, United Nations Special Rapporteur on Extreme Poverty and Human Rights." Accessed January 16, 2019. https://www.ohchr.org/EN/NewsEvents/Pages/DisplayNews.aspx?NewsID=22533&LangID=E.

Appalachian Land Ownership Task Force. 1983. *Who Owns Appalachia? Landownership and Its Impact*. Lexington: University Press of Kentucky. Accessed January 18, 2019. https://uknowledge.uky.edu/upk_appalachian_studies/8.

Ball, Richard A. 1968. "A Poverty Case: The Analgesic Subculture of the Southern Appalachians." *American Sociological Review* 33 (6): 885–895. doi:10.2307/2092681.

Balz, Dan. 2017. "Rural America Lifted Trump to the Presidency. Support is Strong, but not Monolithic." *Washington Post*, June 17. https://www.washingtonpost.com/politics/rural-america-lifted-trump-to-the-presidency-support-is-strong-but-not-monolithic/2017/06/16/df4f9156-4ac9-11e7-9669-250d0b15f83b_story.html?noredirect=on&utm_term=.a2cb730bef7d.

Berry, Chad, Phillip J. Obermiller, and Shaunna L. Scott, eds. 2015. *Studying Appalachian Studies: Making the Path by Walking*. Urbana: University of Illinois Press. https://www.jstor.org/stable/10.5406/j.ctt1hd18n2.

Billings, Dwight, and Anne E. Kingsolver, eds. 2018. *Appalachia in Regional Context: Place Matters*. Lexington: University Press of Kentucky.

Blackley, David J., Cara N. Halldin, and A. Scott Laney. 2018. "Continued Increase in Prevalence of Coal Workers' Pneumoconiosis in the United States, 1970–2017." *American Journal of Public Health* 108 (9): 1220–1222. doi:10.2105/AJPH.2018.304517.

Brashear, Ivy. 2019. "On the ASA and JD Vance." *Rabble Lit*. Accessed January 6, 2019. https://rabblelit.com/2018/06/01/on-the-asa-and-jd-vance-ivy-brashear/.

Burawoy, Michael. 2003. "Revisits: An Outline of a Theory of Reflexive Ethnography." *American Sociological Review* 68 (5): 645–679. doi:10.2307/1519757.

Catte, Elizabeth. 2018a. "Passive, Poor and White? What People Keep Getting Wrong about Appalachia." *The Guardian*, February 6. https://www.theguardian.com/us-news/2018/feb/06/what-youre-getting-wrong-about-appalachia.

Catte, Elizabeth. 2018b. *What You Are Getting Wrong about Appalachia*. Cleveland, OH: Belt Publishing.

Coombs, Wayne. 2018. "Analysis: The Pharmaceutical Colonization of Appalachia." *The Daily Yonder*, February 7. https://www.dailyyonder.com/analysis-pharmaceutical-colonization-appalachia/2018/02/07/23595/.

Duncan, Cynthia M., ed. 1992. *Rural Poverty in America*. New York: Auburn House.

Edelman, Marc. 2018. "Sacrifice Zones in Rural and Non-Metro USA: Fertile Soil for Authoritarian Populism." *OpenDemocracy* (blog), February 18. https://www.opendemocracy.net/marc-edelman/sacrifice-zones-in-rural-and-non-metro-usa-fertile-soil-for-authoritarian-populism.

Edsall, Thomas. 2018. "Opinion: Why Don't We Always Vote in Our Own Self-Interest?" *New York Times*, July 19. https://www.nytimes.com/2018/07/19/opinion/voting-welfare-racism-republicans.html.

Fisher, Stephen L., ed. 1993. *Fighting Back in Appalachia: Traditions of Resistance and Change*. Philadelphia, PA: Temple University Press.

Fisher, Stephen L., and Barbara Ellen Smith, eds. 2012. *Transforming Places: Lessons from Appalachia*. Urbana: University of Illinois Press.

Fraser, Nancy, and Axel Honneth. 2003. *Redistribution or Recognition?: A Political-Philosophical Exchange*. London: Verso.

Gaventa, John. 1977. "Appalachian Studies from and for Social Change." *Appalachian Journal* 5 (1): 23–30.

Gaventa, John. 1980. *Power and Powerlessness: Quiescence and Rebellion in an Appalachian Valley*. Urbana: University of Illinois Press.

Gaventa, John. 1987. "The Poverty of Abundance Revisited." *Appalachian Journal* 15 (1): 24–33.

Gaventa, John. 2006. "Finding the Spaces for Change: A Power Analysis." *IDS Bulletin* 37 (6): 23–33.
Gaventa, John. 2018. "The Power of Place and the Place of Power." In *Appalachia in Regional Context: Place Matters*, edited by Dwight Billings, and Anne E. Kingsolver, 91–110. Lexington: University Press of Kentucky.
Giridharadas, Anand. 2018. *Winners Take All: The Elite Charade of Changing the World*. New York: Alfred A. Knopf.
Glen, John. 1988. *Highlander: No Ordinary School, 1932–1962*. The University Press of Kentucky. Hall, Madeline Isabella, and Savannah Drummer. 2016. "Planning and Action: The Appalachian Land Study 2016." *Liken Knowledge* (blog), November 29. http://likenknowledge.org/2016/11/29/planning-and-action-the-appalachian-land-study-2016/.
Harrington, Michael. 1997. *The Other America*. New York: Simon and Schuster.
Harris, Dylan M., and James McCarthy. 2018. "Revisiting Power and Powerlessness: Speculating West Virginia's Energy Future and the Externalities of the Socioecologial Fix."
Hay, Fred J., and Mary Reichel. 1997. "From Activist to Academic: An Evolutionary Model for the Bibliography of Appalachian Studies." *Journal of Appalachian Studies* 3 (2): 211–229.
Jones, Sarah. 2018. "Whose Appalachia Is It, Anyway?" *The New Republic*, May 8. https://newrepublic.com/article/148315/whose-appalachia-it-anyway.
Jordan, Miriam. 2018. "ICE Came for a Tennessee Town's Immigrants. The Town Fought Back." *The New York Times*, June 11. https://www.nytimes.com/interactive/2018/06/11/us/tennessee-immigration-trump.html.
Karp, Matt. 2018. "51 Percent Losers." http://jacobinmag.com/2018/11/midterm-elections-reconstruction-du-bois.
Kelly, Amy. 2017. "Diversifying Appalachian Coal-Dependent Communities: A Case Study Using Participatory Action Research for Community Engagement." MSc thesis, Kansas State University.
Lewis, Helen M., Linda Johnson, and Donald Askins, eds. 1978. *Colonialism in Modern America: The Appalachian Case*. Boone, NC: Appalachian Consortium Press.
Lukes, Stephen. 1974. *Power: A Radical View*. London: Macmillan.
MacGillis, Alec, and ProPublica. 2016. "The Original Underclass." *The Atlantic*, September. https://www.theatlantic.com/magazine/archive/2016/09/the-original-underclass/492731/.
Mellnik, Ted, Lauren Tierney, and Kevin Uhrmacher. 2018. "The Geography of Voting – and Not Voting." *Washington Post*, October 26. https://triblive.com/politics/politicalheadlines/14218227-74/the-geography-of-voting-and-not-voting.
Patterson, Brittany. 2019. "Coal Comeback? Coal at New Low after Two Years Under Trump." *Resource*, February 1. http://ohiovalleyresource.org/2019/02/01/coal-comeback-coal-at-new-low-after-two-years-under-trump/.
Porter, E. 2018. "The Hard Truths of Trying to 'Save' the Rural Economy." *New York Times*, December 14. https://www.nytimes.com/interactive/2018/12/14/opinion/rural-america-trump-decline.html.
Scoones, Ian, Marc Edelman, Saturnino M. Borras, Ruth Hall, Wendy Wolford, and Ben White. 2018. "Emancipatory Rural Politics: Confronting Authoritarian Populism." *The Journal of Peasant Studies* 45 (1): 1–20. doi:10.1080/03066150.2017.1339693.
Scott, James. 1985. *Weapons of the Weak: Everyday Forms of Peasant Resistance*. New Haven: Yale University Press.
Scott, James. 1990. *Domination and the Arts of Resistance: Hidden Transcripts*. New Haven, CT: Yale University Press.
Scott, Shaunna. 2008. "The Appalachian Land Ownership Study Revisited." *Appalachian Journal* 35 (3): 236–252.
Smith, Barbara Ellen. 2018. "Transforming Places: Toward a Global Politics of Appalachia." In *Appalachia in Regional Context: Place Matters*, edited by Dwight Billings, and Anne E. Kingsolver, 49–70. Lexington: University Press of Kentucky.
Stoll, Steven. 2017. *Ramp Hollow: The Ordeal of Appalachia*. New York: Hill and Wang.
Thomhave, Kalena. 2018. "West Virginia Teachers Won Their Strike. Now, They're Rebuilding the Local Economy." *The American Prospect*, May 7. https://prospect.org/article/west-virginia-teachers-won-their-strike-now-theyre-rebuilding-local-economy.

Turner, William, and Edward Cabbell. 1985. *Blacks in Appalachia*. Lexington: University of Kentucky Press.
Vance, James David. 2016. *Hillbilly Elegy: A Memoir of a Family and Culture in Crisis*. London: William Collins.
Volcovici, Valerie. 2017. "Trump Seeks to Ax Appalachia Economic Programs, Causing Worry in Coal Country." *Reuters*, March 16. https://www.reuters.com/article/us-usa-trump-budget-appalachia/trump-seeks-to-ax-appalachia-economic-programs-causing-worry-in-coal-country-idUSKBN16N2VF.
Watts, Jonathan. 2018. "Protesters Disrupt US Panel's Fossil Fuels Pitch at Climate Talks." *The Guardian*, December 10. https://www.theguardian.com/environment/2018/dec/10/protesters-disrupt-us-panels-fossil-fuels-pitch-at-climate-talks.
Weller, Jack E. 1965. *Yesterday's People: Life in Contemporary Appalachia*. Lexington: University Press of Kentucky.
Wikipedia. 2018. "Appalachian Studies." *Wikipedia, The Free Encyclopedia*, November 2. Accessed January 16, 2019. https://en.wikipedia.org/w/index.php?title=Appalachian_studies&oldid=866908330.
Wilkerson, Jessica. 2019. *To Live Here, You Have to Fight: How Women Led Appalachian Movements for Social Justice*. Urbana: University of Illinois Press.

The rural roots of the rise of the Justice and Development Party in Turkey

Burak Gürel [ID], Bermal Küçük and Sercan Taş

ABSTRACT
This paper puts forward four main arguments regarding the persistence of significant rural support of the Justice and Development Party (*Adalet ve Kalkınma Partisi*, AKP) in Turkey since late 2002. Firstly, since the previous coalition government implemented the harshest neoliberal measures in the agricultural sector, small farmers do not directly associate neoliberal assault with the AKP administration. Secondly, villagers have utilized both the ballot box and direct action in order to bargain with the AKP. Thirdly, although the AKP government did not fundamentally depart from neoliberalism, the return of agricultural subsidies, significant expansion of social assistance, and rapid infrastructure construction have secured a large rural following for the party. Finally, the AKP government has effectively used coercive methods to prevent the emergence of an emancipatory political alternative.

Introduction

The uninterrupted rule of Recep Tayyip Erdoğan's Justice and Development Party (*Adalet ve Kalkınma Partisi*, AKP hereafter), since the general election on 3 November 2002 represents the peak of Turkish Islamism. Over the last sixteen years, the AKP has significantly transformed the Turkish economy, society and politics. In the economic realm, the AKP privatized the great majority of the state-owned enterprises, completing the job that the (relatively) secular mainstream parties undertook since the 1980s.[1] On the other hand, by supporting the Islamist bourgeoisie much more so than the secular bourgeoisie through various favoritisms, the AKP has made significant progress (although not yet completed) in altering the balance of power in favor of the Turkish bourgeoisie's Islamist wing (Balkan, Balkan, and Öncü 2015; Esen and Gümüşçü 2018). The AKP's transformation of Turkish society and politics runs much deeper than its economic performance. The ruling party has implemented an ambitious project of reconstructing the state and

---

[1] The value of privatized assets increased from 8.2 billion dollars between 1995 and 2003 (Somer 2016, 492) to 59.9 billion dollars between 2003 and 2017 (Diken 2018).

Table 1. AKP's estimated vote share (%), 2007–2015[a].

	2007	2009	2011	2014	June 2015	November 2015
Rural	**50.45**	**40.99**	**51.98**	**47.01**	**48.57**	**54.71**
Urban	45.61	38.37	47.97	43.87	42.85	50.59
Metropolitan	44.06	40.22	44.59	39.32	39.02	42.91

[a]The KONDA survey data define the rural area as an area with a population of less than 5000 people until the 2011 elections and with a population of less than 4000 people until the November 2015 elections. Vote shares include those who did not have a party preference and those intended not to vote at the time of the survey.
Source: KONDA Barometer Survey Estimates (2007–2015).

society on an Islamist basis. To this end, the government has considerably altered public education (Butler 2018); boosted the power of the Directorate of Religious Affairs (*The Economist* 2018); generously supported the schools and hospitals run by Islamist foundations (Demirtaş 2017); and suppressed the secular and leftist opposition. It is difficult to predict the future of Turkish Islamism. However, the AKP's uninterrupted rule and mass support over the last sixteen years are undeniably remarkable successes of the Islamist project, which therefore should be seriously investigated.

This paper analyzes the rural roots of the AKP's political power. Despite rapid urbanization, a quarter of Turkey's population is still rural (World Bank 2018). The AKP's vote share has been consistently higher in the countryside than in the cities (Table 1). The approval of the constitutional amendment in the referendum on 16 April 2017 established a super presidential system without checks and balances. The amendment was passed with a slight majority (51.4 percent), but the share of the yes vote in the rural areas was much higher, estimated to be between 56 percent (Konda 2017) and 62 percent (Yetkin 2017). The snap (parliamentary and presidential) elections on 24 June 2018 provide another evidence of this phenomenon. Erdoğan was elected to president by receiving 52.3 percent of the votes, more than 20 percent higher than his closest competitor. AKP got 42.5 percent of the popular vote, 20 percent higher than the second party.

This paper primarily focuses on the economic factors behind the AKP's strong support in the Turkish countryside for two main reasons. Firstly, the existing literature on Turkish politics has investigated the (strictly) cultural, ideological, and political factors behind the continuity of AKP power in greater detail than other factors. The AKP leadership's crafty use of a mixture of nationalist, Islamist, neo-Ottomanist, and developmentalist discourses; shifting alliances in national[2] and international politics;[3] portrayal of the (both right-wing

---

[2]A detailed analysis of the AKP's making and unmaking of political alliances since 2002 is beyond the scope of this paper, but a brief summary is in order. Based on its alliance with Fethullah Gülen's Islamist organization (which was strongly organized especially in the judiciary and security apparatuses of the state) and pro-Western liberals (who were strong in the media and intellectual circles) against the secular nationalists inside the military and civilian bureaucracy, which continued at least until the end of 2010, the AKP government completed a significant part of its Islamization agenda. AKP's relationship with liberal circles rapidly deteriorated, especially after the suppression of the Gezi protests in June 2013. Following the breakup of Turkish Islamism (between the AKP and Gülenists) at the end of 2013, AKP allied with a sizeable portion of the previously suppressed secular nationalists against the Gülenists. Similarly, AKP negotiated with the Kurdish movement during the so-called 'solution process' between 2012 and 2015. The ultra-nationalist Nationalist Action Party (*Milliyetçi Hareket Partisi*, MHP) repeatedly blamed AKP leadership for treason to the Turkish nation and state because of their participation in the solution process. AKP-MHP relations rapidly improved following the end of the solution process in 2015 and became an open partnership following the failed coup attempt (organized primarily by the Gülenists) on 15 June 2016. This partnership was instrumental in the passing of the constitutional amendment on 17 April 2017 and Erdoğan's reelection to presidency on 24 June 2018.
[3]A few examples may explain the AKP government's unending zigzags in international relations. The then Prime Minister Tayyip Erdoğan and Syrian president Bashar al-Assad openly celebrated their countries' close relations during meetings in 2008 and 2009. However, Turkey provided significant support to anti-Assad opposition during the civil war after 2011.

and left-wing) opposition as treasonous; increasingly intensive use of coercive methods to deal with political dissent; and the resulting political polarization in Turkey have all been scrutinized in sufficient detail in the existing literature.[4] Without denying the importance of these factors, this paper mainly investigates the policies of agricultural subsidization, social assistance, and infrastructure construction as important factors which account for the AKP's mass support in the countryside.

The second reason for this paper's exclusive focus on material factors stems from our disagreement with the great majority of the political opposition in Turkey concerning the nature of the AKP's rural policy. Interestingly, unlike the analyses of the AKP, which generally give primacy to cultural and ideological factors, economic analyses dominate discussions on rural Turkey's trajectory during the AKP period. The great majority of the opposition parties – including the center-left Republican People's Party (*Cumhuriyet Halk Partisi*, CHP) (CHP 2017; Yıldırım 2014), the pro-Kurdish People's Democratic Party (*Halkların Demokratik Partisi*, HDP) (*Cumhuriyet* April 21, 2015), socialist parties and organizations (Halkevleri 2010; ÖDP 2017; TKP 2007), and critical scholars (Alçın 2017; Günaydın 2009, 2016; Oral 2013) – believe that the AKP has waged a war against agriculture and farmers, with the aim of completely de-agrarianizing the country and thereby making it entirely dependent on agricultural imports. A significant portion of news reports published by the leftist and rightist (non-AKP) media paints a similar picture.[5] We disagree with these claims. Though the AKP's agricultural policy is pro-capital and (by and large) neoliberal, its critics' singular emphasis on neoliberalism does not help much to explain its rural support. This critique also risks portraying rural people as staunch conservatives whose political behavior will not change, regardless of the changes in their living standards. We should avoid reducing the question of political hegemony to a narrow question of cultural values.

This paper offers an alternative to existing explanations by identifying the material basis of the AKP's rural support. It points to factors such as rural people's perception of government policies, changes in living standards, and bargains with the government (through street protests and the ballot box), as well as the resulting concessions they have secured.

This paper puts forward four main arguments. Firstly, we argue that since the previous coalition government (1999–2002) implemented the harshest neoliberal measures in the agricultural sector, small farmers do not directly associate neoliberal assault with the AKP administration. Secondly, the lower classes in rural areas have utilized both the ballot box and direct action to bargain with the AKP government. Thirdly, although the AKP government did not fundamentally depart from the neoliberal agricultural orientation (established by the previous government), it has adopted policies (in response to villagers' use of street protest and the ballot box) that have eased the pressure on small farmers and proletarianized villagers –to a certain extent– through the return of agricultural subsidies and the significant expansion of social assistance to low-income groups. Along with continuous economic growth and rapid infrastructural development (such as roads and

---

Escalating tensions between Russia and Turkey (due to their being on opposite sides of the Syrian war) resulted in the Turkish military's downing of a Russian military aircraft on the Syrian border on 24 November 2015. On 25 August 2018, less than three years after the crisis, Turkish Foreign Minister Mevlüt Çavuşoğlu claimed that Russia and Turkey were 'strategic partners.' However, the Turkish government has not stopped its efforts to weaken the Russian-backed Syrian regime. Similar examples can be given with regard to Turkey's relations with all major geopolitical actors since 2002.
[4]For examples of this large and growing body of literature, see Esmer 2019; Keyman 2014; Somer 2016.
[5]For examples of negative media coverage of agrarian change, see Büyüktaş 2016; Erboz 2017; Ertürk 2017.

bridges), the AKP's limited economic redistribution has made both the neoliberal transformation and increasing right-wing authoritarianism more hegemonic. Finally, like all historical experiences of political hegemony utilizing the carrot-and-stick approach, the AKP government has also used increasingly more coercive methods against radical farmer organizations, labor unions, and the socialist left in order to prevent the emergence of an emancipatory (rural and urban) politics in Turkey.

This study combines fieldwork, archival research, quantitative analysis, and review of secondary sources. We conducted semi-structured interviews with 28 people (hazelnut producers, tea producers, and district political party representatives) in the cities of Ordu and Rize in the Eastern Black Sea region of Turkey in 2018. The interviewees included young and middle-aged males. Agriculture is the primary source of income for the majority of our respondents. Most respondents have secondary sources of income such as coffee houses or minibuses, with at least one pensioner family member and one family member employed in the non-farm sectors. We focused on the cases of Rize and Ordu for two main reasons. First, the AKP's vote share has been higher than the national average in these regions (especially in rural areas). Second, farmer complaints and protests in these regions have received widespread media coverage. Hence, Ordu and Rize are cases which exemplify the co-existence of both extreme criticism and extreme support for the government. In addition to fieldwork, we consulted the online archives of the local and national news media and the statistical data provided by various international and national agencies. We also reviewed the academic and policy literatures regarding the agricultural and social policies in Turkey.

This paper consists of eight sections. The second section examines the Turkish case from a comparative-historical perspective. The third section examines the period between 1995 and 2002 as a prelude to the rise of the AKP. The fourth section responds to whether or not the AKP has completely de-agrarianized Turkey and impoverished farmers. The fifth and sixth sections examine the AKP's engagement with (respectively) the hazelnut and tea producers of the Eastern Black Sea region. The seventh section responds to the question of whether or not environmental protests have led to any meaningful change in rural politics. The last section reiterates the main arguments of the paper and discusses their political implications for the future of emancipatory rural politics in Turkey.

The AKP's rural mass support from a comparative-historical perspective

The rise of the AKP is clearly a part of the recent global rise of 'authoritarian populism.' According to the Emancipatory Rural Politics Initiative's framing article (Scoones et al. 2018, 2–3),

> Authoritarian populism … typically depicts politics as a struggle between 'the people' and some combination of malevolent, racialised and/or unfairly advantaged 'Others', at home or abroad or both. It justifies interventions in the name of 'taking back control' in favour of 'the people', returning the nation to 'greatness' … Authoritarian populism frequently circumvents, eviscerates or captures democratic institutions, even as it uses them to legitimate its dominance, centralise power and crush or severely limit dissent. Charismatic leaders, personality cults and nepotistic, familial or kleptocratic rule combined with impunity are common […] features of authoritarian populism.

On the other hand, many left-wing parties and governments (especially in Latin America) are both populist and authoritarian, and therefore fit in this broad definition. Hence, we need to acknowledge the substantial differences between left-wing and right-wing authoritarian populisms (Borras 2019) and that the recent global rise of authoritarian populism is mainly about the rise of the far-right (Gürel 2018). By implementing neoliberal policies, frequently defining its opponents as anti-national and anti-religious enemies, presenting its rule as a historically significant transfer of power from the elites to the people and thereby the end/reversal of (more than a century long) decline of the Muslim Turks, creating a personality cult around its leader, and dramatically weakening the checks and balances mechanisms, the AKP rule is clearly a part of the recent global ascent of the far-right.

A sizable portion of the literature has investigated the rural roots of historically important far-right movements in agrarian class conflicts. Robert Paxton (1997, 154–160; 1998, 13–14), for instance, contextualizes the success and failure of far-right movements within the background of massive farm worker strikes in Germany (1919–1923), Italy (1920–1921), and France (1936–1937). Both the state and fascist paramilitaries helped agrarian capital to crush the strikes. While the continuing effectiveness of state violence minimized the agrarian capital's need for paramilitaries and ruled out a fascist takeover in France, the weakness of the state in the Italian countryside increased the agrarian elites' reliance on fascists and helped Mussolini's swift triumph. In Germany, vigilantes supported by the local authorities broke the agricultural strikes. This agrarian reaction led to the rise of a variety of far-right organizations and later, the Nazis (Grill 1982, 152, 184). Similarly, Walden Bello (2018) shows that agrarian capital's goal of suppressing progressive lower-class mobilizations and the degree of reliance on the violence of state and paramilitary groups were key factors shaping the diverse trajectories of counterrevolutionary movements in Chile, Indonesia, and the Philippines in the second half of the twentieth century.

These insights help us to place the AKP's rural politics in the proper comparative-historical perspective. Although the use of violence is *not* absent in their history, Turkish Islamism generally used non-violent methods of taking power, which clearly distinguishes them from classical fascism. Also, although the AKP government has used coercive methods against its opponents since the beginning of its rule, these practices significantly differ from the cases of fascist agrarian reaction illustrated above. The AKP government has deployed coercive methods against its rightist and leftist opponents. The intensity of such coercive methods increased significantly after the Gezi protests of 2013, which marked the limits of the AKP's Islamist project in attaining its goal through mostly consensual methods. None of these opposition movements are rooted in agrarian class conflict. Moreover, there has not been any significant movement of farm workers or small farmers to force agrarian capital to seek the help of intensive state or paramilitary violence. Hence, increasing authoritarianism in contemporary Turkey cannot be explained by agrarian capital's reaction against the movements of agrarian classes of labor.[6]

On the other hand, we find the literature on the role of welfare provision in the rise of far-right movements very useful in explaining the AKP's persistent rural support. Hence, in

---

[6]On the other hand, although the urban labor movement has not been powerful enough to necessitate paramilitary violence, it has certainly been a factor behind increasing authoritarianism in Turkey. Between 2003 and 2018, the government banned 14 large-scale labor strikes that involved 192,000 workers. Nine of these strike bans took place after 2014 (Hak İnisiyatifi İstanbul 2018). In a speech given to Turkish investors in 2017, the president explained the strike bans:

the Turkish context, class analysis is necessary *not* to explain the agrarian class conflict triggering a far-right reaction in the service of agrarian capital *but* to understand the circumstances in which a dramatic increase in welfare provision enables a far-right party to create a mass base of rural lower classes positioned against the mainstream parties. The global literature on far-right movements shows that although the intensive use of coercion against left-wing rural organizations before and after taking power has been a critical factor, it cannot in and of itself explain the success of the far-right in the countryside, as bidding for political power requires a sufficiently large mass base. In fact, far-right movements and regimes established rural hegemony by keeping some of their redistributive promises without significantly altering the existing class structure. In her comparative analysis of the rural support of fascism, Nazism, and Perónism, Leslie Anderson (2006) underscores the critical role of the partisan-style provision of welfare and other services. In Italy,

> [Fascist] unions, working directly with landlords, delivered rewards and concessions quickly without having to produce changes in the laws, as socialists were working to do [...] Over time it became increasingly clear that it was *financially beneficial to join fascism, but financially unrewarding and downright dangerous to remain a socialist*. (2006, 199–200, emphasis added)

Similar factors played out in the German countryside in the late 1920s and 1930s:

> The Nazis organized soup kitchens and other measures to bring immediate aid to rural folk. They offered credit support and small loans to confront the credit crisis and foreclosure threats. As with the Italian fascists, each of these benefits was restricted to Nazi supporters [...] After gaining national power, [...] material support included further credit support, price support, and a new law that disallowed foreclosures. (Anderson 2006, 202)

Finally, welfare-based partisanship underlined the rural hegemony of Perónist authoritarian populism in Argentina between 1946 and 1955:

> To provinces that supported his movement, Perón delivered roads, schools, electricity, potable water, and public-works projects. The Eva Perón Foundation created a nationwide patronage system whereby provincial supporters could write to Eva for individual material aid such as sewing machine or medicine for a sick child. In the poverty of rural Argentina, such material and development efforts were the first time many rural dwellers had ever received anything from the government. (2006, 205)

As in these historical cases, welfare provision continues to play a key role in winning villagers' support of reactionary politics. In fact, 'in rural settings, we see subsidy policies, social welfare support, and local economic development, alongside trade protection, sovereignty and anti-globalisation narratives, being promoted by right-wing, authoritarian regimes' (Scoones 2018).

We argue that a similar dynamic has underlined the AKP's hegemony in rural Turkey. AKP's success has been based on the combination of 'social neoliberalism' (Dorlach

---

We use the state of emergency for the business people's benefit. Let me ask: Do you encounter any trouble, any delays in the business world [now]? When we assumed power [in 2002], there was [also] a state of emergency in Turkey, but all the factories were facing the threat of strikes. Remember those days. But now, thanks to the state of emergency, we immediately intervene in those workplaces that face the threat of strikes. (Bozkurt-Güngen 2018, 232)

The state of emergency was declared on 20 June 2016, five days after the failed coup attempt, and continued for two more years.

2015; Öniş 2012, 137) and increasing authoritarianism. Social neoliberalism occupies an intermediate position on the spectrum of orthodox neoliberalism on the right and social democracy on the left. It differs from social democracy since its 'social reforms are more uneven and remain coupled with more orthodox economic policies.' By recognizing that 'poverty and inequality require, at least in part, political solutions,' social neoliberalism distinguishes itself from orthodox neoliberalism (Dorlach 2015, 524). What motivates social neoliberalism's sensitivity to the question of poverty is its perception of the serious political risks associated with orthodox neoliberalism. Across the globe, the lower classes have rejected neoliberal policies through street protests, armed insurgencies, revolutions, and the ballot box. By providing a variety of material concessions to low-income groups, a strategy often branded as 'controlled populism' (Güven 2016, 1007), social neoliberalism offers (at least) a temporary political fix to contain the radicalization potential of peasants and workers and to win elections (Dorlach 2015, 521; Öniş 2012, 137).[7]

We argue that the AKP has competently followed a line of social neoliberal policy since 2002. On the one hand, it has followed the orthodox neoliberal prescription by privatizing state-owned enterprises and increasing the precariousness of the labor market. On the other hand, as we show below, AKP has shifted away from the orthodox neoliberal prescription through limited increases of agricultural support and significant expansion of social assistance to the rural and urban poor. In addition, the dramatic expansion of credit, which increased the household debt to GDP ratio from 1.9 percent in 2002 to 22.6 percent in 2013, also helped the AKP to expand its popular base (Bozkurt-Güngen 2018, 228–229, 234). In sum, while the AKP's increasingly coercive methods narrowed the scope of labor empowerment through collective mobilization by workers' and farmers' unions, its social neoliberal policies helped the urban and rural laboring classes' '"disciplining by unmediated/individual incorporation" into the AKP's political project as consumers, credit users and social assistance recipients' (Bozkurt-Güngen 2018, 220). Despite the temporary economic slow-down of 2008–2009, the Turkish economy has not faced catastrophic crisis. GDP per capita (in current US$) increased from $3,660 in 2002 to $12.542 in 2013 and then decreased to $10.540 in 2017. GDP per capita (in constant 2010 US$) rose from $8,003 in 2002 to $14.933 in 2017 (World Bank 2018). This has created enough financial space for the AKP government to follow a social neoliberal line, which has been immensely helpful for its hegemony.[8]

Agricultural policies before the AKP

The foundation of the AKP on 14 August 2001 was a result of the split within the National Vision Movement (*Milli Görüş Hareketi*), the brand name for the tradition of legal Islamist parties in Turkey (a tradition dating back to the early 1970s). The Welfare Party (*Refah Partisi*, RP) represented this political line in the 1990s. Turkish Islamism achieved its first significant successes under the RP in the mid-1990s. The RP won the İstanbul and

---

[7]On the question of the use of welfare provision as an apparatus of political containment and mobilization of the poor, also see Yörük 2012.
[8]As the Turkish economy currently enters into its severest downturn since 2001, the AKP will certainly face a formidable challenge to pursue social neoliberalism as before. We briefly discuss this in the last section, but a detailed discussion of the prospects of the AKP and its opponents in the light of the ongoing economic crisis is beyond the scope of this paper.

Ankara metropolitan municipality elections on 27 March 1994. It received 21.38 percent of the popular vote and won the general elections on 24 December 1995. A large portion of the founders of the AKP held important positions in the RP such as top party officials, ministers, deputies, and mayors. Tayyip Erdoğan was the mayor of the İstanbul metropolitan municipality between 1994 and 1998.

Six months after the 1995 election, the RP formed a coalition government with the center-right True Path Party (*Doğru Yol Partisi*, DYP). The RP-DYP coalition remained in power between June 1996 and June 1997. Agricultural producer support (as percent of gross farm receipts) increased from 25.5 percent in 1996 to 31.6 percent in 1997 (OECD 2018a). Hence, small farmers did not have much reason to criticize the RP. On 28 February 1997, Turkish military command used the threat of a coup to force the RP-DYP government to accept a series of secular reforms aiming to prevent the further rise of Islamism. Following that intervention, the alliance of the military command, the secular bourgeoisie (including those controlling the majority of the mass media), and the leaders of major labor unions put heavy pressure on the government, which brought it to collapse six months later. Both the rural and urban poor viewed it as a grave injustice to a government composed of devout people working for their interests. The popularity of Tayyip Erdoğan – who was imprisoned for four months in 1998 after reading an Islamic poem during an RP demonstration, stripped from his post as the mayor of İstanbul, and banned from the parliamentary elections of 2002– rapidly increased.

Later developments consolidated the masses' positive outlook on Islamists. The coalition government of the center-left Democratic Left Party (*Demokratik Sol Parti*, DSP), the ultranationalist Nationalist Action Party (*Milliyetçi Hareket Partisi*, MHP), and the center-right Motherland Party (*Anavatan Partisi*, ANAP) remained in power between May 1999 and November 2002. Two of the three severest economic crises of the post-1980 period (1994, 1999, and 2001) occurred during the rule of the DSP-MHP-ANAP coalition. Compared to 1998, the GDP per capita contracted by one-quarter in 2002 (World Bank 2018). The crises of 1999 and 2001 forced the government to draw loans from the IMF, which were conditional on the implementation of a neoliberal policy package, including drastic cuts to the agricultural support expenditures. World Bank Vice President, Kemal Derviş, was launched into the seat of the Minister of Economic Affairs in March 2001, with a mission to guarantee strict implementation of the neoliberal reforms. Derviş quickly became the symbol of neoliberal orthodoxy and foreign economic influence. Agricultural support (as percent of gross farm receipts) decreased from 36.4 percent in 1999 to 32.3 percent in 2000, and 16.8 percent in 2001. Its increase to 26 percent in 2002 (OECD 2018a), did not meaningfully alleviate the damage done to small farmers. The Tobacco Law of 2001 eliminated state procurement of tobacco and resulted in the decline of tobacco-producing households from 583,400 in 2000 to 401,200 in 2002. The Sugar Law of 2001 implemented similar measures (Aydın 2010, 163–172). In 2002, the DSP-MHP-ANAP coalition eliminated previous forms of government support to agriculture and adopted a direct income support policy that provided cash assistance to farmers cultivating less than 50 hectares. Direct income support was provided to everyone documenting farmland ownership, regardless of whether they actually cultivated or not. In other words, it cut the historically close link between government support and agricultural production. Its primary aim was to contain the risks stemming from the neoliberal assault on small farmers and their resulting rapid proletarianization (Gürel 2014, 348–350).

The neoliberal assault against small farmers and workers made the DSP-MHP-ANAP government very unpopular. Many worker and farmer protests took place in 2001 and 2002 (Gürel 2014, 370–371). Although mainstream media did not side with the protestors, media coverage of mass disappointment and protests was much broader than today and negatively impacted public opinion of government policies. As a result, the coalition crumbled, and an early election was scheduled for 3 November 2002. The combined vote shares of the coalition parties declined from 53.4 percent in 1999 to 14.7 percent in 2002 (Turkish Statistical Institute 2012). One of the notable features of the election campaign in 2002 was the inclusion of Kemal Derviş in the list of deputy candidates of the center-left CHP, which revealed the party's neoliberal orientation once more. More importantly, it also demonstrated the CHP's utter incompetence with regard to understanding the mood of the lower classes at that time. Erdoğan's AKP, established only a year earlier, received 34.3 percent of the popular vote, followed by the CHP, which received only 19.4 percent of the popular vote (Turkish Statistical Institute 2012). The AKP controlled the parliamentary majority and formed a government on 19 November 2002.

The AKP's social neoliberalism in rural Turkey

The AKP government has not changed the neoliberal course of agricultural policy. The transition of Turkish agriculture from a smallholder-based to an agribusiness-based structure has continued unabated. Employment of wage labor and contract farming become increasingly prevalent relations of agricultural production. On the other hand, the government has introduced a series of policies that have helped to make the neoliberalization process relatively acceptable among small farmers and proletarianizing villagers. Since the AKP inherited a very low support base (in terms of agricultural support, economic growth performance, and political popularity) from the previous government, these policies have helped the party to broaden its rural support base.

The AKP government brought back producer support for crop production and animal husbandry in 2004 (Güven 2009). Rather than simply returning to older policy, the party has since liberalized the support policy (Keyder and Yenal 2013, 60). Agricultural regions of Turkey were divided into basins, listing the (suggested) competitive advantage of each basin's products and distributing subsidies and other forms of financial support accordingly. An increasing portion of agricultural support has since been given to the production of certified organic products. The basin-based support policy favors the medium- and large-scale producers over smaller ones (Gürel 2014; Oral 2010; Yıldırım 2017a). Nevertheless, the total amount of agricultural support has increased. The level of agricultural support in Turkey was significantly below the OECD average in 2001 and 2002, and has been consistently above it since 2003 (OECD 2018a).[9] The ratio of irrigated area to total agricultural area did not decline (12.6 percent in 2002 and 13.5 percent in 2014). Although Turkey's agricultural dependency has increased (the value of imports of agricultural and animal products in 2017 is 5.6 times that of 2002, whereas the volume of exports in 2017 is 3 times that of 2002), major indicators of agricultural production have not declined (Turkish Statistical Institute 2018). The index (2004–2006 = 100) of crop production

---

[9] On 20 February 2018, the government announced that it would cover half of the gasoline expenditure of farmers (*Sabah* February 20, 2018).

increased from 94.2 in 2003 to 119.3 in 2016, that of livestock production increased from 83.7 to 163.7, and of that of food production increased from 93.7 to 134.4 within the same period (World Bank 2018).[10] The average annual growth rate of agricultural value added was 1.3 percent between 1969 and 2002 and 2.6 percent between 2003 and 2016. The average annual growth rate of value added per worker in agriculture was 4 percent between 1991 and 2002 and 4.9 percent between 2003 and 2016.[11] In sum, although the growth performance of Turkish agriculture has not been remarkable, the available evidence does *not* support the popular claim of a sharp agrarian crisis in the AKP era.

The AKP government has also implemented a series of social policy reforms to consolidate and expand its support base among the poor. Here, we define 'poor' broadly, including the unemployed population, low-income farmers, and full-time and part-time workers in low-wage jobs. The AKP's social policy programs include means-tested provisions of in-cash and in-kind assistance specifically targeting those below the official poverty rate. However, assistance is often given to those who do not fall below the poverty line. In fact, similar to other countries such as China (Chen, Pan, and Xu 2016) and Mexico (Ramírez 2017), the caseworkers of the Ministry of Family and Social Security in Turkey maintain a significant degree of discretion of defining who is poor and who needs assistance. Many people receive assistance despite being above the official poverty rate (Aytaç 2014, 1218–1219). Similar to the use of social assistance to contain political radicalization in other countries, the AKP government has used social assistance in order to contain the Kurdish movement (Yörük 2012). Public officials explicitly stated that they might consider freezing social assistance to families whose members participate in street demonstrations supporting the Kurdish movement (*Milliyet* October 30, 2008). More often, social assistance has been used to increase the AKP's support base among the poor to win elections.

The share of social expenditure in Turkey's GDP increased from 7.7 percent in 2000 to 10.3 percent in 2005 and 13.5 percent in 2014 (OECD 2018b).[12] The ratio of households receiving public social assistance ('all in-kind and in-cash transfers from the general government budget to poor households, except for retirement pensions and tax repayments') doubled within just a decade, from 15.8 percent in 2002–2003 to 30.7 percent in 2010–2011. The same figure more than doubled in the countryside in the same period: from 31 percent to 67.8 percent for the 'landed subsistence peasants,' from 13.9 percent to 55.6 percent for 'landless subsistence peasants,' from 18.2 percent to 41.5 percent for 'agricultural laborers', and from 25 percent to 64.5 percent for the 'rural unemployed.' Moreover, the combined ratio of public and private social assistance in household income rose from 15.5 percent to 16.4 percent for landed subsistence peasants, from 7.2 percent to 18.8 percent for landless subsistence peasants, from 3.9 percent to 9.4 percent for agricultural workers, and from 51.2 percent to 61.4 percent for the rural unemployed (Bahçe and Köse 2017, 588).[13]

While the level of income inequality has not changed and wealth inequality has increased (Torul and Öztunalı 2018), the social assistance boom has reduced absolute

---

[10] Livestock has been the most problem-ridden sector during the AKP era. The number of cattle and volume of red meat production were stagnant until the early 2010s. However, they have since steadily increased. The production of other major livestock products (chicken meat, egg, milk, and honey) has increased in the entire AKP period (Turkish Statistical Institute 2018).
[11] Authors' calculations based on World Bank 2018.
[12] This is significantly below the OECD average of 21 percent (OECD 2018b).
[13] For specific definitions of these rural groups see Bahçe and Köse 2017, 592–595.

Table 2. The AKP's vote share (%) in Ordu.

General elections		Local elections		Constitutional referendums		Presidential elections	
2002	41.5	2004	40.2	2010	63.47	2014	66.98
2007	55.8	2009	42.5	2017	61.88	2018	65.13
2011	60.2	2014	52.6				
June 2015	53						
November 2015	63.1						
June 2018	48.7						

Sources: Hürriyet 2018; www.secim.haberler.com; www.secim-sonuclari.com; Turkish Statistical Institute 2012.

(rural and urban) poverty in Turkey over the last 16 years (World Bank 2018). In other words, although the main beneficiary of the AKP's economic policy is the Turkish bourgeoisie (especially its Islamist wing), its social policy has made limited improvements to the living standards of low-income groups. This has contributed to the AKP's hegemony in poor neighborhoods and villages.

The AKP's hegemony over hazelnut producers

In 2015, Turkey produced about two-thirds of the world's total hazelnut export (Turkish Statistical Institute 2016). Rural areas surrounding the city of Ordu (located in the eastern Black Sea region) supply one-third of Turkey's hazelnut production (T.C. Gümrük ve Ticaret Bakanlığı Kooperatifçilik Genel Müdürlüğü 2017). Small and medium-sized farms dominate hazelnut production. Because opposition parties, journalists, and scholars have continuously claimed that government policies harm hazelnut production and small producers' interests (CHP 2016; İnce 2012), the AKP's consistently strong electoral performance in Ordu is a puzzle deserving of careful attention (Table 2).

Class struggle in the hazelnut sector occurs on two main levels. The first level includes the struggle of farmers and capital over the market price. Farmers demand prices significantly higher than those traders/exporters/corporations prefer to give. The Union of Hazelnut Sales Cooperatives (*Fındık Tarım Satış Kooperatifleri Birliği*, often called *Fiskobirlik*), founded in 1935, is a quasi-public entity. On the one hand, it represents all hazelnut producers and collects membership fees from them. On the other hand, it has acted as a government institution in regulating the hazelnut market. From the mid-1960s to the mid-2000s, Fiskobirlik purchased hazelnuts from its member cooperatives on behalf of the government treasury at pre-determined prices. Fiskobirlik has also processed hazelnuts in its factories and marketed them in national and international markets (Fiskobirlik 2017). On the other hand, private capital –of both Turkish and foreign agribusinesses– has been an important player in the hazelnut sector. Fiskobirlik and government agencies have taken agribusiness interests into account when setting purchase prices. However, due to the significant bargaining power of farmers, capitalist interests have not unilaterally determined hazelnut prices. Historically, political concerns have been important in price determinations. During the 1960s and 1970s (the height of social movements and influence of the radical left), hazelnut producers organized many meetings and demonstrations. As in the rest of the country, the radical left was harshly suppressed in the region after the coup of 1980.

On the second level of class conflict, farmers' interests clash with those of farm workers. Although the average farm size is small, the picking of hazelnuts during summer months often requires outside labor. The great majority of farm workers come from the Kurdish-majority region of southeastern Turkey, especially since the forced migration policy of the 1990s, which quickly displaced and urbanized the Kurdish peasants (Yörük 2012). The wages of Kurdish farm workers are very low, and they lack decent working conditions, as well as social protection. As a result of the long history and increasing intensity of the Kurdish question, class antagonism between Turkish farmers and Kurdish proletarians involves an important ethnic dimension.[14] Given the significant weakening of the radical left – the only force, which could act against chauvinism among the Turkish farmers– the ethnic dimension of agrarian labor relations has continuously swayed the politics of Turkish farmers in a right-wing nationalist direction. During our fieldwork in Ordu in 2018, farmers told us that they support the government's nationalist stance.

As in other parts of the Turkish countryside, economic crises and the neoliberal assault between 1999 and 2001 paved the way for the AKP's first election victory in Ordu in 2002. Nevertheless, soon after the election, farmers began to believe that the government was favoring the interests of the hazelnut exporters. The strong influence of Cüneyd Zapsu (the owner of Balsu Gıda, a hazelnut exporting company) on the AKP leadership became the personal target of farmers' criticisms (*Cumhuriyet* June 26, 2003). Major opposition parties openly blamed the government for the betrayal of hazelnut producers (*Cumhuriyet* August 3 & 22, 2003). More importantly, the AKP did not have control over top management of Fiskobirlik at that time. Fiskobirlik executives openly criticized the government for the low prices and held meetings with the representatives of opposition parties (*Cumhuriyet* August 15 & 24, 2003). Fiskobirlik also struggled with serious financial difficulties at the time. Its management requested government assistance for its credit applications to public and private banks, but the government refused. As a result, Fiskobirlik frequently delayed its payments to farmers for past purchases. The public perceived this as the AKP's punishment of Fiskobirlik for its refusal to side with it (Ekşi 2006; Karpat 2006). In the early 2000s, criticisms of the AKP's policies (both inside and outside the party) were much more explicit than it is today. Several AKP officials heavily criticized the hazelnut policy in 2003 (*Cumhuriyet* August 3 & 9 & 15 & 16, 2003).

Mass dissatisfaction regarding hazelnut prices continued over the next few years, finally culminating in 2006, the first year that the AKP government left the power of price setting entirely to the authority of hazelnut exporters. For the first time in the history of the Turkish republic, hazelnut harvest season began without the government's declaration of a minimum procurement price (*Cumhuriyet* August 11, 2006), which slashed the market price almost in half. Ordinary farmers, Fiskobirlik, The Chamber of Agriculture (*Ziraat Odası*), The Farmers' Union (*Çiftçi-Sen*), and opposition parties opposed the move (*Cumhuriyet* July 29 & August 30, 2006). Growing farmer dissatisfaction led to a series of protests. Things finally erupted on July 31. About 100,000 hazelnut producers coming from different parts of the eastern Black Sea region gathered for a protest meeting in Ordu. After the meeting, protestors blocked the Ordu-Samsun highway for about eight hours before being dispersed by the gendarmerie and police forces. Many protestors and security

---

[14]For detailed fieldwork-based analyses of the relationship between Turkish farmers and Kurdish farm workers in different regions of Turkey, see Duruiz 2015; Pelek 2010.

forces were wounded (*Hürriyet* July 31, 2006). This is one of the largest farmer protests in modern Turkish history. Small-scale farmer protests (also involving the members of the local branches of the AKP) continued in Ordu in the following months (*Cumhuriyet* September 7 & 10, 20-22, 2006, April 5 & 8, 2007).

Although the great majority of protesting farmers did not sway towards the radical left, the radical left's organizational efforts in the region should not be overlooked. The Union of Hazelnut Producers (*Fındık Üreticileri Sendikası*, Fındık-Sen), founded in 2004, played a significant part in organizing small farmers and participating in farmer protests (Fındık-Sen 2017). Some socialist organizations such as the Freedom and Solidarity Party (*Özgürlük ve Dayanışma Partisi*, ÖDP), the People's Houses (*Halkevleri*), the Socialist Democracy Party (Socialist Democracy Party, SDP), and the Communist Party of Turkey (*Türkiye Komünist Partisi*, TKP) have also worked in the region. The ÖDP organized a march of hazelnut producers from Trabzon to Ankara in the summer of 2006 (*Cumhuriyet* July 25 & October 1, 2006). However, such efforts have not been effective for three main reasons. First, the politics of the radical left in Turkey has not yet recovered from the twin shocks of the military coup of 1980 and the collapse of the Eastern Bloc in 1989–1991. Second, above-mentioned ethnic division of farm labor shifted the politics further towards the nationalist right. Finally, the AKP government has been very careful in containing the radical left by all means possible. More than a decade after its foundation, Fındık-Sen's legal status as a union has still not been completely recognized. Leftist activists are under significant pressure. For example, despite their lack of political influence, socialist activists were the primary targets of police arrests following the July 31 protest (*Cumhuriyet* August 18, 2006).[15]

Farmer protests were alarming signals for the AKP before the general election on 22 July 2007. Political polarization between Islamists and secularists increased before the election. Abdullah Gül, the then second most important figure of the AKP, was chosen to be the presidential candidate of the party. The AKP claimed enough seats in the parliament to elect him. However, secular opposition (represented by the CHP in the parliament and numerous minor Kemalist groups outside the parliament) campaigned against Gül's presidency, which led the constitutional court to freeze the election process. On 27 April 2007, the military's top command issued an online statement blaming the government for the erosion of secularist foundations of the Turkish state. Hence, the July 2007 election became a political battle of decisive importance. The AKP had to win the election, ideally by increasing its vote share, in order to cut the Gordian knot.

The AKP swayed towards a more populist-leaning hazelnut policy in 2007. During the first half of 2007, the government paid all its debts to farmers (for crop procurement and compensation of the losses caused by natural calamities such as drought and frost). Moreover, these 2007 payments were made in advance (*Cumhuriyet* April 9, 2007). More importantly, on July 9, less than two weeks before the election, the government announced a 28.7 percent increase in the minimum price. Both the Fiskobirlik management and the local branches of the Board of Agriculture praised this decision (*Cumhuriyet* July 10, 2007). Finally, small farmers and proletarianized villagers viewed the AKP's social policy

---

[15]The weakness of the center-left CHP is another factor behind the AKP's regional power. As a hazelnut producer in the Ulubey district of Ordu told us, 'The people can't benefit from the other side [center-left]. There was Ecevit before, but now there is no one.' Bülent Ecevit was the most popular leader of the center-left in the 1970s. He was the prime minister of the DSP-MHP-ANAP government between 1999 and 2002. Ecevit died in 2006.

positively (*Cumhuriyet* July 24, 2007). As a result, the AKP won 55.8 percent of the votes in July 2007.

After the electoral victory of 2007, Fiskobirlik management did not have much choice but to surrender to the AKP. In turn, the AKP swiftly took control of the organization (Yıldırım 2007). Given the historical importance of Fiskobirlik in the hazelnut sector, its control by the AKP represented a decisive victory and helped the party to further its hegemony in the region. Over the years, the government has since transformed Fiskobirlik into a branch of the Soil Products Office (*Toprak Mahsulleri Ofisi*, TMO), which has allowed for more direct government control over the hazelnut sector. In our fieldwork in Ordu, we observed that farmers no longer mention Fiskobirlik. They only refer to the TMO when discussing the government's procurement policy. The farmers stated that the AKP government is not responsible for the decline of Fiskobirlik. According to one interviewee,

> The liquidation of Fiskobirlik has nothing to do with the AK Party government. Fiskobirlik went bankruptcy. The state can't sustain it. People want jobs from the state, but it cannot do this. Even if the AK Party government goes, the state will not establish factories.

This discourse is strikingly similar to the post-1980s pro-privatization discourse of blaming public enterprises for inefficiency and corruption.

Important changes have taken place in the hazelnut market in recent years. After buying Oltan Gıda (a Turkish trading company) in 2014, Ferrero (an Italian agribusiness) achieved market dominance. Like Ferrero, the Singaporean Olam Gıda became a major player after purchasing Progıda (a Turkish trading company) in 2011. Cüneyd Zapsu's Balsu Gıda is the third largest player in the hazelnut market (*Dünya* November 20, 2011; Yıldırım 2017c). Greater market dominance of these companies has decreased the state's capacity to influence hazelnut prices, but the AKP has continued using pricing to win elections. Just before the critical constitutional referendum of April 2017, for instance, the government announced that the TMO was going to purchase a significant quantity of hazelnuts from farmers in order to prevent its price from falling below 10 Turkish liras per kilogram (Yazan 2018; Yıldırım 2017b). As one farmer in Ordu told us, 'They are giving the subsidies in such critical periods, right before the elections or in March when all the producers go broke … They throw something at the people and the people jump on it.'

AKP's hegemony over tea producers

Attempts at expanding tea production around the city of Rize in the eastern Black Sea region date back to the late nineteenth century. Since then, the volumes of tea produced have increased gradually, and Turkey has become the world's sixth largest exporter of processed tea in 2016. Rize is currently the most prominent tea-producing city with 131,443 tea producers supplying 61.8 percent of all national production (ÇAYKUR 2016). Until 1984, there was a state monopoly in the tea sector. The state controlled the tea sector through TEKEL until 1971, when the General Directorate of Tea Enterprises (*Çay Kurumu*, ÇAYKUR) was founded as the only state-owned monopoly enterprise. In 1984, the restriction on the private investment in the sector was removed along with other liberalization reforms. The private sector started to invest in the procurement, packaging, and distribution of tea. However, despite the increasing private investments in the tea sector by national and transnational corporations, ÇAYKUR is still the most powerful actor in the procurement

Table 3. AKP's vote share (%) in Rize.

General elections		Local elections		Constitutional referendums		Presidential elections	
2002	44	2004	46.4	2010	76.04	2014	80.57
2007	53.66	2009	46.80	2017	75.06	2018	76.92
2011	69.06	2014	67.9				
June 2015	66.76						
November 2015	75.88						
June 2018	64.85						

Sources: CNN Türk 2018; www.secim.haberler.com; www.secim-sonuclari.com; Turkish Statistical Institute 2012.

and distribution of tea. In 2016, ÇAYKUR purchased 53.1 percent of all tea produced. Despite the long debates over its privatization, ÇAYKUR has been excluded from the privatization program. In 2017, it was transferred to the newly created Turkey Wealth Fund (ÇAYKUR 2018).

As Table 3 demonstrates, the AKP has been dominant in Rize since 2002. The continuation of subsidization is an important factor behind this success. Purchases by the ÇAYKUR did not decrease and subsidy payments continued (T.C. Gıda, Tarım ve Hayvancılık Bakanlığı 2017). In addition to existing support mechanisms, the government has recently started to encourage producers to shift to organic tea production.

Our fieldwork in Rize in 2018 revealed that delayed payments, favoritisms in quota arrangements and corruption in ÇAYKUR in previous periods were major problems for producers. Almost all interviewees expressed their satisfaction with the current management of ÇAYKUR. One of them said,

> Now, there is an appointment-based system. No nepotism. The state still does not purchase all the tea we produce. But the volume that will be purchased is pre-determined at the beginning of the season. The AK Party brought this system.

Another producer stated,

> In the 1990s, ÇAYKUR was out of cash and not able to purchase tea from us. But today, it is. This government came to power and gave the money. Tea prices decreased, but at least we can see our future today.

Especially the memory of the 2001 crisis is still very alive among the producers, when they talk about the developments in the AKP period. A producer from the İyidere district stated,

> The 2001 crisis affected us adversely. ÇAYKUR had gone to pot. When Erdoğan came to power, he put ÇAYKUR in order. Both the workers and the tea producers did not trust ÇAYKUR. Now, a producer gets his money ten days after he delivers his tea.

In 2009, the AKP government drafted a neoliberal law aiming to weaken ÇAYKUR, increase the power of private agribusiness companies in tea production and trade, and hasten the transformation of small tea producers into contract farmers. In response to small producers' strong opposition, the government did not push for the legislation of the draft law (Genç 2016, 271–279). In short, similar to the case of Ordu, the Rize case shows the importance of AKP's bargaining with villagers in its persistent rural support.

Construction and infrastructural investments in the region have also increased significantly. New highways, airports, bridges, housing estates, schools, hospitals, and mosques have been constructed. Although the AKP has not solved the unemployment problem, the rise of construction and infrastructural investment has increased the employment prospects for the lower classes and provided a (limited) opportunity for upward mobility.[16] This is also the case in Rize. One of our interviewees stated, 'I had an old junky car 15 years ago. Now, I have six cars today. I am working in construction in addition to producing tea. The construction sector has developed in Rize.' As lands are fragmented into smaller pieces, producers diversify their income by seeking jobs in the service sector, opening coffee houses, barber shops, grocery shops, etc. Almost all households have at least one retired person who contributes to the household income. Improvements in the welfare system and social assistance are also effective mechanisms behind the high popular support for the AKP government. One of the tea producers stated, 'Today, there is no difference between the public and private schools.'

The expansion of social assistance, in addition to welfare investments, has become effective in encouraging producers' support for the AKP government. In addition to the effective use of social assistance and welfare mechanisms among the producers, the responsibility for poverty is associated with the lack of individual effort rather than the problem of the government policies. In other words, producers who support the AKP government perceive poverty as an individual problem caused by the individuals themselves in a context where social assistance and welfare mechanisms are sufficiently advanced. A tea producer stated, 'They are helping the elderly. They are giving coal to the needy ... There is no one poor in Rize. People who know how to do things, people who work are not poor.'

Rural politics in the context of construction, mining, and energy booms

The construction, mining, and energy sectors have been important engines of economic growth and symbols of rule during the AKP period (Adaman et al. 2018; Arsel, Akbulut, and Adaman 2015). In the Black Sea region, constructions of fossil fuel and hydro-electricity plants have generated popular resistance in rural areas such as Gerze (Sinop), Cerattepe (Artvin), Fındıklı (Rize), Hemşin (Rize), Fatsa (Ordu), and Cide (Kastamonu). However, these resistances have not led to a significant change in their residents' political dispositions. In April 2018, just two months before the snap elections, district organizations of four major parties (including the government party AKP's district organization) and 12 village headmen made a joint declaration demanding the suspension of the construction of hydro-electricity plants in Hemşin (*Evrensel* April 9, 2018). Despite this seemingly wide consensus against hydropower plants, Erdoğan took 65.9 percent of the popular vote in Hemşin in June 2018 (*Sabah* June 24, 2018). The case of Gerze is similar. AKP received 44.5 percent of the popular vote in the 2007 elections. Protests by villagers and urban activists against the construction of a coal power plant in Gerze began in 2008 and peaked in 2011 (Arsel, Akbulut, and Adaman 2015, 4). This did not change the political landscape, however. AKP received 48.5 percent of the vote in 2011, 44.5

---

[16]Walden Bello (2018, 43) identifies a similar process in Thailand in the 2000s:

> The complex character of Thaksin's rural mass base stemmed from the fact that the spread of capitalist production relations and the commercialization of land had contradictory effects, impoverishing some while providing an opportunity for others, including people who were able to access the pro-Thaksin government support to help them build small businesses. Both losers and winners appeared to come together in support of Thaksin.

percent in June 2015, 53.4 percent in November 2015, and 53.7 percent in 2018 (http://www.secim-sonuclari.com).

The incompatibility between environmental protests and political preferences[17] is partly related to the fact that the outcomes of environmental and resource policies usually become visible in the long run and therefore do not immediately affect political dispositions (Adaman and Arsel 2010, 329). Increasing land prices due to construction and extraction boom also affect people's perceptions. The construction of the Ordu-Giresun and Rize-Artvin airports triggered land price increases in the region, which in turn encouraged locals to sell their farms (*Hürriyet* July 5, 2015). Local people positively view land price increases. One interviewee from the İyidere district of Rize stated: 'Now we have constructions [...] constructions of hospitals, roads and hydropower plants. People are selling their lands. They pay well. I also sold my land for a high price.' Similarly, villagers' (partially realized) expectations of high compensation for their land acquisitioned by the state weakened the resistance against the construction of the Yusufeli Dam in Artvin (Evren 2016, 282).

The individual interest in rent increase resonates with the narrative of national development, which is deeply rooted in the imagery of the Turkish state. The AKP government has presented the construction and extraction boom as a manifestation of successful economic development (Arsel, Akbulut, and Adaman 2015). In some cases, protest movements against hydropower plants caused local populations to react. Local people staged demonstrations showing their support to hydropower projects in the Kalkandere district of Rize city in 2009 (*Pazar53* May 22, 2009) and Cide district of Kastamonu city in 2010 (*Haberler.com* December 21, 2010). The anti-hydropower activists were blamed for posing a threat to economic development. During our fieldwork in Rize and Ordu, we also observed the prevalence of this developmentalist narrative among the AKP supporters. One of our interviewees expressed his support of hydropower plants by saying, 'we are producing our own energy and reducing our foreign dependency.' Interestingly, national identity of the actors also shapes the distributive expectations of the villagers. For instance, following the retreat of the two international consortiums due to local resistance, Turkish state became the main investor of the Yusufeli Dam project. Local people then stopped resistance and started to bargain with state officials over compensation (Evren 2016, 270). Regional identities also matter. For example, the involvement of businessmen from Trabzon is seen as a reason of the weakness of resistance against hydropower plants in Trabzon located in the Eastern Black Sea region (Hamsici 2011, 83).

Finally, the consent-making mechanisms discussed throughout this paper are also at play in hydropower projects. Job creation through power plants and companies' investments in local infrastructure (such as repairing village mosques) resulted in such consent in Rize and Kastamonu. Sometimes, companies contact villagers' city-dwelling relatives to garner approval for their projects. One company, for example, donated money to the village compatriot association located in İstanbul in order to gain the villagers' approval of a hydropower project in a village of Kastamonu. Finally, government investment also facilitates the completion of new projects. The case of Düzce, a city in the Western Black Sea region, is instructive in this regard. The Marmara Earthquake of

---

[17]Based on the International Social Survey Program's 2010 survey data, Ali Çarkoğlu (2017, 172) concludes that environmental issues have 'little electoral importance' in Turkey. Our analysis confirms this conclusion.

1999 damaged the local economy. Local villagers believe that the AKP government's economic investments allowed the region to recover more rapidly and therefore do not resist the hydropower projects.[18]

Results and prospects

Four main conclusions can be drawn from our study. First, since the center-left and center-right parties lost much of their credibility during the 1990s, and because two severe economic crises and a harsh neoliberal assault took place during the DSP-MHP-ANAP coalition period (1999–2002), a large proportion of small farmers and proletarianized villagers do not directly associate the AKP with the unpopular neoliberal policies. Second, as the cases of Ordu and Rize reveal, the rural masses have not been entirely silent since 2002. They have used both protests and the ballot box as mechanisms of negotiation with the government. Third, although the AKP has not shifted away from neoliberalism, it has selectively used the agricultural support mechanism to maintain its support base among small farmers. More importantly, by expanding the coverage and quantity of social assistance, the AKP has sustained its support among the poor and proletarianized villagers. Along with continuous economic growth and rapid infrastructural development, these practices have helped the AKP to maintain a relatively positive perception among the rural masses. Finally, the AKP government has continuously used coercive measures to prevent the emergence of emancipatory alternatives.

Although this study paints a generally bleak picture regarding rural politics in contemporary Turkey, the intention is not to disseminate pessimism. This paper shows that the rural masses have not been entirely passive and have managed to win tangible material concessions from the AKP. Nevertheless, it is also clear that the great majority of rural protestors have continuously supported the AKP, and the left has remained weak and marginal. As the world is currently witnessing the rise of far-right politics of various sorts, there is no magic formula to solve this political problem in Turkey, but there are some key arguments to be made for the discussion and practice of a new emancipatory rural politics. First, the left should stop reading agrarian change during the AKP period as a simple process of de-agrarianization and impoverishment. As we have seen, the process has been much more complex. Also, Turkey has *not* witnessed an economic crisis comparable to those in 1999 and 2001. Finally, rural masses have received a significant degree of material concessions from the AKP. In short, people are *not* acting entirely irrationally.

On the other hand, the dynamics discussed in this paper may change in the near future. The Turkish economy is currently entering its worst crisis during the AKP era (and maybe one of the worst crises in the history of the republic) (Akçay and Güngen 2018). Maintaining the current levels of agricultural subsidies, social assistance, job creation, and credit-driven household consumption, let alone their expansion, will be extremely difficult for the government. In other words, AKP's social neoliberalism is bound to face significant constraints in the near future. On the other hand, it should be noted that the last crisis brought the AKP to power, and there is absolutely no reason to expect that the current

---

[18]Information given in this paragraph is based on e-mail communications with Ayşe Nal Akçay (September 25&26 2018), who has conducted her dissertation research on resistance to hydropower plants in Turkey. For similar observations, see Hamsici 2011, 19–20.

crisis would empower a progressive alternative. Although increasing authoritarianism has narrowed down the scope for political dissent, the left cannot avoid its responsibility of building a united pro-labor political alternative in the context of the current crisis. This includes organizing campaigns in order to give voice to economic problems of the laboring classes and to demand greater agricultural support expenditure, the creation of new jobs, and stronger social protection. Short-term campaigns waged by a small handful of organizations will not work. Instead, a large-scale and united effort is needed in order to place economic problems and demands at the forefront of politics – the only potentially effective act that might break authoritarian right-wing hegemony over the lower classes.

Given the fact that former Kurdish peasants who were displaced in the early 1990s currently comprise the great majority of seasonal farm workers and a sizeable minority of the urban workers in Turkey, they are critical actors for any class-based rural alternative. However, neither the Kurdish movement nor the socialist movement has achieved any significant progress in organizing seasonal farm workers. Although the recent narrowing down of political space for open dissent is certainly an important factor, pinning this failure on state repression alone would be an unconvincing explanation, as the situation was not significantly better before the AKP rule. Overall, there is no shortcut to overcome the current political impasse without the existence of a broad anti-capitalist coalition requiring strict organization and close monitoring of day-to-day class-based politics.

As shown above, the dramatic expansion of social assistance has helped the AKP's hegemony over large sections of the laboring classes. The government controls enormous economic resources, and at least in the realm of social assistance, no political force can compete with it. Hence, progressive forces should not engage with such competition because they cannot win. They should, however, take this issue very seriously and establish strong mechanisms of material and economic solidarity as a backbone for their united political efforts.[19]

Acknowledgements

We would like to thank the Emancipatory Rural Politics Initiative (ERPI) for the small grant that facilitated our research and KONDA Research and Consultancy for sharing their political survey data with us. We also thank Ali Rıza Güngen, Ayşe Nal Akçay, Deniz Sert, Eylem Taylan, three anonymous reviewers for JPS, and the participants of the ERPI 2018 International Conference in The Hague for their helpful critiques and suggestions about this paper. We are thankful to Alper Yıldırım and Alper Şükrü Gençer for their research assistance.

Disclosure statement

No potential conflict of interest was reported by the authors.

---

[19]As Cihan Tuğal (2017, 226) notes,

> It is only through the activities of a leading sociopolitical organization that potentially anti-capitalist practices can become and/or remain anti-capitalist. A new benevolent path, therefore, would seek to discover charitable ethics and practices that would enhance the self-organization of the poor (even if the original donors are rich and some of the volunteers are from the propertied classes).

Although we think Tuğal underestimates the rich donors' negative influence on solidarity organizations, we entirely agree with him that material solidarity activities should be an indispensable part of anti-capitalist politics.

ORCID

Burak Gürel http://orcid.org/0000-0002-1666-8748

References

Adaman, F., and M. Arsel. 2010. "Globalization, Development, and Environmental Policies in Turkey.' In *Understanding the Process of Institutional Change in Turkey: A Political Economy Approach*, edited by T. Çetin, and F. Yılmaz, 319–335. New York: Nova Publishers.

Adaman, F., M. Arsel, and B. Akbulut. 2018. "Neoliberal Developmentalism, Authoritarian Populism, and Extractivism in the Countryside: The Soma Mining Disaster in Turkey." Emancipatory Rural Politics Initiative Conference Paper No. 63.

Akçay, Ü, and A. R. Güngen. 2018. Lira's Downfall is a Symptom: The Political Economy of Turkey's Crisis. Accessed October 5, 2018. https://criticalfinance.org/2018/08/18/liras-downfall-is-a-symptom-the-political-economy-of-turkeys-crisis/.

Alçın, S. 2017. Tarımda tasfiye politikası! *Evrensel*. August 31.

Anderson, Leslie E. 2006. "Fascists or Revolutionaries? Left and Right Politics of the Rural Poor." *International Political Science Review* 27 (2): 191–214.

Arsel, M., B. Akbulut, and F. Adaman. 2015. "Environmentalism of the Malcontent: Anatomy of an Anti-Coal Power Plant Struggle in Turkey." *The Journal of Peasant Studies* 42 (2): 371–395.

Aydın, Z. 2010. Neo-liberal Transformation of Turkish Agriculture." *Journal of Agrarian Change* 10 (2): 149–187.

Aytaç, S. E. 2014. "Distributive Politics in a Multiparty System: The Conditional Cash Transfer Program in Turkey." *Comparative Political Studies* 47 (9): 1211–1237.

Bahçe, S., and A. H. Köse. 2017. "Social Classes and the Neo-Liberal Poverty Regime in Turkey, 2002–2011." *Journal of Contemporary Asia* 47 (4): 575–595.

Balkan, N., E. Balkan, and A. Öncü. 2015. *The Neoliberal Landscape and the Rise of Islamist Capital in Turkey*. New York: Berghahn Books.

Bello, W. 2018. "Counterrevolution, the Countryside and the Middle Classes: Lessons from Five Countries." *The Journal of Peasant Studies* 45 (1): 21–58.

Borras, S. M. 2019. "Agrarian Social Movements: The Absurdly Difficult but Not Impossible Agenda of Defeating Right-wing Populism and Exploring a Socialist Future." Journal of Agrarian Change (Forthcoming).

Bozkurt-Güngen, S. 2018. "Labour and Authoritarian Neoliberalism Under the AKP Governments in Turkey." *South European Society and Politics* 23 (2): 219–238.

Butler, D. 2018. With more Islamic Schooling, Erdoğan Aims to Reshape Turkey. January 25. Accessed June 1, 2018. https://www.reuters.com/investigates/special-report/turkey-erdogan-education/.

Büyüktaş, O. 2016. "Tarımda milli çöküş … Hayati ürünler üretilmiyor." *Cumhuriyet*, September 15.

Chen, J., J. Pan, and Y. Xu. 2016. "Sources of Authoritarian Responsiveness: A Field Experiment in China." *American Journal of Political Science* 60 (2): 383–400.

CHP. 2016. "CHP Fındık raporu: "Fındığımıza sahip çıkıyoruz". Accessed January 5, 2018. https://www.chp.org.tr/Public/0/Folder//24374.pdf.

CHP. 2017. Cumhuriyet Halk Partisi bakliyat raporu: "Yozgat tarımına sahip çıkıyoruz". Accessed January 5, 2018. https://www.chp.org.tr/Public/0/Folder//27677.pdf.

Cumhuriyet. Newspaper website. http://www.cumhuriyet.com.tr/.

Çarkoğlu, A. 2017. "Environmental Concerns in Turkey: A Comparative Perspective." In *Neoliberal Turkey and its Discontents: Economic Policy and Environment Under Erdoğan*, edited by F. Adaman, B. Akbulut, and M. Arsel, 147–174. London and New York: I.B. Tauris.

ÇAYKUR. 2016. Çay Sektörü Raporu 2016. Accessed February 21, 2018. http://www.caykur.gov.tr/CMS/Design/Sources/Dosya/Yayinlar/142.pdf.

ÇAYKUR. 2018. Accessed February 21, 2018. http://www.caykur.gov.tr/Pages/Kurumsal/KurumHakkinda.aspx?ItemId=6.

Demirtaş, S. 2017. Turkey: Toward a More Religious, Less Secular Social Order? August 5. Accessed June 1, 2018. http://www.hurriyetdailynews.com/opinion/serkan-demirtas/turkey-toward-a-more-religious-less-secular-social-order-116358.

Diken. 2018. AKP'nin özelleştirme karnesi: 14 yılda 60 milyar dolarlık satış yapıldı. April 10. Accessed June 1, 2018. http://www.diken.com.tr/akpnin-ozellestirme-karnesi-14-yilda-60-milyar-dolarlik-satis-yapildi/.

Dorlach, T. 2015. "The Prospects of Egalitarian Capitalism in the Global South: Turkish Social Neoliberalism in Comparative Perspective." *Economy and Society* 44 (4): 519–544.

Dünya. Newspaper website. https://www.dunya.com/.

Duruiz, D. 2015. "Embodiment of Space and Labor: Kurdish Migrant Workers in Turkish Agriculture." In *The Kurdish Issue in Turkey: A Spatial Perspective*, edited by Z. Gambetti, and J. Jongerden, 289–308. London and New York: Routledge.

Ekşi, O. 2006. Bir fındığın içini … *Hürriyet*. July 11.

Erboz, F. 2017. "Tarımda korkutan tablo." *Yeniçağ*, September 13. Accessed January 3, 2018. http://www.yenicaggazetesi.com.tr/tarimda-korkutan-tablo-172549h.htm.

Ertürk, A. E. 2017. "İthal cenneti olduk." *Sözcü*, December 30. Accessed January 3, 2018. http://www.sozcu.com.tr/2017/ekonomi/ithal-cenneti-olduk-2153004/.

Esen, B., and S. Gümüşçü. 2018. "Building a Competitive Authoritarian Regime: State-Business Relations in the AKP's Turkey." *Journal of Balkan and Near Eastern Studies* 20 (4): 349–372.

Esmer, Y. 2019. "Identity Politics: Extreme Polarization and the Loss of Capacity to Compromise in Turkey." In *Democracy Under Threat? A Crisis of Legitimacy*, edited by Ursula Van Beek, 121–146. Cham: Palgrave MacMillan.

Evren, E. 2016. "Bir baraj karşıtı mücadelenin yükselişi ve düşüşü: Yusufeli Barajı projesi ve hidro-kalkınmanın zaman-mekân siyaseti." In *Sudan sebepler*, edited by C. Aksu, S. Erensü, and E. Evren, 269–287. İstanbul: İletişim.

Fındık-Sen. 2017. Accessed January 3, 2018. https://findiksen.wordpress.com/2017/10/26/findik-sen/.

Fiskobirlik. 2017. Accessed December 1, 2017. http://www.fiskobirlik.org.tr/hakkimizda/.

Genç, F. 2016. "Neoliberal dönüşümün çay evresi." In *Değişen Karadeniz'i Anlamak*, edited by D. Yıldırım and E. Haspolat, 257–280. Ankara: Phoenix.

Grill, J. H. 1982. "The Nazi Party's Rural Propaganda Before 1928." *Central European History* 15 (2): 149–185.

Günaydın, G. 2009. *Tarım ve kırsallıkta dönüşüm: Politika transferi süreci AB ve Türkiye*. Ankara: Tan Kitabevi.

Günaydın, G. 2016. Türk tarımı böyle tasfiye edildi. August 20. Accessed January 15, 2017. https://www.karasaban.net/turk-tarimi-boyle-tasfiye-edildi-gokhan-gunaydin/.

Gürel, B. 2014. "Türkiye'de kırda sınıf mücadelelerinin tarihsel gelişimi." In *Marksizm ve Sınıflar: Dünyada ve Türkiye'de sınıflar ve mücadeleleri*, edited by S. Savran, E. A. Tonak, and K. Tanyılmaz, 303–385. İstanbul: Yordam.

Gürel, B. 2018. The Third Great Depression and the Rise of the Far-Right: Experiences from Turkey. April 25. Accessed April 25, 2018. https://www.opendemocracy.net/burak-g-rel/third-great-depression-and-rise-of-far-right-experiences-from-turkey.

Güven, A. B. 2009. "Reforming Sticky Institutions: Persistence and Change in Turkish Agriculture." *Studies in Comparative International Development* 44 (2): 162–187.

Güven, A. B. 2016. "Rethinking Development Space in Emerging Countries: Turkey's Conservative Movement." *Development and Change* 47 (5): 995–1024.

Haberler.com. 2010. December 21. Accessed October 5, 2018. https://www.haberler.com/loc-vadisi-koylulerinden-hes-e-destek-2428319-haberi/.

Hak İnisiyatifi İstanbul. 2018. Olağanüstü hal koşullarında grev hakkı raporu. April 23. Accessed October 5, 2018. https://hakinisiyatifi.net/wp-content/uploads/2018/05/HAKinisiyatifi_OHALde_Grev_Raporu.pdf.

Halkevleri. 2010. 'Tarım, gıda egemenliği, beslenme hakkı' atölyesi çağrısı. Accessed January 5, 2017. http://www.halkevleri.org.tr/bilim-arastirma/tarim-gida-egemenligi-beslenme-hakki-atolyesi-cagrisi.

Hamsici, M. 2011. *Dereler ve isyanlar*. 2nd ed. Ankara: NotaBene.
Hürriyet. Newspaper website. http://www.hurriyet.com.tr/.
İnce, S. 2012. Fındık üreticisi AKP'ye mecbur mu? Birgün-Pazar. August 19.
Karpat, B. 2006. "Fiskobirlik gerçekleri." *Birgün*, July 11.
Keyder, Ç, and Z. Yenal. 2013. *Bildiğimiz tarımın sonu: Küresel iktidar ve köylülük*. Istanbul: İletişim.
Keyman, E. F. 2014. "The AK Party: Dominant Party, New Turkey, and Polarization." *Insight Turkey* 16 (2): 19–31.
KONDA. 2007–2017. KONDA Barometer Surveys.
Milliyet. Newspaper website. http://www.milliyet.com.tr/.
ÖDP (Özgürlük ve Dayanışma Partisi). 2017. 15 Yılda tarımda yıkım raporu: Tarımda yıkıma, yağmaya, talana hayır. Accessed December 8, 2017. http://portal.odp.org.tr/wp-content/uploads/2017/03/TARIMRAPOR.pdf.
OECD. 2018a. OECD Data. Accessed January 5, 2017. https://data.oecd.org/agrpolicy/agricultural-support.htm#indicator-chart.
OECD. 2018b. OECD.Stat. Accessed June 1, 2017. http://stats.oecd.org/Index.aspx?datasetcode=SOCX_AGG.
Öniş, Z. 2012. "The Triumph of Conservative Globalism: The Political Economy of the AKP Era." *Turkish Studies* 13 (2): 135–152.
Oral, N. 2010. Tarımda doğrudan gelir desteği bitti, sıra havza bazlı modelde. January 12. Accessed March 17, 2016. https://m.bianet.org/biamag/tarim/119405-tarimda-dogrudan-gelir-destegi-bitti-sira-havza-bazli-modelde.
Oral, N., ed. 2013. *Türkiye'de tarımın ekonomi-politiği 1923-2013*. İstanbul: Notabene.
Paxton, R. O. 1997. *French Peasant Fascism: Henry Dorgères's Greenshirts and the Crisis of French Agriculture, 1929–1939*. Oxford: Oxford University Press.
Paxton, R. O. 1998. "The Five Stages of Fascism." *The Journal of Modern History* 70 (1): 1–23.
Pazar53. 2009. HES'e destek, basına tepki. May 22. Accessed October 5, 2018. http://www.pazar53.com/hese-destek,-basina-tepki-11580h.htm.
Pelek, D. 2010. "Seasonal Migrant Workers in Agriculture: The Case of Ordu and Polatlı." Master's thesis., Boğaziçi University, Atatürk Institute for Modern Turkish History, İstanbul.
Ramírez, V. 2017. "Wellbeing and Relationships in Public Policy: The Officer-Recipient Relationship in the Oportunidades-Prospera Programme in Mexico." Ph.D. thesis., University of Bath, Bath.
Sabah. Newspaper website. https://www.sabah.com.tr/.
Scoones, I. 2018. Ongoing Conversations: Realising an Emancipatory Rural Politics in the Face of an Authoritarian Populism. March 24. Accessed March 29, 2018. https://www.opendemocracy.net/ian-scoones/ongoing-conversations-realising-emancipatory-rural-politics-in-face-of-authoritarian-pop.
Scoones, I., M. Edelman, S. M. Borras Jr, R. Hall, W. Wolford, and B. White. 2018. "Emancipatory Rural Politics: Confronting Authoritarian Populism." *The Journal of Peasant Studies*. doi:10.1080/03066150.2017.1339693
Somer, M. 2016. "Understanding Turkey's Democratic Breakdown: Old vs. New and Indigenous vs. Global Authoritarianism." *Southeast European and Black Sea Studies* 16 (4): 481–503.
T.C. Gıda, Tarım ve Hayvancılık Bakanlığı. 2017. Çay işletmeleri verileri. Accessed June 1, 2018. https://www.tarim.gov.tr/sgb/Belgeler/SagMenuVeriler/CAYKUR.pdf.
T.C. Gümrük ve Ticaret Bakanlığı Kooperatifçilik Genel Müdürlüğü. 2017. *2016 Yılı Fındık Raporu*. Ankara: T.C. Gümrük ve Ticaret Bakanlığı.
The Economist. 2018. Turkey's Religious Authority Surrenders to Political Islam. January 18. Accessed June 1, 2018. https://www.economist.com/europe/2018/01/18/turkeys-religious-authority-surrenders-to-political-islam.
TKP (Türkiye Komünist Partisi). 2007. Seçim Bildirgesi.
Torul, O., and O. Öztunalı. 2018. "On income and wealth inequality in Turkey." *Central Bank Review*. doi:10.1016/j.cbrev.2018.06.002.
Tuğal, C. 2017. *Caring for the Poor: Islamic and Christian Benevolence in a Liberal World*. London and New York: Routledge.

Turkish Statistical Institute. 2012. *General Election of Representatives Province and District Results 2011, 2007, 2002, 1999, 1995, 1991*. Ankara: Turkish Statistical Institute.
Turkish Statistical Institute. 2016. Basın odası haberleri. November 8. Accessed February 7, 2017. http://www.tuik.gov.tr/basinOdasi/haberler/2016_112_20161108.pdf.
Turkish Statistical Institute. 2018. Temel İstatistikler. Accessed October 5, 2018. http://www.tuik.gov.tr/UstMenu.do?metod=temelist.
World Bank. 2018. World Bank Open Data. Accessed January 5, 2018. https://data.worldbank.org/.
Yazan, A. 2018. Seçim 2018: Karadeniz'in can damarı fındık sandığa ne kadar yansır? June 17. Accessed October 5, 2018. https://www.bbc.com/turkce/haberler-turkiye-44511790.
Yetkin, M. 2017. "The First Survey after Turkey's Polls Gives Striking Results." *Hürriyet Daily News*, April 20.
Yıldırım, A. E. 2007. Fiskobirlik yönetimi AKP'ye geçti. December 5. Accessed May 7, 2016. http://www.aliekberyildirim.com/2007/12/05/fiskobirlik-yonetimi-akpye-gecti-2/.
Yıldırım, A. E. 2014. "Cumhuriyet'in 100. yılına doğru, yeni tarım düzeni … ." *Dünya*, December 10.
Yıldırım, A. E. 2017a. "Tarımda girdi odaklı destekleme modeline geçilecek." *Dünya*, February 2.
Yıldırım, A. E. 2017b. "Devletin fındığa müdahalesi." *Dünya*, April 20.
Yıldırım, A. E. 2017c. "Fındıkta şirket egemenliği." *Dünya*, September 7.
Yörük, E. 2012. "Welfare Provision as Political Containment: The Politics of Social Assistance and the Kurdish Conflict in Turkey." *Politics and Society* 40 (4): 517–547.

Rural rage: right-wing populism and Patriot movement in the United States

Spencer Sunshine and Chip Berlet

ABSTRACT

In the United States, right-wing populism is a major factor in national politics, as evidenced by the election of Donald Trump as President of the United States in 2015. Right-wing populism is defined by an appeal to 'people' (usually white, heterosexual Christians) to rebel – against both liberal 'elites' from above and 'subversives' and 'parasites' from below – by engaging in a hardline brand of conservative politics. There are a variety of right-wing populist political currents in the U.S. One of the most visible is the contemporary 'Patriot' movement, which is the successor to the Armed Citizens Militia movement which swept the across the nation in the 1990s. Today, the core Patriot movement groups are united by an interpretation of the Constitution that derides federal power (especially regarding environmental regulations, public lands, and progressive taxation) and advocates for a radical brand of right-wing decentralization. This opposition to federal government policies is framed in a way that inflames preexisting White, Christian nationalism (including anti-immigrant xenophobia and Islamophobia), as well as Christian Right support for patriarchy and opposition to LGBTQ rights.

Introduction

Right-wing populist movements are flourishing around the globe. They base their political claims on constructions of national identity which must, by design, include and exclude people based on ethnicity, religion, race, gender identity, class, or political beliefs (Betz 1994; Taras 2009, 2012; Mudde and Kaltwasser 2014, 2017; Abromeit 2016; Scoones et al. 2018). The election of Donald Trump as President of the United States in 2016 involved complex relationships linking right-wing populism to pre-existing organized White supremacy, Christian nationalism, and white nationalism (Berlet and Lyons 2000; Hardisty 1999; Neiwert 1999, 2003, 2009, 2015).

And U.S. right-wing populism shares many core features with similar movements in Europe as well as with populist nationalist movements around the world (Wodak 2015; Müller 2016; Baier, Canepa, and Himmeltoss 2017). Central to this is a ritualized demonization of an 'other' seen as unravelling the threads that weave together the idealized unified 'traditional' national culture and the core ethnic stock. In the United States this is referred to as Nativism (Higham [1955] 1972).

Margaret Canovan (1981, 294) argues that all forms of populism 'involve some kind of exaltation of and appeal to "the people," and all are in one sense or another anti-elitist.' A populist movement uses 'populist themes to mobilize a mass constituency as a sustained political or social force' (Berlet and Lyons 2000, 4). Since the United States was founded, a variety of populist movements have appeared on the both political left and right. These have swept through rural America, engaging farmers and ranchers – but have also appeared in the cities by appealing to the industrial and wage-based working class, as well as finding followers among small entrepreneurs and the urban-suburban salaried middle classes (Berlet and Lyons 2000; Kazin 1995; McMath 1993). Catherine McNicol Stock notes that, 'the roots of violence, racism, and hatred can be and have been nourished in the same soil and from the same experiences that generate ... movements for democracy and equality' (Stock 1996, 148).

The current populist revolt in the United States is in part due to the economic stratification of society. Ninety percent of Americans between 1980 and 2012 received no rise in salary while dividends from a rising GDP rose dramatically for the top 10% (Economic Policy Institute 2014; Political Research Associates 2017). Since the election of President Ronald Reagan in 1980, the 1% has enriched itself while pushing most of us into a downward spiral of exported jobs, lower wages, unsafe working conditions, and tax breaks for the wealthy. Government social services such as public health and food stamps have been slashed. Public works projects, from bridges to sewers, have been gutted. Shifting tax dollars to private charter schools has strangled public education.

This process has been happening in communities of color for decades. Now it is front-page news, and research shows it is devastating White working class – and even middle-class – communities (Chen 2015; Devega 2015). The growth of right-wing populist anti-government movements in the Midwest and Rocky Mountain states in the late 1970s and early 1990s shadowed two collapses of the farm economy, and the resulting anxiety and fear in hard-pressed communities which saw farm families being squeezed off land owned by them for generations (Davidson 1996).

In both periods organized White supremacist groups interacted with apocalyptic survivalists and right-wing populists to spawn many militant quasi-underground formations. These movements included some people who called themselves 'Patriots' or formed armed insurgent groups such as Armed Citizens Militias (Gallaher 2003). Patriot movement groups base much of their analysis on the earlier work of the right-wing and conspiratorialist John Birch Society, which wraps patriotic symbols and references around right-wing libertarian complaints about 'big government' (Zaitchik 2010). The movement incorporates various forms of economic libertarianism which claim that federal government regulations and programs will pave 'The Road to Serfdom' (Hayek [1944] 1960).

For some of the U.S. right-wing ideologues in the 1950s, the collectivism of labor unions and 'big government' inevitably led to totalitarian tyranny like that under Hitler's Nazi genocidal form of fascism and Stalin's brutal repressive communism. This was implied in Hayek's 1944 book *The Road to Serfdom*, which was based in part on the theories of his ally, economist Ludwig von Mises. But neither Mises nor Hayek had any control over the spread of right–wing conspiracy theories about the Democrats and increased government spending that flourished in the 1950s and 1960s in the US (Hofstadter 1965). Nor could they envision this conspiracism overlapping with Christian apocalypticism in the United States and buttressing the Patriot movement (Berlet 2017a, 131–173). However, 'Reaganomics' was ostensibly based on their theories; and 'President Ronald Reagan honored the work of both men, as did President George H. W. Bush. Moreover … the Tea Party and Fox News idolized' Hayek and Fox News pundit Glenn Beck 'caused Hayek's *The Road to Serfdom* ([1944] 1960) to become a national best seller in 2010' (Lindley and Farmelant 2012, 132). Hayek's economic theories were used to defend opposition to civil rights and affirmative action (Katznelson 2017).

But the historical record shows that the militias are not unusual. The United States has seen a number of right-wing, armed insurgent groups throughout its history (Lyons 2017, 2018). Most have used some sort of 'populist' rhetoric. The most noted and lethal of such groups was the Ku Klux Klan (KKK), founded after the U.S. Civil War. The Klan claims five core periods of activism: 1865–1871, 1920–1925, 1950–1965, 1980–1988, and the present time. Patriot movement groups have often intersected with groups further to their right, in particular members of the racist and antisemitic Christian Identity sect. For example, a farm crisis in the late 1970s and 1980s caused widespread bankruptcies in small farms. Members of Posse Comitatus, which had been founded by a Christian Identity minister, successfully wooed a part of the protest movement that arose. And activists who belonged to this religious sect were influential in the Patriot movement throughout the 1990s (Stern 1996).

In the 1990s, the militia movement spread over the United States. It became notorious when two movement members bombed the Oklahoma City federal building in 1995, killing 168, but the movement itself continued through 2001. And between 2014 and 2016, there were four Patriot movement armed occupations and standoffs in rural areas: two at mines, and two involving ranchlands. Rural imagery involving the Wild West, an emphasis on wrenching public lands out of federal hands and giving control to local authorities, and appeals to workers in rural industries (especially miners, loggers, and ranchers) are consistent propaganda themes (Ambler 1980; Larmer 2016; Thompson 2016). Western states with high levels of public federal land ownership have tended to have vibrant Patriot movement activism. Residents of poor rural areas are receptive audiences to the movement's claims that the federal government cannot control public lands, enforce environmental laws, regulate mining claims, or grant grazing permits.

Contemporary right-wing populist movements in the United States are clustered into two models of activism: first, partisan political activism in support of right-wing politicians in the Republican Party and some smaller right-wing political parties and groups; second, insurgent political and social movements (which are suspicious of both the Republican and Democratic Parties) that believe the current government might be controlled by subversive and treacherous elites (Lyons 2018). In this latter group, many social movement activists may either vote for the most militant right-wing politicians in the Republican Party, vote for third party candidates, or abstain from voting.

There is a 'rural consciousness' in the United States that is exploited to forge a 'politics of resentment' which scapegoats 'less deserving social groups' who are portrayed as parasitic – rather than being the victims of 'broad social, economic, and political forces' (Cramer 2016, 9). Central to this process is 'producerism,' a rhetorical tool built around a conspiracy theory of history that in the United States encourages racist, xenophobic, antisemitic, heteropatriarchal, and other forms of bigoted narratives (Kazin 1995, 35–36, 52–54, 143–144; Herman 1997; Berlet and Lyons 2000, 4–6). It is often visually portrayed as a vice squeezing the middle class (Berlet 2017b; Allen with Abraham 1971).

This resentment is shared in different formulations across the United States (Alexander 2017). For example, Republican Presidential Candidate Mitt Romney, running against Democrat Barack Obama in 2008, spoke of the 'Makers' versus the 'Takers,' and claimed 47% of the U.S. population was composed of the 'Takers' (Gupta and Fawcett 2018; DiBranco and Berlet 2016). Obama's 2008 election enraged some conservatives who were angered by a black liberal president. Conspiracy theories also became prominent across the right, including the notorious 'Birther' allegations which falsely claimed that Obama was not born in the United States (Berlet 2010; Public Policy Polling 2009). A more general climate of Islamophobia and anti-immigrant xenophobia also was growing internationally as the politics of resentment took center stage (Taras 2009, 2012).

The Patriot movement sprang back to life very suddenly at the end of 2008, with new organizing forms and groups. Observers of right-wing movements have offered several factors for the movement's dramatic revival. They include the 2008 economic collapse; the federal bank bailouts and economic stimulus package which followed were particularly egregious to a movement which opposed almost all government regulation of the economy and trafficked in conspiracy theories about the role of finance capital. The rise of the Tea Party and Sarah Palin's 2008 candidacy for vice president at the same time showed the strength of angry populist resentment in the Republican base, which rejected the party's neoconservative managerial approach to the economy and international relations (Scher and Berlet 2014). The Republican's aggressive foreign policies (including the Afghanistan and Iraq wars and occupations), commitment to transnational free trade agreements, and acceptance of LGBTQ rights also helped to alienate the right-wing populists. All of this happened as a series of right-wing populist movements grew across Europe and elsewhere starting in the mid-1990s (Betz 1994; Betz and Immerfall 1998; Taras 2009). Activists and scholars had been warning about this trend in the United States for over two decades (Hardisty 1999; Berlet and Lyons 2000; Durham 2000; Chomsky 2010).

American exceptional peculiarities

White nationalism

In June 2015, Dylann Roof – a young white man – came to a bible study group at a historically black church in Charleston, South Carolina. Before murdering nine people by shooting them at point-black range, he told them, 'I have to do it. You rape our women and you're taking over our country. And you have to go'. Roof's attack was at the Emanuel African Methodist Episcopal Church. By the early 1800s, it was at the center of black resistance to slavery in Charleston, according to Gerald Horne. Horne believes that Roof inherited the fear of murderous blacks raping White women from a common historic narrative of White supremacy inspired in part by slave rebellions in the 1800s (Horne 2015). Black people, Roof feared, threaten the existence of the White race; therefore, he wanted the nation to be a White nation. Roof was acting out the ideology of White supremacy in support of White nationalism (Berlet 2015a, Horne 2015).

The term 'White Supremacy' is often used by scholars and activists to describe a constellation of racist ideologies and practices. (There is no consensus on the use of different terms by scholars and activists who study right-wing politics; even the authors of this study use the terms differently). For this paper, we will use the following terms to separate the concept into component parts:

- **White Nationalism** claims that the essence of the United States as a nation is carried exclusively in the social, cultural, economic, and political practices of early European settlers.
- **White Superiority** is the specious idea that White people are a uniquely talented 'race.'
- **White Supremacist System** refers to the systems, structures, and institutions of a nation that give White people special privileges and powers, whether or not they want these privileges or harbor a dislike of people from other races.
- **Organized White Supremacist Groups** are social and political organizations with the goal of ensuring White people exercise power over people of color. These may work through legal means inside of the democratic system as it exists now to maintain or increase the 'White supremacist system'; advocate forming an all-White state; or seek to exterminate or expel people of color. These groups almost always rely on antisemitic conspiracy theories for a theoretical core, and often display intense misogyny.

Biologists reject the popular concept of 'race.' The perception of biological racial differences, however, plays a central role in historic and current power relationships in our nation. The original British settlers, who were followed by northern Europeans, assumed that White Anglo-Saxon Protestants (WASPS) were a superior racial and religious community. These days a muted – sometimes coded – version of White nationalist claims are routinely broadcast on cable TV news and AM radio talk shows.

Until the Civil War the United States was governed by a White supremacist system and was a form of White nationalism. This was true legally, but also in the dominance of the political, cultural, social, and economic arenas of public life. The post-war Reconstruction period was a brief interlude, and in 1868 the 14th Amendment to the U.S. Constitution was passed; it granted birthright citizenship, which made the freed slaves U.S. citizens. The White racist backlash to allowing black Americans legal rights spawned the Ku Klux Klan, an armed terrorist group that throughout its history has killed black people as well as those working for civil and human rights, regardless of their background. The struggle for equality for all has continued to this day, frequently lurching between successes and losses. It is made more complicated as the racial categories themselves are also fluid; they change, contract, and expand. As Noel Ignatiev (1995) shows in *How the Irish Became White*, a group that at one point in U.S. history was considered non-White can later include members who express support for White supremacy. In its most moderate form, White nationalism assumes all citizens need to 'act White' by being willing to adopt the behavior, ideologies, culture, social arrangements, and preferred economic practices common to middle- and upper-class White people. The rhetoric of White nationalism and organized White supremacy can be very similar. Groups such as the Ku Klux Klan and neonazis press for very aggressive measures – which have included murdering people of color; civil rights advocates; LGBTQ people; mixed-race couples; and religious minorities like Jews, Muslims, and Sikhs. The neonazi movement in the US is still active today (Langer 1990).

Organized White supremacist leader David Duke explains White nationalism this way:

> I think the basic culture of this country is European and Christian and I think that if we lose that, we lose America ... I don't think we should suppress other races, but I think if we lose that White – what's the word for it – that White dominance in America, with it we lose America. (Berlet and Quigley 1995; Bridges 1994)

Compare this to Pat Buchanan, who regularly appears as a pundit on national television. Buchanan refers to a looming 'culture war,' and says:

> The question we Americans need to address, before it is answered for us, is: Does this First World nation wish to become a Third World country? Because that is our destiny if we do not build a sea wall against the waves of immigration rolling over our shores ... Who speaks for the Euro-Americans, who founded the USA? ... Is it not time to take America back? (Berlet and Quigley 1995; Bridges 1994)

White nationalism is a system of power that shapes our daily activities and is extolled not only by organized supremacist groups and armed insurgents, but also major media figures and political leaders. When we talk about institutional racism, this is what we mean: the institutions, systems, and structures of power that give White people unfair advantages – even when they personally reject the idea of racism.

As the first black U.S. president, Obama was a lightning rod for White nationalist rhetoric. One of those murdered in Charleston was the church's pastor, Reverend Clementa Pinckney. He also served as a South Carolina state senator and was an acquaintance of Obama. President Obama traveled to Charleston and led the congregation in singing 'Amazing Grace' after an 'extraordinary' eulogy (Follman and West 2015). Obama also said 'the apparent motivations of the shooter remind us that racism remains a blight that we have to combat together.' He noted that 'we have made great progress, but we have to be vigilant because it still lingers. And when it's poisoning the minds of young people, it betrays our ideals and tears our democracy apart' (Lee and Rios 2015).

It would be easy to dismiss racist White nationalism as limited to fringe groups on the extreme edges of civil society, but this is sadly not true. Organized White supremacist groups do not cause prejudice in the United States – they exploit it. What we clearly see as objectionable bigotry surfacing in racist social and political movements is actually the magnified form of oppressions that swim silently in the familiar yet obscured eddies of 'mainstream' society. Racism, sexism, and hostility toward LGBTQ people (Burack 2008), immigrants and refugees, Muslims, and Jews still persists as forms of supremacy that create oppression. Thus, these forms of prejudice defend and expand inequitable power and privilege – whether or not there is activity by organized White supremacist groups.

Prejudice is an ideology while discrimination is an act. Colette Guillaumin suggests it is important to realize that ideologies generate activities. Ideologies shape the actions of individuals, groups, movements, and societies (Guillaumin 1995; Noël 1994). Thus, in the United States, the ideological notion of White superiority and the lingering ideologies embedded in an inherited White supremacist system results in White nationalism being practiced consciously or unconsciously in our daily routines (Guillaumin 1995; Noël 1994). And it saturates the country's politics – from the major political parties to right-wing populists and armed insurgent factions.

A conspiratorial storyline often added by White nationalist ideologues paints a picture of betrayal and subversion of the 'American Dream' by parasites picking the pocket of 'productive' citizens. The 'parasites' are often portrayed as people of color or immigrants. Sometimes this bigoted narrative is linked to the claim that treacherous plotters in the government are secretly planning to impose a totalitarian tyranny. This government conspiracy message is spread by the John Birch Society, Glenn Beck, Alex Jones, the late Tim LaHaye, and others. And the neo-Nazi form of White supremacy goes even further: it revolves around a core of antisemitism while advocating a messianic national rebirth as the opposition to what is sees as a society in decay (Postone 1980; Griffin 1991).

Antisemitism has a long and ugly history in the U.S. Auto magnate Henry Ford circulated tracts drawn from the antisemitic hoax document, The Protocols of the Elders of Zion (Bronner 2000; Cohn 1967; Silverstein 2000). In the 1950s a group inside the US Army began to investigate the 'Jewish Threat' (Bendersky 2000). In the United States, interactions between the left, the right, conspiracy theories, anticommunism, and antisemitism can be complex (Berlet 1988, 1989, 1992a, 1992b, 1992c, 1993a).

Apocalyptic millennialism: fears of subversion in the U.S. Christian right

Christian Right voters mobilized to elect Ronald Reagan President in 1980 (Hardisty 1999). Central to U.S. Christian Right mobilizations of political and social movement constituencies was opposition to gay rights and abortion (Berlet 1993b; Guillaumin 1995; Hardisty 1999; Young-Bruehl 1996). In 2008, the Christian Right opposed the election of Democrat Barack Obama (Toslon 2008a, 2008b). Many of these devout Christians have absorbed apocalyptic narratives from religious sources. During the Presidential administration of Barack Obama (2009–2017), 15% of Republican voters in New Jersey told pollsters in his first year in office that they thought it was possible Obama might be Satan's agent on Earth, known as the Antichrist. An additional 14% were *sure* of it (Public Policy Polling 2009). What can possibly explain these startling statistics?

These and other surveys over many decades reveal that domestic and foreign policies in the United States are shaped in part by conservative Protestant evangelicals (and a few Catholics) who view history as an existential battle between Godly Christians and evil forces in league with Satan (Clarkson 1997; Diamond 1989, 1995, 1997, 1998; Domke and Coe 2008; Kintz 1997; Martin 1996; Phillips 2006). This is more likely among the most doctrinaire wing of U.S. evangelicalism, the fundamentalists (Marty and Appleby 1994; Melling 1999). This influence on politics is not likely to vanish any time soon (Black 2016) and is part of a larger longstanding millenarian phenomenon internationally (Worsley 1968).

Protestant evangelicals and fundamentalists have historically connected apocalyptic prophecies in the Bible's book of Revelation to current political and social events (Boyer 1992; Fuller 1995). Robert C. Fuller notes that trying to match real life political figures with the evil Antichrist (prophesied as the sidekick of Satan in Revelation) became something of an 'American obsession' in certain circles. Elaine Pagels quips, 'Satan has, after all, made a kind of profession out of being the "other"' (1996, xviii).

Christians who use apocalyptic timetables sometimes justify an attempt to seize control of secular society and 'purify' it, and thus hasten the end of time when Jesus returns in triumph (Quinby 1994, 1997, 1999). The idea of welcoming the End Times is known as the impulse to 'hasten the eschaton' (Baumgarten 2002, 230–233; Frankel 1991, 210–211; Henze 2011, 161; Sarris 2011, 260). In Greek, *eschaton* means 'last.' This End Times impulse to control secular society is present in contemporary America (Barron 1992). This all may seem obscure to many readers, but the role of apocalyptic frames and timetables is important inside large portions of the three 'Abrahamic' religions: Judaism, Christianity, and Islam (Berlet and Aziz 2003). Most Christians do not buy into this precise scenario – but millions – perhaps tens of millions – take seriously the possibility that the End Times are near, and that the battles that rage in the Middle East might be part of the war between good and evil prophesied in the book of Revelation.

It is easy to overlook the roots of a longstanding fear of a socialist or communist takeover in the United States (Heale 1990, 1998; Navasky 1980). For many Christian evangelicals and fundamentalists, communism and anarchism were literally tools of the devil. According to Frank Donner, 'Bolshevism came to be identified over wide areas of the country by God-fearing Americans as the Antichrist come to do eschatological battle with the children of light,' as prophesied in Revelation. Although based in Christianity, this apocalyptic anticommunist worldview developed a 'slightly secularized version,' explains Donner, and it was 'widely shared in rural and small-town America,' where leaders of evangelical and fundamentalist groups regularly 'postulated a doomsday conflict between decent upright folk and radicalism – alien, satanic, immorality incarnate' (Donner 1980, 47–48).

Apocalyptic Biblical prophecy warning of conspiracies in high places during the 'End Times' played a major role in right–wing Protestant movements between World War I and World War II. It also helped frame the rhetoric used by the leading spokesmen for what Ribuffo calls the 'Protestant Far Right:' William Dudley Pelley, Gerald B. Winrod, and Gerald L. K. Smith (Ribuffo 1983).

It is the drive to bring heaven to Earth that sparks the activist form of apocalypticism and spawns a wide variety of utopian religious, political, and social movements (Berlet 2008; Landes and Katz 2011; Scafi 2006). This is because dualistic apocalyptic narratives long ago slipped away from Christian religious theology and began to influence secular belief systems and ideologies in the United States in what some scholars refer to as a culture of conspiracy theories (Goldberg 2001; Barkun 2003).

Conspiracy theories are a narrative form of demonization and scapegoating and are central to both right-wing populism and fascism (Berlet and Lyons 2000). They goad people into action by naming the evil threat and attaching it to a need to act because 'time is running out.' This is the classic apocalyptic timetable. Robert C. Fuller (1995) sees a connection between millennialist expectation and the societal use of demonization and scapegoating, especially in terms of the public identification of Satan's evil End Times agent – the Antichrist.

> Many efforts to name the Antichrist appear to be rooted in the psychological need to project one's 'unacceptable' tendencies onto a demonic enemy. It is the Antichrist, not oneself, who must be held responsible for wayward desires. And with so many aspects of modern American life potentially luring individuals into nonbiblical thoughts or desire, it is no wonder that many people believe that the Antichrist has camouflaged himself to better work his conspiracies against the faithful. (Fuller 1995, 168)

Fuller notes that 'Over the last two hundred years, the Antichrist has been repeatedly identified with such "threats" as modernism, Roman Catholicism, Jews, socialism, and the Soviet Union' (Fuller 1995, 5). Mooney (1982) looked at an early example of this process in *Millennialism and Antichrist in New England, 1630–1760*.

Perhaps due to an unusually large percentage of Protestant Christian evangelicals and fundamentalists in the United States, there is a cornucopia of apocalyptic titles with a focus on preparing for a confrontation with evil. Examples of Protestant apocalyptic literature in post-WWII America include *Approaching Hoofbeats: The Four Horsemen of the Apocalypse* by the well-known Rev. Billy Graham (1983) and *Apocalypse: The Coming Judgment of the Nations* (JR Grant, 1994). A book credited by several authors as sparking a renewed interest in millennialism among Christian Fundamentalists is *The Late Great Planet Earth* by Hal Lindsey and CC Carlson (1970); which was followed by *The Terminal Generation* (Lindsey and Carlson 1976). Lindsey also penned *Satan Is Alive and Well on Planet Earth* (1972); *The 1980s Countdown to Armageddon* (1981); and the novel *Blood Moon* (1996). The magazine *Midnight Call* (Ongoing Serial) is a typical example of Protestant apocalyptic expectation.

A prolific scribe in the apocalyptic genre is Christian family counselor Tim LaHaye (1975, 1980, 1982). As the year 2000 approached, LaHaye wrote *Revelation Unveiled* (1999). When it was clear that the end of time had not happened, LaHaye and David A. Noebel published *Mind Siege: The Battle for Truth in the New Millennium* (2000). LaHaye gained international fame when beginning in 1995, he and writer Jerry B. Jenkins produced a series of more than a dozen books in the 'Left Behind' series of novels that have sold more than 70 million copies (LaHaye and Jenkins 1995). Scholarly critiques of LaHaye's theology include Gorenberg (2000) and Frykholm (2004).

The politicized religious view of politics in the United States by conservative Christian evangelicals and fundamentalists with millennial expectation need to be taken seriously by scholars, journalists, and activists. The concept of this sort of politics with religious-like fervor emerges in the late 1920s. A key theorist of these militant political processes was Eric Voegelin, whose essays were collected and published in 1952.

Land conflicts in the rural West

The Western frontier

To understand rural conflicts in the Western states, it is important to consider that many of the participants – regardless of their actual professions – cast themselves in the role of farmers and ranchers who see the federal government as a distant and annoying force (Ambler 1980). In doing so, they 'recycle old Western fantasies' of resistance and rebellion (Larmer 2016).

Sagebrush rebellion

The roots of opposition to federal public land holdings and regulations go back the early 1900s, when the federal government first started reserving public lands and water rights (Larmer 2016; Thompson 2016; Swearingen, Schimel, and Wiles 2018). The 'Sagebrush Rebellion' started in 1976, when the federal government finally stated it would retain the remaining public lands it held from the original western expansion of the country. Legislators in the western states, where most of these lands were, made unsuccessful attempts to gain control of the lands. These politics appeared again during with the 'county supremacy' movement during the Clinton Administration, which sought to curtail public land grazing, mining, and logging. His use of the controversial Antiquities Act, which also placed more restrictions on public lands, also spurred opposition.

Finally, the election of Obama brought on the latest iteration of the movement, with renewed calls for public land transfers to states or counties, and rising anti-federal sentiment, such as that exhibited by the Malheur occupation (discussed below).

Extractive resource industries and 'wise use'

Starting in the late 1970s, a coalition of various right-wing political, social, religious, and corporate leaders set out to create a 'New Right' in the United States to roll back what they considered 'Big Government' intrusions into the society (Himmelstein 1990; Diamond 1995). In 1988, Ron Arnold, a writer for a logging industry publication, presided over the '1988 Multiple Use Strategy Conference' which organized an anti-environmentalist social movement (Ramos 1995, 1997). This became known as the 'Wise Use' movement (Arnold and Gottlieb 1993; Burke 1993; Helvarg 1997; Wise Use Resource Collection 2018). According to Tarso Luís Ramos (1997),

> On the heels of the conference, Arnold's group published a manifesto, The Wise Use Agenda, which includes an index of over two hundred organizations that attended or supported the conference and 'mandated' the publication of the agenda. The index includes various resource corporations and associations, including Boise-Cascade, Du Pont, Exxon, Georgia Pacific, Louisiana-Pacific, Nevada Cattlemen's Association, Washington Contract Loggers Association, and Western Forest Industries Association. The index also lists activist groups, such as the National Center for Constitutional Studies, which seeks to institute biblical law in the United States, and the American Freedom Coalition, a Unification Church front group in which Arnold was deeply involved.

Arnold explains that he first studied scholarly social movement theories based on leftwing movements, and converted them to create a movement on the right. Arnold says he tried to tamp down calls for armed confrontations, which he says he also opposes in current rural movements on the Right (author Berlet interview with Arnold, 2018).[1] However, Ramos argues that 'bullying, threats, and conspiracy theories' have always been 'alive and well in the Wise Use movement,' and that under the banner of Wise Use there have been acts of violence (author Berlet, interview with Ramos 2018).

Patriot movement oppositional organizing

There exists in the United States an overlapping series of right-wing oppositional movements, which consist of national organizations, media outlets, and diffuse activists who sometimes form structured groups and sophisticated media outlets (Kintz 1997; Kintz and Lesage 1998). Sara Diamond (1989, 1995, 1998) refers to the broad sector as 'Americanist' movements with the Christian Right sector engaged in 'spiritual warfare' against liberals (1989, 1995, 1998). These self-described patriotic movements in the United States are overwhelmingly shaped by twentieth century anti-communism and Cold War politics (Berlet and Lyons 2000, 287–304). They share similarities with earlier xenophobic movements such as Nativism in the late 1800s and the '100 Percent Americanism' of the 1920s (Berlet and Lyons 2000, 85–103; Berlet 1988, 1989). The Populist movement in the late nineteenth century was primarily progressive, but some activists embraced conspiracy theories about Jews, Freemasons, or Catholics. Cas Mudde (2017) points out

---

[1] See also: Arnold and Gottlieb (1993).

various historical popular U.S. Nativist movements, groups, and campaigns: the 'Know Nothing' movement, an 1850s anti-Catholic movement; the 1920s and 1950s Ku Klux Klan; the John Birch Society, which formed in 1958; and George Wallace's 1968 and 1972 presidential runs. James Aho (1990, 2016) uses the term 'Christian Patriots' to specifically analyze the movement that combines Americanist patriotic beliefs with the claim that America is a Christian Nation, and weaves in conspiracy theories that consider the U.S. government to be illegitimate. For almost all participants, this involves claims of a conspiracy which is either openly antisemitic, or derived from antisemitic narratives.[2]

Basic patriot movement beliefs

One of the most well-known Americanist movements today is the Patriot movement. It uses the trappings of the U.S. political tradition – including patriotic symbols and appeals to founding documents and structures – to forward a conspiracy theory-driven version of right-wing populism. Despite outward appearances, theoretically it has little relationship to the liberal tradition that the United States was founded on. The movement seeks to implement a radical form of decentralization to advance right-wing economic, social, and cultural aims. This includes dismantling almost all aspects of federal government regulation of the economy, such as the minimum wage, as well as civil rights guarantees for historically oppressed groups (Burghart and Crawford 1996; Katznelson 2017; Kimmel and Ferber 2000). Despite lip service to the Constitution, it is common for the movement to deny that Muslims deserve First Amendment protections for their religion (Sunshine 2016).

Some commentators incorrectly refer to movement members as 'anarchists' (Conroy 2017). But the Patriot movement appeals to the authority of county sheriffs, county commissions, and the U.S. Constitution for legitimacy – institutions which are incompatible with all varieties of anarchism. And while movement members seek to abolish most of the federal government's structure, they want to keep certain parts. Although the details vary among participants, typically this includes activities related to the military, foreign affairs, immigration control, and laws guaranteeing private property and unregulated markets. Local governments will be able to reject federal laws, essentially rendering them optional.

The movement uses several different tactical approaches. The most well-known is the formation of militias and other paramilitary forms. The Three Percenters, for example, were founded in 2008 by a 1990s militia movement veteran who wanted to create a new kind of paramilitary that could avoid infiltration by law enforcement (Sipsey Street Irregulars 2009). These paramilitaries have engaged in a number of high-profile confrontations with federal authorities.

The movement frequently uses ideas based on 'nullification,' originally formulated by pro-slavery advocates in the 1830s, which holds that lower-level governments can reject the rules of higher-level ones (Levitas 2002). The doctrine of 'county sheriff supremacy,' which advocates that county sheriffs can decide which laws are constitutional (and hence enforced), is an example of this. So is 'coordination,' which is a term that appears in some federal land use acts, but is interpreted by the Patriot movement to

---

[2]For an earlier analysis see Hofstadter (1965).

claim that counties and other local governments can veto federal law use rules (Sunshine 2016, 29–32). Another example promoted by the movement is 'jury nullification,' where trial jurors are told they can decide guilt or innocence based on their own beliefs, and not the law.

In addition to paramilitaries, the movement has set up structures that ape governmental functions. These include Committees of Safety, which are activist organizations that claim to have the powers of a county government. There are also a number of self-proclaimed judges, juries, and sheriffs (Sunshine 2016). Another common belief in the Patriot movement, based on an idiosyncratic reading of Article 1, Section 8, Clause 17 of the U.S. Constitution, is that the federal government is only allowed to own what is known in movement jargon as 'ports, forts, and ten square miles' of Washington, DC. Movement members who follow this line of reasoning do not acknowledge the federal government's power to regulate grazing, mining rights, or logging rights on federal lands – since they do not acknowledge the government's right to assert jurisdiction and control these lands (Sunshine 2016). These fictional legal positions were invoked to support the armed Patriot confrontations in both Nevada and Oregon (detailed below).

Sovereign Citizens, a subset of the Patriot movement, adhere to a series of arcane legal arguments which hold that the current U.S. government is illegitimate. They believe they can opt out of paying taxes and other obligations by declaring themselves to be a different – 'sovereign' – citizen. Their ideas originate in Posse Comitatus movement, which spun legal fantasies that combined an idiosyncratic reading of the U.S. Constitution, English common law, and White supremacist interpretations of the Christian Bible (Levitas 2002; Zeskind 2009). In courts, Sovereign Citizens have claimed they are immune from everything from traffic laws and zoning regulations, to child support orders and kidnapping, and even theft and murder. Unsurprisingly, none of their central contentions have been accepted by mainstream legal scholars or the judicial system.[3]

The masculinist warrior motif is central to Patriot movements in the United States (Berlet 2004b; Gibson 1994, 1997; Kimmel and Ferber 2000; Lembke 1998, 2003). Originally these movements were exclusively for men, although the Ku Klux Klan did have a women's auxiliary that sewed robes. A small number of women participated in the 1990s militias, if they had a reputation for handling guns expertly and safely – which men often were not required to prove. And while over the decades most leaders have been men, the militia movement was organized nationally using online resources developed by Linda Thompson (Berlet and Lyons 2000, 292).

Rural economic crises

The 1970s and 1980s

In the late 1970s a serious and devastating farm crisis bankrupted thousands of small farms, and transnational agribusiness swooped in to buy them out. The crisis was caused by Federal Reserve interest rate increases, rising petroleum and input prices,

---

[3]The term Posse Comitatus comes from Latin, and refers to 'the bodily force of the county,' as in a body of men assigned power over a county. The term 'county' is derived from the territory under the control of a Medieval Count; and the leader of the force of men would be a Sheriff. The term 'Sheriff's Posse Comitatus' was used by the founders of the movement. The common translation of Posse Comitatus as 'Power of the County' lacks this explanatory information (Southern Poverty Law Center n.d.; Berlet 2018).

and the cessation of grain sales to the Soviet Union following the U.S. invasion of Afghanistan (Davidson 1996; Greider 2000) Additionally, the wave of mergers and acquisitions which started with Reagan-era deregulation enabled a concentration of economic power in large urban areas – to the detriment of non-agricultural industries in both rural areas and small cities (Cramer 2016; Alexander 2017).

This led to the farmers protest movement; its main group, the American Agriculture Movement, organized a 'tractorcade' protest of farmers in Washington, DC in 1977 and 1979. However, the White supremacist group Posse Comitatus, as well as followers of the right-wing cult leader Lyndon H. LaRouche, Jr., became involved in the movement and spread a conspiratorialist message that scapegoated Jewish bankers as the cause of farm crises. They were able to attract a number of disgruntled farmers, although the majority rejected the most bigoted allegations and violent tactics being promoted (Levitas 2002, 168–182). Nonetheless, antisemitic and racist contentions became a regular topic of discussion in the farm belt for several years. And so while few farmers joined organized White supremacist groups, there was sometimes an appreciation of the fact that these White supremacist groups were paying attention to the hardships created by the collapsing family farm economy (Berlet 1986; Corcoran 1995).

Despite the Patriot movement's hostility to federal programs, rural areas receive a disproportionately large share of federal and state-level expenditures – meaning the urban zones, where wealth has become more consolidated in past decades, are effectively subsidizing them. On the other hand, the collapse of family farms and the growth of giant agribusiness has meant that these federal dollars seldom reach the bank accounts of local farm families. The global agribusiness sector is huge (McMichael 1998). The multi-national giant agribusiness Cargill is singled out by Brewster Kneen (1995, 2002) as a major exemplar of this trend that accelerated farm crises over many decades. 'Cargill is building the kind of industrial agricultural systems it can best profit by,' explains Kneen, 'not necessarily the one that serves the farmers or the public best [nor] the system that ensures everyone everywhere is adequately nourished' (2002, viii). Suicide rates in the farm belt rose along with reports of abuse and mental illness during the downward spirals.

As right-wing populist groups spread conspiracy theories in the farm belt, for the most part corporate media and policy makers ignored the plight of the residents as they saw their way of life devastated (Davidson 1996; Dyer 1997; Neiwert 1999). As one song sung to raise funds for the annual 'Farm Aid' concert put it, these rural farm families were being 'weeded out' (M. Roche, Roche, and Roche 1985). Farm Aid, which originated during the crisis, is an ongoing effort to raise funds to save the family farm and provides a website that explains the issues. In part, Farm Aid seeks to challenge those elements of the protest movement that blamed the farm crises on elaborate conspiratorialist theories involving international Jewish bankers and their minions who they falsely claim control the U.S. banking system through manipulating the Federal Reserve. These theories have circulated since the 1930s; they were popularized by the White supremacist Eustace Mullins in the 1950s and spread by Posse Comitatus in the 1970s and 1980s (Berlet and Lyons 2000, 194–195).

1990s: armed citizens militias
The Armed Citizens Militias are a part of the broader Patriot movement; in the 1990s they spun off the movement as an armed wing. The militias were locally based armed

paramilitaries which vowed to resist a looming New World Order and other nefarious and non-existent conspiracies alleged to be goals of the federal government (Berlet and Lyons 2000, 287–304; Berlet 2004a, 2004c). The militias took many of their basic political positions and organizing forms from the Posse Comitatus (Levitas 2002; Berlet 2004a), and most conducted armed training exercises at rural encampments. The rapid expansion of the militias occurred around 1993, after a second wave of the devastation of many rural economies (Gibson 1994; Berlet and Lyons 1995; Van Dyke and Soule 2002; Berlet 2004c). The specific instances which spurred the movement were anger over Ruby Ridge and Waco (see below) – as well as the 1993 Brady Bill, which established tighter gun controls (Hamm 1997; Freilich, Pienik, and Howard 2001; Levitas 2002; Zeskind 2009). The movement became infamous in 1995 when two members, Terry Nichols and Timothy McVeigh – the latter of whom was tied to its neonazi wing – bombed the Alfred P. Murrah Federal Building in Oklahoma City, killing 168 people (Hamm 1997; Berlet and Lyons 2000). Contrary to many reports, the militia movement continued to grow for at least a year after the bombing, reaching its peak in 1996 (Southern Poverty Law Center 2001).

The militia movement was ignited by government errors and abuses of power during confrontations that resulted in needless deaths at the Weaver family cabin in Ruby Ridge, Idaho, and the Branch Davidian compound in Waco, Texas. Randy Weaver and his wife Vicki and their children, who lived in a remote location in the mountains, were adherents of Christian Identity (Berlet and Lyons 2000, 290–291). The discovery by the Weavers of a secret government surveillance team quickly escalated into a deadly 1992 shoot-out in which a federal marshal, and Weaver's wife and son, were killed. Randy Weaver and a friend were wounded (Hamm 1997).

The Branch Davidian compound in Waco, Texas was a Christian fundamentalist church and survivalist retreat. In 1993, their leader David Koresh was decoding Revelation as an End Times script and preparing for the Tribulations (Samples et al. 1994; Reavis 1995; Tabor and Gallagher 1995). In this apocalyptic timetable many Christian evangelicals (and their more doctrinaire and literal cousins the fundamentalists) argue over the exact timetable heralding the imminent return of Jesus of Nazareth, seen by Christians as the son of God. In some readings of the Bible's Book of Revelation, Jesus returns, there is a confrontation (called the Tribulations), and when this is over, only true Christians are saved, while an angry God vanquishes and eliminates all non-believers.

It is likely that Koresh and his followers believed that the government forces might be agents of Satan in the End Times (ibid). The U.S. government failed to comprehend that the Davidian worldview was part of a rising tide of millennialist expectations generated by the approach of the calendar year 2000. A series of miscalculations by government analysts in April 1993 cost the lives of eighty Branch Davidians (including twenty-one children) and four federal agents (Hamm 1997).

After Ruby Ridge and Waco, the Armed Citizens Militia Movement quickly spread through all fifty states. There were over 200 militia units by the mid-1990s, with between 20,000 and 60,000 active participants at its peak. The broad Patriot movement influenced as many as five million Americans, who shared its belief that the government was manipulated by subversive secret elites that planned to use law enforcement or military force to repress political rights (Berlet and Lyons 1995, 2000, 287–304). Martin Durham (2000, 146) observed that the militia-style Patriot movement was 'divided in strategy and exhibits both authoritarian and libertarian impulses' and that 'aspects of each have the potential to bring its adherents into conflict, sometimes bloodily, with a federal government that they see as a threat to their rights and a servant of their enemies.'

During this period, there were widespread fears that the U.S. federal government was about to impose a draconian tyrannical dictatorship using jack-booted thugs delivered in black helicopters sent by the United Nations (Berlet and Lyons 2000, 287–304; Berlet 2004a, 2004c, 2005, 2009a, 2009b). John Keith Akins likened militia conspiracy theory to an ideological octopus.

> In this analogy, the body of the octopus represents the New World Order theory; each tentacle represents a specific concern, such as firearm ownership, abortion, or prayer in schools. Each tentacle of this octopus reaches into a pre-existing social movement, yet each connects with the others at the body, the New World Order. (Akins 1998, 144–145)

In the United States, these theories have been openly discussed on network television, and by elected representatives on the state and federal level (Berlet 2009b). Using conspiratorialist and producerist rhetoric, the militias identified numerous scapegoats. Each unit, and in some cases each member, could pick and choose targets. These included: federal officials and law enforcement officers, abortion providers and pro-choice supporters, and environmentalists and conservation activists. In a few cases, militias also targeted Jewish institutions, LGBTQ organizers, people of color, immigrants, and other vilified targets (Stern 1996; Southern Poverty Law Center 2001; Southern Poverty Law Center n.d.).

At its peak in 1996, the number of militia units reached 858, according to the Southern Poverty Law Center. The numbers dropped each year after that, and by 2000 there were only 194 units (Southern Poverty Law Center 2001). After the November 2000 presidential election of Republican George W. Bush and the September 11, 2001 terrorist attack, their voices faded to a murmur.

The 2008 banking collapse

For most Americans the word 'collapse' holds more resonance, but the Federal Reserve likes to call what happened to the economy in 2008 a 'recession.' In one article, the Federal Reserve Bank in Kansas City, Kansas, in the heart of the farm belt, reported that 'Recession Catches Rural America.' After claiming that in rural economies in 2008 'the financial crisis was less severe than on Wall Street,' the authors admitted that the 'foundations of rural economic strength in 2008 – high commodity prices, robust export activity, and rising ethanol demand – were crumbling' (Henderson and Akers 2015, 65). According to Lorin Kusmin, 'rural employment in mid-2015 was still 3.2% below its pre-recession peak in 2007' (2015). In some rural areas there was a 'backlog of vacant and abandoned properties' continuing through at least 2014 (Chuck Wehrwein, quoted in Housing Assistance Council 2014a). A detailed look shows that between 2000 and 2012, rural home ownership declined as follows: White Not Hispanic –0.5%; Hispanic –1.0%; Native American –2.9%; and African American –5.2% (Housing Assistance Council 2014b).

The Patriot movement's 2008 revival was closely associated with the rise of the Tea Party movement, which emerged at about the same time (Altemeyer 2010; Cox and Jones 2010; Scher and Berlet 2014). Tea Partiers supported right-wing Republican candidates against the alleged 'socialism' of the Democratic Party, but several studies also showed antipathy toward immigrants and people of color (Berlet 2010, 2012; Burghart and Zeskind 2010; Parker 2010). Over time Christian Right participation in the Tea Party increased. Ann Burlein (2002) has explained how the Christian Right and White supremacy can converge. The Tea Party idea originated with supporters of uberlibertarian Ron Paul, but the franchise was scooped up by conservative billionaires who funded trainings and rallies around the country. Over time Christian Right activists played a leading role in local Tea Party groups, helping shift the focus to a toxic blend of Nativist, anti-immigrant, and anti-Muslim rhetoric coupled with homophobia and anti-abortion propaganda (Berlet 2012; Scher and Berlet 2014). By 2015 the Tea Party grassroots was heavily populated by organized White supremacists (Burghart and Zeskind 2010).

Folks who support the Tea Party and other right-wing populist movements are responding to rhetoric that honors them as the bedrock of American society (Hochschild 2016). These are primarily middle- and working-class White people with a deep sense of patriotism who bought into the American dream of upward mobility. Now they feel betrayed. Trump and his Republican allies appeal to their emotions by naming scapegoats to blame for their sense of being displaced by 'outsiders' and abandoned by their government (Scher and Berlet 2014).

Contrary to some reports, the Tea Party activists, despite garbled language and unsupported accusations, had reasons to be angry. As author Berlet put it:

> They see their jobs vanish in front of their eyes as Wall Street gets trillions. They see their wages stagnate. They worry that their children will be even less well off than they are. They sense that Washington doesn't really care about them. On top of that, many are distraught about seeing their sons and daughters coming home in wheelchairs or body bags. (Berlet 2010)

Emotions matter in building all social movements, and have specific meanings in 'Right-Wing America' (Kintz 1997). The linkage of emotion and politics are at the heart of a multi-year study of rural right-wing conservatives by Arlie Russell Hochschild (2016), who moved to Louisiana for several years and conducted conversations with Tea Party members in the South, where the movement was strongest. Many she spoke with had long doubted that Obama was American; even after the publication of his long-form birth certificate, some still suspected he was a Muslim who harbored ill will toward America. Hochschild observed that this set of beliefs was widely shared among people who otherwise seemed reasonable, friendly, and accepting. How, she wondered, could we explain this? Hochschild's premise is that all political belief is built on a set of emotions that shape a deep internalized narrative story that writes a script for people's political beliefs and voting actions. Previous scholarship has pursued similar lines of inquiry into right-wing social movements, especially in the U.S. South (A. Wilson 1996, 2013; Hardisty 1999; Durham 2000; A. Wilson and C. Burack 2012).

The role of Islamophobia

The Islamophobic ideas that Hochschild documented were not limited to the Tea Party. After Barack Obama's 2008 election, the internet was flooded with conspiracy theories about his alleged subversion and treachery. They claimed that he was, alternately: a secret Muslim; not a citizen of the United States – and so his election as president should be overturned; a puppet of a cell of Jews and Communists in Obama's Chicago neighborhood; and/or was the tool of a New World Order plot to establish a North American Union (Berlet 2009a).

These claims recycled longstanding attacks on progressive politicians and public figures in the United States as being secret Jews or communists, or both; for example, they were directed in the 1930s and 1940s at President Franklin D. Roosevelt (Dilling 1934, 1936, circa 1941). However, it was Donald Trump who moved Islamophobia into the center of U.S. political discourse (Berlet 2015b). A common Islamophobic claim is that Islam is not a religion with varying interpretations, but instead is a violent, subversive, and unified political ideology (Berlet 2011, 2012, 2013; Esposito and Kalin 2011; Lean and Esposito 2012; Taras 2009, 2012). U.S. Muslims are often described in right-wing media as secret sleeper cells, who have infiltrated the country in order to lay plans for a takeover. Even attempts by Muslims to assert democratic rights are portrayed as attempts at subversive infiltration of legal systems in Europe and the United States. Islamophobes in the United States cast Muslims as being in alliance with a 'politically correct' Left, and together they conspire to destroy the nation from within (Cincotta 2010, 2011). This conspiracy theory is often packaged with the claim that there is an attempt in the United States to establish Sharia Law.

In many ways, contemporary Islamophobia in the United States uses many of the same narratives of subversion that can found in prior antisemitic or anticommunist rhetoric tracked by scholars. These ideas are widespread in the Patriot movement as well.

When right-wing populists use the narrative claiming Muslims are terrorists, they are engaging in a psychological projection. Polls show that many Americans assume that Muslims carry out the majority of terrorist acts in the United States. But studies show that between 2008 and 2016, 'White Nationalist Perpetrators' carried out 115 violent incidents, while 'Muslim Perpetrators' were involved in sixty-three incidents (Neiwert 2017; Neiwert et al. 2017; Valverde 2017). In 2018, a major study showed that 'almost two-thirds of the terror attacks in the United States' during a year of study 'were carried out by right-wing' perpetrators (Morlin 2018).

Patriot movement: 2008 to present

In the 1990s, the Militia movement's reputation was damaged by its ties to organized White Supremacist groups. The resurgent Patriot movement publicly distanced itself from these associations, which may have been the result of a self-conscious shift in attitude and/or a reframing for public relations. It also prefers to traffic in the more socially acceptable Islamophobic conspiracism rather than recycled antisemitism. So while it remains an overwhelmingly White, Christian, right-wing project, today's Patriot movement can dodge accusations of White supremacy and antisemitism more easily then in the past. Current prominent Patriot movement figures who have links to organized racism are usually members of the older movement, such as Richard Mack (founder of the Constitutional Sheriffs and Peace Officers Association) and Larry Pratt (founder of the Gun Owners of America). While many of the Patriot movement's goals were consciously formulated as racist positions by the Posse Comitatus – especially the notion that county sheriffs could ignore laws they deemed to be unconstitutional – these tactics are given a different reasoning by today's activists. Nonetheless they retain the same potential effects.

The Patriot movement also uses an inside/outside political strategy. At same time that is has formed armed units and parallel governmental structures, and has encouraged government employees to follow its reading of the U.S. Constitution, it also has made inroads into the Republican Party. Especially in the western U.S. states like Oregon, Washington, Nevada, Utah, and Idaho, some city and county officials, including county sheriffs, are movement adherents. There are also openly sympathetic elected state officials. In 2017 in Multnomah County, Oregon (which includes Portland), the Republican Party passed a resolution approving the use of Oath Keepers and Three Percenters as security (Shepherd 2017; J. Wilson 2017). In Oregon in 2016, after the Malheur occupation (detailed below), several Patriot movement candidates ran for office, although with limited success. But many activists were elected as Precinct Committee People, the lowest level position in the party. At least five Patriot movement activists and sympathizers were elected to either state party positions or as delegates to the national convention at the Oregon Republican Party's June 2016 convention. And in 2017, one of these, paramilitary leader Joseph Rice, ran for head of the state party – although he came in a distant second (Sunshine 2016, 55–56; 2017b).

Organizational clusters

The Patriot movement is very decentralized, and is divided up into different organizations and identities. For example, Armed Citizens Militias, similar to the ones in the 1990s, still exist, primarily in rural areas. In addition to the militias, core Patriot factions include the following:

- The Oath Keepers are a membership-based organization that recruits former and current members of the military, law enforcement, and first responders (although others can join as associate members). They swear they will not help implement ten unconstitutional government orders – which are mostly staple right-wing conspiracy theories about coming concentration camps and foreign invasions.
- The Three Percenters started as a decentralized paramilitary to provide an alternative to the more structured militias. Individuals can declare themselves as Three Percenters, but local and national groups exist as well. The groups draws their name from the disputed claim that only 3% of colonists fought in the American Revolution, implying that a small minority can successfully wage an armed revolutionary struggle. More recently, some Three Percenter groups have become more traditionally organized local political groups, albeit ones that are heavily armed.
- The Constitutional Sheriffs and Peace Officers Association (CSPOA) seeks to recruit county sheriffs and other law enforcement to the Patriot movement. Their founder, Richard Mack, believes that county sheriffs can decide which laws are constitutional, and therefore should be enforced.

All of these groups have members who advocate defying federal laws they think are unconstitutional, and most are armed with guns. They frequently carry lethal weapons openly at public rallies, such as knives, pistols, and long guns (including semi-automatic rifles). Patriot groups regularly find allies among Tea Party groups, the John Birch Society, Gun Owners of America, the Tenth Amendment Center, and the American Lands Council – the latter of which is funded by the fossil fuel billionaires Charles and David Koch to promote the transfer of public lands out of federal hands to encourage exploitation by extractive industries (Taylor 2017). Across several sectors and factions is a conspiratorial shared belief about U.S. Constitutional Law referred to as Sovereign Citizen ideas, which is discussed above.

Guns and armed land use conflicts

Internally, the most important issue for the Patriot movement is an aggressive defense of unrestricted gun rights, even though the United States has some of the loosest gun ownership laws among the industrialized countries. The Three Percenters, for example, refuse to accept any new restrictions on private firearm ownership (Vanderboegh 2009). One of the early projects of the CSPOA was the publication of a list of 485 sheriffs who it claimed, 'have vowed to uphold and defend the Constitution against Obama's unconstitutional gun measures' (Constitutional Sheriffs and Peace Officers Association 2014). The first of the Oath Keepers 'Ten Orders We Will Not Obey' is: 'We will NOT obey orders to disarm the American people' (Oath Keepers, n.d. a). Despite the centrality of this issue to the movement, however, its most popular issue has been armed interventions into public lands conflicts.

The first high-profile armed land use conflict from the revived movement was in 2014 and involved Nevada cattle rancher Cliven Bundy, who was accurately described in the media as an 'anti-government activist' who lived near the aptly named town of Bunkerville, Nevada (Egan 2014). Bundy had refused to pay grazing fees on public lands, and when federal agents came to seize his cattle, hundreds of Patriot movement paramilitaries came to his ranch and engaged in an armed standoff (Sunshine 2016). The confrontation pitted heavily armed federal agents at the gates of corrals where several hundred Bundy cattle had been rounded up, against men with assault rifles on an interstate overpass and hundreds of protesters in a dry riverbed below (Egan 2014). Bundy follows a version of conspiratorial political Mormonism that is intertwined with Patriot movement beliefs, popularized by writers like W. Cleon Skousen, himself close to the John Birch Society (Sunshine 2016). Far from being marginalized, these views are aired on television and radio in the United States by popular media figures such as Glenn Beck (Lind 2010; Zatchik 2010; History News Network 2010).

The second major armed conflict started on 2 January 2016, when a small group of armed men – led by Cliven Bundy's sons Ammon and Ryan Bundy, as well as Arizona rancher LaVoy Finicum – seized the Malheur National Wildlife Refuge headquarters in Oregon (Sunshine 2016). The occupation lasted 41 days and resulted in Finicum's death. The initial issue involved two local ranchers who had received unusually stiff sentences under a terrorism act for arsons that burned federal land to aid grazing (Anti-Defamation League 2016). Soon, however, the occupiers started to demand that the federal government relinquish the refuge lands entirely. Self-proclaimed judges and courts were established at the refuge, and the armed occupiers unsuccessfully tried to convince local ranchers to renounce their federal grazing permits (Sunshine 2016).

Some early media reports from the Oregon confrontation had trouble sorting out the beliefs of the Patriots. These two armed actions by the Bundy family ended up with no direct consequences for them. The family members were acquitted by the jury in the Oregon trial. Charges were dismissed in the Bunkerville trial, when a judge found that there were flagrant government abuses of the constitutional processes (Levin 2018).

This hobbled the campaigns of environmental groups who had pressed state agencies and the federal government to prosecute land grabs and intimidation. According to Kierán Suckling, executive director of the Center for Biological Diversity, 'it's just a horrific outcome ... an absolute disaster. This is going to empower both the militia and the politicians who want to steal America's public lands' (Carney 2018; Levin 2018).

Nativism: anti-immigrant and anti-refugee activism

Today's Patriot movement does not organize by making overt appeals to White racial purity, which is the ideological hallmark of the organized racist movement. While individual Patriot movement members have associations with organized racist groups, they are fairly small in number and not usually in leadership positions. The Patriot movement's relationship to the organized White supremacist movement is a complicated dance. The John Birch Society presented itself as separate from organized racism, but derived many of its ideas from antisemitic conspiracy theorists, and many racist leaders (including Tom Metzger, Willis Carto, and William Pierce) got their start in the group. William Potter Gale, the founder of Posse Comitatus, was a Christian Identity minister. And this racist legacy directly continued for decades. The authors estimate that in the 1990s, perhaps a quarter of militia movement groups were involved in explicitly White supremacist politics – although sometimes these positions were challenged by other movement members.

Today most Patriot movement groups adopt a 'colorblind' approach and say they are not racist. The Oath Keepers bylaws specifically bar members from belonging to an openly racist group (Oath Keepers, n.d. b). But starting in February 2017, the Oath Keepers, Three Percenters, and other Patriot movement groups appeared at several rallies across the U.S. with 'Alt-Right' and other related political actors. These have included fascists and White Nationalists such as Identity Evropa (Europa) and the League of the South (Lyons 2017; Lyons 2018). Other rallies attended by Patriot movement groups include those opposed to the removal of Confederate memorials in the South, and the nationwide Islamophobic 'March Against Sharia' in June 2017. The Oath Keeper leadership denounced the organized racists involved in these events, but continued to act in concert with them through July 2017 (Sunshine 2017a). Militia groups – although notably not the Oath Keepers – also attended the violent 'Unite the Right' rally in Charlottesville, Virginia on 12 August 2017, where they claimed to be a neutral party. However their uniformed followers, armed with semi-automatic rifles, guarded the perimeter of the fascist-led rally and faced counter-protestors.

And while the Patriot movement tries to separate itself from organized White supremacy, it nonetheless radiates an implicit White nationalism. But since it does not verbalize it, and even goes to some lengths to deny it, what is this unspoken underlying structure? The movement directly engages in issues whose successful outcome would both support maintaining White racial demographics at current levels and stymy the redistribution of social and economic power across racial lines. The groups the Patriot movement addresses its appeals to also reflect its implicit White nationalism. For example, its appeals to farmers and ranchers are limited to farm operators – who are 96% White. But the migrant labor workforce, which obviously includes a high number of undocumented workers, is completely ignored (Sunshine 2016, 33–34).

Some of this is the logical conclusion of utilizing approaches and tactics established by White supremacists to thwart laws that ensured civil rights. Anti-immigrant organizing and Islamophobia are central issues for the Patriot movement, helping solidify its links to the mainstream Republican Party as it has shifted right on these issues under Trump. This is true even though Christian evangelicals reported many reasons for voting for Trump in 2016 (Renaud 2017; Silk 2017).

In one notorious action, the Oath Keepers sent members to Murrieta, California, in 2014, to help block buses carrying immigrants – including children – being taken to a detention center. The Patriot movement is closely linked with vigilante border patrols as well. The patrols tend to be independent groups without formal affiliations to larger organizations, but individuals are often activists in the broader Patriot movement. A number of them are Three Percenters, and several border patrol activists travelled to Oregon to take part in the Malheur occupation (Bauer 2016; Sunshine 2016, 42).

The Oath Keepers also embrace this approach. One article on their national website says that 'many' 'Third World immigrants and refugees' have 'later proven to harbor terrorist intentions,' and therefore allowing them entry 'is a form of assisted national suicide.' Migration is fueled by 'various subversive agencies and foundations striving to "consume the host" with "seedlings"' [i.e. the United States and immigrants, respectively]. In turn, organizations supporting immigrant rights are often said to be controlled by liberal financier George Soros (Codrea 2015). In other right-wing media, Soros often is tabbed as the leader of an international Jewish conspiracy (Cherry 2016).

Islamophobia is rampant in the Patriot movement, largely replacing the epistemological role open and coded antisemitism played in the 1990s militia movement (Sunshine 2016, 28). In 2014, Oath Keepers leader Stewart Rhodes wrote that Mexican drug cartels are taking over towns on the U.S. border, while ISIS members 'freely' cross into the country (Diffey 2014; see also Haas 2016). Arizona's John Ritzheimer was a well-known Islamophobic organizer who came to Oregon as part of the Malheur occupation. In October 2015, he had organized a 'Global Rally for Humanity' which targeted Muslims (Neiwert 2015). Another participant at the Malheur occupation, Blaine Cooper, made a video of himself wrapping pages of the Koran in bacon and setting them on fire (Boddyxpolitic 2014). The 3% of Idaho group deployed armed members to Burns, Oregon during the Malheur occupation to gain publicity for themselves and build support for the Patriot movement. In 2015, they had held a number of public rallies in Boise and Twin Falls, Idaho opposing the potential settlement of Syrian refugees.

This activism that opposed the resettlement of refugees fleeing the civil war in Syria was a combination of two Nativist strains coming together: anti-immigration and Islamophobia (Sunshine 2016, 73–74; Sunshine et al. 2016). In contrast to the otherwise libertarian economics – but pandering to their base – some Patriot movement activists have claimed that refugees should not be allowed in the country because they argued that federal funds that supported them should go to veterans instead. Their slogan was 'Vets Before Refugees' (Sunshine 2016, 28).

Patriot movement activists also like to compare themselves to Civil Rights movement activists. At his trial for leading the Malheur occupation, Ammon Bundy compared his armed actions to Martin Luther King, Jr.'s protest activities (Brown 2016). Stewart Rhodes made similar claims, saying 'Ammon Bundy's occupation of an empty building is essentially the same as civil-disobedience sit-ins that the political left has engaged in for decades, from anti-war and Civil Rights protesters in the 60s and 70s' (Rhodes 2016). Richard Mack claimed that during the Civil Rights movement, constitutional sheriffs could have protected Rosa Parks and that, 'Today, that constitutional sheriff does the same for Rosa Parks the gun owner, or Rosa Parks the rancher, or Rosa Parks the landowner, or Rosa Parks the homeschooler, or Rosa Parks the tax protester' (Thompson 2016). This ignores the historic fact that local southern sheriffs were pillars of the resistance against the Civil Rights movement, and were notoriously linked to the Ku Klux Klan (Wade 1987; McVeigh 2009). Mack's argument gets even more bizarre when one takes into consideration that the idea of empowering the county sheriff to decide what laws were constitutional was originally formulated to encourage them to nullify federal Civil Rights laws.

Conclusions

A sense of unease over the future of the United States was prevalent during the 2016 presidential election. Both democratic socialist Bernie Sanders and right-wing populist Donald Trump gained large followings in comparison to the neoliberal candidates in both the Democratic and Republican parties. But, especially with his victory, Trump's immigrant bashing, rabid Islamophobia, bellicose ultra-nationalism, authoritarianism, and embrace of conspiracy theories undermined the mainstream of the Republican Party – and its base has shifted dramatically to the right (Altemeyer 2016; DiBranco and Berlet 2016). Since before the election of President Obama in 2008, right-wing media fed unverified claims to major national media outlets such as Fox News and scores of right-wing AM radio talk shows. This 'fake news' flooded the Internet and especially social media (Benkler et al. 2017; Berlet 2017b). By 2019, President Donald Trump was spreading conspiracy theories about Democrats and the Left on an almost daily basis (Murphy 2016; Hellinger 2019).

Even the 'mainstream' media took notice of the messaging sophistication of the loose network called the Alternative Right. Dubbed the Alt-Right, it was described as a:

> ... weird mix of old-school neo-Nazis, conspiracy theorists, anti-globalists, and young right-wing internet trolls – all united in the belief that white male identity is under attack by multi-cultural, 'politically correct' forces. (*The Week* 2017)

A key figure behind Alt-Right is Steve Bannon, who was a pit bull at the rabidly right-wing Breitbart News website. Bannon became a top advisor to Republican Presidential candidate Donald Trump (J. Wilson 2017). It was later revealed that a Bannon-affiliated stealth propaganda-generating media company had been hired by the Trump campaign to surreptitiously suppress voter turnout for Democratic Presidential nominee Hillary Clinton as part of a strategy bankrolled by a snake pit of shadowy right-wing funders and Russian intelligence agencies.

This has mainstreamed the views held by the Patriot movement and created a fertile organizing climate both for it and other right-wing populists. There are multiple audiences being targeted and complex factors shaping the messaging content (Giroux 2017). The rhetoric of right-wing populism is a core component of fascism – old and new (Berlet 2005; Griffin 1991; Snyder 2017a, 2017b, 2018). This requires a new public conversation (initiated by Snyder) concerning the relationships linking antisemitism (and other forms of demonization) to right-wing populism and neo-fascism. Demonization of an 'other' can lead to 'scripted violence' (Berlet 2014). The resulting violence is called 'Stochastic Terrorism' because the specific identities of the actual perpetrators and targets are unpredictable (Hamm and Spaaij 2017).

Patriot movement groups were active on the streets in 2017, 2018, and 2019, joining the frequently violent pro-Trump street rallies which are also attended by organized White supremacists. And although the Patriot movement's tactics are still fringe, they are also inching toward the mainstream under Trump's presidency. While not exclusively a rural phenomenon, the current right-wing populist backlash against diversity and human rights has established a strong foothold in the United States in rural areas with economies based on farming, ranching, the timber industry, and mining. In April 2017 the Farm Aid website published an article warning of another 'Looming Crisis on American Farms' (Harvie 2017). The article warned: Farmers are enduring a multiyear slump in crop and livestock prices that is pushing many to the financial brink. Since 2013, America's farmers and ranchers have weathered a 45% drop in net farm income, the largest three-year drop since the start of the Great Depression.

The strain in today's farm economy is no accident; it's the result of policies designed to enrich corporations at the expense of farmers and ranchers. If the American family farmer is to survive, farm policy needs a massive shift in direction – one that delivers fair prices to farmers that allow them to make a living. With the cascading crises of the Trump Administration, once again the plight of family farmers and rural Americans has been plowed under the media gaze.

Too often media reports of new research into the Trump phenomenon, the rise of the Right in the United States, or the relationships between right-wing populism and neofascism, promote mono-causal explanations. This is media publicity glitter and is often pegged to a new book or news report. This is distracting us from a deeper and more historically grounded and complicated analysis that can be traced back decades if not to the original founding settlers. No single individual, book, organization, or movement created the massive cluster of right-wing forces in the United States (Hardisty 1999). Explanations about Trump's election and the post-war rise of the right should consider race, gender, and class (Dibranco and Berlet 2016). White racism and anti-immigrant xenophobia were clearly the salient factors for many White Trump voters. Research after Trump's election showed that both White racial antagonisms and fears or the actual experience of economic downward mobility were both statistically significant. Christopher Parker and others established the statistical data regarding White racial antagonism in a series of studies starting with the Tea Party (Parker 2010; Parker and Barreto 2010; Parker 2013).

After Trump's election, Shannon Monnat and David Brown (2017) found that while place of residency 'mattered in the 2016 U.S. presidential election' it was clear that 'rural, suburban, or urban residence per se was not necessarily the causal factor' to consider, but rather 'the disproportionate distribution of adverse economic, health, and social conditions in some rural towns and small cities is an important key to understanding the 2016 election results.' In addition to racism and economic anxiety, antipathy toward abortion rights and the LGBTQ movements were also significant factors (Human Rights

Campaign 2016; Gayle 2018). The environment has suffered as well. Kierán Suckling, executive director of the Center for Biological Diversity, said after Trump was elected:

> Donald Trump is a disaster for public lands, wildlife and climate. But America is a nation of laws, not men, and virtually all his environment-destroying policies run contrary to our nation's bedrock environmental laws. In the face of Trump's disturbing authoritarianism, the Center for Biological Diversity today redoubles its commitment to upholding the rule of law and the right of all Americans to clean air, clean water, healthy forests, rivers and deserts, and thriving wildlife. (Center for Biological Diversity 2016)

Sociologists have shown that right-wing movements tend to flourish when power and prestige are seen as being threatened in political, economic, and/or social arenas (McVeigh 2009; McVeigh, Cunningham, and Farrell 2014). Cas Mudde, a leading scholar of global right-wing populism, warns us to pay attention not just to right-wing movements in the streets, but also the attacks on human rights, civil society, and democracy from inside the federal governments. Mudde (2017) says we should

> focus on all aspects of the populist radical right challenge, including from inside the political establishment, not just on the populism of the outsiders. Because under the cover of fighting off the 'populists,' the political establishment is slowly but steadily hollowing out the liberal democratic system.

Disclosure statement

Portions of this study were originally published by and financially supported by Political Research Associates and the Rural Organizing Project, as well as various journalistic publications as cited. Sections of this study are based in part on previous published works by the authors and are noted as appropriate in the text. The authors are influenced by the prior work of Margaret Canovan, Jean V. Hardisty, Matthew N. Lyons, and Cas Mudde, among others.

Funding

This work was supported by Political Research Associates.

ORCID

Chip Berlet http://orcid.org/0000-0002-4997-9614
Spencer Sunshine http://orcid.org/0000-0003-4498-6185

References

Abromeit, John. 2016. *Transformations of Populism in Europe and the Americas: History and Recent Tendencies*. London: Bloomsbury Academic.

Aho, James A. 1990. *The Politics of Righteousness: Idaho Christian Patriotism*. Seattle: University of Washington Press.

Aho, James A. 2016. *Far-Right Fantasy: A Sociology of American Religion and Politics*. New York: Routledge.

Akins, John Keith. 1998. "God, Guns, and Guts: Religion and Violence in Florida Militias." Ph.D. diss., University of Florida.

Alexander, Brian. 2017. *Glass House: The 1% Economy and the Shattering of the All-American Town*. New York: St. Martin's Press.

Allen, Gary, with Larry Abraham. 1971. *None Dare Call it Conspiracy*. Rossmoor, CA: Concord Press. For 'vice' graphic from book, see http://www.researchforprogress.us/topic/38852/vice-squeezing-the-middle-class.

Altemeyer, Robert. 2010. "Comment on the Tea Party Movement." April 20. http://home.cc.umanitoba.ca/~altemey/drbob/Comment%20on%20the%20Tea%20Party.pdf.

Altemeyer, Bob. 2016. "Donald Trump and Authoritarian Followers." *The Authoritarians*, July 18. https://theauthoritarians.org/donald-trump-and-authoritarian-followers.

Ambler, Marjane. 1980. "The Sagebrush Rebellion: Misdirected dynamite." *High Country News*, February 22: 2. http://s3.amazonaws.com/hcn-media/archive-pdf/1980_02_22.pdf.

Anti-Defamation League. 2016. "Anatomy of a Standoff." www.adl.org/assets/pdf/combating-hate/Anatomy-of-a-Standoff-MalheurOccupiers.pdf.

Arnold, Ron, and Alan Gottlieb. 1993. *Trashing the Economy: How Runaway Environmentalism Is Wrecking America*. Bellevue, WA: Free Enterprise Press.

Baier, Walter, Eric Canepa, and Eva Himmeltoss, eds. 2017. *The Left, the People, Populism: Past and Present*. Transform 2017. London: Merlin.

Barkun, Michael. 2003. *A Culture of Conspiracy: Apocalyptic Visions in Contemporary America*. Berkeley: University of California.

Barron, Bruce. 1992. *Heaven on Earth? The Social & Political Agendas of Dominion Theology*. Grand Rapids, MI: Zondervan.

Bauer, Shane. 2016. "I Went Undercover with a Border Militia. Here's What I saw." *Mother Jones*. November/December. http://www.motherjones.com/politics/2016/10/undercover-border-militia-immigration-bauer.

Baumgarten, Albert I., ed. 2002. *In Apocalyptic Time: 2000*. Vol. 86, Numen Book Series, Series Editor, W. J. Hanegraaff. Leiden: Brill. https://brill.com/abstract/book/edcoll/9789047400561/B9789047400561_s002.xmlBendersky.

Bendersky, Joseph W. 2000. *The 'Jewish Threat': Anti-Semetic Politics of the U.S. Army*. New York: Basic Books.

Benkler, Yochai, Robert Faris, Hal Roberts, and Ethan Zuckerman. 2017. "Breitbart-Led Right-Wing Media Ecosystem Altered Broader Media Agenda." *Columbia Journalism Review*, March 3. http://www.cjr.org/analysis/breitbart-media-trump-harvard-study.php.

Berlet, Chip. 1986. "White, Right, and Looking for a Fight: Has Chicago been Targeted by a New Alliance of White Supremacists?" *Chicago Reader* 15 (39).

Berlet, Chip. 1988. "Cardinal Mindszenty: Heroic Anti-Communist or Anti-Semite or Both?" *The St. Louis Journalism Review*, April, pp. 10–11, 14.

Berlet, Chip. 1989. "Trashing the Birchers: Secrets of the Paranoid Right." *Boston Phoenix*, July 20, pp. 10, 23.

Berlet, Chip. 1992a. "Re-framing Dissent as Criminal Subversion." *CovertAction Quarterly*, no. 41, Summer, 35–41.

Berlet, Chip. 1992b. "The Great Right Snark Hunt: Some Notes on the Secular-Humanist Conspiracy for World Domination." *The Humanist*, September–October, 14–17, 36.

Berlet, Chip. 1992c. "Friendly Fascists." *The Progressive*, June, pp. 16–20.

Berlet, Chip. 1993a. "Big Stories, Spooky Sources." *Columbia Journalism Review*, May–June, 67–71.

Berlet, Chip. 1993b. "Marketing the Religious Right's Anti-Gay Agenda." *CovertAction Quarterly*, Spring, 46–47.

Berlet, Chip. 2004a. "Militias in the Frame." Review Essay Mentioning Four Books on the Militia Movement of *Contemporary Sociology,* by Chermak, Crothers, Freilich, and Gallaher. *American Sociological Association* 33 (5): 514–521.

Berlet, Chip. 2004b. "Mapping the Political Right: Gender and Race Oppression in Right-Wing Movements." In *Home-Grown Hate: Gender and Organized Racism*, edited by Abby Ferber. New York: Routledge.

Berlet, Chip. 2004c. "Militias in the Frame." Review Essay Mentioning Four Books on the Militia Movement of *Contemporary Sociology*, by Chermak, Crothers, Freilich, and Gallaher. *American Sociological Association* 33 (5): 514–521.

Berlet, Chip. 2005. "When Alienation Turns Right: Populist Conspiracism, the Apocalyptic Style and Neofascist Movements. In *Trauma, Promise and the Millennium: The Evolution of Alienation*, edited by Lauren Langman and Devorah Kalekin Fishman, 115–144. Lanham, MD: Rowman and Littlefield.

Berlet, Chip. 2008. "The United States: Messianism, Apocalypticism and Political Religion." In *The Sacred in Twentieth Century Politics: Essays in Honour of Professor Stanley G. Payne*, edited by Roger Griffin, Matthew Feldman, and John Tortice, 221–257. Basingstoke, UK: Palgrave Macmillan.

Berlet, Chip. 2009a. "Fears of Fédéralisme in the United States: The Case of the 'North American Union' Conspiracy Theory." *Fédéralisme Régionalisme* 9 (1). https://popups.ulg.ac.be/federalisme/document.php?id=786.

Berlet, Chip. 2009b. *Toxic to Democracy: Conspiracy Theories, Demonization and Scapegoating*. Somerville, MA: Political Research Associates.

Berlet, Chip. 2010. "The Roots of Anti-Obama Rhetoric." In *Race in the Age of Obama*, edited by Donald Cunnigen, Marino A. Bruce, Vol. 16, 301–319. Bingley: Research in Race and Ethnic Relations, Emerald Group Publishing Limited.

Berlet, Chip. 2011. "Taking Tea Parties Seriously: Corporate Globalization, Populism, and Resentment." *Perspectives on Global Development and Technology* 10 (1): 11–29. http://booksandjournals.brillonline.com/content/10.1163/156914911x555071.

Berlet, Chip. 2012. "Collectivists, Communists, Labor Bosses, and Treason: The Tea Parties as Right-Wing Populist Countersubversion Panic." *Critical Sociology* 38 (4): 565–587.

Berlet, Chip. 2013. "From Tea Parties to Militias: Between the Republican Party and the Insurgent Ultra-Right in the US." In *Right-wing Radicalism Today: Perspectives from Europe and the US*, edited by Sabine Von Mering and Timothy Wyman McCarty. Abingdon: Routledge.

Berlet, Chip. 2014. "Heroes Know Which Villains to Kill: How Coded Rhetoric Incites Scripted Violence." In *Doublespeak: Rhetoric of the Far-Right Since 1945*, edited by Matthew Feldman and Paul Jackson. Stuttgart: ibidem-Verlag.

Berlet, Chip. 2015a. "From the KKK to the CCC to Dylann Roof: White Nationalism Infuses Our Political Ideology." *Washington Spectator*, August 1. https://washingtonspectator.org/from-the-kkk-to-the-ccc-to-dylann-roof/.

Berlet, Chip. 2015b. Corporate Press Fails to Trump Bigotry. *Fairness and Accuracy in Reporting*. September 17. https://fair.org/home/corporate-press-fails-to-trump-bigotry/.

Berlet, Chip. 2017a. "Hayek, Mises, and the Iron Rule of Unintended Consequences." In *Hayek: A Collaborative Biography: Part IX: The Divine Right of the 'Free' Market*, edited by Robert Leeson, 131–173. Cham: Springer International Publishing: Palgrave Macmillan.

Berlet, Chip. 2017b. "Conspiracy Theory Graphic: Vice Squeezing the Middle Class." https://doi.org/10.6084/m9.figshare.7479362.

Berlet, Chip. 2018. "Sovereign Legal Theories." https://www.researchforprogress.us/topic/844/sovereign-legal-theories/.

Berlet, Chip, and Nikhil Aziz. 2003. "Culture, Religion, Apocalypse, and Middle East Foreign Policy." December 4. https://rightweb.irc-online.org/culture_religion_apocalypse_and_middle_east_foreign_policy/.

Berlet, Chip, and Matthew N. Lyons. 1995. "Militia Nation." *The Progressive*, June, 22–25.

Berlet, Chip, and Matthew N. Lyons. 2000. *Right-Wing Populism in America: Too Close for Comfort*. New York: Guilford Press.

Berlet, Chip, and Margaret Quigley. 1995. "Theocracy & White Supremacy: Behind the Culture War to Restore Traditional Values." In *Eyes Right! Challenging the Right Wing Backlash*, edited by Chip Berlet, 15–43. Boston: South End Press.

Betz, Hans–Georg, and Stefan Immerfall, eds. 1998. *The New Politics of the Right: Neo–Populist Parties and Movements in Established Democracies*. New York, NY: St. Martin's Press.

Betz, Hans-Georg. 1994. *Radical Right-Wing Populism in Western Europe*. New York: St. Martin's Press.

Black, Amy. 2016. "Evangelicals and Politics: Where We've Been and Where We're Headed." National Association of Evangelicals. https://www.nae.net/evangelicals-and-politics.

Boddyxpolitic. 2014. "A Message to Muslims Islam, and President Obama Blaine Cooper Burns the Quran Islam Roast." *YouTube* video, 4:29, posted by 'Boddyxpolitic,' May 13. www.youtube.com/watch?v=zPaECrZ6H7k.

Boyer, Paul S. 1992. *When Time Shall Be No More: Prophecy Belief in Modern American Culture*. Cambridge, MA: Belknap/Harvard University Press.

Bridges, Tyler. 1994. *The Rise of David Duke*. Jackson, MS: University Press of Mississippi. 245.

Bronner, Stephen Eric. 2000. *A Rumor About the Jews: Antisemitism, Conspiracy, and the Protocols of Zion*. Oxford: Oxford University Press.

Brown, Karina. 2016. "The Bundy Gang Is Found Not Guilty." *Willamette Week*, October 27. http://www.wweek.com/news/2016/10/27/the-bundy-gang-is-found-not-guilty.

Burack, Cynthia. 2008. *Sin, Sex, and Democracy: Antigay Rhetoric and the Christian Right*. Albany, NY: State University of New York Press.

Burghart, Devin, and Robert Crawford. 1996. "Guns and Gavels." Coalition for Human Dignity, Portland, Oregon.

Burghart, Devin, and Leonard Zeskind. 2010. *Tea Party Nationalism: A Critical Examination of the Tea Party Movement and the Size, Scope, and Focus of Its National Factions*. Kansas City, MO: Institute for Research & Education on Human Rights. https://www.irehr.org/2010/10/12/tea-party-nationalism-report-pdf.

Burke, William Kevin. 1993. "The Wise Use Movement: Right-Wing Anti-Environmentalism." https://www.politicalresearch.org/1993/06/05/the-wise-use-movement-right-wing-anti-environmentalism.

Burlein, Ann. 2002. *Lift High the Cross: Where White Supremacy and the Christian Right Converge*. Durham, NC: Duke University Press.

Canovan, Margaret. 1981. *Populism*. New York: Harcourt Brace Jovanovich.

Carney, Eliza Newlin. 2018. "Fara Fiasco: Congress Swings at Manafort, Hits Environmentalists." *The American Prospect*. September 20. https://prospect.org/article/fara-fiasco-congress-swings-manafort-hits-environmentalists.

Center for Biological Diversity. 2016. Statement on Election of Donald Trump. https://www.biologicaldiversity.org/news/press_releases/2016/donald-trump-11-09-2016.html.

Chen, Michelle. 2015. "Now White People Are Dying from Our Terrible Economic Policies, Too." *The Nation*, November 6. http://www.thenation.com/article/now-white-people-are-dying-from-our-terrible-economic-policies-too/.

Cherry, Tyler. 2016. "Breitbart Uses Nazi-Inspired Anti-Semitic Rhetoric in George Soros Attack." *Media Matters for America*, November 28. https://www.mediamatters.org/blog/2016/11/28/breitbart-uses-nazi-inspired-anti-semitic-rhetoric-george-soros-attack/214641.

Chomsky, Noam. 2010. Transcript from "What Went Wrong: A Q & A with Noam Chomsky." A Z Video Production.

Cincotta, Thomas. 2010. "*Platform for Prejudice*: How the Nationwide Suspicious Activity Reporting Initiative Invites Racial Profiling, Erodes Civil Liberties, and Undermines Security." Political Research Associates. https://www.politicalresearch.org/resources/reports/full-reports/platform-for-prejudice/.

Cincotta, Thomas. 2011. "*Manufacturing the Muslim Menace*: Private Firms, Public Servants, & the Threat to Rights and Security." Political Research Associates. https://www.politicalresearch.org/resources/reports/full-reports/manufacturing-the-muslim-menace/.

Clarkson, Frederick. 1997. *Eternal Hostility: The Struggle between Theocracy and Democracy*. Monroe, ME: Common Courage.

Codrea, David. 2015. "Red-Green Axis Spells Out Danger Threatening to Destroy the Republic." *Oath Keepers*. August 24. https://www.oathkeepers.org/red-green-axis-spells-out-danger-threatening-to-destroy-the-republic.

Cohn, Norman. 1967. *Warrant for Genocide: The Myth of the Jewish World Conspiracy and the Protocols of the Elders of Zion*. London: Serif.

Conroy, J. Oliver. 2017. "They Hate the US Government, and They're Multiplying: The Terrifying Rise of 'Sovereign Citizens.'" *Guardian*, May 15. https://www.theguardian.com/world/2017/may/15/sovereign-citizens-rightwing-terrorism-hate-us-government.

Constitutional Sheriffs and Peace Officers Association. 2014. "Growing List of Sheriffs, Associations and Police Chiefs Saying 'No' to Obama Gun Control." Original post February 1. http://web.archive.org/web/20140110081510/http://cspoa.org/sheriffs-gun-rights. List updated August 12, 2015, showing a total of 485 Sheriffs, http://web.archive.org/web/20150812112805/http://cspoa.org/sheriffs-gun-rights.

Corcoran, James. 1995. *Bitter Harvest: The Birth of Paramilitary Terrorism in the Heartland*. New York: Penguin.

Cox, Daniel, and Robert P. Jones. 2010. "Religion and the Tea Party in the 2010 elections." October 5. https://www.prri.org/research/religion-tea-party-2010/.

Cramer, Katherine J. 2016. *The Politics of Resentment: Rural Consciousness in Wisconsin and the Rise of Scott Walker*. Chicago: The University of Chicago Press.

Davidson, Osha Gray. 1996. *Broken Heartland: The Rise of America's Rural Ghetto*. Iowa City: University of Iowa Press.

Devega, Chauncey. 2015. "Dear White America: Your Working Class is Literally Dying—and This is Your Idea of an Answer?" *Salon*, November 6. http://www.salon.com/2015/11/06/dear_white_america_your_working_class_is_literally_dying_and_this_is_your_idea_of_an_answer/.

Diamond, Sara. 1989. *Spiritual Warfare: The Politics of the Christian Right*. Boston: South End Press.

Diamond, Sara. 1995. *Roads to Dominion: Right-Wing Movements and Political Power in the United States*. New York: Guilford Press.

Diamond, Sara. 1997. "Political Millennialism within the Evangelical Subculture." In *The Year 2000: Essays on the End*, edited by Charles B. Strozier and Michael Flynn, 206–216. New York: New York University Press.

Diamond, Sara. 1998. *Not by Politics Alone: The Enduring Influence of the Christian Right*. New York: Guilford Press.

DiBranco, Alex, and Chip Berlet. 2016. "Republican Ideological Shift Election 2016." Paper Presented at a roundtable at the Annual Meeting of the American Sociological Association, Seattle, WA, 2016. Online at *Progressive Movements Commons*. http://www.progressivemovements.us/now/446/resource-page-sections/studies-and-reports/republican-ideological-shift-election-2016.

Diffey, Larry. 2014. "Obama Must Be Impeached and Removed to Stop His 'Amnesty' of Illegals." *Oath Keepers*. November 20. www.oathkeepers.org/obama-must-be-impeached-and-removed-to-stop-his-amnesty-of-illegals.

Dilling, Elizabeth. 1934. *The Red Network: A 'Who's Who' and Handbook of Radicalism for Patriots*. Chicago, IL: By the author.

Dilling, Elizabeth. 1936. *The Roosevelt Red Record and its Background*. Kenilworth, IL: By the author.

Dilling, Elizabeth. 1941 [circa]. *New Dealers in Office*. Indianapolis: The Fellowship Press.

Domke, D. S., and Coe, K. M. 2008. *The God Strategy: How Religion Became a Political Weapon in America*. Oxford: Oxford University Press.

Donner, Frank J. 1980. *The age of Surveillance: The Aims & Methods of America's Political Intelligence System*. New York: Alfred Knopf.
Durham, Martin. 2000. *The Christian Right, the Far Right and the Boundaries of American Conservatism*. Manchester: Manchester Univ. Press.
Dyer, Joel. 1997. *Harvest of Rage: Why Oklahoma City Is Only the Beginning*. Boulder, CO: Westview.
Economic Policy Institute. 2014. "The Top 10 Charts of 2014." http://www.epi.org/publication/the-top-10-charts-of-2014/.
Egan, Timothy. 2014. "Deadbeat on the Range." *The New York Times*, April 18. https://www.nytimes.com/2014/04/18/opinion/egan-deadbeat-on-the-range.html.
Esposito, John L., and Ibrahim Kalin. 2011. *Islamophobia: The Challenge of Pluralism in the 21st Century*. Oxford: Oxford University Press.
Follman, Mark, and James West. 2015. "Watch President Obama Break into 'Amazing Grace' during His Extraordinary Charleston Eulogy." *Mother Jones*, June 26.
Frankel, J. 1991. *Jews and Messianism in the Modern Era: Metaphor and Meaning*. New York: Oxford University Press.
Freilich, Joshua D., Jeremy A. Pienik, and Gregory J. Howard. 2001. "Toward Comparative Studies of the U.S. Militia Movement." *International Journal of Comparative Sociology* 42 (1-2): 163–210.
Frykholm, Amy Johnson. 2004. *Rapture Culture: Left Behind in Evangelical America*. New York: Oxford University Press.
Fuller, Robert C. 1995. *Naming the Antichrist: The History of an American Obsession*. New York: Oxford University Press.
Gallaher, Carolyn. 2003. *On the Fault Line: Race, Class, and the American Patriot Movement*. Lanham, MD: Rowman & Littlefield.
Gayle, Caleb. 2018. "From Abortion to Affirmative Action, How Trump's Supreme Court Pick Could Change America." *The Guardian*, June 30. https://www.theguardian.com/law/2018/jun/30/supreme-court-trump-pick-abortion-affirmative-action.
Gibson, James William. 1994. *Warrior Dreams: Paramilitary Culture in Post-Vietnam America*. New York: Hill and Wang.
Gibson, James William. 1997. "Is the Apocalypse Coming? Paramilitary Culture After the Cold War." In *The Year 2000: Essays on the End*, edited by Charles B. Strozier, and Michael Flynn. New York: NYU Press.
Giroux, Henry A. 2017. *The Public in Peril. Trump and the Menace of American Authoritarianism*. Basingstoke: Taylor & Francis.
Goldberg, Robert Alan. 2001. *Enemies Within: The Culture of Conspiracy in Modern America*. New Haven: Yale University Press.
Gorenberg, Gershom. 2000. *The end of Days: Fundamentalism and the Struggle for the Temple Mount*. New York: The Free Press.
Greider, William. 2000. "The Last Farm Crisis." *The Nation*, November 20.
Griffin, Roger. 1991. *The Nature of Fascism*. New York: St. Martin's Press.
Guillaumin, Colette. 1995. *Racism, Sexism, Power and Ideology*. London: Routledge.
Gupta, Arun, and Michelle Fawcett. 2018. "Romney Appeals to White Tribalism in Ohio." In *Trumping Democracy: From Reagan to Alt-Right*, edited by Chip Berlet. New York: Routledge. Forthcoming.
Haas, Ryan. 2016. "Militant Website Creator David Fry: 'I'm Not ISIS.'" *Oregon Public Broadcasting*, January 13. www.opb.org/news/series/burns-oregon-standoff-bundy-militia-news-updates/oregon-militant-website-creator-david-fry-im-not-isis.
Hamm, Mark S. 1997. *Apocalypse in Oklahoma: Waco and Ruby Ridge Revenged*. Boston: Northeastern University Press.
Hamm, Mark S., and Ramón Spaaij. 2017. *The Age of Lone Wolf Terrorism*. New York: Columbia University Press.
Hardisty, Jean V. 1999. *Mobilizing Resentment: Conservative Resurgence From the John Birch Society to the Promise Keepers*. Boston: Beacon.
Harvie, Alicia. 2017. "Fact sheet: A looming crisis on American farms." Farm Aid, April 13, https://www.farmaid.org/blog/fact-sheet/looming-crisis-american-farms/.
Hayek, F. A. von. 1960 [1944]. *The Road to Serfdom*. Chicago, IL: University of Chicago Press.

Heale, M. J. 1990. *American Anticommunism: Combating the Enemy Within, 1830–1970*. Baltimore, MD: Johns Hopkins University Press.

Heale, M. J. 1998. *McCarthy's Americans: Red Scare Politics in State and Nation, 1935–1965*. Athens: University of Georgia Press.

Hellinger, Daniel C. 2019. *Conspiracies and Conspiracy Theories in the Age of Trump*. Palgrave MacMillan.

Helvarg, David. 1997. *The War Against the Greens: The 'Wise-Use' Movement, the New Right, and Anti-Environmental Violence*. San Francisco, CA: Sierra Club Books.

Henderson, Jason, and Maria Akers. 2015. "Recession Catches Rural America." Federal Reserve Bank of Kansas City. https://www.kansascityfed.org/OomQl/Publicat/ECONREV/PDF/09q1Henderson.pdf.

Henze, Matthias. 2011. *Jewish Apocalypticism in Late First Century Israel: Reading 'Second Baruch' in Context*. Tübingen: Mohr Siebeck.

Herman, Didi. 1997. *The Antigay Agenda: Orthodox Vision and the Christian Right*. Chicago: University of Chicago Press.

Higham, John. [1955] 1972. *Strangers in the Land: Patterns of American Nativism 1860–1925*. New York, NY: Atheneum.

Himmelstein, Jerome L. 1990. *To the Right: The Transformation of American Conservatism*. Berkeley: University of California Press.

History News Network. 2010. "HNN Special: A Symposium on Jonah Goldberg's Liberal Fascism." Includes short essays by Berlet, Feldman, Goldberg, Griffin, Ledeen, Neiwert, and Paxton.

Hochschild, Arlie Russell. 2016. *Strangers in Their Own Land: Anger and Mourning on the American Right*. New York: The New Press.

Hofstadter, Richard. 1965. "The Paranoid Style in American Politics." In *The Paranoid Style in American Politics and Other Essays*. New York: Alfred A. Knopf.

Horne, Gerald. 2015. *Confronting Black Jacobins: The United States, the Haitian Revolution, and the origins of the Dominican Republic*. http://public.eblib.com/choice/publicfullrecord.aspx?p=4044666.

Housing Assistance Council. 2014a. "Is the Housing Crisis Over? And How Did it Impact Rural America?" *Rural Voices* 19 (2). http://www.ruralhome.org/component/content/article/150/947.

Housing Assistance Council. 2014b. "The Housing Crisis and Its Wake in Rural America." http://prezi.com/bdolfys2hibs/the-housing-crisis-and-its-wake-in-rural-america/?utm_campaign=share&utm_medium=copy.

Human Rights Campaign. 2016. "Trump's Timeline of Hate." January 20. https://www.hrc.org/timelines/trump.

Ignatiev, Noel. 1995. *How the Irish Became White*. New York: Routledge.

Katznelson, Ira. 2017. "Making Affirmative Action White Again." *New York Times*. August 12. https://www.nytimes.com/2017/08/12/opinion/sunday/making-affirmative-action-white-again.html.

Kazin, Michael. 1995. *The Populist Persuasion: An American History*. New York: Basic Books.

Kimmel, Michael, and Abby L. Ferber. 2000. "'White Men Are This Nation': Right-Wing Militias and the Restoration of Rural American Masculinity." *Rural Sociology* 65 (4): 582–604.

Kintz, Linda. 1997. *Between Jesus and the Market: The Emotions that Matter in RightWing America*. Durham, NC: Duke University Press.

Kintz, Linda, and Julia Lesage. 1998. *Media, Culture and the Religious Right*. Minneapolis, MN: Univ. of Minnesota Press.

Kneen, Brewster. 1995. *Invisible Giant: Cargill and Its Transnational Strategies*. London: Pluto Press. [Has material not in the 2nd edition].

Kneen, Brewster. 2002. *Invisible Giant: Cargill and Its Transnational Strategies*. 2nd ed. London: Pluto Press. [Has material not in the 1st edition].

Kusmin, Lorin. 2015. "Rural America in the Post-Recession Years." USDA. December 8. https://www.usda.gov/media/blog/2015/12/08/rural-america-post-recession-years.

LaHaye, Tim. 1975. *Revelation: Illustrated and Made Plain*. Grand Rapids, MI: Zondervan.

LaHaye, Tim. 1980. *The Battle for the Mind*. Old Tappan, NJ: Fleming H. Revell.

LaHaye, Tim. 1982. *The Battle for the Family*. Old Tappan, NJ: Fleming H. Revell.

LaHaye, Tim, and Jerry B. Jenkins. 1995. *Left Behind: A Novel Of The Earth's Last Days*. Vol. 1, *Left Behind* series. Wheaton, IL: Tyndale House Publishers.

Landes, Richard Allen, and Steven T. Katz. 2011. *The Paranoid Apocalypse: a Hundred-Year Retrospective on the Protocols of the Elders of Zion*. New York: New York University Press.
Langer, Elinor. 1990. "The American Neo-Nazi Movement Today." Special Report. *The Nation*, July 16–23.
Larmer, Paul. 2016. "Modern Sagebrush Rebels Recycle Old Western Fantasies." *High Country News*, January 25, http://www.hcn.org/issues/48.1/modern-sagebrush-rebels-recycle-old-western-fantasies.
Lean, Nathan Chapman, and John L. Esposito. 2012. *The Islamophobia Industry: How the Right Manufactures Fear of Muslims*. London: Pluto Press.
Lee, Jaeah, and Edwin Rios. 2015. "Obama to US Mayors on Guns: 'We Need a Change in Attitude. We Have to Fix This.'" *Mother Jones*, June 20. https://www.motherjones.com/politics/2015/06/obama-mayors-charleston-gun-violence-speech-video/.
Lembke, Jerry. 1998. *The Spitting Image: Myth, Memory, and the Legacy of Vietnam*. New York: NYU Press.
Lembke, Jerry. 2003. *CNN's Tailwind Tale: Inside Vietnam's Last Great Myth*. Lanham, MD: Rowman & Littlefield.
Levin, Sam. 2018. "Stunning Victory for Bundy Family as all Charges Dismissed in 2014 Standoff Case." *The Guardian*. January 8. https://www.theguardian.com/us-news/2018/jan/08/bundy-family-charges-dropped-nevada-armed-standoff.
Levitas, Daniel. 2002. *The Terrorist Next Door: The Militia Movement and the Radical Right*. New York: Thomas Dunne Books/St. Martin's Press.
Lind, M. 2010. Glenn Beck's Partisan Historians: The Academics Behind the Progressivism-as-fascism meme. *Salon*, April 5. http://www.salon.com/2010/04/06/glenn_beck_s_historians/.
Lindley, M., and J. Farmelant. 2012. "The Strange Case of Dr. Hayek and Mr. Hayek." *Journal of Social and Political Studies* 3 (2). University of Allahabad, Department of Political Science. https://www.academia.edu/3252760/.
Lyons, Matthew N. 2017. *Ctrl-Alt-Delete: An Antifascist Report on the Alternative Right*. Montreal: Kersplebedeb Publishing. More details at https://matthewnlyons.net/books-articles-and-speeches.
Lyons, Matthew N. 2018. *Insurgent Supremacists: The U.S. far Right's Challenge to State and Empire*. Oakland: PM Press / Montreal: Kersplebedeb Publishing.
Martin, William. 1996. *With God on Our Side: The Rise of the Religious Right in America*. New York: Broadway Books.
Marty, Martin E., and R. Scott Appleby, eds. 1994. *Accounting for Fundamentalisms*. Chicago, IL: The University of Chicago Press.
McMath, Robert C., Jr. 1993. *American Populism: A Social History 1877–1898*. New York: Hill and Wang; Farrar, Straus & Giroux.
McMichael, Philip. 1998. "Global Food Politics." *Monthly Review* 50 (3): 97–111.
McVeigh, Rory. 2009. *The Rise of the Ku Klux Klan: Right-Wing Movements and National Politics*. Minneapolis: Univ. of Minnesota Press.
McVeigh, Rory, David Cunningham, and Justin Farrell. 2014. "Political Polarization as a Social Movement Outcome: 1960s Klan Activism and Its Enduring Impact on Political Realignment in Southern Counties, 1960 to 2000." *American Sociological Review* 79 (6): 1144–1171.
Melling, Philip. 1999. *Fundamentalism in America: Millennialism, Identity, and Militant Religion*. Edinburgh: Edinburgh University Press.
Monnat, Shannon M., and David L. Brown. 2017. "More Than a Rural Revolt: Landscapes of Despair and the 2016 Presidential Election." *Journal of Rural Studies* 55: 227–236.
Mooney, Michael Eugene. 1982. "Millennialism and Antichrist in New England, 1630–1760." PhD. Diss., Syracuse University.
Morlin, Bill. 2018. "Study Shows Two-Thirds of U.S. Terrorism Tied to Right-wing Extremists." *Southern Poverty Law Center*. https://www.splcenter.org/hatewatch/2018/09/12/study-shows-two-thirds-us-terrorism-tied-right-wing-extremists/.
Mudde, Cas. 2017. *The Far Right in America*. Basingstoke: Taylor & Francis Ltd.
Mudde, Cas, and Cristóbal Rovira Kaltwasser. 2014. *Populism in Europe and the Americas: Threat or Corrective for Democracy?* Cambridge: Cambridge University Press.

Mudde, Cas, and Cristóbal Rovira Kaltwasser. 2017. *Populism: A Very Short Introduction*. New York: Oxford University Press.
Murphy, Tim. 2016. "How Donald Trump Became Conspiracy Theorist in Chief." *Mother Jones*. November/December. http://www.motherjones.com/politics/2016/10/trump-infowars-alex-jones-clinton-conspiracy-theories/#.
Müller, Jan-Werner. 2016. *What Is Populism?* Philadelphia: University of Pennsylvania Press.
Navasky, Victor S. 1980. *Naming Names*. New York: The Viking Press.
Neiwert, David A. 1999. *In God's Country: The Patriot Movement and the Pacific Northwest*. Pullman, WA: Washington State University Press.
Neiwert, David A. 2003. "Rush, Newspeak and Fascism: An Exegesis." Online essay. Accessed February 29, 2004. http://dneiwert.blogspot.com.
Neiwert, David A. 2009. *The Eliminationists: How Hate Talk Radicalized the American Right*. Sausalito, CA: PoliPointPress.
Neiwert, David A. 2015. "Militiamen Plan to Bring Guns to Mosques around Nation in 'Global' Protest of Islam." Southern Poverty Law Center. October 9. www.splcenter.org/hatewatch/2015/10/09/militiamen-plan-bring-gunsmosques-around-nation-global-protest-islam.
Neiwert, David. 2017. "Trump's Fixation on Demonizing Islam Hides True Homegrown US Terror Threat." *Reveal*, June 17. https://www.revealnews.org/article/home-is-where-the-hate-is/.
Neiwert, David, Darren Ankrom, Esther Kaplan, and Scott Pham. 2017. "Homegrown Terror." https://apps.revealnews.org/homegrown-terror/.
Noël, Lise. 1994. *Intolerance: A General Survey*. Montreal: McGill-Queen's University Press.
Oath Keepers. n.d. a. "Orders We Will Not Obey." *Oath Keepers*. https://www.oathkeepers.org/declaration-of-orders-we-will-not-obey.
Oath Keepers. n.d. b. "Bylaws of Oath Keepers." *Oath Keepers*, www.oathkeepers.org/bylaws.
Pagels, Elaine. 1996. *The Origin of Satan*. New York: Vintage.
Parker, Christopher S. 2010. *Multi-State Survey on Race & Politics*. Seattle: University of Washington, Institute for the Study of Ethnicity, Race and Sexuality. http://depts.washington.edu/uwiser/racepolitics.html.
Parker, Christopher S. 2013. *Change They Can't Believe in: The Tea Party and Reactionary Politics in America*. Princeton, NJ: Princeton University Press.
Parker, Christopher S., and M. A. Barreto. 2010. "Exploring the sources and Consequences of Tea Party Support." Paper presented at the conference on Fractures, Alliances and Mobilizations in the Age of Obama: Emerging Analyses of the 'Tea Party' Movement, Center for the Comparative Study of Right–Wing Movements, University of California, October 22, Berkeley, CA.
Phillips, Kevin. 2006. *American Theocracy: The Peril and Politics of Radical Religion, Oil, and Borrowed Money in the 21st Century*. New York: Viking.
Political Research Associates. 2017. "Economic Justice." http://www.politicalresearch.org/tag/economic-justice/.
Postone, Moishe. 1980. "Anti-Semitism and National Socialism: Notes on the German Reaction to 'Holocaust.'" *New German Critique* 19: 97–115.
Public Policy Polling. 2009. "Extremism in New Jersey." Public Policy Polling, September 16. http://publicpolicypolling.blogspot.com/2009/09/extremism-in-new-jersey.html.
Quinby, Lee. 1994. *Anti-Apocalypse: Exercises in Genealogical Criticism*. Minneapolis: University of Minnesota Press.
Quinby, Lee. 1997. "Coercive Purity: The Dangerous Promise of Apocalyptic Masculinity." In *The Year 2000: Essays on the End*, edited by Charles B. Strozier and Michael Flynn. New York: New York University Press.
Quinby, Lee. 1999. *Millennial Seduction: A Skeptic Confronts Apocalyptic Culture*. Ithaca, NY: Cornell University Press.
Ramos, Tarso. 1995. 'Wise Use in the West.' In *Let the People Judge: Wise Use and the Private Property Rights Movement*, edited by John Echeverria, and Raymond Booth Eby, 82–118. Washington, DC: Island Press.
Ramos, Tarso. 1997. "Wise Use." Extremists and the Anti-Environmental Lobby: Activities since Oklahoma City. Western States Center. http://www.politicalresearch.org/tag/wise-use/.

Reavis, Dick J. 1995. *The Ashes of Waco: An Investigation*. New York: Simon & Schuster.
Renaud, Myriam. 2017. "Myths Debunked: Why Did White Evangelical Christians Vote for Trump?" Divinity School, University of Chicago. January 19. https://divinity.uchicago.edu/sightings/myths-debunked-why-did-white-evangelical-christians-vote-trump.
Rhodes, Stewart. 2016. "Jan 15. 2016 – Warning to U.S. Military and Federal LEOS: Do Not Follow Orders to 'Waco' Ammon Bundy Occupation, or Risk Civil War." *Oath Keepers*. https://www.oathkeepers.org/critical-warning-to-u-s-military-and-federal-leo-do-not-follow-orders-to-waco-ammon-bundy-occupation-in-oregon-or-you-risk-starting-a-civil-war/aco-ammon-bundy-occupation-in-oregon-or-you-risk-starting-a-civil-war.
Ribuffo, Leo P. 1983. *The Old Christian Right: The Protestant Far Right from the Great Depression to the Cold War*. Philadelphia: Temple University Press.
Roche, Maggie, Terre Roche, and Suzzy Roche. 1985. The Roches: "Weeded Out." *Another World*. [Album] Warner Brothers. Used by permission.
Samples, Kenneth, Erwin de Castro, Richard Abanes, and Robert Lyle. 1994. *Prophets of the Apocalypse: David Koresh & Other American Messiahs*. Grand Rapids, MI: Baker Books.
Sarris, Peter. 2011. *Empires of Faith: The Fall of Rome to the Rise of Islam, 500-700*. Oxford: Oxford University Press.
Scafi, Alessandro. 2006. *Mapping Paradise: A History of Heaven on Earth*. Chicago: University of Chicago.
Scher, Abby, and Chip Berlet. 2014. "The Tea Party Moment." In *Understanding the Tea Party Movement*, edited by Nella van Dyke, and David S. Meyer. London: Ashgate.
Scoones, Ian, Marc Edelman, Saturnino M. Borras, Ruth Hall, Wendy Wolford, and Ben White. 2018. "Emancipatory Rural Politics: Confronting Authoritarian Populism." *The Journal of Peasant Studies* 45: 1–20. doi:10.1080/03066150.2017.1339693.
Shepherd, Katie. 2017. "Multnomah County Republican Party Approves Oath Keepers and Three Percenters as Private Security." *Willamette Week*. http://www.wweek.com/news/2017/06/30/multnomah-county-republican-party-approves-oath-keepers-and-three-percenters-as-private-security/.
Silk, Mark. 2017. "Religious Assessments of Trump v. Obama." *Religion News*, April 18. https://religionnews.com/2017/04/18/religious-assessments-of-trump-v-obama.
Silverstein, Ken. 2000. "Ford and the Führer." *The Nation*, January 6. Investigative Fund of the Nation Institute.
Sipsey Street Irregulars. 2009. "What Is a 'Three Percenter?'" http://sipseystreetirregulars.blogspot.com/2009/02/what-is-three-percenter.html.
Snyder, Timothy. 2017a. *On Tyranny: Twenty Lessons from the Twentieth Century*. Booklet.
Snyder, Timothy. 2017b. "Timothy Snyder Speaks, Episode 4: Sadopopulism." https://www.youtube.com/watch?v=oOjJtEkKMX4/.
Snyder, Timothy. 2018. *The Road to Unfreedom: Russia, Ukraine, Europe*. New York: Crown. See video lecture at https://www.youtube.com/watch?v=oOjJtEkKMX4.
Southern Poverty Law Center. 2001. "The rise and decline of the 'Patriots.'" *Intelligence Report*. Summer. 6–8. https://web.archive.org/web/20040307042459/http://www.splcenter.org/intel/intelreport/article.jsp?pid=355.
Southern Poverty Law Center. n.d. Sovereign Citizens Movement. https://www.splcenter.org/fighting-hate/extremist-files/ideology/sovereign-citizens-.
Stern, Kenneth S. 1996. *A Force upon the Plain: The American Militia Movement and the Politics of Hate*. New York: Simon & Schuster.
Stock, Catherine McNicol. 1996. *Rural Radicals: Righteous Rage in the American Grain*. Ithaca, NY: Cornell University Press.
Sunshine, Spencer, with Jessica Campbell and Daniel HoSang, Steven Besa, and Chip Berlet. 2016. *Up in Arms: A Guide to Oregon's Patriot Movement*, Scappoose, OR and Boston, MA: Rural Organizing Project and Political Research Associates. http://www.politicalresearch.org/up-in-arms.
Sunshine, Spencer. 2017a. "The Growing Alliance between Neo-Nazis, Right Wing Paramilitaries and Trumpist Republicans." *Colorlines*. June 9. https://www.colorlines.com/articles/growing-alliance-between-neo-nazis-right-wing-paramilitaries-and-trumpist-republicans.

Sunshine, Spencer. 2017b. "Peas in an Oregon pod: Right-Wing paramilitaries and the GOP." Political Research Associates. July 7. http://www.politicalresearch.org/2017/07/07/peas-in-an-oregon-pod-right-wing-paramilitaries-the-gop.

Swearingen, Marshall, Kate Schimel, and Tay Wiles. 2018. "Timeline: A Brief History of the Sagebrush Rebellion: An Interactive, Year-By-Year Look at the Current Insurgency." January 17. https://www.hcn.org/articles/a-history-of-the-sagebrush-rebellion.

Tabor, James D., and Eugene V. Gallagher. 1995. *Why Waco? Cults and the Battle for Religious Freedom in America*. Berkeley: University of California Press.

Taras, Ray. 2009. *Europe Old and New: Transnationalism, Belonging, Xenophobia*. Lanham, MD: Rowman & Littlefield.

Taras, Ray. 2012. *Xenophobia and Islamophobia in Europe*. Edinburgh: Edinburgh University Press.

Taylor, Chris. 2017. "Big Coal Burns Bright at ALEC Conference." Center for Media and Democracy. http://www.exposedbycmd.org/2017/07/20/big-coal-burns-bright-alec-conference.

Thompson, Jonathan. 2016. "The Rise of the Sagebrush Sheriffs." *High Country News*, February 2. www.hcn.org/issues/48.2/the-rise-of-the-sagebrush-sheriffs.

Tolson, Jay. 2008a. "The Role of Religion in This Year's Election." *US News and World Report*. June 24. https://www.usnews.com/news/campaign-2008/articles/2008/06/24/the-role-of-religion-in-this-years-election.

Tolson, Jay. 2008b. "The Evangelical Vote: How Big Is It Really?' *US News and World Report*. September 24. https://www.usnews.com/news/campaign-2008/articles/2008/09/24/the-evangelical-vote-how-big-is-it-really.

Valverde, Miriam. 2017. "Were Militia Groups in Charlottesville Better Equipped than Virginia State Police?" *PolitiFact*, 18 August. https://www.politifact.com/truth-o-meter/article/2017/aug/18/virginia-governors-claim-about-militia-weapons-and/.

Vanderboegh, Mike. 2009. "What is a 'Three Percenter'?" February 17. http://sipseystreetirregulars.blogspot.com/2009/02/what-is-three-percenter.html.

Van Dyke, Nella, and Sarah A. Soule. 2002. "Structural Social Change and the Mobilizing Effect of Threat: Explaining Levels of Patriot and Militia Organizing in the United States." *Social Problems* 49 (4): 497–520.

Voegelin, Eric. 1952. *The New Science of Politics*. University of Chicago Press.

Wade, Wyn Craig. 1987. *The Fiery Cross: The Ku Klux Klan in America*. New York: Simon and Schuster.

Wilson, Angelia R. 1996. *Below the Belt: Religion, Sexuality and Politics in the Rural South*. England: Cassell.

Wilson, Angelia R. 2013. "The Southern Strategies: Preaching, Prejudice and Power." *American Review of Politics*.

Wilson, Angelia R., and Cynthia Burack. 2012. "'Where Liberty Reigns and God is Supreme': The Christian Right and the Tea Party Movement." *New Political Science* 34 (2): 72–190.

Wilson, Jason. 2017. "Portland Republican Says Party Should Use Militia Groups after Racial Attack." *Guardian*. May 29. https://www.theguardian.com/us-news/2017/may/29/portland-attack-republican-james-buchal-militia-groups.

Wise Use Resource Collection. 2018. Political Research Associates. http://www.politicalresearch.org/tag/wise-use.

Wodak, Ruth. 2015. *The Politics of Fear: What Right-Wing Populist Discourses Mean*. Los Angeles: SAGE.

Worsley, Peter. 1968. *The Trumpet Shall Sound: A Study of 'Cargo' Cults in Melanesia*. 2nd, augmented, ed. New York: Schocken Books.

Young-Bruehl, Elisabeth. 1996. *The Anatomy of Prejudices*. Cambridge, MA: Harvard University Press.

Zaitchik, Alexander. 2010. *Common Nonsense: Glenn Beck and the Triumph of Ignorance*. Hoboken, NJ: Wiley.

Zeskind, Leonard. 2009. *Blood and Politics: The History of the White Nationalist Movement from the Margins to the Mainstream*. New York: Farrar, Straus & Giroux.

⨁ OPEN ACCESS

Neoliberal developmentalism, authoritarian populism, and extractivism in the countryside: the Soma mining disaster in Turkey

Fikret Adaman, Murat Arsel and Bengi Akbulut

ABSTRACT
While state-society relations in Turkey have historically been top-down and *coups d'état* periodically interrupted democratic politics, the recent authoritarian turn under Erdoğan is remarkable. Two dynamics are especially salient. First, Erdoğan and his AKP have been particularly effective in deepening the neoliberalisation of economy and society. Their policies have created a new form of neoliberal developmentalism, where solutions to all social ills have come to be seen as possible through rapid economic growth. Second, they have intensified the transformation of the countryside, where new forms of dispossession and deagrarianisation open the way to an unprecedented extractivist drive. Together, neoliberal developmentalism and extractivism have resulted in growing social dissent. The eruption of anger after the Soma coal mining disaster that killed 301 miners is one such case. The paper shows how Erdoğan and the AKP use populist tactics (ranging from an uptick in nationalist discourse to the provision of 'coal aid' in winter) to assuage their critics. Where these prove inadequate, an increasingly violent crackdown on social dissent is being deployed in the name of peace and order as the country remains in a state of emergency since the attempted coup of July 2016.

1. Introduction

Three hundred and one men perished in the worst mining disaster in Turkish history at the Soma underground coal mine on 13 May 2014. Rushing to the area to supervise the rescue efforts and to comfort the devastated community, the then Prime Minister Erdoğan adopted a tone that was marked by its combination of defiance and fatalism. In response

---

This is an Open Access article distributed under the terms of the Creative Commons Attribution-NonCommercial-NoDerivatives License (http://creativecommons.org/licenses/by-nc-nd/4.0/), which permits non-commercial re-use, distribution, and reproduction in any medium, provided the original work is properly cited, and is not altered, transformed, or built upon in any way.

DOI: 10.4324/9781003162353-7

to a question regarding which authorities should be seen as responsible for such a tragic loss of life, he began by reading from a list of mining disasters around the world, quoting death tolls recorded mainly in mid-19th and early-twentieth century England as well as a few major episodes from the 1950s and 1960s in China and Japan. He then employed the relatively obscure Islamic term *fitrat*[1], which has since become a colloquialism to ridicule his haplessness in the face of this tragedy to chide the journalists for not recognizing that large scale deaths are an inherent and inevitable aspect of coal mining.

Failed to be assuaged by these words, the residents of the town of Soma fiercely protested Erdoğan and his large entourage (as others coming to join the protests from the region were blocked by security from entering the town) and the Prime Minister was forced to take refuge in a shop in order to escape the angry townspeople. Adding to the state's tone-deaf reaction, one of Erdoğan's aides was photographed literally kicking a man that was knocked down by security forces who were charging the demonstrators with their batons. Even though the people of Soma had voted for Erdoğan's Justice and Development Party (the AKP in its Turkish acronym) at a rate that exceeded the national average, the town then turned against Erdoğan and his government as the disaster was not seen as a mere accident, let alone one that was inherent to the business of coal mining. Wasn't it true that a local MP (from the main opposition party) had called for an investigation into safety concerns at the Soma mining site just two weeks prior the tragedy – only to be rejected by the AKP? Wasn't it true that the heat in the galleries had increased to alarming levels before the accident, yet activities were allowed to continue? Wasn't it true that the rescue operation was poorly executed due to lack of preparation? Wasn't it true that the private company running the site had been one of the *enfants bien-aimés* of the AKP?[2] Finally, although not explicitly mentioned, wasn't it also true that the locals were forced to switch from an agrarian lifestyle to mining after a series of policies that had all but destroyed the viability of peasant agriculture in the area?

Taken together, these rhetorical questions point towards the inconvenient truth that the Soma disaster was a long time coming. Ersoy (2017) is therefore correct when he describes the tragedy with reference to Gabriel García Márquez's famous (1981) novel *Chronicle of a Death Foretold*, where a homicide that will take place in a small town is already known by all residents but no one dares to do anything to prevent it.[3] Similarly, while living with the knowledge that a major disaster was in the making, thousands of men every day went down to the mines and most of the ones that survived continue to do so today. The first goal of this paper is therefore to provide an explanation for this choice within the context of Erdoğan's authoritarian populism, one that builds on structural dynamics of the political economy of development in Turkey.

Another inconvenient truth is that the fury of the Soma community in the days following the disaster did not translate into a lasting political movement or even a sustained electoral 'punishment' of Erdoğan. In fact, the protests gradually faded and the people of Soma supported Erdoğan and his AKP anew in numbers that once again outstripped

---

[1] Originally an Arabic word that does not have an exact equivalent in English, *fitrat* denotes the inherent nature of a person or a thing.
[2] This line of accusations has led many to coin the term "murder" for the incident (see, e.g., Williams 2014; Bracke 2016), as opposed to the term "accident" that the government and the pro-government media have opted for. In this article the terms "disaster" and "tragedy" have been used interchangeably in the interest of using less loaded terminology.
[3] This vision is shared by many reports written on the disaster: Türkiye Barolar Birliği (2014); Türk Sosyal Bilimler Derneği Çalışma Grubu (2016); Boğaziçi Üniversitesi Soma Araştırma Grubu (2017).

the national average in the 2017 referendum on constitutional changes to strengthen the powers of the presidency.[4] The second goal of the paper is therefore to account for the acquiescence of the Soma community with Erdoğan's rule in the aftermath of the mining disaster or, in other words, to demonstrate how authoritarian populism can continue to generate a semblance of societal legitimacy.

In tackling these two questions, our goal is 'to understand, but not judge' (Scoones et al. 2018, 3) the decisions and actions of the Soma community as part of a structural framework. Our proceeding analysis locates the genesis of the Soma disaster and its surprising denouement within three interrelated dynamics: the rise of authoritarian populism, neoliberal developmentalism, and extractivism. They have not only been ascendant around the world in recent years but have effectively defied a left-right divide by manifesting themselves in diverse political economic settings. Their co-emergence can be located at the intersection of neoliberal capitalism's crises of accumulation – which became all too evident at the time of the Great Recession – and inequality. These global crises have had pronounced – and differentiated – national effects, often leading to another crisis for national states, that of legitimacy. Extractivism and authoritarian populism, which have emerged as parts of attempts to shore up waning legitimacy, are essentially the different sides of the same coin. Where possible, charismatic leaders have sought to pump some dynamism into faltering economies by intensifying extractivist processes. As and when further extraction has failed to deliver or, as in the case of Soma, exacerbated other existing issues, they have turned to authoritarianism. In that sense, both extractivism and authoritarian populism are best seen not as exceptions to neoliberal developmentalism but as contemporary features.

The paper develops this argument further by exploring the two questions above within the context of Soma. In response to its first question regarding why workers sought jobs and continued to work in a highly risky mine, the paper explores the impacts of neoliberal developmentalism on the agricultural sector in Turkey to argue that peasants from the Soma region were pushed out of their agrarian livelihoods. The specific manifestation of neoliberal development in its overwhelming focus on extraction and construction, both of which are linked to the energy sector, formed the pull factors that drew (semi)proletarianized workers into the Soma mine. The paper also argues that the lax standards regarding workplace safety and the informalization of the labour force which further coerced them into working in unsafe conditions were structural features of the coal mining sector which prioritized increased production over all other concerns. All in all, peasants-turned-miners in the Soma region did not have much to rely on to counter neoliberal policies that have been transforming their rural lives and offering them jobs in the extractives sector. Put simply, despite appearing to choose to work in an evidently dangerous workplace, it is more appropriate to argue that long-term economic policies compelled them to become miners. It is this absence of a real alternative that also partly explains why the post-disaster scenario failed to exact a price on Erdoğan or his AKP. To the extent that there was an initial burst of political possibility, this was extinguished by

---

[4]The results are particularly significant since the referendum was widely interpreted as a test of Erdoğan's popularity in a particularly turbulent moment in Turkey, marked not simply by an attempted *coup d'état* in July 2016 but also the oppressive crackdown against all forms of political dissent that varnished his authoritarian credentials.

a combination of authoritarian actions (e.g. tear gassing of demonstrators) and populist moves (e.g. paying out exceptionally large compensation to families of the victims of this specific disaster even when thousands of others go unnoticed). Our understanding of these dynamics in the context of Soma are relevant for contemporary Turkish politics not because Soma was an exception but because its experience is increasingly normalized in various ways across the country.

While our aim in tackling these questions is not operationalising a Gramscian theoretical framework *per se*, we ground our understanding of legitimacy and its distinction from authoritarian populism firmly within it. Following his famous formulation of hegemony as 'consent backed by coercion', the Gramscian literature emphasizes the role of active consent and legitimacy for the state's claim to govern, which the ruling groups seek to acquire through a combination of material and ideological practices of intellectual, moral, and political leadership as well as persuasion (Gramsci 1971). Hegemony is thus differentiated from domination, yet it is never absolute and always prone to crises. The hegemonic function of the state breaks down when dominant groups fail to establish effective moral-ideological leadership and active consent (Gramsci 1971; see also Poulantzas 1978). Gramscian scholars discuss the breakdown of the state's hegemonic function especially within the context of transition to exceptional state forms. Most notably Poulantzas (1978) elaborates on state forms that emerge when societal consent cannot be established via organic links between the state and the society, and a repressive state apparatus, increased bureaucratization, and a heavier reliance on material concessions to subordinate classes are substituted in their place.

Following this literature, we use the concept of authoritarian populism to demarcate its difference from a hegemonic project which is based on the acquisition of active consent, and to highlight that it implies the breakdown of a claim to rule backed by societal legitimacy. While heightened use of authoritarian measures signifies reliance on coercion (rather than consent) to maintain the state rule, populist policies represent heavier dependence on the distribution of material concessions to secure support. Extractivism, on the other hand, serves as the supposed vehicle of economic growth, which becomes a pressing political objective within this context as it enables the distribution of (populist) material concessions. Extractivism and authoritarian populism thus emerge as parts of attempts to shore up waning legitimacy, as we claim above. Perhaps more importantly, the Gramscian framework illuminates a vast 'grey' area between a successful hegemonic project based on societal legitimacy and an open contestation of state rule. That state rule can still be maintained by a heavier reliance on a repressive state apparatus and/or material concessions attests to this. In other words, the absence of visible social opposition cannot be taken as evidence of societal legitimacy, but rather likely to represent some mix of less visible forms of contestation and acquiescence. Within the context of Soma, the dynamics that have displaced peasants from agriculture into mining (the 'push' and 'pull' factors we refer below) are critical in accounting for the acquiescence that fills that grey area.

In the next section, we characterize the broad contours of the contemporary global moment that led to the emergence of authoritarian populism, also discussing some of their specificities in the Turkish context. This is followed by a narrative of 'push' and 'pull' factors that resulted in peasants from the region becoming miners and the ways in which a lax safety system was allowed to persist even when disaster was clearly in the making. The penultimate section discusses the underlying reasons as to how Erdoğan's authoritarian populism 'works'. The concluding section argues that, within the context of Turkey, authoritarian developmentalism is itself animated and sustained by the country's long-established economic growth fetish, which has its roots deep into Turkey's post-Ottoman transition process and which the AKP has been particularly adept at weaponizing to sustain its rule.

2. Authoritarianism, neoliberal developmentalism, and extractivism

The tragedy of Soma was shaped at the confluence of three related dynamics, namely the rise of authoritarian populism, extractivism, and neoliberal developmentalism. The global (re)emergence of authoritarian populism is surprising because the post-1989 world was meant to be showcasing the triumph of neoliberal ideology not just in economics but also through the spread of electoral democracy. While elections as a mechanism have proven durable, they have recently delivered a surprising cast of charismatic but authoritarian leaders that include Erdoğan, Modi, and Trump. Coming to the power on similarly demagogic platforms that made reference to past national glories and the promise to return to greatness, most of these leaders have made a rejuvenated state a key ambition. The resulting political reality however is far from a 'democratic' state as these leaders have been equating any criticism of their political performance to the subversion of state power, enacting heavy-handed policies aimed to stifle political dissent and press freedom.

The rise of authoritarian populism around the world defies easy classification across the left-right spectrum, demonstrated by the rise of Rafael Correa and Evo Morales in Latin America as part of the 'left turn' that promised to construct the 'Socialism of the twenty-first century' (Arsel, Hogenboom, and Pellegrini 2016) as well as the rise of Narendra Modi in India who effectively used demagogic nostalgia to sell a vision of a resurgent Indian superpower (Ravindran and Hale 2017). The examples of countries experiencing a combination of authoritarianism and populism in different guises go beyond these and certainly include the Phillippines (Thompson 2016), Hungary (Buzogány 2017), and the United States (Koch 2017), among others. It is important in this context not to use the term authoritarian populism mechanistically, without paying due attention to historic processes setting the stage for these leaders to emerge. For instance, Rafael Correa's rise to authoritarianism came after a particularly pronounced period of political instability where a decade saw seven different presidents. Evo Morales' election was a watershed in the Bolivian history as he became the first indigenous president in a country whose majority indigenous population had been governed by those who were not only not indigenous themselves but often showed active disdain towards them (Schilling-Vacaflor and Eichler 2017). Thus, it is necessary to take a more historicized approach that recognizes how unique circumstances contributed to the emergence of these leaders so as to avoid both the analytical pitfall of using the concept of populism simplistically as a pejorative and the political trap of resigning to the continued abuses of power by these leaders because they position themselves as a defence against an *ancien régime* that lacked legitimacy for other reasons.

In fact, the rise of authoritarian populism on both the left and the right of the political spectrum has been in response to the crises of neoliberalism, which have manifested themselves in faltering accumulation and growing socio-economic inequality. The dominant economic model for the spate of populist leaders that came – and continue to come – to power have been extractivism (and, in many cases, a renewed focus on infrastructure construction), which can create the illusion of dynamic economic growth. The resources in question are different in various contexts. From oil to minerals to the 'agro-extractivism', a new regime of accumulation where novel alliances between state and corporate actors (some of which are state-owned themselves) have intensified the speed and expanded the reach of commodity extraction. This made it possible for these administrations to boost economic growth rates and, to a certain extent, create employment opportunities for the segments of society that have been disfavoured by neoliberalism as well as populist distribution of material concessions to them as mechanisms to garner political support substituting for active consent. While even left-leaning proponents of this extractivist approach shied away from effective wealth redistribution to address societal inequality, extractivism has made it possible for them to achieve a degree of redistributive economic growth. Put differently, the type of policies enabled by extractivism are populist mainly because they do not aim at genuine socio-economic transformation.

It is important to note in this regard that the unsustainability of extractivism has been challenged forcefully by authoritarian populist leaders. This has been done either by reference to the alleged superiority of the commodity that is being extracted – e.g. agro-extraction of biofuel as a substitute to fossil fuels or mining of copper for use in putatively sustainable electric cars – or in the name of the authoritarian leader who claims for himself green credentials, such as Erdoğan himself who argued that he – not the activists in the now famous Gezi Park uprising – is the 'true environmentalist' (Arsel, Adaman, and Akbulut 2017). Nevertheless, in the face of sustained criticism of extractivist practices both left- and right-leaning authoritarian populist leaders have not shied away from targeting activists and generally creating an unsafe environment for them, as manifested by the increases in the incarceration and assassination of activists in recent years. As discussed below, authoritarianism of course goes beyond direct and physical coercion and can characterize state-society relationships overall.

Neither the involvement of the state in extractivism nor its populist guise has meant, however, that neoliberalism has been side-lined. Rather, assuming a more 'developmentalist' outlook – for instance, Trump's allusions to the US becoming a 'Third World' country – neoliberalism's appeal to the supremacy of the logic of economistic calculations gets extended to the national level through arguments that all manners of social ills can be addressed only through rapid economic development (Madra and Adaman 2018). As such, neoliberal developmentalism makes use of state power in its various guises – from planning to cronyism to outright corruption – to achieve and sustain continued economic growth at all costs, including the sacrifice of ecological integrity, erosion of democratic norms, and oppression of societal resistance (Harvey 2005; Klein 2008).[5]

---

[5]We define neoliberalism as a drive towards *depoliticization* of the social and political realm through its *economization* (Madra and Adaman 2014, 2018). By assuming that human beings comprehend and affirmatively respond to economic incentives, neoliberalism is understood as aiming to solve all social and political problems by creating appropriate economic incentives. Once human behavior is conceptualized as a form of cost-benefit calculus, neoliberalism can accommodate a range of theoretical and political positions with diverse policy implications, including those that can be identified as state interventionism. Within this general framework, neoliberalism has historically always promoted growth as an essential element to "all our social and political ends" (Rodrik 2017).

Erdoğan's ascent and persistent hold on power epitomize the ways in which authoritarian populism, extractivism, and neoliberal developmentalism come together. The rise of his AKP (in 2002) was rightly celebrated as part of the normalization of the country, which had not only suffered periodic *coups d'état* but also witnessed the forceful suppression of public piety in the name of secularism. The latter was indeed one of the founding principles of the state, whose founders – chiefly among them Mustafa Kemal who later took the surname of Atatürk, the father of Turks – had diagnosed the slow decline and demise of the Ottoman Empire as a function of Islam's purported resistance to science and technology in particular and Western modernity in general. Secularism was therefore not only a political posture; it was also seen as a prerequisite to national economic development, which would only be possible if the model of the advanced industrial West could be emulated without interference from (putatively backward) Islamic values. That the AKP, formed mainly by political outsiders coming from 'traditional' quarters of the other country who had been at the receiving end of 'civilizational' policies of the modernization drive of the state, overcame various attempts of the country's twin centres of power, the civilian bureaucracy, and military chiefs, to win elections repeatedly and comfortably did therefore signal a sea change in Turkish politics (Özden 2014; Özden, Akça, and Berkmen 2014; Özselçuk 2015; Özden, Bekmen, and Akça 2018).

The AKP did also bring with it a series of political liberalization measures. Most symbolically, in a context where there remained a constitutional ban on 'traditional' headgear, which prevented women from the wearing of the *türban* (headscarf), pious women had been kept out of university education and right of public sector employment as teachers, doctors or lawyers. The repeal of such restrictions were therefore signs of much needed progress in terms of civil rights. Not all such instances of liberalization under Erdoğan's rule have been maintained, and there have been dramatic reversals in political and civil liberties especially since the attempted *coup d'état* of July 2016. For instance, the steps taken towards recognizing the rights of the Kurdish community have unfortunately proven to be short-lived and have since been replaced with a new and even more draconian regime of oppression. In a related vein, hundreds of thousands of public sector employees including academics have been sacked without due process, thousands have been locked up with spurious charges in a crackdown on dissent that put journalists, intellectuals, and non-governmental organization activists behind bars without recourse to meaningful judicial remedies. Nevertheless, the AKP and Erdoğan were able to secure surprisingly persistent credibility with certain segments of the society, tempering their authoritarianism with populism.

While the populism – economic as well as otherwise – of the AKP was always part of its appeal, its authoritarianism was neither predestined nor inevitable. The main mechanism for the AKP to garner and maintain legitimacy has been through its economic policies which, as the story of the Soma mine will demonstrate in more detail, simultaneously created precarity and offered its (temporary) solution. The AKP had come to power at the height of a political crisis that bankrupted the credibility of the existing political parties that had failed to chart a stable path from the country's long-standing patrimonial state tradition (where social ills would ultimately be the responsibility of the *devlet baba* [father state]) towards the laissez-faire system of neoliberalism. The main rupture that came with the AKP was its ability to 'successfully' implement the neoliberalizing policies Turkey had for twenty years attempted to implement.

These policies not only further marginalized a wide array of communities – the peasants, the elderly, the unemployed, etc. – by undermining their ability to gain a foothold in the new economy, they also punched holes through the already meagre safety nets that existed. Instead, the AKP was able to offer a booming economy[6] in which jobs in construction, extraction, and the informal sector were widely available. These jobs – and the infrastructural improvements they brought – combined with the overturning of decades old restrictions on religious practices formed the basis of the AKP's populism. This was buttressed with a strategy of redistributing the benefits of the economic boom whose long term sustainability is very much questioned (Adaman et al. 2014) mainly through social assistance, which, together with the promise of employment, made up the material backbone of the AKP's populism (Sayarı 2011; Bozkurt 2013). In Gramscian terms, these practices represented mechanisms of establishing consent via distribution of material concessions to subordinate classes, on which the AKP came to rely more heavily on as its hegemonic project increasingly ran into crises.

However, the 2008 financial crisis and related disillusionment with the country's prospects of EU membership made it much harder to keep this precarious system going. Not only the global economy was no longer favourable to the type of investment boom required for the continuation of extraction and construction, societal dissent in the face of environmental and social costs of the AKP's economic model[7] also began to mount. The authoritarian and centralizing turn of the AKP emerged in response. The primary target of the AKP's authoritarianism and populism often overlapped in those segments that had been suffering the negative impacts of neoliberal policies all along, which may seem ironic at first sight but is fully consistent with the Gramscian policy tools of consent and coercion.[8]

3. Chronicle of a tragedy foretold

The fatal tragedy at Soma occurred when a fire spread in the galleries after a wall collapsed and exposed self-burning coal, producing a lot of heat and fumes that trapped hundreds of miners inside the mine. Almost all the miners and engineers working in the mine were aware of the presence of self-burning coal. The temperature in the galleries had already increased drastically, warning systems indicated carbon monoxide (CO) and carbon dioxide (CO_2) levels above the standard levels in the days before the tragedy, but no serious measures were taken to mitigate the situation.

> A month or so before the accident the temperature in the tunnels started to rise steadily. We were sweating like hell. Then, a continuous headache and an upset stomach ... When I went to the doctor, he gave me a painkiller ... and no further inquiry. At the end, the coal we extracted turned out to be warm, even hot, indicating that there must be a fire somewhere ... But they

---

[6]Akbulut and Adaman (2013) provides an account of the consent-building trajectory of Erdoğan through growth; see also Arsel (2005) for a similar perspective.
[7]The title of Yeşilyurt-Gündüz's (2015) article in *Monthly Review* speaks for itself: "The 'New Turkey': Fetishizing Growth with Fatal Results"; see also Adaman and Arsel (2005, 2010, 2013).
[8]See *Neoliberal Turkey and its Discontents: Economic Policy and the Environment under Erdoğan* (Adaman, Akbulut and Arsel 2017), which discusses how the AKP's policies have had a detrimental impact on the environment, sustainability, and the long-term health of the Turkish economy, arguing that environmental conflicts in Turkey are not merely about the environment but intersect with contemporary politics of religion, ethnicity, gender, and class within the context of top-down, modernising economic development.

said 'keep extracting', and that is what we did. (32-year-old miner with an experience of 9 years; interviewed 11 July 2014)

When the fire and the fumes began to spread, and thus the gravity of the situation was realised, an immense rescue operation was organised. However, a number of factors made these efforts ineffective:[9] lack of proper air circulation, increased number of miners working in each shift beyond the mine's capacity, lack of safe rooms for miners to take refuge in during emergencies, and improper guidelines for mine evacuation in case of an emergency. It was in such a setting that the disaster unfolded, made all the more tragic by the fact that the mining site had already passed all government inspections.

This section chronicles the steps towards the tragedy, explaining the decision of mining workers through factors that pushed them out of their fields and pulled them into the mines, which account in significant part for the acquiescence that marked the aftermath of the disaster. These push and pull factors were a direct result of the AKP's economic policies that were built around extraction, construction, and populism. They were also directly responsible for the unsafe work environment that prevailed in the Soma mine.

3.1. The push factor

When the Turkish Republic was formed in 1923 over the remnants of the Ottoman Empire, it was mainly an agrarian country with more than three quarters of the population residing in rural areas (and the share of the agricultural sector in the total employment was even higher). Despite the late-blooming of Turkish industrialisation and the accompanying urbanisation circa the 1950s that started to reduce the importance of the countryside, the development of agriculture continued to be seen until 1980 as the main precondition of the country's overall development. The function of the rural sector was seen instrumentally as a supplier of ingredients to mainly the food-processing industry as well as a food provider to urban centres. Thus, the agricultural sector continued to be heavily subsidised during this time (through *inter alia* cheap credits for mechanisation, support price policies, subsidies for agricultural inputs, and above all a protectionist trade regime), enabling farmers to enjoy considerable immunity to fluctuations in the market. Consequently, erosion of peasant practices and the hegemony of market rationality in agriculture were not so significant in this era (Keyder and Yenal 2011). However, with Turkey's shift to neo-liberal policies (the starting date is usually taken as January 1980 – see, e.g. Öniş and Şenses 2009), the role of rural players started to weaken, the influence of international players such as the IMF and the World Bank began to grow stronger, and a market ideology (whose main manifestation was in the removal of agricultural subsidies) was promoted as the only path to enhancing efficiency.

Although liberalisation policies in the agricultural sector began to be implemented initially back in 1994, they truly kicked off with the so-called 'Agricultural Reform Implementation Project (ARIP)' in 2001. ARIP, a World Bank initiative, aimed at 'reducing subsidies, substituting a support system for agricultural producers, and agro-industries, with incentives to increase productivity, responsive to real comparative advantages'

---

[9]For a thorough analysis of the emergency and disaster management for the Soma case, see Demiroz and Kapucu (2016).

(World Bank n.d.). Its main component targeted the subsidised crop pricing mechanism (together with a set of institutions that were charged with specific functions, e.g. state-owned purchasing cooperatives) which was seen as a severe deviation from the logic of the market mechanism and whose elimination would more or less automatically result in enhanced efficiency. ARIP in their stead suggested implementing a direct income support system to financially help the countryside (for an eight-year period).[10] Although the subsidised pricing system was open to a patron-client type of relationship[11], the suggested system opened the way for big corporations, domestic and international, to enter the sector and establish a near monopsony in some crops and localities. With regard to direct income support, the system was based to compute the level of the support exclusively as a function of land size, which by and large ended up in making the poor poorer and the rich richer (see, e.g. Akder 2010).

Thus, with the ending of the national developmentalist era that heavily supported the agricultural sector and farmers, through successive waves of 'structural' reforms and measures, with ARIP having given the *coup de grace*, the social and economic transformation of the rural sector became visible. With a diminished price support system, repealed subsidies and lessened credit opportunities, farmers by and large were left to confront the market forces (national as well as international – see Aydın 2010), which brought about important implications for not only farmers' living and production conditions but population dynamics as well (Keyder and Yenal 2010, 2011, 2013; see also Aydın 2010; İlkkaracan and Tunalı 2010).

The villages of Soma (and those of Akhisar, a neighbouring town) were historically known as agricultural sites and the dynamics described above played out much the same way there as well. The main crop of the region had been tobacco; its production began to decrease quite drastically, first with the liberalisation policies, and then with ARIP. Production levels in Soma dropped drastically from around 2,500 to 500 tons per year from the 2000s till the year of the tragedy (see Figure 1). In the neighbouring town of Akhisar, production levels fell from 12,000 to around 3,500 tons in the same time period. These sharp declines also reflected the situation across the country: a decrease from 290,000 to 62,000 tons (Institute of Statistics of Turkey).

Former tobacco producers in the villages around Soma mostly shifted to olive production (see Figure 2) as the area and the infrastructure did not provide many options. But olive production was not sufficient to lift their income to satisfactory levels; and since olive production is much less labour-intensive than tobacco production, many people – especially the young men from around Soma – had little choice but to look for jobs in the town or city centres, totally or partially disengaged from agricultural production. In short, the policies implemented after 1994 resulted in de-peasantisation in Soma, which accounts for the push of the peasants into wage labour.

---

[10]The ARIP project has been subject to inquiry in the academic circles. Çakmak (2004) provides an early assessment; Akder (2010) focuses on its overall evaluation; Keyman (2010) contextualises the Project within a larger state-society relationship; Çakmak and Dudu (2010) discusses the sectoral and micro implications; İlkkaracan and Tunalı (2010) considers the rural labour market in the post-ARIP era; Çalışkan and Adaman (2010) deciphers the logic of neoliberal agricultural reform initiatives in general.
[11]Such relations did lead to some perverse outcomes, such as the cases in which purchase of low quality tobacco and nuts that could only be disposed of by burning. These occasions were covered by the media as signs of corruption in the state sector.

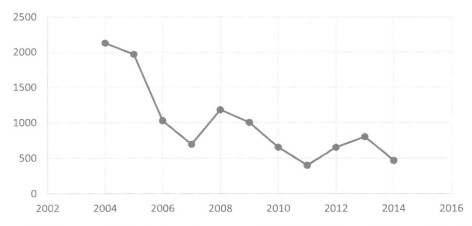

Figure 1. Tobacco production in Soma (tons per year) 2004–2014. Source: Institute of Statistics of Turkey.

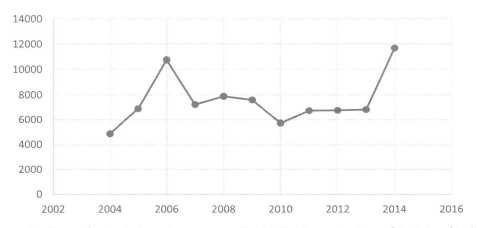

Figure 2. Olive production in Soma (tons per year) 2004–2014. Source: Institute of Statistics of Turkey.

3.2. The pull factor

With the advent of the Erdoğan era, energy was declared as one of the main industries the country should target. One of the critical objectives set out in *The Tenth Development Plan* that covers the 2014–2018 period is to increase the installed capacity of electricity power plants by 35 percent from 58,000 MW to 78,000 MW in five years – a rather challenging task (Ministry of Development n.d.).[12] Despite the country's vast potential for sustainable sources (e.g. wind, solar) and energy gains through efficiency enhancement, Erdoğan has a continued appetite for coal-fuelled thermal plants due to vast domestic coal reserves and thermal plants' relatively cheap technology – if externalities created mainly in the form of green-gas emissions are not taken into account. Approximately one-third of the electricity

---

[12]Erdoğan's words, said almost four years before the disaster, are to be noted: "The more a country consumes electricity the stronger it is, the faster it advances in the path of development. It means that the wheels in the factories are turning, that production in our enterprises is on the rise, that household consumption is increasing, that technology use is spreading in the entire country" (Erdoğan: Akarsular satılmıyor 2010). See also Akbulut and Adaman (2013).

generated has lately been produced at coal-fuelled thermal power plants in the country, and the AKP has been determined to rely on this trajectory. It should not come as a surprise, therefore, that roughly one year after the Soma tragedy, the Ministry of Energy and Natural Resources 'proudly' announced that Turkey would quadruple its coal-fuelled power plants by 2020 (Adaman and Arsel 2016).[13]

In addition to thermal power plants, coal has also been used by the industry and by households, where alternative energy sources (e.g. natural gas) are rather unaffordable. At this junction it is equally important to note that between 2003 and 2015, some 19.2 million tons of coal were distributed for free to 'families in need'. All combined, the total annual coal production has been fluctuating around 60 million tons in the past several years, the bulk of which was excavated from only a few coal mining sites (Soma being one of them). However, domestic production has been falling short in satisfying the total demand. Thus, an additional amount of coal, of around 30 million tons per year, has been imported – almost all of it being used in electricity production (imported coal in the last years corresponding to more than half of the coal used to this end). It requires simple mathematics to realise that this planned increase in coal-fuelled thermic plants will, *ceteris paribus*, further raise the already high levels of imported coal (not to mention the additional demand increase arising from the growing population and economy). And this is indeed where the problem is feared to occur. Increased import figures for coal are destined to jeopardise the already shaky position of the current account deficit.[14] It is worth remembering that *The Tenth Development Plan* also included another critical objective: 'To reduce the current account deficit to a reasonable permanent level'. The logical conclusion, therefore, was that domestic production should be increased, and this was certainly on the Erdoğan government's to-do list.

As in other areas (e.g. the construction sector, most notably housing and inter-city roads), the government invited the private sector to take on greater responsibility in coal production. There were already privately-owned mining sites, but these were rather small in size. The new vision was to keep state ownership intact and subcontract its operation to the private sector. This was based on the *redevance* mechanism, where the state would lease the mine to a private company with the guarantee to purchase the produced coal. Given this incentive scheme, private companies, including *Soma Kömür AŞ* that was operating the site where the tragedy occurred, opted for the obvious path of increasing production levels, mainly relying on labour-intensive techniques, without paying much attention to prevention, mitigation, and preparedness in case of a major mine incident.[15] The employment figure in the mining sector in the Soma region had therefore increased sharply in Soma, reaching the number of 15 thousand miners (see Figure 3; for a similar emphasis, see Çelik 2016). This was possible because the law entrusted the companies operating the mines the task of ensuring the

---

[13] It is worth noting that Erdoğan's appetite to increase the energy production at home has been behind the country's increased investment in energy production sources other than coal-fuelled thermal ones as well, including the nuclear one. The country's first nuclear power plant, at Akkuyu, commenced construction in April 2018; a Franco-Japanese consortium is to build the second one at Sinop – see Akbulut, Adaman, and Arsel (2017).
[14] Turkey's high current account deficit, largely attributed to structural factors, has been at the core of macroeconomic policy discussions in recent years; see Kara and Sarıkaya (2014).
[15] Those interviewed miners in the region by and large stated that, some variances notwithstanding, the supervisory role of the state has rather been poor in the mining area at large, hence not backing the claim that the regulation was softened solely in *Soma Kömür AŞ* due to alleged strong ties between Ankara and the company.

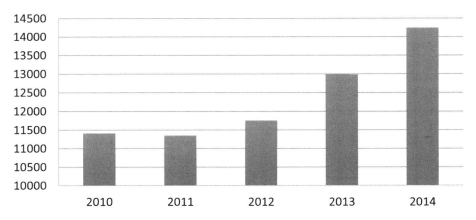

Figure 3. Number of miners in Soma 2010–2014. Source: Soma Municipality Strategic Plan.

implementation of appropriate safety measures, a task that was conveniently left unfilled in this case. That the company could get away with this choice was because the state by and large failed to duly perform its supervisory role. The rest is history; or, as was the case in Gabriel García Márquez's murder, the tragedy was already predestined.

Thousands of men were no longer able to make a living in the countryside and were thus looking for jobs that did not require much human capital, preferably in the formal sector and somewhere near their homes. For such opportunities, they were ready to shoulder considerable safety risks. The words of a 55-year-old farmer-turned into-a miner are representative of many more in the region:

> Before the 2000s, even though I already got a family with two kids, I was able to make my living through agriculture and animal husbandry. But then the state dropped its support, and that is when we found ourselves in hunger. I looked for jobs other than the mining one, as I knew it was risky. But I could not, as – at the age of forty – I had no knowledge other than agriculture and no degree other than the primary school one. I was hopeless. At the end I had to go to mining as it was offering job security. (interviewed 12 July 2014)

The mining sites in the Soma region were mainly operated by established private firms that offered formal contracts. Given the high prevalence of informality in the country (close to one out of three workers [see, e.g. Başlevent and Acar 2014]), that would be an important asset – for it meant job and income security, retirement rights, better health service, and possibility of credit and mortgage borrowing. These jobs did involve high risk and adverse working conditions; but given that the only other options were either unemployment (which does *not* come with unemployment salary/basic income) or working without security and insurance in the informal sector most likely far away from home, many chose to be miners. Some even opted to remain in their countryside houses, commuting to and from the mining site, but others preferred to move to the Soma town (which of course increased the cost of living [e.g. rents] but came with additional benefits [e.g. schooling opportunities for children]).

In other words, the choice was more than simply an economic one. Most young miners interviewed revealed that if a young man from the region did not have a formal job (and the mining industry was offering the bulk of these formal positions), he could not get the approval from the family of the woman he wanted to marry (given the existence of strong, hierarchical and patriarchal relations in the rural areas). The following quotation can be heard with slight variations from many miners in the region:

> Till I went to [serve the compulsory] military service at the age of 18, I was living with my parents in the village, earning our living through agriculture – we were poor but self-sufficient. When I got back [from the military service], I wanted to get married, at which point I realised that, with insufficient and volatile income flows coming from the village, I would have no chance to get my wish realised. And the mining sector was – and still is – the only option in the region. Thus that is what I did. It is vital for a family to have job security, pension scheme, health insurance, and the likes. You can also get loans easily. (27-year-old miner with an experience of six years in mining; interviewed 11 July 2014)

3.3. Work environment and social policies

The above two sections have argued that the de-peasantisation of Soma due to neoliberal economic policies created a workforce willing to take on the difficult job of working in coal mines and the drive to increase coal production made sure that there was an ample supply of jobs.[16] The pressure to produce ever more coal – from the intertwining needs of the state and the private sector – and the availability of cheap labour alone did not alone create the tragedy. For that an additional spark was needed, which came from Turkey's weak attention to working conditions and work safety, characterised by the preventable death of four workers on a daily basis (Sivil Sayfalar 2016). Within these grim conditions, the mining sector is considered to be one of the worst ones in that regard (Buğra 2017).

The mining sector, especially the Soma mining site, corresponds to a specific market form (oligopsony), where labour demand is small while the labour supply large, giving the few mining companies the power to adopt a hiring mechanism. That mechanism emerged as the so-called *dayıbaşı*[17] system, a kind of multi-layered subcontracting formation (Ercan and Oğuz 2015; Çelik 2016, 2017). *Dayıbaşı*, viz. the team leader, is a man trusted by the company, and experienced in mining. These men are well paid, with additional incentives connected to quantity produced. They are given the power to choose their own teams; and in most cases, they rely on their acquaintances, mostly locality-related. This mechanism created a kind of feudal relationship between them and young newcomers, who had not much of a say and could not voice their complaints. *Dayıbaşı* is given the incentive to push production and workload beyond safety limits, which would leave the team with little to question, let alone resist. A 25-year-old young miner's words resonate the fate of many other new starters into the sector:

> I managed to get the job [in the mining site] through a close friend of my uncle, with whom I also happen to be somehow familiar. He was acting as the team leader, and was like an older brother, even a father, for me. He taught me mining, what I should do and what I should not do. If he said 'keep working', even if I felt something hazardous, I would – with no question … When it [the tragedy] happened, I was on my leave; he and many colleagues of mine perished … Well, thinking retrospectively, I think he was taking too much of a risk. (interviewed 12 July 2014)

---

[16]This said, however, we openly acknowledge Arrighi's (1970) seminal point that neither the push factor should be read as a *total* de-ruralisation, nor the pull factor as a *full* proletarianisation; the relationship between agrarian transformation and labour supply (in industry and service sectors) may well not be a linear one.
[17]Literally, "head uncle".

Most young workers, while they felt the increasing danger, could not do much about it because their team leaders – whose authority was built on more than employment relationships – were asking them to ignore the signs.

It is worth recording that the very existence of an informal sector that pays little attention to work safety has been an important factor for the formal sector in relaxing their own safety standards. As in the case of 'bad money drives out good', low safety standards would become the norm, and the formal sector would resist demands to increase safety measures by threatening to switch to informality if pushed further. Meanwhile, state organs whose responsibility is to check and control working conditions would find themselves trapped as well: on the one hand, they have not much to say to the formal side as they are aware that there is little they can do concerning the standards in the informal; on the other hand, the hegemony to attain high growth figures at any cost have engulfed them as well.

The workers' union too had not much power and even less interest in raising safety concerns related to the mining site (Ercan and Oğuz 2015). At any rate, when the overall picture is considered, the power of labour unions had already been curtailed across most of the country following the shift to neoliberalism, which was initially implemented during the three years under a military regime following the 1980 *coup d'état* (Adaman, Buğra, and İnsel 2009; Çelik 2013). The final parameter that led to the tragedy was the position of mining engineers who were responsible for safety in the galleries. Mostly new graduates, these young people found themselves trapped in the system as well. Because they also had not much outside options (and were well paid, most with incentives related to the production level), they by and large accepted the terms of the company, viz. keeping silent on the likely consequences of the overload and lack of preventive measures. Be that as it may, those engineers who were near the collapsed wall seem to have rushed to the area so as to contain the fire rather than try to escape, but alas the fire proved to be uncontrollable.

4. Explaining the AKP's survival in Soma

The death of so many miners made Soma an especially visible manifestation of the conditions of contemporary Turkey, demonstrating the destructiveness of the confluence of extractivism, authoritarian populism, and neoliberal developmentalism. The aftermath of the tragedy itself is instructive since the AKP, after having been heavily criticised by the people of Soma, has managed to survive in the town. This is not to suggest that the disaster did not take at least a momentary toll on the popularity of the party. As Table 1 below shows, there was indeed a dip in the AKP's share of votes in both Soma and across the country in the general election of June 2015. While the underlying causes of this

Table 1. AKP's share of votes in Soma and nationally.

	Soma %	Turkey %
2007 General election	51.2	46.7
2011 General election	52.8	49.8
2015 June general election	39.9	40.8
2015 November general election	49.7	49.5
2017 Referendum	53.1	51.4

decline are complex and beyond the scope of this paper, it would not be far fetched to assume that the Soma disaster contributed to the AKP's national decline at that moment. However, the more significant outcome here is found in the fact that this is the only election out of five in the past 10 years when the AKP's performance in Soma is worse than its national percentage. Yet this relative decline is fairly meagre, staying within a few percentage points. More importantly, by November of the same year, the AKP was able to regroup not just nationally but in Soma as well.

The first relevant factor is the growing authoritarianism of the state under Erdoğan's presidency. Critical voices about the Soma disaster have been 'successfully' quashed at the national as well as local levels. Tellingly, many political rallies organized to protest the AKP's record relating to the Soma disaster ended up with the protestors getting tear gassed and dozens of them being arrested. For instance, 36 individuals were detained pre-emptively in the days following the disaster by the town police. Eight of these were lawyers who were suspected of having travelled to Soma to protest the situation. They were all treated harshly, receiving physical and verbal abuse, leading them to complain that they were detained in a sports complex like 'Victor Jara', who was imprisoned and murdered in a stadium during the Chilean *coup d'état* of 1973. Using the 'state of emergency' declared in the area as a legal cover, the police chief pronounced that 'provocative acts' would not be tolerated in such an 'anguished and sensitive period' ('OHAL ilan edilen Soma'da' 2014). This heavy-handed treatment of all dissent is of course not unique to the Soma case and has been on the increase since the AKP's rule took a turn towards authoritarianism. The state of emergency declared after the attempted *coup d'état* of 2016 has not only given the state even more power to silence dissent but has also opened up the possibility of overriding existing legal mechanisms (e.g. environmental impact assessments) that can be used to stop the implementation of new extraction or construction projects. The ongoing crackdown on civil and political rights has all but destroyed oppositional dynamics in contemporary Turkish politics, with countless cases of activists, campaigners, and 'ordinary citizens' feeling the brunt of unjustified and excessive state power.[18]

As mentioned earlier, the populism and the authoritarianism of the AKP often converge on the same segments of the society. To this end, a huge support campaign has been organised shortly after the mining disaster, led by the government as well as affiliated media and NGOs. Apart from the standard compensations given within the legislative structure to the families of those miners who lost their lives, the organised

---

[18] According to *World Justice Project (WJP) Rule of Law Index* (which measures countries' rule of law performance across eight factors: constraints on government powers, absence of corruption, open government, fundamental rights, order and security, regulatory enforcement, civil justice, and criminal justice) of 2017–2018, Turkey ranks as 101st out of 113 countries (World Justice Project 2017). A special mention has to be made, nevertheless, of the assault on the free press. Since the attempted *coup d'état* of July 2016, several newspapers and TV channels have been shut down with "decrees with the power of law" that are essentially dictates issued by Erdoğan and his inner circle (KHK in its Turkish acronym). Hundreds of journalists have been arrested and many have been sacked from their positions by newspaper owners worried about incurring Erdoğan's wrath. As many of Turkey's major news outlets are owned by industrialists do business either directly with the state or with Erdoğan's cronies in the economy, most have chosen the path of self-censoring and the others have been overtly or covertly threatened with tax audits and other possible means of retaliation and forced to moderate their criticisms. It is not surprising, therefore, that media coverage of the tragedy, Soma (especially the ongoing court against the responsible personnel of the mining company) in particular and the mining sector in general, as well as on other work-related losses, has been marginalised through time. Although in few places commemorations are being held at the anniversary days, the Soma tragedy is as of today by and large a *passé* event.

help amounted to two flats and 156,566 TL (approximately € 50,000) per family, job opportunities to one family member in the public sector, as well as scholarships for their children; following the tragedy and the call for support, in-kind goods (from food items to toys to clothes) were also poured into affected families. Furthermore, the Cabinet decreed that all debts of small businesspeople from the region to state-owned financial enterprises (such as *Halk Bank*) would be postponed without interest for a year (Hangül 2014). Many other banks followed suit, cancelling the debts of families who lost members in the accident and offering other measures to ease the debt burden of their customers from the region (Demir 2014). These efforts have certainly consolidated the AKP's populist countenance. And only a few dared to question why thousands of other families who have lost their loved-ones to work-related accidents were not offered similar support.[19]

Despite Erdoğan's protests that such deaths are inherent to the business of mining, there have also been improvements made in the regulatory framework. Although criticised by many as too little and too late, the government made some improvements in the mining sector concerning the labour processes of miners and the safety standards in mining activities. It was only after the Soma mining tragedy (as well as another major one in November 2014 just six months after Soma, at the Ermenek mining site, where 18 miners lost their lives) that the AKP finally decided to sign the International Labour Organisation's (ILO) convention concerning safety and health in mines (which had entered into force in 1998). Given the high prevalence of informality in the country, including the mining sector, and given the continued pressure to increase domestic coal extraction, to what extent these improvements will be sustained remains to be seen. But at any rate, the government has succeeded to give the signal that the mining sector has been rectified.

Another dimension of the failure of the initial anger to coalesce into a more established political posture can be seen in the inability of opposition political parties and other local forces to exercise effective leadership in the area. For instance, attempts to form an alternative workers' union failed, mainly because of internal fights. Opposition political parties were not able to articulate an alternative strategy to prevailing neoliberal climate. The lack of alternatives is not merely in terms of actual employment possibilities, though this is certainly the case. For instance, after six months of suspended activities during when the miners' salaries were paid by the state, the mining company had decided on the grounds of safety concerns to close down some sites, thus terminating the employment of 2,853 miners. Those affected by these proposed cuts fiercely opposed this decision, most of them indicating that irrespective of the level of risks they were ready to go back to the galleries. This desperate reaction prompted a member of parliament from the main opposition party to remark that the workers were given a choice between dying in the mine or dying from hunger (Yıldırım and Şen 2014).

Nevertheless, the remarkable absence of sustained political reaction from the residents of Soma cannot be explained only in relation to a combination of authoritarian and

---

[19] A caveat is to be made that offering jobs in the public sector to one member of the affected families in Soma was generalised recently (as of 21 May 2018) to cover other mining incidents that occurred during the period between 10 June 2003 till the Soma disaster, which indeed shows how a particularised solution can sometimes lead to the formulation of new demands by larger sections of the working community and thus bring more – albeit partial – concessions ('Madende hayatını kaybedenlerin yakınlarının' 2018). We are thankful to one of the referees who drew our attention to this point.

populist measures from the state. Furthermore, Soma is not unique in such a political stance: examples of similarly puzzling 'quiescence' have been the focus of many other studies (e.g. Akbulut, Adaman, and Arsel 2017; Arsel, Pellegrini, and Mena forthcoming), including Gaventa's (1980) seminal work on West Virginia coal mining communities. Despite the strength of Gaventa's explanation that power operates through complex and sometimes unseen channels to thwart potential acts of revolts, the example of Soma differs not because all instances of state and capital dominance in Turkey are in the open but because almost a century of state-led developmentalism in Turkey has succeeded in constructing a society which – even at the moment of revolt – recognizes itself in the state and in its modernizing ambition. In other words, even when the legitimacy of the state in a particular moment or instance might be diminished – as was the case around the time of the Soma disaster – the legitimacy of the idea of the state as the vanguard of Turkish development remains unassailable. In fact, the Turkish state's hegemonic project depended on this very notion, as it acquired consent through the promise of modernisation via economic growth – as if corresponding to the general interest of the society (Akbulut 2011; Akbulut, Adaman, and Arsel 2018).

At a broader level, there remains a lack of alternative to the dominant discourse of the state that Turkey is destined to renew its lost national greatness, last experienced at the height of the powers of the Ottoman Empire. This nationalist posture brings with it a certain economic logic, lending credence to calls to such goals as 'energy independence'. Absent a critical discussion of why increases in energy consumption are seen as a sign of national progress and why such increases have to be enabled by the cheapest and dirtiest technologies available at home, oppositional forces in Turkey have failed to challenge the twin forces of extraction and construction. In the absence of an alternative narrative, the AKP and Erdoğan have been able to contain societal dissent through a combination of populism and authoritarianism.

5. Conclusion

Neither the Soma disaster nor the authoritarian populism that created the conditions for its genesis and its surprisingly calm aftermath can be seen as inevitable. This paper has argued that they have all been underwritten by an economic development imperative, which Erdoğan and the AKP have used even more successfully than past administrations. Both authoritarianism and populism (as well as their combined manifestation) have been deployed particularly boldly in times when economic development failed to materialize at a sufficiently fast pace or failed to create sufficient buy-in from poor and marginalized segments of society. Borrowing from a Gramscian framework, they represent mechanisms of establishing support within a context marked by the breakdown of a hegemonic project mobilising active consent. It is therefore ironic that both the beneficiaries and the victims of authoritarian populism are those who continue to legitimize a system that is structurally geared to impoverish them. This was the case of the Soma miners who were first forced off their agrarian lifestyles and then into certain death in a coal mine that was run without concern for health and safety so as to maximize production. While the death of the 301 miners is of course lamentable, the real tragedy is the fact that the 'accident' was a structural feature of the Turkish economy.

While the tragic spectacle of Soma has resulted in an at least temporary societal pushback and certain improvements in worker safety, demonstrating once again that the 'squeaky wheel gets the grease' (Orta Martinez, Pellegrini, and Arsel 2018), it is important to reflect more broadly on the argument that these deaths are a structural feature of the economic model. As mentioned earlier, Turkey experiences four preventable deaths of workers daily. Just as the death of 301 miners cannot be explained away with the concept of *fıtrat*, this predictable death toll cannot be explained away as examples of 'industrial accidents'. They represent a particularly lethal form of 'slow violence' (Nixon 2011) that has not galvanized even a temporary backlash or a questioning of their underlying dynamics.

It is this absence of societal pushback that allows the normalization of the 'drip, drip, drip' of individual tragedies that characterise the fundamental threat of authoritarian populism. As the support of certain segments of society is secured via the promise of jobs, the delivery of 'free' coal, or the unrolling of ever faster and more glamorous transport networks, the sustenance of alternative visions and associated forms of dissent that cannot be contained by authoritarian forces becomes increasingly crucial. The ultimate question posed by the tragedy of Soma is, therefore, how to cultivate the emancipatory potential of radical forces who will need to organize – intellectually, programmatically as well as physically – to break out of the vice-like grip of authoritarian populism towards a counter-hegemonic project. Within the context of Turkey, this preparatory work necessarily implies rethinking the country's fetishism of economic growth.

Acknowledgements

The authors are grateful for the comments and suggestions made at various stages of this work by Önsel Gürel Bayralı, Banu Can, Coşku Çelik, Orkun Doğan, Fethiye Erbil, Nuri Ersoy, Sumru Tamer and Zafer Yenal, though dissociating them from any views expressed. Two of the authors have paid multiple visits to the Soma region, starting right after the disaster, interacting with different institutions and organizations as well as miners' families including those who have been directly affected by the disaster. We are equally thankful to them, even though their names have not been mentioned for understandable concerns. Some of these visits were conducted within the project of *Boğaziçi University's Soma Inquiry Report* (2017), which is the outcome of the desk- and field-work conducted by a group of faculty and students of the University, with organizational support from the Rectorate. The authors would also like to acknowledge the team's contribution in the formation of the ideas in this article.

Disclosure Statement

No potential conflict of interest was reported by the authors.

References

Adaman, Fikret, Bengi Akbulut, and Murat Arsel, eds. 2017. *Neoliberal Turkey and its Discontents: Economic Policy and the Environment Under Erdoğan*. London: I.B. Taurus.

Adaman, Fikret, Bengi Akbulut, Yahya M. Madra, and Şevket Pamuk. 2014. "Hitting the Wall: Erdoğan's Construction-Based, Finance-led Growth Regime." *The Middle East in London* 10 (3): 7–8.

Adaman, Fikret, and Murat Arsel, eds. 2005. *Environmentalism in Turkey: Between Democracy and Development?* Aldershot: Ashgate.

Adaman, Fikret, and Murat Arsel. 2010. "Globalization, Development, and Environmental Policies in Turkey." In *Understanding the Process of Economic Changes in Turkey: An Institutional Approach*, edited by Tamer Çetin, and Yılmaz Feridun, 319–335. New York: Nova Science Publishers.

Adaman, Fikret, and Murat Arsel. 2013. "Environment." In *The Routledge Handbook of Modern Turkey*, edited by Metin Heper, and Sabri Sayarı, 317–327. London: Routledge.

Adaman, Fikret, and Murat Arsel. 2016. "Climate Policy in Turkey: A Paradoxical Situation?" *L'Europe en Formation* 380: 26–38.

Adaman, Fikret, Ayşe Buğra, and Ahmet İnsel. 2009. "Societal Context of Labor Union Strategy: The Case of Turkey." *Labor Studies Journal* 34 (2): 168–188.

Akbulut, Bengi. 2011. "State Hegemony and Sustainable Development: A Political Economy Analysis of Two Local Experiences in Turkey." PhD thesis, University of Massachusetts, Amherst.

Akbulut, Bengi, and Fikret Adaman. 2013. "The Unbearable Appeal of Modernization: The Fetish of Growth." *Perspectives: Political Analysis and Commentary From Turkey* 5: 14–17.

Akbulut, Bengi, Fikret Adaman, and Murat Arsel. 2017. "The Radioactive Inertia: Deciphering Turkey's Anti-Nuclear Movement." In *Neoliberal Turkey and its Discontents: Economic Policy and the Environment Under Erdoğan*, edited by Adaman Fikret, Bengi Akbulut, and Murat Arsel, 124–134. London: I.B. Taurus.

Akbulut, Bengi, Fikret Adaman, and Murat Arsel. 2018. "Troubled Waters of Hegemony: Consent and Contestation in Turkey's Hydropower Landscapes." In *Water, Technology and the Nation-State*, edited by Filippo Menga, and Erik Swyngedouw, 96–114. London: Routledge Earthscan.

Akder, Halis A. 2010. "How to Dilute an Agricultural Reform: Direct Income Subsidy Experience in Turkey (2001-2008)." In *Rethinking Structural Reform in Turkish Agriculture: Beyond the World*

Bank's Strategy, edited by Barış Karapınar, Adaman Fikret, and Gökhan Özertan, 47–62. New York: Nova Science Publishers.

Arrighi, Giovanni. 1970. "Labour Supplies in Historical Perspective: A Study of the Proletarianization of the African Peasantry in Rhodesia." *The Journal of Development Studies* 6 (3): 197–234.

Arsel, Murat. 2005. "Reflexive Developmentalism? Toward an Environmental Critique of Modernisation." In *Environmentalism in Turkey: Between Democracy and Development?*, edited by Fikret Adaman, and Murat Arsel, 15–34. Aldershot: Ashgate.

Arsel, Murat, Fikret Adaman, and Bengi Akbulut. 2017. "'A Few Environmentalists'? Interrogating the 'Political' in the Gezi Park." In *Neoliberal Turkey and its Discontents: Economic Policy and the Environment Under Erdoğan*, edited by Fikret Adaman, Bengi Akbulut, and Murat Arsel, 191–206. London: I.B. Taurus.

Arsel, Murat, Barbara Hogenboom, and Lorenzo Pellegrini. 2016. "The Extractive Imperative in Latin America." *The Extractive Industries and Society* 3 (4): 880–887.

Arsel, Murat, Lorenzo Pellegrini, and Carlos Mena. Forthcoming. "Maria's Paradox: Oil Extraction and the Misery of Missing Development Alternatives in the Ecuadorian Amazon." In *Immiserizing Growth: When Growth Fails the Poor*, edited by Ravi Kanbur, Richard Sandbrook, and Paul Shaffer. Oxford: Oxford University Press.

Aydın, Zülküf. 2010. "Neo-liberal Transformation of Turkish Agriculture." *Journal of Agrarian Change* 10 (2): 149–187.

Başlevent, Cem, and Ayşenur Acar. 2014. "Recent Trends in Informal Employment in Turkey." *Yıldız Social Science Review* 1 (1): 77–88.

Boğaziçi Üniversitesi Soma Araştırma Grubu. 2017. *Boğaziçi Üniversitesi Soma Araştırma Grubu Raporu*. Edited by Ersoy Nuri. Istanbul: Boğaziçi Üniversitesi Yayınları.

Bozkurt, Umut. 2013. "Neoliberalism with a Human Face: Making Sense of the Justice and Development Party's Neoliberal Populism in Turkey." *Science & Society* 77 (3): 372–396.

Bracke, Sarah. 2016. "Is the Subaltern Resilient? Notes on Agency and Neoliberal Subjects." *Cultural Studies* 30 (5): 839–855.

Buğra, Ayşe. 2017. "Türkiye'nin Sosyal Politikaları ve Soma Felaketi." In *Boğaziçi Üniversitesi Soma Araştırma Grubu Raporu*, edited by Ersoy Nuri, 185–202. Istanbul: Boğaziçi Üniversitesi Yayınları.

Buzogány, Aron. 2017. "Illiberal Democracy in Hungary: Authoritarian Diffusion or Domestic Causation?" *Democratization* 24 (7): 1307–1325.

Çakmak, Erol H. 2004. "Structural Change and Market Opening in Agriculture: Turkey towards EU Accession." *ERC Working Papers in Economics* 04/10.

Çakmak, Erol H., and Hasan Dudu. 2010. "Agricultural Policy Reform in Turkey: Sectoral and Micro Implications." In *Rethinking Structural Reform in Turkish Agriculture: Beyond the World Bank's Strategy*, edited by Barış Karapınar, Fikret Adaman, and Gökhan Özertan, 63–86. New York: Nova Science Publishers.

Çalışkan, Koray, and Fikret Adaman. 2010. "The Logic of Neoliberal Agricultural Reform Initiatives: Perspectives and Consequences." In *Rethinking Structural Reform in Turkish Agriculture: Beyond the World Bank's Strategy*, edited by Barış Karapınar, Fikret Adaman, and Gökhan Özertan, 87–104. New York: Nova Science Publishers.

Çelik, Aziz. 2013. "Trade Unions and Deunionization During Ten Years of AKP Rule." *Perspectives: Political Analysis and Commentary From Turkey* 3: 44–48.

Çelik, Coşku. 2016. "Soma'da İşçileşme Süreçleri." *Evrensel*, May 13, 2016. https://www.evrensel.net/haber/279977/somada-iscilesme-surecleri.

Çelik, Coşku. 2017. "Kırsal Dönüşüm ve Metalaşan Yaşamlar: Soma Havzası'nda İşçileşme Süreçleri ve Sınıf İlişkileri." *Praksis* 43: 785–810.

Demir, Serkan. 2014. "Bankalar Kredi Borçlarını Siliyorlar," *Banka Kredileri*, May 16. https://www.banka-kredileri.com/bankalar-kredi-borclarini-siliyorlar/.

Demiroz, Fatih, and Naim Kapucu. 2016. "Emergency and Crisis Management: The Soma Mine Accident Case, Turkey." In *The Routledge Handbook of Global Public Policy and Administration*, edited by Thomas R. Klassen, Denita Cepiku, and T. J. Lah, 207–216. London: Abingdon.

Ercan, Fuat, and Şebnem Oğuz. 2015. "From Gezi Resistance to Soma Massacre: Capital Accumulation and Class Struggle in Turkey." *Socialist Registar* 51: 114–135.

Erdoğan: Akarsular satılmıyor. 2010. *Sabah*. August 11. https://www.sabah.com.tr/gundem/2010/08/11/erdogan_akarsular_satilmiyor.
Ersoy, Nuri. 2017. "İşleneceğini Herkesin Bildiği Bir Cinayetin Öyküsü." In *Boğaziçi Üniversitesi Soma Araştırma Grubu Raporu*, edited by Nuri Ersoy, 81-108, Istanbul: Boğaziçi Üniversitesi Yayınları.
García Márquez, Gabriel. 1981. *Crónica de una Muerte Anunciada*. Barcelona: Debolsillo.
Gaventa, John. 1980. *Power and Powerlessness: Quiescence and Rebellion in an Appalachian Valley*. Urbana and Chicago: University of Illinois Press.
Gramsci, Antonio. 1971. *Selections From the Prison Notebooks*. Edited by Quintin Hoare and Geoffrey Nowell-Smith. London: Lawrence & Wishart.
Hangül, Hamide. 2014. "Soma esnafına kredi ertelemesi: Soma'daki maden kazası nedeniyle zarar gören Soma ve Kırkağaç esnafının kredi borçları ertelendi. Halkbank ve Türkiye Esnaf ve Sanatkarlar Kredi Kooperatifleri borcu 1 yıl faizsiz ötelendi." *Yeni Şafak*, August 3. https://www.yenisafak.com/amphtml/politika/soma-esnafina-kredi-ertelemesi-673788.
Harvey, David. 2005. *A Brief History of Neoliberalism*. Oxford: Oxford University Press.
İlkkaracan, İpek, and İnsan Tunalı. 2010. "Agricultural Transformation and the Rural Labor Market in Turkey." In *Rethinking Structural Reform in Turkish Agriculture: Beyond the World Bank's Strategy*, edited by Barış Karapınar, Fikret Adaman, and Gökhan Özertan, 105–148. New York: Nova Science Publishers.
Kara, Hakan, and Çağrı Sarıkaya. 2014. "Current Account Deficit in Turkey: Cyclical or Structural?" Koç University-TÜSİAD Economic Research Forum Working Paper Series, no 1420.
Keyder, Çağlar, and Zafer Yenal. 2010. "Rural Transformation Trends and Social Policies in Turkey in the Post-Developmantalist Era." In *Rethinking Structural Reform in Turkish Agriculture: Beyond the World Bank's Strategy*, edited by Barış Karapınar, Fikret Adaman, and Gökhan Özertan, 11–28. New York: Nova Science Publishers.
Keyder, Çağlar, and Zafer Yenal. 2011. "Agrarian Change Under Globalization: Markets and Insecurity in Turkish Agriculture." *Journal of Agrarian Change* 11 (1): 60–86.
Keyder, Çağlar, and Zafer Yenal. 2013. *Bildiğimiz Tarımın Sonu: Küresel İktidar ve Köylülük*. Istanbul: İletişim.
Keyman, Fuat E. 2010. "Modernization, Globalization and Development: The State Problem in Turkey." In *Rethinking Structural Reform in Turkish Agriculture: Beyond the World Bank's Strategy*, edited by Barış Karapınar, Fikret Adaman, and Gökhan Özertan, 29–46. New York: Nova Science Publishers.
Klein, Naomi. 2008. *The Shock Doctrine: The Rise of Disaster Capitalism*. Toronto: Vintage.
Koch, Natalie. 2017. "Orientalizing Authoritarianism: Narrating US Exceptionalism in Popular Reactions to the Trump Election and Presidency." *Political Geography* 58: 145–147.
'Madende hayatını kaybedenlerin yakınlarının kamuda istihdamı ile ilgili duyuru'. 2018. *Memurlar.net*, May 21. https://www.memurlar.net/haber/750221/madende-hayatini-kaybedenlerin-yakinlarinin-kamuda-istihdami-ile-ilgili-duyuru.html.
Madra, Yahya M., and Fikret Adaman. 2014. "Neoliberal Reason and its Forms: De-Politicisation Through Economisation." *Antipode* 46 (3): 691–716.
Madra, Yahya M., and Fikret Adaman. 2018. "Neoliberal Turn in the Discipline of Economics: Depoliticization Through Economization." In *SAGE Handbook of Neoliberalism*, edited by Damien Cahill, Melinda Cooper, Martijn Konings, and David Primrose, 113–128. London: Sage.
Ministry of Development. n.d. "Tenth Development Plan 2014–2018." http://www.mod.gov.tr/Lists/DevelopmentPlans/Attachments/4/Brochure%20of%20Tenth%20Development%20Plan%20(2014-2018).pdf.
Nixon, Rob. 2011. *Slow Violence and the Environmentalism of the Poor*. Cambridge, MA: Harvard University Press.
OHAL ilan edilen Soma'da 36 kişi gözaltına alındı. 2014. *Evrensel*. May 17. https://www.evrensel.net/haber/84442/ohal-ilan-edilen-somada-36-kisi-gozaltina-alindi.
Orta Martinez, Marti, Lorenzo Pellegrini, and Murat Arsel. 2018. "'The Squeaky Wheel Gets the Grease'? The 'Conflict Imperative' and the Slow Fight Against Environmental Injustice in Northern Peruvian Amazon." *Ecology and Society* 23 (3): 7.
Öniş, Ziya, and Fikret Şenses. 2009. *Turkey and the Global Economy*. London: Routledge.

Özden, Barış Alp. 2014. "The Transformation of Social Welfare and Politics in Turkey: A Successful Convergence of Neoliberalism and Populism." In *Turkey Reframed: Constituting Neoliberal Hegemony*, edited by İsmet Akça, Barış Alp Özden, and Ahmet Berkmen, 157–173. London: Pluto Press.

Özden, Barış Alp, İsmet Akça, and Ahmet Berkmen. 2014. "Antinomies of Authoritarian Neoliberalism in Turkey: The Justice and Development Party Era." In *Turkey Reframed: Constituting Neoliberal Hegemony*, edited by İsmet Akça, Barış Alp Özden, and Ahmet Berkmen, 189–209. London: Pluto Press.

Özden, Barış Alp, Ahmet Bekmen, and İsmet Akça. 2018. "Passive Revolution: Beyond a Politicist Approach." *Development and Change* 49 (1): 238–253.

Özselçuk, Ceren. 2015. "'İktidar Boşluk Kabul Etmez': AKP'nin Hizmet İdeali ve Polülizm Üzerine." In *Türkiye'de Yeni İktidar Yeni Direniş: Sermaye-Ulus-Devlet Karşısında Yerelötesi Müşterekler*, edited by Yahya M. Madra, 81–95. Istanbul: Metis.

Poulantzas, Nicos. 1978. *State, Power, Socialism*. London: Verso.

Ravindran, Tathagatan, and Charles R. Hale. 2017. "Rethinking the Left in the Wake of the Global 'Trumpian' Backlash." *Development and Change* 48 (4): 834–844.

Rodrik, Dani. 2017. "The Fatal Flaw of Neoliberalism: It's Bad Economics." *The Guardian*, November 14, 2017. https://www.theguardian.com/news/2017/nov/14/the-fatal-flaw-of-neoliberalism-its-bad-economics.

Sayarı, Sabri. 2011. "Clientelism and Patronage in Turkish Politics and Society." In *The Post-Modern Abyss and the New Politics of Islam: Assabiyah Revisited: Essays in Honor of Şerif Mardin*, edited by Faruk Birtek, and Toprak Binnaz, 81–94. Istanbul: Bilgi University Press.

Schilling-Vacaflor, Almut, and Jessika Eichler. 2017. "The Shady Side of Consultation and Compensation: 'Divide-and-Rule' Tactics in Bolivia's Extraction Sector." *Development and Change* 48 (6): 1439–1463.

Scoones, Ian, Marc Edelman, Saturnino M. Borras Jr., Ruth Hall, Wendy Wolford, and Ben White. 2018. "Emancipatory Rural Politics: Confronting Authoritarian Populism." *The Journal of Peasant Studies* 45 (1): 1–20.

Sivil Sayfalar. 2016. Rakamlarla Türkiye'de İş Kazaları ve İşçi Ölümleri. http://www.sivilsayfalar.org/2016/05/02/rakamlarla-turkiyede-is-kazalari-ve-isci-olumleri/.

Thompson, Mark R. 2016. "The Specter of Neo-Authoritarianism in the Philippines." *Current History* 115 (782): 220–225.

Türkiye Barolar Birliği. 2014. *Soma Maden Faciası Raporu*. Ankara: Türkiye Barolar Birliği Yayınları.

Türk Sosyal Bilimler Derneği Çalışma Grubu. 2016. "İki Yılın Ardından Soma Maden Faciası." http://tsbd.org.tr/wp-content/uploads/2017/01/somaraporu11Nisan.pdf.

Williams, Chris. 2014. "It Was Murder, Not an Accident." *SocialistWorker.org* https://socialistworker.org/2014/05/19/it-was-murder-not-an-accident.

World Bank. n.d. "Agricultural Reform Implementation Project (ARIP)." http://projects.worldbank.org/P070286/agricultural-reform-implementation-project-arip?lang=en&tab=overview.

World Justice Project. 2017. "WJP Rule of Law Index."https://worldjusticeproject.org/our-work/wjp-rule-law-index/wjp-rule-law-index-2017%E2%80%932018.

Yeşilyurt-Gündüz, Zuhal. 2015. "The 'New Turkey': Fetishizing Growth with Fatal Results." *Monthly Review* 67 (2): 40–53.

Yıldırım, Taylan, and Banu Şen. 2014. Soma'da 2 bin 800 işçinin işine son verildi. *Hürriyet*. December 1. http://www.hurriyet.com.tr/gundem/somada-2-bin-800-iscinin-isine-son-verildi-27686653.

The vanishing exception: republican and reactionary specters of populism in rural Spain

Jaume Franquesa

ABSTRACT
In contrast to the dominant European tendency, the 2008 economic crisis and the ensuing austerity in Spain led to the emergence of left populist movements that have kept authoritarian populism at bay. However, those progressive movements have made few inroads in the countryside, potentially ceding this ground to reactionary politics. But if the specter of reaction haunts the countryside, I also suggest that this specter coexists with emancipatory possibilities. To examine these, I discuss a rural protest movement against extractive practices that developed in the early 2000s. This movement, I argue, provides valuable insight into how feelings of abandonment can be given a class-conscious, popular democratic expression.

> Whether one calls them fascist, authoritarian populist or counterrevolutionary, there is no doubt that angry movements contemptuous of liberal democratic ideals and practices and espousing the use of force to resolve deep-seated social conflicts are on the rise globally. (Bello 2018, 21)

As Walden Bello argues, far-right populism has been gaining momentum across the world in recent years. In Europe, although by no means new, it seems to have found fertile ground in the context of economic crisis and austerity policies. And yet, as a recent *Foreign Affairs* article, revealingly titled 'The Spanish Exception', argues: 'One country seems immune to it all: Spain' (Encarnación 2017). How are we to explain Spain's alleged immunity to this authoritarian wave? In this article I defend a straightforward answer to this puzzle: authoritarian populism has been kept at bay by a series of popular democratic (or as I prefer to call them: 'republican') populist movements that have offered a potentially emancipatory response to the disenfranchisement and dispossession experienced by large sectors of the Spanish population. Nonetheless, I also argue that this situation should not be taken for granted: the risk that authoritarian populist movements develop and crystallize is high in the current political conjuncture, which is particularly open and unstable.

In this respect, it should be noted that these republican movements have a had a poor penetration in the Spanish countryside. I shall suggest that this circumstance, which reflects a growing divide between city and country and the political isolation of the latter, makes rural Spain particularly vulnerable to the spread of right-wing populism. This hypothesis gains strength once we observe the growing impoverishment and marginalization experienced by large sectors of the Spanish rural population. Thus, I entertain that the specter of reaction haunts the countryside, but I also argue that this specter coexists with republican possibilities.

This paper is divided into four parts. In the first one, I examine the current Spanish political conjuncture, and argue for the need to read it through a relational perspective attentive to the *longue durée* of Spanish politics in order to assess the popular democratic movements that have emerged in recent years. In the second one, I explore the effects of crisis and austerity in the Spanish countryside, arguing that it has exacerbated an already ongoing process of slow dispossession with objective (impoverishment, land concentration) and subjective (feelings of abandonment, erosion of self-esteem) dimensions.

In the third part I take on the issue of emancipatory rural politics. To do so I move to Southern Catalonia, a region where I have been conducting ethnographic fieldwork[1] since 2010 (Franquesa 2018). I examine how in that region a broad movement – popularly known as the 'Southern revolt' – against land (and water and green) grabbing was able to reveal, and combat, the uneven ecological foundations of an unfair, territorially and class-inflected structure of accumulation and political domination. Although the Southern revolt peaked in the first years of this century, its echoes are still noticeable today in a region that has politically moved to the left since the turn of the century. Southern Catalonia and the Southern revolt thus offer a telling example of how feelings of abandonment in the countryside can be given a popular democratic expression.

Finally, I conclude this paper by dwelling on the thin but all-important line that separates republican (or 'left wing' or 'popular democratic') from reactionary (or 'right wing' or 'authoritarian') populism. I do so by examining the role that the morally charged idiom of dignity has played in recent years in the formation of political subjectivities in Spain. Thus, whereas this idiom offers an opportunity to bridge the existing political divide between country and city, connecting urban and rural experience and consciousness, recent developments make clear that it can also become a mobilizing rhetoric for authoritarian populism. Both republican and reactionary specters can hide behind, and eventually thrive through, the demand for dignity.

The Spanish exception

Narratives about Spain's exceptionality within Europe are not new (see, for instance, Swyngedouw 2015). During the better part of the nineteenth and twentieth centuries these

---

[1]The bulk of this fieldwork was carried out between 2010 and 2014, totaling 11 months. Research was aimed at building an ethnographically situated history of how Southern Catalans have related with energy facilities from the 1960s to the present. Fieldwork included interviews, participant observation and documentary analysis in local archives. I interviewed local mayors and administration officials, activists, peasant leaders, wind farm developers, environmentalist leaders, wine producers, nuclear workers and landowners affected by energy infrastructure. Among other activities, participant observation involved attending marches, demonstrations and activist meetings, visiting electricity-producing facilities, wine cellars and farming cooperatives, and accompanying farmers in their daily routines, as well as participating in the rich festive calendar of the region.

narratives – epitomized in famous mantras such as 'Spain is different' and 'Europe ends at the Pyrenees' – pointed towards some essential deficiency: Spain's marginal position within Europe, the country's archaic and oppressive political structure (which Franco's dictatorship epitomized), its incapacity to modernize its productive base, and so on. Nonetheless, with the death of the dictator (1975) and entry into the European Union (1986) the situation changed quite radically: Spain became a 'normal' European country, a liberal democracy firmly inserted within the Western European landscape. And yet, it was precisely in that historical moment that the specter of the far right made a comeback to the heart of Europe (Stolcke 1995), now under the guise of what Stuart Hall called 'authoritarian populism' (Hall 1985). Since then, authoritarian populism has continued to grow, especially since 2008, being, in Don Kalb's words, 'the traumatic expression of material and cultural experiences of dispossession and disenfranchisement' (2011, 1). In sum, over the course of half a century, Spain's alleged exceptionality has undergone a complete reversal: the country is now identified for its imperviousness to far-right temptations and, presumably, the health of its democratic values and institutions.

Yet the 'Spanish difference' should be neither overstated nor taken for granted. We should first disentangle the two different rationales that political scientists bring forward to justify Spain's exceptionality. The first one underscores the electoral weakness, and consequent parliamentary irrelevance, of far-right parties since the 1980s (see, for instance, Arzheimer 2009). True and important as it is, this parliamentary irrelevance needs to be qualified with two major, interrelated caveats. First, the recent memory of the Francoist regime has historically acted as an obstacle for the emergence of openly authoritarian parties and movements. But, second, far-right factions and ideologies have found easy refuge in the Partido Popular, a party founded by Francoist cadres that has ruled the country for the better part of the last two decades (1996–2004 and 2011–2018) (Casals 2011).

A second strand of literature approaches Spain's alleged exceptionalism in a way that is more relevant to the subject of this paper. The title of a recent scholarly report neatly captures the thrust of this argument: 'The Spanish exception: the failure of right-wing populist groups *despite* unemployment, inequality and immigration' (González Enríquez 2017, my emphasis). A comparable argument can be found in Alonso and Rovira Kaltwasser, when they write that even if 'in contemporary Spain there is a real demand for populist radical right parties ... the Great Recession has not improved the electoral odds of the populist radical right as such but rather facilitated the emergence of leftist populist forces' (2015, 21). As these quotes suggest, the alleged absence of far-right populism in Spain is understood as an anomaly, which the authors explain away by pointing to a series of relevant institutional factors – such as the electoral system and the existence of regional party systems (Alonso and Rovira Kaltwasser 2015) – and more dubious cultural traits – such as the Spaniards' weak attachment to their national identity and their supposed Europeanism (González Enríquez 2017, 10–13).

We may observe that the construction of this anomaly is premised on the juxtaposition of two one-sided assumptions. The first one is economistic, assuming a mechanical relation between certain objective economic factors (economic crisis, unemployment, etc.) and the rise of populist movements (for a critique, see van der Linden 2018). The second, culturalist one, assumes that populist movements should by default be located on the right, that is to say, that far-right *ideas* such as anti-immigration, xenophobic and anti-EU discourses will strike a chord among the disenfranchised masses even if they may go against their class interests.

Here, I will argue for the need to abandon this juxtaposition of one-sided approaches and instead adopt what Don Kalb calls a 'relational approach,' attentive to how shifting fields of class power 'generate a history of clashes, victories and defeats, including memories and amnesias, which then form the background for broad-based populist sensibilities' (Kalb 2009, 294). A relational approach thus invites us to dismiss notions of mechanical causation to explore in historical perspective the dialectical interplay between objective economic conditions and political subjectivities. As importantly, it invites us to move away from a cold sociological analysis in order to place politics center stage, insisting on the need to remain open to affects and to the creative capacity of political praxis. This praxis is the key to understanding Spain's exceptionality. Indeed, I will actually suggest that the emergence of 'left populism' is not a concomitant circumstance or a byproduct of an anomalous process, but rather its main explanation: authoritarian populism has not unfolded because the emergence of a popular democratic response to austerity has kept it at bay.

This response has taken two main expressions, both possessing a broad social base: Catalan *sobiranisme* – the movement demanding a Catalan independence vote[2] – and, more importantly, the anti-austerity movement that emerged after what is known as the *indignados* uprising – the peaceful, semi-spontaneous gathering of a mostly young, middle-class crowd in the main urban squares of the country on 15 May 2011. This event triggered a very notable cycle of protest, giving rise to, or strengthening, a series of anti-austerity organizations (such as the *Plataforma de Afectados por la Hipoteca* [the Platform for Mortgage Victims]) and political parties, most notably Podemos.

Both movements can rightly be considered populist, especially if we define populism not so much through its contents but as a kind of strategic practice: 'The deliberate political act of aggregating disparate and even competing and contradictory class and group interests and demands into a relatively homogenized voice, i.e. "us, the people", against an "adversarial them" for tactical or strategic political purposes' (Borras, forthcoming, 4). Borras pointedly adds that if we adopt this perspective, populism must be viewed 'not [as] an "either/or" question … [but as] *a matter of degree*' (Borras, forthcoming, 5). Indeed, this populist premise is central to Podemos' political strategy, based on the construction of a discursive apparatus aimed at 'building a people' in opposition to the corrupt 'elites' who defrauded them (Errejón and Mouffe 2015). Although trying to distance itself from the populist label and its negative connotations, Catalan *sobiranisme* has followed a similar strategy, premised on structuring a subject ('the Catalan people') whose demand to peacefully and democratically decide its own fate is denied by the Spanish state, therefore posited as an adversarial, undemocratic and illegitimate 'them'.

Nonetheless, whereas it is relatively simple to see why these movements may be deemed populist, explaining why they are forms of *left* populism is a more cumbersome

---

[2]*Sobiranisme* includes, but cannot be reduced to nor should it be confused with *independentisme* (the political movement aiming to achieve the secession of Catalonia from Spain). *Sobiranisme* is larger, broader and more plural than *independentisme*, both in its position towards the political status of Catalonia and in the range of issues in its agenda. On the one hand, not all *sobiranistes* are *independentistes*, that is to say, not all those political actors and forces that claim that Catalans have the right to hold an independence vote are in favor of Catalan independence. On the other hand, whereas *independentisme* tends to restrict political debate to discussing the path towards Catalan independence, *sobiranisme* insists that this discussion needs to be placed within a broader emancipatory project putting social and economic demands center stage.

task, especially considering how common the parallelisms and connections between right- and left-wing populisms are.[3] To shed light on this issue, it may be useful to follow Bello's (2018) suggestion to situate political movements within the historical unfolding of the dialectic between revolution and counterrevolution. For this, Bello (2018) argues, we need to adopt a broad definition of revolution that includes historical processes of radical, democratic reform able to empower broad sectors of the popular classes. Let's thus have a necessarily quick look at the *longue durée* of Spanish politics.

Longue durée: the dialectic between revolution and counterrevolution

A look at Spain's political history during the nineteenth and twentieth centuries reveals a cyclical regularity. Periods of decentralization, economic reform and extension of democratic rights intersperse amid a general panorama of elite dirigisme, clientelism and authoritarianism. If the first represent moments of political openness and class fluidity, the latter represent political closure and class consolidation. For the sake of brevity, I will call the former, democratizing periods 'republican' and the latter, reactionary periods 'authoritarian'. Although admittedly reductionist, this bipartite scheme will allow us to visualize the dialectic between revolution and counterrevolution that articulates Spain's political trajectory.

The republican interludes, glorified by the Spanish Left, are brief: the *Sexenio democrático* (or 'six democratic years', 1868–1874), the Second Republic (1931–1939) and the *Transición* (the period, roughly 1973–1982, covering the latter years of the dictatorship up until the consolidation of a democratic regime). Authoritarian periods, such as the *Restauración* (1874–1923) and Franco's dictatorship (1938–1975), usually extend for three to five decades.[4]

All republican periods have been politically turbulent and unstable, features that sometimes extend to the preceding years (for example, 1919–1931). The turbulence and instability that characterize these periods express both the political and class fluidity that made them possible and the reactionary tendencies that strove to annul the promise of democratization and change that republican periods portended. Indeed, in the origin of each authoritarian period we can find some counterrevolutionary foundational act or set of events justified in the need to eliminate the risk of social revolution and aimed at controlling the state apparatuses and restoring the *status quo ante* in order to reestablish class power, defend the economic interests of the elites and discipline the working classes. The result is a new authoritarian period, generally resistant to change and quite stable, which tends to get eroded over time as the accumulated changes in the country's political economy realign its class structure. As Bello (2018) suggests, the politically volatile middle classes tend to be the decisive social sector making both revolution (democratization) and counterrevolution (reaction) possible.

It is also important to underline that, within each category, the memory of the preceding period tends to have an important role in the following one. This is especially obvious

---

[3] For opposite views on the emancipatory, transformative potential of left-wing populism, see Fassin (2017) and Mouffe (2018).
[4] This dialectic can be extended back to the first two thirds of the nineteenth century, albeit with a quicker turnover: 'The history of Spain between 1808 and 1874 is a succession of attempts to advance through the democratic path ... which were ultimately frustrated by as many blowbacks ... with a balance of 15 years of democratizing attempts against 66 of counterrevolution' (Fontana 2007, 433).

with the republican periods. Each republican period remains in the memory of the left as an unfulfilled agenda and a repository of political possibilities – what Bloch (1991) would call an *uncompleted past* – that reemerges in the subsequent republican period (Izquierdo Martín and Sánchez León 2010). A last historical constant should be highlighted. The coming about of republican periods has been characterized by the convergence and (often uneasy) alliance between (radical and moderate) left progressive movements and federalizing demands emanating from some non-Castillian regions (such as Galicia, the Basque Country and, especially, Catalonia). This helps explain why in counterrevolutionary processes the curtailment of social rights tends to go hand in hand with administrative centralization and cultural uniformization efforts.[5]

In the light of the scheme that I just proposed, how should we characterize the contemporary constitutionalist, liberal democratic period, known as *Regime of 78* (in reference to the passing of the current constitution in 1978)? At least in part for the sake of clarity, I propose that we classify it as authoritarian. Such a perspective is contentious: not only is it problematic to class it together with a military dictatorship, but it should also be stressed that the Regime of 78 has created levels of political freedom, administrative decentralization and social protection that are quite unprecedented in Spanish history. However, two further considerations justify my interpretation. First, in the origin of the Regime of 78 revolution and restoration mixed in intricate ways, thus emerging as what Gramsci (1971, 106–120) called a *passive revolution*.[6] Indeed, the *Transición* was secured from above: that is to say, the current regime emerged as a reaction against the political openness of the *Transición*, articulated through a series of *transactions* between elites (epitomized in the 1977 *Pactos de la Moncloa*) oriented towards fencing off popular democratic reforms and demands in order to preserve the economic *status quo* and bury the memory of the Civil War (Naredo 2001). Second, over time, the Regime of 78 has grown progressively less democratic and more authoritarian. Indeed, since the mid-1990s there has been a slowdown in the rhythm of democratic conquests, and in some cases a clear rollback, while economic inequality has increased in parallel to the creation of a financialized economy that allowed for the hardening of class hierarchies. A result of this process has been the consolidation of a political-cum-economic power nucleus operating through mechanisms of rent extraction supported by clientelist, and often corrupt, practices knitting together corporate capital and the political party system (Narotzky 2016).

Authoritarian tendencies within the Regime of 78 have accelerated in the aftermath of the 2008 economic crisis. While joblessness, precariousness and private indebtedness augmented at an unprecedented rhythm, the Spanish government and EU institutions implemented an austerity program that dismantled welfare provisions, eroded workers' rights and socialized corporate debt (especially beneficial for banks and electricity companies, the traditional stalwarts of political-cum-economic power). The crisis revealed that promises of social reproduction and middle-class aspirations could not be maintained anymore for wide segments of the population.

---

[5]Or, in Brais Fernández's formulation, 'why Galician, Basque and … Catalan independentists are – together with the "Reds" – the enemies par excellence which the Spanish Right's project is built around' (Fernández 2018).
[6]'Whereby social struggles find sufficiently elastic frameworks to allow the bourgeoisie to gain power without dramatic upheavals … [so that] the efforts of the traditional classes … prevent the formation of collective will' (Gramsci 1971, 115). Thus, popular projects are sidelined and remain *incomplete*.

The popular democratic response (2011–2016)

It is in this context that the left populist response emerged. The *indignados* movement did not blame the duress that Spaniards were experiencing on migration, but on a corrupt structure of accumulation that only benefitted a few. As their slogans said: 'They do not represent us' and 'This is not a crisis; it is fraud.' The key characteristic of the 15-M was its capacity to 'fram[e] the democratic struggle as a radical redistribution of power, which should necessarily lead to a distribution of wealth' (Palomera 2018, 79). The afterlives of the *indignados* – most notably Podemos and the electoral coalitions currently ruling most Spanish major cities (Madrid, Barcelona, Valencia, Coruña, Cádiz, etc.) – achieved a tremendous capacity for social mobilization and high levels of electoral support. Although the immediate geographical reach of Catalan *sobiranisme* is far more restricted, its impact over Spain's political life and its capacity to call into question the existing institutional arrangement may have been greater. Indeed, in Catalonia, the pillars of the Regime of 78 (such as a stable, imperfectly bipartisan, party system; sacralization of the crown and the constitution; and the triumphalist narrative of the *Transición* as a foundational myth) have been shattered in less than a decade.

The uneasy relationship that both movements, which possess distinct historical trajectories, maintain with each other is clear evidence of their differences – a circumstance, I should note in passing, that also extends to the interior of two movements that contain a diversity of political sensibilities and projects. Yet despite their differences, the two are popular democratic, non-authoritarian movements that, in a context of growing authoritarianism and economic-cum-political crisis, promote a democratic extension of civic empowerment (Pastor 2016). The two are also characteristically 'republican': they seek to undermine (and in many cases overcome) the Regime of 78; they are anti-monarchical; and they seek historical precedent in earlier republican periods. Indeed, both movements re-enacted previous struggles, injecting into the country's political life, as Ernesto Semán's says in reference to Argentinian Peronism, 'the plebeian surge, the heretical, collective demand for dignity and workers' rights that seems to be perpetually ready to call into question certain social and cultural hierarchies' (Semán 2018, 126).

Since 2011, these two movements have been the main popular forces in the streets of Spain, and their activities have largely determined the country's political agenda during this period. In parallel, the imperfect bipartisan system upon which the Regime of 78 was constructed has been seriously undermined. But the stalwarts of this system have not remained passive. The growth of Podemos and what is often described as the 'Catalan challenge' provided the justification for the growth of the government's authoritarianism, which took shape in a context in which the division of powers has eroded, almost all big media outlets have closed ranks with the regime, and the main economic powers have heralded a visceral opposition and disdain to the two movements. Antentas (2017a) labeled the government's strategy *offensive resistentialism*. Resistentialist because it was aimed at avoiding the possibility that the context of political fluidity would give rise to a democratic, republican opening; 'offensive' because it was not merely reactive, but also reactionary: it did not seek to preserve the *status quo* but to roll back the extension of democratic freedoms. Indeed, to the dismantling of welfare provisions, we must add, among others, the increased protagonism in the political process of the judicial system, an emphasis on 'law-and-order' that has curtailed protest and freedom of expression (epitomized in the *Ley Mordaza*), and the attempts to recentralize the administrative apparatus.

Moreover, the increasing authoritarianism of the Partido Popular's government took place alongside the quick rise of its parliamentary ally, Ciudadanos, a neoliberal party that presents itself as the nemesis of Podemos. Ciudadanos' electoral appeal seems to rest on an ambiguous, even nebulous, ideology that combines ultra-nationalist rhetoric, pro-market jargon, and a coded xenophobic discourse, together with the image of a young leader who allegedly embodies the apolitical, meritocratic modernization which Ciudadanos promises to bring forth. The fact that this ideological mix attracted large numbers of mostly young, urban, middle- and working-class Spaniards constituted the first evidence that a new form of 'authoritarian populism' oriented to fend off the republican surge was in the making (Alabao 2018).

The end of the exception?

The period between 2011 and 2016 can be defined as one of emergent republicanism or, at least, as one in which the possibility of a democratic opening gained strength. However, in 2016 and 2017 the republican opening stalled, giving rise to a complex situation.

On the one hand, in recent years and months the two republican movements have encountered serious obstacles: Podemos' inability to widen its electoral support became clear in 2016, and, in 2017, the Catalan roadmap to independence collapsed, revealing the movement's strategic shortcomings. The reasons behind this regression have to do both with developments in the international arena – such as Syriza's 'capitulation', unexpected electoral results (Brexit, Trump's victory, etc.) and the EU's glacial response to Catalan demands – as well as with internal contradictions within both movements – such as the important, but waning, role of conservative nationalism within *sobiranisme* and Podemos' abjuring of the left-right political axis (Charnock, Purcell, and Ribera-Fumaz 2012). These contradictions are not unrelated to the ambivalently demos-phobic, state-centric (Badiou 2016) attitudes of both movements: their bet to play the political game within the institutional sphere has translated into a certain distrust towards, and desire to control, the popular ferment on which their force is based (Antentas 2017b). In fact, the blowbacks have revealed the limitations of the populist premise that the two movements, and especially Podemos, heralded. The hypothesis that a powerful narrative and charismatic leadership would lead to the fast seizure of power through electoral means has not only proven to be incorrect, it has also led to a palpable fading of the popular enthusiasm that animated these movements and to their progressive moderation.

Recently, we have seen strong evidence that the political volatility that has shaken Spain since the outset of the economic crisis is far from over. In the spring of 2018, a parliamentary no-confidence vote – supported, among others, by all left-wing and Catalan parties – surprisingly ousted the conservative government, and led to the election of a new Prime Minister from the nominally social-democratic party, the PSOE. It is unlikely that the new government will be able to create a new (but continuist) stable framework, for this would require some sort of federalist reform and a new period of sustained economic growth. In any event, right-wing parties will likely try to avoid such a settlement by resorting to increasingly authoritarian discourses and populist strategies, as evidenced by the recent election of the young Pablo Casado to lead the Partido Popular. As Rodrigo

Amírola argues, Casado's strategy, partly inspired in the success of Cuidadanos, is clearly populist, aiming to assemble 'a new moral majority that goes beyond left and right ... by mobilizing strongly conservative sectors in order to foment political polarization' (Amírola 2018). In just a few weeks, Casado has made clear the platform through which he aims to achieve this goal: war against so-called peripheral nationalisms (Catalan, Basque and Galician), visceral disdain to feminism (rebranded as 'gender ideology'), and a revamped anti-immigration discourse, peppered with neoliberal proposals (lowering taxes, especially on the wealthy) and due reverence to the historical pillars of Spanish nationalist conservatism (church, army, fatherland, and king). This is eerily similar to the discourse of Vox, a neofascist political party that has experienced a sudden rise in popularity in recent months. These events likely 'mark the end of the so-called Spanish exception' (Fernández 2018).[7]

It is too early to say whether the years 2016–2018 signaled the closure of the republican opening and the triumph of reaction, or whether they should simply be seen as an impasse marked by the resistance of a sclerotic regime. The outcome will depend, in the first place, on the ability of the republican movements to rejuvenate, extend and strengthen their base, and, above all, to develop strategic alliances; in the second place, on the success that the forces of reaction will have in promoting the emergence of forms of authoritarian populism. This tension will also be played out in the Spanish countryside.

The countryside

If, as I suggested, the period 2011–2016 contained the germ of a new republican period, it would also be the case that it introduced an absolute historical novelty with respect to its republican predecessors: the countryside has been little more than a non-presence in the recent political cycle.[8]

The anti-austerity movement is overwhelmingly urban: its rhetoric and style, its symbols, its agenda, they all are quintessentially urban. Catalan *sobiranisme* is less univocal, and it certainly has strong support in the Catalan countryside, but rural issues play a minimal part in its agenda and the political battle seems to be focused on widening its social base in urban Catalonia. This invisibility is further nurtured by media descriptions of the effects of the crisis, which tend to focus on urban contexts: both crisis and austerity and the response to it are presented as having an urban face. It is not difficult to detect behind this urban bias the hardwired, implicit assumption that rural dwellers are conservative (with a small c) and poorly organized (the infamous 'sack of potatoes'), and that change, therefore, can only come from the metropolitan areas.

This political divide between country and city is very problematic. On the one hand, it imposes limits on the reach of emancipatory politics. On the other hand, it tends to conceal the worsening of life conditions in rural Spain and its potential political effects. This worsening of life conditions is especially evident in three processes that I will now examine: depopulation, land concentration and impoverishment.

---

[7]As I finish the revisions to this article, on 2 December 2018, Vox has obtained 11% of the vote in the Andalusian election, thus entering a (regional) parliament for the first time ever and therefore confirming beyond any doubt that the exception is over.

[8]The *Sindicato Andaluz de Trabajadores*, allied with the left sectors of both movements, is the one very notable exception to the countryside's post-crisis political invisibility.

Depopulation, land concentration and impoverishment

The Spanish countryside suffered an abrupt process of rural exodus between 1955 and 1975. This process of depopulation left a durable imprint in the consciousness of rural dwellers, generating widespread feelings of abandonment and hopelessness (Sevilla Guzmán 1979). Although depopulation has decelerated since the 1980s, rural Spain keeps losing population and getting older, especially in the northern half of the peninsula. A recent report (Recaño 2017) suggests that close to 2000 municipalities (about 20% of the Spanish total) are at risk of disappearing. Indeed, a new genre of TV program and monograph (e.g. del Molino 2017) has popularized the idea of rural Spain as a romanticized 'Empty Spain.' Emptiness qua irrelevance is replacing the old stigma of ignorance and backwardness, further distancing the urban dweller from the quotidian reality of the countryside.

In parallel, the Spanish countryside has experienced a remarkable process of land concentration. As Franco, Borras, and van der Ploeg (2013) suggest, this process is generalized all over Europe, representing one of the faces that land grabbing has taken on the continent. According to Eurostat, between 1999 and 2009 the number of agricultural holdings in Spain decreased by 23%, whereas the agricultural area shrank by 9%. In the same period, large holdings (over 100 hectares) grew in number and became larger, whereas the amount of agricultural land in the hands of corporations increased by more than 20%, reaching 11% of the country's total. Whereas these transformations would seemingly confirm modernization theory-informed visions of agrarian differentiation, such an explanation tends to ignore the role that mechanisms of extra-economic coercion (state and EU policies, financialization, real estate pressure, etc.) have played in land concentration processes.

Moreover, changes in the agricultural sector only reveal a part of the challenges that Spanish rural territories have been facing.[9] The data that I have just presented cover an interval (1999–2009) that largely coincides with what I have elsewhere (Franquesa 2017) called the *Second Miracle*: the bubble-led cycle of economic growth that Spain experienced between 1995 and 2007. The two most visible processes of this cycle were the massive construction of private housing and the public and private construction of infrastructure such as roads, high-speed trains, airports, cultural facilities and power stations (Aguilera and Naredo 2009). Inflation of real estate assets was the lifeblood of the Second Miracle, generating rents that were captured by a bundle of real estate, construction and financial interests (López and Rodríguez 2011). The reproduction of this accumulation pattern required an incessant extension of the frontier of ground rent valorization,[10] fueled by cheap credit, public subsidies, rezoning mechanisms and corrupt deals that rarely benefitted the original owners of the land. Despite its geographical unevenness, it is hard to overemphasize the impact of this real estate and construction frenzy over the bulk of the Spanish countryside: land artificialization, the re-ordering of land uses, the privatization of public and communal lands and natural resources, speculation and

---

[9]For a synthesis of the transformations of Spanish agriculture and their effects on rural land and territories since the turn of the century, see Arnalte, Moreno, and Ortiz (2013) and Soler and Fernández (2015).
[10]On the concept of ground rent and rent capture, see the classic work of Smith (1990) and the recent contribution of Andreucci et al. (2017).

land-price increases.[11] Indeed, it seems fair to argue that the Second Miracle worked as a land grab, especially if we adopt a definition of land grabbing that loosens the emphasis on ownership to place it on the capture of *control* over resources and the re-ordering of land uses (Franco, Borras, and van der Ploeg 2013). I will return to this point in my discussion on Southern Catalonia.

But if the Miracle eroded the control of rural dwellers and farmers over their environment – and consequently over their reproductive strategies – it is fair to say that the impact of the ensuing crisis over their livelihoods has been even deeper. Current urban-rural income differentials are large. Indeed, it is not rare for the income of rural dwellers to be less than half that of the inhabitants of the respective provincial capital (Sánchez 2017). This situation is in large part the result of the uneven effects of the Miracle and the ensuing crisis over rural and urban territories. Thus, for instance, according to Idescat (the Catalan statistical institute) whereas in the early 1990s the average individual income in Catalan rural agrarian counties was slightly above that of Barcelona's postindustrial, working-class neighborhoods (the old urban 'red belts'), nowadays it is clearly below (Franquesa 2018, 2015–16). The crisis has thus impoverished rural Spain both in relative and in absolute terms.

This impoverishment is especially troublesome for smallholders and, by extension, for the regions where family agriculture, often practiced on a part-time basis, is more prominent (Arnalte, Moreno, and Ortiz 2013). Economic crisis and austerity have led to the erosion of state provisioning and the loss of industrial and state jobs in rural areas, thus undermining the complementary sources of income that are critical for the reproduction of smallholding agriculture (Moragues-Faus 2014). Furthermore, the extension of precarity jeopardizes the complex bundle of relationships of trust between households through which land is cultivated, as well as the forms of subjectivity on which those relationships, and by extension the future of these areas, depend. Southern Catalans often refer to this form of subjectivity as 'self-esteem.' The term encompasses a broad range of ideas: believing in your product and investing in it; maintaining affective relations with your land, your neighbors and the broader territory; developing initiatives that create new revenue opportunities; transmitting to your children the desire to stay and make a living in the area; and so on.

Slow dispossession and angry people

Altogether, the transformations I have just described – depopulation, land concentration and farming deactivation, urban and infrastructural encroachment, impoverishment – can be seen as a general process of *slow* dispossession, nurturing feelings of abandonment and hopelessness – the further erosion of self-esteem. My use of the adjective 'slow' – borrowed from Nixon (2013) – indicates the unspectacular, gradual and mundane character of dispossession here, which also helps to explain the inattention that this process receives in the broader public debate. Yet it is fair to assume that the objective and subjective conditions that I have described for the Spanish countryside constitute a fertile hummus for the emergence of authoritarian populism in this part of the country. Indeed, although so far rural disenfranchisement has not turned into organized anger, it is worth noting that

---

[11]Between 1995 and 2008, the average price of agricultural land more than doubled – from 5200 to 11,010 euros per hectare (Soler and Fernández 2015, 88–93).

an insightful analyst such as Fernando Fernández has recently spoken of the risk of Le Penization in the Spanish countryside:

> A year and a half ago, an agrarian organizer told me that he was worried because his bases reacted to their problems in increasingly more conservative ways, and because he found it increasingly difficult to introduce broader issues and debates. ... Since then I have observed a worrying political trend among certain sectors of the rural world who, feeling belittled and attacked, react by closing towards their own principles and evolve towards positions that have nothing to do with the defense of the rural world. ... More and more frequently I hear loaded conversations in the bar, the market and the fiestas that suddenly move from defending hunting and the need to control the fauna to a ferocious attack against environmental organizations and a defense of Spain and its traditions. I am worried to see Francoist flags in demonstrations demanding irrigation ... Where has the effort of the last decades in favor of food sovereignty and a lively, open, fraternal rural world gone? (Fernández 2017, 27)

Fernández fears that we may be witnessing an authoritarian populist movement *in statu nascendi*. This movement, he observes, understands itself as reacting against abstract enemies, most notably 'environmentalists' and 'the urban society', posited as the antagonists of the rural dwellers and their interests. Fernández offers a double explanation for the emergence of this movement. First, he points at the Left's historical inability to engage with the plight of the rural world and its unwillingness to understand the agrarian economy and, especially, family farming. This would open the way for the emergence of a Le Pen-style populism that would find its social base among pensioners, rural workers, and small and middle farmers, rather than among large landowners and the agroindustry, more favorable to the *status quo* and supportive of so-called market liberalization.

Indeed, the second key explanation has to do with the activity of a series of right-wing rural organizations, loosely connected with the Partido Popular and, increasingly, to Vox (see Fernández and Jerez 2018). These organizations have recently undertaken an effort to organize rural discontent, creating a movement called 'In defense of the rural world and its traditions' that emphasizes identity questions and posits urban environmentalists as its nemesis. Fernández admits that whether this will give place to some sort of full-fledged form of authoritarian populism in rural Spain is uncertain, yet the activist warns us that rural Spain is politically up for grabs. This view is congenial with my argument that the poor penetration of contemporary republican movements in the countryside opens a real opportunity for the emergence of authoritarian populism. In this respect, the analogy with the French National Front is apposite. For although the emergence in Spain of an independent, agrarian-focused, rural form of authoritarian populism is highly unlikely, the FN provides a revealing example of how far-right discourses and ideologies can be successfully ruralized (Ivaldi and Gombin 2015). Indeed, it seems fair to assume that the Partido Popular's incipient authoritarian populist strategy will target the rural voter, especially in those parts of the country where the party is dominant (such as central and western Spain, and probably extending to the south). It may also be a telling fact that Casado is the only national leader *not* born and raised in a major metropolitan center.

Southern Catalonia: a permanent revolt against all sorts of grabs

In their panoramic discussion of the global rise of authoritarian populism, Scoones et al. (2018) argue that the countryside not only provides the breeding ground for regressive political forces, but may also offer progressive alternatives in the form of emancipatory rural politics and struggles. In this section I briefly discuss one such struggle in Southern Catalonia; it came to be known as the Southern Revolt, and it unfolded in the first years of the century, opposing a series of hydraulic and energy projects and defending a model of endogenous economic development.

Following the classification suggested by Strijker, Voerman, and Terluin (2015; see also Woods 2008) we may describe it as a form of 'spontaneous rural protest.' 'Spontaneous', to be clear, does not signal lack of organization, but absence of political party or union direction. 'Rural', in contrast to 'agrarian', indicates that the range of actors and issues involved went beyond – though they certainly included – farmers and strictly agrarian problems, tackling a large variety of questions, from the defense of local livelihoods and landscapes to the critique of the country's hydrological and energy policies – but also of those local actors who were complicit with them. In so doing, the Southern Revolt developed a practical, ecologically-informed understanding of the role that the country-city division plays in the social division of labor and value in Spain. The Southern Revolt gave a unified voice to the region, vindicating a local identity rooted in peasant practices and a shared experience of marginalization, blaming this marginalization on a 'them' composed by all those actors – from the government to construction and electricity companies, but also local caciques – that had historically benefitted from it. Thus, as I will argue in the conclusions, the Southern Revolt can be located within a larger tradition of progressive agrarian (or rural) populism, which, while involving multiclass alliances, is, as Borras (forthcoming) argues, necessarily class-conscious.

A new productive function

In the 1960s–70s, while Spain was experiencing an accelerated, industrialization-led process of urbanization and economic modernization, Southern Catalonia's agrarian economy collapsed. As Southern Catalonia was losing its population, and thus becoming a place 'with no productive function' (Smith 2011) in modern Spain, the region was targeted for a new economic specialization: providing water and energy to urban Spain. Government and private electricity companies eyed the region, first projecting a series of dams and hydroelectric stations, and later (in the 1970s and 1980s) as many as seven nuclear power plants. Southern Catalans resisted this process from the outset (Garcia 1997). Thanks to this resistance they were able to force the withdrawal of several projects, including two dams and three nuclear plants. The peak of this struggle took place in the late 1970s, in the context of the *Transición*, largely becoming the face of the pro-democracy struggle in Southern Catalonia. Opposition to these projects was especially strong among those social sectors depending on agriculture and, to a lesser extent, fishing. The then-nascent progressive agrarian unions played a decisive role in this struggle.

Southern Catalan land (and water) became useful for capital and state's interests at the same time that the region's labor was deemed redundant. A series of actors, from agrarian organizations to the antinuclear movement, but also some sectors of the church, led the opposition to this process, framed as a defense of the local means of livelihood. It thus corresponded with what Martínez Alier's (2003) calls 'environmentalism of the poor', a defense of the local environment understood as a means of livelihood. It also possessed a strong republican, democratizing component, opposing and aiming to supersede unelected power structures, such as the electricity companies – dismissively labeled the 'new masters' – and vertical agrarian unions and Francoist mayors, together with their clientelist networks. These actors, accused of 'serving the new masters', were the main advocates of energy facilities, as well as their main beneficiaries, enjoying, for instance, privileged access to good jobs in the nuclear plants.

The country's pantry and sink

Resistance against extraction in Southern Catalonia experienced a strong rebirth at the turn of the century as a result of the coincidence of a series of proposed infrastructure projects. On 4 February 2001, the streets of Móra, the small commercial capital of the three northern counties of Southern Catalonia – Priorat, Ribera, and Terra Alta – hosted the largest demonstration that has ever taken place in the region. In front of 25,000 peaceful demonstrators, a simple banner read: 'Stop aggressions to the territory.' It was signed 'The Platforms,' a term that, in Spain, identifies local civic organizations convened to oppose a specific localized development and operating through an assembly-based, nonhierarchical structure. The four self-identified 'Southern Platforms' that organized the Móra demonstration formed in the previous two years in response to three kinds of infrastructure projects. The Platforms of Terra Alta and Priorat opposed the proposal of the Catalan government that positioned the two counties at the center of wind farm development. The Platform of Ribera opposed several projected waste and energy facilities, most notably Enron's plan to build a natural gas combined-cycle power plant in Móra. And the Southern Catalan section of the state-wide Platform in Defense of the Ebro (PDE) opposed the National Hydrological Plan (PHN, in its Spanish acronym), a governmental plan of hydraulic infrastructure that hinged on the transfer of water from the Ebro River to Barcelona and the Spanish Levant (Valencia and Murcia).

The Móra demonstration is widely seen as the inaugural event for an unprecedented cycle of mobilization, popularly known as the Southern Revolt. This revolt gathered a numerous and diverse social base, triggering a reconfiguration of the political balance of forces within the region, which has kept shifting to the left to this day. In contrast to the 1970s and 1980s, agrarian organizations played a secondary role in the Southern Revolt, a circumstance that reflected the fact that agriculture had ceased to be the main source of revenue for a significant part of the local population. Whereas during the *Transición* the conflict was framed as one of traditional (farming, fishing) versus modern economy (power plants), this time around the conflict emerged between two diverging economic development models.

The platforms defended a model based on what they called 'endogenous economic development,' where the farming base of the area and of many household economies would be strengthened by adding distinction to local production (mostly, high-scale wine) and complementary activities (fundamentally, tourism). 'Endogenous', thus, did not mean autarkic or self-sufficient, i.e. delinked from market circuits. It rather referred to the possibility of drawing on local (or endogenous) resources – the people, landscapes and agrarian produce of the region – to achieve a more favorable engagement with those circuits. Beyond the generation of new economic opportunities, the goal was thus to build a development model that afforded a larger degree of control to the local population. As activists insisted, this project of endogenous economic development wanted to combat hopelessness and relied on 'generating self-esteem.' In contrast, the second model defended that the region should deepen its specialization as an extractive hub. Once again, it had its main advocates among conservative mayors, who supported the government's view that the area was a 'lagging' region that could only develop by hosting ever-new energy projects, which would generate tax revenues, rents, and a few jobs to the local economy. This second model enjoyed limited support among the local population, as the declining support to pro-extraction mayors in successive electoral contests evidenced.

The platforms developed a fairly sophisticated understanding of the broader political economic dynamics that converted their region into a site of extraction. In an interview conducted during my fieldwork, in 2010, a leading activist of the PDE (the largest and most powerful of the Southern platforms) described what united the different platforms, and thence the spirit of the revolt, in the following terms: 'We are sister struggles, we all fight against a development model that makes us peripheral: a pantry for water and energy, and a waste dump for what the country does not want.' Furthermore, although the platforms emerged as a reaction to a series of projects, they were able to go beyond a merely defensive attitude. This is most obvious in their proposals for what they called a New Culture of Water and a New Culture of Energy. With these proposals, the platforms made clear that they were not NIMBY (Not In My Back Yard) organizations.

The New Culture of Water presented itself as a new socioenvironmental paradigm for water management, calling for conservation and the democratization of water politics in front of the traditional top-down approach that saw water as a bulk resource to be managed through large-scale infrastructure (Arrojo 2006). Importantly, the activists of the PHN dispelled the idea that the conflicts around water were mere conflicts between regions or between the country and the city. This was not, they argued, a struggle for water between, say, Southern Catalan and Murcian peasants, or between rural Southern Catalans and Barcelona's working classes. Against the government's argument, which depicted Southern Catalans as selfish citizens depriving their fellow countrymen of water, the PDE took pains to emphasize that the water sent to Barcelona and the Spanish Levant would not serve urban dwellers and small farmers, but would instead benefit a select few in the thriving real estate and tourist sectors, as well as a non-sustainable agroindustry predicated upon cheap water and cheap migrant labor.

Similarly, the New Culture of Energy emphasized the need to decouple economic development from energy use, demanded the closure of nuclear plants, and proposed a distributed energy system where smaller power plants closer to the point of consumption would progressively substitute large power plants owned by the traditional utilities. In this sense, they criticized the way renewable energy was being developed (top-down planning and corporate ownership), suggesting that it worked as a form of what Fairhead, Leach, and Scoones (2012) call 'green grabbing'. This is illustrated with the recurrent complaint that Southern Catalan farmers, echoing a long trajectory of struggle, wage against wind farm developers: 'They have become the (new) masters.'

Against the Second Miracle and its ecological regime

The Southern Revolt had its maximum strength between 2000 and 2004, the peak years of the Second Miracle. Indeed, the Southern Revolt was one of the largest of a series of conflicts against infrastructure projects (airports, golf courses, waste dumps, seaside resorts, etc.) that mushroomed in Spain, with a very strong presence in Catalonia. There, local activists, although their platforms tended to operate independently, identified their struggles as part and parcel of a countrywide 'movement in defense of the territory' (Alfama et al. 2007).

This may in fact be read, using Polanyian language (Polanyi 2001), as a countermovement, an unplanned social defense against a structure of accumulation based upon a frenetic use and abuse of space and nature. The housing bubble, the ecological degradation of the seaside, the dramatic underuse of new, large-scale infrastructure such as airports, power plants, and high-speed trains – as well as the corruption that accompanied these projects – are all part of the present-day consequences, a damning testament to the Second Miracle's effects on Spain's environment. So is the ongoing crisis and the austerity measures that the government and the EU imposed on the Spanish citizenry in order to facilitate debt repayment.

As the epicenter of this countermovement, the Southern Revolt made clear that the Second Miracle was a deeply ecological process. It constituted what Moore (2015) calls an 'ecological regime', a notion that refers to durable sets of relations (from patterns of governance to class structures, among others) organizing the metabolism – that is to say, the material exchanges between humans and the environment – of any given political-economic order. These relationships are not external but a central constitutive element of that order.

As mentioned earlier, the key element of the Second Miracle was the spatial expansion of the frontier of ground rent valorization, allowing for the inflation of real estate assets, the overgrowth of the construction sector, and fabulous financial profits for banking and related sectors – as well as an unprecedented escalation of private and corporate indebtedness. All the big winners of the Second Miracle – banks, electric utilities, construction companies, and the real estate sector – engaged in a construction binge, funded by cheap credit and focused on residential units and large-scale infrastructure. Whereas traditional core areas (big cities, the seaside) became central to this activity, the Second Miracle pushed the frontier into peri-urban areas and the entirety of the Mediterranean coast. The 'rest' of the country was *iterated* as a periphery. Thus, the expansion of the frontier of ground rent valorization, combined with the increasing metabolic demands of an economic system highly reliant on increasing flows of energy and water, put added pressure to peripheries such as Southern Catalonia. The Southern Revolt was a struggle against using the area as tap and sink for that wasteful metabolism, and in so doing it revealed the contradictions and socioenvironmental injustice on which it was based.

These contradictions lie at the heart of the debate between development models. For the construction of infrastructures required a certain kind of *value relation*. It needed territories beyond the frontier of ground rent valorization that could be further *cheapened*, a term that I use in the double sense proposed by Moore: 'One is a price moment: to reduce the costs of working for capital, directly and indirectly. Another is ethico-political: to cheapen in the English language sense of the word, to treat as unworthy of dignity and respect.' (Moore 2017, 600). Indeed, infrastructure development needed land with a low market value as much as people who felt and could be treated as unworthy, unable to claim a higher value for their land and their lives and willing to accept those facilities that other territories did not want. The model of endogenous development aimed to challenge this value relation, positing the local territory as a valuable (as opposed to 'cheap') element, both in market terms – that is to say, as the potential base for the making of livelihoods – and a source of self-esteem.

Rural populism and emancipatory rural politics

As I have argued all throughout this paper, the poor penetration of anti-austerity movements in the countryside signals a weakness in these movements' capacity to expand their social base and geographical reach. Yet as importantly, it also undermines their capacity to analyze the Spanish reality and, by extension, to propose emancipatory projects. In this respect, the Southern Revolt teaches us two main lessons: the urgency to develop an ecologically informed understanding of the city-country division, and the need to couple the critique of austerity with an equally ruthless critique of the economic bonanza that preceded it, understanding its 'slow' dispossessing effects.

In the first place, by neglecting the countryside, left populist movements in Spain at best downplay and at worst ignore the city-country (and center-periphery) relationship that underpins the existing structures of accumulation and domination. This, in turn, becomes a burden for introducing ecological questions in the emancipatory agenda. Indeed, as a certain Marxist tradition – represented by authors such as Gramsci (1957), Williams (1973) and Lefebvre (1978) – has argued, and the practice of the Southern Revolt shows, any successful emancipatory project must not only understand, but aim to supersede, the division between country and city that has been, and continues to be, central to the reproduction of capital and state. The ecological dimension of the structures of accumulation and domination becomes especially visible in peripheral areas such as Southern Catalonia, for that peripherality expresses an economic and ecological extraction – based upon and sustaining political marginalization – that is inseparable from the practice, experience and identity of the region's inhabitants.

In the second place, the popular democratic movements that have tried to break with the *status quo* since 2011 have focused their critique on the crisis and austerity policies. They have denounced the undemocratic character of these policies, as well as their dispossessing effects upon the urban middle classes that form their backbone. Yet the emergence of the Southern Revolt and similar rural movements in the preceding decade make evident that dispossessing dynamics were central to the cycle of accumulation that preceded and provoked the crisis. Furthermore, the Southern Revolt also criticized and revealed the authoritarian tendencies that gave stability to the Regime of 78, especially evident in the hydrological projects put forward by PSOE and PP. Something similar can be said about *Nunca Mais*, the movement that emerged in Galicia after the Prestige's oil spill in 2003. A broad, successful, left populist movement must take into consideration such a broad range of dispossessing processes and the authoritarianism that underpinned them in order to understand the divergent subjectivities to which they have given place over time.

Dignity: on morality, relationality, and class

Borras (forthcoming) argues that the historical – and ongoing – debate among left scholars on agrarian populism can help analyze (and build) progressive populist movements.[12] This

---

[12] For recent installments on this debate, see Bernstein (2018), van der Ploeg (2018) and White (2018).

debate has tended to polarize between so-called Chayanovian or (neo-)populist and Marxist (or Leninist) positions: whereas the former celebrate the political imagination of populism and its capacity to mobilize disparate social groups, the latter tend to criticize it as a romantic movement that privileges moralizing understandings of 'the people' while ignoring class analysis. The key, Borras argues, is to find common ground between these two positions, retaining the populist impulse while enriching it with the Marxists' keen understanding of class dynamics, in order to advance to a *class-conscious left-wing populism*.

In this concluding section I contribute to this debate by exploring how moral discourses intervene in the construction of populist movements. I do so by focusing on the notion of dignity and its role both in the Southern Revolt and in the more recent popular democratic movements. Whereas the centrality achieved by this notion makes patent the ability of the latter movements to grasp and mobilize emergent affects and 'structures of feeling' (Williams 1973), it also signals the limitations of a strategy that has been largely discursive. In and of themselves, moralizing discourses are insufficient unless they are related to class experiences (Franquesa 2016). Otherwise they can easily be captured by right-wing populism.

Southern Catalan dignity

Dignity was central to the Southern Revolt's discursive apparatus. This can be appreciated in a manifesto issued in 2007 by a group of organizations opposing a new series of energy projects (more wind farms, a nuclear waste storage facility, and a natural gas submarine deposit). The authors wrote:

> Until recently, we put up with everything like submissive subjects. … But since 2000, with the struggle against Enron and the PHN, we gained our dignity and learned to organize and make ourselves respected. Never again resignation … We are not submissive subjects anymore, we are citizens who have learnt how to struggle and we will struggle for our future. (Plataformes de les Terres de l'Ebre 2007)

This quote underscores that the Southern Revolt created politically active subjects, and it does so by contrasting dignity and resignation. During the last decades, dignity has been the main idiom through which Southern Catalans have opposed their marginalization and the conversion of their land into tap and sink of the accumulation process. Indeed, dignity should be understood as the central element of a local 'theoretical framework' – to use Narotzky's (2016) expression – aiming to explain but also to disrupt the value relations that both sustain and result from a particular political economic structure. This structure allows for the extraction of profits from the area, *cheapening* its inhabitants and their possessions, most notably land. Or, to put it in Gidwani's (2012) terms, turning them into 'waste': what the law of value needs to devalue or cheapen (in the full sense of the term) in order to produce economic value.

This demand for dignity takes two different, although often overlapping, forms. First, it emerges as indignation, a fiery reaction against passively accepting the denial of one's own dignity. Indignation draws on, reinforces and gives political character to self-esteem; it constitutes the opposite of resignation and deference and thus combats a fatalistic passivity. Indignation, then, emerges as an attempt to reproduce a resistant subjectivity that has informed a long history of peasant struggle, thus recalling an *uncompleted past* (Bloch 1991) of making autonomous peasant livelihoods and of being citizens who fully participate in the political process. The second form emerges as an assertion of dignity, understood as worth. It claims the value of Southern Catalans and their possessions, especially of their land, and of the region as a whole. The demand of dignity is an attempt to preserve – but also to construct and perform – certain possessions, a struggle against dispossession: being able to make a living and stay in place, preserving the value of land, maintaining local networks of solidarity, preserving some control over the labor process and household reproduction.

The Southern Revolt was able to put the moral strength of the notion of dignity at the service of its populist strategy, using it to build an opposition between a 'we' (the Southern Catalan people) and a 'them' (all those who benefit from a political economic structure that peripheralizes the area and its inhabitants). But we should also note that in Southern Catalonia the notion of dignity has obvious class undertones. Beyond its explicit political uses, the term is rarely used in the region. But there is a glaring exception: Southern Catalans often emphasize the dignity of being a *pagès*, a Catalan word – cousin of the French *paysan* – that means peasant or family farmer. Yet I should point out that in Southern Catalonia the term is applied to anyone who feels an attachment with the agrarian economy, anyone who wishes to make a living *in* (and not simply *off*) the land.[13]

The point that I am trying to make, therefore, is that the Southern Revolt's demand for dignity underpinned a populist strategy that was class-conscious. For in the region the notion is crucially linked to the everyday struggle for survival, a struggle to be a *pagès* which we could describe, using van der Ploeg's phrasing, as 'a struggle for autonomy and improved income within a context that imposes dependency and deprivation' (van der Ploeg 2013, 61). The demand for dignity, thus, connects disenfranchisement and dispossession with broader political economic structures, while anchoring the region's plight and struggle within a deeper trajectory of political and quotidian struggle.

Dignity beyond Southern Catalonia: the limits and openness of dignity

More recently, the claim for dignity has been a powerful undercurrent of popular democratic struggles. Indeed, the anti-austerity movement emerged as indignation (the *indignados* movement), and ongoing initiatives such as the Dignity Marches followed, organized by a coalition of unions and left organizations to demand 'bread, roof, and work'. In 2015, Pablo Iglesias, the leader of Podemos, argued in a political rally: 'We are the only reasonable possibility to recover our dignity' (Europa Press 2015). On 2 October 2017, in the aftermath of the police's repression of the Catalan self-determination vote, the cover of the newspaper *Ara* had just two words: 'Shame and Dignity' (*Vergonya i Dignitat*). A few days later, Xavier Domènech, a leader of the Comuns (the main Catalan afterlife of the *indignados* movement) tweeted: 'October 1st was the dignity of a plural and diverse people that affirmed itself in the face of repression.' The examples are multitudinous.

---

[13]This semantic extension runs in parallel to the declining importance of agriculture in the area, and is commensurate with the Southern Revolt's above-mentioned shift from strictly agrarian to rural concerns.

During the first decade of the century, the idiom of dignity was central to the political discourse of movements – such as the Southern Revolt, but also the Galician *Nunca Máis*, with its 'Manifesto da dignidade' – that felt mistreated and abandoned, largely left out of the body politic. After 2011, the idiom traveled from the rural periphery to the city squares, a move that reflected that a growing section of the urban working- and middle-classes felt left behind. Crisis and austerity curtailed their middle-class aspirations and threatened to expulse them from the mechanisms of hegemony and to render them 'people with no productive function.'

This sequence of events shows the strength of the notion of dignity, its capacity to assemble people with different life experiences. But we should not fool ourselves. The demand for dignity and the experience of indignation are not patrimony of the Left. As several authors have noted (e.g. Riley 2013), the force of the demand for dignity is its disruptive capacity, its ability to call into question the existing liberal order. Yet that disruptive capacity can be mobilized in a popular democratic direction or in an authoritarian populist one.

This latter possibility can be appreciated in a political rally that the movement 'In defense of the rural world and its traditions' (the movement that Fernando Fernández identified as containing the seed of a rural authoritarian populism) organized in September of 2017 in Córdoba. In this rally, attended by 40,000 people, the organizers gave a speech complaining about nature preservation laws and the animal rights movement, arguing that they were causing 'unease and indignation' in the rural world. And they continued by saying: 'Today a new alliance is born, a new way of fighting for the rural world and its traditions. And, with it, the rural world inaugurates a new way of fighting for its dignity and its interests' (Pedrosa 2017). Indeed, the ferment for an authoritarian populism with a rural base speaking in the language of dignity is in place. If the mostly urban-based, popular democratic movements that have set the political agenda in recent years do not increase their effort to reach the countryside, this ferment will grow.

It thus seems fair to say that in order to be hegemonic, any popular/populist movement must come to embody a fight for dignity. Yet dignity is a largely empty concept, which simply asserts the presence and value of a group that feels disenfranchised. Whether this morally loaded concept takes a republican or a reactionary direction largely depends upon the contents that it is given and the social groups that articulate it and are summoned by it. If republican movements are to make inroads in the countryside, they have to connect the feelings of indignation with a broader analysis – oriented to a more equal and fraternal future – of the political economic dynamics that are at the base of those affects. This is what makes dignity republican. Otherwise rural dwellers are likely to find their self-esteem through an exclusionary notion of dignity underpinning a reactionary program. Easier said than done, of course. Yet I would argue that this is what the Southern Revolt did. And yet the spirit of the Southern Revolt is growing weaker in Southern Catalonia. The crisis is making Southern Catalan livelihoods more and more fragile, and with that precarity, solidarity gets strained, self-esteem weakens, and the energy to reproduce a resistant subjectivity feels increasingly quixotic. And in the face of these tendencies, the specter of reaction grows stronger.

Acknowledgements

I am grateful to the Wenner-Gren Foundation (Hunt Fellowship, Gr. 8732) and to the Humanities Institute and the Baldy Center Center for Law and Social Policy at the University at Buffalo-SUNY for supporting parts of the research on which this paper is based. Part of this paper was written while enjoying a visiting professorship (2018–19) in the Department of Anthropology at the University of Barcelona; I am grateful to the colleagues in Barcelona for their warm welcome and for providing a collegial and friendly atmosphere. I also thank three anonymous reviewers from the *Journal of Peasant Studies*, its editor Jun Borras, as well as Gavin Smith and Marion Werner, for their insightful comments on this manuscript. Finally, I thank the colleagues from the Emancipatory Rural Politics Initiative (ERPI) group for initiating research on authoritarian populism and the rural world.

Disclosure statement

No potential conflict of interest was reported by the author.

Funding

I am grateful to the Wenner-Gren Foundation (Hunt Fellowship, Gr. 8732) and to the Humanities Institute and the Baldy Center Center for Law and Social Policy at the University at Buffalo-SUNY for supporting parts of the research on which this paper is based.

ORCID

Jaume Franquesa http://orcid.org/0000-0001-8416-2792

References

Aguilera, Federico, and José Manuel Naredo. 2009. *Economía, poder y megaproyectos*. Taro de Tahíche: Fundación César Manrique.
Alabao, Nuria. 2018. "El peligro 'populista' de Cs está en Vallecas o El Raval." *Ctxt: Revista contexto* 170, 23 May. http://ctxt.es/es/20180523/Firmas/19842/Cs-Ciudadanos-Madrid-Barcelona-CSOA-ciudad-Nuria-Alabao.htm.
Alfama, Eva, Àlex Casademunt, Gerard Coll-Planas, Helena Cruz, and Marc Martí. 2007. *Per una nova cultura del territori? Mobilitzacions i conflictes territorials*. Barcelona: Icaria.
Alonso, Sonia, and Cristóbal Rovira Kaltwasser. 2015. "Spain: No Country for the Populist Radical Right?" *South European Society and Politics* 20 (1): 21–45.
Amírola, Rodrigo. 2018. "Reino de España: ¿Populismo de derechas?" *Sin permiso*, 18 August. http://www.sinpermiso.info/textos/reino-de-espana-populismo-de-derechas.
Andreucci, Diego, Melissa García-Lamarca, Jonah Wedekind, and Erik Swyngendouw. 2017. "'Value Grabbing': A Political Ecology of Rent." *Capitalism Nature Socialism* 28 (3): 28–47.
Antentas, Josep M. 2017a. "¿Proyecto de República o República imaginaria?" *Viento Sur*, 31 November. https://vientosur.info/spip.php?article13161.
Antentas, Josep M. 2017b. "Imaginación estratégica y partido." *Viento Sur* 150: 141–150.
Arnalte, Eladio, Olga Moreno, and Dionisio Ortiz. 2013. "La dimensión del proceso de ajuste estructural en la agricultura española." In *La sostenibilidad de la agricultura española*, edited by José Gómez-Limón and Ernest Reig, 117–154. Almería: Cajamar.
Arrojo, Pedro. 2006. *El reto ético de la nueva cultura del agua: Funciones, valores y derechos en juego*. Barcelona: Paidós.
Arzheimer, Kai. 2009. "Contextual Factors and the Extreme Right Vote in Western Europe, 1980–2002." *American Journal of Political Science* 53 (2): 259–275.

Badiou, Alain. 2016. "Twenty-Four Notes on the Uses of the Word 'People'." In *What is a People?*, edited by Alain Badiou, Pierre Bourdieu, Judith Butler, Georges Didi-Huberman, Sadri Khiari, and Jacques Rancière, 21–31. New York: Columbia University Press.

Bello, Walden. 2018. "Counterrevolution, the Countryside and the Middle Classes: Lessons from Five Countries." *The Journal of Peasant Studies* 45 (1): 21–58.

Bernstein, Henry. 2018. "The 'Peasant Problem' in the Russian Revolution(s), 1905–1929." *Journal of Peasant Studies* 45 (5–6): 1127–1150.

Bloch, Ernst. (1962) 1991. *Heritage of Our Times*. Cambridge: Polity Press.

Borras, Saturnino M. Forthcoming. "Agrarian Social Movements: The Absurdly Difficult but Not Impossible Agenda of Defeating Right-Wing Populism and Exploring a Socialist Future." *Journal of Agrarian Change*.

Casals, Xavier. 2011. "La nova dreta populista i 'l'enigma espanyol'." *L'espill* 38: 82–91.

Charnock, Greig, Thomas Purcell, and Ramon Ribera-Fumaz. 2012. "Indígnate!: The 2011 Popular Protests and the Limits to Democracy in Spain." *Capital & Class* 36 (1): 3–11.

del Molino, Sergio. 2017. *La España vacía*. Madrid: Turner.

Encarnación, Omar G. 2017. "The Spanish Exception: Why Spain Has Resisted Right-Wing Populism." *Foreign Affairs*, 20 July.

Errejón, Íñigo, and Chantal Mouffe. 2015. *Construir pueblo: Hegemonía y radicalización de la democracia*. Barcelona: Icaria.

Europa Press (Murcia edition). 2015. "Iglesias, orgulloso de ser hijo del 15-M: 'Somos la única posibilidad razonable de recuperar nuestra dignidad'." http://www.europapress.es/murcia/noticia-iglesias-orgulloso-ser-hijo-15m-somos-unica-posibilidad-razonable-recuperar-dignidad-20150515232627.html.

Eurostat. "Agricultural Census in Spain 2000–2010." Accessed 1 December 2018. https://ec.europa.eu/eurostat/statistics-explained/index.php?title=Archive:Agricultural_census_in_Spain.

Fairhead, James, Melissa Leach, and Ian Scoones. 2012. "Green Grabbing: A New Appropriation of Nature?" *Journal of Peasant Studies* 39 (2): 237–261.

Fassin, Éric. 2017. *Populisme: Le grand ressentiment*. Paris: Textuel.

Fernández, Fernando. 2017. "¿Está aumentando la extrema derecha en el medio rural?" *Soberanía Alimentaria* 30: 26–28.

Fernández, Brais. 2018. "Spain's New-Old Monster." *Jacobin*. https://jacobinmag.com/2018/11/spain-vox-far-right-franco-partido-popular-podemos.

Fernández, Fernando, and Ariel Jerez. 2018. "VOX a la conquista del mundo rural." *Público*, 23 November. https://blogs.publico.es/mundo-rural/2018/11/24/vox-a-la-conquista-del-mundo-rural/.

Fontana, Josep. 2007. *Historia de Espana: La época del liberalismo*. Vol. 6. Barcelona: Crítica/Marcial Pons.

Franco, Jennifer, Saturnino M. Borras Jr., and Jan Douwe van der Ploeg. 2013. *Land Concentration, Land Grabbing and People's Struggles in Europe*. The Hague: Transnational Institute.

Franquesa, Jaume. 2016. "Dignity and Indignation: Bridging Morality and Political Economy in Contemporary Spain." *Dialectical Anthropology* 40 (2): 69–86.

Franquesa, Jaume. 2017. "El compromiso antropológico a partir del Segundo Milagro: desmitificar lo real y rescatar lo posible." In *Antropologías en transformación: Sentidos, compromisos y utopías*, edited by Teresa Vicente, Maria Albert, Pilar Espeso, and María José Pastor, 39–64. Valencia: Alfons el Magànim.

Franquesa, Jaume. 2018. *Power Struggles: Dignity, Value and the Renewable Energy Frontier in Spain*. Bloomington, IN: University of Indiana Press.

Garcia, Xavier. 1997. *Catalunya tambe té sud*. Barcelona: Flor del Vent.

Gidwani, Vinay K. 2012. "Waste/Value." In *The Wiley-Blackwell Companion to Economic Geography*, edited by Trevor J. Barnes, Jamie Peck, and Eric Shepard, 275–288. Maldon, MA: Wiley-Blacwell.

González Enríquez, Carmen. 2017. "La excepción española: El fracaso de los grupos de derecha populista pese al paro, la desigualdad y la inmigración." Working Paper 3/2017 of the *Elcano Royal Institute*.

Gramsci, Antonio. (1926) 1957. "The Southern Question." In *The Modern Prince & Other Writings*, 28–51. New York: International Publishers.

Gramsci, Antonio. 1971. *Selections from the Prison Notebooks.* Edited and translated by Quentin Hoare and Geoffrey N. Smith. New York: International Publishers.
Hall, Stuart. 1985. "Authoritarian Populism: A Reply." *New Left Review* 151: 115–124.
Idescat (Institut d'estadística de Catalunya). "Renda bruta familiar disponible territorial." Accessed 1 December 2018. https://www.idescat.cat/pub/?id=rfdbc.
Ivaldi, Gilles, and Joël Gombin. 2015. "The Front National and the New Politics of the Rural in France." In *Rural Protest Groups and Populist Political Parties*, edited by Dirk Strijker, Gerrit Voerman, and Ida Terluin, 243–263. Wageningen: Wageningen Academic Publishers.
Izquierdo Martín, Jesús, and Pablo Sánchez León. 2010. "El agricultor moral: Instituciones, capital social y racionalidad en la agricultura española contemporánea." *Revista española de estudios agrosociales y pesqueros* 225: 137–169.
Kalb, Don. 2009. "Headlines of Nationalism, Subtexts of Class: Poland and Popular Paranoia, 1989–2009." *Anthropologica* 51 (2): 289–300.
Kalb, Don. 2011. "Introduction." In *Headlines of Nation, Subtexts of Class: Working Class Populism and the Return of the Repressed in Neoliberal Europe*, edited by Don Kalb and Gabor Halmai, 1–36. Oxford: Berghahn.
Lefebvre, Henri. 1978. *De l'État. Volume 4: Les contradictions de l'état modern (la dialectique et/de l'état).* Paris: PUF.
López, Isidro, and Emmanuel Rodríguez. 2011. "The Spanish Model." *New Left Review* 69: 5–29.
Martínez Alier, Joan. 2003. *The Environmentalism of the Poor: A Study of Ecological Conflicts and Valuation.* Cheltenham: Edward Elgar.
Moore, Jason W. 2015. *Capitalism in the Web of Life: Ecology and the Accumulation of Capital.* London: Verso.
Moore, Jason W. 2017. "The Capitalocene, Part I: On the Nature and Origins of Our Ecological Crisis." *The Journal of Peasant Studies* 44 (3): 594–630.
Moragues-Faus, Ana. 2014. "How is Agriculture Reproduced? Unfolding Farmers' Interdependencies in Small-Scale Mediterranean Olive Oil Production." *Journal of Rural Studies* 34: 139–151.
Mouffe, Chantal. 2018. *For a Left Populism.* London: Verso.
Naredo, José M. 2001. *Por una oposición que se oponga.* Barcelona: Anagrama.
Narotzky, Susana. 2016. "On Waging the Ideological War: Against the Hegemony of Form." *Anthropological Theory* 16 (2–3): 263–284.
Nixon, Rob. 2013. *Slow Violence and the Environmentalism of the Poor.* Cambridge, MA: Harvard University Press.
Palomera, Jaime. 2018. "Austerity Wars: The Crisis of Financialization and the Struggle for Democracy." In *The Global Life of Austerity: Comparing beyond Europe*, edited by Theodoros Rakopoulos, 74–90. Oxford: Berghahn.
Pastor, Jaime. 2016. "La reforma constitucional, Catalunya y Podemos." *Viento Sur*, 21 December 2016. http://vientosur.info/spip.php?article12032.
Pedrosa, Yolanda. 2016. "El mundo rural existe y lo demuestra en la calle." *Cordoba hoy*, 30 September 2016. http://www.cordobahoy.es/album/la-ciudad/mundo-rural-existe-demuestra-calle/20170930171959033628.html.
Plataformes de les Terres de l'Ebre. 2007. "Ja n'hi ha prou." http://www.plataformaterraalta.com/manifest%20mani%20tortosa.htm.
Polanyi, Karl. (1944) 2001. *The Great Transformation: The Political and Economic Origins of Our Time.* Boston: Beacon.
Recaño, Joaquín. 2017. "La sostenibilidad demográfica de la España vacía." *Perspectives Demogràfiques* 7: 1–4.
Riley, Stephen. 2013. "The Function of Dignity." *Amsterdam Law Forum* 5 (2): 90–106.
Sánchez, Raúl. 2017. "De Zahínos a Pozuelo: El mapa de la renta media en España muestra la brecha entre el campo y la ciudad." *Eldiario.es*, 18 October 2017. https://www.eldiario.es/economia/brecha-riqueza-pueblo-municipios-poblados_0_698531032.html.
Scoones, Ian, Marc Edelman, Saturnino M. Borras Jr., Ruth Hall, Wendy Wolford, and Ben White. 2018. "Emancipatory Rural Politics: Confronting Authoritarian Populism." *The Journal of Peasant Studies* 45 (1): 1–20.

Semán, Ernesto. 2018. "Populism is Not in the Air (But Maybe It Should Be)." *International Labor and Working-Class History* 93: 125–134.

Sevilla Guzmán, Eduardo. 1979. *La evolución del campesinado en España: Elementos para una sociología política del campesinado*. Barcelona: Península.

Smith, Neil. 1990. *Uneven Development: Nature, Capital and the Production of Space*. London: Blackwell.

Smith, Gavin. 2011. "Selective Hegemony and Beyond-Populations with 'No Productive Function': A Framework for Enquiry." *Identities* 18 (1): 2–38.

Soler, Carles, and Fernando Fernández. 2015. *Estructura de la propiedad de tierras en España: Concentración y acaparamiento*. Bilbao: Mundubat.

Stolcke, Verena. 1995. "Talking Culture: New Boundaries, New Rhetorics of Exclusion in Europe." *Current Anthropology* 36 (1): 1–24.

Strijker, Dirk, Gerrit Voerman, and Ida Terluin, eds. 2015. *Rural Protest Groups and Populist Political Parties*. Wageningen: Wageningen Academic Publishers.

Swyngedouw, Erik. 2015. *Liquid Power: Water and Contested Modernities in Spain, 1898–2010*. Cambridge, MA: MIT Press.

van der Linden, Marcel. 2018. "Workers and the Radical Right." *International Labor and Working-Class History* 93: 74–78.

van der Ploeg, Jan D. 2013. *Peasants and the Art of Farming: A Chayanovian Manifesto*. Halifax, NS: Fernwood Publishing.

van der Ploeg, Jan D. 2018. "Differentiation: Old Controversies, New Insights." *The Journal of Peasant Studies* 45 (3): 489–524.

White, Ben. 2018. "Marx and Chayanov at the Margins: Understanding Agrarian Change in Java." *The Journal of Peasant Studies* 45 (5–6): 1108–1126.

Williams, Raymond. 1973. *The Country and the City*. Oxford: Oxford University Press.

Woods, Michael. 2008. "Social Movements and Rural Politics." *Journal of Rural Studies* 24: 129–137.

Understanding the silent majority in authoritarian populism: what can we learn from popular support for Putin in rural Russia?

Natalia Mamonova

ABSTRACT
This study distinguishes and challenges three main assumptions/shortcomings regarding the silent majority – the majority of the 'ordinary', 'simple', 'little' people, who are the main supporters of authoritarian populism. The silent majority is commonly portrayed as (1) consisting of 'irrational', 'politically short-sighted' people, who vote against their self-interests; (2) it is analysed as a homogeneous group, without attempting to distinguish different motives and interests among its members; (3) existing studies often overlook the political economy and structures of domination that gave rise to authoritarian populism. I address these shortcomings while analysing the political behaviour of rural Russians, who are the major supporters of Vladimir Putin. I reveal that the agrarian property regime and power relations in the countryside largely define the political posture of different rural groups. Less secure socio-economic strata respond more strongly to economic incentives, while better-off villagers tend to support the regime's ideological appeals. Furthermore, Putin's traditionalist authoritarian leadership style appeals to the archetypal base of the rural society – namely, its peasant roots – and, therefore, finds stronger support among the farming population. Finally, this study reveals that collective interests prevail over individual interests in the voting behaviour of rural dwellers, who support the existing regime despite the economic hardship it imposes upon them.

1. Introduction

Authoritarian populism[1] has been spreading across the world. Its main features are a coercive, disciplinary state, a rhetoric of national interests, populist unity between 'the people'

---

[1]The contemporary literature uses a variety of terms – 'authoritarian populism', 'populist authoritarianism', 'right-wing populism', 'national populism' – to describe the ongoing political processes. However, as Borras (2018) rightly noted, most of these populist movements have a strong tendency towards authoritarianism, it is just matter of degree. The

and an authoritarian leader, nostalgia for 'past glories' and confrontations with 'Others' at home and/or abroad. The rise of authoritarian populism is primarily linked to recent political events, such as Donald Trump's election, the Brexit referendum, Erdoğan's power grab in Turkey, and the entry of right-wing political parties into many European parliaments. Meanwhile, in Russia, a similar type of governance has existed for quite some time. There are ongoing debates on whether Vladimir Putin's rule can be characterised as authoritarian populism (Oliker 2017; Yudin and Matveyev 2017; Lassila 2018). However, regardless of their position, all scholars agree that Putinism and populism have much in common and that Putin's governance and popularity are 'admired by populist leaders as well as right-wing extremists' (Oliker 2017, 19). In this study, I do not take sides in the debates on authoritarian populism in Russia, but rather look for explanations for the popular support of its main features: authoritarian leadership, a strong state, nostalgia for 'past glories', and 'us' versus 'them' rhetoric.

The supporters of authoritarian populism are often referred as the 'silent majority'[2'] – the majority of the 'ordinary', 'simple', 'little' people, whose interests are often overlooked in favour of the 'vocal minority' of the economic and political establishment (Lassiter 2011). For its support for authoritarian populist leaders, the silent majority is commonly portrayed by progressive media and experts as 'naive people' or 'blind crowds', who vote against self-interests as they are not sophisticated enough to resist the propaganda they encounter (Rancière 2013; Inglehart and Norris 2016).

In this study, I look beyond the common assumptions about popular support for authoritarian populism. In particular, I distinguish and challenge the three following shortcomings in the contemporary debates on the silent majority: (1) the popular support for authoritarian populism is commonly portrayed as irrational and against self-interests; (2) the silent majority is discussed as a homogeneous group, and there is no attempt to distinguish different motives and interests within that group; (3) debates on authoritarian populism often overlook the political economy and structures of domination that triggered/provided the ground for the emergence of this political movement.

I investigate social, economic and political factors that influence rural Russians' support for the authoritarian regime of Vladimir Putin. Rural dwellers are the key political actors in Putin's Russia: their electoral support and relatively high turnout at presidential, parliamentary and regional elections[3] have contributed to the regime's durability for more than 17 years (Zubov 2017; Mamonova 2016a; Vasilyeva 2015). However, their political views and preferences are largely overlooked in Russian studies literature[4], which portrays them as politically silent, conservative, propaganda-ridden, reluctant to engage in open contestations, and having no influence on the ongoing political processes (see Granberg and Sätre 2016 on the 'othering' of rural Russians).

This study brings the ordinary rural Russians in the spotlight and sees them not simply as passive victims of propaganda (although propaganda does play an important role[5]). It

---

present study uses the term 'authoritarian populism' to emphasise the authoritarian character of this movement, which is especially pronounced in present-day Russia.
[2]The term is borrowed from Richard Nixon's populist speech during the Vietnam War.
[3]The turnout is significantly higher for presidential elections than for regional and parliamentary elections.
[4]With some exceptions such as Mamonova 2016a, 2016b, Mamonova and Visser 2014.
[5]The state-controlled media (primarily, federal TV channels) is the main instrument of state propaganda. Russian rural dwellers watch television for an average of 246 min per day, which is 20 min longer than inhabitants of small cities, and 30 min longer than residents of large cities (Poleekhtova 2010).

aims to understand the underlying motives, needs and incentives that define rural dwellers' support for Putin's authoritarian governance. Here, I follow Taylor's (1998) argument that 'any regime reflects the needs of the society under which it had originated' (Taylor 1998, 223). By understanding the reasons behind the popular support for Putin's governance, we can better understand the Russian regime and its durability.

Furthermore, this study contributes to the emerging literature on authoritarian populism and the rural world. Recent studies revealed a strong rural constituency of many authoritarian populist movements (Borras 2018; Scoones et al. 2018). Populist parties are rising by tapping into discontent in the countryside and exploiting rural resentment against elites, migrants and ethnic minorities. In order to curtail this dangerous political trend and to build positive alternatives, we need to understand – not judge – the supporters of authoritarian populism, asking why it is that various rural dwellers are often strongly behind reactionary populist positions (Scoones et al. 2018).

The present analysis is based on my primary qualitative data, obtained during fieldwork in several villages in the Moscow region[6] during August and November 2017, and public opinion survey data, conducted by Levada-Center during November-December 2017. The primary qualitative data was collected for the purposes of this study and focused on motives, incentives and underlying processes of rural support for authoritarian populism. In total, 21 semi-structured in-depth interviews were conducted with various rural dwellers: commercial and subsistence farmers, rural workers, farm directors, civil servants, pensioners and other social groups. This data is complemented with additional data from my previous fieldwork in the Moscow, Vladimir and Stavropol regions during 2013-2015. Elements of critical discourse analysis are used to analyse the primary qualitative data.

The public opinion survey data was obtained from a database of Levada-Center – a Russian independent non-governmental polling and sociological research organisation. Levada-Center provided me with survey data on public attitudes towards authoritarian leadership in Russia, the populist unity between the president and the ordinary people, the neoimperialist foreign policy, nostalgia for the Soviet past and other features of authoritarian populism. The data (sample size: 1600) contains socio-economic characteristics (gender, age, occupation, education, income), and geographical characteristics (urban, rural settlements), which allowed me to distinguish several rural socio-economic groups and analyse their political opinions.

The paper is structured as follows. The next section (section 2) presents the existing theoretical assumptions about popular support to authoritarian populism and discusses their limitations. Section 3 briefly introduces the political situation in Russia and provides the current arguments for and against referring to Putinism as authoritarian populism. Section 4 discusses the relations between the structures of political authority and agrarian

---

[6]It should be noted that the Moscow region is not a typical Russian region. Its proximity to Russia's capital leads to higher living standards for its residents and better access to alternate sources of information. However, the support for Putin in the Moscow region is in line with the national average, as shown by the results of the 2018 Presidential Elections (Golos 2018). The fieldwork sites were selected in the most remote areas of the Moscow region to lessen Moscow's impact on rural lifestyle. Nevertheless, it would be wrong to argue that the findings of this qualitative study are generalisable to the entire country. Instead, the goal of this analysis was to depict the variety of motives, needs and incentives that determine villagers' support for Putin in one particular place. However, I believe that many detected trends could be found in other villages across Russia, as supported by the results of my previous fieldwork in the Vladimir and Stavropol regions. Furthermore, the primarily qualitative data was complemented with the public opinion survey data of Levada-Center. This survey was carried out among 1600 people in 136 localities of 52 of the country's regions, in order to guarantee the representability of the sample.

property regimes in Russia. Section 5 distinguishes different socio-economic groups in Russian rural society and explores their political positions regarding various elements of authoritarian populism. Section 6 examines the notion of the 'self' in villagers' self-interests. The concluding Section 7 answers the question posed in the title – 'what can we learn from popular support for Putin in rural Russia?'

2. Three assumptions/shortcomings in understanding the popular support for authoritarian populism

Authoritarian populism is not a new phenomenon. This term was developed by Hall (1980, 1985) to explain the policy of Margaret Thatcher that provided a right-wing solution to the economic and political crisis in Britain. It characterises 'a movement towards a dominative and "authoritarian" form of democratic class politics – paradoxically, apparently rooted in the "transformism[7]" of populist discontents' (Hall 1985, 118). Among the main features of authoritarian populism, Hall distinguished: a strong and interventionist state, a shift towards a 'law-and-order' society, populist unity between people and the power bloc, an embrace of nationalist over sectional interests, and an anti-elite movement. The concept of authoritarian populism was criticised by Jessop et al. (1984) for its ambiguity and problematic coupling of the notions of 'authority' and 'people': 'sometimes its authoritarian, disciplinary, coercive pole is emphasised, sometimes its populist, popular, and consensual pole' (Jessop et al. 1984, 35).

However, the very same contradiction between 'authoritarian' and 'populism' makes this concept suitable to explain the current crisis of liberal democracy, when authoritarian leaders find support among the ordinary people – the silent majority – whose interests used to be overlooked in favour of the 'vocal minority' of the economic and political establishment. The authoritarian populist leaders promise to 'bring back control' in favour of 'the people', returning the nation to 'greatness' or 'health' after real or imagined degeneration attributed to malevolent, racialised and/or unfairly advantaged 'Others' at home and/or abroad (Scoones et al. 2018). This political movement favours strong individual leadership over diplomatic negotiations, nationalist interests over cosmopolitanism, protectionism over cooperation across borders, xenophobia over multiculturalism, traditional over progressive values (Inglehart and Norris 2016).

In many countries, authoritarian populism has a strong rural base (see Gonda [2018] on rural support for Orbán's party in Hungary; Gürel et al. [2018] on Erdoğan's popularity among small-scale farmers in Turkey; Gaventa [2018] on rural communities voting for Trump in the USA). The rural silent majority is the most dramatically affected by the development of neoliberal capitalism in the countryside. The commoditisation of land and nature, massive resource extraction, multinational corporations' control over the agrifood system, and the dispossession of rural communities from productive resources have caused poverty among many smallholders and farmers, exacerbated socio-economic inequality, and created the 'relative surplus population' that spreads across rural, peri-urban and urban areas (Hall, Scoones, and Tsikata 2015; Edelman, Oya, and Borras 2013; Li 2010). Many right-wing populist parties use the ongoing crisis in the countryside to

---

[7]Transformism is Gramsci's term for the process when, in order to create or sustain a historic bloc, the dominant class has to make concessions to the subordinate social forces, giving them a material interest in its maintenance.

gain popular support among the rural population. Thus, the French far-right party Front National has recently re-formulated its political programme to focus more on agrarian values and farmers' interests (Ivaldi and Gombin 2015). The Swedish extreme-right party Sweden Democrats put defending the interests of farmers and forest owners at the very top of its agenda (Ferrari 2018).

While the supply-side of authoritarian populism (i.e. the strategic appeals of its leaders and the programmes of populist parties) have received considerable public and academic attention (Lubarda 2018; Ferrari 2018; Inglehart and Norris 2016; Strijker, Voerman, and Terluin 2015), little is known about the demand side of this phenomenon. Below I distinguish the main assumptions/shortcomings in contemporary literature about the popular support for authoritarian populism.

First, *the supporters of authoritarian populism are portrayed as 'simple', 'irrational' people, who vote against self-interests and are not sophisticated enough to resist the propaganda they encounter*. The 'apparent irrational support of the working class' for the authoritarian populism of Margaret Thatcher was mentioned by Jessop et al. (1984, 35). Recently, Peters (2017, 1) called the election of Donald Trump 'against all logic and humanism'. Vladimir Putin's popularity among ordinary Russians is often attributed to 'the state propaganda and societal fears and Soviet complexes' (Amelyushkin 2014). Certainly, the role of propaganda transforms societal attitudes in every country it is applied, but if the 'propagandistic message does not have an archetypal base [in a society], it is inefficient and most likely will be rejected by the society' (Valiev 2017).

The difficulty of explaining the popular support for authoritarian populism makes many experts and scholars refer to this support as 'irrational' or 'illogical'. At the recent British Psychological Society Lecture, professor Reicher addressed this issue from a political psychology perspective. He argued that the people's vote for authoritarian populist leaders does not seem 'irrational' and 'against self-interests' if we understand the nature of the 'self' in the self-interests. The self-concept comprises three fundamental components: the individual self, the relational self, and the collective self. The individual self-identity is generated through the feeling of belonging to, and identification with, a particular group or nation; therefore, the interests of the collective (national) self are equally important to individual self-interests. At certain moments of time (usually during crises) people put collective interests above personal interests, and vote as a nation not as individuals. Then, the collective elements of national identity become important parts of an individual's definition of the self and how he/she views the world and his/her own place in it. Reicher (2017) argued that authoritarian populist leaders are the 'entrepreneurs of identity' – they generate popular support by appealing to the people's 'endangered' collective identity, and claim to share and defend this identity. Therefore, in order to explain the popular support for authoritarian populism, we need to understand the nature of the self in the silent majority's self-interests.

Second, *the supporters of authoritarian populism are analysed as a homogeneous group, and there is no attempt to distinguish different motives and interests within it*. When talking about the supporters of authoritarian populism, experts and scholars often use aggregated concepts – such as 'the ordinary people', the 'silent majority', 'masses', 'crowds' – that emphasise the homogeneity of its members. This generalisation stems from the fact that authoritarian populism is an ideology that considers society to be ultimately separated into two homogeneous and antagonistic groups – 'the pure people'[8] and 'the corrupt elite' (Mudde 2017).

By adopting the populist discourse about the homogeneous people with common interests, scholars tend to overlook different interests within the silent majority. Thus, in their analysis of 268 populist political parties in 31 European countries, Inglehart and Norris (2016) aimed to reveal whether the societal support for populist movements can be explained by the economic insecurity perspective or by the cultural backlash thesis. The economic insecurity perspective emphasises the consequences of profound changes transforming the workplace and society in post-industrial economies. According to this view, less secure social strata – so-called left-behinds – are heavily affected by economic insecurity and social deprivation and, therefore, are more vulnerable to anti-establishment, nativist, and xenophobic feelings, blaming 'Others' for stripping prosperity, job opportunities, and public services from 'Us'. Meanwhile, the cultural backlash thesis explains popular support for authoritarian populism as a reaction to progressive cultural change. According to this position, the societal transformation to post-materialist values (primarily, cosmopolitanism and multiculturalism) has triggered a retro backlash, especially among older generations, who 'feel strangers from predominant values in their own country, left behind by progressive tides of cultural change which they do not share' (Inglehart and Norris 2016, 5).

The analysis of Inglehart and Norris (2016) revealed that demographic and social controls suggest that populist support in Europe is generally stronger among the older generation, men, the less educated, the religious, and ethnic majorities. The authors concluded that the cultural backlash thesis is the most suitable to explain the popular support for authoritarian populism. Meanwhile, the results of their empirical analysis in regard to economic parameters were 'mixed and inconsistent'. Populists do indeed receive great support from less well-off and those who have experienced unemployment. However, in terms of occupational class, populist voting was strongest among the 'petty bourgeoisie', not unskilled manual workers. Moreover, populist parties received less support among those whose main source of income came from social welfare benefits (Inglehart and Norris 2016). This contradictions cannot be reconciled if the authors try to apply one theory to explain the motives of the entire group of populist supporters. We need to study the silent majority as a composition of different socio-economic strata with different interests.

This brings us to the third shortcoming in the contemporary debates on authoritarian populism: *the existing analysis often overlooks the political economy and structures of domination that triggered/provided the ground for the emergence of authoritarian populism*. This limitation was already pointed out by Jessop et al. (1984) in their critique of Hall (1980), who focused primarily on ideological and discursive aspects of authoritarian populism.

The classic studies have demonstrated the existence of interrelations between the structures of political authority and agrarian property regimes (Marx and Engels 1967; Moore 1966; Skocpol 1979; Rueschemeyer, Stephens, and Stephens 1992). Moore (1966) argued that the preservation of the peasantry leads to an emergence of authoritarian

---

[8]Inclusionary populists describe 'the people' as everyone within the national borders who is not part of the elite. Exclusionary populists define 'the people' as excluding not only the elite, but also other groups of people – i.e. ethnic and cultural minorities, immigrants, etc. – who are portrayed as 'anti-national' or 'alien' (Margulies 2016).

regimes, as the landed class needs a repressive state to help with surplus extraction. Meanwhile, the bourgeoisie is the main agent of democracy, as economic development driven by capitalist interests in competition with each other brings about political freedom and democratisation of the society (Moore 1966). Marxists, on the contrary, believed that bourgeois democracy proclaims the rule of the people, but, in fact, only protects the interest of capitalist class (Lenin, Marx).

Rueschemeyer, Stephens, and Stephens (1992) argued that democratic development in the countryside depends on: the balance of power among different rural classes and class coalitions; benefits and losses that classes could expect from extensions of political inclusion; and their ability to organise themselves and engage in collective action to defend their own interests. According to these authors, 'independent family farmers in small-holding countries were a pro-democratic force, whereas their posture in countries or areas dominated by large landholdings was more authoritarian. Peasants living on large estates remained by and large unmobilised and thus did not play a role in democratisation. Rural wage workers on plantations did attempt to organise and, where they were not repressed, they joined other working-class organisations in pushing for political inclusion' (Rueschemeyer, Stephens, and Stephens 1992, 247). Therefore, the typical rules in agrarian societies that feature the peasant mode of production have been autocracy and oligarchy (Rueschemeyer, Stephens, and Stephens 1992). Even today, Kurtz and Barnes (2002) revealed that a larger rural population with peasant-like features correlates with lower levels of democracy.

Thus, in order to explain the emergence of an authoritarian regime that enjoys popular support, we need to understand the agrarian property regime and power relations in the countryside.

3. Is there authoritarian populism in Russia?

A number of analytical discussions on contemporary populist movements include Russia as an example of authoritarian populism (Stroop 2017; Reicher 2017). Some experts even believe that Putin was the first who discovered a breach in the modern liberal democracy and created an authoritarian regime that enjoys popular support by 'making empty populist promises and using the political short-sightedness and irresponsibility of the ordinary people' (see discussion by Yudin and Matveyev 2017).

Putin, indeed, followed the same path as some Western populists – he came to power through elections and then proceeded to centralise. He built a political regime that has a number of authoritarian populist features: strongman authoritarian leadership, coercive disciplinary state power, traditionalist and nationalist (sometimes xenophobic) appeals in domestic and foreign policies, demonstrative attacks on 'disloyal' elites, and popular support among ordinary Russians. However, Putin did not come to power in 2000 on a populist platform and his first two presidential terms were based on a programme of economic modernisation and neoliberal development. The beginning of his rule coincided with rising oil prices, which boosted Russia's economic growth. The global financial crisis that hit the country in 2008 triggered growing dissatisfaction among many Russians who experienced a decline in earnings. People became more critical to systematic corruption and started doubting the government's ability to manage the economy. The crisis also 'undercut whatever vestiges of support remained for the neoliberal, globalisation, and pro-Western model of economic development' (Chaisty and Whitefield 2015, 167).

In response to the growing social discontent, Putin's third and fourth presidential terms (from 2012 onwards) involved more direct engagement with nationalist issues, and took 'a conservative direction, with greater prominence given to themes of order and the need to protect the state' (Chaisty and Whitefield 2017, 169). Putin has used the Tsarist and Soviet legacies in order to develop patriotism and a unified sense of Russian identity and to create positive historical parallels to justify the state's policy toward internal opposition and external enemies (Mamonova 2016a, 326). The idea of a strong – nearly sovereign – leader who has the power to intervene in any political process and decision making is often portrayed by the state-controlled mass media as the only efficient way to rule the country. Besides that, the Orthodox Church – which has recently gained a strong political and spiritual influence over Russian society – plays an important role in generating people's loyalty and obedience to the country's authoritarian leadership.

In one of my studies, I argued that Putin's governance (re-)established naive monarchist principles in the state-society relations: the president plays the role of an intercessor and benefactor for the ordinary people, while all problems are blamed on 'disloyal' and 'evil' elites, who deliberately misrepresent and misinform the president. Indeed, Putin regularly demonstrates his benevolence and closeness to ordinary Russians (i.e. his shirtless pictures on fishing trips, staged meetings with provincial residents, the annual TV question-and-answer session 'Hotline with the President', etc.). From time to time, Putin demonstratively punishes 'disloyal' elites to maintain his image of the 'just and impartial ruler'. However, the business elites are the backbone of Putin's regime and his demonstrative punishments are aimed at maintaining the elites' loyalty and satisfying anti-elite sentiments of ordinary Russians (Mamonova 2016a).

The ambivalent relations between Putin and elites are one of the reasons against calling the Russian regime 'populism' (Oliker 2017; Yudin and Matveyev 2017). Oliker (2017, 16) argued that 'anti-elite and anti-corruption campaigns, and popular feeling, are fundamentally different in Russia, where corruption is simply more accepted as part and parcel of the system, than in Europe'. Another reason against Russian populism is the depoliticisation of ordinary Russians. According to Yudin and Matveyev (2017), while populist leaders in other countries are aimed at mobilising and politicising their supporters, Putinism is based on the demobilisation and depoliticisation of the Russian population. The regime endorses peoples' 'non-interference in the affairs of those who are above'.

However, demobilisation and depoliticisation are not necessarily in opposition to populism. According to Norman (2018), populist movements often substitute 'rule by the people' with 'rule for the people', which is embodied in their leader and, thereby, curbs broad political participation. Furthermore, the anti-elitist discourse is essential for the 'populists-in-opposition', who critisise the ruling elite in order to gain the support of the ordinary people and, thereby, obtain leading positions in the government. Meanwhile, the 'populists-in-government' (which is the case in Russia) use populist rhetoric and practices to maintain the status quo, therefore, the anti-elite/establishment discourse is less pronounced in their campaigns (Makarenko 2017).

The present paper does not take sides in the debates on Russian populism but rather aims to examine why rural dwellers support the following features of the regime: authoritarian leadership, a strong state, populist unity between the people and the president,

Table 1. Rural dimension of popular support for Putin's governance.

	Moscow	Large cities (> 500 K people)	Medium cities (100-500 K people)	Small towns (< 100 K people)	Rural settlements	Total
Support/Positive attitude to V. Putin	60%	62%	65%	63%	70%	64%
Belief that Russia needs strong authoritarian governance	18%	41%	37%	43%	45%	40%
Regret about the USSR's collapse	61%	55%	54%	60%	61%	58%
Support for Putin's neoimperialist foreign policy (protection from the West, return of global respect)	18.8%	20%	18.3%	18.2%	14%	17.7%
Appreciation for the charismatic features of V. Putin, the 'real muzhik' (man of the ordinary people)	23.3%	17%	19%	17.9%	18%	18.5%
Belief that V. Putin represents the interests of *ordinary* Russians	11.6%	18%	18.6%	14.4%	18%	16.1%

Note: All but the first row in the table is based on Levada-Center data, collected during November – December 2017; data for the first row, 'Support/Positive attitude to V. Putin', was taken from the Public Opinion Foundation (2017) report.

nostalgia for past glories and confrontation with 'Others'. There is a strong rural bias in the popular support for the authoritarian rule of Putin. Table 1 displays selected results from public opinion surveys, categorised by type of settlement. It demonstrates that rural dwellers are the major supporters of Putin's regime: 70 percent of Russian villagers have a strong positive attitude towards the president, which is six percent above the national average. Likewise, rural Russians are those who most believe that their country needs strong authoritarian governance, but also those who support Putin's neoimperialist foreign policy the least (an issue which will be discussed later). They also score high for appreciating the populist image of Putin as a 'real muzhik' (real man – man of the people) and believe that the president represents the interests of ordinary Russians.

Rural dwellers constitute nearly 30 percent of the total population (Rosstat 2017). Moreover, many residents of small towns and town-like settlements are not very different from rural dwellers 'in terms of lifestyle, consumption pattern, and socio-political orientations and beliefs'. Together with villagers, they represent more than 50 percent of the population (Gudkov and Dubin 2002, 1). This largely conservative social array 'has a decisive influence on the course of changes in the country' (Gudkov and Dubin 2002, 1).

4. Agrarian structure and the lack of pro-democratic rural forces

In order to understand the popularity of Putin's governance in rural areas, it is important to, first, understand the socio-economic structure of the contemporary rural society. Here, I follow Rueschemeyer, Stephens, and Stephens (1992), who argued that different rural classes exhibit different political tendencies in the struggle for democracy. The political posture of class actors depends on: the balance of power among different rural classes; benefits and losses that classes could expect from extensions of political inclusion; and their ability to organise themselves and engage in collective action to defend own interests. According to this position, peasants are least prone to democratic movements, as their dependence on subsistence farming makes them resilient to economic shocks and, therefore, less interested in political inclusion. Rural proletariats are relatively pro-democratic if they are able to mobilise themselves and join other working-class organisations in pushing for democratic governance. The most pro-democratic force is the group of individual family farmers in small-holding countries, as their economic activities require free competition that, in its turn, requires democratic government. Meanwhile, large agroholdings would require a repressive state to help with surplus extraction. Certainly, the class structure[9] is not so definite in contemporary Russia; however, this approach provides an explanation for the general tendencies of different rural groups towards or against democracy.

In the Soviet period, all farmland and productive resources belonged to collective and state farm enterprises (kolkhozy and sovkhozy), where the majority of the rural population were employed. However, rural dwellers were not absolute proletarians: in addition to their wage-work, they conducted subsidiary farming on their household plots of 0.2 ha on average, which they were allowed to own since the late 1930s. This highly productive food production was 'outside the state planning and procurement system' (Wegren 2005, 8) and preserved a number of peasant features (see Humphrey 2002 on 'Soviet peasant'). The private subsidiary farming was seen by some experts as an indication that – once Soviet-era restrictions on private production were lifted – rural dwellers would establish commercial family farms.

After the collapse of the Soviet Union in 1991, the new Russian government initiated land reform measures aimed at distributing kolkhozy's and sovkhozy's land to rural dwellers by means of land share certificates for private farming. However, due to the absence of financial resources and informational support, fragmented and often non-functioning markets, and the rural dwellers' unwillingness to leave the collectives, the majority of land recipients did not become farmers (Pallot and Nefedova 2007). The restructured kolkhozy and sovkhozy experienced severe financial difficulties in free market conditions, and, as result, many villagers lost their jobs. The transition period of the 1990s was characterised by economic and political instability, deep rural poverty, and high unemployment. Many rural residents, especially young people, 'voted with their feet' and moved to cities. Those who remained in the villages became highly dependent on subsistence farming on their household plots.

Putin's rise to power in the year 2000 has changed the direction of agricultural reform: the previous state programmes of private farming development were curtailed, and the main state support was directed towards the reestablishment of large-scale industrial agriculture, albeit in neoliberal guise. Land sales were legalised in 2002, which brought oligarchic capital to the countryside. Russian oligarchs and foreign investors bought (or rented) land shares from the rural population and established modern agricultural enterprises. In his analysis of the land reform, Wegren (2009, 143) wrote: 'Russia's land reform did not deliver on early intentions in that large farms continue to use most of Russia's agricultural land. Individuals have not become "masters of the land". The former large

---

[9]Some Russian scholars argue that class analysis is inappropriate for studying post-socialist transformation, because social stratification cannot be adequately explained by relationship to the means of production (i.e. Clark and Lipset 1991). New forms of social stratification are now discussed: emerging elites (or the 'top 1 percent'), the lower class (or 'precariat'), and many strata in between (Stenning 2005). I partially agree with the existing critique of the class analysis in the Russian context. Therefore, I discuss different socio-economic groups (not classes!) in the empirical sections of my study. However, in this section, I follow the class-based approach of Rueschemeyer, Stephens, and Stephens (1992) that explains how the political economy and structures of domination influence the democratic development in the countryside. This helps to define the material base of democracy in rural Russia (even though class structure is not transparent and rural groups do not share a particular class consciousness).

collective farms were transformed into even larger agricultural enterprises, while the majority of the rural population continue being dependent on semi-subsistent farming at their household plots.

Today large industrial farms control 80 percent of Russian farmland and contribute to 52 percent of the gross agricultural output. Meanwhile, rural households grow staple food for personal consumption and occasional sales at local markets. They produce 35 percent of the total food in Russia by cultivating only 8 percent of the country's farmland. Private farming remains underdeveloped with less than one percent of rural dwellers that can officially call themselves family farmers[10] (Rosstat 2017; All-Russian Agricultural Census of 2016).

The underdevelopment of individual family farmers left the Russian countryside without the main actor pushing for democracy (i.e. liberal democracy under capitalist ideology). Large industrial farms are enjoying state subsidies and patronage, almost as much as their collective predecessors once did. Many former Soviet structures and networks have remained unchanged, which makes the re-emergence of large-scale industrial agriculture to some extent socially accepted. By taking over the collective farmland, new agricultural enterprises have to take over some of the social functions of their predecessors (support to rural areas, productive symbiosis with rural households, employment, albeit at a much smaller scale than it was practiced in the Soviet time). Putin's policy boosted large-scale agricultural production and thereby, indirectly, increased the living standards of rural residents. However, rural poverty and unemployment remain the key problems of the countryside. The majority of rural dwellers continue practicing peasant-like farming, which is subsistence-oriented, based on family labour and traditional farming methods.[11] Although some principles of market economy have emerged in the countryside, the capitalist development *within* rural communities remains rather insignificant. The state support to large agribusiness and overall corruption significantly limits prospects for small-scale rural entrepreneurship and commercially-oriented individual farming (Mamonova 2016b). Moreover, due to the socialist tradition of industrialised agriculture, post-Soviet rural dwellers regard themselves primarily as workers and not as landowners, and therefore, they do not long for commercial family farming (Petrick, Wandel, and Karsten 2013).

Collective action is very limited in rural Russia. Waylen (2010) argued that the Soviet legacies of state intervention caused the post-Soviet population's reluctance to undertake organised (formal) initiatives to improve their wellbeing. Furthermore, the majority of the rural population tend to distrust independent civil organisations and collective initiatives. As a result, there are hardly any civic organisations or social movements that could defend the interests of smallholders and represent them in the political arena (Mamonova and Visser 2014).

---

[10]Commercial family farmers produce about 10% of gross domestic agricultural output.

[11]There are longstanding debates on the persistence versus disappearance of the peasantry under capitalism. Marxist thinkers argue that peasants tend to differentiate into the bourgeoisie and the proletariat, and, therefore, disappear as a class. Agrarian populists, on the contrary, argue that peasants preserve their mode of production and lifestyle, and, thereby, provide a sustainable alternative to capitalist agriculture (see Mamonova 2016b for a detailed discussion of these two approaches). Russian scholars traditionally follow the disappearance thesis because of the socialist history of collectivisation, expropriation, and forced industrialisation that aimed at the erosion of the peasantry as a class. However, recent research has demonstrated that many peasant features were preserved and even reinforced by the capitalist developments in rural Russia and other post-socialist countries (Mamonova 2016a; Dorondel and Şerban 2014).

Thus, the largest part of Russian rural society is stuck between socialism and capitalism, and has preserved a number of peasant features in their household farming. Under such circumstances, the domination of large-scale agriculture, lack of free market competition, and little stimuli for collective action have made villagers seek state patronage instead of political inclusion.

5. Explaining Putin's popularity among different socio-economic groups

In Table 2, I distinguished different socio-economic groups for the purposes of this study, based on the available data. The division of rural dwellers into small-scale food producers, rural labourers, pensioners, and jobless groups is primarily guided by their self-identification and their degree of dependence on subsidiary farming. However, they all conduct small-scale farming at their household plots and are reported in the Agricultural census as 'rural households' (see an elaborate description below Table 2). Rural groups are listed in descending order from the most secure to the least secure socio-economic strata.

Furthermore, it should be noted that the percentages in the table represent the share of people who support Putin *because of* particular reasons, i.e. his authoritarian leadership, foreign policy, etc. (not just a share of people who support his authoritarian leadership or foreign policy). The same principle is used for the explanation of people's regret about the USSR's collapse. Respondents were allowed to give multiple answers choosing among many options, which resulted in relatively low percentage value. Although the difference between the answers of various groups is often insignificant (usually just a few percentage points), it is still possible to observe variations in the groups' response to the elements of authoritarian populism.

Column A 'Support/Positive attitude to Putin' indicates that the most supportive groups are less secure social strata – pensioners, rural labourers, jobless, small-scale food producers. They were heavily affected by economic insecurity and social deprivation during the post-socialist transition period. Their support can be partly explained by the economic insecurity perspective, as discussed later in this paper. Farm managers and rural specialists also score quite high in their support/positive attitude to Putin – these are the members of rural communities who benefited the most from Putin's regime (I should note that land investors, businessmen and authorities – i.e. the rural establishment – are not discussed here). The commercial family farmers and rural entrepreneurs are least positive about Putin and his authoritarian governance. To some extent, this confirms the previous section's argument that commercial family farmers are the main pro-democratic force.

It is also interesting to mention that Putin is more popular among women than men, and that women are more likely to believe that Russia needs authoritarian governance. Some Russian experts explain Putin's popularity among women by the president's machismo (Sperling 2014). However, Table 2 shows that Putin's 'real man' image is less popular among women than men. The present study does not explicitly address the gender differences due to the space limit. However, it should be noted that, during the interviews I carried out, rural women expressed very traditional patriarchal views on family: they stressed the dominant role of a husband, who protects and takes care of his submissive wife and children. They often used this idea to explain what kind of leadership their country needs. A more thorough research is required to understand the role of gender in the popular support for authoritarian populism.

Table 2. Various rural groups and their support for different features of authoritarian populism in Russia

Categories:	Support/ Positive attitude towards Putin	Authoritarian governance		Populist unity between the ordinary people and the president		Nostalgia for the 'past glories'		Economic reasons		The benevolent president – evil elites		Regret about the collapse of the USSR	Share in rural population (approx, author's calculations)
		Believe that Russia needs authoritarian governance (not Putin per se)	Support Putin as he is a strong (authoritarian) leader	Support Putin as he is a 'real muzhik' (man from the people)	Believe that Putin represents the interests of the 'ordinary people'	Regret the USSR collapse because people lost the feeling of belonging to a 'great global power'	Support Putin because of his foreign policy that returned global respect towards Russia	Regret the destruction of the USSR economic system, and the reorganisation of kolkhozy and sovkhozy	Support Putin as he brought economic stability, improved living standards, ensured pensions are paid on time	Believe that Putin is misinformed about the situation in the country	Support Putin as he is a fair and honest man		
No. of columns	A	B	C	D	E	F	G	H	I	J	K	L	M
Rural groups:													
Farm managers/ specialists	62.5%	43.9%	16.0%	18.0%	17.0%	32.7%	16.6%	54.9%	6.6%	41.0%	5.9%	52.6%	1–5%
Commercial family farmers/rural entrepreneurs	55.3%	46.1%	8.0%	14.6%	13.3%	31.0%	12.0%	58.1%	3.1%	35.6%	4.2%	47.3%	0.5–6.3%
Rural labour (main income from wages)	71.3%	37.1%	16.3%	17.7%	16.4%	26.7%	14.0%	60.2%	6.4%	42.0%	12.0%	61.0%	35–40%
Small-scale food producers (main income from farm activities)	67.7%	49.5%	17.3%	19.0%	18.0%	27.6%	13.0%	67.6%	6.0%	39.5%	11.8%	61.0%	40–45%
Pensioneers	77.6%	51.8%	11.5%	17.3%	18.4%	32.0%	12.8%	56.0%	6.3%	40.0%	13.0%	87.3%	26%
Jobless	67.0%	45.0%	20.2%	18.5%	17.4%	28.4%	11.8%	55.9%	5.5%	38.5%	8.1%	50.5%	10–15%
Gender:													
Male	60.2%	43.9%	15.0%	19.5%	16.0%	31.0%	14.0%	61.2%	5.1%	41.0%	6.6%	59.9%	46%
Female	78.3%	46.1%	15.0%	16.5%	18.4%	30.5%	14.8%	52.8%	6.6%	41.0%	10.5%	62.1%	54%
Average for rural areas	70%	45%	15%	18%	17%	31%	14%	57%	5.9%	41%	8.6%	61%	
Average for Russia	64%	40%	15.6%	18.5%	16.6%	36%	17.7%	54%	5%	41.5%	7.3%	58%	

Note: This table is largely based on the data from a public opinion survey, conducted by Levada-Center in November-December 2017 (columns B – L). The sample size was 1600, of which 30% were rural residents (the same proportion as in the total Russian population). The survey data was categorised by socio-economic parameters (gender, age, occupation, education, income), and geographical location (urban, rural residence), which allowed me to distinguish 6 rural socio-economic groups (that represent the largest groups in the rural society and are important for my study). I faced a major difficulty in distinguishing the group of 'small-scale food producers' as the survey questionnaire did not contain this category for respondents' self-identification. The closest category was a 'house keeper/housewife'. The categories 'Authoritarian governance', 'Populist unity ...', 'Nostalgia for the past glories', 'Economic reasons' and 'The benevolent president – evil elites' combine at least two variables. The variables represent either one of the most popular answers, or most related ones. I do not use negative answers in this analysis (although they were available) in order to focus primarily on the *supporters* of Putin's regime and investigate the reasons for their support.
Column A is calculated based on the data from the report of the Public Opinion Foundation (2017). The Public Opinion Foundation provides the data on the degree of people's positive attitude to Putin, which is distributed by age, education, income (*not* occupation) and rural-urban divide. Here too, I distinguished the same rural socio-economic groups and applied a rural coefficient. Therefore, although the percentages in column A might be not fully accurate, they reflect the general trends and can be used for the purpose of this study. Column M is also very suggestive, as no exact data is available. The share of 'commercial family farmers/rural entrepreneurs' is indicated based on the research of Skalnaya and Burykin (2009), who argued that up to 6.3% of rural households are commercially-oriented, but not all of them are registered as commercial farms. The size of the 'farm managers/specialists' group was calculated based on data from the All-Russian Agricultural Census of 2016. The share of 'rural labour' is calculated based on rural employment rates minus the share of the 'farm managers/specialists' group, corrected according to various scholars' estimations of a real rural employment/unemployment rate in rural Russia. The share of the 'jobless' percentage was calculated accordingly. The share of 'pensioners' was estimated based on the data from Rosstat (2017).

5.1. Authoritarian governance and democracy with adjectives

In the early 1990s, many Russians were enthusiastic about democracy and supported democratic reforms hoping that the post-socialist transformation would bring a better life to many. However, the economic and political turmoil of the 1990s disillusioned many Russians with liberal democracy, which became associated with instabilities and uncertainties. Pensioner Vitaly (69), who used to be a combine driver at a former kolkhoz, does not believe in democracy for ordinary people, but describes it as a means of wealth accumulation by elites:

> Democracy belongs to those who have large wallets. They have democracy. We do not know what democracy is. Maybe, democracy does not exist at all. There is a ruling elite [that follows the principle]: you give to me – I give to you. That is what they call a democracy.[12]

The negative associations with democracy are shared by 13 percent of the population, and 24 percent think that this form of government is not for Russia. They prefer a strong economy over a good democracy. The majority of the population still believes that democracy is needed, but they refer to a unique Russian form of democracy, which is associated with a strong state that takes care of the people, economic stability, law and order, free elections, and protection from illegitimate (external) interference in state affairs (commonly known as 'sovereign democracy'[13]). The interview data indicated that liberal democracy finds its stronger adherents among commercial family farmers, while the majority of rural dwellers are in favour of sovereign democracy with its ideas of a strong state. Therefore, Putin's consolidation of state power is not seen by the majority of rural Russians as contradictory to democracy. Former kolkhoz milkmaid Maria (67) sees the state power centralisation as a positive outcome of Putin's presidency, supported by the votes of ordinary people:

> Maria: I voted for Putin and continue voting for him. Not only me, but many people in the village raise both of their hands for him [*note*: totally support him].
>
> I: But the centralisation of state power happened during Putin …
>
> Maria: Yes of course! It is right. I think this is very positive. We at least began to live normally. We lived well under Brezhnev and under Putin.[14]

Villagers' perceptions of elections did not change significantly since the collapse of the Soviet Union. Similarly to the Soviet elections, when all candidates were members of the Communist Party, the contemporary regime of Putin eliminates all real political alternatives, but still needs elections to legitimise its power and to create the image of democratic governance. As a result, the majority of rural dwellers see elections more as a symbolic act of expressing loyalty and their approval of Putin's performance, instead of a democratic choice between different candidates. There is a significant difference in societal attitudes to presidential elections and those for regional/local authorities. If

---

[12]Interview conducted on 09-11-2017 in the Gravornoe village, Istra district, Moscow region.
[13]The advocates of 'sovereign democracy' challenge the applicability of the western liberal type of democracy in the Russian context. They believe that the 'democratic tradition is not something that can be introduced to Russia from abroad; rather, it is a value hard won by our people [that reflects] national values and traditions [...] on par with such values as freedom and justice' (Kokoshin 2006).
[14]Interview conducted on 10-11-2017 in the Sumarokovo village, Ruza district, Moscow region.

voting in the presidential elections is an expression of loyalty, the regional and local elections are rather seen as a civic duty with no impact on actual politics. Farmer Nikolai (65) has this to say about local elections in his village:

> People go to the polls by inertia. It is like as a duty. Elections, elections! You get a postcard. A beautiful postcard! There is a flag painted; they addressed me personally: "Nikolai Alexandrovich, come to the polls".[...] But my voice defines nothing. They [local authorities] have their own agenda.[15]

The inability of the ordinary people to influence the decision making at local and regional levels creates a desire for a strong and powerful leader who can rein in corrupted authorities and bring order to the country. Nearly a half of rural dwellers believe that Russia needs authoritarian governance (in the original questionnaire, it was formulated as 'Do you believe that Russia needs a "strong arm"?' (column B)). Even individual family farmers and rural entrepreneurs, who are the most critical to the existing regime, support this idea. Besides the failure of bottom-up democracy, there might also be a rural/peasant dimension in the popular support for authoritarian governance. This interview with small-scale food producer Sergey (61) highlights an interesting comparison between a traditional peasant family and the country's leadership:

> Russia – it used to be mostly a peasant country. How is a peasant family organised? There should be a *khozyain*[16] [a good household leader, master]. Otherwise, the household will fall apart. There should be only one bear in a den. And everyone should listen to him. A strongman should lead the family [...] The state is a family but at a large scale.[17]

Therefore, it may not only be a coincidence that traditionalist (patriarchal) ideas about power and domination found particular support among those rural groups who are engaged in individual farming: commercial family farmers, small-scale food producers, jobless, pensioners (although I should note that pensioners' support for authoritarian governance is mainly attributed to their strong nostalgia for the Soviet past). Meanwhile those who have wage jobs (farm managers, specialists and rural labourers) are less supportive of traditionalist ideas about the country's leadership.

5.2. Unity between the ordinary people and the president (against the corrupted elites)

Elections in the countryside are different from urban areas in that rural voters are primarily guided by the candidates' personal characteristics, not by pre-election political campaigns and programmes (Petrov 2013). Indeed, many respondents in this study stressed the importance of Putin's strong and heroic traditional masculinity and his charismatic leadership, but they are not interested in the political programme of his party. The image of Putin as a representative of the ordinary people is highly popular among rural dwellers,

---

[15] Interview conducted on 10-11-2017 in the Sumarokovo village, Ruza district, Moscow region.
[16] The word 'khozyain' was first mentioned in the *Domostroy* (Domestic Order) – the 16th-century Russian set of household rules, instructions and advice pertaining to various religious, social, domestic, and family matters in Russian society. According to the Domostroy, the main qualities of a good khozyain were discernment, knowledge of the practical side of the matter, and concern for the material and especially moral position of subordinates.
[17] Interview conducted on 11-11-2017 in the Sumarokovo village, Ruza district, Moscow region.

especially among less economically secure rural strata (see columns D and E). In the interview for this study, unemployed villager Vladimir (58) stresses which of the president's features he appreciates the most:

> How nicely he treats the ordinary people! He knows [everything] inside and out. I like him very much. He can answer any question. And he does not look whether you are poor or a millionaire. He talks to everyone.[18]

In his public appearances, Putin shows that he does not only support the ordinary people, he is also one of them – a real '*muzhik*' (a real man, a man of the people). It is interesting to note that the word 'muzhik' literally means a peasant man in Tsarist Russia. Although the peasant meaning of 'muzhik' is less common nowadays, Putin's 'real muzhik' image is especially popular among small-scale food producers (column D), who also score very high on traditionalist (patriarchal) understandings of power and domination (column B). This might suggest that the popular image of Putin appeals to the archetypal base of the rural society, namely its peasant roots.

Although Russian rural dwellers are not traditional peasants, the Tsarist peasant belief in a just and impartial ruler and evil officials, who deliberately misinform and misrepresent the ruler, is still quite common in the countryside. Column J shows that more than 40 percent of rural dwellers believe that Putin is misinformed about the situation in the country. The myth of a benevolent president and evil officials is ardently maintained by the regime (mainly through mass media that portrays Putin as fair and just, in contrast to the corrupted authorities) and by the president himself, who acts as a defender and benefactor of the ordinary people when he visits rural regions (Mamonova 2016a). This myth contributes to the regime's stability – all the wrongdoings are blamed on the political and economic elites, while Putin's authority is not challenged. Many of Putin's supporters share this belief. This interview with pensioner Natalia (81) is representative:

> Putin is a good man. He increased our pensions ... He makes it better for people, but you cannot be a warrior when you are alone in the field. He cannot cover everything. The local authorities are those who do things wrongly.[19]

However, in some cases, it is difficult to distinguish whether people faithfully believe in the myth of a benevolent president and evil officials, or intentionally exploit it in their own interests. In my study on naive monarchism and rural resistance in contemporary Russia (Mamonova 2016a), I analysed different types of rural protests in the name of Putin. I revealed that many villagers strategically use this myth in their grievances: they frame their dissents within the official discourse of deference and express their loyalty to the president to shield themselves from repressions. At the same time, they deliberately exploit the gap between the rights promised by the president and the rights delivered by local authorities, demanding that the latter fulfil their obligations. Whether sincere or strategic, these rural politics largely maintain the status quo and the populist image of Putin as a protector of the ordinary people's interests against the interests of corrupted elites.

---

[18]Interview conducted on 09-11-2017 in the Gravornoe village, Istra district, Moscow region.
[19]Interview conducted on 20-07-2014 in the Rasshevatskaya village, Novoalexandrovsk district, Stavropol Krai.

5.3. Economic versus geopolitical reasons

Significantly more Russians support Putin for his foreign policy that 'returned global respect to the country' than for his economic achievements at home (columns G, I). However, if we examine the differences between rural responses and the national average (the two last rows of Table 2), we see that villagers are less excited about Putin's neo-imperialist foreign policy and more positive about his domestic economic achievements. This is not because Putin's domestic policy is more successful in the countryside, on the contrary – poverty in rural areas is twice as high as in urban areas (Bondarenko 2012). However, the point of comparison for many rural residents is the transition period of the 1990s. Lyudmila (54), who works at a large agricultural enterprise, refers to the interruptions in the payment of wages[20] during the 1990s to justify her support for Putin:

> As for me, I am for Putin. With him, we started receiving salaries. Before, we worked without salaries. Once, we did not receive salaries for seven months. I remember I did not go to a shop for three months. We planted our household plot with potatoes. That's how we survived. (I: When did the situation begin to change?) With Putin. With him, we started seeing the light.[21]

The economic reasons for popular support have been declining since the economic crisis of 2008; in contrast, Putin's foreign policy enjoys societal support, especially after the annexation of Crimea in 2014. Even those who are very skeptical about Putin's regime are positive about his geopolitical achievements. An interview with pensioner Mikhail (69) is representative:

> Mikhail: I do not support Putin's domestic policy. I have a pension of 9000 rubbles [note: approx. 120 Euros]. Can you survive with this pension?! Luckily, I have a good household with a big glasshouse, I can manage. But what about those who live in urban areas?!
>
> I: What do you think about the foreign policy?
>
> Mikhail: I support it. Although I think Putin should be tougher with these … so to say 'foreign friends[22]'. We need to implement harder sanctions against them. We should close our borders and work for a domestic market only. So that they would not have access to us. […].[23]

Russia's sanctions on food imports from a number of western countries[24] receive quite high support among rural dwellers (especially among the non-farming population), who welcome the further development of domestic agriculture and food self-sufficiency. There is comparatively little evidence that rural dwellers support Russia's geopolitical conflict with the West because of neo-imperialist sentiments. Column F shows that many fewer villagers regret their country's loss of 'great global power' status after the collapse of the Soviet Union, than the country average. Besides that, the importance of Russia's 'great global power' status declines with a decrease in the respondents'

---

[20]More than half of the Russian workforce experienced some form of interruption in the payment of wages during 1994-1997.
[21]Interview conducted on 10-11-2017 in the Sumarokovo village, Ruza district, Moscow region.
[22]In this context, the respondent refers to western countries / countries' leaders.
[23]Interview conducted on 09-11-2017 in the Gravornoe village, Istra district, Moscow region.
[24]Russia's food sanctions have been in force since 2014. They were initiated in response to the Western sanctions over Russia's annexation of Crimea and military interventions in Eastern Ukraine.

socio-economic security, while the importance of economic reasons increases (see columns F and H). The interviews for this study revealed that the majority of rural dwellers support Putin not for returning the 'great power' status to their country, but for protecting it from the dangerous 'Others', represented by the western countries. The collapse of the Soviet Union and the harsh transition period are often ascribed to the foreign influence. Villager Sergey (51) blames the United States – Russia's long-term geopolitical adversary – for his country's troubles in the past and today:

> All our problems come from Americans. Americans – *they* paid Gorbachev to dissolve the Soviet Union. [...] They ruined us then, and want to ruin us now. They cannot get enough! They need to seize someone, start a war – and our guys resist.[25]

The confrontation with the 'Others' abroad is part of the re-generating Russian national identity, which was in a deep crisis during the transition period (Light 2003). The next section discusses the role of national identity in defining the 'self' in the self-interests of rural voters.

6. Against self-interests?

The supporters of authoritarian populism are commonly portrayed as 'naive', 'ignorant' people who vote against self-interests. Certainly, rural Russians are more conservative and less exposed to alternative political views; however, it would be wrong to conclude that rural Russians naively believe in all the myths of Putin's regime. In public discourses, people often blame authorities for economic problems and widespread corruption; however, in more private conversations, some of them also acknowledge the president's responsibility. The following focus group discussion with rural dwellers is indicative. A group of former sovkhoz workers has been applying to the court for many years to demand a compensation for their land shares, which they lost during the illegal acquisition and deliberate bankruptcy of their sovkhoz. However, they are unable to get a fair resolution:

> Woman 1: And who did this? It was during Putin. So, it was his will. The courts are not fools – they fulfilled his order. Putin could not be uninformed about this. I doubt that ... Then, there was Medvedev [as the president]. Useless! Now Putin again.
>
> Woman 2: And wherever he speaks, he does not talk about rural areas – nothing. Silence. Like nothing is going on here.
>
> I: For whom will you vote in the next presidential elections?
>
> Woman1: Despite everything – for Putin. He is experienced.
>
> Woman 3: It won't go our way, anyway ...
>
> Woman 4: I also voted and continue voting for Putin, although I know that this [corruption and injustice] is the result of his dealings. It is impossible that the *khozyain* does not know what is going on in his country.[26]

---

[25]Interview conducted on 08-11-2017 in the Gravornoe village, Istra district, Moscow region.
[26]Interview conducted on 30-05-2013 in the Purschevo village, Balashikha district, Moscow region.

This group discussion demonstrates that rural Russians vote for Putin *not because of his domestic policy, but despite it*. What makes the people, who personally suffer from Putin's regime, ignore their individual interests and repeatedly vote for Putin? This can be explained by several factors. First, the majority of rural dwellers have the so-called 'underdog' mentality (see Scott 1990). Rural socio-economic marginalisation has exacerbated the sense of inferiority and pessimistic views of the future among villagers, who found themselves in the bottom ranks of Russian society and have hardly any economic or political power to influence the status quo. The subordinate position of rural dwellers makes them accept the world as it is, with its injustices and inequalities. The phrase 'It won't go our way, anyway' confirms this argument.

Furthermore, the ignorance of individual self-interests in the villagers' voting behaviour can be attributed to the national identity that requires 'self-sacrifice' for the sake of the so-called 'collective values' (see Gudkov 2017). Historically, the Russian national identity has developed in an active conflict between the Westernising ideology (characterised by western rationalism, materialism and individualism) and the Slavophile ideology (which stresses Russia's uniqueness based on autocracy, traditionalism and isolationism). After the collapse of the Soviet Union, Russia went down the Westernising path of development; however the western ideas of private property, market relations, and liberal democracy did not work out for the benefit of all. Putin's rule is characterised by a shift towards a more traditionalist Slavophil episteme, which took place in the discursive sphere of Russian society (Chebankova 2017). Interestingly, the Slavophil ideology used to consider the Russian peasant commune an uncorrupted representation of an ideal (spiritual) community model, and the autocracy as the most suited form of government to rule over this community. Certainly, the idea of the peasant commune is not directly used in contemporary Russian discourse on the distinctive path of development; however, its traditionalism and nativism might appeal more strongly to the rural communities that still bear some peasant roots.

Besides autocracy and traditionalism, Russia's collective self-identification also includes the idea of Russia as the 'great nation'. According to a recent poll of Levada-Center (2017), 64 percent of respondents are confident that the Russian people are 'a great nation with a unique/special role in the world's history'. National greatness is associated with statehood and its glory and, therefore, implies the ignoring of individual rights and interests in the face of national (state) interests (Gudkov 2017). Under this ideology, the Western world is perceived as the dangerous 'Others' that block Russia's path towards becoming a 'great nation' with its 'high-profile place in the world'.

Certainly, Russia's quest for great-power status in the international arena can be referred to as 'imperial nationalism' (Arnold 2016). However, for many ordinary Russians, Putin's foreign policy is more associated with the restoration of justice and the protection of Russia's sovereignty and national right to a distinctive path of development. Sergey (46) – a manager at a large agricultural enterprise – explained why Russian people put the country's geopolitical interests above their personal wellbeing:

I: What is more important for you – Russia's domestic or foreign policies?

Sergey: I think that the pride for the country is the main thing.

I: Does this mean, it comes before the economic concerns?

Sergey: Yes, it does. You know, we Russians – we can complain about life, but when the misfortune happens – we all rise to protect our motherland. This is the mentality. This is, perhaps, the democracy. Each country has its own democracy. This is our feature.[27]

8. Conclusion

In this study of rural Russians' political behaviours, I tried to address the main shortcomings in the existing debates on the popular support for authoritarian populism. In particular, I looked beyond the common assumption that the supporters of authoritarian populism are 'simple', 'irrational' people, who vote against self-interests as they are not sophisticated enough to resist the propaganda they encounter. I argued that propaganda does play a role in shaping the perceptions of Russian villagers, however, if the propagandistic message does not have an archetypal base, it will be inefficient and most likely rejected by society.

In this paper, I tried to identify the roots of rural support for Putin. I discovered a number of traditionalist peasant features that influence people's choice for strongman leadership, an authoritarian state and other elements of authoritarian populism. Thus, I revealed that Putin's traditionalist authoritarian leadership style appeals to the villagers' imaginary of a traditional peasant family structure and the characteristics of an ideal household leader. I also showed that the tsarist peasant myth of a benevolent ruler and evil officials is still used in state-society relations in contemporary Russia. Furthermore, I argued that the main national idea about Russia's distinctive path of development – which is based on autocracy, traditionalism and isolationism – is historically grounded in the Slavophil idealisation of traditional culture and patriarchal values of the Russian peasantry. Thus, even though rural Russians are not traditional peasants, a number of conservative peasant values are still preserved in the countryside, which make villagers more responsive to the traditionalist authoritarian appeals of Putin's regime.

In the title of this paper, I raised the question: what can we learn from the popular support for Putin in rural Russia? The Russian case is quite different from other parts of the world characterised by the rise of authoritarian leadership. Nevertheless, it is possible to distinguish some common trends and draw several conclusions.

First, this study has shown that the agrarian property regime and power relations in the countryside largely define the political posture of different rural groups in Russia. The underdevelopment of individual family farmers has left the Russian countryside without a main actor pushing for democracy. At the same time, the majority of rural dwellers have little stimuli for collective action because of the socialist legacy of state interventions in rural affairs, and due to their dependence on semi-subsistence farming and symbiotic relations with large farms. These factors resulted in a situation where the majority of villagers seek state patronage instead of political inclusion. This situation is quite typical for post-socialist countries with underdeveloped individual family farming. Thus, Ivanou (2018) argued that Belorussian peasants often prefer the state-guaranteed stability at the expense of civil liberties.

Second, this study demonstrated that the silent majority is not a homogeneous group, and that different socio-economic groups have different interests and motives to support

---

[27] Interview conducted on 12-11-2017 in the Sumarokovo village, Ruza district, Moscow region.

regressive populist forces. I revealed that less secure socio-economic strata respond more strongly to economic incentives, while better-off villagers are more likely to support the ideological appeals of the regime. Furthermore, this research showed that populist support in Russia is generally stronger among the older generation, the less well-off, and women. The latter finding deviates from the general trend in global populism, where the typical supporters are older males (Inglehart and Norris 2016). This discrepancy requires further investigation based on a careful examination of the class, gender, ethnic and cultural-religious dimensions of rural constituencies.

Third, this study argued that the silent majority is not so naïve and irrational. For example, I revealed that villagers' economic perceptions are very subjective and play an important role in people's justification of their support for an authoritarian leader. The bitter memories of the post-socialist transition period (when the Yeltsin government implemented harsh neoliberal reforms in agriculture) make rural Russians perceive Putin's more conservative, but still neoliberal, economic policies in a much more positive light. Similar societal perceptions of government agricultural policies were discussed by Gürel, Küçük, and Taş (2018) in their study of rural support for Erdoğan's party in Turkey. These authors revealed that Erdoğan's government is not associated with the neoliberal assaults on small-scale farmers despite the fact that it did not deviate from the previous government's neoliberal policy. By blaming the problems on the previous government and implementing modest support to rural households, Erdoğan's party managed to maintain continuous loyalty and support among rural Turks.

Furthermore, I revealed that many rural Russians do not share naïve illusions about Putin, who is obtrusively portrayed by the state-controlled mass media as a benevolent president and intercessor of the ordinary people, whereas all failures are blamed on elites and authorities. However, villagers often intentionally use this populist discourse in their grievances to make their protest less risky. Despite knowing about Putin's responsibility for the corruption and economic recession in the countryside, villagers nevertheless continue voting for him. I argued that rural Russians support Putin not because of his domestic policy, but despite it. This can be compared to the United States, where Trump's supporters voted for him not because of his sexism and racism, but despite them (Reicher 2017). At certain moments (usually during crises), people can turn a blind eye on some (even obnoxious) features of the regime or leader in order to support other presumably more important values and ideas that their government or leader represents.

Finally, this study revealed that the popular support for Putin's governance results from the failure of liberal representative democracy, similarly to many other countries characterised by the rise of authoritarian populism. The inability of Russian villagers to influence the decision making at local and regional levels creates a desire for a strong and powerful leader who can rein in corrupted authorities and bring order to the country. This study showed that many people willingly sacrifice some of their democratic freedoms in favour of political and economic stability. They, however, perceive their sacrifice as a true manifestation of their democratic choice. Therefore, in order to curtail authoritarian populism and to build positive alternatives, we need to understand what is wrong with the liberal democracy, and why more and more people support the so-called 'democracies with adjectives', such as 'sovereign democracy' in Russia, or 'illiberal democracy' in Hungary.

Acknowledgements

This paper was written during my fellowship at the Institute for Advanced Studies 'New Europe College' in Bucharest. I am very grateful for the Institute's financial support, which allowed me to carry out the most recent round of fieldwork in Russia and to write this paper. I also would like to thank my colleagues from the Swedish Institute of International Affairs (Utrikespolitiska institutet) for their comments and suggestions on earlier versions of my paper. Furthermore, I am very grateful to the colleagues from Levada-Center in Moscow, who shared with me the results of their public opinion survey. I would like to thank the Russian studies scholars Dr. Greg Yudin, Dr. Alexander Nikulin and Dr. Svetlana Basukova for their valuable comments and feedback on my ideas for this paper. And, finally, I thank Prof. Jun Borras and other colleagues from the Emancipatory Rural Politics Initiative (ERPI) group for initiating the research on authoritarian populism and the rural world, of which this paper is a part.

Disclosure statement

No potential conflict of interest was reported by the author.

Funding

This work was supported by Pontica Magna Fellowship Program, New Europe College.

References

All-Russian Agricultural Census of 2016. Results. Accessed 1 February, 2018. http://www.vshp2016.ru/.

Amelyushkin, K. 2014. Putin's Ratings are Kept on Propaganda and Soviet Complexes. Accessed 1 April, 2018. https://ru.delfi.lt/opinions/comments/obozrevatel-rejtingi-putina-derzhatsya-na-propagande-i-sovetskih-kompleksah.d?id = 65644666.

Arnold, R. 2016. *Russian Nationalism and Ethnic Violence: Symbolic Violence, Lynching, Pogrom and Massacre. Series: Europa Country Perspectives*. London: Routledge.

Bondarenko, L. 2012. "Poverty in Rural Russia." *Otechestvenniye Zapiski* 6 (51). Accessed 05 January 2019, http://magazines.russ.ru/oz/2012/6/12b.html.

Borras Jr., S. M. 2018. "Understanding and Subverting Contemporary Right-Wing Populism: Preliminary Notes from a Critical Agrarian Perspective." *The ERPI Working Paper Series*. Accessed 25 October, 2018. https://www.tni.org/files/article-downloads/erpi_cp_47_borras.pdf.

Chaisty, P., and S. Whitefield. 2017. "Putin's Nationalism Problem." In *Ukraine and Russia. People, Politics, Propaganda and Perspectives*, edited by A. Pikulicka-Wilczewska, and R. Sakwa, 165–173. Bristol: International Relations.

Chebankova, E. 2017. "Vladimir Putin: Making of the National Hero." In *Ukraine and Russia. People, Politics, Propaganda and Perspectives*, edited by A. Pikulicka-Wilczewska, and R. Sakwa, 173–183. Bristol: International Relations.

Clark, T. N., and S. M. Lipset. 1991. "Are Social Classes Dying?" *International Sociology* 6 (4): 397–410.

Dorondel, S., and S. Şerban. 2014. "A Missing Link: The Agrarian Question in South-East Europe." In *The Agrarian Question in South-East Europe*, edited by I. Popescu, 7–30. Bucharest: MARTOR.

Edelman, M., C. Oya, and S. M. Borras Jr. 2013. "Global Land Grabs: Historical Processes, Theoretical and Methodological Implications and Current Trajectories." *Third World Quarterly* 34 (9): 1517–1531.

Ferrari, C. A. 2018. "Populist Strategies, Right-Wing Political Parties and Ideological and Land Questions in Chile and Sweden." *The ERPI Working Paper Series*. Accessed 25 October, 2018. https://www.tni.org/files/article-downloads/erpi_cp_13_alarcon_ferrari_0.pdf.

Gaventa, J. 2018. "*Local Rural Alternatives to Trump in the USA.*" Presentation at the ERPI International Conference on 'authoritarian populism and the rural world', The Hague, March 17-18.

Golos. 2018. Map of Regional Electoral Divisions in Russian Presidential Elections. Accessed 21 October, 2018. http://2018.golosinfo.org/.

Gonda, N. 2018. "Championing Change in Rural Hungary. The Role of Emancipatory Subjectivities in the Construction of Alternatives to Illiberal Authoritarian Populism." *The ERPI Working Paper Series*. Accessed 25 October, 2018.

Granberg, L., and A. M. Sätre. 2016. *The Other Russia: Local Experience and Societal Change*. London: Routledge.

Gudkov, L. 2017. "Peculiarities of Russian Populism." *Herald of Public Opinion. Data. Analysis. Discussion* 1-2 (124): 91–105.

Gudkov, L., and B. Dubin. 2002. Rural Life: Rationality of Passive Adaptation. Accessed 11 December, 2017. http://ecsocman.hse.ru/data/280/985/1219/05gudkov-23-37.pdf.

Gürel, B., B. Küçük, and S. Taş. 2018. "Rural Roots of the Rise of the Justice and Development Party in Turkey." *The ERPI Working Paper Series*. Accessed 25 October, 2018. https://www.tni.org/files/article-downloads/erpi_cp_57_gurel_kucuk_tas.pdf.

Hall, S. 1980. "Popular-Democratic Versus Authoritarian Populism." In *Marxism and Democracy*, edited by A. Hunt, 157–185. London: Laurence and Wishart.

Hall, S. 1985. "Authoritarian Populism: A Reply to Jessop et al." *New Left Review* 151: 115–124.

Hall, R., I. Scoones, and D. Tsikata, eds. 2015a. *Africa's Land Rush: Rural Livelihoods and Agrarian Change*. Oxford: James Currey.

Humphrey, C. 2002. "Subsistence Farming and the Peasantry as an Idea in Contemporary Russia." In *Post-socialist Peasant?*, edited by P. Leonard, and D. Kaneff, 136–159. New York: Palgrave.

Inglehart, R., and P. Norris. 2016. Trump, Brexit, and the Rise of Populism: Economic Have-Nots and Cultural Backlash, HKS Working Paper No. RWP16-026. doi:10.2139/ssrn.2818659. Accessed 25 October, 2018.

Ivaldi, G., and J. Gombin. 2015. "The Front National and the New Politics of the Rural in France." In *Rural Protest Groups and Populist Political Parties*, edited by D. Strijker, G. Voerman, and I. Terluin, 243–264. Wageningen: Wageningen Academic Publishers.

Ivanou, A. 2018. "How Far Does 'Lukascism' Go? Insights into Moral and Political Economies of Vjetnam and Other Belarusian Villagers." *The ERPI Working Paper Series*. Accessed 25 October, 2018) https://www.tni.org/files/article-downloads/erpi_cp_7_ivanou.pdf.

Jessop, B., K. Bonnett, S. Bromley, and T. Ling. 1984. "Authoritarian Populism, Two Nations and Thatcherism." *New Left Review* 147: 32–60.

Kokoshin, A. 2006. "Real Sovereignty and Sovereign Democracy." *Russia in Global Affairs* 4 (2006). Accessed 12 June, 2018. http://eng.globalaffairs.ru/number/n_7338.

Kurtz, M., and A. Barnes. 2002. "The Political Foundations of Post-Communist Regimes." *Comparative Political Studies* 35: 524–553.

Lassila, J. 2018. "Putin as a Non-populist Autocrat." *Russian Politics* 3 (2): 175–195.

Lassiter, M. 2011. Who Speaks for the Silent Majority? Accessed 17 July, 2018. http://www.nytimes.com/2011/11/03/opinion/populism-and-the-silent-majority.html.

Levada-Center. 2017. Velocode Moods in Russia Have Reached the Historical Maximum. Accessed 23 July, 2018. https://www.levada.ru/2017/12/21/velikoderzhavnye-nastroeniya-v-rossii-dostigli-istoricheskogo-maksimuma/.

Li, T. M. 2010. "To Make Live or Let Die? Rural Dispossession and the Protection of Surplus Populations." *Antipode* 41 (1): 66–93.

Light, M. 2003. "In Search of an Identity: Russian Foreign Policy and the End of Ideology." *Journal of Communist Studies and Transition Politics* 19 (3): 42–59.

Lubarda, B. 2018. Homeland Farming? The Two Faces of Right-Wing Populism in Agriculture and Forging Alliances for Emancipatory Change in Hungary. *The ERPI Working Paper Series*. Accessed 25 October, 2018. https://www.tni.org/files/article-downloads/erpi_cp_11_lubarda.pdf.

Makarenko, B. 2017. "Populism and Political Institutions: A Comparative Perspective." *Herald of Public Opinion. Data. Analysis. Discussion* 1-2 (124): 15–28.

Mamonova, N. 2016a. "Naive Monarchism and Rural Resistance in Contemporary Russia." *Rural Sociology* 81 (3): 316–342.

Mamonova, N. 2016b. "Rethinking Rural Politics in Post-socialist Settings: Rural Communities, Land Grabbing and Agrarian Change in Russia and Ukraine." PhD diss., Erasmus University Rotterdam, The Hague.

Mamonova, N., and O. Visser. 2014. "State Marionettes, Phantom Organisations or Genuine Movements? The Paradoxical Emergence of Rural Social Movements in Post-Socialist Russia." *Journal of Peasant Studies* 41 (4): 491–516.

Margulies, B. Populism: A Field Guide. Political Studies Association. Accessed 19 October, 2018. https://www.psa.ac.uk/insight-plus/blog/populism-field-guide.

Marx, K., and F. Engels. (1848) 1967. . *The Communist Manifesto*. London: Penguin.

Moore, B. 1966. *Social Origins of Dictatorship and Democracy: Lord and Peasant in the Making of the Modern World*. Boston: Beacon.

Mudde, C. 2017. The Power of Populism? Not Really! Accessed 11 May, 2018. https://www.huffingtonpost.com/cas-mudde/the-power-of-populism-not_b_9226736.html.

Norman, L. 2018. "*What's the Problem with Populism?*" Paper presented at the research seminar of the Swedish Institute of International Affairs, Stockholm, March 21.

Oliker, O. 2017. "Putinism, Populism and the Defence of Liberal Democracy." *Survival* 59 (1): 7–24.

Pallot, J., and T. Nefedova. 2007. *Russia's Unknown Agriculture: Household Production in Postsocialist Rural Russia*. Oxford: Oxford University Press.

Peters, M. A. 2017. "The End of Neoliberal Globalisation and the Rise of Authoritarian Populism." *Educational Philosophy and Theory* 50 (4): 323–325.

Petrick, M., J. Wandel, and K. Karsten. 2013. "Rediscovering the Virgin Lands: Agricultural Investment and Rural Livelihoods in a Eurasian Frontier Area." *World Development* 43: 164–179.

Petrov, A. 2013. *From Putin to Putin: Siberian Electoral Preferences in the Presidential Elections in Russia*. Irkutsk: Irkutsk State University.

Poleekhtova, I. A. 2010. "Dynamics of the Russian TV-Audience." *Sociological Research* 1: 66–77.

Public Opinion Foundation. 2017. V.Putin: Rating, Attitude, Work Assessments. Indicators of Attitude Towards the Head of State. Accessed 22 April, 2018. http://fom.ru/Politika/10946.

Rancière, J. 2013. The People are Not a Brutal and Ignorant Mass. Accessed 25 April, 2018. http://www.versobooks.com/blogs/1226-the-people-are-not-a-brutal-and-ignorant-mass-jacques-ranciere-on-populism.

Reicher, S. 2017. *Trust the People! On the Psychology of Authoritarian Populism*. London: British Academy/British Psychological Society Lecture. delivered on 14 September 2017.

Rosstat. 2017. Russia in Figures 2017. Statistical Handbook. Accessed 22 June, 2018. http://www.gks.ru/free_doc/doc_2017/rusfig/rus17e.pdf.

Rueschemeyer, D., E. H. Stephens, and J. D. Stephens. 1992. *Capitalist Development and Democracy*. Chicago: University of Chicago Press.

Scoones, I., M. Edelman, J. Borras, R. Hall, W. Wolford, and B. White. 2018. "Emancipatory Rural Politics: Confronting Authoritarian Populism." *The Journal of Peasant Studies* 45 (1): 1–20.

Scott, J. C. 1990. *Dominance and the Arts of Resistance: Hidden Transcripts*. New Haven: Yale University Press.

Skalnaya, M. M., and D. E. Burykin. 2009. "Methodical Approaches to the Classification of Small-scale Producers in Rural Areas." *Bulletin of the Personnel Policy, Agricultural Education and Innovation* 11: 35–38.

Skocpol, T. 1979. *States and Social Revolutions*. Cambridge: Cambridge University Press.

Sperling, V. 2014. *Sex, Politics, and Putin: Political Legitimacy in Russia*. New York: Oxford University Press.

Stenning, A. 2005b. "Where is the Post-Socialist Working Class? Working-class Lives in the Spaces of (Post-)socialism." *Sociology* 39 (5): 983–999.

Strijker, D., G. Voerman, and I. Terluin. 2015. *Rural Protest Groups and Populist Political Parties*. Wageningen: Wageningen Academic Publishers.

Stroop, C. 2017. Between Trump and Putin: The Right-Wing International, a Crisis of Democracy, and the Future of the European Union. Accessed 13 April, 2018. http://www.politicalresearch.org/2017/05/11/between-trump-and-putin-the-right-wing-international-a-crisis-of-democracy-and-the-future-of-the-european-union/#sthash.Nhl4hhVW.dpbs.

Taylor, C. 1988. "The Hermeneutics of Conflict." In *Meaning and Context: Quentin Skinner and his Critics*, edited by J. Tully, 218–228. Cambridge: Polity Press.

Valiev, A. 2017. What are Russians Proud of and Why Does the "Electoral Swamp" Go After the Winner. Accessed 11 June, 2018. http://ru.rfi.fr/rossiya/20171222-chem-gordy-rossiyane-i-pochemu-elektoralnoe-boloto-idet-za-pobeditelem.

Vasilyeva, N. 2015. Few Jobs and Little Hope, But Rural Russia Sticks with Putin. Accessed 28 February, 2018. https://globalnews.ca/news/2217219/few-jobs-and-little-hope-but-rural-russia-sticks-with-putin/.

Waylen, K. 2010. *The Implications of Local Views and Institutions for the Outcomes of Community-Based Conservation*. London: The University of London.

Wegren, S. K. 2005. "From Communism to Capitalism? Russia's Agrarian Relations in the Twentieth Century and Beyond." In *Rural Adaptation in Russia*, edited by S. K. Wegren, 1–38. London: Routledge.

Wegren, S. K. 2009. "Russia's Incomplete Land Reform." *Russian Analytical Digest* 64 (09): 2–5.

Yudin, G., and I. Matveyev. 2017. A Politician Without the People. Is it Right to Refer Putin as a Populist? Accessed 21 April, 2018. https://republic.ru/posts/82802.

Zubov, M. 2017. Detailed Analysis of Putin's Future. Accessed 14 February, 2018. http://www.mk.ru/politics/2017/05/04/putina-razlozhili-po-polochkam-eksperty-predskazali-ego-budushhee.html.

Authoritarian populism in rural Belarus: distinction, commonalities, and projected finale

Aleh Ivanou

ABSTRACT
The paper inspects how agrarian debates apply to rural Belarus. Following the 'persistence versus disappearance' debate, it finds the moral economy alongside request for change. Pursuing the 'adaptation versus resistance' debate, it spots adaptability and exclusion of those failing to adapt. Here 'lukascism' surfaces resting on constructing the 'other'. A rare case of agrarian populism employed by top authority, lukascism is otherwise humdrum. Proclaiming some principles of the moral economy while disregarding others, inconsistent lukascism undercuts the 'coexistence scenario' of households with large-scale farming. Change avoidance is a commonplace foretelling lukascism's finale: its appeal is limited by the older generation..

Researchers of post-Soviet transformation often explain aversion to capitalist reforms as framed by the moral economy, a historical cultural continuity of peasant conservatism opposing land privatisation and other reforms (Wegren 2006). However, in Belarus, it is the authoritarian populist regime that blocks the reforms avowedly following 'old ways' on the people's behalf.

Many changes have occurred in post-Soviet Belarusian countryside contributing to its commercialisation and villagers' impoverishment while neither affecting the state ownership for land nor dominance of state-directed large farm enterprises (post-kolkhozy/sovkhozy). If it is a transition, then where to? How do the villagers consider the actual changes, and how would they respond to capitalist reforms when the authoritarian dictatorship discontinues?

I apply the agrarian and peasant studies framework to actual and prospective rural advancements toward agrarian capitalism in Belarus. After providing a background information, and upon reviewing the literature and methodology, the paper proceeds with three arguments (economic, cultural, political) about villagers' ability to face capitalism.

DOI: 10.4324/9781003162353-10

Situating Belarus in the rural world

Rural Belarus is worth scholarly attention, presently directed at such much larger post-Soviet countries as Russia, Ukraine, and Kazakhstan (the three largest post-Soviet agricultural producers – Visser and Spoor [2011]). Belarus used to be the Soviet Union's 'assembly shop' and has retained its industrial (largely outdated) specialisation. However, it is also a regionally important exporter of agricultural produce. Potentially, it is even more important given its large farmland acreage per capita (0,9 hectares), of which about half is arable land (BelAgroBelarus n.d.). Using snatches of information, 22 percent (2.1 million) of Belarusians still reside in the countryside, reduced by 10 percent since 1996 (by 56 percent since 1938), in around 23,000 rural settlements inhabited by several to several thousand residents. The agricultural sector employs 0.3 million (1.1 million in 1996).

Belarus is an 'actually existing socialism' (using Humphrey's [2002, 12], expression). It forgoes a 'resolute refusal to abandon values and expectations associated with socialism' that Humphrey (2002, 12) finds in countries pursuing market reforms. Belarus is also an instance of what Burawoy (2002) calls 'transition without transformation'. Despite being listed among countries in transition, Belarus retains its Soviet social structures, especially in the village. However, there are significant changes in the structure and operation of rural entities, income differentiation and labour migration that signal the arrival of agrarian transition, primarily over disintegration of the system of kolkhozy/sovkhozy that until recently have changed only superficially in organisational terms, but that significantly shrunk economically. It invokes the agrarian question.

Theoretical framework: agrarian question

The agrarian question concerns the economic and political consequences of the introduction of capitalist relations into a traditional, self-sufficient peasant agriculture (Bernstein 2004). There is then an argument of what follows the agrarian transition under capitalism: in terms of subjective orientations, declining agricultural activities, and reducing self-sufficiency. The disappearance versus persistence argument then ensues: whether the peasantry disappears by splintering into bourgeoisie and proletariat – a position by Marxists (e.g. Lenin [1964] 2004), or otherwise peasants persist by retaining their production and lifestyles, as populists argue (e.g. Chayanov [1925] 1966)?

The Marxists' position is not uniform either. Marx ([1867] 1977) and Lenin ([1964] 2004) saw peasant farming as doomed under capitalism, to be replaced by capitalist agriculture. They found peasants unable representing themselves as a class and therefore inert. At the same time, they saw rural labourers as untied by prejudice and property, and therefore revolutionary (Marx [1852] 1963). Kautsky's ([1899] 1988) minority opinion was that peasant farms might persist for some time if they retain access to land (though typically not enough for their subsistence), by proceeding with land cultivation but increasingly relying on selling their labour and gradually becoming extinct. Modern class-based theorists (e.g. Bernstein 2004) update the classical ideas to address the neoliberal capitalism, and they treat instances of rural resistance as manifestations of a class struggle against capitalist dispossession and inclusion into industrialised agriculture. Overall, Marxists agree that the peasant production will inevitably be ousted by the capitalist agriculture.

Conversely, agrarian populist thinkers advocate 'the persistence thesis' in that the peasantry withstands the onslaught of capitalism owing to its moral economy, being able to subsist with a little and being self-exploitative. The agrarian populist approach is espoused by some social movements striving to mobilise peasants against dispossession and inclusion in the capitalist production (Scoones et al. 2018).

A major feature of the populist approach is the moral economy concept, primarily consisting of ideas by Thompson (1971), Scott (1976) and Chayanov ([1925] 1966) (see Edelman [2005] discussing their relative input). Thompson (1971) considered the moral economy found among the 18th-century English consumers' opposing profiteering and immoderate commercial extraction in food markets. Scott (1976) studied the moral economy of peasants in Vietnam and emphasised their values and customs, of what was for them just, tolerable exploitation and what was otherwise. Most important for this paper given its proximate focus, Chayanov's ([1925] 1966) input concerned Russian peasant household dynamics, family farming being a backbone of society, peasant economy and self-exploiting subsistence provision (drudgery), disdain for commerce and excessive accumulation, and either fighting capitalism openly or resisting it on a daily basis (Chayanov [1925] 1966). Overall, the literature on peasants' moral economy premises on that peasants oppose change.

Authoritarian populisms: lukascism

Longstanding social cohesion bonded by rural moral economies weaken in former Soviet countries, often leading to authoritarian populism (Mamonova 2018). The term applies to situations when '"authoritarian closure" [i]s given "the gloss of populist consent"' (Hall 1985, 116). For Scoones et al. (2018), authoritarian populism is a strategy for winning and exerting state power, pitting a uniform and virtuous people against unrighteous elites and dangerous 'others'. Borras (2018, 8) argues that authoritarian populism is often supported by people despite their embrace of the moral economy when they untypically 'take the risk of throwing support to something new'. I argue that people voting for an ascending authoritarian populist still look for something familiar. Such was the case of A. Lukašenka who came to power in Belarus on the wave of disappointment with democracy and fear of the market, by promising a Soviet-lookalike patron-client arrangement.

I want to term Lukašenka's authoritarian populism as lukascism[1] (no initial capital). I emulate both Hall (1988), who introduced Thatcherism as authoritarian populism, and whoever coined the 'Chavismo' term. Lukascism warrants a separate name not as a standalone type but as a discernible phenomenon within the 'global authoritarian populist axis' (Edelman 2018, 8), in its post-Soviet Russia-adjoining segment. Making it distinct is its penchant to look for legitimation in agrarian populism.

If we try to attribute lukascism to the two broad clusters of populism (Canovan [1981]; discussed in Borras [2018]), then by informing the populist dictatorship, lukascism certainly relates to the 'political populism' cluster, while it heavily draws on moral economy principles from the 'agrarian populism' cluster, as intellectual agrarian socialists would normally draw. However, due to its contradictory character (inherent to all contemporary populist politics – Scoones et al. 2018) and certain primitivism, it is pointless situating

---

[1]Previously, 'lukascism' was in colloquial use as a pejorative term consonant to 'fascism'. I give it a precise meaning.

lukascism within the ideational range of agrarian populisms by Byres ([1979]; discussed in Borras [2018]).

Lukašenka's 'top-down agrarian populism' comes by way of his specific political charisma. Like N.Khrushchev in the Soviet past and unlike other post-Soviet leaders, Lukašenka is a 'tough agrarian'. He spares no time and public funds to revive agriculture and village, although they remain unprofitable and hopeless – probably because these efforts are informed by a desire to retain power. Despite few people left in rural areas on the 24th year of Lukašenka's presidency and despite the elections are regarded to become a fiction, villagers are still considered his reliable electorate. 'If we give the land into private hands, how will we control the election process in the countryside?', Lukašenka asked *načaĺstva* (folks-up-top) in 1998 (Karbalievič 2018). Lukascism would subscribe to a viewpoint that it is villagers with landed property who are revolution-prone (Wolf 1969), rather than landless peasants are (as believed by Paige [1975]). Displaying its sensitivity to the moral economy, lukascism is nonetheless beset and shaped by worries in line with the class-based approach – a w(W)olf in a lamb's skin of sorts.

In Belarus of 1994 vintage, Lukašenka, a former director of a loss-making sovkhoz achieved his elevation and since then relies on a clientelism legitimised using a moral economy discourse. Lukašenka understands folk archetypes, public idolatry for the harvest of grain, and the importance of subsistence. For 24 years, Lukašenka holds televised conference calls with *načaĺstva* during sowing and harvesting campaigns, goes through the fields in peasant embroidery, poses for cameras in a harvester, hand harvests potatoes (accompanied by his sons, government members, and sports luminaries) on his garden allotment in his posh presidential residence (he also keeps a cow). He thus plays on old archetypes and the fear of famine, deep-sitting in the culture and mass consciousness of the older generation (Cyhankoŭ and Karbalievič 2017).

Lukascism is anti-capitalist and rural essentialist. It targets the assumed aversion of people to the market and profit, a penchant for equality and for hard work, and reverence to land. Exploiting the archetypes, lukascism for many years promises a uniform wage equivalent to US$ 500. It abuses people's respect for hard work by imposing a tax on the jobless by calling them 'do-littles'. It employs the traditional concern over unused land to justify the ploughing of radioactively contaminated areas for an additional, risk-laden yield of grain. It appeals to people's anticipated right to subsistence and solidarity obligations: it conditions the former on the latter, making people sanction each other in a vain expectation of the promised.

Mamonova (2016b) uses the concept (neo)patrimonialism to explain why rural dwellers ask Putin for patronage and portray him as the 'tsar'. 'Early' Lukašenka was probably aiming at something different when he publicly admired the 'German order' that, according to him, 'peaked' under Hitler. However, later the propaganda betted on the 'tsardom' line, such as by putting in public use an affectional '*bac'ka*', to imply both Father-the-Tsar and patriarch of a peasant family. More recently, Lukašenka started publicly referring to his smaller son as the heir to his presidency. This way lukascism engages naïve monarchism, ingrained in Russians (Mamonova 2016a) and Belarusians.

At a 1996 referendum, Belarusians succumbed both to lukascism and naïve monarchism and ditched their right to elect local government. Since then, Lukašenka forms his 'vertical power structure', or *načaĺstva* unaccountable to the people, where lower echelons are accountable to the higher echelons and to the ruler. Eke and Kuzio (2000) erroneously define the regime in Belarus as 'authoritarian sultanism', because 'sultan' is not tied by any value system, and loyalty to him is based on fear and rewards. In the absence of feedback from citizens (except for complaints concerning housing and utilities), lukascism nonetheless always does 'on public request' rather than waywardly. Lukascism is also not about fear-motivated *načaĺstva*. For all their ostentatious loyalty to Lukašenka and studied helplessness regarding the ordinary people's problems (together constituting a 'politics of appearances' – Byres 2018), *načaĺstva* is led by personal profit in managing the land and assets (not via property rights but through physical access) and wrangling public money.

Contemporary village: questions, arguments and scenarios

Belarusian rural population is politically apathetic and unwilling to defend their interests in open protest. Alcoholisation, nonexistent self-government and landed property, and bleak life perspectives make them disinterested in the results of their work and powerless before *načaĺstva*. Herewith, the countryside remains patriarchal and intolerant of 'unjustified' dependency regarded as social parasitism.

It was the historical experience of Belarus within the Russian Empire (1795–1917) that led to such centrepiece of its moral economy as the redistributive commune with its land-and-labour complex (e.g. Bartlett 1990). While the Belarusian countryside followed the general trends in the Russian Empire and later the Soviet state (1905 reforms, 1917 revolution, civil war, NEP, collectivisation, expropriation of kulaks etc), its specificity has been said to be a proclivity for even more equal distribution of material resources and land. Thus, Belarusian historians have stressed recently that, relative to the then Russia and Ukraine, there were no wealthy people in historic Belarus, and that prior to its annexation by the Russian Empire (when Belarus was part of The Grand Duchy of Lithuania and Rzecz Pospolita) local gentlemen were observed tilling the land like any ordinary peasant would do but with a sword at their side (Drakakhrust 2017). However, such comparisons of past configurations using patchy evidence might be inaccurate: current researchers have a penchant for national revivalist sentiments and their sometimes obvious desire to separate Belarus from Russia.

Still looking for definitive characterisations of present-day villagers, I ask if we can call them peasants. Belarusian villagers do not possess Shanin's (1973) peasantry four facets any properly: household as a primary social unit, subsistence based on land and animal husbandry, allegiance to a culture of small rural communities, and subjection to external power. Except for the last facet, the match is only partial amidst the habitual dependency on large-scale farming. A new rurality approach, summarised by Mamonova (2016b) to include 'multifuctionality' and 'pluriactivity', presented as eternal attributes of the peasant household, might allow calling the Belarusian villagers peasants, but Bernstein (2007) still considers this approach as mistaken and referring to survival strategies of labouring classes and to creeping proletarianisation.

Focusing on political consequences of the agrarian transition, I consider rural responses to the changes either taking place or pending in Belarus. Wegren (2006) says that the 'cultural continuity/peasant conservatism' argument ignores peasants' nonresistant responses. Besides resistance, Kerkvliet (2009) distinguishes such types of everyday politics as support, compliance, modifications, and evasions.

There is a debatable issue of pilfering at post-kolkhozy being either an additional source of subsistence (Mamonova and Visser 2014) or an intentional act of disagreement (Nikulin 2009). Naïve monarchism might also be seen as an everyday rural politics of support and compliance (Mamonova 2016b), whereby people consider the top authority as the intercessor against the lower branches. In Belarus, the classical scheme 'Tsar versus boyars' appears as 'President versus *načaĺstva*': given their treatment of ordinary people, *načaĺstva* assumes the role of 'those to be protected from'. In turn, it is only rational for the people to address their aspirations directly to Lukašenka bypassing 'helpless' *načaĺstva*, which is tantamount to a not-so-naïve monarchism (discussed for Russia in Mamonova [2016a]).

Naïve/not-so-naïve monarchism is paradigmatically close to rumours and the holy foolery. Alongside non-compliance, pilfering, and foot-dragging, rumour spreading is a hidden form of rural resistance (Scott 1985). Here most active is a simulacra form of the 'holy fools'. This often came to the fore of public life in the proverbial Russian world in its darker days and was intimately related to Russian Orthodox tradition. A paradigm of marginality, a holy fool nonetheless actively engages with the community, administers social order, and denounces the public authority (Hunt and Kobets 2011). Furthermore, Mamonova (2016b) considers food self-provisioning and exchange as a type of everyday rural politics not subsumed by everyday resistance, compliance, and indifference but representing an alternative to the post-kolkhozy-dominated food system.

The aforementioned forms of rural politics are unable to challenge the existing order – but might provide rural dwellers with a means to remedy local injustices, as shown for other post-Soviet contexts by Mamonova and Visser (2014). Moreover, a core argument nowadays is that adaptation prevails resistance to post-communist rural transition because many rural dwellers put their interests over a community's interest (Mamonova 2016b). There is then a pertinent issue: what happens to those rural households that do not adapt, such as when they neither adapt nor resist. Since in many cases it implies marginalisation, this issue clearly speaks to a central question in analysing populism (Scoones et al. 2018): who is excluded?

Finally, there is a coexistence scenario of rural people with large-scale farming by using its resources (Kerkvliet 2009). Understood as a long-term adaptation and as a prognosis, coexistence echoes the Kautsky's ([1899] 1988) point and asks whether this condition is lasting. Awaiting in-depth examination in the empirical section, it should be mentioned that the coexistence in Belarus is obstructed since 2004, when a presidential decree to discipline (prevent pilfering in) the countryside was passed and largely disabled symbiotic relations with post-kolkhozy: since then, few people in the village keep cows and run a large subsistence farm. Ultimately, there is an expert conclusion in that coexistence scenarios are possible only under the clearly defined land rights (Mamonova 2016b). Summing up, the Belarusian village appears ill-fitting the coexistence scenario, and hence cardinal changes are imminent.

Methodology

This is a narrative study that the author considers as currently the only way to research Belarusian society. No reliable survey data and statistical information exist for the

Belarusian countryside. The Belarusian state is notoriously 'preempting' (Silitski 2005), here to imply that it uses its monopoly on information to release numbers that would flatter and fit its political course.

Independent social data collection is a challenge in Belarus, where it is formally constrained (Korf 2012), and where informal prohibitions are even more absolute. The habitually self-restraining Belarusian villager would rather not speak to a stranger. The author was not a stranger due to family roots in Juravičy, the study site.

The author spent most of 2016 and summer months in 2017 in Juravičy and adjacent smaller villages (Kalinkavičy District, Homieĺ Region) doing participant observation and semi-structured in-depth interviews ($N = 100$) with mostly randomly chosen (but in several instances specially targeted) local residents involving various questions ranging from their households' daily routine to their vision of the future of Belarusian villages. The interviews have been carried out in dialectal Belarusian, but all transliterations are done using literary Belarusian (even referring to Mr. A. Lukašenka but not to Chernobyl), as a matter of the author's national priorities.

Even though the research concerned only one territorial cluster of settlements, the study is representative of the Belarusian countryside, since the present-day organisation of land and labour is fairly uniform throughout rural Belarus, attributable to the state land monopoly. Situated in the Belarusian south-east and next to Chernobyl, the area could be very dissimilar due to radiation – however, not for now, and the paper partly explains the reason.

The approach involved structure-focused interpretations of rural life intended to establish functional relations and a post-structuralist and discursive view of reality. Wherever the focus is on cultural elements, the text becomes ethnographic. Ensuring the objectivity is this qualitative study's conformability with findings by other researchers of the region and from elsewhere.

A methodological difficulty in addressing authoritarian populism relates to its eclectic nature (resulting in contradictory politics – Scoones et al. 2018) – its penchant to straddle both sides (class-based versus agrarian populist) of the agrarian argument. Another difficulty is that large-scale farming is pertinent both to capitalism and socialism, thus obscuring the idea of the agrarian transition in post-Soviet settings.

In what follows, I propose the case study of village Juravičy with a focus on a particular family prominent for moral economy traditions, three arguments regarding such behavioural traits currency throughout the population, and my conclusions.

Empirical setting: Juravičy

Juravičy was the first place in Belarus settled by humans: its primitive man sites date back to the Palaeolithic 26,000 years ago and feature remnants of mammoths, the then central component of subsistence for local hunter-gatherers. The local story of initially off-farming subsistence thus outstrips the textbook ten-millennia crises-replete history of farming subsistence (Edelman 2005).

Juravičy was first described around 1430 as an oasis in the Paliessie marshlands inhabited by subsistence farmers. Situated next to an East–West trade route, it was invaded and pillaged by Mongols and Tartars, and later by Napoleonic, Russian, German, Bolshevik and Polish forces. Ultimately, the Soviets transformed the local life by forced collectivisation.

The latest dramatic impacts came first with WWII, then in 1986 (Chernobyl catastrophe) and in 1991 (collapse of the USSR). There followed nearly three decades of economic and social travails, manifest in the protracted disintegration of the local kolkhoz and depopulation. Recently, Juravičy numbered 633 villagers (in 251 households), whereas it had been home to six times that number in the 1930s.

Two Juravičy villagers

During my study in 2016–2017, where the moral economy was concerned, the key role in Juravičy was played by an elderly couple known by their unusual nicknames Vjetnam and his wife Vjetnamka. They were both in their eighties. They have spent most of those years in Juravičy, having grown up separately in two outlying smaller villages. Though unrelated to the Vietnamese nation, the couple coincidentally hit the right note with the Vietnam-focused research by Scott (1976). This childless couple embodied an authentic moral economy still to be found in Belarusian Paliessie. The nickname 'Vjetnam' dated back to the early 1960s, to the man's first encounter with the local kolkhoz. It happened when the newlyweds came to live in Juravičy in a house that they received as her dowry. The man's first assignment of putting a horse to the cart went awry and he was behind his colleagues in a kolkhoz coachmen team. A born wisecracker, he explained his coming late to the unit's gathering place by that other workers were locals, while 'he came from Vietnam, where there [wa]s a war'. This lame excuse was nothing unusual at the time when Soviet people were overwhelmed by propaganda on the collective struggle for social justice across the globe. The nickname attached to him for the rest of his life, but the reason behind his missing skills in approaching the horse was the absence of horses in his native village. Paradoxically, he was a grandson of a rich farmer who owned many horses but who was eventually recognised by the Soviet power as kulak, dispossessed and sent together with his large family to their certain death in the Gulag. Only one daughter, Vjetnam's mother, was able to survive. No less paradoxical, this and other grandsons of successful farmers who were deprived of crucial skills and means have become part of a silent support base of the Soviet regime and subsequent lukascism.

Despite his modest education and unassuming career of a kolkhoz general labourer, Vjetnam was a local moral authority. This is evident from the fact that for many years he served as a church acolyte and the bearer of the icon during Orthodox church processions. However, it was mostly Vjetnamka who has propelled the couple to the centre of the village moral economy. Accustomed from her childhood to charity, caring for others, and acquiring daily bread by the sweat of her brow, she has lived up to these principles. As an active communicator and ardent narrator, Vjetnamka daily spread the lore of her native village Lomuš (resettled after the Chernobyl catastrophe) that in her stories played the role of a lost Avalon of moral economy. There, she said, people had been 'in kindness to each other' (u laske), friendly and mutually supportive – especially after WWII, when, in the absence of tractors or horses, five-six women had been pulling a plough. Lomuš dwellers formed a close-knit community so much so that they were 'deluging the village' (tapili sialo) with their song. They helped each other, and nobody would ever accept a kopek for this. It seemed that they often worked hard for hard-working sake, which clearly was part of their idea of drudgery[2].

---

[2]There is an objection that Chayanov's idea of drudgery was that it was the point after which people stopped working, and that the Lomuš women apparently accepted the necessity of hard work and kept working, which is different. As a

In Juravičy, Vjetnamka used to be a chef in the local school canteen (and was awarded a Soviet medal for her achievement) but was juggling that job with keeping a large household, including the mandatory several cows/pigs/poultry. The lion's share of the household products has been given away. Vjetnam and Vjetnamka in principle helped each and everyone. There were always some helpers for their household routine, and many came to help with harvesting the couple's large subsistence plot. Despite their advanced age and failing health, it was only recently that they have given up their last cow, regretting themselves turning into 'do-littles'. Vjetnamka also referred to herself as *pustalga*, meaning a bird kestrel in Belarusian but consonant with 'emptiness'. The couple named their life-long hard-working using a verb encountered often in my interviews: '*haravać*'. It meant to be in sorrow, or to be involved in drudgery, in Chayanovian English-language scholarship. The couple occasionally referred to themselves, and others like them, as *horapašnyja*, an endemic word splicing 'sorrowing' and 'harrowing'.

How representative was such life-long selfless devotion? As mentioned previously, there are attempts to substantiate national superiority in terms of an equalising moral economy based on the anecdotal evidence of local gentry working in their gardens. The Juravičy couple themselves could provide similar anecdotal evidence. They shared a joking recollection of how they had allowed *baciuška* (the local Orthodox priest) to have his vegetable beds within their fertile subsistence plot and then kept telling puzzled passers-by that they had been so godly a family for the priest to do their household chores. Even though this older couple appears to embody ideas of an economically moral peasantry, this needs testing for the larger population by triangulating their experiences with economic, cultural, and political arguments. In the following, I employ this triangulation not only to define the spread and mutual correlation of the attitudes inculcated by class-based and populist approaches but also to delineate the timeframe for the present-day rural status quo and for the hold of lukascism.

Local economy's rationale: need or accumulation?

Juravičy post-kolkhoz was decaying and laying off workers. It supplied all its produce to the state at fixed low prices, while the Soviet-time kolkhoz had enjoyed more freedom managing its assets and cheap machinery supplied by the state: tractors were available at 'a kilo for a rouble' (a 'Belarus' tractor weighing three tons had a fixed price of 3,000 Soviet roubles, twenty monthly wages). Even when Juravičy kolkhoz did not need spare parts, the latter were nonetheless pressured upon it. Recently, a tractor costed the equivalent of US$ 8–15,000 (80–150 monthly wages), and Juravičy post-kolkhoz had to lease tractors from the state; spare parts and fertilisers were also very expensive. Juravičy villagers doubted that the relative stability of the past would return, as they remembered that the kolkhoz had begun to fall into disrepair long before the collapse of the USSR.

The households' economy was declining and disassociating from local issues. Instead of becoming individual farmers they looked for occasional construction work in cities. Villagers accepted any job and were ready to travel long-distance, mostly to Russia. Even when they did bring their hard-earned money back to the village (often they were swindled by

---

counterclaim, the peasant habits and practices that once had inspired Chayanov's ideas were later ruthlessly bent by the repressions of the 1930s (Chayanov himself fell victim to) and afterward.

employers), they could spend it on drink, partly out of ignorance of how to apply the money for something worth-while (echoing Visser [2010] on post-Soviet villagers having lost cultural tradition of entrepreneurship), but also due to an insufficiency of market institutes and sheer absence of the land market.

Economic processes caused depopulation. Recurrent phrases expressed the cycle: 'the village dies'; 'no jobs, few people left, few children [119 aged under eighteen, by official count]', contrasting with the erstwhile 'buzzing village' when thriving local enterprises had been staffed by the many local residents, and larger local households served subsistence requirements of large families. It was Chernobyl in 1986 that the exodus of local people started, and large swathes of local lands became unusable, tantamount to another negative synergistic effect.

In this situation what could rejuvenate the village? The current extent of drudgery ('*haravać*') in agricultural work was not high. Locals clung to the view that 'the village is where one has to toil', but, in practice, not many households engaged in intense tilling of the land. Few households kept a cow, selling extra milk to the state procurers at fixed low prices or giving it to relatives and friends. If the household finally decided to stop keeping the cow(s), it alleviated other household work, such as haymaking. Thus another combination of low fertility and unattractive procurement prices produced a decline of household agricultural activities.

The land tenure system could support only small-scale, subsistence production. Next-to-house subsistence allotments did not exceed 0.25 ha of only moderately fertile land (ridden with the risks associated with spotty soil-bourne radionuclide content) and could provide staple food to a small family. By law, the local post-kolkhoz (the agricultural land's administrator) could provide up to a hectare to a villager claiming it for agricultural pursuits, but in practice, the post-kolkhoz would only give badlands.

Prospects of larger, business-scale ventures, or 'farming' (in the official definition), attracted only a few people. To be entitled to receive a larger land plot (up to 100 ha) involved a lengthy process of state registration of a peasant farm enterprise, and it also required a starting capital to prove the claimant's consistency and ability to pay the corresponding taxes. State credits were mostly inaccessible and feared even when offered. In the absence of landed property, villagers had nothing in terms of collateral. Their weather-beaten wooden houses had little commercial value amid many vacant constructions remaining deserted after the death of their owners. Whoever risked investing their money (painstakingly earned elsewhere) eventually dealt with the purchasing agents and fixed low prices. Most importantly, starting your business required connections.

In Juravičy, there was only one villager, informally referred to as Jaroś, who has positioned himself well for the farmer's role. His business was comparable in scope to the local post-kolkhoz, and the latter occasionally asked Jaroś to help with seed material, machinery, and money to pay wages. Jaroś started as a perestroika-period (the late 1980s) cooperator by buying a kolkhoz-decommissioned tractor 'Belarus' for 300 roubles, when many could do the same. However, his subsequent business path could not be copied by each and everyone. His sister married a German, who supported Jaroś first entrepreneurial attempts, and he was said to have established ties with *načaĺstva*. His daughter has become the public prosecutor for the administrative district where Juravičy is located. Such factors of business success were essential in Belarus. Not only was red tape a block, but strenuous efforts were required to protect a business from forcible takeover by *načaĺstva* and from numerous state inspectorates that readily fined and extorted.

Addressing the economic differentiation, with Jaroś at the top of the income hierarchy, the poorest category were people (roughly, every third from the 369 working-age villagers) suffering alcohol addiction and eking out an existence by herding villagers' cows to the pasture in the summer and rendering help to local pensioners throughout the cold period. Two categories were scraping a living quite uniformly: locally employed (50–60, seasonally variable) and pensioners (164). There were also some self-employed people who were able to earn money in Russia. Another asset was privately owned agricultural machinery: the work on subsistence plots that traditionally had been performed manually with the use of horsepower, and more recently received mechanised assistance from the kolkhoz, was now often performed using privately owned machinery. Their owners were highly regarded due to their economic independence, and the increasingly elderly population made their service increasingly sought-after.

The economic hierarchy did not automatically translate into a social hierarchy. However, social and economic cohesion in Juravičy was gradually deteriorating. The erstwhile camaraderie, cemented by kolkhoz team-working, has now been replaced by aloofness of individual breadwinning. The penchant for mutual help was least evident among younger-generation villagers, and it was markedly higher among 'those of old hardening'. It is the latter who most actively communicated and shared their household products.

Vjetnam's household was one example of the above: despite their modest consumption, they planted extensively, to be harvested attracting volunteer helpers, and to be given away. This behaviour by older and physically frail people might be explained by their fear of losing their social network and by adherence to the old customs. However, even for the older people, the advent of mechanised cultivation and harvesting made the non-monetary-based mutual help increasingly redundant. All the locals unconditionally helped in emergencies. However, the idea to do something together came to villagers 'only as innermost thoughts'. It is thus impossible to compare the role in the village of those typically older people who espoused self-abnegation, toiling and giving away their products (representative of the economy of need) and the relative weight of typically younger villagers acting in line with the economy of accumulation. Besides the unfortunate economic circumstances, what other factors prevent its successful development and which is a way out? The ensuing analysis of firstly cultural barriers and then political openings might suggest the village destinies with more certainty. Reviewing the cultural barriers, most of which have been raised by populism, I eventually indicate a social group that has been left behind these barriers, or excluded (a central element in analysing populism – Scoones et al. [2018]) under the current conjuncture, and why.

Cultural barriers: who is excluded?

Since moral economy involves values, the question is which values are predominant and acceptable in a rural community. Are they morally charged barriers (that ultimately constitute 'culture'[3] and particular moral economies – Orlove [1997]) to commerce, wealth and

---

[3]'Culture is what we know about what people like us do' (Ulrich-Schad and Duncan 2018, 7).

landed property, to risk and to otherness? I address a number of social determinants to understand which of them stipulate exclusion.

Attitude to landed property is a matter of social justice. Elderly descendants of the repressed and dispossessed in Juravičy did not want any restitution. This can be explained by their declining years and Soviet collectivism that has replaced skills of proprietorial independence over their lifetime involvement in collective farming. My interviewees were content with only using the land, presently in plenty and uncontested.

Regarding the attitude to private economic pursuits, there was no conflict between Jaroś (symbolising the economy of accumulation) and the collective 'Vjetnam' (standing for the economy of need). The attitude to Jaroś was positive (*jon haruje*: he is in sorrow/sheds tears on land) and even condescending ('let him pull and plough if he wants!'). Vjetnamka called Jaroś *horapašnyj* (working without letup). In his own turn, Jaroś did not prevent anyone from attending a local fishy lake that he leased from the state. Jaroś discerned 'what can be turned into a commodity, and of what natural or commonly held resources can be appropriated for private use and profit', using Edelman's (2005, 332) words regarding such practices. The treatment of Jaroś reflected the public respect for hard work, making people turn a blind eye to his privileges arising from being well-connected to the state.

Addressing the emotional sphere of fears as a source of cultural barriers translated into risk aversion, such recurrent fears as an apprehension to lose subsistence in Juravičy was perceptibly grounded in villagers' experience. Lending weight to the importance of subsistence, Vjetnam told a shocking story of how his undernourished small brother had died during WWII of a mere fright (that caused abdominal spasms) when a neighbouring boy had put on a discarded German gas mask and had appeared at their house window. The awareness of food-related death was all-pervasive in this Chernobyl-affected region, but there were other apprehensions that sidelined radio-phobia: 'Beware not the radiation that you eat [with food] but the one that eats you' (to imply *načaĺstva*), to be addressed later.

Often fears refuted sweeping generalisations about 'traditional' aptitudes and aversions. In her turn, Vjetnamka has depicted stigmatisation of her fellow villagers from Lomuš once resettled to the nearby but less affected by Chernobyl fallout village Azaryčy. Locals kept the newcomers at bay and refused to queue with them to buy bread in the local store (in the late 1980s – the time of severe shortages and queues). The resettled saw it as an ultimate injustice and *tapili sialo* (kept inundating the village with tears). Given that čarnobyĺcy (people from Chernobyl-affected areas) were met much more amicably elsewhere, I explain the 'Azaryčy fear' by this village's tragic history: by the Winter of 1943, the Wehrmacht turned this Belarusian village into a death camp, where 20,000 peaceful residents died from camp fever, intentionally spread with a view to contaminate the advancing Soviet troops (Khatyn Memorial n.d.). Since Azaryčy villagers had proceeded to die from camp fever, it is no wonder that in the late 1980s they were afraid of the then unheard pestilence, radiation (by 2017, radiation has rather become part of the folklore, as above). Using Azar's (2018, 2) terminology from the Boomtown's contaminated water account, the Azaryčy queuing involved a clash of two toxic uncertainties, each producing 'a specific within-group consciousness'. The Azaryčy story also evokes a discussion initiated by Verdery's (1996) 'etatization of time', whereby the socialist state wielded control by arresting peoples' bodies in queues. The Azaryčy story corroborates Mincyte's (2012, 49) opposing view of queuing as a rare chance to have 'experience of social time' in 'the context of shrinking public sociality, weakening common rituals, and ever-increasing social isolation'.

A transience of fears is related to risk-taking and is evident in Juravičy villagers' courage in treating neighbours suffering from tuberculosis and HIV. Villagers were cautious to them but also sympathetic and suggestive that sufferers were not guilty of their decease, and should be treated rather than blamed. Quite expectedly, Vjetnam's family were most compassionate: when a local woman with terminal-stage AIDS could not care for herself, they took her to their house and cared for, and then buried using their own and 'crowd-sourced' money. When I asked Vjetnamka to explain, she told me a story from her childhood in Lomuš: a female relative suffering from tuberculosis visited the family but was reluctant to share family meals (at the time, a traditional way was to eat from the same dish) – but the father insisted, following his usual instruction to the children: 'somebody else's illness is not catching'. Vjetnamka and other older people uphold the principles of never rejecting anyone (in contrast to authoritarian populists' 'strong man' talk pitting insiders against outsiders [Scoones et al. 2018] espoused by lukascism). In their turn, younger villagers defied 'traditional' fears by bravely entering the capitalist labour market in the city but most often came back to their village.

Trust and treatment of otherness was the sphere where lukascism was most active both in exploiting the traditional disdain for gain and undermining public trust in various 'others'. For many years since Chernobyl, owing to international organisations and with the Belarusian state permitting it grudgingly, children from Juravičy periodically recuperated in host families in Italy. Their parents invoked these trips but had 'mixed feelings' rather than were they unreservedly grateful: they were confused by Italian host families presumably motivated by tax exemption, as villagers learned from a certain 'documentary investigation' on Belarusian TV. However, it was arguable whether lukascism secured its monopoly for benevolence by striking the right note with the supposedly traditional aversion to capitalism or in many cases it just met a widespread cynicism, scepticism and appetite for conspiracy theories (Professor Chris Pickvance, personal communication, 19 December, 2016).

My interviews gave evidence of the mistrust of the outside world inculcated exactly using rural peoples' liking for fables. Recurrent in local folklore was a 'provenance' myth of the Colorado potato beetle dating back to the 1950s: it linked the beetle invasion of Soviet territory to American imperialists seeking to undermine potato harvests. This myth is still widespread in Belarus, having been adorned with local details: its Juravičy-specific version involved kolkhoz herders who had seen a plane dropping sacks with never-before-seen striped beetles. The mistrust of the outworld based on such myths sometimes left people disoriented before global warming. Besides the acquisitions in terms of new crops that they enjoyed in the warmer climate, there was a downside in terms of new pests, such as a certain omnivorous 'black fly' eating currents, raspberry, and even apple bloom, and making villagers wonder as to its future spread and appetites. As one occasional visitor to Juravičy who had been on a work contract in Venezuela (a fruit of Lukašenka-Chaves friendship at the time much vaunted by state propaganda) identified the pest as the Venezuelan 'flying ant'. This update made local people clueless, unable to explain the pestilence by 'machinations of imperialism'.

> 'Mixed feelings' and disorientation were not the only product of populism. There was also racial exclusion and genocide. For five years, two dozen houses in Juravičy have been

occupied by Roma families. Unlike other new-comers (Ukrainian refugees and several Tajik-Belarusian families) who were treated equally with fellow Belarusians, the attitude to Roma was uniformly negative. The prejudice concerned theft, swindle, and drug-selling. Most of these accusations were ungrounded, and villagers finally admitted it. The only blame which appeared solid to the locals and determined the exclusion of Roma was their 'not working'. This implied their ability to remain self-sufficient without tilling subsistence allotments and staying away from the post-kolkhoz or construction sites in the city. On a daily basis, Roma took bags with some cheap merchandise to a town thirty kilometres away, but peddling was not considered as valid work by locals. What was more, Roma kept receiving social pensions, they received medical treatment, and their children attended school ('because of free lunches there', as locals supposed).

Roma sometimes tried to achieve rapprochement with locals, but in vain, even though the two groups had plenty in common. Older Roma, like their Belarusian peers, bewailed the disappearance of the traditional community; and the younger Roma families also shared most problems with any other family in the village, and even worse – many children in Roma families implied frequent addressing the authorities, where they met the same ineffectiveness on top of prejudice. Even though Roma were excluded from the village community without being excluded from the social welfare and healthcare, their exclusion was furnished by the authoritarian state via its populist instruments (like the 'decree on do-littles') that referred to the still persistent popular ideas discriminating honourable versus dishonourable labour, and to the special attitude to land that in practice splintered rural community along ethnic and racial lines. The world is like a village, and 'in Appalachia rich and poor people would tell us there are the good families who work and the bad families who "draw" benefits rather than work. These stigma stick, despite evidence that they are not accurate' (Ulrich-Schad and Duncan 2018, 7).

The present exclusion of Roma in Juravičy is a reminder of the horrible consequences of similar traditionalism during WWII: Juravičy could be the only Belarusian settlement where local collaborators (rather than Nazi) organised the holocaust of their Jewish neighbours (Studzinskaja 2017) and nearly four hundred Jews died, in entire families. Nowadays, older villagers remember their Jewish neighbours as very good people, remarking in passing that Jews have never tilled the land. At the time, this objection was probably strong enough and served Belarusian neighbours to 'define the boundaries of a moral community' (expression by Snyder [2016]) that could prompt local scoundrels to action. The moral boundary drawing mechanism is presently employed in Juravičy to construct Roma as objectionable and to marginalise them. This historical parallel suggests a darker side of the moral economy that might turn reactionary.

Prospects for political settlement: resistance or adaptation?

Like elsewhere in Belarus, the local community in Juravičy was not institutionalised, with only moral and informal leaders. Nobody ever asked my interviewees about their views aside from their regular participation in elections – commonly rigged, in their opinion. No regular contacts (such as to discuss local issues) occurred between the authorities and villagers, save for shortly prior to and on election days. It might seem that these people were stuck-in-the-mud and had no preferences to voice, but my interviewees invariably turned out to be intelligent and concerned. Speaking to a night watch at the post-kolkhoz depot positioned next to its gates, I was astonished to hear a phrase from Confucius: 'Even the guard at the gate has his own opinion, but who is interested in the opinion of the guard at the gate?' However, when my interviews touched upon independent decision-making and collective action, people were disconcerted. Most interviewees had no idea how to revive the village. When asked to apply an imagined 'investment' money to the local economy or infrastructure, they were at loss, having no experience dealing with public funds.

As mentioned, popular wisdom urged caution to *načalstva* above the heed to radiation. People distinguished between *načalstva* and Lukašenka. Typically older villagers still believed in Lukašenka's ability to relieve the country from need, and yet they feared changes (Lukašenka promised 'no reforms'). They expressed hopes that Lukašenka would last as long as they lived. And they wished Lukašenka to force the youth into work – fully realising that there were virtually no (paid) jobs in the country and thus obliging young people to do drudge work. Younger villagers were mostly reticent, self-censoring and afraid of saying anything 'in excess' about Lukašenka.

Regarding *načalstva* and its deliberate failure in duties, interviewees spared no words. The local council chairman was appointed rather than elected, and probably for this reason unsupportive and as somebody acting to enable 'right' results at the elections and prevent social unrests than in line with his direct responsibilities. The latter featured putting the settlement to rights and meeting older villagers' common request to re-measure/trim their subsistence plots to correspond their actual land usage and to cut their land tax, tiny as it was ('because people love justice'). Probably by force of the habit, villagers commonly suspected the chairman (originally from another village) of thwarting the locals. However, locals never risked direct confrontation.

Resisting the non-accountable *načalstva* took two concrete forms: rumours and holy fools (Scott 1985; Hunt and Kobets 2011). Rumours in Juravičy were generated by villagers gathering next to the local store over discussing TV news. While the Soviet regime had ensured local interpretation of its 'political course' (via ubiquitous political propaganda briefings), present-day Belarusian villagers were left to their own devices. On such occasions, villagers concentrated on sugar-coating TV pictures of rural life, causing their indignation and invariably blaming *načalstva*, who kept misinforming Lukašenka.

Communicating and interpreting the extra-local information was different from spreading the unambiguous local news. Juravičy-based holy fool Andrej mostly communicated the guileless local message. In line with holy fools' perceived proximity to death (and thus to god, in villagers' mindset), he was a harbinger of bad news. He also carried the icon at the head of funeral processions and kept his primitive records of village deaths along with their causes that could put to shame the official statistics, which has been suspected of downgrading the mortality rate and cancer accidence in this Chernobyl-affected area.

Having assumed the holy foolery, Andrej inevitably assumed its constituent part of public intercessor (compensating for the lack of overt and rightful resistance by other villagers). Capable of saying anything in their face and often performing in a scandalous form, he pressed the local council to abide by their duties. Andrej was no fool and realised much of his social function: 'If we keep silent, Juravičy will die', he said. Even though resistance via rumours and holy fools had bleak prospects for any real emancipation, these forms nonetheless conveyed public protest, unlike the 'pilfering from post-kolkhoz'.

While the latter has been regarded as 'everyday' resistance in Russia (Nikulin [2009] criticised by Mamonova and Visser [2014]), indicating a disjuncture was Belarusian villagers' differentiating pilfering and stealing (from post-kolkhoz in both cases).

In Juravičy, villagers initially denied involvement in any such practice but getting more open conversationally, they admitted that 'everyone was pilfering from the kolkhoz'. None of my interviewees recognised in their pilfering any opposition to the Soviet regime. Explanations of these episodes either fitted the 'abundance and good husbandry argument' ('because people worked hard and always produced in excess of the [government-assigned] plan') or some liberally interpreted Biblical rationale, as in a local saying 'to be next to the river without being able to drink' reminiscent of passages from the Exodus 7 and the 'next-to-a-well' talk by Jesus and the Samaritan woman.

The tradition of pilfering has outlived the kolkhoz: post-kolkhoz mechanisers drained diesel fuel for their private ('coincidentally' diesel) cars; night watchmen could take a modicum of grain; and a local care worker for the elderly jokingly remarked that at such a work you could only pilfer time (take your time most literally). There was still a glaring mismatch between the kolkhoz and the post-kolkhoz: during my interviews, people differentiated their pilfering from the commercial-level theft by *načaĺstva*. The popular explanation of this disparity positioned *načaĺstva* not only to steal but also to sell the stolen, whereas common people could only take a modicum to meet their household's pressing needs. Such pilfering suggested an adaptation, rather than 'everyday' resistance: locals did consider the post-kolkhoz as their common endowment and tolerated each other's measured tapping into this public domain.

There has been no shortage of conjecture about what could prompt Belarusians to political action, such as a recurrent claim that they may agitate if they finally discover the extent of Soviet repression and dispossession. My interviews and observations in Juravičy suggested that villagers were too averse to social conflicts to be effective politically. For instance, Vjetnam never resisted the Soviet regime despite his knowing the grandfather family's lot. During WWII, Soviet guerilla fighters waywardly killed his father, who had been saying 'do not hurt anybody and fear nobody'. Later, Vjetnam refused revenge saying merely 'outlived but unforgotten' (*perabytno ale ne zabytno*).

Aside from agency-related non-conflictual dispositions, there are structural factors contributing to the quiescence. Juravičy villagers' access to natural resources was so far quite liberal and their social differentiation was insignificant. Another structural factor inhibiting resistance was that power petered out towards the bottom of the Belarusian hierarchy of power: it was simply inexpedient demanding anything, for instance, from the local council.

Blocking a resistance was also a dismissal by people residing on this radioactively contaminated land of their initial 'toxic consciousness' without forming a distinct contamination-mediated political culture (Azar 2018). This happened under the influence of what Van Dyck and Arora (2018) in a different context called 'tactic of purification' and de-problematisation of facts – of the objective radiological situation by the Belarusian authorities. It might be the case that when Belarus embarks on capitalist reforms Belarusian villagers will collectively defend their moral economy. However, the Juravičy case suggests that it is more likely going to be a picture of the adaptation.

Conclusions

Based on an empirical study of rural households' responses to the entrenching monopoly of state-controlled large-scale agriculture, the paper positions Belarusian village and agriculture both within post-socialist rural politics and global agrarian debates. The paper depicts the post-Soviet rural Belarus with its continuing monopoly of state-run large-scale farming, patrimonial governance, and the unsettled lives of rural characters. It finds intermingled in the Belarusian village those people who abide by principles of the moral economy and those seeking to regenerate their lives. The classical 'persistence versus disappearance' debate is of theoretical relevance in this case: determining whether Belarusian villagers are peasants by definition would not add much definitiveness about their destinies.

Much more practically important is how the 'adaptation versus resistance' debate is resolved. The paper argues that Belarusian villagers are not averse to capitalist reforms, often pro-market oriented, and highly adaptive. An inclusive privatisation of land would create conditions for further adaptation and protection of the owners from state incursions on their rights. The analysis of adaptive behaviours also concerns those who might be seen as either not adapting (via algorithms commonly considered as 'befitting') or adapting differently. The paper shows that these people are subject to exclusion, largely furnished by authoritarian populism that rests on pitting people against the 'other'.

The coexistence scenario invokes the Kautsky's ([1899] 1988) point on the deferred capitalist change-over, and its consideration acquires a prognostic quality. After the 2004 ('anti-pilfering') decree, Belarusian village is not prone to coexist under the current conjunction that fails to support the small-scale people's farming. Like other populisms, lukascism is inconsequential: while proclaiming some principles of the moral economy it disregards others, thus undercutting the coexistence.

The paper discusses lukascism as a separate phenomenon within the worldwide authoritarian populism. Turning to the classical debate on the consequences of agrarian transition by class-based theorists and agrarian populists, it presents lukascism as a rare case of agrarian populism used by top authority. Instead of being espoused by egalitarian intellectuals seeking liberation for peasants by protecting them from changes, the paper shows what happens when this rhetoric is taken up by authoritarian demagogues to retain their personal power and staving off development opportunities for the country.

For many years, lukascism has exploited the peasant moral economy. However, the older generation of villagers, maintaining a particular allegiance to old traditions, regrettably passes away[4]. Pitching solidarity obligations against subsistence rights does not work with younger generations, as the mismatch 'between what is being conjured or promised and what is delivered' (expression by Borras [2018, 6]), is obvious to them. Rural Belarus is thus on the verge of changes.

Acknowledgements

The author is grateful to Gordon Pirie, Chris Pickvance, and Bruce Grant who advised him on the initial text and who had played a decisive role in his becoming a researcher. He would never dare to focus on the Belarusian countryside without a research stay with the Roosevelt House Pubic

---

[4]January 2018, Aliaksandr Kupryjenka ('Vjetnam') died.

Policy Institute. The author is indebted to five anonymous reviewers who considered the paper at its various stages. He understands that the paper would never materialise without Oane Visser, Natalia Mamonova, Jun Borras, and Marc Edelman.

Disclosure statement

No potential conflict of interest was reported by the author.

ORCID

Aleh Ivanou http://orcid.org/0000-0002-6908-2353

References

Azar, R. 2018. "Boomtown Poison: Political Culture Under the Shadow of Lead Poisoning in West Texas." ERPI (Emancipatory Rural Politics Initiative) Working Paper Series. Accessed 29 June 2018. https://www.tni.org/en/article/erpi-2018-conference-papers-international.

Bartlett, R. 1990. *Land Commune and Peasant Community in Russia: Communal Forms in Imperial and Early Soviet Society*. London: Palgrave Macmillan.

BelAgroBelarus. n.d. "Sel'skoye khozyaystvo Belarusi" [Agriculture of Belarus]. Accessed 17 September 2018. http://aw.belal.by/russian/prof/prof.htm.

Bernstein, H. 2004. "Changing Before Our Very Eyes: Agrarian Questions and the Politics of Land in Capitalism Today." *Journal of Agrarian Change* 4 (1-2): 190–225.

Bernstein, H. 2007. "*Capital and Labour From Centre to Margins*." Keynote address for the conference: living on the margins: vulnerability, exclusion and the state in the informal economy, Stellenbosch, 26–28 March.

Borras Jr, S. M. 2018. "Understanding and Subverting Contemporary Right-wing Populism: Preliminary Notes from a Critical Agrarian Perspective." ERPI (Emancipatory Rural Politics Initiative) Working Paper Series. Accessed 29 June 2018. https://www.tni.org/en/article/erpi-2018-conference-papers-international.

Burawoy, M. 2002. "Transition Without Transformation: Russia's Involuntary Road to Capitalism." In *Locating Capitalism in Time and Space: Global Restructurings, Politics and Identity*, edited by D. Nugent, 290–310. Stanford: Stanford University Press.

Byres, T. J. 1979. "Of Neo-Populist Pipe-Dreams: Daedalus in the Third World and the Myth of Urban Bias." *Journal of Peasant Studies* 6 (2): 210–244.

Canovan, M. 1981. *Populism*. London: Junction Book.

Chayanov, A. V. [1925] 1966. *The Theory of the Peasant Economy, Edited by D. Thorner et al.* Manchester: Manchester University Press.

Cyhankoŭ, V., and V. Karbalievič. 2017. "Navošta nam svoj uradžaj, kali impartnaje liepš?" [Why do we have a harvest, when imported is better?] RFE/RL, August 23. https://www.svaboda.org/a/ci-patrebna-belarusi-svaja-selskaja-haspadarka/28693000.html.

Drakakhrust, Yu. 2017. "Što pryniesla Bielarusi Kastryčnickaja revaliucyja?" [What the October Revolution has brought to Belarus?] RFE/RL, October 6. https://www.svaboda.org/a/28836488.html.

Edelman, M. 2005. "Bringing the Moral Economy Back in … to the Study of 21st-Century Transnational Peasant Movements." *American Anthropologist* 107 (3): 331–345.

Edelman, M. 2018. "Sacrifice Zones in Rural and Non-metro USA: Fertile Soil for Authoritarian Populism." ERPI (Emancipatory Rural Politics Initiative) Working Paper Series. Accessed 29 June 2018. https://www.tni.org/en/article/erpi-2018-conference-papers-international.

Eke, S. M., and T. Kuzio. 2000. "Sultanism in Eastern Europe: The Socio-Political Roots of Authoritarian Populism in Belarus." *Europe-Asia Studies* 52 (3): 523–547.

Hall, S. 1985. "Authoritarian Populism: A Reply to Jessop et al." *New Left Review* 151: 115–124.

Hall, S. 1988. *The Hard Road to Renewal: Thatcherism and the Crisis of the Left*. London: Verso.

Humphrey, C. 2002. "Does the Category 'Postsocialist' Still Make Sense?" In *Postsocialism: Ideals, Ideologies and Practices in Eurasia*, edited by C. M. Hann, 12–15. London: Routledge.

Hunt, P., and S. Kobets. 2011. *Holy Foolishness in Russia: New Perspectives*. Slavica Publishers: Bloomington.

Karbalievič, V. 2018. "Pochemu agropromyshlennyy kompleks v Belarusi—eto politika." [Why the agro-industrial complex in Belarus is politicised]. Zaŭtra tvajoj krainy, July 23. http://www.zautra.by/art.php?sn_nid=28659.

Kautsky, K. [1899] 1988. *The Agrarian Question*. London: Zwan Publications.

Kerkvliet, B. J. 2009. "Everyday Politics in Peasant Societies (and Ours)." *Journal of Peasant Studies* 36 (1): 227–243.

Khatyn Memorial. n.d. "Ozarichy, Kalinkovichy Region." Accessed 17 September 2018. http://www.khatyn.by/en/genocide/ccs/ozarichi/.

Korf, V. 2012. "V Belarusi zapretili sotsiologicheskiye issledovaniya?" [Social research banned in Belarus?] Liberal Club, 6 July. http://liberalclub.biz/en/blogs/v-belarusi-zapretili-sociologicheskie-issledovaniya.

Lenin, V. I. [1964] 2004. *Development of Capitalism in Russia*. Honolulu, Hawaii: University Press of the Pacific.

Mamonova, N. 2016a. "Naïve Monarchism and Rural Resistance in Contemporary Russia." *Rural Sociology* 81 (3): 316–342.

Mamonova, N. 2016b. "Rethinking Rural Politics in Post-socialist Settings: Rural Communities, Land Grabbing and Agrarian Change in Russia and Ukraine." PhD diss., Erasmus University Rotterdam.

Mamonova, N. 2018. "Understanding the Silent Majority in Authoritarian Populism: What can we Learn from Popular Support for Putin in Rural Russia?" ERPI (Emancipatory Rural Politics Initiative) Working Paper Series. Accessed 29 June 2018. https://www.tni.org/en/article/erpi-2018-conference-papers-international.

Mamonova, N., and O. Visser. 2014. "State Marionettes, Phantom Organisations or Genuine Movements? The Paradoxical Emergence of Rural Social Movements in Post-Socialist Russia." *Journal of Peasant Studies* 41: 491–516. doi:10.1080/03066150.2014.918958.

Marx, K. [1852] 1963. *The Eighteenth Brumaire of Louis Bonaparte*. New York: International Publishers.

Marx, K. [1867] 1977. *Capital. Volume 1*. New York: Vintage.

Mincyte, D. 2012. "How Milk Does the World Good: Vernacular Sustainability and Alternative Food Systems in Post-Socialist Europe." *Agric Hum Values* 29: 41–52.

Nikulin, A. 2009. "The Oligarkhoz as Successor of Post-kolkhoz." Paper presented at the Max Planck Institute for Social Anthropology, Halle/Saale, n.a.

Orlove, B. 1997. "Meat and Strength: The Moral Economy of a Chilean Food Riot." *Cultural Anthropology* 12 (2): 234–268.

Paige, J. 1975. *Agrarian Revolution: Social Movements and Export Agriculture in the Underdeveloped World*. New York: Free Press.

Scoones, I., M. Edelman, S. M. Borras Jr, R. Hall, W. Wolford, and B. White. 2018. "Emancipatory Rural Politics: Confronting Authoritarian Populism." *Journal of Peasant Studies* 45 (1): 1–20.

Scott, J. C. 1985. *Weapons of the weak: Everyday Forms of Peasant Resistance*. New Haven, CT: Yale University Press.

Scott, J. 1976. *The Moral Economy of the Peasant: Rebellion and Subsistence in Southeast Asia*. New Haven: Yale University Press.

Shanin, T. 1973. "The Nature and Logic of the Peasant Economy 1: A Generalisation." *Journal of Peasant Studies* 1 (1): 63–80.

Silitski, V. 2005. "Preempting Democracy: The Case of Belarus." *Journal of Democracy* 16 (4): 83–97.

Snyder, T. 2016. "A New Look at Civilian Life in Europe under Hitler (An Iron Wind: Europe Under Hitler by Peter Fritzsche)." NYT, November 22. http://www.nytimes.com/2016/11/22/books/review/a-new-look-at-civilian-life-in-europe-under-hitler.html?hp&action=click&pgtype=Homepage&clickSource=story-heading&module=mini-moth&region=top-stories-below&WT.nav=top-stories-below.

Studzinskaja, I. 2017. "Byli i praviedniki, i zdradniki. Ci vinavatyja bielarusy ŭ Halakoście?" [There Were Both Righteous People and Traitors. Were Belarusians Involved in the Holocaust?] RFE/RL, March 2. https://www.svaboda.org/a/28342587.html.

Thompson, E. 1971. "The Moral Economy of the English Crowd in the Eighteenth Century." *Past and Present* 50: 76–136.

Ulrich-Schad, J. D., and C. M. Duncan. 2018. "People and Places Left Behind: Work, Culture and Politics in the Rural United States." ERPI (Emancipatory Rural Politics Initiative) Working Paper Series. Accessed 29 June 2018. https://www.tni.org/en/article/erpi-2018-conference-papers-international.

Van Dyck, B., and S. Arora. 2018. "Tactical Alliances: Science-Based Authoritarian Populism." ERPI (Emancipatory Rural Politics Initiative) Working Paper Series. Accessed 29 June 2018. https://www.tni.org/en/article/erpi-2018-conference-papers-international.

Verdery, K. 1996. *What was Socialism and What Comes Next?* Princeton: Princeton University Press.

Visser, O. 2010. "Insecure Land Rights, Obstacles to Family Farming and the Weakness of Protest in Rural Russia." *Laboratorium* 2 (2): 275–295.

Visser, O., and M. Spoor. 2011. "Land Grabbing in Post-Soviet Eurasia: The World's Largest Agricultural Land Reserves at Stake." *Journal of Peasant Studies* 38 (2): 299–323.

Wegren, S. 2006. *The Moral Economy Reconsidered: Russia's Search for Agrarian Capitalism*. New York: Palgrave.

Wolf, E. 1969. *Peasant Wars of the Twentieth Century*. New York: Harper and Row.

Land grabbing and the making of an authoritarian populist regime in Hungary

Noémi Gonda

ABSTRACT
How do authoritarian populist regimes emerge within the European Union in the twenty-first century? In Hungary, land grabbing by oligarchs have been one of the pillars maintaining Prime Minister Orbán's regime. The phenomenon remains out of the public purview and meets little resistance as the regime-controlled media keeps Hungarians 'distracted' with 'dangers' inflicted by the 'enemies of the Hungarian people' such as refugees and the European Union. The Hungarian case calls for scholarly-activist attention to how authoritarian populism is maintained by, and affects rural areas, as well as how emancipation can be envisaged in such a context.

Introduction

In the discourse of the Hungarian authoritarian populist government, new 'enemies' of the people constantly pop up like in a shooting game at an amusement park. The 'dangers' that they represent are taken up by the media, which is controlled by the ruling power. Among the latest 'enemies' are refugees, the investor George Soros, NGOs, and the European Union. Parallel to, and under cover of this 'distraction', the regime is consolidating itself economically and politically via land grabbing by and for national oligarchs and 'pocket contract' foreigners.

Land rights have been propelled into the global spotlight as vital for achieving the United Nation's Sustainable Development Goals (SDGs) and have been extensively discussed in academia and activist circles, in particular on the pages of this journal. Scholars and activists have been especially interested in understanding how increased competition for land has led to evictions, the privatization of natural resources, and human rights violations, thereby threatening equitable natural resource management across the Global North and South (e.g. Borras et al. 2011; Daniel 2011; De Schutter 2011; Hernandez-Arthur and Grainger

2016; McMichael 2012; Peluso and Lund 2011; White et al. 2012; Zoomers 2010). Securing the land-tenure rights of farmers has therefore become a core concern of international development donors, development research institutes, human rights activists, farmers groups, and local government agencies alike. Yet in several countries whose political regimes have become more authoritarian, the process of (re-)making the state has recently involved agricultural land grabbing by the regime itself. Land grabbing in these cases entails the transfer of control over agricultural land from smallholder farmers to national-scale entities and to the regime's supporters, with a clear agenda of promoting the regime's control and power. In order to advance our understanding of how authoritarian populist regimes arise and maintain themselves, an effort that is at the heart of the Emancipatory Rural Politics Initiative (ERPI), there is an urgent need to explore in more depth these processes of promoting authoritarian regimes' power through land grabbing, a relationship insufficiently addressed in most literature to date.

In this article, I examine agricultural land grabbing at the domestic level in Hungary, a country that has recently undergone significant political changes at both the governmental and societal levels. I explore how recent political regime shifts have altered state involvement in land tenure. My aim is to contribute to discussions on the extent to which domestic agricultural land-grabbing processes are inserted into broader governance struggles over power relations and identities, ultimately leading to the development and maintenance of authoritarian populism. With this goal in mind, I discuss how state-supported land grabbing by both Hungarian elite oligarchs and 'pocket-contract' foreigners helps sustain the authoritarian populist regime in Hungary. After presenting my theoretical and methodological approaches, I argue, first, that changes in land tenure are both a key rural driver and an important outcome of Prime Minister Orbán's electoral victories (2010, 2014, 2018). Second, I show how populist narratives that generate 'subjects' – whether the lazy *Roma*, the valiant *Magyar*[1] farmer, or the meddling EU – combine to generate a particular authoritarian political dynamic, with strong rural dimensions. Third, I highlight how emancipatory initiatives are contesting these subjectification processes, as people in the countryside begin engaging through new forms of agency. In my analysis, the latter discussion provides an opportunity for a conceptual rethinking of emancipation in oppressive contexts.

Theoretical and methodological approaches

How have changes in rural land ownership affected domestic politics, and how have they created the context for the rise of authoritarian populism with its clear rural origins under Orbán's regime? This is the core question this paper asks, which then prompts us, scholar-activists, to think in new ways about emancipation in this type of context.

Many studies discuss land grabbing as the source of state power. For example, academic debates on agricultural land grabbing often focus on how capital accumulation drives processes aimed at controlling natural resources in regions where they are still available (e.g. Borras et al. 2012; De Schutter 2011). Other research examines land grabbing's consequences for food security, employment, and welfare (e.g. Jiao, Smith-Hall, and Theilade 2015; McMichael 2012). In these debates, the state is frequently discussed according

---

[1]*Magyar* means Hungarian in Hungarian.

to a Manichean perspective: either as a weak 'target' state, which does not have the capacity to resist the pressures from foreign and domestic agricultural businesses, or as a 'host', which facilitates land accumulation by providing infrastructure and financial support to large farm enterprises. However, the strategic use of domestic land grabbing and land-grab related conflicts in generating and maintaining state power has not been discussed enough in contemporary literature. Because land grabbing remains an urgent socio-environmental concern, especially in countries where democracy is under threat, I address this gap by re-situating discussions of domestic land grabbing and land-grab related conflicts as part of a broader question of democratic governance.

Land grabbing tends to be discussed as a North to South (e.g. White et al. 2012; Zoomers 2010) and South to South (e.g. Hall 2011) phenomena of 'accumulation by dispossession' (Harvey 2004). Scholarly work on domestic land grabs, understood as national land forcibly acquired by investors, is less common both in the South (exceptions are Lavers 2012 on Ethiopia, Levien 2011 on India) and the North (exceptions are Desmarais et al. 2015 on Canada, Visser and Spoor 2011 on former Soviet countries). This gap is more than merely geographical: it makes researchers and activists focus on land grabbing through an international lens rather than on democratic land governance within states, and particularly within *certain* political regimes that strategically use domestic land grabbing and land-grab related conflicts to consolidate authoritarianism.

Additionally, there is an insufficient focus on the role of the European Union in enabling (or impeding) land grabbing, in particular in post-socialist states. The roles of transnational companies in land grabbing are often highlighted. However, the contribution of regional rural development institutions and policies, while sometimes cited (Transnational Institute 2013), are insufficiently known. European development institutions are increasingly questioned (Hulme 2016; Pe'er et al. 2014) on their roles (e.g. enabling development for whom? At what social and environmental price?). Therefore, it is timely to understand not only the role of the EU's Common Agricultural Policy (CAP) in potentially facilitating the expansion of industrial farms to the detriment of Europe's small producers but also in contributing to the maintenance of authoritarianism within its own borders.

Finally, this discussion is timely as there has clearly already been a recent and notable proliferation of what Scoones *et al.* call authoritarian populist regimes since the start of the twenty-first century (2017). This is a cause of worry, particularly for rural areas, as can be seen by the large mobilization around the ERPI research effort, initiated in 2017 by the International Institute of Social Studies (ISS) in the Netherlands. Researchers and civil society are increasingly interested in understanding authoritarian rural politics and envisioning how democratic alternatives can emerge. My article aims to strengthen ERPI's efforts in this direction.

The concept of power is central to my analysis. But 'power relations' is not an easy concept to operationalize. Thus, I use authority (the recursive processes through which power relations are accepted as legitimate; [Sikor and Lund 2009]), intersectional subjectivities (the ways people are brought into relations of power in specific subject positions based on differences such as gender, class, and ethnicity), and emancipation as analytical lenses through which to understand power relations. I see authority as constantly (re)produced or challenged 'through the process of successfully defining and enforcing rights to community membership and rights of access to important resources' (Lund 2016, 1199) such as land. Given this, land governance turns out to be as much about the processes of authorization of power actors (Lund 2016, 1221) and the governing of citizens (Valdivia 2008) as anything else. Hence, I start from the idea that struggles to control land politics will reveal the tenets of how authority works and how the exercise of authority generates specific exclusions and inclusions, rights, and permissions to use land – in short, power relations. Thus, in my discussion of authority, I ask to what extent (if any) are authoritarian regime-making processes enabling or impeding agricultural land grabbing and *vice versa*, and how the regime uses land-grab related conflicts to assert its power. Analyzing the Orbán regime's land politics will highlight how exclusions and oppressions are (re)produced and how they may become integrated in broader governance systems that are ultimately maintaining his authoritarian regime.

But looking at power relations as simply struggles over authority misses key dimensions of how the exercise of power always contains both oppressive *and* emancipatory possibilities (Ahlborg and Nightingale 2018). Intersectional subjectivities captures the possibility that people may adopt the subject position they are 'supposed to' or challenge it while they are enrolled in everyday affairs, including land governance and land conflicts. The intersectional lens enables me to explore the social differences that emerge from everyday practices (Nightingale 2011) of relating to both the land (e.g. via agricultural activities) and the regime (via complying with or resisting its discourses, its measures and policies), and to ultimately discuss how we might envision and promote the development of emancipatory land governance regimes that can contribute to challenging exclusions based on social differences such as gender, class, and ethnicity.

In addition, the focus on subjectivities allows me to discuss the possible moments in which the norms that influence the constitution of subjects (especially the subjugated ones) are broken. As Butler claims, norms must not be understood as operating in a deterministic way. Rather, '[n]ormative schemes are interrupted by one another, they emerge and fade depending on broader operations of power' (2009, 4). The conceptual focus on subjectivities helps to show the possibilities for emancipation to emerge as subjectivities change (Butler 1997; Sundberg 2004) and particular groups of people refuse the subject position they are assigned. This focus is useful to developing a new analytics of emancipation in particularly oppressive contexts.

With this threefold focus on (1) authority (how rural authority is shifting under the Orbán regime), (2) subjectivities (how rural subjects are changing), and: (3) emancipation (how opportunities for emancipation open up and close down), my ultimate aim is to reveal how the authoritarian regime and its citizen subjects are made in relation to each other, how resources like land as well as land conflicts are vital to their making, and what the possibilities are for creating more democratic relations. I raise the strategic question about emancipatory possibility given Orbán's dominance and his hold on the rural areas.

My analysis relies upon my long-term engagement in rural Hungary, which began in 2000 when I first undertook a sociological study of the North-Eastern wine-making region of Tokaj. I also draw upon information gathered over many years from my Hungarian network of activists who endeavor to envision and support alternatives to Hungarian authoritarian populism. My engagement in this network was especially strong between 2011 and 2017 when I lived in Hungary. To write this article, I also undertook an additional three months of complementary research in Hungary during 2017–18. This included participant observation in debates concerning this article's topic, many informal discussions with Hungarians and people living in Hungary during important moments such as just before and after the 2018 elections, and thirteen qualitative interviews with researchers, journalists, activists, and policy-analysts, as well as staff of environmental organizations. I also reviewed secondary sources on the topic such as policy documents, research publications, blogs, and newspaper articles. One important limitation is that I did not talk directly with farmers to write this article, as extensive fieldwork is just about to be undertaken. While my conclusions should be considered preliminary for this reason, the conceptual approach and the empirical findings nevertheless serve to highlight the need to continue and deepen this debate. In light of the global tendency towards a rise in authoritarian populist regimes, there is an urgent need for scholar-activists to systematically engage with the ways in which the development of such regimes is linked to the depletion of natural resources and, in particular, land grabbing for speculative purposes.

Discussion: the politics of domestic land grabbing in authoritarian populist Hungary and the possibilities for emancipation

Authority

Using state-owned land and European subsidies to constitute the pro-regime oligarchy

In Hungary, agriculture has been instrumentally used by the Orbán regime to both please and control its oligarchs by making them owners of the land. The climax was reached in 2015 when the Orbán regime took a great quantity of agricultural land that had been owned by the Hungarian state and privatized it that year via a 'thunderstorm' process that mainly benefitted the oligarchy. The agricultural sector attracted oligarchs and oligarchs-to-be for two main reasons. First, agriculture is an important economic sector in Hungary that has been receiving considerable amounts of European subsidies representing potential economic benefits in the short term. Second, land prices are likely to increase significantly in the medium term following the end of the moratorium that once limited the possibilities of foreign land ownership in Hungary. Thus, the agricultural sector has been an important carrot of the Orbán regime because it can potentially make its owners rich in both the short and long terms.

The Hungarian state's ownership of this great quantity of agricultural land, prior to 2015, is a legacy of the communist era and of the post-communist land tenure system, which was based on long-term leases. Indeed, after the fall of communism in 1989, a relatively large proportion of land – representing 23 per cent of the country's overall land in 2014 – remained in the hands of the Hungarian state. According to Ángyán's study (2015), which uses 2014 data from the Hungarian Central Statistical Office, this corresponded to 1.7 million hectares of productive land owned by the state, of which 500,000 hectares were arable land, 1.2 million hectares were forested, and the rest were so-called non-productive land, such as protected areas (Ángyán 2015; Hungarian Central Statistical Office 2014). The dismantling of state-owned socialist farms in the late 1980s and early 1990s was followed by agrarian reform via the distribution of compensation vouchers to former owners of expropriated land. Only the original receiver of the voucher could in theory use it to purchase agricultural land (Hartvigsen 2014). Despite this restriction, the commercialization of compensation vouchers happened in such a way that it favored wealthy Hungarian actors interested in investing in land rather than former cooperative workers (Roszík 2011; Szabó 2013); the first oligarchs – some of them still present in the agricultural sector today – started to constitute their wealth during that period of the early 1990s. Despite this phenomenon that contributed to the increasing polarization of agrarian society from the 1990s onwards, the agrarian structure remained relatively fragmented until 2015 with the presence of many smallholder farms, at least in comparison to other European countries (Hartvigsen 2014). This was essentially due to the fact that the state-owned large tracts of land that were leased out to producers via long-term agreements.

The commercialization of most state-owned lands, conceived with the objective of ending this long-term lease-based land tenure system, was announced by the government in August 2015. The intent was to complete the process by the end of 2015 via what several of my interviewees describe as a 'thunderstorm' process, which, most importantly, took place in the midst of a refugee crisis whose handling fueled a politics of fear that 'conveniently' kept Hungarian people's minds occupied. Of course, the strategy for establishing a new land tenure system had been prepared earlier. Some lease contracts had been given to national oligarchs and their family members two to three years prior to 2015 so that they could easily benefit from the land commercialization process that (in theory) was supposed to prioritize the leaser over any other potential buyer. According to former Fidesz (Orbán's party) MP József Ángyán, the regime's supporters had been warned before Orbán won the 2014 elections that this would happen in the case of his victory; thus, they were given ample time in particular to collect the requested liquidities for their entrance and/or consolidation within the Hungarian land market. It is precisely this lack of liquidities that impeded most smallholder land-leasers to buy the land they had been farming for decades.

The significance of the Hungarian agricultural sector is clearly evident when one compares Hungarian statistics with those of the EU 28. According to a report by the Hungarian Agricultural Ministry, the Institute of Agricultural Research, and the National Agricultural Chamber (Bene et al. 2016), the country has the fifth most important proportion of agricultural land in relation to its total size within the EU 28, and the second most important proportion of arable land. Indeed, 58 per cent of the country's 9.3 million hectares are under agricultural cultivation, of which 80 per cent is arable land and 15 per cent is grasslands. The proportion of arable land is higher than the EU 28 average, where 42 per cent of the total area is agricultural and 25 per cent is arable land. In 2016, there were 415,800 individual farms in Hungary, 12.3 per cent less than in 2013 (Bene et al. 2016). However, the agricultural area grew in this same period with an additional 256,000 hectares on top of the 5,372,000 hectares of 2013, which is a sign of rapid land concentration: it is mostly very small farms, of less than 4 hectares, that disappeared between 2013 and 2016 (minus 30.4 per cent). This, I argue, is in large part due to the 2015 land privatization.

Agricultural subsidies and rural development funding within the framework of the CAP have been important for the regime's oligarchs. Hungary is receiving in the 2014–2020 period a total of 12.4 billion euros; this figure represents 3.19 per cent of the total CAP budget – one of the highest shares in comparison with other EU countries (Bene et al. 2016). Prior to 2015, CAP payments made land lease contracts economically interesting, and after 2015, the ownership was economically desirable because of speculation on land prices. The subsidy payment in 2014 was around € 240 per hectare of land, which was a significant amount for those who leased large quantities of land (Krasznai Kovács

2015). It was all the more significant when viewed in relation to the average price for which the state leases land: approximately € 100 per hectare (interview with a staff member of a Hungarian environmentalist organization, October 2017). Hence, even if one did little with the leased land, he/she would receive a benefit of more than a 100 € per hectare by declaring it land under agricultural cultivation.

Those that were close to the regime and who leased agricultural lands often did not even cultivate it. Some pro-Orbán leasers (often illegally) sub-contracted the original leaser or a neighboring farmer to take care of their plots, while others just left them fallow. As one of my interviewees told me, these types of irregularities were not detected by CAP controllers. Instead, they were facilitated by the fact that CAP-related controls are often biased in Hungary; their implementation is the responsibility the Agricultural and Rural Development Agency (*Mezőgazdasági es Vidékfejlesztési Hivatal*), which, instead of randomly choosing the producers to be controlled often chooses them from among the farmers who 'don't agree [with the regime]', as one of my interviewees put it. Additionally, in Hungary, the system to control the distribution and use of subsidies works in such a way that it is depersonalized and rendered apolitical, especially towards the 'upper spheres' (Krasznai Kovács 2015). Thus, when the fines are distributed for (rightly or wrongly identified) non-compliances with EU requirements and farmers complain, the government is not blamed for the supposedly unjust implementation of the system as the street-level bureaucrats claim that they are not responsible for the procedures; rather, their critiques point to the inadequacy of the European policy. The latter reinforces Orbán's anti-EU rhetoric at the same time that it contributes to hiding the oppressions generated by the way CAP-related procedures are implemented in Hungary (Krasznai Kovács 2015), and in particular how CAP contributes to strengthening the pro-Orbán oligarchy.

The EU subsidies, initially designed to develop the new members' economies, went instead to oligarchs, and not only in Hungary; in Macedonia and Poland they have been, to a certain extent, linked with the development of authoritarian populist regimes via benefitting their allies. In Macedonia, Otten (2013) described this phenomenon in the wine-making region of Tikveš. In Poland, oligarchs have been acquiring land for speculative purposes and benefitting from EU subsidies; meanwhile land prices started increasing with the 2016 lapse of the moratorium on foreign ownership (van der Ploeg, Franco, and Borras 2015).

Despite a lack of official studies, it is clear that there has been a massive land transfer to oligarchs and oligarchs-to-be and that the decline of smallholder farming in Hungary is, to a great extent, related to this dynamic of land grabbing by and for oligarchs. Ángyán's investigations (Ángyán 2015, 2016, 2018) in seven Hungarian counties (made public on the Web to denounce governmental abuse) show this connection. Reflective of what happened in most parts of the country is the case of the county of Csongrád in South-East Hungary. Ángyán's recent report (Ángyán 2018) shows that twenty-seven stakeholders – mostly those close to Fidesz – obtained 70 per cent of the land put up for auction during the 2015 land privatization process. Smallholders (who obtained farms of less than 20 hectares) received less than nine per cent of the territory put up for auction. Calling the process an 'auction' has contributed to governmental propaganda; in fact, among the 12,000 hectares of land 'put up for auction', in reality, nearly 65 per cent was distributed without being auctioned, despite the government's narrative about the need to establish land prices via market mechanisms. Land transactions were organized in such a way that they impeded real auctions from taking place; local smallholders who had already been farming for decades in the region were unable to compete for their own plots or for additional neighboring ones as the government promoted the commercialization of large plots (more than twenty hectares) with starting prices that smallholders could not afford. Moreover, they were not given sufficient time to arrange credit. Additionally, intimidation, threats, and other non-documented but often mentioned mechanisms, forced smallholders to withdraw from engaging in the auctions. As a result, most people who acquired land through these auction processes, despite being described by the government propaganda as 'local producers', were not farmers in reality: they were, among other professions, teachers, merchants, pharmacists. They had in common that they were speculators and supporters of the regime.

The process described above has contributed to the creation and consolidation of the pro-Orbán oligarchy. One of its key figures is Sándor Csányi, the wealthiest person in Hungary (Forbes 2017), a businessman and banker who is not only a shareholder in the Hungary-based multinational oil and gas company, MOL group, he is also the exclusive owner of the Hungarian food manufacturer BONAFARM which is in the process of becoming an inevitable actor in the Hungarian agricultural and food processing scene. At a lower scale, the oligarchic system consolidates itself by involving family members of pro-regime figures. For example, in the county of Csongrád, the group of people that won the third biggest area of land in the auction (514 hectares) is related to János Lázár, ex-minister of Orbán and current Fidesz MP; the group includes his father, uncle, and several cousins (Ángyán 2018).

Land speculation and the consolidation of privileges
The 1994 Law LV, known as the land moratorium, stipulated that foreign citizens, legal entities, or any other organization without legal personality could not, until its expiration (which happened in 2014, essentially due to pressure by the EU), acquire ownership of arable land or any natural reserve in Hungary. In addition, even a private Hungarian citizen could only acquire up to a maximum of 300 hectares or 6000 golden crowns (*Arany Korona*) of value (Téglási 2013).

The average price of a hectare of land in Hungary is 1 million Hungarian Forints (HUF), which is equivalent to € 3,300, while in the Netherlands, a hectare of land costs thirty-five times that much – approximately € 115,000 (Ángyán 2015). The 2015 'thunderstorm' commercialization of formerly state-owned land attracted most wealthy Hungarians, like the previously mentioned Sándor Csányi, to buy land without the aim of using it to produce agricultural goods. These Hungarian oligarchs are speculating on the fact that within a short time period the EU will start an infringement procedure against Hungary thereby obligating the country to liberalize its land market. That moment will bring more wealth to the wealthiest Hungarians, who will happily sell their land to foreigners. In addition, Orbán will most probably blame the EU to explain to his supporters why so many foreigners will get hold of Hungarian land so quickly, thus fueling the anti-EU and anti-foreigner sentiments of his right-wing voters.

The reasons for Orbán's rural support
Land has been key in the development of Hungarian authoritarian populism under the Orbán government, starting with the 2010 elections. Land has not lost its importance

since then, but its role has changed. In 2010, Orbán used the scandals that had emerged just a few months before the elections on land grabbing by foreigners to ally the countryside. He built upon a nationalist rhetoric that stated that Hungarian land should go to Hungarians, and he held out the prospect of a socially sensitive rural development policy that would not only support existing smallholder farmers but would also lease out state-owned land to young Hungarian families. The latter families were discursively constructed as the dynamic, albeit traditional, neo-rurals who would engage in diversified production of *háztáji* (small-scale, backyard, good quality, traditionally Hungarian) agricultural products that would be sold through short circuits such as farmers markets. This discourse was bolstered by the fact that, by then, the Hungarian state already owned a great quantity of land, and Orbán declared publicly that that would continue: the 'State will buy rather than sell land' (Ángyán 2015).

This perspective, which appealed to so many smallholder farmers, was supported by the fact that (1) at that time, Hungary had a land moratorium and (2) it had a national rural strategy, written in 2010, that included a social program intended to develop small-scale diversified family farming by repopulating rural areas with young families. These two instruments could theoretically be qualified as potentially emancipatory for rural areas, even though one of them (the rural development strategy) was developed only with the express aim of winning the 2010 elections. Their example shows how progressive instruments can so easily be co-opted by authoritarian regimes, but also how difficult it is for emancipation to emerge from within the state. Equally important, they show how these kinds of instruments can appear as emancipatory and favorable for smallholder farmers while in fact serving the interests of pro-regime elites and fueling a nationalist rhetoric.

Orbán strategically used the conflicts that rose concerning the non-respect of the land moratorium to gain rural voters in 2010. Land moratorium was supposed to guarantee that only Hungarians would become agricultural land owners in Hungary and to impede land concentration by setting maximums for farm superficies per owner. In reality, while the moratorium did limit, to a certain extent, land speculation over relatively cheap Hungarian land by foreigners with much higher purchasing power than Hungarian citizens, it contributed to the rise of the so-called 'pocket contracts'. Originally used to describe land deals with foreigners that omitted the date of purchase, and that were kept 'in the pocket' until the moratorium was lifted, the expression has been generalized to describe contracts utilized to overcome the existing legal restrictions (Fidrich 2013). According to Roszík (2011), more than 1 million hectares of land had been acquired by foreigners via 'pocket contracts'; the foreign owner (which in many cases was a Western-European company) usually relied on Hungarian foremen who would 'lend' their names for the contract(s) (Fidrich 2013; Roszík 2011). As for the surface limit, it has usually been overcome by using family members' names to acquire extensions of thousands of hectares (Ángyán 2015).

The 2010 national rural strategy (*nemzeti vidékstratégia*) for the 2012–2020 period also played an important role in Orbán's electoral victory in 2010. The strategy, which was a reason for many Hungarian smallholders, environmentalists, and justice activists to be hopeful, rightly describes itself as innovative in comparison with former Hungarian rural policies. On the website that still bears the logo of the Ministry of Rural Development (*Vidékfejlesztési Minisztérium*) that has been dismantled since then, it explains the innovative character of the strategy, with the arguments that its goal is an integral rural development policy that gives priority to the development of family farming instead of monocultural mass production, that favors a type of agriculture based on quality production, a fragmented agricultural structure, as well as environmentally and landscape-friendly management.[2]

Ángyán, who had been a respected professor in a Hungarian agricultural university and a popular figure in agricultural union circles, developed this strategy upon Orbán's request to help his campaign in the countryside. He became State Secretary of Agriculture after Orbán's victory in 2010. His rural development strategy, had it been implemented, could have been rightly described as emancipatory, democratic, and socio-environmentally just. Unfortunately, the strategy ended up in the dustbin while Ángyán, its ideologue, resigned from his position after realizing that he had been merely used as an instrument for the campaign (Interview with József Ángyán, October 2017).

The strategy's central pillar was the so-called demographic land program (*demográfiai földprogram*) aimed at increasing the quantity of state-owned land and leasing it long-term to families and young people who would live and work on the farm and who would be willing to raise two or more children (Ángyán 2015). This program would have made land accumulation and speculation increasingly difficult while, on the other hand, it would have strengthened diversified family farming and attracted young people to the countryside. Equally important for Fidesz, the program would have meshed well with the populist right-wing rhetoric about 'land to Hungarians', Hungarian rural traditions, and the need for Hungarians to have more children – a point of convergence that Fidesz used to have with Hungary's second most popular political party: the extreme-right-wing Jobbik.

However, unlike Jobbik's platform, Fidesz's politicians no longer assert that Hungarian land should go to Hungarians (Lubarda 2018). On the contrary, the political program of the party refers to the interests of Hungarian agriculture *in general* and of farmers *within Europe* and *globally*. This focus on Hungarian agriculture, rather than on Hungarian farmers, reinforces the hypothesis that the regime's speculative plans regarding land are aimed at generating wealth for its oligarchs and were prepared prior to Orbán's first election in 2010. Put somewhat differently, what has been at stake for the regime was to make Hungarian agriculture more valuable in the global context while getting rid of smallholder farmers without however losing their votes.

In 2014 and 2018, Orbán and Fidesz no longer needed the type of instruments they had used in 2010 to win the support of rural voters. In addition to a careful mediation of Orbán's image as a 'man of the people and the countryside' (Wilkin 2016, 55), in 2011, a new electoral law was accepted by the Hungarian Parliament that was at that time ruling with a majority of Fidesz MPs (in alliance with the conservative Christian Democrats KDNP). As explained by Kovács and Vida (2015), in the countryside, the clear political winner of the 2014 elections was the radical nationalist party Jobbik, but it did not challenge Fidesz's victory due to the electoral system change. They explain:

> The analysis of the 2014 pattern of voting showed that (…) even though Fidesz-KDNP lost more than 570,000 voters compared to the 2010 elections, a drop of 8.2 percent, given the extreme disproportionality of the new electoral system led only to a drop of only 1.3 percent of the seats. (Kovács and Vida 2015, 63)

---

[2] www.videkstrategia.kormany.hu; My translation.

A similar explanation is valid for Fidesz's 2018 victory (with 49 per cent of the votes) with the difference being that by 2018, Fidesz had, in addition, gathered a significant proportion of usual far-right-party Jobbik voters (Jobbik received 19 per cent of the votes in 2018), especially in poor rural areas. The ruling party was indeed extremely popular among the poorest: Fidesz scored over 80 per cent in the most disadvantaged villages (Juhász and Molnár 2018b). A majority of the *Romas* (representing approximately 6–7% of the Hungarian population) also voted for Orbán's party. While there are no quantitative studies that break down votes according to ethnicity, my interviewees claim that in rural areas, approximately 90 per cent of *Romas* voted for Fidesz. It is also in the poorest regions and in the countryside where FIDESZ's anti-refugee narrative has found an audience of increasingly impoverished rural populations receptive to simplistic and racialized explanations for their economic hardships.

Ironically, those most excluded in Hungarian society have been precisely the ones who most contribute to maintaining the forces that create and reproduce their oppressions:

> The most frequently mentioned reasons [for the fact that the poor and *Roma* massively vote for Fidesz] (…) [are] the Public Work Scheme (PWS) and its relative popularity, the neo-feudal dependence on the government and local rulers, the effective governmental campaign focusing on fears about migration and Fidesz's domination of the media market in the countryside. (Juhász and Molnár 2018a)

The PWS is indeed an illustrative example of the Orbán government's social model and how it became the 'symbol of subservience, as mayors, notaries and minority leaders decide who is and who is not allowed to partake in the scheme' (Bertelsmann Stiftung 2018, 23). The PWS provides work for unemployed and often unskilled people for a monthly wage that is significantly lower than on the primary labor market. The average number of monthly participants in the PWS had been steadily increasing before the 2018 elections: it was 178,852 in 2014, 208,127 in 2015, and 224,812 in the first ten months of 2016 (Bertelsmann Stiftung 2018, 23). PWS has also contributed to improving the statistics on poverty and unemployment: this improvement has often been mentioned in Fidesz's political campaign.

Furthermore, according to my interviewees, the contract with the Russian company Rosatom is going to take the relay in providing the necessary liquidities for Orbán to keep not only his oligarchs but also his poorer voters content once the state has no land to lease and no CAP payments to manipulate. Indeed, in 2015, Rosatom was given an impressive € 12.5 billion contract to build two additional reactors to the nuclear power plant in the Hungarian town of Paks (Dunai 2017), something that made no sense in a country whose environmental characteristics allow not only for more environmentally friendly but also cheaper alternatives to nuclear power via renewables (Greenpeace 2017). As one of my interviewees stated:

> [from 12.5 billion €—the price tag of the project] if you have only 1 per cent corruption rate, which is extremely low, then you are already able to finance everybody (…). [In addition], Hungary needs loans to finance its pension system and health system and you cannot get loans for that—you can get loans for power plants—and with that loan, you are able to subsidize other things (…) [the government's] rhetoric is that Hungary doesn't have a stable enough renewable energy supply and that's why we have to have [the nuclear power plant in] Paks. [In reality, Orbán's problem with renewables is that they] lack this point of central control [which is needed for the authoritarian system to maintain itself]. (Interview with a Hungarian expert in environmental policies, September 2017)

The situation highlights how money from speculative land-grabbing, but also corruption within energy projects, can help support political elites and, in the meantime, subsidize welfare redistribution, both key elements for maintaining authoritarian populism. Thus, authority under the Orbán regime is working in such a way that the most excluded support a system that could not be maintained without these exclusions. These processes have been mobilizing different measures such as the rural development strategy, the land moratorium, and the PWS that had significant effects on the Hungarian countryside and its people. In particular, they have assigned specific people certain subject positions that are likely to reinforce the regime's authority. In the next section, I discuss some of these positions as a way to start thinking about emancipation.

The shifting 'subjects' of Hungarian authoritarian populism

The politics of land grabbing that underpin Hungarian authoritarian populism have mobilized, one after the other, the subjectivities of the young smallholder; the dynamic, neo-rural farmer; and the poor *Roma* rural populations living on welfare, and have recently put forward a new figure that fits well with the profile of the national oligarchs: that of the post-European feudal *Magyar* producer.

The young, dynamic, rural Hungarians who used to be the central subjects in the political narrative prior to the 2010 election, and who were supposed to be the main beneficiaries of the never-implemented rural development strategy, have been progressively replaced in the public discourse on the 'backwards' and poor countryside with the figure of the lazy *Roma* living on welfare (Schwarcz 2012). And indeed, as Krasznai Kovács (2016, 175) highlights, there is a distinctly racist underpinning to the regime's rationale when it comes to implementing programs like the already mentioned PWS:

> One of the key driving rationales for this [welfare] programme by the majority *Fidesz* government who instigated it is to 'make gypsies work', to break the 'dependency' of local communities on the state, as traditionally (so the political rhetoric goes), gypsies have become too lazy to work and 'milk' the system in a calculating, targeted way.

While the narrative is about breaking the dependency on the state, the regime's logic is to create and maintain dependency so that the poor and the *Romas* continue voting for Fidesz.

Recently, the *Romas*' 'issues' lost some of their importance in the governmental discourse as it started focusing on the need to defend the Hungarian borders from international refugees. However, the racist underpinnings of Fidesz's political program is still manifest in many 'social' measures so that the *Romas*' exclusion is maintained. For example, it is part of Orbán's rhetoric to make the Hungarian nation strong 'again' by encouraging Hungarian women (sic) to have more children. Extremely conservative policy measures support this by inciting women to become housewives and fulltime mothers. But *Romas*, who usually have more children than non-*Romas* in Hungary, face many obstacles to accessing the related support: their children are clearly not the ones that in the regime's narrative are called upon to populate Hungary and make it 'great'.

In the countryside, with the decreasing importance of EU subsidies to maintain the oligarchy, a new figure is progressively appearing: what I call the post-European *Magyar* farmer. The post-European *Magyar* farmer is the oligarch, the aristocrat of a new feudal system, the neoliberal entrepreneur who will capitalize on Hungary's agricultural assets, some of its national products ('*Hungarikums*'), and the cheap labor force to be found in the Hungarian *hinterlands*, while speculating on land prices, positioning themselves in the agro-industry sector and in parallel selling plots to foreigners. According to my interviewees, who are familiar with the debates taking place within the Parliament, this will be enabled by a future rural policy architecture that gives the power to organize the agricultural sector to big integrator agricultural companies such as Csányi's BONAFARM. This is the opposite of the never-implemented rural development plan discussed above, as it uses land as a pure commodity rather than as a source of social, historical, and cultural wealth related to a nation's well-being and its democratic development.

Of great worry for biodiversity, is that national lands with a protected status will follow the fate of agricultural lands. In 2015 there was a failed intent of the government to turn over the management of protected areas from nature conservation organizations to the national land portfolio management institute (*Nemzeti Földalap Kezelő szervezet-NFA*) – an organization driven by economic rather than conservation interests (Benedetti 2015). Opposition by organizations such as WWF in Hungary, Birdlife Hungary, and the Hungarian Association for Environmental Protection (*Magyar Természetvédők Szövetsége*) ultimately contributed to a presidential veto of the initiative. However, several of my interviewees believe that Orbán has only temporarily backed out on this point. Now that he won the 2018 elections, he will probably undertake the privatization of protected areas, too.

In sum, in the course of its development, Hungarian authoritarian populism has relied on the construction of different subjects and subject positions to, in the end, divert attention from the exclusionary politics of land grabbing by national oligarchs and the role of corruption in supporting the system (including to support the welfare policies that maintain the dependent poor). To challenge the regime, the first step, to which I tried to contribute above, was to understand its development, on what grounds it lies, which subject positions it puts to the fore and which others are hidden, and how its pillars are likely to evolve in the future. The next challenge is to think about emancipation in this context.

Emancipation

Emancipatory subjectivities and the need for alliances

Permaculture, seed exchange initiatives, and farmers markets are growing in Hungary; however, even when they are put in place by people who otherwise oppose the regime, few rationalize them as initiatives that could challenge authoritarian populism. As Scoones et al. highlight, because so many initiatives fail to fuel radical transformation, scholar-activists have an important role in helping local communities come together with the global community 'to reimagine rural spaces and democracy, underpinned by emancipatory politics' across scales and places (2017, 12). Indeed, as they state:

> The radical potential of these local, rooted alternatives (…) may only be realised when they are connected to a wider debate about political transformation, in rural spaces and beyond. This in turn requires situating practical grounded 'alternatives' in a broader historical, social and political context, where deepening, linking and scaling up become essential. (Scoones et al. 2017, 11)

According to my interviewees who are working on alternatives, people who might be described as the Hungarian *bobos* (*bourgeois-bohemians*) could become key actors in a potentially transformational process. These young, educated Hungarian women and men – who are either neo-rural (people of urban origin who have recently settled in the countryside) or interested in becoming ones and implement environmentally and socially friendly production and living practices – have one important strength: they are informed and connected. Moreover, their production models do not require large amounts of land and they currently fall outside of the regime's main focus and narrative. They could play a central role in challenging authoritarian rural politics via scaling-up emancipatory initiatives and making them the basis for democratic emancipatory politics, conceptualized through an emancipatory political rationality. Via the Internet, not only can they access the information that the Hungarian government tries to hide from its citizens by controlling the media, they can also establish solidary connections with initiatives abroad as well as benefit from the support of the half a million (mostly young) Hungarians who fled the country because of the lack of economic and social opportunities in contemporary Hungary. These dissidents, to whom I also belong (most of them being opposed to the regime), can be of great support for those in Hungary ready to soil their hands and boots to engage in the construction of emancipatory rural politics. Hence, the Hungarian *bobos* allied over a common political project with Hungarian consumers in Hungary and beyond, and the model of production and consumption that they convey makes them potential subjects and agents of Hungarian emancipatory rural politics. *Bobos*, however, need to build alliances with the oppressed groups: smallholders, *Romas*, and women who do not want to have children with the objective of 'making Hungary great again', among others. We scholars and activists should help them to creatively design the concrete steps towards a clear emancipatory political project.

Emancipatory initiatives need to be scaled up

There have been many small and less-small triggers that have led to mobilizations against the regime, even if, in the end, they have not significantly challenged its solidity. Some of these have already been successful, such as the already mentioned campaign to stop the government from privatizing the management of conservation areas. The case of the Kishantos Rural Development Centre is another symbolic example. The center has been working for more than twenty years on 452 hectares of state-owned land leased out to implement an organic show farm that functions in partnership with a folk high school. The government decided to end the center's lease contract in 2012 and to thereby open up the possibility of other 'local producers' obtaining lease contracts. In reality, the 'local producers' who ended up winning those contracts were not 'local'. Often, they were not even 'producers'. According to Ángyán, they were a conventional 29,00 hectares agricultural firm, a businessman, a mayor who is not farming, farmers from dozens of kilometers away, as well as a company specialized in construction. After getting the lease contract in 2012, they got the right to buy the land in February 2016 from the state (Ángyán 2016). A mobilization demanding that the government reverse this process and give the land back to its former users – the organic farm and the folk school – took place (Greenpeace 2014) in the midst of violence. Indeed, some of the new leasers spread chemical products on the until-then organically produced plots, thereby destroying productions. A lawsuit was brought against the Hungarian state, where it was rejected in 2016 by Hungary's constitutional court (where the government has its agents); it was then taken to the European Court with the help of Greenpeace Hungary. The Kishantos case has yet to be resolved, but it shows how the emancipatory rural subjectivities of organic farmers allied with environmentalist organizations can challenge the regime's authority. Scholar-activists need clearer strategies to find out how to support these types of initiative and to help them become examples and triggers with which to challenge authoritarian populism.

The importance of emotions in thinking about emancipation
I argue that emotions can help us think about democratic alternatives, radical political transformations, and a novel project of living life in common in the type of context described in this article. Indeed, as highlighted by Singh, emotions are the openings through which new ways of living life in common will emerge: they can 'contribute to the emergence of novel collective subjectivities that animate a new politics of life and modes of being' (2013, 197). The Hungarian regime is currently trying hard to create artificial enemies, fear, and intolerance within Hungarian society. To counter this and produce new and democratic ways of living life in common, there is a need to produce new subjectivities based on positive emotions that are not manipulated by the regime. Among these emotions are those that may be triggered by initiatives that promote healthy ways of living and producing, such as the *bobos* are doing. Those who are subjugated by the regime and their allies need to refuse subject positions such as the 'lazy *Roma*', 'the blamed recipients of subsidies', or the 'mothers who will make Hungary great again' and to, instead, claim emancipatory ones for themselves and the society – as have the smallholders who very recently contributed to imagining the Hungarian countryside as a democratic and dynamic place. Similarly, scholar-activists need to support the emergence of such emancipatory subjectivities, both individual and collective.

While waiting for the spark
Putting the Hungarian situation in perspective with situations in other places can be enlightening, especially for those who think that there is no way out from Hungarian authoritarianism 'unless the system implodes or rots due to its own moral decadence, similar to what happened once with the Roman Empire', as stated by one of my interviewees. Another of my interviewees, who is involved in the degrowth movement in Europe, stressed that Hungarians tend to think that emancipatory rural politics are more likely to occur in places other than Hungary. However in Hungary, more so than elsewhere in Europe, there is still some land in the hands of the state, and there is a culture of appreciating the local, the *háztáji*, the traditional. These elements could be creatively used to trigger positive emotions for building an emancipatory rural political project because they fit with small-scale farming and democratic organizations (but can nevertheless become dangerously co-opted as much by nationalist stances as by emancipatory ones). In addition, it was not long ago that the intention was there to develop a rural strategy based on visions of small-scale farming, cooperation, and agro-ecology – a strategy that would be supported by a majority of local farmers as the former State Secretary for Agriculture who designed the strategy discovered when he 'toured' the country looking for farmers' support in 2010. Although temporarily silenced, intimidated, and oppressed by current Hungarian rural politics, some of these farmers are still out there, hopefully waiting for the spark that will lead to emancipatory changes. This spark can start anywhere: from the mobilisations in January 2019 against a new alienating labor law to the expulsion of the Central European University from

Hungary. For this reason, we all need to be ready to overthrow the regime and contribute to re-constructing a new, democratic state.

Conclusion

Speculation on agricultural land by and for oligarchs has been a key driver to consolidate the authoritarian populist regime in Hungary and to create its subjects. While land grabbing via 'pocket contracts' with foreigners was conveniently used by Fidesz to win the election in 2010, the significance of land grabbing by and for national oligarchs in maintaining the authoritarian populist system (including after the 2014 and 2018 elections) remains mostly invisible. In particular, the role played by national oligarchs in the processes that render the poorest and most marginalized populations vulnerable is discursively hidden, while blame is placed on those most excluded, such as *Romas* living on welfare. This, in the end, diverts attention from the oppressive and exclusionary politics of land grabbing by and for national oligarchs.

The EU's land policy and CAP are fueling Hungarian authoritarian populism, even as the EU is conveniently blamed by the government and its allies for being anti-Hungarian. Land market liberalization promoted by the EU is favoring land grabbing motivated by speculation on land prices. This was denounced by Fidesz when it motivated foreign land grabbers to acquire land in Hungary via 'pocket contracts', but the same policy is now favored by national oligarchs to enrich themselves and to indirectly maintain the authoritarian system. Second, the CAP as well as the push by the EU to end the 2004 land moratorium are facilitating and encouraging land grabbing by oligarchs.

Understanding how domestic land-grabbing and related conflicts have been used by the Orbán regime to develop and maintain authoritarian populism is a key topic for scholar-activists concerned by the recent 'authoritarian turn' in many places of the world, and in Europe in particular. While this type of land-grabbing has been written about (e.g. Ángyán 2015; Fidrich 2013; Greenpeace 2014; Szabó 2013), its importance, and the precise mechanisms through which it works, is under-theorised in both international academic spheres and within Hungarian scholar-activist circles as it gets diluted among other important topics such as the lack of a free press in Hungary, Orbán's racist refugee policy, his anti-EU rhetoric, or his anti-gender-equality stances.

Despite the oppressive context, a myriad of emancipatory initiatives exist, each of which could become the spark needed to initiate emancipation. People are brought into relations of power through specific subject positions, but the subjectification process is always contested, always in the making. This is key for scholar-activists because it offers hope. However, the moments in which emancipation might emerge need to be better known, understood, discussed and built-upon, so as to inspire the social imaginary – of scholar-activists and subject populations – of what is possible in terms of breaking free from subjugated positions and mobilizing for an emancipatory rural politics.

Acknowledgements

The author is grateful for the constructive suggestions made by the Journal of Peasant Studies reviewers, Balsa Lubarda and the participants to the conference on Authoritarian Populism in the

Rural World (The Hague, March 2018) on previous versions of the article. The Department of Environmental Sciences and Policy at Central European University must also be acknowledged for their supporting role as well as the author's family who took care of her children while she was doing doing research and writing up this paper.

Disclosure statement

No potential conflict of interest was reported by the author.

Funding

This research is supported by FORMAS, the Swedish Research Council for sustainable development (mobility grant No. 2018-00442).

ORCID

Noémi Gonda http://orcid.org/0000-0002-1261-8380

References

Ahlborg, Helene, and Andrea Nightingale. 2018. "Theorizing Power in Political Ecology: The Whereof Power in Resource Governance Projects." *Journal of Political Ecology* 25: 381–401.
Ángyán, József. 2015. Állami földprivatizáció – intézményesített földrablás – 2015 [State-led land Privatisation- Institutionalised Land Grabbing- 2015].
Ángyán, József. 2016. Állami földprivatizáció- intézményes földrablás (2015–2016) II. Megyei elemzések. Fejér Megye [State-led land Privatisation- Institutionalised Land Grabbing (2015–2016). II. County-level Analysis. The County of Fejér].
Ángyán, József. 2018. Állami földprivatizáció- intézményes földrablás (2015–2016) II. Megyei elemzések. Csongrád Megye [State-led Land Privatisation- Institutionalised Land Grabbing (2015–2016). II. County-level Analysis. The County of Csongrád].
Bene, Enikő, Németh Szilvia, Kálmán Ákos, Keszthelyi Szilárd, Berczi Ildikó Ehretné, Boldog Valéria, and Páll Zsombor. 2016. *A Magyar Mezőgazdaság és Élelmiszeripar számokban A Magyar Mezőgazdaság és Élelmiszeripar számokban* [The Hungarian Agriculture and Food Industry in Numbers]. Edited by Szabolcs Vágó, and Zsombor Páll. Budapest, Hungary: *Nemzeti agrárgazdasági kamara* [National Agricultural Chamber].
Benedetti, Lisa. 2015. "Hungary's nature in peril." *Birdlife International*. https://www.birdlife.org/europe-and-central-asia/news/hungary's-nature-peril, Accessed February 5 2018.
Bertelsmann Stiftung. 2018. *BTI 2018 Country Report – Hungary*. Gütersloh: Bertelsmann Stiftung.
Borras, Saturnino M., Jennifer C. Franco, Sergio Gómez, Cristóbal Kay, and Max Spoor. 2012. "Land Grabbing in Latin America and the Caribbean." *Journal of Peasant Studies* 39 (3–4): 845–872. doi:10.1080/03066150.2012.679931
Borras, Saturnino M., Ruth Hall, Ian Scoones, Ben White, and Wendy Wolford. 2011. "Towards a Better Understanding of Global Land Grabbing: An Editorial Introduction." *Journal of Peasant Studies* 38 (2): 209–216. doi:10.1080/03066150.2011.559005
Butler, Judith. 1997. *The Psychic Life of Power: Theories in Subjection*. Stanford, CA, USA: Stanford University Press.
Butler, Judith. 2009. *Frames of War*. London, New York: Verso.
Daniel, Shepard. 2011. "Land Grabbing and Potential Implications for World Food Security." In *Sustainable Agricultural Development: Recent Approaches in Resources Management and Environmentally-balanced Production Enhancement*, edited by Mohamed Behnassi, Shabbir A. Shahid, and Joyce D'Silva, 25–42. Dordrecht: Springer Netherlands.

De Schutter, Olivier. 2011. "How not to Think of Land-Grabbing: Three Critiques of Large-Scale Investments in Farmland." *Journal of Peasant Studies* 38 (2): 249–279. doi:10.1080/03066150.2011.559008

Desmarais, Annette Aurélie, Darrin Qualman, André Magnan, and Nettie Wiebe. 2015. "Land Grabbing and Land Concentration: Mapping Changing Patterns of Farmland Ownership in Three Rural Municipalities in Saskatchewan, Canada." *Canadian Food Studies / La Revue canadienne des études sur l'alimentation* 2 (1): 16–47.

Dunai, Marton. 2017. "Rosatom's Paks Nuclear Project in Hungary Delayed." *Reuters*, October 6, 2017. Accessed January 2 2017. https://www.reuters.com/article/us-rosatom-hungary-nuclearpower/rosatoms-paks-nuclear-project-in-hungary-delayed-idUSKBN1CB2FT.

Fidrich, Robert. 2013. "Hungary. The Return of the White Horse: Land Grabbing in Hungary." In *Land Concentration, Land Grabbing and People's Struggles in Europe*, edited by Jennifer C. Franco, and Saturnino M. Borras Jr, 128–147. Amsterdam: Transnational Institute.

Forbes. 2017. "33 leggazdagabb magyar 2017" [33 richest Hungarians 2017]. *Forbes*, Accessed January 3 2017. https://forbes.hu/extra/33-leggazdagabb-magyar-2017/.

Greenpeace. 2014. "Fighting a Government-assisted Land Grab with #peoplepower in Hungary." Accessed January 5 2018. http://www.greenpeace.org/international/en/news/features/Fighting-a-government-assisted-land-grab-with-peoplepower-in-Hungary/.

Greenpeace. 2017. Paks II zsákutca, a jövő a megújulóké [Paks II is a dead end, the future is renewables].

Hall, Ruth. 2011. "Land Grabbing in Southern Africa: The Many Faces of the Investor Rush." *Review of African Political Economy* 38 (128): 193–214. doi:10.1080/03056244.2011.582753

Hartvigsen, Morten. 2014. "Land Reform and Land Fragmentation in Central and Eastern Europe." *Land use Policy* 36 (Supplement C): 330–341. doi:10.1016/j.landusepol.2013.08.016

Harvey, David. 2004. "The 'New Imperialism': Accumulation by Dispossession." *Actuel Marx* 35(1): 71–90.

Hernandez-Arthur, Simon, and Matt Grainger. 2016. *Costudians of The Land, Defenders of our Future. A new era of the Global Land Rush*. Oxfam.

Hulme, David. 2016. *Should Rich Nations Help the Poor?* Cambridge, UK: Polity Press.

Hungarian Central Statistical Office. 2014. *Mezőgazdaság* [Agriculture]. Budapest, Hungary: Hungarian Central Statistical Office.

Jiao, Xi, Carsten Smith-Hall, and Ida Theilade. 2015. "Rural Household Incomes and Land Grabbing in Cambodia." *Land Use Policy* 48: 317–328. doi:10.1016/j.landusepol.2015.06.008

Juhász, Attila, and Csaba Molnár. 2018a. "The Role of the Government's Social Policies in the Stability of the Orbán Regime." *Political Capital*. Accessed 10 January 2019. http://www.politicalcapital.hu/kereses.php?article_read=1&article_id=2309.

Juhász, Attila, and Csaba Molnár. 2018b. *Szolidaritás és jóléti sovinizmus a magyar társadalomban: Adalékok az Orbán-rezsim szociálpolitikájának megértéséhez* [Solidarity and Welfare Chauvinism in the Hungarian Society: Additional thoughts to Undertand the Orbán rEgime's Social Policy]. Budapest, HU: Political Capital Friedrich Ebert Stiftung.

Kovács, Zoltán, and György Vida. 2015. "Geography of the new Electoral System and Changing Voting Patterns in Hungary." *Acta Geobalcanica* 1 (2): 55–64. doi:10.18509/AGB.2015.06

Krasznai Kovács, Eszter. 2015. "Surveillance and State-making through EU Agricultural Policy in Hungary." *Geoforum; Journal of Physical, Human, and Regional Geosciences* 64 (Supplement C): 168–181. doi:10.1016/j.geoforum.2015.06.020.

Krasznai Kovács, Eszter. 2016. "The 'Differentiated Countryside': Survival Strategies of Rural Entrepreneurs." In *Rethinking Life at The Margins. The Assemblage of Contexts, Subjects and Politics*, edited by Michele Lancione, 169–181. Oxon, New York: Routledge.

Lavers, Tom. 2012. "Patterns of Agrarian Transformation in Ethiopia: State-mediated Commercialisation and the 'Land Grab'." *Journal of Peasant Studies* 39 (3–4): 795–822. doi:10.1080/03066150.2012.660147

Levien, Michael. 2011. "Special Economic Zones and Accumulation by Dispossession in India." *Journal of Agrarian Change* 11 (4): 454–483. doi:10.1111/j.1471-0366.2011.00329.x

Lubarda, Balsa. 2018. "Homeland Farming? The two Faces of National Populism and the Conceptualization of Sustainable Agriculture in Hungary." ERPI 2018 international conference authoritarian populism and the rural world, The Hague, The Netherlands.

Lund, Christian. 2016. "Rule and Rupture: State Formation Through the Production of Property and Citizenship." *Development and Change* 47 (6): 1199–1228.

McMichael, Philip. 2012. "The Land Grab and Corporate Food Regime Restructuring." *Journal of Peasant Studies* 39 (3–4): 681–701. doi:10.1080/03066150.2012.661369.

Nightingale, Andrea J. 2011. "Bounding Difference: Intersectionality and the Material Production of Gender, Caste, Class and Environment in Nepal." *Geoforum; Journal of Physical, Human, and Regional Geosciences* 42 (2): 153–162. doi:10.1016/j.geoforum.2010.03.004

Otten, Justin. 2013. "Wine Mafia and the Thieving State: Tension and Power at the Crossroads of Neoliberalism and Authoritarianism in 21st Century Macedonia." *Anthropology of East Europe Review* 31 (2): 2–18.

Pe'er, G., L. V. Dicks, P. Visconti, R. Arlettaz, András Báldi, T. G. Benton, S. Collins, et al. 2014. "EU Agricultural Reform Fails on Biodiversity." *Science* 344 (6188): 1090–1092.

Peluso, Nancy Lee, and Christian Lund. 2011. "New Frontiers of Land Control: Introduction." *Journal of Peasant Studies* 38 (4): 667–681. doi:10.1080/03066150.2011.607692

Roszík, Péter. 2011. A fenntartható birtokpolitika megvalósíthatóságának akadályai (közte a zsebszerződések).

Schwarcz, Gyöngyi. 2012. "Ethnicizing Poverty Through Social Security Provision in Rural Hungary." *Journal of Rural Studies* 28 (2): 99–107. doi:10.1016/j.jrurstud.2012.01.022

Scoones, Ian, Marc Edelman, Saturnino M. Borras, Ruth Hall, Wendy Wolford, and Ben White. 2017. "Emancipatory Rural Politics: Confronting Authoritarian Populism." *Journal of Peasant Studies*, 1–20. doi:10.1080/03066150.2017.1339693.

Sikor, Thomas, and Christian Lund. 2009. "Access and Property: A Question of Power and Authority." *Development and Change* 40 (1): 1–22. doi:10.1111/j.1467-7660.2009.01503.x

Singh, Neera M. 2013. "The Affective Labor of Growing Forests and the Becoming of Environmental Subjects: Rethinking Environmentality in Odisha, India." *Geoforum; Journal of Physical, Human, and Regional Geosciences* 47: 189–198. doi:10.1016/j.geoforum.2013.01.010

Sundberg, Juanita. 2004. "Identities in the Making: Conservation, Gender and Race in the Maya Biosphere Reserve, Guatemala." *Gender, Place & Culture* 11 (1): 43–66. doi:10.1080/0966369042000188549

Szabó, Rebeka. 2013. "Hungarian Land-grabbing: Family Farmers vs. Politically Backed Oligarchs." *Green European Journal* 5 (2013): 26–30.

Téglási, András. 2013. "The Protection of Arable Land in the Basic Law of Hungary with Respect to the Expiring Moratorium of Land Acquisition in 2014." *Acta Universitatis Brunensis Iuridica* 442: 2442–2465.

Transnational Institute. 2013. "Land Concentration, Land Grabbing and People's Struggles in Europe." In *Hands Off the Land. Take Action Against Grabbing*, edited by Jennifer C. Franco, and Saturnino M. Borras Jr, 233. Amsterdam: Transnational Institute.

Valdivia, Gabriela. 2008. "Governing Relations between People and Things: Citizenship, Territory, and the Political Economy of Petroleum in Ecuador." *Political Geography* 27 (4): 456–477. doi:10.1016/j.polgeo.2008.03.007

van der Ploeg, Jan Douwe, Jennifer C. Franco, and Saturnino M. Borras. 2015. "Land Concentration and Land Grabbing in Europe: A Preliminary Analysis." *Canadian Journal of Development Studies / Revue Canadienne D'études du Développement* 36 (2): 147–162. doi:10.1080/02255189.2015.1027673

Visser, Oane, and Max Spoor. 2011. "Land Grabbing in Post-Soviet Eurasia: The World's Largest Agricultural Land Reserves at Stake." *Journal of Peasant Studies* 38 (2): 299–323. doi:10.1080/03066150.2011.559010

White, Ben, Saturnino M. Borras, Ruth Hall, Ian Scoones, and Wendy Wolford. 2012. "The new Enclosures: Critical Perspectives on Corporate Land Deals." *Journal of Peasant Studies* 39 (3–4): 619–647. doi:10.1080/03066150.2012.691879

Wilkin, Peter. 2016. *Hungary's Crisis of Democracy: The Road to Serfdom*. Lanham, Bouder, New York, London: Lexington Books.

Zoomers, Annelies. 2010. "Globalisation and the Foreignisation of Space: Seven Processes Driving the Current Global Land Grab." *Journal of Peasant Studies* 37 (2): 429–447. doi:10.1080/03066151003595325

Authoritarian populism and neo-extractivism in Bolivia and Ecuador: the unresolved agrarian question and the prospects for food sovereignty as counter-hegemony

Mark Tilzey

ABSTRACT

The new economic flows ushered in across the South by the rise of China in particular have permitted some to circumvent the imperial debt trap, notably the 'pink tide' states of Latin America. These states, exploiting this window of opportunity, have sought to revisit developmentalism by means of 'neo-extractivism'. The populist, but now increasingly authoritarian, regimes in Bolivia and Ecuador are exemplars of this trend and have swept to power on the back of anti-neoliberal sentiment. These populist regimes in Bolivia and Ecuador articulate a sub-hegemonic discourse of national developmentalism, whilst forging alliances with counter-hegemonic groups, united by a rhetoric of anti-imperialism, indigenous revival, and livelihood principles such as *buen vivir*. But this rhetorical 'master frame' hides the class divisions and real motivations underlying populism: that of favouring neo-extractivism, principally via sub-imperial capital, to fund the 'compensatory state', supporting small scale commercial farmers through reformism whilst largely neglecting the counter-hegemonic aims, and reproductive crisis, of the middle/lower peasantry, and lowland indigenous groups, and their calls for food sovereignty as *radical* social relational change. These tensions are reflected in the marked shift from populism to authoritarian populism, as neo-extractivism accelerates to fund 'neo-developmentalism' whilst simultaneously eroding the livelihoods of subaltern groups, generating intensified political unrest. This paper analyses this transition to authoritarian populism particularly from the perspective of the unresolved agrarian question and the demand by subaltern groups for a radical, or counter-hegemonic, approach to food sovereignty. It speculates whether neo-extractivism's intensifying political and ecological contradictions can foment a resurgence of counter-hegemonic mobilization towards this end.

DOI: 10.4324/9781003162353-12

Introduction: neo-extractivism, authoritarian populism, and the unresolved agrarian question – BRICS and the Latin American 'Pink tide'

China's, and to a lesser degree Brazil's, emergence as key sites of capital accumulation has opened up a space for other states in the global South to re-assert more nationally-based capitalist development or, at least, for national (what we here term 'sub-hegemonic') fractions of capital to selectively displace global Northern dominance, embodied in hegemonic transnational neoliberalism. This has coincided with widespread disenchantment with neoliberalism in the global South, and in Latin America particularly. The boom in primary commodity prices stimulated particularly by China's growth has enabled sub-hegemonic fractions of national capital to ally with non-capitalist (what we here term 'counter-hegemonic') class forces to install a wave of centre-left, and characteristically populist, regimes in Latin America particularly (known as the 'pink tide') (Spronk and Webber 2015). Although this 'tide' is now on the ebb elsewhere in Latin America[1], Bolivia and Ecuador have been, and remain, exemplars of such populist regimes, both states pursuing neo-developmentalist policies on the basis of neo-extractivism stimulated and enabled largely by Chinese capital accumulation. Both states have also exhibited, however, a marked shift over the last few years from populism to authoritarian populism. This being so, one of the principal concerns of this paper is to ask how a populist project transmutes into one of authoritarian populism.

While the rise of the BRICS sub-imperium affords the wider enabling global context for this populist conjuncture, its direct political basis lies in the widespread resistance in Latin America, particularly from the 1990s, to the socially polarizing consequences of neoliberalism and to the progressive loss of national sovereignty (including sovereignty over food) that accompanied the deepening of 'extroverted' dependent development (Veltmeyer and Petras 2000). Bolivia and Ecuador are representative of states where popular forces, comprising peasants, semi-proletarians, proletarians and landless, indigenous groups, and more endogenously oriented class fractions of the bourgeoisies, have succeeded, with varying degrees of success, in resisting and displacing the dominance of the 'disarticulated alliance' of the national landed oligarchy and trans-nationalized capital (Spronk and Webber 2015; Petras and Veltmeyer 2011). What both states have in common is a new commitment to greater state guidance and interventionism in the economy, a greater formal or substantive commitment to national food sovereignty, and the introduction of social programmes to alleviate the severe income disparities characteristic of the neoliberal era. Funds for the latter, however, are predicated on the proceeds of the 'new' extractivism, not only of mineral and fossil-fuel resources, but also of agri-fuels, offered by the emergence of sub-imperial states, notably China in the case of Ecuador, and Brazil in the case of Bolivia (Davalos and Albuja 2014) (with China increasingly influential in Brazilian agri-food dynamics, however, particularly in respect of soya production, although still a minor player by comparison to investments from the global Northern imperium [Oliveira 2018]).

The 'post-neoliberal' era in Bolivia began in 2005 with the election, as the country's new president, of Evo Morales, the leader of the coca growers' union. His party, MAS (*Movimiento al Socialismo*), was closely linked to, indeed was an outgrowth of, the emergent indigenous, anti-colonial, and populist social movements that had coalesced in opposition

---

[1]The recent presidential election in Mexico suggests an exception to this trend.

to the neoliberal reforms of the 1990s, and had culminated in the anti-neoliberal uprising of October 2003 leading to the flight from the country of President Sánchez de Lozada (Hylton and Thomson 2007). This broad coalition of peasant, indigenous, and worker organizations formed the *Pacto de Unidad* (Unity Pact) which was essential in Morales' rise to power and became integrated, to varying degrees, within the new regime (Fabricant 2012; McKay, Nehring, and Walsh-Dilley 2014; Webber 2015). Unlike the AP (*Alianza País*) in Ecuador, therefore, MAS was not created as a vehicle simply to move a president into power. Rather, MAS defined itself as a political instrument of its constituent social movements, relying heavily on mobilizational politics (Riofrancos 2017). Presciently, however, neither Morales nor his Vice-President Garcia Linera saw their assumption of power as entailing a fundamental alteration of capitalist social-property relations. Rather, 'it was expected to modify the rules of neoliberal capitalism in favour of a state that would work to improve the welfare of *all* its citizens, especially the poor rural and urban indigenous majority, through redistributive policies and social programmes' (Hylton and Thomson 2007, 133). This, then, was to be a regime that pursued a sub-hegemonic, national-popular – or populist – programme of reformism (see below), placating its counter-hegemonic constituency through welfarism and anti-imperial rhetoric, and soothing the landed oligarchy through accelerated agri-food extractivism and effective exemption from the terms of the agrarian reform.

In the case of Ecuador, the period leading up to Rafael Correa's 2006 election as the country's president saw its social movements presenting a powerful challenge to the prevailing neoliberal paradigm. Correa's anti-neoliberal, and anti-imperialist campaign, much like that of Morales in Bolivia, drew centrally on this social unrest, and its eventual success depended on the support of the country's social movements (Becker 2008). Prior to 2006, the *Mesa Agraria* (a coalition of four peasant/indigenous organizations) had signed an agreement with Correa in which he gave a commitment, upon election, to initiate an 'agrarian revolution' based on the demand of the peasant movement for food sovereignty, a demand centred on the democratization of land and water access, and upon state resources for the revival and stimulation of the 'peasant' economy (Giunta 2014; Henderson 2017). The most important force behind the 2005 coup against the then incumbent neoliberal regime, however, was a group known as the *forajidos*, middle-class sectors of Quito (Clark 2017), and these subsequently became an important political force behind Correa's 2006 presidential bid. Unlike Morales, therefore, Correa (replaced as president by Lenín Moreno in 2017) lacked deep roots in civil society and social movements, and sought actively to demobilize peasant and indigenous activism once in power (De la Torre 2013). Accordingly, Ecuador's AP represents a much more technocratic, Keynesian project than is the case with Bolivia's MAS (Le Quang 2016). Presciently, however, like Morales it was never Correa's' intention to challenge capitalist social-property relations. Again, this was to be a national-popular reformist regime. Its populism pivoted on the nationally-focused bourgeoisies' and petty bourgeois class fractions' easy co-optation of the 'progressive' (mainly upper peasant) tendency within the food sovereignty movement through support for small farm productivity enhancements, the neutralization of the more 'radical' tendency through social welfare payments funded through extractivism, and the placation of the landed oligarchy through its exemption from the 'agrarian revolution' (Herrera Revelo 2017).

Thus, while there are indeed differences of detail between Bolivia and Ecuador, the structural similarities between these two national-popular regimes are compelling. Since the assumption of power by, respectively, MAS and AP, both Bolivia and Ecuador have been pursuing neo-developmentalist policies predicated on neo-extractivism (Davalos and Albuja 2014). This neo-developmentalism, as neo-extractivism, is contradictory both 'politically' and 'ecologically', however. Politically, it comprises a populist *reformism* that attempts to address selected symptoms of capitalist contradiction, notably poverty and inequality, through redistributive policies, whilst failing to address their structural causes, based as these are on highly unequal access to the means of production. Populist reformism may be understood by means of the Gramscian concept of *passive revolution*, entailing reform from above, led by nationally-oriented fractions of capital, but, crucially, in alliance with proletarians, peasants and indigenous people (Robinson 2017; Webber 2017b). Ecologically, these regimes are contradictory since they pursue unsustainable policies of both energy and mineral extraction, and of productivist, export agriculture, not only for purposes of capital accumulation, but also, crucially, in order to fund redistributive social programmes and infrastructure development (McKay 2017; Tilzey 2018a). In both Bolivia and Ecuador, largely due to continuing opposition from an entrenched landed oligarchy and their governments' increasing collusion with transnational capital in the search for export earnings, relatively little progress, consequently, has been made with respect to addressing the structural bases of poverty and inequality – that is, the agrarian question of land redistribution in favour of the semi-proletariat and landless, and the confirmation of land rights with respect to indigenous groups (Giunta 2014; Spronk and Webber 2015). In this way, a percentage of revenues from primary resource extraction, via ground rent, has been diverted to social programmes to placate the semi-proletariat and urban proletariat, leading to an uneasy compromise, embodied in these populist regimes as 'compensatory states' (Gudynas 2012), between (counter-hegemonic) subaltern classes, the nationally-focused (sub-hegemonic) bourgeoisie, and the continuing (hegemonic) power of the landed oligarchy, often in alliance with transnational capital. The key to the coherence of these populist regimes lies, materially, in the distribution of wealth (via state welfarism) beyond their core political constituencies (the upper peasantry, small farmers, nationally oriented bourgeoisie) to the semi-proletariat and proletariat, even as the means of production of these latter continues to attenuate before the pressures of capital accumulation (Carrión and Herrera Revelo 2012). It lies, discursively, on the basis of the deployment of legitimating measures such as the construction of a 'national consensus or alliance for progress' and an attendant demonization of all those resisting or opposing such 'progress', often vilified as 'imperialist stooges' (Webber 2017b).

Over the last decade, the coherence of such populism has come under increasing strain as these neo-extractivist regimes have failed to meet the key objectives of their erstwhile constituencies of support amongst indigenous groups and semi-proletarian/landless peasantry, particularly (Veltmeyer 2014; Webber 2015). Tensions focus around access and rights to the means of production, and the neo-developmentalist preoccupation with economic growth and welfarism as a means of *bypassing* the need to address the *structural* causes of land poverty and insecurity of land tenure. Food/land sovereignty is thus a highly contested discourse, deriving initially from re-assertions of national sovereignty as a counter-narrative to neoliberalism, but now often appropriated by neo-developmentalism to mean national food provisioning by productivist means. This discursive tension is expressed in the constitutionalization of food sovereignty in Bolivia and Ecuador (Tilzey 2018a). The appropriation of food sovereignty discourse by these neo-extractivist regimes is increasingly contested by peasant/indigenous movements seeking a 'post/alternative developmental' (Vergara-Camus 2014) model of cooperative social relations founded on the principle of *buen vivir* [2](Giunta 2014; Tilzey 2016). The irony here is that the populist governments of Bolivia and Ecuador have invoked *buen vivir* to legitimate further capital accumulation by means of a national-popular programme of 'embedding' extractivism through the 'compensatory state'. As the dependency of welfare on extractivism becomes ever more entrenched, however, and the latter ever more corrosive of the original alternative developmental aims of counter-hegemonic movements, so have the populist regimes of Bolivia and Ecuador become more authoritarian, deploying a variety of 'legal' and extra-legal mechanisms to close down opposition to mineral and agri-food extractivism (Carrión 2016; Svampa 2016, 2017).

This paper proposes to further explore and to explain these dynamics, encapsulated in the question: How is it that a populist project becomes an authoritarian populist one? Despite the considerable significance of this issue, particularly when related, as we suggest here, to the contradictory dynamics of the state-capital nexus, it has been an infrequently acknowledged one in recent debates about populism. Given this significance but relative neglect, this paper attempts to undertake four principal tasks:

- To articulate a coherent theoretical framework to explain populism and the shift to authoritarian populism;
- To analyze the transition, in both states, from populism to authoritarian populism;
- In so doing, to throw light on the contradictions of the peripheral state-capital nexus which, we argue, underlie and propel this transition, paying particular attention to the agrarian question;
- To ask whether alternative and sustainable 'modes of production' are available, how these might arise from the contradictions of authoritarian populism and neo-extractivism, and which social forces might bring them about.

In order to fulfil these aims, the paper proposes, in the following section, to delineate what we might mean by populism and authoritarian populism, and to articulate a set of theoretical tools to enable us to do this. This section will suggest that populism and authoritarian populism have their causal bases in the contradictions of capital accumulation and class struggle in the state-capital nexus, and, specifically, in the peripheral state-capital nexus. The paper will then apply these theoretical propositions to the case studies of Bolivia and Ecuador. The section following will distil out the dynamics of authoritarian populism and neo-extractivism on the basis of the case studies, arguing that their contradictory character pivots around the unresolved agrarian question. This agrarian question asks whether a transition to industrial capitalism 'with equity' is possible 'politically' and 'ecologically', or whether the peripheral state-capital nexus is necessarily incapable of securing 'growth with jobs'. If the latter, then the agrarian question cannot be resolved in favour of capitalism, and the swelling ranks of the semi-proletariat are likely to demand an

---

[2]*Buen vivir* and *vivir bien* are used as synonyms, although the former is used preferentially in Ecuador and the latter in Bolivia.

alternative, and non-capitalist, form of 'development'. Finally, the paper explores which classes and political strategies might foment social-relational change towards a non-capitalist alternative, paying particular attention to the experience of the MST in Bolivia.

Developing a conceptual framework: Gramsci, Poulantzas, *trasformismo*, and reformism

In order to explain the dynamics of populism and the shift to authoritarian populism, this paper develops new theorization which integrates Political Marxism (Brenner 1977, 1985; Mooers 1991; Wood 1995, 2009), neo-Gramscian International Political Economy (Cox 1993, Bieler and Morton 2004), Regulation Theory (Boyer and Saillard 2002, Jessop and Sum 2013), and Poulantzian state theory (Poulantzas 1978).[3] The paper also has affinities with the important work on imperialism and sub-imperialism of Ruy Mauro Marini (see Marini 1972, 1973).[4] In this paper, then, 'class struggle', capital, and the state remain central and dialectically related analytical categories. These 'political' dynamics of 'structured agency' (Potter and Tilzey 2005) are conjoined to the 'ecological' dynamics of biophysical resource 'sources' and 'sinks' (and related and discounted 'costs' and loss of livelihood which are located increasingly in the global South) through political ecology (Tilzey 2018a). These analytical tools also enable the key parameters of the agrarian question, the peasantry, and food security/food sovereignty within capitalism to be defined as approximately state-level trends within the global centre-periphery structure. Here the state, despite differential power and capacity between core and periphery and the global disciplining force of capitalism/imperialism, is seen to remain the key medium for the regulation and institutionalization of social-property relations and, hence, for the understanding of social relational change (Tilzey 2018a, 2018b).

Poulantzas (1978) is particularly useful, since for him the state is itself a social relation, comprising the condensation of the balance of class forces in society. Here, the state provides the institutional space for various fractions of the capitalist class, in addition possibly to other classes, to come together and form longer-term strategies and alliances, while simultaneously, the state disorganizes non-capitalist classes through various means of co-optation and division. This theoretical approach enables us to capture the key dynamic of populism as the means, particularly, of re-establishing legitimacy of the state-capital nexus, following its de-legitimation during the neoliberal period, by means of reformism as neo-developmentalism. As populism encounters the contradictions of its neo-extractivist foundations in the periphery – growing opposition from marginalized constituencies, and increased difficulty of funding welfare policies with the commodity price slump – so does populism become increasingly authoritarian.

---

[3]This approach stands in contrast to 'populism' in agrarian political theory, represented by McMichael (2013) and van der Ploeg (2008), with its elision of class amongst the 'peasantry', its radical under-theorization of the state, and its assumptions regarding the full trans-nationalization and unity of capital. It does concur with agrarian 'populism', however, in its concern for the ecological dimension and its advocacy of agroecology and food sovereignty, the latter on its 'radical' definition (Tilzey 2018a). It stands also in contrast to 'orthodox' Marxism, represented for example by Bernstein (2010), with its class reductionism, its instrumentalist view of the state, its reification of developmentalism, and its failure to comprehend the profound importance of the ecological dimension.
[4]In his treatment of imperialism, Marini saw peripheral super-exploitation of labour, and export-oriented capitalism as necessary to sustain industrial capitalism and high consumption in the centre. In his treatment of sub-imperialism, he saw dependent economies like Brazil seek to compensate for the drain of wealth to the imperium by developing their own exploitative (sub-imperial) relationships with even more peripheral neighbouring economies, such as Bolivia.

De la Torre (2013) describes 'populism' as an approach to politics which depicts it as a struggle between the 'people' and some malign elite or set of elites. Here, the 'people' is imagined as a homogeneous body sharing interests and an identity which are embodied in a leader whose mission is to save the nation. Populism includes previously excluded groups, while fostering majoritarian understandings of democracy which do not always respect the rights of the opposition or the institutional fabric of democracy. For de la Torre, it is the progressive erosion of the latter that leads to an authoritarian regime. While all this is true, we suggest that the loss or abuse of 'liberal rights' (de la Torre's focus), although important, is but a reflection of the deepening of the contradictions between capital accumulation, the legitimation of capitalism through 'welfarism', and the continuing process of primitive accumulation through the expropriation of lowland indigenous peoples and the progressive proletarianization of the lower peasantry. The contradictions of the latter are exacerbated by capital accumulation as extractivism, since this fails to afford any 'compensation' for loss of land in the form of employment (see McKay 2017). The only alternative for many under the resulting conditions of precarity is reliance upon 'welfare', which, as a political 'safety valve', serves only to deepen the populist regimes' commitment to further extractivism, welfare's source of funds.

Populism may be said to represent a distinctive structural episode in capitalism's dynamic spiral (typically conditional upon the introduction of a significant level of representative democracy) that is marked by a deterioration in the conditions of accumulation and, *particularly*, of legitimation for a liberal/neoliberal/trans-nationalizing regime of accumulation.[5] Thus, populism and its close counterpart, nationalism, emerged in response to the crises of globalizing liberalism in the late nineteenth century (culminating in the First World War) and in the late 1920s and 1930s (culminating in the Second World War), and now in response to the contradictions of neoliberalism (Brass 2000, 2014; Tilzey 2018a). Since populism elides the causal basis of capitalist contradiction (both 'political' and 'ecological'), the transition to authoritarianism is immanent in its configuration from the outset, particularly in peripheral states, where contradictions cannot, in contrast to the core states, be easily externalized by means of 'spatio-temporal fixes' (Tilzey 2016).

Populism represents the attempt by certain classes/class fractions to exploit a crisis of accumulation, and particularly of legitimacy, to expand its own interests politically, and hence economically, by means of enlarged accumulation opportunities for its core constituency. It does this by forming an historic bloc (Gramsci 1971) or alliance of interests beyond its core constituency in order to 'capture' the state in the first instance, and subsequently to stabilize it by re-establishing its legitimacy, through reformist measures, amongst the classes adversely affected by the prior crisis that gave rise to populism. Typically, populism invokes nationalism in opposition to 'internationalism' and externally oriented capital (that is, neoliberal and trans-nationalized fractions of capital), and elevates national/ethnic/racial identity above that of class (Brass 2000, 2014). For populism, then, it is not capitalism per se that is the problem, but rather 'foreign', 'big', 'corporate', or transnational capital. It is not difficult to see, then, how populism overlaps with national, 'progressive', or indeed 'populist' understandings of food sovereignty, wherein the emphasis is

---

[5]Offe and Lenhardt (1976) articulated the twin structural problems of capitalism as: a) the driving imperative to uphold the process of accumulation, and b) the demands of social actors which need, to a certain degree, to be fulfilled in order to maintain legitimacy. This insight was later translated into Regulation Theory's dual concepts of 'regime of accumulation' and 'mode of regulation'.

above all upon the 'small', the 'local', and an essentialized 'peasant way' that elides class differentiation in its opposition to the 'corporate' food regime (McMichael 2013).

Because it is neoliberal and trans-nationalized fractions of capital, hegemonic within the peripheral capitalist state, which have forfeited legitimacy through their failure to spread the 'benefits' of capital accumulation beyond a tiny minority, and actually to exacerbate the poverty and precarity of the majority, it is the more nationally-oriented and petty bourgeois (sub-hegemonic) fractions (for example, the upper peasantry) which see the opportunity, in alliance with subaltern (potentially counter-hegemonic) groups, to displace the ruling oligarchy in order to secure political power and accumulation opportunities for themselves in the name of 'national development'. Initially, this bloc may be at loggerheads with the oligarchy, but soon realizes that a line of least resistance may be to make use of revenue generating opportunities afforded by externally-oriented capital via the expansion of ground rent appropriated by the state and redistributed as welfare/benefit schemes to its counter-hegemonic constituency. This 'left' populism may thus become progressively more centrist as dependency upon extractive capital increases, while the oligarchy, in turn, softens its own stance as it sees the benefits of the taming of radicalism, continued accumulation opportunities, and de facto exemption from land reform measures. This process is best described by Gramsci's (1971) concept of *trasformismo*.

As the promised 'agrarian revolution' fails to materialize in a form beneficial to subaltern classes, however, and extractivism simultaneously erodes or destroys the livelihoods of these same groups and provides few compensating jobs (and the populist 'glue' of welfarism remains precariously dependent on high primary commodity prices), so does counter-hegemonic unrest grow, and the populist compact begins to fray. This tension is expressed in the progressive shift to authoritarian populism.

It is the legitimation dimension of reformism that is inextricably associated with populism, entailing a significant expansion in the numbers of those benefitting from capital accumulation either through welfarism or through Keynesian-style infrastructure projects. Here *trasformismo* (Gramsci 1971) is a key concept and dynamic (see Webber 2017a, 2017b). *Trasformismo* is a process that works to co-opt potential leaders of subaltern social groups. By extension, *trasformismo* can serve as a strategy to assimilate and domesticate potentially dangerous ideas by adjusting them to the policies of the dominant coalition and can, thereby, obstruct the formation of class-based organized opposition to established political power (Cox 1993). In this way, 'early phase' subaltern mobilization capabilities, that is the mobilizations against neoliberalism during the 1990s and the first decade of the new millennium in the cases of Bolivia and Ecuador, are progressively repressed, circumscribed, or co-opted, while the political capacity of certain dominant class fractions is gradually restored, as has occurred in the last decade. Passive revolutions, as *trasformismo*, entail the implantation of a mode of domination predicated on conservative reformism (sustaining capitalism) disguised in the language of earlier (counter-hegemonic) subaltern mobilizations, thereby securing a passive consensus of the dominated classes. Rather than a restoration of the *status quo ante*, passive revolution entails a 'molecular' transformation (Gramsci 1971) in the balance of class forces, progressively eviscerating, by co-optation, the capacities of counter-hegemonic forces for self-organization, fomenting passivity and demobilization through reformism, and controlling such subaltern mobilization as still occurs (Webber 2017b). Passive revolutions, in the case of

Bolivia and Ecuador, thus involve neither total restoration of the old order as desired by the hegemonic landed oligarchy (in this case, peripheral neoliberalism or 'disarticulated' accumulation), nor radical revolution as proposed by counter-hegemonic forces. Rather, they involve a dialectic of revolution/restoration, transformation/preservation, in which a sub-hegemonic, populist bloc placates the oligarchy, on the one hand, while co-opting the popular masses on the other. In Bolivia and Ecuador this has been secured by the Correa/Morales regimes restoring the *legitimacy* of capitalism by a reformist/'left' populist process of distributing some of the proceeds of extractive accumulation to those otherwise most disadvantaged by that very same process of accumulation.

Thus, reform may be defined as a state intervention, as passive revolution, that is stimulated by a developmental crisis, in this case peripheral neoliberalism, and is: first, evidently short of revolution (in which case the dominant mode of production, capitalism, would be overthrown, as would also the capitalist state); and, second, is not dependent on sheer repression. Reformism, attempts, therefore, in parlance of Regulation Theory, to construct a 'flanking' mode of regulation to 'embed' a somewhat modified regime of accumulation but, crucially, without subverting capitalist social-property relations themselves. In this, then, reformism has much in common with Keynesian (in essence populist) 'solutions' to capitalist crises (see Tilzey 2017 for discussion).

There are two types of reforms that are of fundamental relevance to securing and reproducing capitalism in the face of its contradictions with respect to the peripheral state-capital nexus.

- Reforms associated with crises of accumulation. In the periphery, this is not a problem in itself for trans-nationalized capital since the under-consumption crisis is located primarily in the core countries (Tilzey 2018a). Similarly, under-production crisis in the conditions of production does not appear imminent. Rather, the problem lies with the exclusion of other fractions of capital, notably national bourgeoisie and small commercial farmers, from the accumulation nexus of the 'disarticulated alliance';
- Reforms associated with crises of legitimacy. Here the elements that create legitimacy are: first, the existence of a petty bourgeoisie, this providing the material basis for the ideology of liberal capitalism, and of the meritocratic, enterprising, and 'sovereign' individual; the ability of certain fractions of the working class to enter into social democratic arrangements for the improvement of wages and working conditions under the ideology of state planning and the welfare state (or the 'compensatory state' in its latest iteration). Legitimacy reforms, in response principally to the poverty generating policies of neoliberalism, are arguably the most important motivation behind reformism in the Bolivian and Ecuadorian cases, and take the form of 'embedding' capitalism and the creation of a petty bourgeoisie (the upper peasantry, for example) and the co-optation of some parts of the working class and semi-proletariat through populism.

In embarking on reform programmes, the state operates under two principal constraints, both relevant to dynamics of reformism in our case studies:

- A constraint determined by the degree of legitimacy of the state. To implement its reformist policies, the state needs to secure, via populism, the support of different social classes and fractions of classes that comprise its constituency;

- A constraint imposed by the fiscal capacity of the state. The reformist capacity of the state is limited by its capacity to generate a public budget on the basis of tax revenues or the ability to take on debt. As we shall see in the case of Bolivia and Ecuador, the legitimacy of the current regimes has been founded on redistributive policies involving social security, health, and welfare payments to those sectors of society most marginalized by neoliberalism. The monies employed to this end depend upon revenues originating in the sphere of production, most especially through extractivism, via ground rent. It is thus clear that political protests against resource extraction potentially have an impact of the state's fiscal capacity and upon those groups benefitting from it. As such protests grow, so is the state's response likely to become increasingly authoritarian.

Reformism in the current conjuncture also has referents in previous rounds of reform, in Bolivia from the 1950s until the neoliberal era (1952–1985), and in Ecuador during much shorter episodes of developmentalism, especially during the 1970s. In both countries, agrarian reformism was, firstly, an attempt to generate a more 'articulated' model of development (De Janvry 1981), and secondly, with legitimacy concerns uppermost, a means of containing peasant political pressures both through direct control of peasant organizations, and through the legislation of mild land reform projects intended to eradicate semi-feudal estates from the agrarian structure and to redistribute some land, inadequately, to the peasantry (Conaghan 1988; Webber 2017a). This effectively induced the transformation of semi-feudal estates into capitalist enterprises of the oligarchy, while limited redistribution of land created an incipient sector of capitalized family farms, thus bridging, through the establishment of a politically stable petty bourgeoisie, the historical gap between *minifundio* and *latifundio*. The remaining peasantry became, in the main, semi-proletarians, selling their labour on the new capitalist estates or on the urban market. The agrarian question thus remained unresolved from the perspective of the peasantry, and it was this unresolved question that underpinned the renewed agrarian protest that erupted from the 1990s in response to neoliberalism (Veltmeyer and Petras 2000).

Below we present case studies of agrarian class dynamics, the state-capital nexus, and the transition from populism to 'authoritarian populism' in Bolivia and Ecuador.

Bolivia

An important source of anti-neoliberal protest derived from the parlous condition of the largely indigenous peasantry in Bolivia, particularly the middle and lower peasantry. Thus, rural class structure in Bolivia is characterized by very considerable concentration of land in the hands of an agrarian oligarchy, located particularly on the most productive land in the eastern lowlands. This oligarchy is juxtaposed to large numbers of landless and land-poor peasants. Some 400 individuals own seventy per cent of productive land, whilst there are two and a half million landless peasants in a country of nine million people (Enzinna 2007; Webber 2015). Between these two groups is located a class of rich or upper peasants (small commercial farmers), comprising a key political constituency for Morales and one which has benefitted from, and grown during, the period of MAS rule (Webber 2017b).

A key aim of the *P. de Unidad* (see above) was the implementation of a programme of agrarian reform to address the plight of the land-poor, landless, and largely indigenous peasantry, principally by means of land expropriation and redistribution to these groups (McKay, Nehring, and Walsh-Dilley 2014). This formed a central pillar of a radical constitution, formally embodying plurinationalism and indigenous autonomy within the state to a degree that did not have a real counterpart in the Ecuadorian case. Again, unlike Ecuador, unprecedented numbers of women, indigenous people, and members of the working-class were appointed to high positions in government, reflecting the status of MAS as a direct outgrowth of its indigenous/peasant/proletarian base (Farthing 2017). Thus, the first policy aim of the 2006 'Agrarian Revolution' was to entail the distribution of state-owned land and redistribution by expropriation of land not serving a 'socio-economic function' in respect of indigenous peoples and peasant communities (Fabricant 2012).

This programme of land redistribution, unfortunately, has largely failed to happen, so that the main beneficiaries of this reform have been the small commercial farms of the upper peasantry, the crucial petty bourgeois constituency for the MAS populist reformists (Colque, Tinta, and Sanjines 2016). Moreover, the agrarian oligarchy of the eastern lowlands has been left essentially intact (Fabricant 2012; Webber 2015). Thus, superficially, the agrarian reform appeared to be successful, with more than 31 million hectares being titled and over 100,000 of those titles being distributed to 174,249 beneficiaries (INRA 2010; Redo, Millington, and Hindery 2011; McKay, Nehring, and Walsh-Dilley 2014). However, crucially, 90 per cent of titled land has 'been endowed by the state and is composed entirely of forest reserves' (Redo, Millington, and Hindery 2011, 237). Thus, less than ten per cent of land in the reform sector has actually been redistributed to those who need it most. So, while the 'Agrarian Revolution' was 'intended' to challenge the prevailing and highly unequal agrarian structure, it has failed to do so.

This reluctance to implement the first policy aim of the 'Agrarian Revolution' has been reinforced since 2010, with a concern by the MAS government to focus on land registration and titling at the expense of expropriation and redistribution (Colque, Tinta, and Sanjines 2016; Webber 2017b).[6] The power of the landed oligarchy remains unchallenged, therefore, while the process of peasant differentiation into a growing class of small commercial farms, on the one hand, and increased semi-proletarianization and landlessness, on the other, has accelerated (Webber 2015; Colque, Tinta, and Sanjines 2016). The greatest achievement of the 'Agrarian Revolution' has been the introduction of TCOs (*Tierras Comunitarios de Origen*) and the legal recognition of indigenous territories in the highlands and lowlands, a phenomenon which, nonetheless, is shot through with contradictions (see Webber 2017b). Land registration, entailing the conferral on individuals of absolute property rights, has facilitated the legal consolidation of a stratum of small-scale capitalized peasants (upper peasantry). This applies particularly to the 'intercultural' sector, that is, migrant Quechua and Aymara peasants from the *altiplano* to the *Oriente*, small-scale, but capitalist, producers of commercial export crops such as coca, soy, and quinoa (Colque, Tinta, and Sanjines 2016, 218). With consolidation of its legal and economic position, this commercial upper peasantry makes use of the deteriorating status of the middle/

---

[6]Detailed data concerning land registration and title according to types of property (agrarian classes) are presented in Colque, Tinta, and Sanjines 2016.

lower peasantry by purchasing its labour power. As noted, it is this stratum of commercial peasantry which represents the core political constituency of the MAS and the pivot point of its populist discourse.

The result of land registration has been the emergence of a tripartite structure of agrarian social-property relations, where before there was more of a dualism between the agrarian oligarchy and the peasant semi-proletariat, with the third, and novel, element comprising the consolidating class fraction of small commercial farmers. Thus, the hegemonic class remains the agrarian oligarchy, controlling the bulk of land, surplus value production, and land rent. The sub-hegemonic class comprises the small commercial farm sector, which, however, is not so much independent but rather deeply integrated into larger value chains of agro-industrial development (Colque, Tinta, and Sanjines 2016; Webber 2017b). Moreover, claims made for this sector's key role in expanding the national production of food staples ring hollow, since this period has seen a significant rise in the import of wage foods, further undermining national food security and the economic viability of the middle/lower peasantries (Colque, Urioste, and Eyzaguirre 2015; Ormachea Saavedra 2015). The counter-hegemonic class of the semi-proletariat and landless within this tripartite structure is either 'functional' with respect to the first two in terms of supplying wage labour or a reserve army of potential labour (exerting downward pressure on wages and the costs of production), or it comprises a 'surplus' rural population excluded from the requirements of agrarian capital accumulation (Colque, Tinta, and Sanjines 2016; McKay 2017).

Politically, the agrarian oligarchy was entrenched in the state between 1996 and 2006. This neoliberal 'disarticulated alliance' fragmented during the openly antagonistic episode of Morales' first administration (2006–2009). Following the failed civic coup attempt by the Santa Cruz agrarian oligarchy, this hegemonic group forged a renewed alliance with the post-2010 Morales regime, together with the sub-hegemonic fraction of small-scale capitalist farmers. This populist alliance now comprises the central pillar of support for Morales (Colque, Tinta, and Sanjines 2016). The sub-hegemonic fraction, as noted, comprises the upper peasantry, now highly influential within CSUTCB (*Confederación Sindical Única de Trabajadores Campesinas de Bolivia*), an organization which has been deeply integrated into the state under Morales (Colque, Tinta, and Sanjines 2016). The sub-hegemonic fraction is now influential in a wide spectrum of public institutions such as INRA (*Instituto Nacional de Reforma Agraria*), CAN (*Comunidad Andina de Naciones*), and MDRyT (*Ministerio de Desarrollo Rural y Tierra*) (Webber 2017b). Rather than the transformation of rural social-property relations and the capitalist state, this infiltration of upper peasant fractions into the state apparatus has engendered, as suggested by Gramscian *trasformismo*, the decapitation of subaltern organizations and the circumscription of their mobilization capacity.[7] Thus, an agrarian reform which might have benefitted the landless and the land-poor majority remains in abeyance and in direct contradiction with the class interests of the Morales government's principal allies (Almaraz 2015).

---

[7] One of the clearest political patterns to have emerged over the 'progressive' cycle is the bureaucratization of social movement actors through their entry into the bourgeois state apparatuses. Rather than transforming state institutions, the institutions have systematically transformed the movements. The problem of bureaucracy is not merely one of inherited structures of the '*ancien regime*' or of the recalcitrance of 'old order' civil servants. Rather, it is a question of subaltern movement representatives themselves being transformed into impediments to change once received into the institutionality of the capitalist state. This bureaucratic layer of subaltern movement representatives begins to live off the state they are ostensibly intending to transform, such that their own material reproduction comes to depend on the preservation of the status quo (Thwaites Rey and Ouviña 2012; Zibechi 2016a; Webber 2017b).

The agrarian question of the peasant majority thus remains unresolved and raises the vexed question of how long the populist compact can endure while the promise of redistributive land reform remains unfulfilled. The material base of this compact, beyond the core class alliance of its hegemonic and sub-hegemonic fractions, has been secured thus far by means of welfarism through the 'compensatory state', premised on the proceeds of extractivism.[8] The Morales regime thus pursues a tortuous path between the generation of increased social precarity through its policies of extractivism, whilst mitigating such precarity by means of revenue from that same extractivism. As this fragile equilibrium is disrupted by the combined effects of increased social precarity and decreased ability to fund welfarism (through decrease in commodity prices since 2014, particularly), so will Morales' populism become increasingly authoritarian in complexion. Indeed, Morales' authoritarian leadership increasingly has the character of *caudillismo* (Thwaites Rey and Ouviña 2012; Zibechi 2016a, 2016b; Webber 2017b), where a personality cult elevates the president as indispensable history-maker through his 'extraordinary' abilities, while the protagonism of the subaltern classes upon which his power rests is commensurately demoted.[9] Here also policy-making is technocratized and de-politicized, and policies enforced against opposition through recourse to the police and army.

Indeed, the extractivist policies of Morales have given rise to a destabilizing process of class struggle characterized by a veritable wave of protest and social resistance (Veltmeyer and Petras 2014; Webber 2015). In the last few years, a large number of movements and struggles have been calling into question the extractivist-export model and its attendant violence and environmental devastation wrought primarily by transnational (imperial and sub-imperial) capital in conjunction with the Bolivian agrarian oligarchy and small commercial farm sector. This has resulted in the fragmentation of the Unity Pact, with CIDOB (Confederation of Indigenous Peoples of Bolivia) and CONAMAQ (National Council of *Allyus* and *Markas* of *Qullasuyu*), for example, splitting in 2011 (Viaña 2012; Webber 2017b). In response, the MAS has striven to disable and delegitimate the capacity of these organizations independently to represent indigenous groups.

By means of the compensatory state, the Morales government has constructed a structure of legitimacy, or in other words 'flanking' measures, to support renewed capital accumulation through extractivism (Orellana 2011). This represents an attempt to embed capitalism through income and infrastructure measures for low-income groups founded on a narrative of communalism and cooperation as *vivir bien*. In this way, the MAS government had, until recently, temporarily stabilized the contradiction between the accumulation and legitimation functions of the capitalist state.[10] Morales restored legitimacy by placating counter-hegemonic groups during the period 2006–2009. He then proceeded (2010-date) to re-focus on capital accumulation to the benefit of the

---

[8]Thus, for example, poverty in Bolivia between 2001 and 2012 decreased from 58.6% of the population to 44.9% (Colque, Urioste, and Eyzaguirre 2015).

[9]Zibechi (2016b) indicates that the problem with *caudillismo* is that it is a culture of the right, functional to those who want to substitute the protagonsim of those from below with those from above. It is a political and cultural operation of legitimation, at the cost of emptying out the content of collective actors. It is a conservative, elitist politics which reproduces oppression instead of superseding it.

[10]In building consensual hegemony in this way, the Morales regime could, according to Akram-Lodhi (2018) (after Hall [1985]), actually be described as 'authoritarian populist' in its first phase. The subsequent loss of consensual hegemony and slide into increased authoritarianism/violence could then be described in some ways as, in his terms, 'right-wing populist nationalism'. This does not really explain, however, why populism in its first phase should be termed 'authoritarian' – hence we prefer to use the terms as defined by Scoones et al. (2018).

agri-food oligarchy, the upper peasantry, and transnational extractive capital to the neglect of the semi-proletarian and indigenous majority (Webber 2017b). With progressive loss of support from these counter-hegemonic fractions, another legitimation crisis now beckons. With the de-legitimation of extractivism, the proletariat, lower and middle peasants, and indigenous groups are increasingly unruly, advocating a model of the cooperative society beyond capitalism. The Morales reformist regime is thus encountering the constraint defined by a legitimacy deficit and this is manifest in the turn to increasingly authoritarian and repressive policies in respect of counter-hegemonic class fractions. Meanwhile, the fiscal capacity of the state is predicated on a Faustian bargain with extractivism, a mode of accumulation that, while providing a short-term revenue windfall for populism, actively, and perhaps fatally, compromises the ecological basis for constructing longer-term livelihood sovereignty for Bolivians as 'real citizens'.[11]

Ecuador

Historically, land ownership and distribution has been highly concentrated and unequal in Ecuador, with the majority of the peasantry having insufficient access to land to meet family subsistence needs throughout the year (Brassel, Herrera, and Laforge 2008). Indeed, this remains the case today despite over ten years of rule by the left-leaning regimes of Rafael Correa and Lenín Moreno and it constitutes one of the principal contradictions for the continued reproduction of the populism on which they are founded (Carrión and Herrera Revelo 2012; Martinez 2014, 2017). Such lack of access to land on the part of the peasantry, and a pattern of 'disarticulated' capitalist development, fed widespread anti-neoliberal agrarian protest during the 1990s, protest which had, moreover, a strong indigenous inflection (Becker 2008). This, in turn, created electoral space for the rise of Correa's populism in the first decade of the new millennium, enabled, fiscally, by the new Chinese search for fossil fuels, minerals, and agro-exports, and that state's willingness to both shoulder the burden of Ecuador's external debt and extend credit (Bonilla 2015). As noted, the most important force behind the 2005 coup against the then incumbent neoliberal regime were the *forajidos* (Clark 2017), and these subsequently became an important political force behind Correa's 2006 presidential bid. Presciently, such nationally-focused bourgeoisies and petty bourgeois class fractions could relatively easily co-opt the 'progressive' (mainly upper peasant) tendency within the food sovereignty movement through support for small farm productivity enhancements, whilst neutralizing the more 'radical' tendency through social welfare payments as subsistence supplement disbursed by what was to emerge as the 'compensatory state' (Henderson 2017).[12]

Correa did, however, fulfil one of his central campaign promises to subaltern classes in April 2007 with the convocation of a national constituent assembly. Correa's political dependence on the food sovereignty movement in the form of the *M. Agraria*, enabled the latter to secure the institutionalization of many of its central demands, specifically, state support for the distribution of land to the peasant sector, and its complement by

---

[11] See for example McKay (2017) on the devastating ecological and health impacts of agro-extractivism in the *Oriente*.
[12] This has been complemented by increased employment, often on large public infrastructure projects, with unemployment falling from over 10% in 2006 to under 5% in 2016, while poverty has decreased by 38% over the same period (Davalos and Albuja 2014; Henderson 2017; Peña 2017).

affordable credit and state-funded training (Clark 2017). For reasons of legitimacy, the Correa regime was obliged to recognize these broad demands of food sovereignty and to integrate them, rhetorically, into its project. It has subsequently become evident, however, that Correa has been happy to implement some of the reformist ('progressive') demands of food sovereignty from the sub-hegemonic fraction, whilst failing to deliver on the 'radical', or counter-hegemonic, agenda of land redistribution (Henderson 2017; Tilzey 2018a). This possibility was feasible, however, precisely because of the discursive breadth of, and lack of clarity in, food sovereignty discourse, enabling Correa differentially to fulfil commitments that accorded with national food sovereignty, and the stimulation of productivity for expanded accumulation amongst the class fractions of the upper peasantry.

As in the case of Bolivia, small-scale capitalists and petty commodity producers are thus seen to co-exist quite happily alongside the large agro-exporters, on whom the government relies in no small part for foreign exchange earnings (Carrión and Herrera Revelo 2012; Martinez 2017). Other than the goal of securing greater national food security in key wage foods (the key definition of food sovereignty for the Correa and Moreno regimes, and one which has been met in significant degree through productivity improvements among smaller producers), the Correa/Moreno conception of food sovereignty does not accord with the key peasant movement demands of land redistribution, sustainability, and the promotion of agroecological production. As Henderson (2017) indicates, there is increasing anxiety amongst peasant leaders concerning the government's success in consolidating, through populism, power and legitimacy amongst broad swathes of the population[13], including agrarian populations, despite a signal failure to address the highly unequal distribution of land. This success is due, of course, to Correa's, and latterly Moreno's, emphasis on those elements of food sovereignty discourse – improvements to the wellbeing, productivity, and competitiveness of the upper/middle peasantry – that conform to their neo-developmental model (Clark 2017; Henderson 2017). Meanwhile, the lower peasantry, through their wage dependency, benefit from enhanced welfare payments through the 'compensatory state', income flowing from the proceeds of neo-extractivism (Davalos and Albuja 2014). In this, as in the Bolivian case, the Correa and now Moreno regimes have encouraged not only agri-food extractivism but, perhaps even more importantly, mineral and fossil-fuel extractivism, located primarily in the *Oriente*, and undertaken increasingly by Chinese capital (Carrión 2016). Indeed, Chinese loans have underwritten the Correa/Moreno 'compensatory state', and their repayment requires the current administration to maximize extractivism to obviate default (Bonilla 2015). Meanwhile, such extractivist activities are wreaking ecological and social havoc in the *Oriente* particularly (Arsel 2016; Carrión 2016), raising profound questions concerning the desirability, and certainly sustainability, of the neo-extractivist strategy. But the beneficiaries of neo-extractivist revenue, revenue directed to small farmers as credit and to semi-proletarians as welfare, are, in the main, spatially distanciated

---

[13]De la Torre (2013) notes that the state is co-opting social movements and taming civil society whereby citizens are being turned into passive and grateful recipients of the leader's benevolent and technocratically engineered policies. This is part of a clear trend towards *caudillismo* and authoritarianism. In contrast to Bolivia, however, it is not so much the case of social movement leadership being co-opted into the state apparatus but rather of the membership being politically beguiled by strategically targeted policies and welfare disbursements. The result has been to progressively divorce social movement leaders from their mass base in the case of organizations such as FENOCIN (see below), CONAIE (*Confederación de Nacionalidades Indígenas del Ecuador*), and Ecuarunari (Confederation of the Peoples of the *Kichwa* Nationality of Ecuador).

from its direct ecological and social impacts. The Correa/Moreno regimes have, through due attention to their legitimacy roles through the 'compensatory state', thus cleverly muted opposition from these quarters. At the same time, opponents of extractivism are derided and denigrated as 'terrorists' and enemies of the 'citizens' revolution' symptomatic of an increasingly authoritarian turn in populist discourse and practice (De la Torre 2013). Indicative of this trend, was the arrest, in 2017, of hundreds of indigenous/*campesino* demonstrators for protesting peacefully against the oil and mining policies of the regime. These protests were a response to the declaration by the government of a state of emergency in Morona Santiago province in the *Oriente*, where the regime has deployed military and police forces to displace and dispossess, forcefully, Shuar indigenous people whose territory occupies land earmarked for mining projects (Riofrancos 2017).

Extractivism complements productivism, and food security can, according to Correa and Moreno, be secured through improved productivity on existing holdings, without the need to expropriate and divide large properties (Carrión and Herrera Revelo 2012; Henderson 2017). The production and reproduction strategies of middle and upper peasantry, such as those characteristic of coastal province smallholders, for example, are significantly more dependent on commodity markets than the semi-proletarian peasants who predominate in the Andes. The latter, typically, seek more land and institutional support for agroecology to bolster subsistence production, this acting primarily as a wage subsidy for their highly semi-proletarianized livelihood strategies (Martinez 2017). The Correa/Moreno strategy of improving the productivity and 'efficiency' of small farmers on the basis of expanded petty commodity production, and of re-centring the state ('re-statization') as the driver of development (Herrera Revelo 2017; Tilzey 2018a), represents a response to the historically neglected demands of the middle/upper peasantry, a fraction particularly well represented in the coastal provinces (Henderson 2017). Unsurprisingly, Correa/Moreno policies receive widespread support amongst this constituency. By contrast to their Andean, semi-proletarian counterparts, therefore, who seek more land as a wage subsidy and subsistence guarantee against adversity in the labour market, a labour market on which their reproductive strategies overwhelmingly depend, the small commercial farm sector is not concerned with land redistribution (Tilzey 2018a). Through the implementation of rural policy that improves their productivity and market competitiveness, Correa and Moreno have gathered considerable support from the sub-hegemonic small farm commercial sector. As we have seen, this has helped to legitimize their regimes and their national market-focused policies. By the same token, these policies have served to weaken those leaders of counter-hegemonic organizations, located principally in the Andes, who continue to demand structural land reform and the rejection of market-based 'solutions', whether nationally-focused or neoliberal in character (Carrión and Herrera Revelo 2012).

Since their apogee in 2006, when they helped propel the state in an anti-neoliberal direction, peasant organizations have been obliged increasingly to adopt reactive responses to a government that has, in part, institutionalized their demands, *selectively* co-opted their leadership, and progressively appropriated their discourses and mass bases of organizational support (Becker 2012; Henderson 2017). With demands historically based on anti-government and anti-neoliberal foundations, the rise of Correa and the neo-developmentalist state, with 're-statization' a key feature of its governance and anti-neo-liberalism key to its discourse and (in part) policy, has rendered these claims increasingly redundant. With much of their discourse, and key elements of their policy, at least with respect to the middle/upper peasantry, now appropriated by the Correa/Moreno administrations, many peasant/indigenous organizations have become disempowered (Herrera Revelo 2017).

These policies and payments have progressively neutralized the counter-hegemonic tendencies in organizations such as FENOCIN (*Federación Nacional de Organizaciones Campesinas, Indígenas y Negras*).[14] Thus, from 2013 onwards, as Henderson (2017) documents, FENOCIN's discourses and political strategies have changed significantly as it has become once more a vocal supporter of Correa and his 'Citizens' Revolution'. Rather than calling for the radical transformation of Ecuador's agrarian structure through mass expropriation and redistribution as the foundation of a 'food sovereign' nation (on its 'counter-hegemonic' definition), the organization's current leadership uses food sovereignty, according to its reformist definition, as a political tool to negotiate projects and resources for its membership from within Correa's 'anti-neoliberal', but national capitalist, project, including measures to 'revitalize' the productivity of 'peasant' agriculture – that is, making the petty bourgeois peasantry more competitive. By re-centring the state as the driver of economic and social development, Correa's project has responded to a number of key national-popular demands of the peasant organization's memberships for protective mechanisms against more globalized competition in the agri-food sector (together with ancillary welfare measures for semi-proletarianized peasants), and, in so doing, has weakened the food sovereignty movement's more counter-hegemonic demands for an alternative, anti-capitalist model as articulated by key peasant leaders (Herrera Revelo 2017). Again, the concept of *trasformismo* does much to explain these trends.

It is moot, however, whether, or for how long, this populist compact can endure. The fiscal capacity of the reformist state is dependent upon the inherently unsustainable, and time-limited, revenue windfall that derives from neo-extractivism. Whether through progressive exhaustion of the resource base ('second', ecological, contradiction) or through a collapse in the commodity boom as a result of accumulation crisis in China ('first', political, contradiction) (Tilzey 2018a), or a combination of both, Ecuador's model of neo-developmentalism, like Bolivia's, is built on shifting sands. If and when revenues from extractivism begin to dry up, the short-term consumer boom, the welfare payments, and the class alliances that go with them, are likely to unravel. At this point, the populist/reformist regime will encounter the limits of its legitimacy, and, indeed, we have already entered a period of increased violence and authoritarianism in response to enhanced protests against extractivism in the *Oriente*, particularly.[15] Also, we may speculate whether, at this point, the counter-hegemonic movements will regain the membership unity, and the force, that lay behind their original vision of radical food sovereignty.

---

[14]FENOCIN was founded as FENOC in the 1960s. Its roots lie in the Catholic Church's attempts to draw support away from the Communist affiliated FEI (*Federación Ecuatoriana de Indios*). In the 1970s, FENOC broke with the church and assumed a more radical, socialist position. In the 1990s, after one name change, it assumed its current name to reflect the incorporation of indigenous and Afro-Ecuadorian communities into its membership. FENOCIN, a member of La Via Campesina, emphasizes an interculturality that embraces Ecuador's diversity and strives to unify all poor people into a struggle to improve their quality of life, democratize the country, and build a sustainable and equitable system of development (Becker 2012).

[15]Indeed, a 'regrouping' of counter-hegemonic social movements was already apparent in 2012 with the Plurinational March for Life, Water, and Dignity from the southern province of Zamora Chinchipe to the capital Quito in protest against the opening of the Mirador copper mine, operated by the Chinese-owned company Ecuacorriente (Becker 2012).

Beyond the impasse of authoritarian populism: food sovereignty as counter-hegemony

As we have seen from the case studies presented, populism, as a national-popular programme of development, pursues a form of redistributive capitalism, focusing on the accumulation needs of its core sub-hegemonic constituency, while using the proceeds of neo-extractivism (generated largely by the oligarchy and transnational capital) to placate counter-hegemonic classes through welfarism. This enables the structural bases of inequality and poverty to be temporarily by-passed or mitigated, but only at the cost of deepening the political and ecological contradictions of extractive capitalism. As these contradictions deepen, exacerbated by 'jobless' growth and high dependency on external markets, so does social unrest grow commensurately. The response of the ruling bloc is a turn to increasing authoritarianism to push through its programme of accelerated commodification and destruction of the biophysical foundations for sustainable living (*buen vivir*) in the name of short-lived growth and consumerism.

Under these conditions, a de-legitimation of 'left' populism threatens, and a resurgent right, 'flying the flag of nationalism' (Malamud 2017) is poised to take over the baton of authoritarian populism (Herrera Revelo 2017). As 'left' populism moves to the right and the right itself invokes national populism, it becomes increasingly difficult to distinguish the two variants of authoritarian populism, both premised on a programme of neo-extractivism. If, in neglecting the structural foundations of inequality and poverty, 'national-popular' populism leads inevitably to authoritarianism and not to *buen vivir*, what might the latter comprise and which political strategy(ies) might best realize its imaginary?

In addressing the first question, we have already noted that *buen vivir* has perhaps been most associated with 'populist agrarianism', post-developmental/alternative developmental, or a 'progressive' approach to food sovereignty (see Escobar 1995; Esteva and Prakash 1999; Mies and Bennholdt-Thomsen 2000). This tends to be espoused by the 'sub-hegemonic' class fractions of the commercial upper peasantry and is characterized by the elevation of scale, ecology, and indigeneity at the expense of class and state. The 'radical' or 'counter-hegemonic' position on food sovereignty does indeed accept (in contrast to 'orthodox' Marxism) key elements of the 'alternative development' approach such as a certain degree of autonomy, a focus of 'fundamental needs' realized endogenously, self-reliance through solidarity and reciprocity, 'human-scale' development (household, community, popular social movements), addressing gender and other forms of discrimination (but as related to class rather than divorced from it), and ecological sustainability (Vergara-Camus 2014; Tilzey 2018a). It also recognizes, however, certain limitations of the 'alternative development' approach:

- It lacks a historical perspective able to identify the long-term effects of the insertion of local processes into those at regional, national, and global level;
- By using the undifferentiated categories of 'poor' and 'peasantry', there is no appreciation of the specificity of peasant communities and smallholder production within different national capitalist formations;
- It avoids the issue of power relations between and within classes, ethnic groups, and genders, and resorts to moral criticism rather than recognizing that all forms of

oppression rest on power relations, material and ideological, which can only be tackled through conflict and struggle;
- Its criticism of the 'state-led' model of development, and its lack of a theory of the state, has led to an avoidance of the need to address the state in any broader project of social transformation;
- It tends to over-emphasize processes of social change at the local level, failing to address how local processes of social change are related to regional, national, and global processes and struggles.

Thus, while recognizing the strengths of certain aspects of 'alternative development', the 'radical' or 'counter-hegemonic' approach to food sovereignty emphasizes the need for *transformation in the social relations of production and domination* (Tilzey 2017). This is to draw not on 'orthodox' Marxism, but rather on Marxian-derived schools such as neo-Gramscian IPE, Poulantzian state and class theory, Political Marxism, and Political Ecology.

This 'radical' counter-hegemonic model of food sovereignty enables us to suggest some answers to the second question of political strategy. Here Poulantzas (1978) is again very useful. Poulantzas vitiates the Leninist 'dual powers' approach which seeks to construct workers' councils wholly outside the state, considered (incorrectly) to be entirely a bourgeois instrument. The workers' councils, having achieved critical mass, then 'smash' the state and replace it with a 'dictatorship of the proletariat'. This then becomes Stalinist statism. Poulantzas sees social democracy as also embodying this statism, comprising a profound mistrust of mass initiatives and suspicion of democratic demands. The latter manifests itself in the Bolivian and Ecuadorian cases as reformist passive revolution.

Poulantzas also notes another position akin to post-developmentalism and agrarian populism. According to this conception, the only way to avoid statism is to place oneself outside the state, leaving it as it is and disregarding the problem of its transformation. This aims simply to block the path of the state from outside through the construction of self-management 'counter-powers' at the base – in short, to quarantine the state within its own domain. Poulantzas notes that this appears in the language of the 'new libertarians' (antecedents of post-structuralism and post-developmentalism), for whom statism can be avoided only by breaking up power and scattering it among an infinity of micro-powers. In this case, however, 'the Leviathan-State is left in place, and no attention is given to those transformations of the State without which the movement of direct democracy is bound to fail. The movement is prevented from intervening in actual transformations of the State and the two processes are simply kept running along parallel lines' (Poulantzas 1978, 262). He goes on to suggest that the task, then, is not really to 'synthesize' or stick together the statist and self-management traditions, 'but rather to open up a global perspective of the withering away of the State. This comprises two articulated processes: transformation of the State and the unfurling of direct, rank-and-file democracy.' (Poulantzas 1978, 263). This points strongly towards a *dual strategy* for 'radical' food sovereignty, one that seeks to exploit opportunities for democratic socialism at the local level, whilst simultaneously engaging the state in order to transform capitalist social-property relations at national level.

If this social relational and institutional transformation of the state-capital nexus is the essential prerequisite for livelihood sovereignty, which social forces might bring this about? We suggest that it is the middle and lower peasantries, and indigenous peoples, possibly in alliance with the proletarian precariat, which comprise the main counter-hegemonic agent for emancipatory politics as livelihood sovereignty. This is so because they view access to non-commodified land, the escape from market dependence, and the equitable and ecologically sustainable production of use values to meet fundamental need satisfaction, as the key objectives of social relational transformation (Vergara-Camus 2014). So, although the middle and lower peasantries have indeed become progressively more (semi)-proletarianized under neoliberalism, and subsequently neo-extractivism (Carrión and Herrera Revelo 2012; Webber 2015), they have, contra Bernstein (2014), resisted the adoption of a proletarian class positionality. This is so because, for them, poverty equates to a gradual loss of peasant status, which they consequently seek to reverse. The desire for such a reversal has indeed become ever more insistent as the contradictions of neoliberalism, and now neo-extractivism, have mounted and the proletariat has increasingly acquired the status of a precariat. Access to land, however limited, often provides, under these conditions, the only real element of livelihood security. Thus, struggles in the countryside and in the city often have an essentially peasant character due to the incapacity of disarticulated development or neo-extractivism to provide salaried employment as a viable alternative to secure the means of livelihood. Both peasants and workers seek refuge in the peasant situation, therefore, that is, in the auto-production of use values, to the greatest degree possible, to meet fundamental needs (Vergara-Camus 2014). The rise of indigenous and ecological consciousness since the 1990s, and the simultaneous delegitimation of capitalist modernism[16], have served only to reinforce the hunger for land and aversion to full proletarianization.

Thus, the resolution of the unresolved agrarian question of the peasantry in Latin America, particularly in the current ecologically constrained and increasingly volatile conjuncture, seems, contra Bernstein, more than ever to be, of necessity, agrarian and peasant in nature. In this, the potential for mass mobilization on the part of the middle/lower peasantries, the precariat, and indigenous groups, for an agrarian solution to the contradictions, 'political' and 'ecological', of capitalism (expressed in ongoing primitive accumulation) should not be regarded as unrealistic, as our case studies have suggested. It is evident, however, that the (authoritarian) populist regimes in Bolivia and Ecuador, and *trasformismo* more widely, have the capacity to delay or subvert such mobilizations by co-opting elements of the precariat through welfarism, by fomenting a petty bourgeois consciousness amongst the upper peasantry, and by conserving the power of the oligarchy. It will be important, consequently, for counter-hegemonic forces, in their wish to secure autonomy from market dependence through secure access to the means of production, to confront both 'capitalism from below' and 'capitalism from above' – in short, a dual strategy for livelihood sovereignty.

The MST and emancipatory rural politics as counter-hegemony in Bolivia

The importance of differentiating between reformism (sub-hegemony) and anti-capitalism (counter-hegemony) is well illustrated by the dynamics of the *Movimiento de los Trabajadores Rurales sin Tierra* (MST) in Bolivia (a sister organization of the better-known Brazilian

---

[16]This echoes Gudynas' (2018) call to go beyond modernism (capitalism) for both 'political' *and* 'ecological' reasons.

MST). These dynamics help us to identify a strategy of emancipatory rural politics whereby counter-hegemony, as food and livelihood sovereignty, may be implanted at 'local' level as a form of autonomy (confronting 'capitalism from below'), whilst, simultaneously, recognizing the need to engage the state ('capitalism from above') to secure a more generalized autonomy from capitalism. The MST seems to embody a 'dual strategy' approach, exploiting current opportunities for autonomy where possible, whilst amplifying the struggle for deeper and wider transformation through appropriation and subversion of the modern state itself. It also seems to represent the kind of 'radical' food sovereignty which we have identified in this paper as counter-hegemony. Here, we draw on Fabricant's (2012) ethnography of the MST in the Bolivian *Oriente*, a study that demonstrates the movement's embrace of radical, participatory democracy, and its advocacy of collective ownership of land, drawing on, while 'reinventing', communal traditions inspired by the pre-Columbian *ayllu*.

The formation of the MST in Bolivia was inspired by its sister organization in Brazil. Like the latter, the Bolivian MST has exploited the constitutional requirement for agricultural land to be in productive use. Accordingly, the organization has targeted idle land, owned by members of the agrarian oligarchy, but held largely for purposes of speculation. The state constitution permits the occupation of such land for the purpose of turning it to productive use, through the submission of a petition for legal title. The MST is painfully aware, however, that such autonomy as exists in these small number of successful cases is founded on a fragile legal loophole within a more generalized system of absolute property rights which the capitalist state, including the reformist state of Evo Morales, is committed to uphold. It recognizes, therefore, that a far greater, and more thoroughgoing, transformation of social-property relations is required if its model of *ayllu*-inspired autonomy for the landless and land-poor peasantry is to be more widely implanted.

In these few cases of successful, legalized, land occupations, the MST has built an organizational structure that is democratic and participatory, capable of creating order and holding leaders and rank-and-file to account through collective governance. This is a form of grassroots citizenship, inspired by, but also reconfiguring, Andean principles of autonomy, self-governance, and participatory democracy. This stands in contrast to liberal citizenship as individualism, 'given' to members as a right by the state. The Andean ideal of the *ayllu*, imagined as community-held land and collective forms of governance and control, has become the principal framework for governing MST settlements. These modern *ayllus* are characterized by nucleated settlements, communal landholdings, rotational political and administrative offices, land redistribution, and rural tax collection.

The MST has adapted the *ayllu* model to structure their political organization at the community, regional, and national levels. The state has fractionalized land and territory through a model of citizenship that has assigned absolute property rights to individuals. The MST asserts, by contrast, that complete dominion over land by an individual or group is itself illegitimate. Rather, land is a collective right and should entail stewardship rather than absolute dominion. The occupation of land signifies reclaiming and re-territorializing indigenous/peasant control and autonomy over land and other critical resources. The dynamic relationship between territorial autonomy and the ability to provide a political infrastructure that sustains humanity is designated by indigenous conceptualizations such as *sumak kawsay* (in Kichwa) or *buen vivir*. This 'return to the past' logic provides a sense of territorial and communal security through a form of 'collective' control.

•

The MST's idea of food sovereignty and agroecology is deeply embedded in collaborative and collective forms of production. The MST has revived and politicized essentialized notions of Andean rural culture by establishing *ayni* (reciprocity) and *minka* (exchange) as forms of resistance to the capitalist, large-scale, agro-industrial production of the oligarchy. In their re-appropriation of this cultural model as antithetical to capitalism, the MST affirms the social, collective, and reciprocal forms of production, in which all members of the community benefit from family farming.

Nonetheless, there exist tensions within the MST between those, the majority, who wish to pursue a collectivist ideal, and those, a minority, who wish to acquire title to land on an individual basis, the latter an individualistic and capitalist-driven response to the problem of land inequality. Land petitions, in the latter case, are filed as individual rather than communal requests. This has the potential to undermine the ability of the MST collectively to negotiate for communal land ownership by placing such power in the hands of a few individuals who want simply to buy and sell property. This tension is unsurprising. Peasant and indigenous movements cannot simply 'transition' to a pure collective model given the huge constraints of actually existing capitalism and marginalization with which they have to contend on a daily basis. While the better-off peasantry may wish to pursue the capitalist 'farmer road' ('accumulation from below'), it remains the case that many members tend to adopt, as best they can, 'pieces' of the alternative collective model whilst attempting to optimize survival strategies within actually existing capitalism (Fabricant 2012, 129). The result is a hybridization between pragmatic survival strategies and the striving towards something better, the latter articulated by MST as the *ayllu*. This serves perhaps to highlight the limitations of autonomism as a doctrine that assumes that real change can occur 'without taking power' or, in other words, without addressing the causal basis of poverty, marginalization and ecological despoliation generated by 'capitalism from above', orchestrated by the state. This is recognized by the MST. While seizing all the opportunities available at the local level to secure access to land and institute collective ways of life as food sovereignty, the MST recognizes that the limits to this strategy are defined precisely by the forces of unsustainability that need to be confronted. This confrontation can occur only if the struggle is taken to the state by means of a dual strategy. This is why the MST has taken part in successive Marches for Land and Territory to the state capitals, demanding fundamental change in social-property relations throughout the country, and concomitant change in the nature of the state itself.

Conclusion

The populist regimes of Bolivia and Ecuador have, for the last decade or so, been able to support social welfare programmes only through resource extraction fed principally by the Chinese commodity boom. Welfarism mitigates and dulls pressure from counter-hegemonic movements to implement policies to redistribute land and affirm the right to land as the basis for 'radical' food sovereignty. Consequently, the regimes of Morales and Correa/Moreno have been reluctant to institute sustainable food production and livelihood systems based on land redistribution and security of land rights, precisely because the growth model is premised on the perpetuation of neo-extractivism, and the stimulation of productivist agriculture by the small farm commercial sector. So, while the regimes of Correa/Moreno and Morales relied heavily upon peasant and indigenous support to secure their initial electoral success, and have included constitutional provisions for food sovereignty, substantive implementation of these provisions has fallen far short of expectation (Henderson 2017; Webber 2017a, 2017b), particularly in the case of Ecuador. Consequently, these peasant and indigenous constituencies are becoming increasingly alienated from the governments of Morales and Moreno. Moreover, the current decline in primary commodity prices portends a reduction in government budgets for welfare programmes and, consequently, a threat to the populist compact between sub-hegemonic and counter-hegemonic constituencies. Indeed, as Scoones et al. (2018) suggest, this has coincided with a clear trend towards 'authoritarian populism' in Latin America, as in our case studies both Morales and Moreno concentrate power in their executives, assume the role of 'indispensable' and charismatic leaders of the nation (*caudillismo*), and deploy increasingly draconian measures to quell anti-extractivist protests.

This paper has argued that the only route out of this impasse that is both socially equitable and ecologically sustainable is that of 'radical' food sovereignty, or livelihood sovereignty (Tilzey 2018a). This represents a resolution of the agrarian question in favour of counter-hegemonic forces, comprising the great majority of the citizenry. Choosing this path requires the thoroughgoing transformation and abrogation of capitalist social-property relations towards democratic and devolved common ownership – or better, stewardship – of the means of livelihood (Carrión and Herrera Revelo 2012). Given our previous discussion, a class-relational and political ecological understanding of capitalism appears necessary as a basis for this transformation (see Tilzey 2017, 2018a, 2018b for discussion). Since the alienation of land and labour constitute the quintessence of capitalism, it is the re-appropriation of land by the dispossessed or partially dispossessed, and the retention of land by those fortunate enough to sustain customary access to it, for the co-operative production of use values for society as a whole, that mark the key elements in capital's transcendence and as the basis for future sustainability. Here the transformation of class-relational power through political action within and around the state (that is, seizing opportunities for autonomy at the local level whilst addressing wider social-property relations by confronting the state) – a 'dual strategy' – will be key in expunging exploitative relations and laying the jurisdictional and material foundations for social equity, cooperative organization, and ecological sustainability.

Acknowledgements

This paper is based in part on research undertaken by the author in June, July and August 2015 in Bolivia and Ecuador on the basis of semi-structured interviews conducted with a spectrum of stakeholders connected with agrarian dynamics and food sovereignty in the two states. Interviews were conducted with government departments and agencies, politicians/political parties, peasant/indigenous/farmer/landowner organizations, civil society organizations, and NGOs, whose help and support is gratefully acknowledged. It is also based on a wide-ranging and critical review of the literature related to the above and to the agrarian question, capitalism and state theory more generally, and on the author's prior analytical work in agrarian politics in the global South and North. The research was made possible by CAWR's (Coventry University) Innovation Fund and this support is gratefully acknowledged. An earlier version of this paper was presented as Conference Paper No. 34 at the Emancipatory Rural Politics Initiative 2018 Conference, ISS, The Hague, Netherlands. The paper has benefitted greatly from the helpful comments of two anonymous referees.

Disclosure Statement

No potential conflict of interest was reported by the author.

Funding

This work was supported by Coventry University.

References

Akram-Lodhi, A. H. 2018. "The Promise? Using and Misusing Authoritarian Populism." *Conference Paper No. 6*. ERPI 2018 International Conference: Authoritarian Populism and the Rural World, The Hague, Netherlands.

Almaraz, A. 2015. "Luchas Políticas y Legales por la Tierra en Bolivia: Las Luchas Indígenas y Campesinas en los Dos Ciclos de la Reforma Agraria." In *Recientes Transformaciones Agrarias en Bolivia*, edited by Fundación Tierra, 52–53. La Paz: Fundación Tierra.

Arsel, M. 2016. "Poverty, nature, and post-neoliberal developmentalism: Political economy of the foretold demise of Ecuador's Yasuni-ITT initiative." Paper presented at the American Association of Geographers Annual Meeting, San Francisco, 29 March – 3 April.

Becker, M. 2008. *Indians and Leftists in the Making of Ecuador's Modern Indigenous Movements*. Durham: Duke University Press.

Becker, M. 2012. *Pachakutik! Indigenous Movements and Electoral Politics in Ecuador*. Lanham: Rowman and Littlefield.

Bernstein, H. 2010. *The Class Dynamics of Agrarian Change*. Halifax: Fernwood Publishing.

Bernstein, H. 2014. "Food Sovereignty via the 'Peasant Way': A Sceptical View." *The Journal of Peasant Studies* 41 (6): 1031–1063.

Bieler, A., and A. Morton. 2004. "A Critical Theory Route to Hegemony, World Order and Historical Change: Neo-Gramscian Perspectives in International Relations." *Capital and Class* 82 (Spring): 85–113.

Bonilla, O. 2015. "China's Geopolitical Strategy in the Andean Region." In *BRICS: An Anti-Capitalist Critique*, edited by Patrick Bond, and Ana Garcia, 135–147. London: Pluto Press.

Boyer, R., and Y. Saillard. 2002. *Regulation Theory: The State of the Art*. London: Routledge.

Brass, T. 2000. *Peasants, Populism and Postmodernism: The Return of the Agrarian Myth*. London: Frank Cass.

Brass, T. 2014. *Class, Culture, and the Agrarian Myth*. Chicago: Haymarket Books.

Brassel, F., S. Herrera, and M. Laforge. 2008. *¿Reforma Agraria en el Ecuador? Viejos Temas, Nuevos Argumentos*. Quito: SIPAE.

Brenner, R. 1977. "The Origins of Capitalist Development: A Critique of Neo-Smithian Marxism." *New Left Review* 104: 25–93.

Brenner, R. 1985. "The Agrarian Roots of European Capitalism." In *The Brenner Debate: Agrarian Class Structure and Economic Development in Pre-Industrial Europe*, edited by T. Aston, and C. Philpin, 213–328. Cambridge: Cambridge University Press.

Carrión, A. 2016. "Extractivismo Minero y Estrategia de Desarrollo: Entre el Nacionalismo de los Recursos y los Conflictos Socioterritoriales." In *La Revolución Ciudadana en Escala de Grises: Avances, Continuidades y Dilemas*, edited by M. Le Quang, 181–204. Quito: Editorial IAEN.

Carrión, D., and S. Herrera Revelo. 2012. *Ecuador Rural del Siglo XXI: Soberanía Alimentaria, Inversión Pública y Política Agraria*. Quito: Instituto de Estudios Ecuatorianos.

Clark, P. 2017. "Neo-Developmentalism and a 'Via Campesina' for Rural Development: Unreconciled Projects in Ecuador's Citizen's Revolution." *Journal of Agrarian Change* 17: 348–364.

Colque, G., E. Tinta, and E. Sanjines. 2016. *Segunda Reforma Agraria: Una Historia que Incomoda*. La Paz: Fundación Tierra.

Colque, C., M. Urioste, and J. L. Eyzaguirre. 2015. *Marginalizacion de la Agricultura Campesina e Indigena: Dinamicas Locales, Seguridad y Soberania Alimentaria*. La Paz: Fundacion Tierra.

Conaghan, C. 1988. *Restructuring Domination: Industrialists and the State in Ecuador*. Pittsburgh: University of Pittsburgh Press.

Cox, R. 1993. "Gramsci, Hegemony, and International Relations: An Essay in Method." In *Gramsci, Historical Materialism, and International Relations*, edited by S. Gill, 49–66. Cambridge: Cambridge University Press.

Davalos, P., and V. Albuja. 2014. "Ecuador: Extractivist Dynamics, Politics, and Discourse." In *The New Extractivism: A Post-Neoliberal Development Model or Imperialism of the Twenty-First Century?*, edited by H. Veltmeyer, and J. Petras, 144–171. London: Zed Books.

De Janvry, A. 1981. *The Agrarian Question and Reformism in Latin America*. Baltimore: Johns Hopkins University Press.

De la Torre, C. 2013. "Technocratic Populism in Ecuador." *Journal of Democracy* 24 (3): 33–46.

Enzinna, W. 2007. "All We Want is the Earth: Agrarian Reform in Bolivia." In *Socialist Register 2008: Global Flashpoints, Reactions to Imperialism and Neoliberalism*, edited by L. Panitch, and C. Leys, 217–236. London: Merlin Press.

Escobar, A. 1995. "Imagining a Post-Development Era." In *The Power of Development*, edited by J. Crush, 211–227. London: Routledge.

Esteva, G., and M. S. Prakash. 1999. *Grassroots Post-Modernism: Remaking the Soil of Cultures*. London: Zed Books.

Fabricant, N. 2012. *Mobilizing Bolivia's Displaced: Indigenous Politics and the Struggle Over Land*. Chapel Hill: University of North Carolina Press.

Farthing, L. 2017. "The State of the Left in Latin America: Ecuador and Bolivia After the Pink Tide." *NACLA*. July 19. https://nacla.org/news/.../state-left-latin-america-ecuador-and-bolivia-after-pink-tide

Giunta, I. 2014. "Food Sovereignty in Ecuador: Peasant Struggles and the Challenges of Institutionalization." *Journal of Peasant Studies* 41 (6): 1201–1224.

Gramsci, A. 1971. *Selections from the Prison Notebooks*. New York: International Publishers.

Gudynas, E. 2012. "Estado Compensador y Nuevos Extractivismos: Las Ambivalencias del Progresismo Sudamericano." *Nueva Sociedad* 237: 128–146.

Gudynas, E. 2018. "A Critique of the Idea of Populism and the Urgencies with Authoritarianisms: Some South American Notes on Progressivisms, Development and Alternatives." *Conference Paper No. 75*. ERPI 2018 International Conference: Authoritarian Populism and the Rural World, The Hague, Netherlands.

Henderson, T. 2017. "State-Peasant Movement Relations and the Politics of Food Sovereignty in Mexico and Ecuador." *The Journal of Peasant Studies* 44 (1): 33–55.

Herrera Revelo, S. 2017. "Lecciones del Contradictorio Progresismo en el Ecuador." *Lalineadefuego.Info January* 31: 1–5.

Hylton, F., and S. Thomson. 2007. *Revolutionary Horizons: Past and Present in Bolivian Politics*. London: Verso.

INRA (Instituto de Reforma Agraria). 2010. *La Tierra Vuelve a Manos Indígenas y Campesinas*. La Paz: INRA.

Jessop, B., and N. L. Sum. 2013. *Towards a Cultural Political Economy: Putting Culture in its Place in Political Economy*. Cheltenham: Edward Elgar.

Le Quang, M. 2016. *La Revolución Ciudadana en Escala de Grises: Avances, Continuidades y Dilemas*. Quito: Editorial IAEN.

Malamud, A. 2017. "Qué cosa fuera la patria sin Correa." *Nueva Sociedad*. March 17. http://nuso.org/articulo/que-cosa-fuera-la-patria-sin-correa/

Marini, R. M. 1972. "Brazilian Subimperialism." *Monthly Review* 23 (9): 14–24.
Marini, R. M. 1973. *Dialéctica de la Dependencia*. Mexico: Editorial Era.
Martinez Valle, L. 2014. "La Concentracion de la Tierra en el Caso Ecuatoriano: Impactos en el Territorio." In *La Concentracion de la Tierra: Un Problema Prioritario en el Ecuador Contemporaneo*, edited by A. Berry, L. Martinez Valle, C. Kay, and L. North, 43–62. Quito: Abya-Yala.
Martinez Valle, L. 2017. "Agribusiness, Peasant Agriculture, and Labour Markets: Ecuador in Comparative Perspective." *Journal of Agrarian Change* 17 (4): 680–693.
McKay, B. 2017. "Agrarian Extractivism in Bolivia." *World Development* 97 (September): 199–211.
McKay, B., R. Nehring, and M. Walsh-Dilley. 2014. "The State of Food Sovereignty in Latin America: Political Projects and Alternative Pathways in Venezuela, Ecuador and Bolivia." *Journal of Peasant Studies* 41 (6): 1175–1200.
McMichael, P. 2013. *Food Regimes and Agrarian Questions*. Halifax/Winnipeg: Fernwood Publishing.
Mies, M., and V. Bennholdt-Thomsen. 2000. *The Subsistence Perspective: Beyond the Globalized Economy*. London: Zed Books.
Mooers, C. 1991. *The Making of Bourgeois Europe: Absolutism, Revolution, and the Rise of Capitalism in England, France, and Germany*. London: Verso.
Offe, K., and G. Lenhardt. 1976. "Social Policy and the Theory of the State." In *Contradictions of the Welfare State*, edited by J. Keane, 51–64. London: Hutchinson.
Oliveira, G. 2018. "Chinese Land Grabs in Brazil: Sinophobia and Foreign Investments in Brazilian Soybean Agribusiness." *Globalizations* 15 (1): 114–133.
Orellana, L. 2011. "The National Question and the Autonomy of the State in Bolivia." In *Reclaiming the Nation: The Return of the National Question in Africa, Asia, and Latin America*, edited by S. Moyo and P. Yeros, 235–254. London: Pluto Press.
Ormachea Saavedra, E. 2015. "Pequena y Gran Produccion Agricola Capitalista y Trabajo Asalariado en Bolivia." In *Asalariados Rurales en America Latina*, edited by A. Riella and P. Mascheroni, 165–186. Buenos Aires: CLACSO.
Peña, Karla. 2017. "Will Lenin Moreno Champion Food Sovereignty in Ecuador in Ways Rafael Correa Didn't?" *Upside Down World*. September 20. http://upsidedownworld.org/archives/ecuador/will-lenin-moreno-champion-food-sovereignty-ecuador-ways-rafael-correa-didnt/
Petras, J., and H. Veltmeyer. 2011. *Social Movements in Latin America: Neoliberalism and Popular Resistance*. New York: Palgrave Macmillan.
Potter, C., and M. Tilzey. 2005. "Agricultural Policy Discourses in the European Post-Fordist Transition: Neoliberalism, Neomercantilism and Multifunctionality." *Progress in Human Geography* 29 (5): 581–600.
Poulantzas, N. 1978. *State, Power, Socialism*. London: Verso.
Redo, D., A. Millington, and D. Hindery. 2011. "Deforestation Dynamics and Policy Changes in Bolivia's Post-Neoliberal Era." *Land Use Policy* 28: 227–241.
Riofrancos, T. 2017. "The State of the Left in Latin America: Ecuador and Bolivia After the Pink Tide." *NACLA*. July 19. https://nacla.org/news/…/state-left-latin-america-ecuador-and-bolivia-after-pink-tide
Robinson, W. 2017. "Passive Revolution: The Transnational Capitalist Class Unravels Latin America's Pink Tide." *Truthout*. June 6. https://truthout.org/articles/passive-revolution-the-transnational-capitalist-class-unravels-latin-america-s-pink-tide/
Scoones, I., M. Edelman, S. M. Borras Jr, R. Hall, W. Wolford, and B. White. 2018. "Emancipatory Rural Politics: Confronting Authoritarian Populism." *The Journal of Peasant Studies* 45 (1): 1–20.
Spronk, S., and J. Webber. 2015. *Crisis and Contradiction: Marxist Perspectives on Latin America in the Global Economy*. Chicago: Haymarket Books.
Svampa, M. 2016. *Debates Latinoamericanos: Indianismo, Desarrollo, Dependencia y Populismo*. Buenos Aires: Edhasa.
Svampa, M. 2017. "Populismos latinoamericanos en el fin del ciclo progresista." *PúblicoGT* April 16.
Thwaites Rey, M., and H. Ouviña. 2012. "La Estatalidad Latinoamericana Revisitada: Reflexiones e Hipótesis Alrededor del Problema del Poder Político y las Transiciones." In *El Estado en América Latina: Continuidades y Rupturas*, edited by M. Thwaites Rey, 51–92. Buenos Aires: CLACSO.

Tilzey, M. 2016. "Global Politics, Capitalism, Socio-Ecological Crisis, and Resistance: Exploring the Linkages and the Challenges." *Colloquium Paper No. 14*. Global governance/politics, climate justice & agrarian/social justice: linkages and challenges: An international colloquium 4-5 February 2016. ISS, The Hague, Netherlands.

Tilzey, M. 2017. "Reintegrating Economy, Society, and Environment for Cooperative Futures: Polanyi, Marx, and Food Sovereignty." *Journal of Rural Studies* 53 (July): 317–334.

Tilzey, M. 2018a. *Political Ecology, Food Regimes, and Food Sovereignty: Crisis, Resistance, and Resilience*. London: Palgrave Macmillan.

Tilzey, M. 2018b. "'Market Civilization' and Global Agri-Food: Understanding Their Dynamics and (In)Coherence Through Multiple Resistances." In *Resistance to the Neoliberal Agri-Food Regime: A Critical Analysis*, edited by A. Bonanno, and S. A. Wolf, 64–77. London: Routledge.

Van der Ploeg, J. D. 2008. *The New Peasantries: Struggles for Autonomy and Sustainability in an Era of Empire and Globalization*. London: Earthscan.

Veltmeyer, H. 2014. "Bolivia: Between Voluntarist Developmentalism and Pragmatic Extractivism." In *The New Extractivism: A Post-Neoliberal Development Model or Imperialism of the Twenty-First Century?*, edited by H. Veltmeyer, and J. Petras, 80–113. London: Zed Books.

Veltmeyer, H., and J. Petras. 2000. *The Dynamics of Social Change in Latin America*. London: Palgrave Macmillan.

Veltmeyer, H., and J. Petras, eds. 2014. *The New Extractivism: A Post-Neoliberal Development Model or Imperialism of the Twenty-First Century?* London: Zed Books.

Vergara-Camus, L. 2014. *Land and Freedom: The MST, the Zapatistas, and Peasant Alternatives to Neoliberalism*. London: Zed Books.

Viaña, J. 2012. "Estado Plurinacional y Nueva Fase del Proceso Boliviano." In *El Estado en América Latina: Continuidades y Rupturas*, edited by M. Thwaites Rey, 375–394. Buenos Aires: CLACSO.

Webber, J. 2015. "Revolution Against 'Progress': Neo-Extractivism, the Compensatory State, and the TIPNIS Conflict in Bolivia." In *Crisis and Contradiction: Marxist Perspectives on Latin America in the Global Economy*, edited by S. Spronk and J. Webber, 302–333. Chicago: Haymarket Books.

Webber, J. 2017a. "Evo Morales, *Transformismo*, and the Consolidation of Agrarian Capitalism in Bolivia." *Journal of Agrarian Change* 17: 330–347.

Webber, J. 2017b. *The Last Day of Oppression and the First Day of the Same: The Politics and Economics of the New Latin American Left*. Chicago: Haymarket Books.

Wood, E. M. 1995. *Democracy Against Capitalism: Renewing Historical Materialism*. Cambridge: Cambridge University Press.

Wood, E. M. 2009. "Peasants and the Market Imperative: The Origins of Capitalism." In *Peasants and Globalization: Political Economy, Rural Transformation, and the Agrarian Question*, edited by A. H. Akram-Lodhi, and C. Kay, 37–56. Abingdon: Routledge.

Zibechi, R. 2016a. "Progressive Fatigue? Coming to Terms with the Latin American Left's New 'Coyuntura'." *NACLA* 48 (1): 22–27.

Zibechi, R. 2016b. "El Caudillismo es Cultura de Derecha." *La Jornada*. March 4. https://www.jornada.com.mx/2016/03/04/opinion/018a1pol

Pockets of liberal media in authoritarian regimes: what the crackdown on emancipatory spaces means for rural social movements in Cambodia

Alice Beban, Laura Schoenberger and Vanessa Lamb

ABSTRACT
Cambodia's ruling party cracked down on the press, civil society, and opposition in the lead up to the 2018 national elections. Drawing on interviews with Cambodian journalists who lost their jobs, as well as long-standing research on rural struggles in Cambodia, we argue that the Cambodian state's crackdown on media is part of an ongoing transformation of authoritarian populism that has reduced the space for rural collective action. The state's repression and co-optation of media also signals a change in the ruling party's brand of populist authoritarianism: from simultaneously courting and spreading fear amongst rural voters, to casting rural people aside. The media is a space of both emancipatory and authoritarian potential, and for the journalists who saw themselves as building the post-conflict democratic state, the crackdown signals the loss of a more emancipatory, democratic imaginary. This study contributes to analyses of authoritarianism as practice by drawing attention to the various scales and spaces in which it is produced, enacted, and imagined.

Introduction

The oppositional categories of 'democratic/authoritarian' and 'liberal/illiberal' obscure the pockets of liberalism and democratic norms folded into authoritarian regimes. These can provide temporary spaces for emancipatory politics, and can also be brutally shut down. In the lead up to Cambodia's 2018 national elections, the ruling Cambodian People's Party (CPP) launched a coordinated attack on the political opposition, the press, and civil society groups in an attempt to ensure the party's political survival. The government closed independent media outlets and stripped the opposition party (the Cambodian National Rescue Party [CNRP]) of their parliamentary seats. With no credible opposition, the CPP won every seat in the national assembly, ensuring that Prime Minister Hun Sen retains his status as the world's longest ruling current Prime Minister. Prior to this crackdown, Cambodia had been considered unique in the Southeast Asian region for a relatively free press. Although the environment was risky, and at least 14 journalists have been killed for their reporting since 1992, the existence of media outlets outside the ruling party's control had been a space of political possibility and a vehicle for mobilization for almost half a million Cambodians facing violent land struggles. But this space is fragile. In 2016, independent analyst Kem Ley was gunned down in Phnom Penh two days after speaking on *Radio Free Asia* (RFA) about the control that Hun Sen's family wields over the country's key businesses. RFA, and the stations that broadcasted its coverage, as well as the English daily newspaper, *The Cambodia Daily*, were shut down in late 2017. The remaining four biggest media groups are all affiliated with the government and spread a pro-government viewpoint to nearly 85% of the public (MoM 2016; RSF 2018). As a result of these moves against non-state media, the country's press freedom rankings plunged 10 places in one year, falling to 142nd worldwide (RSF 2018).

In this paper, we argue that the Cambodian state's crackdown on the free press is part of an ongoing transformation of authoritarian populism that has reduced the space for rural collective action: farmers can no longer listen to independent news while harvesting rice; organizers cannot reach out to journalists to cover their plight; and a media landscape is being remade around online platforms that spout state propaganda just as rural activists delete their social media profiles to avoid imprisonment. Cracking down on the free press and co-opting social media spaces appears to be part of a shift to draw support away from oppositional politics and to silence rural resistance to the enrichment of well-connected elites. By ousting independent journalists who illuminated rural struggles, the current moment spells heightened extraction – without apology – from rural areas. And for the Cambodian journalists we interviewed who lost their jobs in 2017, these political shifts signal a 'darkness' brought on not only by the material loss of the news outlets, but also the loss of a democratic imaginary. As state-affiliated media proliferate alongside enhanced state surveillance capabilities and repressive laws, the *possibility* that the country is transitioning to a free press appears ever less likely. The journalists saw themselves as enacting the project of liberal democracy in Cambodia, and in our interviews they pined for a democracy that was never fully realised but had seemed possible.

The journalists' sentiments are powerfully reflected in a recent 'eulogy' for *The Cambodia Daily* newspaper written by 'Sombath', an anonymous Cambodian university graduate. He writes that repression and co-optation of independent media are the marks of a 'diminished' democracy:

> It was you who kept me and other countless Cambodians, who are sick and tired of hearing overpraised statements and one-sided commentary broadcasted on TV, informed of what is really happening in this Kingdom of Endless Wonders … I want to thank you for your insightful stories and information that keep people like me informed and unblind about what the rich and powerful have done at the expense of ordinary Cambodians. I want to thank you for crossing the line, confront[ing] the tyrant, and say[ing] what should be said about the way things work in this country. I want to thank you for enlightening my immature understanding of how a democracy works. You have been at the heart of this UNTAC-sponsored, hopeless and soon-to-be-diminished democracy. (Sombath 2017)

Not only does this eulogy invoke sadness for the 'passing' of the free press; Sombath's post associates the press with education, civil rights, holding those in power accountable, and highlighting the voices of ordinary Cambodians. But print and broadcast media are not inherently liberatory; illiberal and authoritarian regimes use the press to spread propaganda and enable state surveillance. The central role media plays in subverting and enabling authoritarian populist regimes is often neglected in favour of analyses focusing on electoral politics and everyday practices of resistance (Lewis 2013). In the scholarly literature on Cambodia, for example, there is little attention to the varied ways in which rural people resisting land grabs have used different forms of media to publicize their struggles and share information, or the ways that flows of information to and from rural areas are connected to the state's use of media to strengthen the regime and repress activists. However, renewed attention to oppressive or illiberal power relations and authoritarianism (*Journal of Peasant Studies* Forums 2019, 46:3, 2018, 45:1; *Area* 2013, 45:4; *Annals of the American Association of Geographers* 2019, 109:2) are challenging the tendency to view the phenomenon through a state-based lens (Koch 2019), and there is a call for scholars in agrarian studies to understand the media's emancipatory potential and its use as a structure of oppression (Scoones et al. 2018). This paper contributes to this effort by examining media-based practices to produce, enact, and imagine both enhanced structures of oppression and emancipatory potentials. Our interviews with journalists in the aftermath of the crackdown shows that authoritarian closures are closures not just of institutions and people, but also closures of the imagination that entail the power to foreclose alternative imaginings of subjectivity and political arrangements (Koch 2013, 392).

In what follows, we first describe our methodology, which had to be continually adapted in response to the changing political situation. Then, in five subsequent sections, we intertwine empirical material with theoretical insights to develop our focus on journalism as a practice that contributes to democratic imaginaries, and that is also retooled to further authoritarian and populist ends. We first outline the historical context of populist authoritarianism in Cambodia and how this is intertwined with the development of Cambodia's media landscape. Second, we draw on insights from political communications theory to understand the roles different forms of media play in both strengthening rural struggles and sustaining authoritarian regimes. Third, we consider how these processes articulated with local journalistic practices to enact democracy, and we then analyse the implications of the crackdown. Finally, we detail the ways in which spaces for emancipatory politics have been captured by the ruling elite.

Methodology

The research that informs this paper began as a way to understand the 2017 crackdown and to explore what it might mean for rural politics – the focus of our long-standing scholarly engagement in Cambodia. The research team conducted interviews in late 2017 with 15 journalists who previously worked with two of the most important media outlets for rural social struggle: *The Cambodia Daily* newspaper, and *Radio Free Asia Cambodia*. This timing meant that we spoke to people within three to four months of the coordinated crackdown on the press, the shuttering of important institutions, and the loss of these journalists' jobs. All participants were Cambodian citizens and ranged from those whose careers started in the 1990s, to several young reporters who had only recently completed their training. The interviewees covered a range of news beats and job responsibilities, from land disputes and courts reporters, to print, video, and audio editing. To contextualize the accounts given by local journalists, we also draw from our past research with rural people living in land conflict areas (2010-2015), during which people struggling to access and control land and forests explained how they used media to further their efforts (Beban, So, and Un 2017; Lamb et al. 2017; Schoenberger 2017; Schoenberger and Beban 2018; Beban and Schoenberger 2019).

Following considerations for research in places 'haunted by an authoritarian past or abandoning democracy' (Goode 2010, 1055), we carefully designed our study 'with an eye to the broader fields and power relations in which we conduct our research' (Koch 2013, 391). Questions of research ethics were continually negotiated in this context.[1] As the state crackdown on journalists and civil society intensified in late 2017, two Cambodian reporters were imprisoned, foreign journalists and filmmakers were accused of espionage, and civil society organisations with US ties were forced to close. In this quickly changing context, we adapted our original plans that had called for the researchers (three white women) to undertake fieldwork ourselves. Instead, we worked with journalists who had recently been let go when outlets were closed in the crackdown. We did initial interviews ourselves (via video conferencing), then consulted two journalists and hired one as a research assistant (hereafter referred to as 'the RA' for anonymity) after extensive conversations about research ethics, and the need for the journalist to lead the data collection process in ways that would ensure safety for all involved. The RA chose to remain anonymous, rather than join the team as a named researcher for publication. Trust was necessary for participants and the interviewer to speak openly, so our team sought potential interview participants through a snowball method, contacting former colleagues and these colleagues' contacts. The research assistant only spoke with people under conditions of anonymity, conducting interviews in public spaces, or online, in order to maintain the safety of research participants. The research assistant transcribed the interviews, then the team met virtually to discuss the interview transcripts, and to code for emerging themes. Recordings were then destroyed. We are deliberately vague about identifying the journalists' place of work or gender, or the location of the rural people we quote in the article, in order to protect their safety.

Our analysis also makes extensive use of secondary sources, particularly media coverage from newspaper, radio and social media platforms, to understand the ongoing political transformation. In integrating these sources, we acknowledge the multiple functions of social media as a form of knowledge production and as a new arena for the exchange of ideas. Social media was more than a text for analysis in our research; we used it to identify research assistants, to inform changes in the study design, and to understand the reporting on political twists and turns by following local journalists, activists, and commentators on multiple platforms.

Populist authoritarianism and the (un)free press in Cambodia

For more than thirty years, Hun Sen has in many ways been the archetypal populist strongman who 'frequently circumvents, eviscerates or captures democratic institutions, even as [he] uses them to legitimate [his] dominance, centralise power and crush or severely limit

---

[1] The team had an intensive consultation process with the research assistant and other interlocutors in the profession, as well as our colleagues. The research went through an extensive ethics review process at Massey University, New Zealand, including a full hearing with the ethics committee, which one of us attended, and received ethics clearance.

dissent' (Scoones et al. 2018, 3). When the post-Khmer Rouge state was formed under Vietnamese occupation in the 1980s, Hun Sen's Cambodian People's Party (CPP) maintained control by establishing tight surveillance at the village level that prevented resistance, and channelled resources through shifting, informal networks. In the 1990s, two democratic norms – regular elections and a free press – were mandated in the 1991 Paris Peace Agreement and enshrined in the Constitution. In the context of these donor-imposed conditions that facilitated the creation of the UN Transitional Authority in Cambodia (UNTAC), Hun Sen has faced a constant struggle to balance the closure of space for dissent with the need to legitimate his rule through maintaining elections and tolerating, to various degrees, a free press and civil society. This explains the 'pocket of openness' for the free press that is unusual in a region better known for media repression (Schultheis 2018). Press freedom was a cornerstone of the project to instil democracy in the 1990s: The UN created a model radio station, 'Radio UNTAC', to inform Cambodians in the lead-up to the first post-war elections in 1993, and the Japanese government financed the distribution of 346,000 radios throughout rural areas (McDaniel 2007; Strangio 2017).

Hun Sen's politics evolved into a populist authoritarianism in which the CPP combines surveillance and violent censorship with personalised political handouts, promises of post-war stability, and a veneer of democracy through elections and tolerating civil society institutions (Milne 2015; Schoenberger and Beban 2018). Hun Sen must also legitimise his rule to domestic voters through gift-giving practices in rural areas, practices which have grown to an elaborate system of mass patronage and mobilisation (Hughes 2006; Norén-Nilsson 2016). The result is that rural voters have historically been the most consistent supporters of Hun Sen's government. But this system of patronage also depends on profits from the extraction of rural resources. State officials and business elite are given access to lucrative contracts, such as Economic Land Concessions (ELCs), logging and mining licenses, in exchange for their loyalty, thereby remaking rural areas as 'sacrifice zones' (Scoones et al. 2018, 5) for the enrichment of the elite. Land grabbing has had devastating effects in rural areas; 1% of Cambodia's population is said to own as much as 30% of arable land (UNCDS, cited in Neef, Touch, and Chiengthong [2013, 1085], and more than 500,000 farmers have been displaced due to ELC expansion (Human Rights Watch 2013). For rural people who live near ELCs, constant surveillance and the threat of displacement is part of everyday life (Schoenberger and Beban 2018).

However, in the past decade, people struggling to hold onto their land have become more outspoken. From the mid-2000s, new trends in trans-local mobilising emerged, in which community activists organised into social movements with links to NGOs (Beban, So, and Un 2017) and international support networks (Baird 2017), and mobilised in mass marches to the capital city (Schoenberger 2017). Rural people also used the ballot box to express their resistance; in the 2013 National election, following a period of intense land grabbing that took off in the mid-2000s, the opposition gained enormous ground from both urban and rural voters. An uprising following the 2013 election made clear the delicacy of the state's balance of repression and patronage in the face of state elite's capture of rural resources (see Schoenberger, Beban, and Lamb 2018, 8–10 for more detail).

The importance of different forms of media for rural struggle has changed over time as these shifts in Cambodia's regime, alongside changing technology, transform the media landscape. Radio continues to be important for rural people because it is a low-cost medium that does not require literacy or to be connected to the electricity grid, and it can be carried anywhere. Before mid-2017, radio was the most fragmented, or freest, media, with a number of stations run by NGOs or overseas funders, and US government-funded *Radio Free Asia* (RFA) broadcast throughout the country on 15 different radio stations (MoM 2016; Strangio 2017). RFA is funded through a grant from the US Agency for Global Media, so while it is not strictly independent from government control, it has a legislative firewall that bars interference by US government officials, and our interviewees saw the broadcaster as an uncensored, accurate source of news[2].

The radio's role as source of information for isolated rural areas is connected with independent newspapers, as the newspaper scoops were regularly read out on radio. Two English-language newspapers were established during the 1990s: the *Phnom Penh Post*, founded in mid-1992, and *The Cambodia Daily*, in 1993. *The Daily* was established by a private NGO, World Assistance for Cambodia, funded by philanthropist Bernard Krisher. While these newspapers have a small circulation in rural areas (with the print edition reaching about 11% of the population, primarily in urban areas), *The Cambodia Daily* had a greater reach in rural areas because its news features were read out on *Radio Free Asia*, and its English edition, which include weekly language lessons, made it a popular resource for those studying English. Journalists we interviewed repeatedly noted that *The Daily* has a wide reach because 'even if people couldn't read *The Daily*, RFA would report on their stories' (Interviewee #1),[3] showing the ways these two formats combine to engender a culture of information that could transcend various limits on access, such as literacy, foreign language skills, or the availability of newsprint vendors.

The pocket of openness for non-state controlled media has become more constrained over the past decade, as increased reliance on Chinese assistance, which comes with fewer conditions tied to democratisation than Western aid, has reduced the need for the CPP to legitimate its rule through maintaining press openness. The ruling party stepped up press censorship in the wake of the June 2017 sub-national ('Commune') elections, when the CNRP shocked the ruling party by winning almost half the popular vote and gaining 482 commune seats, up from a mere 40 seats in the previous election (*The Cambodia Daily* 2017). *The Daily* and RFA became direct targets of repression. Amendments to the national media code facilitated the CPP's repression of oppositional politics by creating legal grounds for the CPP to shut down more than 30 independent radio stations as well as the long-running newspaper (RSF 2018). The information ministry invoked fear and self-censorship amongst the remaining media outlets by declaring on their website that the closures were 'a warning to all media' and that 'there is no condition that the revoked licenses can be renewed or reissued' (RSF 2018, 10).

As the CPP threaten and close media outlets, they have also bolstered their own propaganda machine on Facebook and through state-owned media. Almost all Khmer-language print and broadcast outlets are now aligned or sympathetic to the CPP and Hun Sen, and tend to project pro-government viewpoints (MoM 2016). TV news consists above all of official ceremonies, Prime Minister's speeches, and military parades

---

[2]However, these rationales were not necessarily widely accepted by Cambodian officials, as one interviewee explained, 'when I interviewed [senior CPP officials], they accused me of serving a foreign radio, the opposition party, or "rebel radio". They said that what we reported opposed the government, that the news was inaccurate and was more about supporting foreign interests and getting aid from the US'.

[3]Interviewees have been given numbered codes, shortened as '#X'. We use the gender neutral 'they' to contribute to maintaining anonymity of participants.

(MoM 2016). Journalists we interviewed critiqued the remaining news outlets that broadcast glowing spectacles of what 'his Excellency' does: 'His Excellency blah-blah-blah visits local people, gives some donations' (#15). This interviewee made the pointed case that rural people do not need to know about Excellencies, they need 'real information' that would help them with land struggles, such as 'how many trucks export wood, how many trucks are stopped and how many people are arrested. They do not want to know that His Excellency goes to build something' (#15).

New state media outlets are fostering Hun Sen's performative style of governing. The Chinese-backed government TV channel, 'Nice TV', for example, which launched in 2017 to great fanfare and generous funding, has as its mission 'covering security matters and national police operations' and 'praising government policy and law enforcement activities' (quoted in RSF 2018). The creation of such a channel in the wake of the media shutdown has the potential to reshape imaginaries and signal the foreclosure of the democratic project. In the place of a model of liberal peace as the endpoint for post-war transformation comes an authoritarian peace built on government control and stability and tied to imaginaries propelled by China and Russia (Barma 2016). We develop an understanding of the media as a space of emancipatory and authoritarian potential in rural Cambodia in the following sections.

Media, authoritarianism, and emancipation

The classical liberal theory of the press has at its core the idea that a free market ensures a free press with a diversity of views, owing allegiance only to the public and able to hold the country's rulers to account; an idea that has, as James Curran notes of the British press, 'been repeated so often it has acquired a seemingly unshakable authority' (2009, 326; see also Stockmann and Gallagher 2011). In post-conflict peacebuilding operations, the establishment of the free press (as a means to an end and an end in itself – an institution that both symbolises democracy and is expected to bring democracy about through holding leaders to account), has become a cornerstone of the liberal peacebuilding project. But continued violence in post-conflict countries has called into question the model of liberal peace, and scholars have grown more skeptical that the media alone could have such an effect (Richmond and Franks 2007; Heder 2012; Öjendal and Ou 2015; Barma 2016). Among a burgeoning literature critiquing the liberal peace, Richmond and Franks (2007, 30) argue that the liberal peace imaginary, or what he terms the 'virtual peace', is fundamentally flawed in its 'hubristic belief that once institutions are provided, populations will simultaneously adopt and benefit from them regardless of local characteristics, culture and priorities'. This critique reminds us that the 'free press' is always a goal – an imaginary to be strived toward. In reality, the press is subject to power plays, corporate lobbying, elite capture, monopolies and state repression (Curran 2009, 327).

Looking at the media – as space and as practice – draws attention to the work done to produce, enact, and imagine both enhanced structures of oppression and emancipatory potentials in ways that contribute to moving beyond normative language of the liberal/illiberal binary (Koch 2013). Contributors to a special issue in *Area* (45.4) argue that the labels of 'authoritarian' or 'illiberal' obscure spaces of openness and closure, and instead choose to use the term 'closed contexts' to focus on the nature of closure and coercion, and to allow for the variety of scales and places at which practices of closure unfold (Koch 2013, 390). Importantly,

> just as 'liberal' techniques of government can be used under despotic regimes, so too are there dubiously pervasive 'pockets' of despotism in many 'liberal' and 'democratic places' (Koch 2013, 392)

Print journalism, radio broadcasts, social media, and text messaging are places and scales at which neat binaries are disrupted in practice. Indeed, just as government technologies of openness and closure are strategically woven together (Belcher and Martin 2013), media institutions and activists are also strategically working to manipulate these spaces for their own ends. What emerges is not necessarily coherent government bodies 'bent on obscurity', but a wide range of situated practices that play out in daily practices (Belcher and Martin 2013).

The theoretical challenge, then, is to go beyond both overly celebratory assumptions of the media as a vehicle for democracy, or overly dire assumptions that the media is simply a tool of the state, to recognise the spaces in which the media can be a vehicle for emancipation and authoritarian closure. Scholars of social movements draw from resource mobilisation theory to show how in particular moments and places, movements are able to gather strength through accessing and manipulating resources, like money, people in government, or distinct pressure points, to communicate their messages (Della Porta and Mosca 2005; Eltantawy and Wiest 2011). But a national media that may be sympathetic to peasant struggle at one point in time may also work to de-legitimise the movement amongst a broad audience if the political situation changes (Teubal 2009). One way to understand how social movements and authoritarian states variously seek to use different forms of media for their own projects of rule and resistance is through media communications theory, which focusses on the relationships formed between media types and users, broadly characterising these as 'vertical' and 'horizontal' (Cardoso, Cunha, and Nascimento 2004; Castells 2007). Vertical relationships are those forms of communication between citizens and the 'center' (and vice versa) – such as rural social movements and the politicians in the capital city, as well as supporters and NGOs abroad – while horizontal relationships are the flows of communication that circulate within and between social movements and rural communities. This language is useful for recognising that media is a field of contestation, an 'agonistic arena' (Rahimi 2011), in which the regime and civil society struggle to gain and spread information and thus to control discourse.

Vertical information flows are critical to both rural social movements and governing authorities. In contexts like Cambodia where information is secretive and the state/corporate elites' roles in resource conflict are deliberately obscured (Schoenberger and Beban 2018), rural activists use the media to gain information, and to speak back to policy makers and to attract potential supporters. For authorities, the tolerance of a partially free press and limited public participation can enable states to demonstrate legitimacy as democracies, while also enabling authorities in urban areas to surveil rural communities and to know what is happening in the margins, particularly when local officials may choose to obscure on-the-ground realities (Mathews 2011; Lewis 2013). Strongman politicians also attempt to control public discourse through constructing their own propaganda in print and broadcast media and increasingly in the social media sphere to directly communicate their messages to the public, often engaging in theatrical politics that celebrates a direct connection between the leader and 'the people' – typically identified in nativist terms against a scapegoated 'other' (Lewis 2013; Gonda 2019; McCarthy 2019). State attempts to control information flows are evident in our interviews with frustrated journalists, who discussed the myriad practices state actors deploy to thwart reporting:

> We meet problems. The government officials do not provide us important documents. They do not want to give us documents because we don't have the law to access information. So, they have excuses for not providing them. And sometimes, we send a request letter and they just keep it somewhere. When we call them, they say they are busy… These kinds of issues keep happening. (#10)

This refusal to give documents was one of many stalling manoeuvres journalists talked about; they also noted officials who required written requests and made journalists wait weeks for permission to meet (#11) or simply hung up the phone when journalists introduced themselves (#4). One interviewee who asked the Chief of the Anti-Corruption Unit for a comment on a story was told, 'you should love your country'. Perhaps most illustrative of the relationship between the free press and governing officials prior to the shutdown is how one journalist summed it up: 'they criticized us, but, sometimes, they also talked to us' (#14).

In comparison with broadcast and print journalism, which are often shaped by vertical transmission facilitated by various institutions, horizontal communications can take many forms, such as covert rumours, face-to-face conversations and meetings, phone calls, collective action and social media groups and postings. These mediums are often thought of as less open to cooptation by authoritarian leaders, although recent trends around social media, like Russian troll farms and the Cambridge Analytica scandal with Facebook, are disrupting assumptions that enhanced internet access would subvert state control over information flows and national discourse (Castells 2007; Stockmann and Gallagher 2011).

Political communications theory enables scholars to understand how rural social movements seek to use the media in different ways to assist their struggle, and to ask what is the difference that difference makes when it comes to being rural. The stakes of the relationship with media are different for a group of people living in a remote land conflict area from those living in a dense urban environment. As Schuler and Truong (forthcoming) suggest, rural groups mobilising via social media may be subject to repression because dispersed populations are easier for state surveillance tools to identify. In comparison, in dense urban areas it is harder to pinpoint the trouble-maker and thus the risks are differently distributed. If rural people reach out to radio broadcasters for help to witness and take their voice to a broader audience, it puts rural activists one step removed from being personally responsible for any future fall-outs. For journalists, however, reporting in rural areas entailed a great deal of risk even before the shutdown, particularly for journalists working on environmental conflicts. Interviewees detailed instances in which they were threatened by government officials and police and arbitrarily detained,

> They chased us. They wanted to know – why are we here, why do we interview people. They harassed and threatened us … They did not allow us to take photos … So, we explained to them [our purpose] … we also wanted to interview [the police] but they said they did not know anything. (#3)

These types of interactions could get very heated:

> They showed me their guns and threatened to crash into me [on the road]. Sometimes they threatened to file a lawsuit against me. (#13)

The journalists said that these types of threats and restrictions of freedom of expression intensified in 2017. One interviewee explained:

> this year, media freedom and security of journalists decreased ... Now I think journalists are not friends or partners anymore with the authorities. They think that independent journalists are their enemy. (#7)

Other interviewees noted that their colleagues had resigned because they were threatened and their homes were surrounded by authorities. But many saw it as their duty to continue reporting, as another said: 'in the 2000s, some journalists were shot and killed ... and recently reporters were arrested ... I'm scared but as a journalist we follow our professionalism' (#8). The ways these journalists spoke of themselves as a perceived enemy, and of the existence of a 'black list' that contained the names of journalists, conjured an imaginary of the authoritarian state's surveillance powers as pervasive, subverting democratic space and potentials.

Journalism as democracy

The journalists' depictions of state violence remind us that we cannot romanticise the role of the press as ushering forth democracy, for this under-emphasises the possibilities for the press to be used for authoritarian ends. But nor is the free press simply a 'facade', 'a virtual front that defers local democracy ... for some mythical liberal future' (Richmond and Franks 2007, 45). For the Cambodian journalists we interviewed, the imaginary of press freedom was both something abstract that they strived towards and something they struggled to enact and translate into their everyday work. They saw independent journalism as a tool to encourage democratic ideas and practices (#13) as well as necessary for developing critical thinking skills and generating new ideas for both the population and governing authorities (#2). Journalists broke this down into clear principles:

> When they listened to RFA ... they will think when RFA talks to three sources. They will think about what the three sources are saying. RFA never judges who is right or wrong, but people can think by themselves. So this is how RFA educates people how to think. (#13)

Another journalist explained, 'democracy, it means that people should know everything, how the country is developing, what they should decide'. They said that during the commune council election, they found that people did not know who the candidates were or anything about their backgrounds, and weren't even able to recognise their faces, and they saw this as evidence of how the media is vital for basic democratic ideas and practices to function (#4).

Through everyday practice, the journalists held onto and widened small spaces of openness in risky circumstances. All fifteen interviewees stressed the importance they placed on including multiple voices, in particular the voices from both political parties, as a core principle of investigative journalism (#2). But these efforts to get two sides of the story in order to show objectivity were frequently thwarted, as members of the ruling party were reticent to speak to independent outlets; as one journalist noted, 'we give opportunity to both sides to comment, but if they don't comment we cannot force them' (#1). The journalists continued to struggle to enact democratic practices but they said it had become more difficult to uphold the journalistic standards they held onto, such as obtaining two viewpoints, in the wake of the 2017 crackdown:

> In the past years, it was easier to report because we had the opposition party and other political parties and analysts. If we could not reach one, we could reach someone else. It is very different now. There is no opposition party. If we want to get a comment to react to another comment, we don't have anyone. It is difficult to contact political analysts and economic analysts. It is difficult to find them for interviewing. (10)

As journalists described the period that the interviewee above terms the 'past years' prior to 2017, they articulated the roles they played in building democracy by forming vital connections with rural activist networks despite the regime's fluctuations between moments of openness and closure (Koch 2013). The most common theme journalists articulated was their role as *'messengers of the people'*. They described how media enables vertical relationships between rural people and the central government, acting as *'connectors'* and *'bridges'* between dispossessed villagers, local and national officials, and NGO staff, and conveying rural people's voices – 'voices that could not reach the public' (#2) – to policy makers by travelling to rural areas and conducting in-depth reporting. As one reporter said proudly, 'any places that people suffer from land dispute or burning houses, RFA went down there to report' (#13). These activities entailed great personal risk for journalists, particularly when covering issues such as land grabbing and illegal logging, and the journalists' described numerous stories of their work to navigate risks in the field in order to get the 'real news' out. One interviewee emphasised their refusal to bend to pressure as 'I only report real news. Real news is real news. Land grabbing is land grabbing. If they are logging, I report logging' (#13). Part of being a professional journalist, one said, was to 'report something that was buried in order to help society' (#11). In these stories, the journalists emphasised the difference that on-the-ground reporting can make to rural land struggles:

> I think that when we report on land dispute with powerful people and government officials, it will send a message to government leaders. Then they will know the matters of the people. So, it means that their resistance is hopeful when reported by media. If they do any action but no media reporting, it is not effective. When we report, the news will reach to authorities as well as the leaders and then they will find a solution. (#6)

In this quotation, the journalist suggests that media works to both bring hope to rural movements by reporting people's resistance, and that the vertical communication from rural areas to government leaders gives the central state information on what is occurring in rural areas and thus encourages solutions. This assumed causal link between reportage and solutions is difficult to prove (and seems dubious in cases in which central state actors are themselves implicated in rural land conflict), but all the journalists pointed to concrete cases of social policy change that they believed the government had introduced in response to media pressure. These included the provincial government stepping in to resolve problems between a rural community and an agribusiness concessionaire (#3), the cancellation of private fishing lots in the Tonle Sap Lake (#10), and the firing of a Secretary of State after a report on his corrupt actions (#2), among other concerns. While it is likely that these policy shifts were the result of multiple factors including timing and broader political pressure, the journalists emphasised these outcomes as the direct result of strong relationships between independent reporters working with rural people in risky, violent circumstances to make their voices heard.

The journalists' discussion of the repression and violence they were subjected to even before the crack-down in 2017 suggests that the crackdown was not a sudden plunge into 'darkness'. There never was a fully free press; rather, what had become 'dark' for these journalists when we talked with them in the aftermath of the state's crackdown was the imaginary of the free press, the *possibility* of this space. The 'darkness' which now befalls Cambodia, according to the journalists, is the closure of the possibility of democratic media, itself the symbol of the broader democracy.

Closures producing a 'dark space' for rural people

From the journalists' vantage point, the ruling party's closure of RFA and *The Cambodia Daily* in 2017 now left only a 'dark place' (#10). Rural people are left 'in the dark ... their voice is lost' because 'they don't know who they can ask to report all these real problems' (#13). The journalists said that in the wake of the crackdown, communities had lost their access to journalists that could travel to rural areas to help with awareness of rural struggles, and rural people were reluctant to go to the media themselves to publicise their struggles because they did not know who to trust. The journalists explained that rural people are now 'fearful ... and concerned for their safety and scared to speak to other reporters' (#9). Journalists also complained that the remaining government-controlled news is 'only fake news and twist news' (#2) that could not be trusted as it did not seek balanced sources. The pervasive theme that emerged was that 'the voices of land dispute communities will no longer reach the public' (#10).

Alongside the closing of space for rural people to make their struggles public, journalists also noted that the media closure made it difficult for rural people to access information. This need for information is crucial in Cambodia's political economy, where much state practice takes place in the secretive, murky realm of informal politico-business networks, and obfuscation and withholding information is one way that state elite maintain control over land and resources (Cock 2016). This lack of information made people 'angry', as one journalist explained,

> They want to know about politics and want to follow up Kem Sokha's arrest, dissolution of the opposition party, and illegal logging. ... victims of land disputes are very disappointed. (#8)

The journalist underlined this point, adding that, 'if the radio hadn't closed, they are more hopeful when they submit petitions'. In other words, rural people need information on the workings of corruption and natural resource extraction and broader trends of political oppression. In addition, this journalist echoed several other interviewees who stressed the material consequences of people lacking the information needed to make important livelihood decisions.

The extent of this loss can be better understood through the voices of rural people we spoke with prior to the shutdown, who spoke about how much they learned from the independent media. They said the radio helped them to understand what was going on around the country so that they could be better informed and potentially use this knowledge when they had their own land disputes. One farmer-activist explained, 'When we listen to RFA, we hear what is happening with the companies in Ratanakiri, in other parts ... [it] gives us ideas about what we can do.' People also echoed the journalists' notion that the print and broadcast media bring hope to people engaged in protracted land struggles:

> [The media] gives people bravery because they hear about other struggles, [and] we can know about other struggles. (farmer, 50s)

> Sometimes I get so mad when I listen to the radio, I want to throw it away. But we must not lose hope. Look at Thailand, they had to fight for 30 or 40 years. (farmer, 50s)

For these people, listening to the radio is an emotional experience that can induce anger as well as hope through the connections people make with other rural struggles and the knowledge that success is possible. Furthermore, the media is important not just because reporters go out into land conflict areas; rural people also use the media as a way to get their message out. Going to the RFA or *The Daily* is a strategy used frequently by community activists in land conflict areas, where local state officials are often not deemed trustworthy or helpful (and may in fact be working for the companies/political elite enacting land grabs), and NGOs may have a scarce presence. Rural activists tend to contact journalists based in Phnom Penh directly by phone, or by visiting them in local towns, and asking for their help. In a focus group at an activist's house, a community struggling to regain their land after being evicted said that contacting media, as well as NGOs and opposition party members, was a key part of their resistance strategy:

> People contacted the Cambodia Daily, the Phnom Penh Post ... A government channel covered it, but the TV of the government shares only 'good information'. The international sources like VoA and RFA share all the problems of villagers, they don't keep information like the others.

Another farmer-activist similarly told us:

> We went to the NGO but they couldn't help because it is the military [who grabbed the land], and people don't want to go to the opposition because then we are labelled opposition. And so we go to the radio RFA and their reporter was here last week. I talked with them and [a woman from the village active in the land protests] talked to them ... now we hope that something will happen, now we wait to see.

As this farmer notes, the role of the radio in providing information about land grabbing was particularly important in remote areas where the presence of NGOs is limited, or in cases where NGOs were reluctant to help. Throughout our research, we have found that it is often isolated communities who rely most on the media to act as an information source and a 'bridge' to make rural concerns public, because these communities may lack relationships with NGOs, and the distance and lack of resources makes it difficult for them to travel to urban areas themselves.

Social media and news online: Capturing spaces for emancipatory rural politics

Alongside the shutdown of traditional media, the Cambodian government has adapted swiftly to discursive contestation on the Internet, producing what MacKinnon (2011) has termed 'networked authoritarianism', a co-optation of Internet-based communication that mirrors the authoritarian state's ability to repress and co-opt other civil society spaces. Many journalists we interviewed talked about online spaces as another site of mounting state co-optation and repression. This disrupts global narratives about the emancipatory potential of the internet (Goldsmith and Wu 2006; Sinpeng 2013). Across the 15 journalists, all were highly critical of the emancipatory potential of social media. This caught our attention because online social media is an important space for Cambodian activists, and the internet is seen as one space that is difficult for the ruling party to close. In the 2000s, the opposition skilfully grabbed onto the opportunities provided by social media – which lies outside of state media licenses – combined with a raging market for discounted smartphones and cheap data plans that launched in the early 2010s. As cell phone ownership spreads to over 50% of the rural population, online news has quickly become Cambodian people's 'go-to' source of information (Meyn 2017). The lines between traditional press/broadcasters and online media are now blurred to some extent, as press outlets distribute their content via social media. Many Cambodians have turned to the online version of Radio Free Asia, followed by 4.7 million, and a growing number of citizen-journalists are starting to cover problems affecting their communities, especially in rural areas (RSF 2018).

But our interviewees suggested that an optimistic view of the emancipatory potential of social media is unwarranted, because much of social media is missing the journalistic integrity and trust that is a hallmark of the democratic spaces the journalists were struggling to build. While the RFA, for example, still has a presence online, the closure of the Cambodia office and arrests of its reporters has limited the broadcasters' ability to report in rural areas. The online space is a confusing proliferation of information. Journalists gave emotive descriptions of social media news as 'fake news' (#2), 'fast news' that is only half true (#5), and 'confusion news' that 'is difficult for people because they do not know which news is real and trustworthy' (#4). These sentiments are similar to analysis of Chinese state social media posts as 'strategic distraction' rather than genuine engagement (King, Pan, and Roberts 2017). The journalists' sense of social media as untrustworthy was juxtaposed with explanations of journalistic integrity and trust built through their everyday practices – the careful analysis of information with sources from different sides of the story that is missing in the 'fast', 'poisonous' social media landscape (#9). One journalist noted that social media platforms like Facebook don't have the resources or ability to break stories or generate scoops (#1) which limits the ability for rural people to use these spaces to share information or to hold officials accountable. Without some of the standard practices of professional journalism – a newsroom, editors, and sources – the information on social media was not at a high enough standard to be considered news for our interviewees:

> I think social media has more impact because some users like the pages of government officials, the prime minister, and party pages, and then they receive information. It is just information but not news. For the media, we collect all the information and then we analyze the information to make the news. (#8)

This journalist's notion of social media as a forum for 'information' but 'not news' points to a noted tendency for social media to act as an 'echo-chamber', where people with similar views gather together, rather than a space where contrary opinions are expressed (McCarthy 2018). On Facebook, the most popular social media platform in Cambodia, the content of newsfeeds are determined by the posts of friends and pages users choose to follow, which are reflective of pre-existing social networks (Schissler 2015). During the critical pre-election period in 2017, Facebook also instituted new algorithms in Cambodia that privileged friends and sponsored content rather than news and organisations' pages, which meant that the pages of independent media and organisations tended not to show up on people's feeds (RSF 2018).

Beyond the limitations of social media as a space for trusted information, the journalists also described how organisations and news websites that are struggling to enact democratic norms and build new spaces for sharing information are facing censorship and violent repression. Prior to the 2018 election, for example, the government blocked 17 independent websites, including RFA, VoA, *Phnom Penh Post*, and even Pinterest (Handley 2018). Government monitoring of social media means people perceive it to be dangerous to use Facebook or other social media to communicate. Reporters we spoke with noted that what people are willing to post has also been transformed:

> If anyone does not listen to [Hun Sen], or stand up against him, then he uses a trick to arrest people and put them in jail ... Local people, politicians, students, they used to give opinions on Facebook. Now they are more quiet because people do not dare to give their opinions on Facebook. They still do it, but they do not strongly criticize. They say things like: 'The government dissolved the opposition, it is not fair'. They don't say something strong like 'it's illegal'. (#15)

We realised the extent of online surveillance and its implication for imaginaries of authoritarianism and how this shapes everyday practices when one of us noticed that a rural activist friend was no longer on Facebook. She later explained that she and other land activists in her community had all deleted their Facebook accounts because they had been threatened with arrest for content they posted. 'It was after [political commentator] Kem Lay was murdered', she said, 'and there was a petition going around Facebook about it. The [government] said it was us that started it, but we didn't, we just shared it'. Other activists maintain a social media profile but say they have stopped posting anything political. In this context, where online surveillance is stepped up and offline gatherings have also been restricted, rural movements must constantly search for new forms of online communication that may not yet be under the surveillance of the state. This ranges from Facebook, to WhatsApp, and now to lesser known platforms that according to activists are more difficult to operate and not as trusted by rural people. Distrust and fear of potential state surveillance punctuated our discussions; although the activists did not know whether the government actually had the capability to monitor all messaging and online content, the spectre of the all-seeing state – what we might term the authoritarian imaginary – overshadowed the democratic potential of online spaces.

New state mouthpieces

The regime has not simply cracked down; the government is also co-opting social media to spread populist discourse. Hun Sen has ramped up the populist image of himself as the leader of 'the people', cultivating his online persona and co-opting social media spaces to bolster his legitimacy amongst the young urban population. Hun Sen's Facebook page has been 'liked' over 9 million times, although the Phnom Penh Post alleges that most come from paid 'click farms' abroad (Nass and Turton 2016). He regularly streams events and speeches live on Facebook, posts photos of himself talking with everyday people and posing with family, and has announced the creation of his own mobile app (Khoun 2016). One Cambodian researcher[4] recently called Hun Sen a 'Facebook Prime Minister', and the long-time opposition leader Sam Raimsy a 'Facebook opposition', battling to control online spaces through performative politics rather than coherent policies.

The government has also launched a pro-government online media outlet and smartphone app, called 'Fresh News', used to spread misinformation and entangle opposition officials in scandal. Since the launch of Fresh News in 2014 – the app media analysts dub the ruling party's 'digital communications arm' – it has spread to more than 2.5 million followers on its Facebook page and associated online sites (Meyn 2017; Fresh News 2018; Nachemson and Mech 2018). During the 2017 crackdown, Fresh News was the first media outlet to publish accusations against the opposition party and ran unsubstantiated articles alleging treasonous acts for weeks before the leader's arrest (Nachemson and Mech 2018). The Fresh News 'recipe' is to draw attention to problems in other countries in order to discredit the West and attack all forms of opposition. Beyond Fresh News, other social media including WhatsApp and Twitter were used prior to the election to spread pro-CPP propaganda and target thousands of voters who found themselves added to groups and text chains (Handley and Kong 2018).

Discussion and conclusion

The idea of an authoritarian peace – which focuses on economic growth and infrastructure without pushing for deep reforms – offers a contrast to the assumptions of the New World Order of the 1990s that envisaged a post-conflict, and post-Cold War, transition to liberal democracies (Barma 2016). This model, according to Barma (2016), defines peace as the reassertion of hierarchical state authority over territory, space, and resources. This outcome is achieved not only through military means, but also through the control of knowledge production and the channelling of economic resources through patronage networks. Significantly, the discourse of authoritarian peace is not limited to individual states, but circulates in sites of international diplomacy, in ways that increasingly challenge the global hegemony of liberal peace. The Cambodian case is suggestive of the ways in which a shift from a model forged in the liberal peace ideals can be transformed into one more aligned with authoritarian peace. The landslide victory of the ruling party in 2018, in the absence of an opposition party or a free press, was seen by one of our participants as indicating that

> the Khmer Rouge in the forest have disappeared, but they appear in Phnom Penh – they use the tactic of the Khmer Rouge. If anyone dares to criticize or say we don't like Prime Minister Hun Sen, they don't sue or file a complaint, they just arrest and send to court. (#15)[4]

This creep of authoritarian Khmer Rouge-like tactics into new spaces, new times, and new imaginaries, is what we have explored in this paper. Hun Sen's crackdown on political opposition and media shows that democratisation is not a predetermined linear pathway, but a process of shifting openings and closures that can just as easily slide deeper into authoritarianism.

Invoking political communication theory, which stresses the media's role in enabling information flows between the public and vertical information to and from the regime

---

[4]Ou Virak, presentation at the Entrenched Illiberalism conference, Australian National University, Canberra, April 9th, 2019.

and citizens, we showed that the media can have multidimensional effects for rural people. A free press can facilitate vertical communication between rural social movements and state actors, holding leaders accountable and enabling the voices of rural people to be heard, as well as spreading information within and between rural and urban communities. But authoritarian leaders also use the media to spread propaganda and control public discourse. Authoritarian regimes may tolerate a semi-autonomous media sphere to understand what is happening in rural communities, and to gain legitimacy with citizens and the international community. This space for media freedom is fragile. The Cambodian case showed that the regime turned to violent repression when public resistance swelled, and when the financial support of China legitimised greater coercion.

The media shutdown means that one key strategy for gathering information, getting messages out via trusted news sources, and holding authorities to account is lost. The Cambodian journalists we hear from in this paper illustrate another dimension of loss. These journalists' rich accounts of the forces reshaping their country are no longer on the front pages of newspapers in offices and on road side stalls, their voices are no longer heard by rural farmers who listen to the radio news 'as if it were music' (#13). For these journalists who see themselves as part of the project of liberal democracy in Cambodia, the 'darkness' of the current political moment is not only the material loss of the independent news outlets, but the loss of a democratic imaginary. The proliferation of state-affiliated media and social media alongside the repression of independent media outlets subverts the journalists' ability to enact democracy through their everyday journalistic practices. It is important to recognise, though, that the journalists' understanding of what quality journalism looks like and their commitment to democratic journalistic norms may also blind them to other projects working to create democratic spaces in rural areas that do not follow the same kinds of journalistic conventions. While the media shutdown has reduced the space for rural social movements to operate, it is not all darkness; rural people are still actively resisting land grabbing, and they are constantly innovating via online communications and offline strategies to undermine state surveillance and communicate across communities and movements.

In our turn to consider social media, our analysis emphasizes that a shift in Cambodia's authoritarian populism is taking shape online. As seen in the creation and use of *Fresh News*, the ruling party harnessed social media to enhance populist rhetoric while simultaneously repressing independent media and restricting the use of social media more generally in Cambodia in 2017-2018. This in many ways disrupts global narratives about the emancipatory potential of the internet. The trend in Cambodia, and across the region in Myanmar and Thailand, is a restriction of social media through a mix of libel suits, censorship, moral policing, and violence (Weiss 2014). At the same time, then, that social media is restricted for some, it is used to cultivate new forms of populism.

Throughout this paper, we aimed to highlight the voices of interviewees in their responses and assessments of the situation in Cambodia. It is important that these actors are not dismissed in narratives that depict Cambodia as inevitably headed to an authoritarian state with no political spaces to manoeuvre. Activists distributed throughout the Cambodian countryside, and their networks of engaged smallholding farmers, remain creative and dynamic in their organising. Journalists committed to democratic practices are now reconfiguring their livelihoods and practices to shape the future media landscape – even as they face violent challenges. Continued research is necessary to understand how these actors reassemble and re-shape their strategies.

Acknowledgments

We would like to thank the hard-working and dedicated RA in this project and all the professional journalists who shared their rich stories, knowledge, and energy with the research team. This research was made possible by an Emancipatory Rural Politics Initiative Small Grant and benefitted from feedback at the 2018 *International Conference Authoritarian Populism and the Rural World*. We would like to thank Wendy Wolford for her constructive feedback and the three anonymous reviewers for their comments.

Disclosure statement

No potential conflict of interest was reported by the authors.

Funding

This work was supported by Emancipatory Rural Politics Initiative Small Grant.

ORCID

Alice Beban http://orcid.org/0000-0001-9618-9669
Laura Schoenberger http://orcid.org/0000-0001-7781-9485
Vanessa Lamb http://orcid.org/0000-0003-1717-6777

References

Baird, I. 2017. "Resistance and Contingent Contestations to Large-Scale Land Concessions in Southern Laos and Northeastern Cambodia." *Land* 6 (16): 1–19.
Barma, N. H. 2016. *The Peacebuilding Puzzle*. Cambridge: Cambridge University Press.
Beban, A., and L. Schoenberger. 2019. "Fieldwork Undone: Knowing Cambodia's Land Grab through Affective Encounters." *Acme* 18 (1): 57–84.
Beban, A., S. So, and K. Un. 2017. "From Force to Legitimation: Rethinking Land Grabs in Cambodia." *Development and Change* 48 (3): 590–612.
Belcher, O., and L. L. Martin. 2013. "Ethnographies of Closed Doors: Conceptualising Openness and Closure in US Immigration and Military Institutions." *Area* 45 (4): 403–410.
Cardoso, G., C. Cunha, and S. Nascimento. 2004. "Ministers of Parliament and Information and Communication Technologies as a Means of Horizontal and Vertical Communication in Western Europe." *Information Polity* 9: 29–40.
Castells, M. 2007. "Communication, Power and Counter-Power in the Network Society." *International Journal of Communication* 1 (1): 1–15.
Cock, A. 2016. *Governing Cambodia's Forests: The International Politics of Policy Reform*. Singapore: NIAS Press.
Curran, J. 2009. "The Liberal Theory of Press Freedom." In *Power without Responsibility: The Press and Broadcasting in Britain*, edited by J. Curran, 326–340. London: Routledge.
Della Porta, D., and L. Mosca. 2005. "Global-net for Global Movements? A Network of Networks for a Movement of Movements." *Journal of Public Policy* 25 (1): 165–190.
Eltantawy, N., and J. Wiest. 2011. "Social Media in the Egyptian Revolution." *International Journal of Communication* 5: 1207–1224.
Fresh News. 2018. Fresh News Officially Launches Website. *Fresh News*, July 30. http://en.freshnewsasia.com/index.php/en/7495-2018-02-19-01-40-28.html.
Goldsmith, J., and T. Wu. 2006. *Who Controls the Internet? Illusions of the Borderless World*. Oxford: Oxford University Press.

Gonda, N. 2019. "Land Grabbing and the Making of an Authoritarian Populist Regime in Hungary." *The Journal of Peasant Studies* 46 (3): 1–20.

Goode, J. P. 2010. "Redefining Russia: Hybrid Regimes, Fieldwork, and Russian Politics." *Perspectives on Politics* 8: 1055–1075.

Handley, E. 2018. "Cambodia Blocks 17 Media Websites before Vote." *Al Jazeera News*, July 28. https://www.aljazeera.com/news/2018/07/cambodia-blocks-17-media-websites-vote-180728103300267.html.

Handley, E., and M. Kong. 2018. "When We Vote, We Expect Change." *Inside Story*, July 30. https://insidestory.org.au/when-we-vote-we-expect-change.

Heder, S. 2012. "Capitalist Transformation by Neither Liberal Democracy Nor Dictatorship." *Southeast Asian Affairs*, 103–115.

Hughes, C. 2006. "The Politics of Gifts: Tradition and Regimentation in Contemporary Cambodia." *Journal of Southeast Asian Studies* 37 (373): 469–489.

Human Rights Watch. 2013. *Cambodia: Land Titling Campaign Open to Abuse*. New York. https://www.hrw.org/news/2013/06/12/cambodia-land-titling-campaign-open-abuse.

Khoun, N. 2016. "Keeping up with Hun Sen? There's a New App for that." *The Cambodia Daily*, January 6. https://www.cambodiadaily.com/news/keeping-up-with-hun-sen-theres-a-new-app-for-that-104519/.

King, G., J. Pan, and M. Roberts. 2017. "How the Chinese Government Fabricates Social Media Posts for Strategic Distraction, not Engaged Argument." *American Political Science Review* 111 (3): 484–501.

Koch, N. 2013. "Introduction - Field Methods in 'Closed Contexts': Undertaking Research in Authoritarian States and Places." *Area* 45 (4): 390–395.

Koch, N., ed. 2019. *Spatializing Authoritarianism*. https://www.jiscmail.ac.uk/cgi-bin/webadmin?A2=CRIT-GEOG-FORUM;436a79be.1906.

Lamb, V., L. Schoenberger, C. Middleton, and B. Un. 2017. "Gendered Eviction, Protest and Recovery: A Feminist Political Ecology Engagement with Land Grabbing in Rural Cambodia." *The Journal of Peasant Studies* 44 (6): 1215–1234.

Lewis, D. 2013. "Civil Society and the Authoritarian State: Cooperation, Contestation and Discourse." *Journal of Civil Society* 9 (3): 325–340.

MacKinnon, R. 2011. "Liberation Technology: China's Networked Authoritarianism." *Journal of Democracy* 22 (2): 32–46.

Mathews, A. 2011. *Instituting Nature: Authority, Expertise, and Power in Mexican Forests*. Cambridge: MIT Press.

McCarthy, G. 2018. "Cyber-spaces." In *Routledge Handbook of Contemporary Myanmar*, edited by A. Simpson, N. Farrelly, and I. Holliday, 117–130. London: Routledge.

McCarthy, J. 2019. "Authoritarianism, Populism, and the Environment: Comparative Experiences, Insights, and Perspectives." *Annals of the American Association of Geographers* 109 (2): 301–313.

McDaniel, D. 2007. "An Awakening in Cambodia." In *Negotiating Democracy: Media Transformations in Emerging Democracies*, edited by I. A. Blankson, and P. D. Murphy, 77–97. New York: State University of New York Press.

Meyn, C. 2017. "The Fresh Prince of Cambodian Media." *Southeast Asia Globe*, June. https://southeastasiaglobe.com/cambodia-fresh-news/.

Milne, S. 2015. "Cambodia's Unofficial Regime of Extraction: Illicit Logging in the Shadow of Transnational Governance and Investment." *Critical Asian Studies* 47 (2): 200–228.

MoM. 2016. *Who Owns the Media in Cambodia?* Phnom Penh: Media Ownership Monitor, Cambodian Center for Independent Media, Reporters without Borders. http://cambodia.mom-rsf.org/en/.

Nachemson, A., and D. Mech. 2018. "Analysts say Government use of Fresh News Fits the Authoritarian Playbook." *The Phnom Penh Post*, October 25. https://www.phnompenhpost.com/national-post-depth-politics/analysts-say-government-use-fresh-news-fits-authoritarian-playbook.

Nass, D., and S. Turton. 2016. "Only 20 Percent of PM's Recent Facebook 'Likes' from Cambodia." *The Phnom Penh Post*, March 9. https://www.phnompenhpost.com/national/only-20-cent-pms-recent-facebook-likes-cambodia.

Neef, A., S. Touch, and J. Chiengthong. 2013. "The Politics and Ethics of Land Concessions in Rural Cambodia." *Journal of Agricultural and Environmental Ethics* 26 (6): 1085–1103.

Norén-Nilsson, A. 2016. "Good Gifts, Bad Gifts, and Rights: Cambodian Popular Perceptions and the 2013 Elections." *Pacific Affairs* 89 (4): 795–815.

Öjendal, J., and S. Ou. 2015. "The 'Local Turn' Saving Liberal Peacebuilding? Unpacking Virtual Peace in Cambodia." *Third World Quarterly* 36 (5): 929–949.

Rahimi, B. 2011. "The Agonistic Social Media: Cyberspace in the Formation of Dissent and Consolidation of State Power in Postelection Iran." *The Communication Review* 14 (3): 158–178.

Richmond, O., and J. Franks. 2007. "Liberal Hubris? Virtual Peace in Cambodia." *Security Dialogue* 38 (1): 27–48.

RSF. 2018. *Cambodia: The Independent Press in Ruins*. Phnom Penh: Reporters without Borders.

Schissler, M. 2015. "New Technologies, Established Practices: Developing Narratives of Muslim threat in Myanmar." In *Islam and the State in Myanmar: Muslim–Buddhist Relations and the Politics of Belonging*, edited by M. Crouch. Oxford: Oxford University Press. https://www.academia.edu/9587031/New_Technologies_Established_Practices_Developing_Narratives_of_Muslim_Threat_in_Myanmar.

Schoenberger, L. 2017. "Struggling Against Excuses: Winning Back Land in Cambodia." *The Journal of Peasant Studies* 44 (4): 870–890.

Schoenberger, L., and A. Beban. 2018. "'They Turn Us into Criminals': Embodiments of Fear in Cambodian Land Grabbing." *Annals of the American Association of Geographers* 108 (5): 1338–1353.

Schoenberger, L., A. Beban, and V. Lamb. 2018. *Authoritarian Rule Shedding its Populist Skin: How Loss of Independent Media in the 2017 Crackdown Shapes Rural Politics in Cambodia* (ERPI No. 70). The Hague. https://www.tni.org/en/publication/authoritarian-rule-shedding-its-populist-skin-how-loss-of-independent-media-in-the-2017.

Schuler, P., and M. Truong. forthcoming. "Connected Countryside: The Inhibiting Effect of Social Media on Rural Social Movements." *Comparative Politics*.

Schultheis, E. 2018. Cambodia Eviscerates its Free Press—And the Whole Region Suffers. *The Atlantic*, July 28.

Scoones, I., M. Edelman, J. Borras, R. Hall, W. Wolford, and B. White. 2018. "Emancipatory Rural Politics: Confronting Authoritarian Populism." *The Journal of Peasant Studies* 45 (1): 1–20.

Sinpeng, A. 2013. "State Repression in Cyberspace: The Case of Thailand." *Asian Politics & Policy* 5 (3): 421–440.

Sombath. 2017. My Testimony on the Shutdown of the Cambodia Daily. *Khmao Blog*, 3 September. https://kmaoblog.wordpress.com/2017/09/03/my-testimony-on-the-shutdown-of-the-cambodia-daily.

Stockmann, D., and M. E. Gallagher. 2011. "Remote Control: How the Media Sustain Authoritarian Rule in China." *Comparative Political Studies* 44 (4): 436–467.

Strangio, S. 2017. "The media in Cambodia." In *The Handbook of Contemporary Cambodia*, edited by K. Brickell, and S. Springer, 76–86. New York: Routledge.

Teubal, M. 2009. "Agrarian Reform and Social Movements in the Age of Globalization: Latin America at the Dawn of the Twenty-First Century." *Latin American Perspectives*, 36, 9–20.

Weiss, M. 2014. "New Media, New Activism: Trends and Trajectories in Malaysia, Singapore and Indonesia." *International Development Planning Review* 36 (1): 6–24.

Confronting agrarian authoritarianism: dynamics of resistance to PROSAVANA in Mozambique

Boaventura Monjane and Natacha Bruna

ABSTRACT
This paper explores how varying degrees of authoritarianism and populism, although not always coinciding, have been intrinsic to the imposition of agrarian policies in Mozambique. Taking the case of ProSAVANA, a highly controversial agrarian development program, we look at how its undemocratic imposition by the state has given rise to a vigorous resistance movement. By tracing a decade of electoral results in selected districts where ProSAVANA is intended to be implemented, we argue that due to its agrarian authoritarian policies which have had negative implications on rural livelihoods, the ruling party, FRELIMO, has recently been losing popularity to the strongest opposition party RENAMO.

1. Introduction

Authoritarianism and undemocratic forms of imposing policies and measures on rural and peasant populations were a norm in colonial and post-colonial Mozambique. This contributed, consequently, to the recurring failures to grasp the nature of the agrarian question[1] in Mozambique in the context of changing regimes from central planning to market-based development policies (Wuyts 2001). Soon after independence in 1975, Mozambique's dominant political party, *Frente de Libertação de Moçambique* – Mozambique Liberation Front (FRELIMO), exhibited undemocratic, and to some extent populist, characteristics with regards to implementing agrarian policies. In the current neoliberal period, however, FRELIMO's regime has come to clearly exercise varying and decreasing degrees of populism combined with authoritarianism when it comes to choosing and imposing agrarian policies. The Triangular Co-operation Programme for Agricultural Development of the Tropical Savannah in Mozambique Project (hereafter referred to as ProSAVANA), is one concrete example.

---

[1]The agrarian question approached in this paper goes in line with the classic definition provided by Byres (1991, 9) where the continuing existence of poverty – and its political consequences – in the country side alongside with substantive obstacles to generate economic development both inside and outside agriculture.

DOI: 10.4324/9781003162353-14

ProSAVANA was first introduced in the beginning of the 2010s, as a developmental project in line with the main agrarian policy of Mozambique, the *Plano Estratégico para o Desenvolvimento do Sector Agrário* (PEDSA – Strategic Plan for the Development of the Agrarian Sector), which aimed to transform the agricultural sector to be more investment and business-friendly (RM 2011). To this end, the main objective of ProSAVANA has been to increase agricultural productivity, targeting 11 million hectares in north-central Mozambique, targeting areas in Niassa, Nampula and Zambézia provinces, a region known as the Nacala Corridor. Importantly, ProSAVANA was initiated and implemented by the Mozambican Ministry of Agriculture and Food Security (MASA), the Brazilian Cooperation Agency (ABC) and the Japan International Cooperation Agency (JICA).

Public disclosure of the Master Plan quickly sparked resistance. This was largely due to the apparent lack of transparency and inclusivity in the planning process, and the apprehension coming from knowledge of the negative impacts of PRODECER, a large scale agricultural development project in Brazil, in the late 70's of the last century (we develop more on PRODECER later). The emergence of a transnational campaign, called '*Campanha não ao ProSAVANA* – No to ProSAVANA Campaign' (hereafter referred to as NPC), came to be central to the resistance process. NPC presented an organized and explicit contestation to not only the ProSAVANA project itself, but the fundamental paradigm of rural development promoted by the project. Parallel to the constitution of the campaign and the resistance movement, FRELIMO was losing electoral support in the region where ProSAVANA is due to be implemented, the Nacala Corridor. The NPC, while demanding the discontinuation of ProSAVANA, also proposed alternatives to rural and agricultural development. This effort not only led to the current 'hibernation' of the project but created space to enable expanded participation of peasants and civil society throughout the decision-making process.

1.1. Key questions and structure of the paper

This paper analyses the process and dynamics of resistance to ProSAVANA as a way of confronting authoritarian imposition of agrarian policies in Mozambique. The main objective is to explore how the varying political regimes and their varying degrees of populism and authoritarianism contribute to the triggering of resistance, particularly looking at how and why the NPC was able to 'succeed' in hibernating ProSAVANA. The paper gives an explanation on how a combination of five elements, in the right timing regarding FRELIMO's popularity and support, were strategically determinant in putting the program on hold: (1) political reactions from below, (2) intersectoral civil society alliance, (3) communication, outreach and media strategy, (4) transnationalization of the struggle, and (5) the proposal of alternatives to dominant narratives. Although these five tactics were strategically executed, opponents of ProSAVANA were sharp in maximizing the existing generalized rural discontent. The decrease in rural votes for FRELIMO across the Nacala Corridor was not an accident, but a result of FRELIMO's strategy and policies on rural development as the paper demonstrates further.

The paper is organized into five main sections. Following Section 1, the Introduction, Section 2 briefly approaches the conceptualization of authoritarianism and populism, and its relation to Mozambique. This section also explores the presence of authoritarianism throughout the inception and early implementation of ProSAVANA. Section 3 examines ProSAVANA: what are its main goals, its components, deficiencies as well as contradictions. Section 4 directly addresses how ProSAVANA was confronted, highlighting the role of the National Peasant Union (UNAC) in the NPC. Lastly, Section 5 has concluding remarks.

1.2. Methods and methodology

This paper is based on data collected from a combination of methods during fieldwork conducted intermittently between 2014 and 2018 in the capital city of Maputo, and in the provinces of Nampula and Zambézia. Unstructured (open) and semi-structured interviews were conducted throughout and directed to multiple stakeholders, such as peasants, peasant union representatives, organizations affiliated with NPC, government officials at district and province levels and ProSAVANA representatives at the provincial level.

Additionally, participant observation was conducted, including participating in public hearings both at district and national levels, visiting ProSAVANA's pilot-projects sites and participating in meetings with the Mozambican civil society at the international, national, provincial and district levels. Lastly, analysis of secondary sources on ProSAVANA – both officially and un-officially (leaked) disclosed documents, public statements and government strategies – was held. Such activities were reinforced by extensive first-hand foundational knowledge by one author who had worked as a staff member of UNAC between 2009 and 2015.

The qualitative primary data was processed through transcription of the interviews and field notes. The body of empirical data was then analyzed using process tracing in order to trace the links between possible causes and observed outcomes (Bennett and George 2005). Validation of preliminary conclusions was conducted in September to November 2018, where the authors discussed their main findings with NPC members.

Table 1. Percentage of total votes per district (elections of 2008 and 2018).

Votes per region		FRELIMO			RENAMO		
Province	District	2008	2013	2018	2008	2013	2018
Niassa	Lichinga	75	66	51	23	n/a	45
	Cuamba	77	70	39	16	n/a	53
	Marrupa	95	91	71	4	n/a	18
Nampula	Nampula City	69	44	32	28	n/a	59
	Ribaue	87	72	46	11	n/a	42
	Monapo	62	70	47	37	n/a	46
Zambézia	Quelimane City	55	33	36	43	n/a	59
	Alto Molocue	67	53	48	31	n/a	47
	Mocuba	73	52	50	24	n/a	45

Notes: In 2013 Renamo boycotted the municipal elections; contestation of electoral processes and previous results were among the different reasons presented by the party leader Afonso Dhlakama.
Source: Comissão Nacional de Eleições (2018) and WLSA Moçambique (2014).

2. Authoritarianism, populism and coercive rural policies in Mozambique

The discussion about authoritarian populism emerged from Poulantzas' discussions on 'authoritarian statism', which was defined as the increase of state control regarding every aspect of economic life, accompanied by a decrease in democracy (Hall 1980). Hall took the concept one step further, identifying 'the set of operations designed to bind or construct a popular consent into these new forms of statist authoritarianism' (Hall 1980, 161), terming it 'authoritarian populism'. The concept emerged from a reflection on the construction of popular consent 'by a historical bloc seeking hegemony, as to harness to its support some popular discontents, neutralize the opposing forces, disaggregate the opposition and really incorporate some strategic elements of popular opinion into its own hegemonic project' (Hall 1985, 118).

Scoones et al. (2017) reintroduced and further explored the concepts of 'populism' and the rising worldwide phenomenon of 'authoritarian populism' within current contexts in the countryside. Nevertheless, in Southern Africa, populism is generally associated with liberation movements that secured political power as governments, using populist stand as a means to legitimize their power by appealing to the continued struggle against foreign domination and thereby marketing themselves as the only true political alternative. When contested politically, they accuse opponents of being remote-controlled agents of imperialism seeking regime change as instruments of foreign agendas (Melber 2018).

Populism is largely a reaction to social dislocations tied to processes of neoliberal globalization (Hadiz and Chryssogelos 2017). What seem to be a common ground among political and state elites in the region is the push for neoliberal agendas in various sectors applying populist strategy and at times authoritarianism. There has been an increase in reactionary politics in some societal sectors in the region, to promote neoliberal neoclassic values and visions. ProSAVANA, as we argue, fits in this trend. If on the one hand ProSAVANA was imposed authoritatively, resistance to it took, in part, progressive populist forms. Some would contest the term 'populist' when referring to progressive approaches and instead use 'popular' (Shivji 2019).

Borras (2019, 3) furthers the discussion of Scoones et al. (2017) by defining populism as 'the deliberate political act of aggregating disparate and even competing and contradictory class and group interests and demands into a relatively homogenized voice, i.e. "us, the people", against an "adversarial them" for tactical or strategic political purposes'.

Borras (2019) distinguishes populism into two types: a right-wing populism, the one that has disdain for democratic institutions, and a more progressive type of populism, namely agrarian populism. Although he uses the term 'right-wing populism' as a proxy for authoritarian populism, he still questions the more fitting term to this concept among the ones used. He conceptualizes agrarian populism as the political bundling of anti-capitalist rurally-based or rural-oriented social groups advocating for a peasant way of alternative development.

Most notably, Borras (2019) describes that the crucial point of analysis is not whether a specific regime is populist or not, but the degree to which the regime is populist. In other words, to what extent is a regime, regardless of its authoritarian nature, populist. It can therefore be conjectured that a regime dynamically oscillates between varying degrees of populism and a persistent high level of authoritarianism throughout time. Evidence of this dynamic can be clearly observed through careful analysis of the historical trajectories characterizing rural Mozambique.

O'Laughlin (1996, 5) summarized post-independence strategies of agrarian transition in three phases:

> The first phase, from 1975 to 1980, was defined by broad-ranging political consensus around the need for a rapid socialization of production and residence through the expansion of state-farms, co-operatives, and communal villages. The second highly contradictory phase, from 1980 to 1983, was defined by FRELIMO's shift to a bureaucratic and hierarchical model of rapid socialist accumulation based almost exclusively in state farms. Goods starvation in rural areas, the stagnation of state farm production, and widening support for the RENAMO opposition movement from South Africa (amongst others) led to a rapid expansion of both the war and parallel markets in rural areas. FRELIMO's strategy in the third phase, beginning with the Fourth FRELIMO Party Congress in 1983, was initially defined as market socialism, but moved rapidly towards increased support for private commercial farming, and the distribution of some state farm land to multinational enterprises, Mozambican commercial farmers and some peasant households.

The first phase referred to by O'Laughlin (1996) is parallel to FRELIMO's rise as the protagonist of the national liberation from colonial rule, as its name itself portrays ('Frente de Libertação Nacional' – National Liberation Front). They showed themselves as the symbol of national resistance, as revolutionary and a savior of the people, winning back the control of the country for the Mozambican people. FRELIMO was represented in the national anthem as 'the guide of Mozambican people' and portrayed, in the 1975 constitution, as 'the leading force of the State and Society'. Additionally, the presence of a charismatic and visionary leader, namely Samora Moisés Machel who served as the first president after independence, who believed in socialist principles, leading the discourse on social change and justice was essential in the attempt to build a positive image for FRELIMO.

Authoritarianism and undemocratic forms of imposing policies and measures taken on rural and peasant populations were a norm in colonial Mozambique. Soon after independence in 1975, some of FRELIMO's agrarian policies exhibited undemocratic characteristics. For example, from a historical perspective, we can refer to the agrarian policies implemented by the revolutionary government of the People's Republic of Mozambique, FRELIMO, namely the *aldeamentos comunais* (villagization) or the communal village policy, which took similar measures as *aldeamentos coloniais*, the colonial villages.

Established in 1968, the colonial villages were believed to have been created as a mechanism to monitor and control rural populations, mostly to avoid contact with FRELIMO, the national revolutionary forces at the time (Coelho 1998). The colonial villages were

> (…) based on a preventive philosophy, sought to bring people together in villages that would enable social progress and, at the same time, avoid contact with subversion, so that they would not be 'contaminated'. (Garcia 2001, 130)

On the other hand, FRELIMO's communal villages aimed to organize a dispersed peasantry in the form of villages. This, however, was also understood as a measure taken to control the peasantry, preventing the population from gaining access to and receiving influence from the *Resistência Nacional de Moçambique* (RENAMO), the anti-FRELIMO government guerrilla group. Assuring FRELIMO to maintain hegemony over the peasantry.

There is a consensus among scholars on the idea that implementation of the communal village policy was directly inspired by the colonial villages (Coelho 1998; Garcia 2001; Lourenço 2010; Monjane 2016a). The majority of communal villages were simply conversions of the old colonial village settlements. Vitor Lourenço (2010) demonstrates how the colonial Portuguese settlements along the main road connecting Mandlacaze and Panda districts in southeastern Mozambique, were simply renamed, with few organizational modifications, when converted into communal villages (2010, 178). FRELIMO was equally criticized as being 'interventionist, authoritarian, and coercive for engaging in projects that belittled customary African practices, forcibly relocating people, or threatening the livelihoods of the peasantry' (Pitcher 2012, 19).

FRELIMO and Samora's discourse was explicitly critical of colonialism, and later on, of the emerging opposition movement (RENAMO). These political discourses consistently included divisive narratives of 'us' against 'them', in which the 'other' changed faces from colonialism to the scourge of colonialism, in the form of 'armed bandits', the RENAMO. Scoones et al. (2017) point out that authoritarian populism is based in depicting politics as a struggle between the people and 'others'. In this case, it would be FRELIMO against colonialism, or FRELIMO against RENAMO. This was the foundation for the construction of FRELIMO's authoritarism and populism. In this context, Mosca (2005, 137) stated that 'Overall, FRELIMO structured society and power based in an authoritarian one-party system, with an ideology that combined populist and orthodox leftist features'.

Going back to O'Laughlin (1996), the third phase was characterized by a process of massive privatization, in the name of economic rehabilitation, supported by the Bretton Woods Institutions. This was represented by the emergence of a market economy in Mozambique, in what was now called a 'democratic' society. The societal acceptance of FRELIMO as the nation's rescuer, sustained through the stigmatization of those who are against it, helped to maintain FRELIMO's populism both in rural and urban areas. Although it has been the ruling party since independence, RENAMO has been systematically contesting and questioning election outcomes, occasionally succeeding in proving irregularities in the processes. Nevertheless, the enduring legitimization of FRELIMO's dominance was a clear feature of authoritarian populism (Hall 1985; Scoones et al. 2017).

We expand our analysis and include the current processes of forced displacement of rural populations (specially the peasantry) from their areas of residence and cultivation to resettlement zones (*reassentamentos*) as a continued state policy of coercive, and therefore authoritarian and undemocratic, regrouping of rural populations in Mozambique (Monjane 2016b).

Throughout history, FRELIMO showed patterns of an authoritarian populist party with relatively high support in the countryside of some provinces due to its role as the revolutionary force and savior of the people. Nevertheless, in the current neoliberal period, we understand FRELIMO's regime as exercising a combination of dynamically changing expressions of populism and persistent presence of authoritarianism when it comes to selecting and imposing agrarian policies.

3. Authoritarism in pushing market-oriented agricultural development: the imposition of ProSAVANA[2]

Nowadays, FRELIMO does not always have the supportive base to exercise its populist character. In reality, Frelimo's popularity has been falling throughout the years. Two main reasons might partially explain the decadence of this very important strategy of the dominant political party in the last decades: (1) colonialism per se is no longer an issue and RENAMO no longer represents a 'threat' to the well-being of the people, which results in the inexistence of a powerful external/internal enemy in the discourses as there is no longer a clear 'other' to blame for[3]; (2) the emergence of a intense feeling of frustration and discontent after decades of authoritarian agrarian policies, adopted and implemented by the government, resulted in land conflicts between capital and the peasantry, localized intensification of poverty and political and military instability; consequently, different segments of the rural and urban population no longer feel represented nor identify themselves with FRELIMO's claims and discourses.

So, Table 1 shows the patterns of electoral votes and the reflection of a loss of popularity by the dominant political party in selected regions. To understand the fall of FRELIMO's popularity, we chose to analyze the results from the most recent elections (municipal elections of 2018) which shows the most recent picture of the manifestation of 'revolt' at the ballot box. The 2008 and 2013 elections happened in a period of time in which the penetration of capital in rural areas started to have major implications – especially related to land grabbing to accommodate resource extraction such as Vale de Moçambique and the whole complex of multinationals investing in coal extraction in Tete province since 2009. So, the ratio Investment/GDP shows an increasing tendency from 2008 to 2018, with a maximum registered in 2014 when total investment represented 55% of the GDP (Instituto Nacional de Estatística 2018). At the national level, the agriculture sector as well as in the 'mineral resources and energy' sector hosted the highest amounts of approved investment in cumulative terms, from 2001 to 2017 (CPI 2017). At the provincial level, investment trends show that Nampula is the second province in the country with the highest amount of approved investment inflow from 2001 to 2017, with cumulative investment of more than 9 billion USD (CPI 2017).

In the table below, we only put forward provinces that were targeted by ProSAVANA. Within each province, we selected three main districts, including the capital of the province, and two essentially rural districts. Additionally, we considered the size of the population (chose most populated areas) and areas in which ProSAVANA's activity/investment/resistance have taken place; but, of course, limited by the availability of data regarding the selected period of election.

As mentioned previously, land conflicts that arose as a result of capital penetration in the countryside were a major issue of contestation within the rural population. The imposition of land-based agricultural investments in specific regions of the country resulted in the expropriation of people's land, especially throughout these three provinces. A number of companies expropriated hundreds of thousands of hectares from local peasants and

---

[2]Detailed analysis of ProSAVANA's discourses, objectives and Master Plan Zero can be explored in the following papers: Funada-Classen (2013a, 2013b), Clements and Fernandes (2013) and Mosca and Bruna (2015).
[3]However, Frelimo Government has been targeting confrontational civil society organizations, throwing unfounded accusation that they serve obscure interests and are external agents.

consequently, a lot of people were displaced. In Zambézia province, Gurué district, by 2017, Portucel Mozambique had occupied the land of more than 2,000 households; in the same district, Hoyo Hoyo expropriated the land of about 800 families (Mandamule and Bruna 2017); in Wakua (in the border area between Nampula and Zambézia) Agribusiness de Moçambique SA, Agromoz, forced the displacement of approximately 1,000 families (Mandamule and Bruna 2017); in Malema district (Nampula province) Mozambique Agricultural Corporation, Mozaco, also forced the displacement of about 1,000 families (UNAC and GRAIN 2015).

In the same period, debates around the implementation of ProSAVANA emerged. The imposition of ProSAVANA as the most important policy for the Nacala Corridor initiated in the 2010s. As previously mentioned, ProSAVANA was drafted, initiated and implemented in a top-down manner. Guidelines, strategies and specific activities were mostly defined by the Ministry of Agriculture (led by José Pacheco, the Minister at the time), along with its Brazilian and Japanese partners, the Brazilian Cooperation Agency (ABC) and the Japan International Cooperation Agency (JICA). Preparatory activities were already taking place even before the Master Plan was published, without the information provided or consultation with the population of people who are to be directly and indirectly affected.

> The ProSAVANA programme, from the beginning, was neither conceived together with the local inhabitants nor was there interest in meeting local needs. Instead, this project was conceived as a way for Japan and Brazil to: work together for achieving UN reform, participate in the new global political/economic structures such as BRICS and G20, and jointly promote commodity production/extraction. (Funada-Classen 2013b, 3)

Despite the Mozambican legislation (specifically the Land Law 19/1997, Decree 31/2012 of resettlements and Law of access to information 34/2014) clearly stating the need for public consultation and consent throughout the process of planning and implementation of any projects requiring the use of land,[4] It was only after public protests and political pressure calling for a more inclusive and transparent process from Mozambican, Brazilian and Japanese civil society that JICA and the Mozambican Government decided to engage in public hearings and consultations throughout the whole target region.

A joint statement published by Civil Society Organizations (Comboni Missionaries 2015), which participated in such public hearings, described the authoritarian character of ProSAVANA's implementation process very clearly. Issues brought up included the belated announcements of the date, time and location for the public hearings, citing an incident when only a couple of weeks' notice was given. This compromised people's access to information, which directly lead to limiting the presence of stakeholders at the hearings. Another issue was how the public hearing process did not cover all of the targeted regions in ProSAVANA. Where public hearings were held, the time was mostly spent on announcements, rather than on open discussion. The hearings predominantly focused on optimistic representations of ProSAVANA, without any mention of social, economic or environmental risks. Questions raised by the public were not fully answered. And

---

[4]For specific cases of acquiring land, community consultations are the first step to be taken. These community consultations or hearings are a legislated form of public participation that ought to be conducted before the implementation of a project or investment as a way to get the 'community' sensibility regarding the plan of investment and consent regarding the use of land (No 3, Article 13 of Land Law 19/1997). In case of reaching community consent to transfer the land to the investor/project, four public consultations are needed to plan and implement the resettlement process of the people who agreed to transfer their land (Article 23 of Decree 31/2012 of Resettlements).

lastly, the presence of an armed policeman in the room suggested the potential to suppress any divergent opinions or positions.

These findings are corroborated by Mosca and Bruna (2015) who report on a public hearing for ProSAVANA that took place on the 12th June in 2015 in Maputo. This gathering was moderated by the then Minister of Agriculture himself, who clearly stated how 'all of the interventions during the debate must be "patriotic". Do not come here with obscurantist agendas'. He further goes on to state his firm commitment for the mission, by stating 'If there is any obstacle, we will run over it and move on with our mission' (Moçambique para todos 2015; Monjane 2015; Mosca and Bruna 2015, 25–26). Mosca and Bruna further highlighted the under-representation of peasants in the meetings and the dominant presence of public workers such as teachers, nurses and the police. Moreover, they report on the accounts of people who were threatened after protesting or showing opposition to the ideas presented in the public hearing (Mosca and Bruna 2015).

As we argue in this paper, ProSAVANA was introduced with a great degree of authoritarianism and sometimes with elements of populism. We demonstrate further that the strategy of its opposition had visible characteristics of agrarian populism.

3.1. What is ProSAVANA?

ProSAVANA's stated aims are to boost agricultural and rural development, targeting an area covering approximately 13% of the country and 17% of the total population. The area is referred to as the Nacala Development Corridor,[5] which lies in a uniquely fertile region, also famous for its endowment of mineral resources. The region also includes the deepest sea port in East Africa, strategically located to allow easy access to Asian markets. This government-led program follows most of the guidelines recorded in Mozambique's Strategic Plan for the Development of the Agrarian Sector (PEDSA). The first drafts of ProSAVANA's Master Plan were written by consultants and experts from JICA, Brazilian Agricultural Research Corporation (Embrapa), FGV and the Mozambican Institute of Agricultural Research (IIAM).

Shankland and Gonçalves (2016), Funada-Classen (2013a), among others assume that ProSAVANA was initially inspired by PRODECER, a Japanese-Brazilian Cooperation Program for the Development of the Cerrado of Brazil. The program began with a joint statement to establish a relationship between the two countries on agricultural development, signed by then Japanese Prime Minister, Kakuei Tanaka, and then President of Brazil, Ernesto Geisel, in September 1974 (Inocêncio 2010). Official project documents regarding ProSAVANA commonly emphasize the biophysical and geographic similarities between the Cerrado and Nacala Corridor as well as their position as centers of economic and political power. Wolford and Nehring (2015), however, emphasize the differences between the two nations, highlighting key differences in the commodification processes of land and labor with relation to capital.

The Mozambican civil society only heard of ProSAVANA after Brazilian media reported on Mozambique giving away extensive farm land for Brazilian soy production (Mello 2011),

---

[5]Connecting Malawi, Zambia and Mozambique up to Nacala Port, located on the coast of the Indian Ocean (approximately 700 km), the Nacala Corridor is one of the six logistic corridors assigned for the implementation of PEDSA and the target for the implementation of ProSAVANA (MASA 2015).

drawing reference to 'Brazil's successful experience'. Detailed information about the project was only revealed to the public after a draft copy of the ProSAVANA Master Plan was leaked in 2013. In a joint statement, a group of Mozambican and foreign civil society groups denounced the project, stating that it 'confirms that the governments of Japan, Brazil and Mozambique are secretly paving the way for a massive land grab in Northern Mozambique' (Justiça Ambiental et al 2013, 1).

An official unclassified powerpoint presentation from the Joint Coordination Committee (JCC) of ProSAVANA was also revealed to Mozambican civil society. Some points highlighted included 'Land Reserve for Investment' and 'Development of Agribusiness' (JCC 2012). Moreover, potential infrastructure development of the Nacala Development Corridor included the renewal of the Nacala Port – the country's deepest port – and the Nacala Railway. The leaked documents confirmed that the main goal of ProSAVANA was to prioritize agribusinesses, promote monocrop production and exports of cash crops (such as soy). Furthermore, all of the activities targeting small to medium scale farmers were related to financialization schemes, which JCC (2012) called 'financial support systems', directly associated with their ability to hold land titles.

3.2. Components of ProSAVANA

The official document of ProSAVANA, namely 'Master Plan Zero' was published by MASA (Ministry of Agriculture and Food Security) in March 2015. Included are three components: (1) ProSAVANA – PD (*Plano Director* or Master Plan) that introduces the main guidelines through which the overall agricultural sector would be improved and modernized, (2) ProSAVANA PI (*Projecto de Investigação* – Research Project) which refers to the intensification of research and technology transfer, and (3) the ProSAVANA PEM (Models of Extension Project) that aims to improve extension activities (MASA 2015).

Under ProSAVANA 'fast impact' pilot projects, some medium to small-scale private companies and peasant associations received credit inflows to develop activities that answered to ProSAVANA's Master Plan guidelines. One of the investing companies, in an attempt to implement the financed project in the Ribaué District, encountered several families that were already established in the area. The area included houses and plots that had been there for more than 10 years; consequently, a land conflict emerged. Even though Article 12 of the Land Law confirms that the land in question belonged to the rural households (since they have been living on those plots for more than 10 years), they were displaced. This process resulted in the expropriation of land, and a loss of houses and cultivated plots.

According to the Director of the Institute of Agrarian Research in Nampula Province,[6] the main activities carried out under ProSAVANA PI included research related to cultivation systems and transfer of technology, testing and introduction of varieties, institutional training, and soil improvement. However, the main target was to introduce and spread the production of soy, in order to feed Mozambique's chicken value chain. In other words, a lot of effort was put into the production of a crop that was not going to directly benefit the local economy nor the diet. Even if it were available, households were not familiar with the crop, nor did they have the knowledge or the means to process it into food.

---

[6]Interview, Director of the Institute of Agrarian Research in Nampula Province, April 2015.

In relation to ProSAVANA PEM, during fieldwork activities, the authors identified and visited two peasant associations (Maria da Luz Guebuza and Namuáli) that received financial support in order to receive a motor pump. While it was intended to be shared, since the machine was too heavy to carry from one location to the other, only one association, the bigger one, got the opportunity to use and benefit from the pump. What resulted was the poorest association ending up with nothing but a debt.

3.3. ProSAVANA deficiencies, contradictions and the Nacala fund

ProSAVANA's Master Plan is far from comprehensive, beginning with the incomplete explanation of their financial resources. The initial discussions regarding the cooperation between Brazil, Japan and Mozambique in the Nacala Corridor required the creation of the Nacala Fund. According to Fundação Getulio Vargas (FVG),[7] the institution which was supposed to manage this fund (specifically in the FVG Projects branch), this was an initiative from FGV, ABC, JICA, Embrapa, FAO, Chamber of Commerce and Industry Brazil-Mozambique, Mozambican Ministry of Agriculture, and 4I. GREEN.

According to FGV, the main objective of the fund was to finance projects that stimulate agricultural development in the Nacala Corridor (FGV 2012), including ProSAVANA. However, throughout the implementation of ProSAVANA pilot-projects and even after the program's hibernation period, it was never made clear how FVG was managing and applying for funds, much less what FVG was planning to do with it in the future. Nevertheless, the Master Plan presents a very brief summary of a preliminary ProSAVANA budget of 9.371.000.000,00 Meticais (or USD133.871.430,00 using an average current exchange rate of 70Mts/USD) (MASA 2015).

The Nacala Fund issue suddenly vanished from official discourses and documents on ProSAVANA after being criticized by civil society for being the main financing vehicle for the big agribusiness projects in the Nacala Corridor. It was revealed that the fund would be registered in the fiscal paradise of Luxembourg (Justiça Ambiental, et al. 2013, 2–3). A ProSAVANA representative in Nampula said however that the idea of the Nacala Fund was introduced by a third party, external to the main ProSAVANA initiatives.[8]

After resistance, there were significant changes in a later version of the Master Plan Zero of 2015. This version attempted to be more inclusive, for example, through the use of 'agroecological' language, mentioning local markets and small to medium scale models of agriculture. Regardless, the response from civil society emphasized how, fundamentally, the text maintained its vision to promote businesses, maintaining the same outlook. This can clearly be inferred from the fact that the revised Master Plan Zero of 2015 did not mention a mechanism for securing land use and access for peasants in the proposed areas.

Mosca and Bruna (2015) further identify gaps in ProSAVANA's Master Plan Zero of 2015: they include (1) not providing resettlement processes or mechanisms to assure that it can be conducted in a fair and sustainable manner while maintaining or improving the quality of lives in communities; (2) not being clear about its environmental, social and economic impacts; (3) being overly optimistic about the capacity of the Government to effectively

---

[7]FVG is a private higher education institute which, according to their mission, aims to develop and disseminate knowledge in the field of public and private businesses.
[8]Interview with Américo Uacequete, Nampula, February 2017.

support a program of this dimension; (4) predicting a fall in the overall contribution of the agricultural sector to the regional GDP (from 42% in 2011 to 24% in 2035), while forecasting an increase in the mineral sector; (5) not reflecting the needs, priorities and aspirations of the peasants; and (6) ignoring possible conflicts between the traditional models and systems of agricultural production and the model presented by ProSAVANA.

In sum, it is clear that the initial effort to implement ProSAVANA has been one that distinctly supports the expropriation of land, the intensification of debt among peasants, and the promotion of crops that do not meet the people's needs. In other words, ProSAVANA's model does not respect customary rights. It marginalizes the needs and aspirations of the peasant and rural populations. As a result, the project fosters higher levels of vulnerability in communities, furthering conflicts and a deepening levels of poverty and food insecurity. This stems from a complete deviation from constitutional rights, land legislation and the constitutional principle of legal pluralism, which states that customary laws should be respected.

Beginning with the lack of transparency and limited participation throughout the entire planning process, combined with the model of development and the guidelines proposed in the Master Plan, ProSAVANA was a wake-up call for the Mozambican National Peasant Union. It resulted in civil society groups of Mozambique, Brazil and Japan joining efforts to initiate and articulate a resistance, based on apprehension for serious social, economic and environmental impacts, mainly surrounding land expropriation of peasants. Such concerns resulted in the formation of the *Campanha Não ao ProSavana* 'No to ProSAVANA Campaign' or NPC.

4. Confronting agrarian authoritarianism

4.1. The rise of the 'no to ProSAVANA campaign': an agrarian 'populist' confrontation

Before the launching of the NPC, there were a number of noteworthy actions taken by civil society organizations, led by the National Peasant's Union (*União Nacional de Camponeses*) or UNAC. Perhaps, the most significant was an open letter addressed to the governments of Brazil, Japan and Mozambique, sent in in May 2013. The letter protested the lack of an inclusive and transparent public discussion concerning ProSAVANA's environmental, social and economic impacts (UNAC et al 2013). The letter was signed by 23 Mozambican organizations and supported by 43 international organizations. The prolonged silence of the three governments following the letter was what triggered the formation of the NPC a year later.

The NPC was launched in June 2014, initially with nine-member organizations: UNAC; the Rural Association for Mutual Aid (ORAM); the Mozambican Human Right League; *Fórum Mulher* and World March of Women; *Justiça Ambiental* (Environmental Justice); *Livaningo;* Academic Action for the Development of Rural Communities (*Acção Académica para o Desenvolvimento das Comunidades Rurais*, ADECRU); Archdiocesan Commission for Justice and Peace of Nampula (*Comissão Arquidiocesana de Justiça e Paz de Nampula*); and lastly, gained strong support from the Mozambique Bar Association (*Ordem dos Advogados de Moçambique*). NPC's main objective was clear: To disable and terminate all ongoing activities and projects related to the ProSAVANA program (ADECRU 2014).

In a statement read during the launching of the NPC, the proponents stated the nefarious and devastating impact that this program would potentially bring to thousands of peasant families residing in the Nacala Corridor. It was added that ProSavana does not represent a solution for Mozambican agriculture, but is simply a solution to meet Japan and Brazilian soy needs (ADECRU 2014). In an interview with the authors, the Director of UNAC stated:

> Firstly, we heard about it (ProSAVANA) through the newspaper Folha de São Paulo that talked about the Minister's intervention regarding the perspective of the development of a program in Nacala Corridor, which had already been developed in Brazil ... This raised some questions among us. For us, the Nacala Corridor is the corridor for food production and supply for the entire area ... and we realize that with the implementation of ProSAVANA, we are going to have serious issues. So, we asked that a group (UNAC and ORAM) go to Brazil to investigate this type of development model. The information received was that it is not worth it.[9]

The uniqueness of the NPC was the assemblage of groups working on diverse issues: agrarianism, gender and feminism, human rights and legalism, environmentalism, faith and academic, unifying in order to defend a particular agrarian cause.

The NPC kept on incorporating more members from diversified sectors within Mozambique, but then started to extend their alliance to the Brazil Agrarian Movements and NGOs, as well as Japanese activists and academics. The campaign soon became a transnational movement.

As JICA was intensifying its support for ProSAVANA, in 2017, members of the NPC sent an open letter to its President, demanding an immediate suspension of JICAS's actions in ProSAVANA. In addition, they called for a revision of JICA's approaches, an acknowledgement of their mistakes, and compensation to repair the damages already caused to victims of the program in Mozambican society (Monjane 2017).

4.2. Actions, strategies and fragmentation

The NPC's strategy has consisted of an overt and organized contestation of specific projects mandating a model of rural development. The actions were specifically targeted at the Mozambican government (Ministry of Agriculture, later Ministry of Agriculture and Food Security), alongside advocacy targeting the Japanese and Brazilian governments.

Public strategic meetings, such as the 'Triangular Peoples Conferences', the most recent in November 2018 in Japan, were held.[10] Some of the actions included occupying public spaces (such as holding protests) and issuing statements and open letters to be used as materials for recurrent tactics. UNAC members in Nampula and Zambézia provinces strategically mobilized citizens to oppose ProSAVANA through regular field visits and meetings with the peasantry living in these provinces.

As the proponents of ProSAVANA continued to face resistance, tactics were used to fragment and isolate opposition. This was done through a voting system which consisted

---

[9]Interview, Luís Muchanga, Director of UNAC, member of NPS campaign, 30 August 2018.
[10]So far, four Triangular Peoples Conferences were held, the first three in Maputo, Mozambique. These conferences bring together peasants (UNAC members) from Nampula, Zambézia, Niassa and Cabo Delgado provinces, activists from NPC member organisations, members of government (i.e, the Ministry of Agriculture himself), academics and members of the press.

of asking which organizations were open to working on revising ProSAVANA PD (Chichava 2016).

This eventually resulted in the fragmentation of Mozambican civil society into two factions: the pro- and anti-ProSAVANA. Those who support the vision of the Master Plan organized themselves into the *Mecanismo de Coordenação da Sociedade Civil para o Desenvolvimento do Corredor de Nacala* (Civil Society Coordination Mechanism for the Development of the Nacala Corridor), or MCSC-CN. The MCSC-CN has since been officially recognized by MASA as its legitimate interlocutor in issues regarding ProSAVANA. This was justified by the fact that most of the MCSC-CN members are based, or are working in, Nampula and Zambézia provinces. MCSC-CN has not integrated local UNAC (at the district and provincial levels) unions.

The other faction are those in the NPC, who have raised critical questions concerning the contradictions inherent in the Master Plan and the model of agricultural development it is predicated on. Their modes of outreach have been through the release of statements in Mozambique media, and holding regular strategy meetings. Apart from activists from the regular participating members, there was the participation of the President and Vice-President of UNAC and a former vice-president of Zambézia Peasant Union.

In the next section, we go over UNAC's foundational roots and principles, paying particular attention to the dynamics of its instrumental participation in the opposition and resistance to ProSAVANA.

4.3. The role of the national peasant union (UNAC)

4.3.1. Roots and constituency

When Mozambique was moving into a market economy through the adoption of IMF and the World Bank programs, peasants in various parts of Mozambique feared a possible disappearance of already established farmers cooperatives. This initiated the national movement to defend the interest of the peasantry.[11] UNAC wanted to represent the voice of peasants, speaking out in defense of their social, economic and political interests, upholding a vision to attain sustainable development, promoting both qualitative and quantitative approaches to self-organization (Article 4, UNAC Constitution).

At the beginning of their establishment in 1987, one of UNAC's top priorities was the political organization and establishment of leaders within the member associations. This was based on the conviction that, in order for a national peasant movement to be politically strong, it should be politically trained.[12]

The relevance of UNAC is recognized starting with its considerable number of members (more than 100,000, according to the accounts announced in its last Electoral Assembly, in 2016), placing it as the largest organized social movement in Mozambique. UNAC is recognized as the organization that officially speaks on behalf of the peasantry in Mozambique. This is regardless of whether those represented by it are actually affiliated to UNAC as members.[13] Hence, the Mozambican Ministry of Agriculture necessarily considers UNAC as their strategic partner (MASA, website 2018).

---

[11]Interview, Ismael Oussemane, honorary president and co-founder of UNAC. March, 2017.
[12]Interview, Ismael Oussemane, honorary president and co-founder of UNAC. March, 2017.
[13]This statement was confirmed on several occasions by government officials themselves, when speaking in meetings with UNAC.

Historically, the first popular organizations in Mozambique, i.e. of women, youth, workers and teachers, were initiated by FRELIMO. It is, therefore, significant that UNAC was one of the few organizations that formed outside the strict boundaries of FRELIMO (Negrão 2002; Monjane 2016). As a national movement, UNAC membership was strongly influenced by the political undercurrents of rural Mozambique. When UNAC was first established, RENAMO supporters dominated rural areas in central and northern regions of Mozambique. On the other hand, those in the southern regions strongly supported FRELIMO. The north's aversion to FRELIMO's policies may have been a key factor preventing FRELIMO from controlling the peasant movement.

UNAC could be seen as the microcosm of the peasantry in Mozambique: diverse, complex and clearly divided politically. Historically the peasantry was at the center of disputes in Mozambique: between the colonial regime and the liberation movement (liberation war); between the state forces and the RENAMO guerrilla (civil war); and today between FRELIMO and RENAMO parties (electoral battles). As Table 1 shows, it is mostly in the countryside where we observe significant fluidity in electoral support between FRELIMO and RENAMO. Differences in political views within UNAC are therefore so evident that it was decided that debates of a political-partisan nature within the movement have to be avoided in order to avoid fragmentation (interview, Ismael Oussemane, 2017).

4.3.2. UNAC and ProSAVANA

At the beginning, UNAC attempted to be intimate with the then Ministry of Agriculture and ProSAVANA officials. This tactic, however, did not succeed in influencing the Government's decisions. Luís Muchanga, the current Director of UNAC, described the initial interactions:

> There was some authoritarianism then, and it was felt in several ways; even in conferences, we (UNAC and the Government) had some clashes, and there were threats, even to the previous President of UNAC ... maybe because there is the assumption that civil society is against the Government, and if the person disagrees with me, even if it is a good idea, there is a blockage, just because it is divergent.[14]

The first UNAC official statement on ProSAVANA was issued in October 2012, after a meeting held in Nampula, which aimed at discussing and analyzing ProSAVANA. It was strongly critical of the program, stating 'we strongly condemn any initiative that calls for the resettlement of communities and expropriation of peasants' land, in order to give way to mega agricultural projects for monocultural production' (UNAC 2012). The statement emphasized that the Provincial UNAC Unions of Nampula, Zambézia, Niassa and Cabo Delgado were skeptical about ProSAVANA. Their statement posed that opposing ProSAVANA was a decision of 'all members of the National Union of Peasants' (UNAC 2012).

It was only later, however, that the movement truly started to engage with its membership base on ProSAVANA, starting mainly with the leaders of district and provincial unions. This implies that the official UNAC position on ProSAVANA was not necessarily reflective of all of its members' deep understanding of the issue. This was evidenced by the lack of

---

[14]Interview, Luís Muchanga, Director President of UNAC, member of NPC, 30 August 2018.

consistency in opinions given regarding ProSAVANA among UNAC members. While the leadership of UNAC provincial unions in Nampula and Zambézia were consistent in their oppositions against ProSAVANA, at the individual level, there were some emerging opinions in favor of it.

Literature on social movements and peasant agency suggests that there is often a distance between movements and their base (Edelman 2017). This can, to some extent, be the case of UNAC, regarding ProSAVANA. It is worth noting, however, that people strongly questioning ProSAVANA at public hearings and consultations were not limited to peasants who are aligned with UNAC and NPC. This shows that opposition to ProSAVANA has been actually wider and beyond the scope of the known actors.

Nonetheless, the participation of UNAC and its leadership role in the opposition to ProSAVANA was essential in giving legitimacy to NPC, even after the fragmentation of civil society into two opposing groups. After a recently held meeting in March 2019, which was convened by the current minister of MASA to reach consensus among civil society and de-hibernate ProSAVANA, both NPC and UNAC (in a separate statement) released statements reiterating their opposing position.

4.4. Key strategies of NPC that resulted in the stagnation of ProSAVANA

The stagnation of ProSAVANA can be explained from a combination of tactics intrinsic to the NPC. We developed these into five elements: (1) active agency from below, (2) inter-sector civil society alliance, (3) communication, publicity and media strategy, (4) transnationalization of the struggle and (5) proposal of alternatives confronting dominant narratives. These elements are considered against a backdrop of external factors which include the political and economic environment within Mozambique and in the external investor countries. We do not claim this set of strategies, some of them mere activities, to be a formula to guarantee 'success' in resisting agrarian authoritarianism. The goal is to show in detail what ProSAVANA opponents have done, in terms of actions and activities, to hibernate it, which is relevant enough to the understanding of the outcome of the resistance process, particularly in the case of Mozambique.

4.4.1. Active agency from below

The debate about the various political reactions from below towards land grabbing, initiated by Borras and Franco (2013), directly relates to the resistance processes regarding the ProSAVANA case. This was the unique factor that quickly brought strength and legitimacy to the opposition of ProSAVANA; and it framed the determination of UNAC to lead the process of resistance. Peasant protests, however, were not limited to UNAC members. This was exemplified during the Mutuale public hearing which took place in Malema District, Nampula Province. A peasant protested against the implementation of ProSAVANA (ADECRU 2015):

> We, in Mutuale, do not want ProSAVANA because this program does not represent the interests of the peasants. We know that with this program, we will lose our land. We know that the peasants will be forced to go ask for land in other places as it is happening now with the people who were expelled from their land when the AGROMOZ company entered, in the Gurué District, Administrative Post of Lioma. Today, those people left there are coming to

ask for places to live here in Mutuale. We do not want to go asking for land in other communities because this will later bring conflict between us

With no satisfactory response from the proponents of ProSAVANA, peasants decided to walkout of the meeting. This was because peasants from this particular area were previously exposed and had access to information translated into their local language in the form of videos and leaflets, which helped them to clearly understand the risks, which shaped their opinions about ProSAVANA.

When asked why he is saying no to ProSAVANA, a peasant member of UNAC, from Muecate district in Nampula province, responded with the following:

> ... from the information that we had access to, regarding Prodecer in Brazil and its impacts, they tried to take away Brazilian peasant's land, and now those projects are being transferred to Mozambique ... Being a less developed country compared to Brazil, we think that we cannot accept that project, one day it will harm us. They occupy extensive areas, so we don't have enough space to do our *machambas* [family farm land], this was one reason to say no to ProSAVANA. We have the capacity to work, but they cannot come and harm us in our life, that lead us to say no to ProSAVANA and we will continue to say so.[15]

Such statements are reflective of UNAC having taken the lead and released a statement of concern at an early stage, allowed political reactions from below to take emerge. Very quickly, local associations, district and provincial unions of UNAC were mobilized. This crippled the efforts for the proponents of ProSAVANA, including local government, to convince the peasantry of its 'benefits'. This strong position of UNAC and peasants on the ground, however, did not quite overcome the authoritarian position of the Mozambican Government. The government remained unphased by protests. This, however, contributed to the extend efforts to cooperate between different sectors of society.

4.4.2. Inter-sector civil society alliance and segregated processes of resistance

The segregation of struggles and movements has been very common among Mozambique civil society groups and has long contributed to the segregated processes of resistance and focus of social change among social movements and activists. Historically, urban-based struggles have had little dialogue with rural-based struggles. Trade unions have had little dialogue with peasant/agrarian organizations. Similarly, advocates of women and gender issues have had very little dialogue with those working on housing, transportation, and environmental issues.

The first notable exception was the Land Campaign (*Campanha Terra*), which was one of the few active inter-sectoral groups to build an advocacy and debate platform to include popular views and defend the interest of the peasantry in the 1997 Land Law. At the beginning, the Land Campaign was not coordinated. According to Negrão (2002, 18) 'there were fundamental concerns covering a wide spectrum of layers and groups of social interests,' bringing together 'churches, associations and cooperatives, non-governmental organizations, academics, politicians and even elements in the private sector, in addition to dozens of incognito honest citizens'. Once the 1997 Land Law was passed, the Land Campaign declined. Nevertheless, the issue of land, particularly losing land for capital grab in Mozambique remained a compelling issue for mobilization.

---

[15]Interview, peasant Member of UNAC Nampula, District of Muecate, February 2017.

Following the Land Campaign, different sectors of the Mozambican civil society created synergies that fed the growth and legitimacy of the fight for environmental, land, agrarian and gender issues as one big and cohesive cause. Following this trend, NPC has arguably been one of the most innovative and effective alliance among different constituencies, which paved the way for ProSAVANA to be perceived as an important national issue, garnering public interest.

This demonstrates that land is a highly sensitive and potent issue in Mozambique. Defending it is associated with people's sovereignty, and losing it triggers memories of colonialism and vulnerability. This makes the agrarian question in Mozambique transversal to many other national concerns. It is important to note that many academics and civil society organizations, including members of parliament, not associated with NPC, also publicly presented critical assessments of ProSAVANA's Master Plan, its discourse and how the program itself was problematically being introduced.

4.4.3. Communication, publicity and media strategy

One of the main strengths of NPC can be attributed to the designing of an effective communication and media strategy. The use of online communication channels, from websites and blogs to social media, as well as local newspapers, has been a dominant tactic. The campaign would publish on a regular basis, and openly disclosed statements, testimonies, articles, videos and images (photos and infographic material) highlighting resistance to ProSAVANA, exposing its negative social and environmental issues. This can be attributed to the extensive communication and media experience held by NPC members, providing effective access to tools and existing networks to disseminate information.

The NPC publications were shared amongst the websites managed by the various participating members not only in Mozambique, but in Brazil and Japan. Social media was also actively utilized, where links to the publications and key messages were shared on the campaign's facebook page, which had more than one thousand followers as of January 2018.[16] Additionally, campaign materials were quickly republished through other media outlet websites, including media organizations such as Pambazuka News (2016). NPS media strategy included getting the issue into local and international mainstream media. As a result, leading international newspapers, such as The Guardian (2014), Neues Deutschland (2018) and Deutsche Welle (2017), published stories mentioning the resistance to ProSAVANA.

4.4.4. Transnationalization of the struggle and solidarity mobilization

The involvement of Brazil and Japan's social movements/civil society in ProSAVANA resistance inspired international solidarity. Almost all of the main Brazilian agrarian movements associate with La Via Campesina Brazil, and a number of progressive NGOs, such as GRAIN, and progressive intellectuals in Japan were supporting the Campaign. Since 2014, a number of activities – such as 'lobbying' meetings in Brazil – have been carried out in their respective countries, as a strategy to put pressure on EMBRAPA in Brazil and JICA in Japan and, wherever possible, to identify allies inside those institutions. This was particularly effective in Japan, where their lobbying and advocacy actions at the parliament level resulted in a strong alliance between Japanese organizations and a left-wing

---

[16]The facebook page was opened in 2016.

parliamentarian who pushed for fierce debates on ProSAVANA. It was through this alliance that ProSAVANA was strongly debated at Japanese parliament.

Institutional impacts in Brazil have been harder to monitor. What is noteworthy, however, is the progressive decline of Brazil's institutional involvement in the current developments of the program. Contributing factors may be the political and economic events that have taken place during the last three years, namely the deepening economic crisis, the impeachment of President Dilma Rousseff, and the election of a right-wing government that openly announced shifting its foreign policy to focus on the Global North.

Regardless, a defining factor is how some Mozambican organizations in NPC have been active members of some of the largest and most radical transnational social movements in the world. In particular, UNAC is a member of La Via Campesina, Fórum Mulher is a member of, and hosting, the World March of Women, and Justiça Ambiental is a member of Friends of the Earth International. With its established global network, these movements are known for their capacity to mobilize global solidarity, attract media attention, and give global visibility to local struggles.

4.4.5. Alternative proposals confronting dominant narratives

UNAC has been credited for establishing a constructive form of resistance led by the people, contesting the model of development proposed in ProSAVANA with a clear proposition of an alternative on the table. To this end, agroecology, as a strategy, has guided UNAC's agenda since the design of its 2011–2015 Strategic Plan.

> We remain firmly committed to peasant farming and agroecology – the foundations of Food Sovereignty – as alternatives to the development of the agricultural sector in Mozambique, which consider all aspects of sustainability and are, in practice, friends to nature. (UNAC 2012)

In its current 2015–2020 Strategic Plan, agroecology is mentioned under the 'Advocating Peasant's Rights' pillar of the plan in which UNAC assumes agroecology as the main mechanism through which food sovereignty is going to be achieved in Mozambique. In almost all statements of NPC, it is made clear that rejecting ProSAVANA was not just an end in itself. Proposals such as Agroecology and Food Sovereignty were given as practical alternatives to what ProSAVANA proposed, which were based on agribusiness, monoculture, land reserves, global markets, and intensified production. In recent years, UNAC has actively been engaging its members in specific educational and training programs on agroecology. Furthermore, the movement has been successful in building an Agroecology School in the Manhiça District (South of Mozambique) and training rural extensionists in agroecology throughout the country (three promoters per province who conduct trainings at the village level). For example, in the Marracuene District, 285 peasants were trained on agroecology as a pilot project. Lastly, exchanging visits and experiences between peasant associations have also been influential in the promotion of alternative narratives of development.[17]

Another experience worth highlighting is the Alfredo Nhamitete Agricultural Association, in the district of Marracuene, Maputo province. Their 280 members produce various food crops, some of which they sell at the local market. Income is shared equally among members (LVC Africa News 2014). Several peasants began an exchange

---

[17]Interview, Renaldo João, peasant member of UNAC, 4 September 2018.

with a peasant organization in Brazil, the Small Farmers Movement (MPA), to rescue seeds that are at risk of extinction, which are deemed to be of greater importance for food sovereignty. This exchange led to increased local seed sovereignty, drastically reducing the cost of seed procurement.

The growing number of peasants at the national level who are practicing agroecology and challenging the large-scale capitalist farming model, like ProSAVANA, should be seen as emancipatory. This combination of words followed by action has given strength to NPC.

4.4.6. External factors: political and global economic environment

A number of factors that were out of the control of the movement and the resistance actors could have directly or indirectly contributed to the strength of the resistance process. At the national level, the rising disapproval of the local government, due to overlapping crises, can be seen as the emergent localized ruptures with the authoritarian populist FRELIMO regime, especially in the areas where ProSAVANA is to be implemented. On an international scale, the political climate, both in Brazil and Japan, should be considered as a potential factor in the stagnation of the program. Additionally, the trends of commodity prices should be analyzed in order to fully understand the behavior of potential investors for ProSAVANA. Although it is difficult to have a comprehensive analysis of how these factors might have influenced the stagnation of ProSAVANA, the important points are summarized.

4.4.6.1. Overlapping crises and the rise of localized government unpopularity.

The process of discussion and resistance to ProSavana was characterized by a parallel emergence of political and military crises that consequently contributed to the escalation of the economic crisis in Mozambique. These events derived from a combination of micro and macro issues of political and economic instability such as unjust resettlements of peasants due to the development of extractive industries and agricultural investments, the uncovering of hidden and illegal public debt involving ministers, along with both the current and former presidents, alongside the rising discontent of the RENAMO Party, and competition over the control of the resource-rich regions. This resulted in recurrent armed conflicts in rural areas. Needless to say, rural inhabitants and peasants were economically affected. The state, however, was slow in controlling this social instability.

As mentioned previously, the localized decrease of FRELIMO's popularity, specifically in rural areas, can be explained by the increased implementation of land-based agricultural investments that resulted in the expropriation of people's land in Zambézia, Nampula and Niassa Provinces, where a number of companies expropriated hundreds of thousands of hectares from local peasants (UNAC & GRAIN 2015; Bruna 2017; Mandamule and Bruna 2017).

As shown in Table 1, FRELIMO has been losing votes since 2008. In 2018, RENAMO got more votes in many of the districts in these three provinces, including Malema District, which was one of the regions where peasants were contesting the most, due to ongoing ProSAVANA activities. It is also important to take into consideration that, for the first time, RENAMO was able to get 49% of the total votes on the national level. This means that for the last decades, FRELIMO's political dominance has been decreasing as RENAMO's has been increasing.

The importance of analyzing the political context in which the process of resistance happened is because it contributed to the increase of awareness of FRELIMO's failure in adopting a socially just development model for both rural and urban contexts. This, then, facilitated and/or motivated the engagement of peasants in the struggle. This fact marked the transformation of the roots of rural Mozambique's typical way of resistance, which had been characterized up to this point by Scott's (1986) everyday forms of resistance until the incorporation of an overt and semi-organized way of protesting as was verified in the case of ProSAVANA.

4.4.6.2. Brazil's political instability and Japanese democracy. As Brazil's political crisis emerged in the last years, the Brazilian Cooperation Agency's (ABC) role in the implementation of ProSAVANA has been decreasing, especially in terms of degrees of involvement in the responses to the program's resistance movement. Contrary to this position, the Japanese Cooperation Agency (JICA) took the lead in attempting to revise the program's Master Plan, claiming to be open, to a certain degree, to negotiate its terms and integrate civil society's demands. They were even willing to finance the formation of an integrated organization to manage all civil society claims regarding the implementation and revision of the Master Plan.

It is relevant to consider the role of the Japanese parliament and democracy in relation to the process of resistance against ProSavana. More than cooperating with the struggle in Mozambique, the pressure exercised by the Japanese civil society towards the Japanese parliament directly reflected on the decision-making process of JICA. This would consequently compel the Mozambican Government to give in, given the power relations existing between the two nations, that of beneficiary and donor. Despite its controversies, the democratic system in Japan is operating at a much higher degree than in Brazil or Mozambique. Hence, the existing 'democratic regime' in Mozambique is less reliable than in Japan.

4.4.6.3. Global economic environment: commodity prices trends. Since ProSAVANA's implementation was contingent upon the support of both internal and external investors, the investment decision would inevitably rely on global trends of commodity prices. The Master Plan identifies two main crops as 'priority crops' to be promoted by the program, namely maize and soya. Looking at the international price of maize (Index Mundi 2019), the trends show high prices for the period between 2011 and 2013, with a peak of approximately 330USD per metric ton between July and August of 2012. This is followed by sharp decreases in late 2013, reaching the lowest point in 2017, priced at 150USD per metric ton.

Regarding the international price of soybeans (Index Mundi 2019), rising prices were observed in the beginning of the 2000s reaching a maximum of 684USD per metric ton in August 2012, a period in which ProSAVANA discussions were still ongoing far from the public eye. This was followed by some fluctuations in price between late 2012 and 2014. In mid 2014 the price started to significantly decrease, until reaching the lowest point in early 2016 at 370USD per metric ton. When taking into account the factors influencing the decision-making process for investors, we could observe a significant decrease in the international price of both priority crops by approximately 50% throughout the period during which the ProSAVANA resistance movement was taking place.

5. Concluding remarks

The failure of grasping the nature of the agrarian question in Mozambique rests in the fact that Mozambique has been governed by a persistent authoritarian regime with oscillating levels of populism, which tended to impose agrarian policies that prioritize large scale investments to the detriment of peasants. The achievement of national independence by a revolutionary force, whose populist claims for ending Portuguese colonial continuities and subsequently fighting a guerilla counter-movement were both used to build and sustain its political power and influence.

This paper highlighted problems surrounding the planning and implementation of Pro-SAVANA, starting with the approaches taken to hold public hearings. This was followed by the deviations of ProSAVANA's Master Plan, its proposed guidelines, which was contributing to the expropriation of land, the intensification of debt among peasants, and the promotion of crops that do not answer to people's needs. The persistent lack of transparency and little or no regard for public participation were at the core of these issues. It was in this context that the resistance process took place with NPC as the leading force and UNAC as the main element of legitimation.

Confronting agrarian authoritarianism may go beyond the intrinsic boundaries of a campaign. There are factors that are beyond the control of a specific movement, but still a determinant for its success. Although FRELIMO lost its popularity because of its own failure to deliver and to meet people's expectations, it reacted with higher levels of authoritarianism and, consequently, it lost a big share of its electoral votes. Nevertheless, we argue that it is important to acknowledge that this kind of rupture in the dominant political force could be a window of opportunity to effectively confront authoritarianism. In this case, progressive populism arose as a strategic response of the resistance process. NPC upheld a clear agenda: demanding that ProSAVANA stop immediately and indefinitely through proposing an alternative model of development.

The set of strategies and tactics that gave strength and cohesion to the NPC, discussed above, was built into a unified agenda against the proposed model of development. The strong ideological bond among all of the transnational members of the campaign allowed them to constitute a narrative of 'us against them', othering, in this case, the proponents of ProSAVANA. Moreover, NPC discourses were highly anti-capitalistic and with a strong position toward an alternative paradigm of development, referred to as the 'peasant way' and 'agroecology'. This is in line with what Borras (2019) called agrarian populism, or a form of progressive populism. The outcomes of the resistance process were not only the current stagnation (not yet a discontinuation) of the ProSAVANA project, but also the expanded space for discussion and participation among peasants and civil society throughout the decision process.

Overall, this paper addressed the process and dynamics of resistance to ProSAVANA as a way of confronting authoritarian imposition of agrarian policies in Mozambique. It portrays how the process of building a unified and coherent resistance movement transformed the Mozambican civil society into a more mature, consolidated and dynamic civil society. Moreover, it argues that by identifying breaks and/or rifts in the authoritarian populist regime, such as the decrease of FRELIMO's popularity, they can be used against the regime itself and increase the effectiveness of the campaign's strategies and give more fluidity for the resistance process itself.

Acknowledgments

The authors wish to thank Mai Kobayashi and Amanda Kobayashi for their kindness in proofreading the manuscript. We are also grateful for the helpful comments of the anonymous reviewers. All possible errors remain ours. The authors would also like to thank the Rosa Luxemburg Foundation and the Institute for Poverty, Land and Agrarian Studies in the context of the Emancipatory Rural Politics Initiative (ERPI) for the small research grant provided.

Disclosure statement

No potential conflict of interest was reported by the authors.

ORCID

Boaventura Monjane http://orcid.org/0000-0002-8944-629X

References

ADECRU. 2014. "Lançada campanha NÃO AO PROSAVANA em Moçambique." *Blog Article*. Accessed March 21, 2019. https://adecru.wordpress.com/2014/06/02/lancada-campanha-nao-ao-prosavana-em-mocambique/.

ADECRU. 2015. "Comunidades rejeitam a implementação do ProSAVANA e abandonam a sala de reunião de auscultação pública em Malema." Accessed March 21, 2019. https://adecru.wordpress.com/2015/04/30/comunidades-rejeitam-a-implementacao-do-prosavana-e-abandonam-a-sala-de-reuniao-de-auscultacao-publica-em-malema/ and https://www.jpic-jp.org/es/w/3547-comunidades-rejeitam-a-implementa-o-do-prosavana-e-abandonam-a-sala-de-reuni-o-de-ausculta-o-p-blica-em-malema.

Bennett, A., and A. L. George. 2005. *Case Studies and Theory Development in the Social Sciences*. Cambrige: MIT Press.

Borras, J. 2019. "Agrarian Social Movements: The Absurdly Difficult but Not Impossible Agenda of Defeating Right-Wing Populism and Exploring a Socialist Future." *Journal of Agrarian Change* 2019: 1–34.

Borras, S., and J. Franco. 2013. "Global Land Grabbing and Political Reactions 'From Below'." *Third World Quarterly* 34 (9): 1723–1747.

Bruna, N. 2017. "Plantações florestais e instrumentalização do Estado em Moçambique." *Observador Rural*. No. 53. Maputo.

Byres, T. J. 1991. The Agrarian Question and Differing Forms of Capitalist Agrarian Transition: An Essay with Reference to Asia. *Rural Transformation in Asia*, 3–76.

Chichava, S. 2016. "A sociedade civil e o ProSAVANA em Moçambique." In *Desafios para Moçambique 2016*, IESE.

Clements, E. A., and B. M. Fernandes. 2013. "Land Grabbing, Agribusiness and the Peasantry in Brazil and Mozambique." *Agrarian South: Journal of Political Economy* 2 (1): 41–69.

Coelho, J. P. B. 1998. "State Resettlement Policies in Post-colonial Rural Mozambique: The Impact of the Communal Village Programme on Tete Province, 1977–1982." *Journal of Southern African Studies* 24 (1): 61–91.

Comboni Missionaries. 2015. Accessed September 18, 2019. https://www.comboni.org/contenuti/107523.

Comissão Nacional de Eleições. 2018. "Autárquicas 2018." Accessed August 8, 2019. http://www.open.ac.uk/technology/mozambique/sites/www.open.ac.uk.technology.mozambique/files/files/Resultados%20e%20mandatos%202018.pdf.

CPI (Centro de Promoção ao Investimento). 2017. Investimento aprovado [Data Base], June, 2017. Maputo: CPI.

Deutsche Welle. 2017. "Moçambique: Investigação à JICA no caso ProSavana vista como conquista na luta contra o projeto." Accessed September 18, 2019. http://www.dw.com/pt-002/mo%C3%A7ambique-investiga%C3%A7%C3%A3o-%C3%A0-jica-no-caso-prosavana-vista-como-conquista-na-luta-contra-o-projeto/a-39648276.

Edelman, M. 2017. *Activists empedernidos e intelectuales comprometidos: ensayos sobre movimientos sociales, derechos humanos y studios lationoamericanos*. Quito: Instituto de Altos Estudios Nacionales.

FGV. 2012. "FGV Projetos e GVAgro lançam Fundo Nacala nesta quarta-feira, em Brasília." Accessed September 18, 2019. https://portal.fgv.br/noticias/fgv-projetos-e-gvagro-lancam-fundo-nacala-nesta-quarta-feira-brasilia.

Funada-Classen, S. 2013a. "Anatomia Pós-Fukushima dos Estudos sobre o ProSAVANA: Focalizando no 'Os mitos por trás do ProSAVANA' de Natalia Fingermann." *Observador Rural* No 6. Observatório do Meio Rural. Maputo.

Funada-Classen, S. 2013b. *Analysis of the Discourse and Background of the ProSAVANA Programme in Mozambique – Focusing on Japan's Role*. Tokyo: Tokyo University of Foreign Studies.

Garcia, F. P. 2001. "Análise global de uma guerra (Moçambique 1964–1974)." PhD., Universidade Portucalense, Porto.

The Guardian. 2014. "Mozambique's Small Farmers Fear Brazilian-style Agriculture." Accessed September 18, 2019. https://www.theguardian.com/global-development/2014/jan/01/mozambique-small-farmers-fear-brazilian-style-agriculture.

Hadiz, V. R., and A. Chryssogelos. 2017. "Populism in World Politics: A Comparative Cross-Regional Perspective." *International Political Science Review* 38 (4): 399–411.

Hall, S. 1980. "Popular-Democratic Versus Authoritarian Populism." In *Marxism and Democracy*, edited by A. Hunt, 157–187. London: Laurence and Wishart.

Hall, S. 1985. "Authoritarian Populism: A Reply to Jessop et al." *New Left Review* 151: 115–124.

Index Mundi. 2019. "Commodity Prices." Accessed September 18, 2019. https://www.indexmundi.com/commodities/.

Inocêncio, M. E. 2010. "PROCEDER and the Wefts of Power in the Territorial Capital in the Cerrado. 2010. 271 f." PhD., dissertation. Doctorate in Humanities – Universidade Federal de Goiás, Goiânia.

Instituto Nacional de Estatística. 2018. Produto Interno Bruto [Data Base], July 2018. Maputo: INE.

JCC. 2012. Triangular Cooperation for Agricultural Development of the Tropical Savannah in Mozambique (ProSAVANA JBM): Support of Agriculture Development Master Plan for Nacala Corridor. Power Point Presentation: The third JCC, Nampula, Mozambique, 2013.

Justiça Ambiental et al. 2013. "Leaked Copy of the Master Plan for the ProSAVANA Programme in Northern Mozambique Confirms the Worst: Civil Society Groups Warn Secretive Plan Paves the Way for a Massive Land Grab." *Civil Society Joint Statement*. Accessed March 20, 2019. https://www.grain.org/media/W1siZilsIjlwMTMvMDQvMzAvMDhfMzZfNDhfN19Db2xsZWN0aXZlX3N0YXRlbWVudF9vbl9NYXN0ZXJfUGxhbl9BcHJpbF8yOV9GSU5BTDIucGRmIl1d.

Lourenço, V. A. 2010. *Moçambique: Memórias sociais de ontem, dilemas políticos de hoje*. Segunda edição ed. Lisboa: ISCTE-IUL.

LVC Africa News. 2014. "Mozambique: 'Agroecological farming came to stay in Marracuene' — say the farmers." Accessed September 24, 2019 https://viacampesina.org/en/mozambique-agroecological-farming-came-to-stay-in-marracuene-says-the-farmers/.

Mandamule, U., and N. Bruna. 2017. "Investimentos, migrações forçadas e conflitos de terra: representações sociais de populações reassentadas no Corredor de Natal." In *Movimentos migratórios e relações rural-urbanas: estudos de caso em Moçambique*, edited by j. Feijó. Maputo: Alcance Editores.

MASA. 2015. "Plano Director para o Desenvolvimento Agrário do Corredor de Nacala em Moçambique." *Esboço Versão* 1–39. (Maputo).

Melber, H. 2018. "Populism in Southern Africa under Liberation Movements as Governments." *Review of African Political Economy* 45 (158): 678–686.

Mello, P. C. 2011. "Moçambique oferece terra à soja brasileira." *Folha de S. Paulo*, August 14.

Moçambique para todos. 2015. "Irritada com ameaças de Pacheco, Sociedade Civil abandona sala de debate." Accessed September 18, 2019. https://macua.blogs.com/moambique_para_todos/2015/06/irritada-com-ameaças-de-pacheco-sociedade-civil-abandona-sala-de-debate.html.

Monjane, B. 2015. "Auscultação pública sobre o ProSAVANA: Ministro exige intervenções 'patrióticas' e activistas abandonam a sala." *Reflectindo sobre Moçambique*. Accessed September 18, 2019. http://comunidademocambicana.blogspot.com/2015/06/auscultacao-publica-sobre-o-prosavana.html.

Monjane, B. 2016a. "Movimentos sociais, sociedade civil e espaço público em Moçambique: uma análise crítica." *Cadernos CERU* 27 (2): 144–155.

Monjane, B. 2016b. "Reagrupar para controlar? Uma análise crítica das políticas Estatais de organização coerciva das populações rurais em Moçambique." *Revista Educação e Políticas em Debate* 5 (1): 84–94.

Monjane, B. 2017. "ProSavana: Mozambique's Civil Society Demands the Immediate Suspension of the Actions of JICA." *The Dawn*. Accessed September 18, 2019. http://www.thedawn-news.org/2017/02/24/prosavana-mozambiques-civil-society-demands-the-immediate-suspension-of-the-actions-of-jica/.

Mosca, J. 2005. *Economia de Moçambique: Século XX*. Lisboa: Instituto Piaget.

Mosca, J., e N. Bruna. 2015. "ProSAVANA. Discursos, práticas e realidades." Observador Rural No 31. Observatório do Meio Rural. Maputo.

Negrão, J. 2002. "A indispensável terra africana para o aumento da riqueza dos pobres." *Centro de Estudos Sociais*. Accessed September 18, 2019. http://www.ces.uc.pt/publicacoes/oficina/ficheiros/179.pdf.

Neues Deutschland. 2018. "Mosambiks Kleinbauern müssen gegen die Interessen der Agrarmultis verteidigt warden." Accessed September 18, 2019. https://www.neues-deutschland.de/artikel/1075801.nd-soliaktion-teilen-macht-satt-umkaempftes-saatgut.html.

O'Laughlin, B. 1996. "Through a Divided Glass: Dualism, Class and the Agrarian Question in Mozambique." *The Journal of Peasant Studies* 23 (4): 1–39.

Pambazuka News. 2016. Accessed September 18, 2019. https://www.pambazuka.org/land-environment/mozambique-government-not-sincere-about-prosavana.

Pitcher, M. A. 2012. *Transforming Mozambique. The Politics of Privatization, 1975–2000*. Cambridge: Cambridge University Press.

República de Moçambique. 2011. *Plano Estratégico para o Desenvolvimento do Sector Agrário (PEDSA)*. Maputo: Ministério da Agricultura.

Scoones, I., M. Edelman, S. M. Borras Jr, R. Hall, W. Wolford, and B. White. 2017. "Emancipatory Rural Politics: Confronting Authoritarian Populism." *The Journal of Peasant Studies* 45: 1–20.

Scott, J. 1986. "Everyday Forms of Peasant Resistance." *The Journal of Peasant Studies* 13 (2): 5–35.

Shankland, A., and E. Gonçalves. 2016. "Imagining Agricultural Development in South–South Cooperation: The Contestation and Transformation of ProSAVANA." *World Development* 81: 35–46.

Shivji, Issa G. 2019. "Sam Moyo and Samir Amin on the Peasant Question." *Agrarian South: Journal of Political Economy* 8: 1–16.

UNAC. 2012. "Pronunciamento da UNAC sobre o Programa Prosavana." *Nampula*, de Outubro 11.

UNAC e GRAIN. 2015. *Os usurpadores de terras do Corredor de Nacala. Uma nova era de luta contra plantações coloniais no Norte de Moçambique*. Maputo: UNAC e GRAIN.

UNAC, et al. 2013. "Open Letter from Mozambican Civil Society Organizations and Movements to the Presidents of Mozambique and Brazil and the Prime Minister of Japan." Accessed Auguest 13, 2019. https://www.grain.org/bulletin_board/entries/4738-open-letter-from-mozambican-civil-society-organisations-and-movements-to-the-presidents-of-mozambique-and-brazil-and-the-prime-minister-of-japan.

WLSA Moçambique. 2014. "Eleições autárquicas de 2013." Accessed August 8, 2019. http://www.wlsa.org.mz/wp-content/uploads/2014/11/Eleicoes2013_anexos.pdf.

Wolford, W., and R. Nehring. 2015. "Constructing Parallels: Brazilian Expertise and the Commodification of Land, Labour and Money in Mozambique." *Canadian Journal of Development Studies/Revue Canadienne D'études du Développement* 36 (2): 208–223.

Wuyts, M. 2001. "The Agrarian Question in Mozambique's Transition and Reconstruction." Discussion Paper, 14. United Nations University.

Populism from above and below: the path to regression in Brazil

Daniela Andrade

ABSTRACT
Brazil has recently shifted from economic growth to recession, from left-wing to far-right politics and from neo-developmentalist to ultra-liberal economic policies. This regressive change in Brazil (and elsewhere) has prompted the need for empirical investigation and emancipatory movement-building, as urged by the Emancipatory Rural Politics Initiative (ERPI). This article responds to the ERPI call by reflecting on the politics of the past. It argues that the road to regression was paved during the tenure of the Workers' Party, when Lula's leadership emerged as representative of interests 'from below' while advancing a political project that protected and nurtured interests 'from above' - a populist ambiguity. By offering an understanding from a class political economy perspective, this article concludes that reinforcing left-wing populism in the face of authoritarianism is unlikely to create a path to emancipation.

Introduction

The Emancipatory Rural Politics Initiative (ERPI), launched in October 2017 by a group of scholars, echoed growing concern over the rise of populist governments around the world, many of which are associated with authoritarian, right-wing and exclusionary politics. In the ERPI framing article, Scoones et al. (2018) make 'authoritarian populism' their primary focus and specify the 'rural world' as the site of their scholarly efforts. As the authors point out, the rural setting has served as both an electoral base for populist leaders and a base for resistance and alternative politics. They argue that the spread of authoritarian populism is not only a reason for concern, but also a call for emancipatory rural politics. Seeking to grasp a better understanding of populism and its authoritarian form, the ERPI has called on scholars to provide insights from their countries of study by considering whether and how the rural context is affected by, contributes, or reacts to populism.

This article focuses on Brazil, a country where the economic and political tide has recently changed. In 2016, Brazil entered a full-blown recession and underwent a hostile impeachment process fueled by a popular uprising that brought to an end not only the mandate of democratically elected president Dilma Rousseff, but also a 13-year period (2003–2016) during which the Workers' Party (*Partido dos Trabalhadores*, PT) was in power. After the impeachment process, policies shifted toward stark economic austerity and the curtailment of labor rights. Such an authoritarian and reactionary U-turn was consolidated in October 2018 with the election of former military officer and congressman Jair Bolsonaro, who openly espoused dictatorial principles, moral conservatism and ultra-economic liberalism. Fear, hate and hope, mobilized by a vicious presidential campaign, boosted his political ascension. All of the above suggest that Brazil has joined the club of right-wing authoritarian populist governments – a setback that has reached the countryside, and in contrasting ways.

It should be noted that 50% of the impeachment votes in the Chamber of Deputies were cast by the so-called Agribusiness Parliamentary Front, which comprised 41% of the total number of serving parliamentarians (Castilho 2017). Still in 2016, this agribusiness caucus voted to shelve a corruption complaint lodged against interim president Michel Temer, saving his mandate. In exchange for their congressional vote, Temer's government committedly fulfilled the agribusiness sector's demands (Castilho 2017).

By contrast, the 'family farm' sector quickly started to experience the bitter effects of authoritarianism and austerity, including direct violence. In its first week in power, the interim government abolished the Ministry of Agrarian Development and eliminated or severely reduced internationally celebrated programs that were providing support and welfare to the rural poor, such as the *Bolsa Família* or the Food Acquisition Program (PAA), among several other setbacks (see e.g. Pericás 2017 and Mitidiero Junior 2018). Perhaps even more alarming was the sharp increase in the number of murders, death threats, murder attempts, instances of torture and imprisonment of rural peoples since the impeachment (CPT 2017).[1]

In face of this political throwback and the quickly deteriorating economic and social conditions in rural areas, agrarian movements and other organized social forces have been confronted with the pressing need to mobilize the masses to contest the drastic cutbacks in public support, as well as to reclaim the loss of political representation in the government. As part of that endeavor, from August 2017 to March 2018, the Landless Workers' Movement (*Movimento dos Trabalhadores Sem Terra*, MST) openly supported former president Luiz Inácio Lula da Silva (Lula, for the PT) during a pre-presidential election caravan that took place across the country. At the time, Lula was the PT's official candidate and topped all opinion polls.

Together, these elements place Brazil at the center of the ERPI problematic, yet with a caveat: the risk that scholarship as well as resistance and mobilization – which together form the primary foci of the ERPI – would focus on recent political changes without sufficient reflection on and learning from the politics of the past. This becomes imperative given the suspicion that the road to regression did not start with the ousting of Rousseff, but was paved during the PT's tenure, when the government enjoyed popular support and

---

[1] Between 2016 and 2017, 132 rural dwellers, many of whom in leadership positions, were murdered – a 100% increase in the average number of murders per year compared with the 2005–2014 period (CPT 2017).

its politics were celebrated for promoting a post-neoliberal and neo-developmentalist project that primarily affected the poor (see Sader 2013). Notably, the rural context was central to the PT's politics. It was not due to misfortune or mere coincidence, but rather to critical political choices that Lula's project was shipwrecked just after the end of the global commodity boom.

Agricultural production and exports, which have undergone widespread expansion since the early 2000s, have played a crucial albeit ambiguous role in the politics of the PT. These were instrumental in bringing back economic stability and growth, enabling the state to sponsor a new type of economic and social progress, which was central in giving rise to and propelling the phenomenon of 'Lulism' (Singer 2009): the identification of Lula as representative of interests 'from below'. Yet agricultural exports were also structural to a state-sponsored pattern of accumulation 'from above', clashing with the PT's claim of promoting a popular political project. The countryside became the backdrop for strategy contradictions that placed the very poor in alliance with the dominant classes. The mystification of this ambiguous form by which the PT secured and exerted power, and represented the interests of its social base, is characteristic of populism.

This phenomenon needs to be carefully understood so that its constitutive flaws and political consequences can be fully exposed and confronted. The first section of this article presents an understanding of populism in light of the class-based political economy; this creates the foundations for the ensuing analysis of Lulism and the PT's politics in three stages. The first stage describes the way in which politics was perceived by the people and how this shaped political outcomes. The second stage examines the economic and social bases of politics, contrasting apparent and concrete social effects. In the final stage, the article reflects on Lula's model of populism to shed light on the recent regressive turn and inform emancipatory politics.

Approaching populism

> […] if social and political aspirations are not disciplined by careful theory and analysis, they will lead to false prescription and to development policies which fail. Theory is not therefore a mere intellectual indulgence, but, at its best, the most 'practical' of activities. (Kitching 1989, 5)

Since the end of the 1990s and throughout the 2000s, several left-leaning governments in Latin America have surfed the commodity boom wave, promoting economic growth and social development (Vergara-Camus and Kay 2017). The so-called 'Pink Tide' governments, notably those in Ecuador, Bolivia and Venezuela, have been associated with left-wing or neo-populism (de la Torre 2016; Andreucci 2017), and in a positive fashion. Echoing such an assessment, Scoones et al. (2018, 3) note that neo-populist governments in the region have been in favor of 'the people', once achieving 'impressive gains in poverty reduction and expanded political recognition and government support for previously marginalised groups'. Their interpretation seems to imply that populism, as long as it is not right-wing and authoritarian, becomes a desirable feature of politics. It is unclear, however, what is meant by the term populism itself. Certainly, not all popular and progressive politics are populist, just as not all populist politics are progressive. The same applies to authoritarian, right-wing, xenophobic or other sorts of (populist) politics.

Drawing from Kitching's opening quote, defining and analyzing populism should not be a mere intellectual indulgence, but rather a practical activity with important political consequences. Even though this article is not the space for extensive theoretical exploration, key conceptual aspects of populism should be reflected upon so that real experiences can be singled out and direct effects exposed. Contrary to the Pink Tide governments mentioned above, the Brazilian government has seldom been associated with populism, even if also being at the forefront of extractivism and neo-developmentalism.

So, what is populism? Why would the PT government, under Lula's leadership, make a case for it? And why does this analysis matter? In light of the political economy, populism is a political phenomenon and, as such, is entrenched in and unfolds into economic and social phenomena, all of which must be reflected upon in the analysis. When conceptualizing populism, it is essential that questions such as who controls what, who does what and who gets what are addressed theoretically.

The political economy of populism

Democratic representation as a system of power, with populism as its fetish

The events of authoritarian populism that the ERPI is concerned with emerged between the cracks of representative democracy – the formal governing system of most capitalist economies, including Brazil. Populism is rooted in relations of representation, which, in the context discussed here, are those between the state (as the representative) and citizens (as the represented).

In a system of representative democracy, citizens have the power to elect (or reject) a government through voting, which not only is a limited way of expressing preferences and demands, but also has a limited scope for participation in decision-making. State representatives are the ones who can effectively express, and decide how to implement, views on public matters. An inevitable disposition of power therefore underlies political representation because of differences in agency and the decision-making capacities of those with concrete needs, interests and demands, and those who voice and realize them on their behalf.

It is therefore important to observe the political roles played by state agency and decision-making power in representing societies whose social organization is based on the monopoly of the means of production by a minority and wage employment of the majority – the basis of the compulsion to purchase labor power (for commodity production for profit) and sell labor power (for material and social reproduction) (Fine and Saad-Filho 2016). This means that, when governing, the state inevitably confronts social interests arising from the (class) position of different groups within capitalist social divisions. State policies will represent, protect and nurture particular social interests while simultaneously remediating, neglecting or undermining others.

State political choices therefore express a class character, whereas maintaining political control of the state denotes the political power of a class over the economy and society. The state's political choices are conditioned by and reflect social disputes over the (re)organization of property, as well as the processes of production, appropriation and accumulation. This is why Wood argues that the state represents the ultimate locus of social force; it is 'the decisive point of concentration for all power in society' (1995, 47).

As she rightly points out, even if ensuring the right to vote for all citizens (regardless of socioeconomic position), the system of representative democracy has been opportune for maintaining the capitalist social order. Exerting 'civic freedom and equality' (1995, 201) does not directly affect the logic (and legitimacy) of private property, market compulsion and the profit maximization imperative forming the capitalist spheres of domination and coercion (1995, 234). Even though democracy in its original and historical sense denotes rule by the *demos*, "the people", representative democracy conceals and legitimizes rule by the dominant (propertied) classes (Wood 1995).

When embedded in state and society relations, populism further conceals the flaws of representative democracy while concurrently exacerbating them. As a corollary, democracy as a whole is perceived to be more transparent, direct, legitimate and just while becoming more arbitrary, personalistic and pernicious to the working class. Unsurprisingly, populist leaders produce deep loyalties and cleavages, polarizing 'their polities and the academic community into those who regarded them as democratic innovators, and those who considered them a threat to democracy' (de la Torre 2017, 195). These tensions have been evidenced in the recent debates on the 'Pink Tide' in Latin America. The next section explains how populism affects political representation in democratic capitalist societies as a way of expanding the view introduced here.

Fetishism and ambiguous politics

What becomes distinctive in relations of representation when populism is embedded, and what is particular to the manifestation of populism itself, is the existence of a *fetish*: the fetish of a genuine popular democratic representation, or even of popular power. Drawing upon Marx's fetishism of the commodity (1992 [1867], Vol. 1, Chapter 1), fetishism is understood as a social perception or a collective construct of social reality (needs, identity, rights etc.), which is formed, on the one hand, from concrete social experiences of people, thereby corresponding to materiality. Yet, on the other hand, it is a perception that obscures, misrepresents and ultimately conflicts with more fundamental aspects of that same social reality at the abstract level – that of social (class) relations. Fetishism is the mystification of social relations, but it is not simply a false or illusory perception of reality, or a phenomenon happening only in people's minds; it is first and foremost a practical phenomenon expressing ideas that correspond to (and shape) concrete forms of appearance of social reality. As such, a fetish is social and historically determined.

Populism is fetishized politics of people's representation, and thus associated with the fetish of 'the people', the 'common good', 'popular will' or general welfare. The fetishization of social matters may prompt discursive, ideological and social unity (mystifying class and other social divisions). By default, fetishized social unity creates an equally mystified social 'other'. Social polarization is part of populism, as are changes in the social correlation of forces and power relations.

In a democratic political system, populism often leads to the seizure of the state, expansion and reproduction of the political power of social representation. A state representative becomes the direct voice of 'the people' and the agent that realizes the popular will. Populism creates leaders (usually male) who are often seen as a 'savior', a 'father', a 'hero' or 'one of us', embodying the collective identity or will (Arditi 2005, 81–83). A fetishized representative has greater public appeal not only as a matter of degree, but also quality. Personal charisma or background, cultural or partisan identity, and rhetorical or discursive devices can reinforce the fetish of representation. These factors help populist leaders to create a direct, unmediated, uninstitutionalized and quasi-personal relation with the constituencies they claim to represent (Weyland 2001, 14).

Laclau, who remains influential in the academic debate on populism, associates this phenomenon with a crisis of hegemonic power. However, drawing from a particular understanding of Gramsci, he circumscribes power and political hegemony to the spheres of discursive and ideological dominance (Laclau 1977), thus taking a partial view on the capitalist forms of domination. A dominant class exerts hegemony through the neutralization of potential resistance or conflicting ideologies of the dominated by articulating some of their views, discourses and demands (1977, 161–62). That way, he conceives of a 'populism of the dominated' (1977, 173–74) when the masses absorb and articulate a popular ideology of their own, thereby challenging, antagonizing and possibly overtaking the elite ideological hegemony. For Laclau, this would be not only desirable, but also necessary to put an alternative political project in place.[2]

The idea of 'people's power' detached from careful theorization can easily become an unproblematic treatment of transformative politics, which is an important aspect of populism itself. First, one should not assume the immediate interest of 'the people' (or the dominated) in defying the capitalist logic of social organization and inherent forms of oppression, differentiation and inequality (Wood 1995). Second, one should be suspicious of transformative politics arising from arbitrary popular unity, subjectively construed.

Third, one should be skeptical of the pursuit of transformative politics through political representation – 'won by proxy or conferred by benefaction' (1995, 103) – instead of through direct collective activity. Yet the populist fetish stalls people's protagonism and disempowers citizens. People become loyal to and reliant on a leadership that they entrust to act on their behalf, thereby widening the gap in agency and decision-making capacities between citizens and state representatives. Promoting social benefits, a populist leader favors the formation of a grateful and obedient mass (Lefort as mentioned in Arditi 2005, 96–97) instead of a critical, politically engaged and combative mass.

Finally, if progressive populism brings people's voices, material aspirations and ideologies to the political stage, and possibly to the top of the political system – thereby overtaking elite hegemony, as in Laclau's view – how does this correspond to the transformation of the (capitalist) patterns of property organization, production, distribution and appropriation? This is the crux of the matter. An ideological ascendancy of the dominated over the state's politics is populist when (and because) it is detached from a correspondent structural transformation on the control of property and market relations, which are the material forms of domination – and the most tangible ones.[3]

Populism makes all the more ambiguous who controls politics, who expresses their will, who drives the political project, who has agency, who holds power, who benefits and who loses. This political ambiguity, with a clear class connotation, forms the backbone of populist politics. As the term 'populism' indicates, this ambiguity is defined in relation to, and from the perspective of, the working class, which is both an agent of the state's political empowerment and a recipient of the state's political decisions. Populism does not enhance

---

[2]For Laclau (1977), socialist ideology is populist in nature. 'Socialist populism', therefore, is not backward, but rather the most advanced form of 'populism of the dominated'.
[3]In the case of progressive and possibly emancipatory politics, the political project, its practice and effects cohere – the antagonism is found in the very class struggle, transforming social and power relations.

working-class agency and decision-making power, nor does it guarantee economic democracy or lead to social emancipation, even though this might appear to be the case.

Grasping the populist fetish requires two levels of analysis. One describes how a leader, social groups and the political agenda are perceived (as 'the people' against 'the elite', for example), and how their relationships, actions and political capacities are shaped as a result. Most descriptions and analyses of populism do just that, which is not unimportant; populism is about perceptions driving political outcomes and playing a key role in the battle for power. A judicious investigation, however, should take a second analytical step to disclose the relationship between the way reality is perceived and the way it is in essence – a task to which a Marxist political economy analysis is devoted (see Fine and Saad-Filho 2016, 4). The analysis should reveal how subjective, fetishized political relationships, such as those among 'the people' or between them and the state and its leaders, correspond objectively as social class relations. Assuming a macro perspective, this article explores broad class relations constituted and conditioned by a state-sponsored pattern of accumulation and development.

2003–2006: the making of a leader of the poor

Brazil, a country for all
(2002 electoral campaign slogan)

Lula contested three presidential elections as a candidate for the PT before he was successful in 2002. Between his first electoral campaign in 1989 and his first term of office, Brazil underwent two mutually reinforcing and constituting transitions (Saad-Filho 2010, 24). The first was a political transition from 20 years of military dictatorship to an era of representative democracy. The second was an economic transition from developmentalism, supported by Import Substitution Industrialization (ISI) policies, to neoliberalism, underpinned by policy and institutional reforms in the early 1990s.

A combination of high interest rates, an overvalued currency, fiscal austerity measures, the privatization of public assets, open trade and capital borders – the cornerstones of the 1990s reforms – transformed the patterns of production, capital accumulation and labor reproduction in the country through a fast-advancing financialization process. The national industrial sector, once the pillar of the developmentalist model, was significantly harmed and with it the industrial workforce; more than two million salaried posts were lost between 1989 and 1999 in the industrial sector alone (Oliveira 2006, 11). In addition to this development, wages depreciated and labor rights were relaxed. As Saad-Filho (2010) remarks, democracy facilitated and legitimized economic changes that fragmented the labor force, repressed trade union activities and increased economic insecurity while creating the conditions for capital accumulation through the expansion and intensification of financial transactions that transferred income (and power) to the financial system.[4]

The new development pattern produced five years of macroeconomic stability and consumption-led growth (1993–1997), followed by five years of multiple crises and a recession (1998–2002), including a balance of payments crisis, currency collapse, the

---

[4]Saad-Filho (2010, 24) argues that democracy was established as 'the political form of neoliberalism in Brazil'. From 1989 onwards, the control and coercion of the working class become 'primarily "economic" rather than "political", as was the case under the dictatorship' (Saad-Filho 2010).

return of inflation, further job cuts and the deterioration of public services. Lula obtained his first electoral triumph on the backdrop of crises – largely blamed on Cardoso's government. His electoral victory also reflected the PT's historical representation of the organized working class struggles, as well as contestations of the neoliberal ruling order.[5]

Lula was elected after securing 61.3% of the vote in the second (runoff) voting round, after having won 46.5% in the first. His votes originated from the social sectors most affected by the neoliberal financialization process. This group of voters, which Saad-Filho and Morais (2018, 109–113) refer to as an 'alliance of losers', was composed of the unionized working class (rural and urban), civil servants, sections of the middle-class population and members of the business community (Saad-Filho and Morais 2018). They were predominantly educated, had higher levels of income, and resided in the most urbanized and industrialized states in the South and Southeast regions (Hunter and Power 2007, 4).

Although his election was celebrated as signifying the long-awaited 'rise of the left', Lula's electoral campaign showed that the PT no longer had the same political and ideological character of the past. The party had toned down its political discourse and adopted a non-confrontational spirit, encapsulated in its all-embracing 'Brazil for all' campaign slogan and in Lula's self-designation as the candidate of 'peace and love'. The party also allied with a center-right party, from which an industrial businessperson was handpicked for the post of vice president. In addition, near the campaign's final stage, Lula addressed the Brazilian people in a letter in which he vowed, if elected, to maintain the orthodox macroeconomic policies of his predecessor – a move considered both pragmatic and politically opportunistic.

Preceding the election, the Brazilian economy was on the verge of collapse, provoked by massive capital flight and domestic currency devaluation. Lula's letter was written in an attempt to appease nervous foreign investors – and the market in general – alarmed by his imminent election. It also served to gain the sympathy of more conservative constituents who had never voted for the PT. As Anderson (2011) noted, Lula had understood that 'it was not just builders and bankers who needed reassurance that he would not do anything unduly radical in power, but – even more crucially – street vendors and slum-dwellers too'.

In brief, Lula's campaign had an ambiguous political identity. Despite creating a glimmer of hope that improvements and political change would follow, it also produced a sense of political disenchantment and skepticism among the radical left and the PT's most politicized base. It was clear that the party had no mandate to carry on the structural changes that once formed its political agenda (Saad-Filho and Morais 2018, 116–117).

In January 2003, when Lula took office, the country was in disarray. Unexpectedly, however, by the end of his first year on the job, he had managed to stabilize the economy. From there, he continued to make steady gains throughout his term of office. In 2006, the year in which Lula was reelected, the country seemed to be ready to 'take off' – the Brazilian miracle was within reach!

Before understanding the basis for and the reach of his administration's economic and social achievements, the next section examines the appeal these achievements have effected – perhaps Lula's most significant political feat.

---

[5]Together with the Workers' Central Union (*Central Única dos Trabalhadores*, CUT), the PT has fought against 'privatizations, outsourcing and the managerial state model. At the same time, they have defended the universalization of public social policies and the state's responsibility to meet social needs' (Sitcovsky 2013, 119, author's translation).

Lulism

> Lula again, with the power of the people
> (2006 electoral campaign slogan)

In 2006, Lula was reelected with 61% of the vote in the second voting round (having secured 48.6% in the first), thereby practically replicating the outcome of the 2002 elections. Yet the overall electoral result concealed a phenomenon that Brazilian intellectual André Singer termed 'Lulism': Lula's rise as a 'leader of the poor'. Lula was rejected by his previous electorate, but was reappointed as president by the vote of a new constituency with very different social features.[6]

Lula's new supporters included the internal bourgeoisie but especially the low and very low-income strata, beneficiaries of the social policies of his first mandate. This time, his constituency formed an 'alliance of winners' (Saad-Filho and Morais 2018, 126). The majority of Lula's voters encompassed a social category that Singer (2009) called the 'sub-proletariat'[7]; they represented the Brazilian workforce majority since the period of neoliberal restructuring (Oliveira 2006, 11), consisting of mainly informal (irregular and unskilled) workers associated with precarious working conditions and poor remuneration – the working poor. These voters came from rural areas and overwhelmingly from the North and Northeast regions of the country.

For the first time in Brazilian history, the very poor voted for a candidate representing the left (Singer 2009, 90). Singer's explanation of the change in the voting pattern of the sub-proletariat is important to this article's argument. For him, this change reflected two characteristics of this social stratum that were met by Lula's inaugural legacy. First, given their poverty, this group had an objective and pressing need for material and social change. Second, and paradoxically, the sub-proletariat, even though desiring change, had a conservative political and moral ethos. Differing from the formal working class, these workers had no protection from unions or their own forms of labor organization, and had little capacity to build it from below (Singer 2009, 87–88); consequently, they were the most affected by strikes or social unrest, for example. As a result, this materially and socially vulnerable group desired change, but largely expected it without political confrontations or social distress. In fact, given their lack of social and political organization, they relied on the state to realize change and provide protection. In the 2006 election, they identified Lula as the leader of such a state who would tackle poverty and inequality without breaking from the established order.

As mentioned above, the PT adopted a non-confrontational strategy in the 2002 campaign, renouncing its radical leftist identity and moderating its discourse and political program. Singer (2009, 99) suggests that, unable to mobilize and shape the sub-proletariat

---

[6] The loss of the previous electorate's support is partially explained by the so-called '*mensalão*' corruption scandal that erupted in 2005. Oliveira (2006, 5) also reminds us that, although voting is compulsory in Brazil, 31% of the electorate either did not vote or cast blank or null votes – the highest rate of electoral indifference in Brazil's democratic history.

[7] Singer adopts the definition of his father, Paul Singer, arguing that the sub-proletariat is a social category that sells its labor power below what is necessary for social reproduction under normal conditions. As survival strategies, this highly heterogeneous group relies on occasional wage work, informal exchange, opportunistic engagement with the economy, state transfers, charity and crime (Saad-Filho and Morais 2018, 196). These authors called them the informal working class, which is the preferable term. The authors also remark that, since the advent of neoliberalism, the dividing line between the informal and formal working class has become increasingly blurred. In parts of the text, I chose to use the 'working poor' because it alludes to both class and the conditions of social reproduction.

through a Left debate and action, Lula transformed them into a political actor by shaping his discourse and political program to their conservatism.

Lula succeeded in achieving economic stability, which was particularly important to the informal, non-unionized workers. But unlike all previous governments, he was able to substantially improve the quality of life of the very poor, particularly by increasing their purchasing power. Such an accomplishment resulted from not only the cash transfer program, the *Bolsa Família*, but also the 24.25% real increase in the minimum wage during his first presidential term (Singer 2009, 92), which strongly impacted the income of families who were relying exclusively on the pension of an elderly household member. Lula's social policies also included the provision of popular credits, support to family farmers, housing, and electricity to remote areas, among others, which altogether enabled an increase in popular consumption, an expansion of the domestic market and the creation of more employment opportunities. His welfare policies were material evidence of his intention and ability to put in place a transformative agenda benefiting the poor (thus serving as a powerful basis for support).

Reaching the poor population through federal programs, Lula delivered a symbolic message: 'the state [or Lula] cares for the lot of every Brazilian, no matter how wretched or downtrodden, as citizens with social rights in their country' (Anderson 2011). As Anderson stresses, the image of a caretaker of the poor became Lula's 'most unshakeable political asset' (Anderson 2011). *Bolsa Família*, despite being managed impersonally – and thus contrasting with the kind of clientelism characteristic of classic populism (Anderson 2011) – had 'immediate and palpable effects on the president's political fortunes' (Hunter and Power 2007, 25). Other social programs, Oliveira (2006, 19) argues, were so poorly managed that they achieved virtually nothing besides reaffirming Lula's strong leadership and caring image.

Singer argues that Lula established an ideological bridge with the conservative sub-proletariat by succeeding in assisting them only by pursuing a weak reformist agenda.[8] Without denying the significance of improved material conditions for vulnerable people under Lula's rule, it is necessary to highlight the emergence of an equally important development: the fetishization of Lula as a representative of the poor. Lula came to embody popular hopes and under his leadership created a sense among the working poor that they had become the main social force in power.

Lula had the same social background as his supporters and incorporated the poor's culture and language. In the past, this was not an asset for him but it became so after his first successful term in office. His personal history as a humble, northeastern, working-class migrant began to affect people's self-esteem, already suggesting an emerging fetish around 'President Lula' (as he is still called today). Such a dynamic increased his credibility as 'the champion of the poor', while expanding his government's legitimacy.

Anderson (2011) remarks that Lula's direct relationship with the masses prevented the media from shaping the political undercurrent in the country, as it had been able to do in the past, when framing Collor as 'the 'Maharajas' hunter' during the 1989 presidential campaign, or Cardoso as the 'inflation tamer' during the 1994 and 1998 campaigns. The 2006

---

[8]Singer's thesis is sophisticated and nuanced. In this article, it is not presented or endorsed in its entirety. 'Lulism' has provoked considerable academic repercussions in Brazil, which this article also reflects on only partially. What I focus on here is the electoral realignment phenomenon and the inception of Lula's leadership over the masses, both of which Singer pointed out and offered convincing historical and contextual explanations for.

election revealed an effective loss of the political power of the media while the masses assumed a protagonist role by effecting political power through voting based on their connection to Lula, not only giving him a second mandate, but also allowing the PT to remain in power for two subsequent elections.

Lulism and populism

According to de la Torre, '[l]eft-wing populists emerged [in Latin America] as a result of widespread popular resistance to neoliberalism' (2016, 63–64). While it holds that the PT came to power as a result of discontent over the effects of neoliberal reforms, Lula's leadership of the marginal masses emerged despite, if not because of, his compliance with the (neoliberal) order. Furthermore, it is precisely the working class disorganization and depoliticization, both deepened by neoliberalism, that together form one of the pillars of Lulism. In Filgueiras' words (2013, 388), Lulism did not originate only as a result of Lula's poverty alleviation policies; more importantly, it reflected the identification of Lula as a representative of those fragmented and disorganized social segments that could not express themselves autonomously and independently in the political arena. Paradoxically, the rise of Lula (and the PT) to power manifested the disempowerment and disorganization of Lula's own class (Oliveira 2006, 11). Even though Lula maintained an organized and critical electoral base – the MST, for example, was part of it – it was insignificant in size.

Contrary to Laclau's idea that 'there is no populism without discursive construction of an enemy' (Laclau 2005, 39), Lula united the electorate using a social conciliation discourse. This does not invalidate the hypothesis of populism, but rather points to the limits of empiricism found in the literature. If Singer is right, social conciliation allowed for the expression of an ideological unity with the working poor, just as an antagonistic discourse could in a different context. Furthermore, in a deeply divided and unjust society such as that of Brazil, social conciliation is no less fetishized than many forms of 'us-and-them' divides.

Lula realized, however, that social conciliation served to aggregate the masses but not to win the elites' trust. Oliveira (2006, 6) stresses that in Lula's first interview after his second electoral victory, he 'complained bitterly of not being the choice of the rich, pointing out that bankers have never earned so much money as under his government'. Lula was right, but chose to frame his election as 'a victory of the poor'. The media subsequently fueled the polarization of the rich and the poor. Of course, the dichotomy was figurative. First, Oliveira (2007) notes that the other half of the electorate was not composed of only the rich. Second, as Lula's statement informs, his administration was not (and not even primarily) supporting only the poor; thus, his election was also a victory of the rich. This, however, remained invisible.

The polarization of rich and poor bears relations with class conflict, but cannot be equated to class struggle (Singer 2013). According to Singer, 'the success of Lulism involved a social solution from above, creating both a depolarization [of capital and labor] and a repolarization [of rich and poor] politics' (Singer 2012, 157 as quoted in Filgueiras 2013, 388, author's translation).

Although Singer would agree that Lulism incorporates several elements of populism, for him, the PT political project was a genuine and complete project of the sub-proletariat with a conservative ethos, that is, an authentic representation of the working poor, able to respond to their needs. In Singer's view, there is no fetish. For him, Lulism could be considered as the politics of the sub-proletariat, even if they only attempted to reconcile with those of the bourgeoisie. In Singer's thesis, Lulism was a successful model in arbitrating the interests of the two essential classes: the bourgeoisie and the proletariat (see Boito 2013).

This, however, is problematic. First, Singer seems to disregard the asymmetries in the power relations between the two essential classes, as noted by Boito (2013). Second, to infer that the PT executed the political project of the sub-proletariat, it is necessary to look at the state's overall politics. This helps to identify where and how the policies aimed at the poor's interests were articulated – and made sense – economically and politically, as part of a broader social context. This is what the next sections examine.

Disclosing the economic basis of the PT's political project

The combating of poverty and social inequality without social confrontation – the basis of Lula's ideological and social project – meant, in practice, having an economic project with two legs: one developmentalist, the other neoliberal. The latter was a continuation of Cardoso's prescription, whereas the former represented the novelty of the PT's strategy. Organic intellectuals of the party (see Pochmann or Sader in Sader 2013) have called the political project 'neo-developmentalist', defending the advancement of a post-neoliberal pattern of development in the country despite the maintenance of the neoliberal macroeconomic orthodoxy. In Sampaio Jr.'s critical view, the PT's neo-developmentalist project intended to

> reconcile the 'positive' aspects of neoliberalism – unconditional commitment to currency stability, fiscal austerity, the search for international competitiveness, the absence of any kind of discrimination against international capital – with the 'positive' aspects of the old developmentalism – commitment to economic growth, industrialization, the regulatory role of the state and social sensitivity. (2012, 679, author's translation)

However, if the combat of social inequality within the established order were two political agendas that did not seem to combine (Singer 2009, 96), developmentalism and neoliberalism were two policy prescriptions that, together, seemed unsustainable, either from the mainstream perspective or from the neo-developmentalist heterodoxy (Morais and Saad-Filho 2011, 523). On the one hand, neoliberal macroeconomic policies impose real limits on growth, industrial competitiveness, public investment, social welfare and state activism, all of which are promoted and expected under developmental policies. On the other hand, the expansion of domestic consumption, imports and public spending, which developmentalism promotes, deteriorate the current account balance, primary fiscal surplus and inflation control, thereby undermining the macroeconomic stability brought about by orthodox policies.

Within the political sphere, developmentalist and neoliberal economic policies were accompanied by a tension between a productivist and a rentier social coalition. The productivist coalition agenda included the control of foreign capital flows, interest rate reduction, domestic currency devaluation, protection of the industry against the 'Dutch disease' and deindustrialization, an increase in public investments in infrastructure and a reduction in inequality (Filgueiras 2013). The rentier coalition, in turn, advocated high interest rates, the free flow of foreign capital, a floating exchange rate, central bank independence and the rejection of state-led income redistribution.

Despite this tense economic and political arrangement, Brazil started to experience an economic upswing, followed by social improvements that were visible during Lula's first term in office. In December 2010, Lula ended his presidential term with an unprecedented popularity level of around 90%. How was he able to reconcile the irreconcilable?

Agricultural exports have a prominent and revealing political role in answering this question. The next section shows that there was no leadership miracle.

Agribusiness and the commodity boom: a political windfall

Agricultural export was critical in lifting the economy out of the stagnation and crisis it faced in the early 2000s. At the end of Lula's first year as president, the agribusiness trade surplus had offset the country's current account deficit, ending the period of macroeconomic instability and producing the first growth cycle, both having a substantial political effect for Lula and the PT. Lula thus reaped the political fruits of a convergence of domestic and international factors.

The productivity increase in the agricultural export sector, which reflected the technological advancement stimulated during Cardoso's last administration, resulted in sizable soya harvests that were traded on the international market not only at exceptional prices, but also under the condition of strong domestic currency devaluation, thereby generating extra revenue. Brazil was in crisis when Lula first came to power, but was ready to feed into and benefit from the global commodity super-cycle driven by emerging markets, particularly China.

Over the course of one year, from 2003 to 2004, the annual GDP growth rate increased from 1.1% to 5.8%, and by the end of 2005, Brazil was experiencing a growth cycle driven mainly by (agricultural) exports (Carvalho 2018). According to Loureiro (2019, 5), between 2003 and 2005, exports corresponded to 42.7% of the rise in aggregate demand against 39.5% and 4.5% of private consumption and investment, respectively.

This externally-driven growth cycle during Lula's first administration unleashed a series of processes that led to a second and virtuous growth cycle with very different characteristics (Loureiro 2019). Together with macroeconomic stabilization and lower inflation, the first growth wave helped to recover the average real salary after mid-2004 (Filgueiras 2013, 398), stimulating an increase in domestic consumption. The extraordinary trade balance surpluses mentioned above stimulated the return of foreign investors to the economy. With investments, production, trade and consumption on the rise, the fiscal budget increased, allowing for the expansion of income redistribution programs and public investments, both of which have an impact on employment opportunities. The improvement in employment and income – through income transfer programs, a minimum wage increase and access to popular credit – further stimulated an increase in consumption. From 2006 to 2012, economic growth was domestically driven, mainly by domestic consumption and investment (Loureiro 2019). Yet this second pattern of growth was not detached from, but rather reinforced by, and partly reliant on, the commodity export sectors.

Several authors claim that the second growth cycle resulted from a state-led policy inflection (Barbosa and Souza 2010) or policy hybridization (Morais and Saad-Filho 2011) characterized by state activism in relaxing macroeconomic policies and pushing forward developmental policies. Politically, the inflection meant alleviating the tensions between the productive and rentier bourgeoisies while benefiting the poor. The extraordinary performance of agricultural exports – this time together with the extractive industry (oil, mining and gas) – partly explains the temporary lift of the policy incompatibility within the PT's political formula. Such a role became evident and possible during Lula's mandates, when commodity prices and international liquidity were exceptional – two contingent and exogenous factors to the national economy.

Carvalho (2018) mentions that the rise in international commodity prices not only increased incentives and resources for investments in the commodity-producing sectors, but also engendered a chain effect for the related sectors, raising government revenues needed for the expansion of public investments. The massive inflow of foreign investment during this period responded to the opportunities in the agricultural sector, the extractive industry and related infrastructure (Gonçalves 2012, 13) – besides the opportunities arising from Brazil's large domestic market.

Many of the investments of the Growth Acceleration Program (PAC), a state investment platform launched in 2006, were also induced by the commodity production sectors. The PAC became a dynamic center of growth in subsequent years (Sitcovsky 2013, 120). Other state initiatives, such as the provision of subsidized loans from the National Development Bank (BNDES) to national corporations, or South-South investments and partnerships, targeted and boosted the primary sector.

The evolution of employment in this period occurred at the base of the Brazilian social pyramid, corresponding to the labor-intensive, low-paid and low-skilled sectors that were driving economic growth, in particular, the service sector, construction and extractive industries (Pochmann 2012). It is important to note that the salary gains, particularly in the service sector, were transferred to the final service costs, resulting in service price inflation (Carvalho 2018). It was only possible to increase income (and consumption) at the base of the pyramid and to retain overall control of inflation because primary commodity exports and foreign investment (both generating a massive inflow of foreign currency) induced exchange rate appreciation (Carvalho 2018). This cheapened imports and prevented price readjustments in the sectors that, unlike services, faced international competition, thereby enabling inflation targets to be met.

Allowing the exchange rate to fluctuate according to market forces was a political choice that had several effects on the patterns of production and trade. While the steady appreciation of domestic currency favored the assemblers of imported industrial inputs, it undermined the internal and external competitiveness of several branches of the national industry. This implied that the increase in domestic consumption (as a driver of growth) was linked to the development of a growing industrial trade deficit. In the mid-2000s, this perverse dynamic could continue, since the trade surpluses of the primary commodity sector compensated for the industrial trade deficit. The primary sector, which exploits cheap and abundant production factors, was highly competitive, regardless of the exchange rate overvaluation.

Maintaining high interest rates was also a political choice that produced unequal and conflicting effects between the productive and rentier bourgeoisie, as well as society at large. It increased the cost of bank credit operations and undermined the domestic capacity of private investments. While some businesses perished, corporate financialized industries (several in agribusiness itself) could expand, relying on external financing, either through intercompany loans, buying and selling equity stakes, or borrowing abroad at favorable rates. The state itself could increasingly rely on external financing, selling public debt bonds with very attractive interest rates leveraged by the Central Bank benchmark rate. In a moment of expansion of the global economy, Brazil became a hub of foreign investment and financial transactions.

That meant that, besides offsetting the industrial trade deficit, primary exports were also remunerating the stocks of foreign capital, both perversely enhanced as a consequence of the growth model (Andrade 2016). Primary exports prevented an immediate erosion of the balance of payments (BoP), public accounts and inflation control (Filgueiras 2013, 37; Carvalho 2018). Therefore, these exports helped to sustain the economic policy inflection that promoted growth leveraged by investment and domestic consumption while maintaining high interest rates, currency overvaluation and a contractionary fiscal policy.

In this particular international context, primary commodity production and exports helped the state promote a concrete, albeit temporary and limited reversal between the neoliberal and neo-developmentalist policy effects on the economy and society, letting the latter stand out – the material basis of Lulism. However, they did not help transform the power asymmetries between the two essential classes in state decision-making, nor did they transform the inequalities in economic and social relations, which form the abstract basis supporting the argument for populism and the fetish of the neo-developmentalist project. The performance of the primary commodity sectors reinforced, deepened, sustained and concealed its structural vulnerabilities and dependencies, which are discussed in the next section.

The development pattern and social relations: deceiving the class mandate received at the polls

The pattern of economic growth and development contributed to the deterioration of the commodities – manufacture composition of the country's trade balance (Morais and Saad-Filho 2011, 523) and enhanced a regressive primary specialization trend in the international division of labor. As the productive structure became less diversified and integrated, reflecting the dismantling of industrial chains since the 1990s, the country entered a fragile path of international market dependence and reliance on exchange rate overvaluation. Depreciating the *real* would make imported products (on which the country came to depend) more expensive, advancing instead of relieving the negative effects on the trade balance, consumer prices and inflation – all of which came to be experienced soon after the end of the commodity boom.

The macroeconomic policies mentioned above stimulated a massive, state-operated transfer of public income – leveraged by the effects of growth on the fiscal budget – to the private sphere of national and international owners of financial assets (Carvalho 2018). In this way, the state limited its capacity to invest and redistribute. The increase of domestic assets owned by foreigners (e.g. state- and private-owned enterprises and services, bonds of public debt, private equity stakes) created a corresponding intensification of income and profit repatriation, or a draining of income and capital. The exchange rate overvaluation further stimulated remittances and foreign speculative investment (Andrade 2016, 11) by increasing their real return when converted back to hard currency.

The patterns and intensity of financial transactions between residents and nonresidents of the country placed a structural burden on the current account of the BoP.

The policy inflection at the basis of the neo-developmentalist project was fragile, depending on and nurturing itself through the primary sector and foreign investment, both contingent to the international context. It was also weak: the economic model was structurally inadequate for attaching domestic demand dynamism to a corresponding industrial, technological dynamism, as well as for linking the fiscal gains to a corresponding expansion in public investment and social redistribution. It promoted a limited convergence of class interests within the bourgeoisie, as well as within the working class, shaped by the constraints of monetary policies and financial dominance.

Instead of neo-developmentalism, the PT promoted a 'reverse developmentalism' (Gonçalves 2012). The structural axis of the (old) national developmentalism had been inverted, inducing a reprimarization of exports, de-industrialization and the import of industrial goods (literally the reversal of import substitution), greater technological dependence and denationalization, a loss of international competitiveness and greater external structural vulnerability – making the Brazilian economy prone to crises (Gonçalves 2012).

Different from the first years of the 2000s, agribusiness exports were no longer a contingent element that helped lift the country out of crisis and launch a neo-developmentalist experience. Agribusiness for exports became endogenous to the state-sponsored pattern of accumulation and integral to the regressive structures of production, trade, consumption and finance. Vergara-Camus and Kay (2017) pointed to the inability of left-leaning governments in Latin America to confront agribusiness power and deal with the state's rentier character. In the case of Brazil, it was not a matter of the government's inability, but rather its direct economic and political reliance on agribusiness and the extractive industry for sustaining its political project.

To avoid these flaws, the entire macroeconomic policy framework would have to change, with a corresponding demise of the rentier coalition's ascendance in policymaking. As Filgueiras and Gonçalves sharply note,

> […] the interest rate in Brazil is not only the classical instrument of monetary policy; it is much more than that. […] it constitutes the fundamental element that structures and at the same time expresses class and power relations. (2007, 180, author's translation)

The patterns of employment creation, earned income distribution and consumption promoted in this period benefited the very poor, albeit at the margins. These patterns also created a (dangerous) double squeeze on the urban middle class and part of the formal proletariat, which was still significantly poor. The latter were users of public services (e.g. health, transport, education), which worsened in terms of quality, cost and service capacity, whereas the former were users of urban services (e.g. restaurants, hairdressers, domestic services, construction) affected by the price inflation resulting from the increase in labor costs. The middle class also experienced a decline in the availability of formal (and better remunerated) employment opportunities. In brief, the neo-developmentalist project increased tensions within the broad working class (while easing those within the bourgeoisie) (Filgueiras and Gonçalves 2007).

Finally, it is important to remember that the income redistribution did not reach the top of the pyramid. It is worth looking at the fostered pattern of asset ownership. Land and natural resource assets, which have a historically narrow basis, became even more concentrated after the 2000s. Comparing land distribution patterns, Teixeira (2011) shows that, between 2003 and 2010, large properties increased by 16% in number and 48.4% in size: an additional 104 million hectares of private property, 70% of which is found in the Amazon region. In 2003, large properties corresponded to 51.6% of the country's total rural property area, compared with 56.1% in 2010; all other property size groupings reduced their share of the total property area.

Concentration also marks the pattern of financial asset ownership. Consequently, several authors have questioned the assertion over decreasing inequality and poverty rates in Brazil (Oliveira 2009; Sitcovsky 2013, 134):

> […] the mere payment of the domestic debt service, around 200 billion *reais* per year, against the extremely modest 10 to 15 billion of Bolsa Família, does not require much theoretical speculation to conclude that inequality is increasing. (Oliveira 2009, author's translation)

Amann and Baer (2012, 420) have asked 'whether further substantial improvements in the distribution of income can be realized in the context of a highly skewed pattern of asset ownership'. Indeed, this brings into question the forms and effectiveness of income redistribution, including cash transfer programs and other social policies, all of which were definitive to the success of the PT in presidential elections. The next section briefly exemplifies how these tensions touched upon the countryside.

The rural staging political tensions and appeasements

In December 2010, the Institute of Agrarian Reform (INCRA) presented statistics showing that, during Lula's terms in office, the Agrarian Reform Program reached its best ever performance in regard to designated area and number of settled families. The well-known scholar Ariovaldo U. de Oliveira contested the statistics, explaining that INCRA aggregated land titling and land regularization with the expropriation and implementation of new settlements. According to his calculations, only 34.4% of the total number of land settlements documented by INCRA between 2003 and 2009 were truly new settlements (Arruda 2011). And in 2011, under Rousseff's administration, the number of settled families reached the lowest point in 16 years (Pericás 2017, 61).

By contrast, the volume of public resources Lula and Rousseff spent on the 'family farm' agricultural sector was without precedent – although significantly lower than the volume spent in large-scale, highly capitalized agriculture – and had an impact on rural income and productivity. The rural credit program (Pronaf) mostly benefited the better-off (small-scale) producers, while programs such as the food procurement program (PAA) or targeted credit for women and youth benefited poorer producers (Sabourin 2007), including most of the beneficiaries of agrarian reform. The number of rural poor decreased by 38.7% between 2003 and 2009 (author's calculation based on DIEESE 2011, 143).

For the MST leadership, agrarian reform itself became a sort of social compensation policy during the mandates of the PT. Mafort (2018, 19), who is part of that leadership, argues that the consolidation of family agriculture occurred at the expense of structural and transformative agrarian reform, class consciousness formation and movement-building. Agrarian reform, which once formed the core of the PT's political project, assumed a different nature during the party's mandate, as did the social struggle for land.

Pericás (2017) presents other interesting figures covering the period in which the economic crisis commenced. In 2012, 70% of the budget allocated to INCRA was cut. During the same period, 42.9% of land reform settlers had abandoned their land, and 35% had illegally transferred their property (Pericás 2017, 60–61). At the start of 2013, 36% of the families in land reform settlement schemes depended on the *Bolsa Família* (Pericás 2017, 59–60). Unsurprisingly, authors such as Filgueiras and Gonçalves (2007) argued that several of Lula's social policies were unable to disarm the structural mechanisms of poverty reproduction. Maintaining the poor in a permanent state of insecurity and dependence, they only functioned as a buffer of social tensions within a liberal project or instruments of political manipulation (Pericás 2017). In the countryside, many programs simply mitigated a state-sponsored erosion of rural social reproduction.

The MST remained critical of the government and politically active during the entire period, but could not escape the effects of populism on its base, which, on the one hand, was at the forefront of the conflict related to agribusiness expansion, and, on the other, was benefiting from several social and income policies. Both dynamics were linked and promoted by the government. The movement was put into a deadlock: structural agrarian reform, its main demand, did not make sense in the PT development model and advanced very little; as a result, the movement lost the power of mobilization. The MST remained politically engaged, but became less effective. To a certain extent, placing more emphasis on the economic-corporate demands of its landed base, which were partly met by public programs, the movement became dependent on Lulism (Almeida 2012) – even if there was a sharp understanding and critique of the development model, its logic and corresponding powers among its ranks.

The irony of Lula's political project in rural areas was having the state capacity to redistribute income, expand credit and other forms of support to the rural working poor tied to the encroachment of capital (and thus, to its legitimacy) on land and natural resources. This signifies that, beyond concessions to the rural poor, social welfare was part and parcel of a vicious social alliance between the poor and the dominant capital – an alliance that deepened structural class contradictions.

Tackling poverty and social inequality were rendered exogenous to capital-labor relations and to the dynamics of income and wealth accumulation that bring them into being. Social programs, such as *Bolsa Família*, could be presented as administrative solutions (with a temporary, immediatist, selective and assistentialist nature), depoliticizing both poverty and inequality (Oliveira 2006, 22). As Sitcovsky observed,

> [t]he intellectuals of the Workers' Party, by presenting the thesis of post-neoliberalism, neo-developmentalism, and arguing for a virtuous growth cycle, [...] created a mystifying [perhaps, fetishized] vision of reality, covering up reprimarization, deindustrialization and the deepening of financialization. Likewise, by declaring the end of extreme poverty through Bolsa Família, and reducing the social phenomenon of poverty to an income issue, they eventually reified it. (2013, 135, author's translation)

The next section resumes the discussion on populism and elaborates on Lula's model.

A new modality of left-wing populism: drawing from above and below

> I am no longer a human being; I am an idea – an idea fused with yours
> (Lula's statement on the day of his arrest, 7 April 2018)

Lula's model of populism is not easy to grasp – it is nuanced. Simple labels fall short in describing, much less analyzing it. Lula and the PT are associated with the left, whose politics is inspired by a critique of capitalism and a corresponding alternative vision. Concerns with poverty, employment, income and working class mobilization have been constitutive of leftist politics. Yet 'populism of the left' does not adequately describe the PT experience in power.

The populism of the left is historically associated with the fetishization of patterns of accumulation from below in which the rural economy assumes central importance. This type of populism is marked by the pursuit of economic and social policies that assume inherent properties of small-scale property and production, family labor, local culture, rural development and nationalism as the bases for social justice, equity, autonomy (rural or national), sovereignty and emancipation. The fetish lies in the fact that none of these – the scale, the family, the locality, the territory or the nation – relate to the causes of capitalist exploitation, poverty or inequality (see Byres 1979; Kitching 1989; and Brass 2000). Consequently, populism from below, even if having a sophisticated political agenda, fails to describe in theory, and to resolve in practice, how forms of (petit commodity, national) production and accumulation are integrated into broader capitalist and international commodity relations. Their politics fail 'the people', in part or in total, leaving unrestrained forms of capitalist exploitation, which in theory they oppose (Kitching 1989, 181–3).

Yet it is likely that populism from below is economically more democratic, mobilizes the grassroots, has a leader that comes from below and calls upon or urges the people to act, rallies supporters, bends the economic elite and so on. However, these and other features should not be inferred theoretically, but rather described empirically. In contemporary Latin America, perhaps Morales in Bolivia could be better described as a leader embodying populism from below. Other examples can be found in the African context, such as Tanzania under Nyerere's rule, where the widespread access to and dependence on land for social reproduction made accumulation from below conceivable as a political project.

Lula's personal history and the social characteristics of the population he mobilized created a sense of a government 'for and from below'. Lula promoted personal ties with the poor, but also catered to their real interests, enabling income redistribution that is a progressive and popular demand. This has been crucial to the way in which Lula and the PT secured and exerted power. However, Lula did not try to implement a model of accumulation from below. His populism therefore belongs to a new modality of populism of the left.

Lula did not attempt to dispute control over the (re)organization of property, production, appropriation and accumulation within society. In his government, the dominant classes (e.g. banks, financiers, multinational corporations, national and international holders of public debt bonds) benefited from structural macroeconomic policies, while the working class benefited from income redistribution measures with essential limits in scope, scale and sustainability, conditioned by the former. The benefits for the working class were short term, selective, restricted and assistentialist. The PT governed for large capital – for the already privileged and powerful. The very expansion of primary exports in this period can be considered a manifestation of a neoliberal, financialized pattern of accumulation from above.

Accumulation from above can be defined as the formation or expansion of (preexisting) dominant capital (or groups of capital) through processes of social income and wealth appropriation (as in the privatization, expropriation, and direct appropriation of public land and resources, in addition to the control of production, trade and finance), for which state command is essential. Neoliberalism is a specific pattern of accumulation from above, assuming a specific form in the Brazilian context. The fetishization of such a type of economics can assume various forms and enable the emergence of populist politics supported and legitimized by the masses.

Populism from above tends to be economically and politically transformative, changing the relations of power within the bourgeoisie and, consequently, the patterns of production, distribution and accumulation. These transformations require economic, social, political and institutional reforms, possibly requiring top-down decision-making, a disciplinary, coercive state, and strong leaders that preach to the masses. President Vargas (1930–1945 and 1950–1954), who led the process of industrialization in Brazil, could be considered an example. Lula did not have these characteristics, and his policies were not as transformative; rather, he maintained and nurtured the material and political basis of neoliberalism through corresponding macroeconomic and social policies, but under the promise of transforming the living conditions of the working poor.

In conversation with Gramsci and Singer, Oliveira (2006) argues that Lulism flipped Gramsci's formula on its head: instead of the moral ascendancy of the possessing over the laboring classes, the dominant was bent, consenting to be led by a representative of the dominated, yet simply to reinforce the structures of their exploitation – a 'hegemony in reverse' (Oliveira 2006). Lula, in turn, conceded to capital as a condition of power.

The myth of his political project relates to the illusion of creating an endogenous growth process yielding social equity (neo-developmentalism) without attempting to renegotiate power and property, rallying popular power in society and state decision-making – a hallmark of populism. The masses were political agents in the instance of elections, expressing preferences, asking, hoping and waiting for support and change; however their political participation was instrumental.

> In some respects, petismo-lulismo represents a far purer populism – the impossibility of a politics based on organized class – than the classic cases of Vargas, Perón and Cárdenas. These were, in various ways, authoritarian forms for the inclusion of the working class in politics [under the tutelage of the bourgeois state]. Today's neo-populism represents not the authoritarian inclusion but the democratic exclusion of those classes from politics. (Oliveira 2006, 19)

Delivering material improvements to the poor without active engagement, Lulism reinforced a passive political actor, allowed or stimulated political lethargy and constrained more ambitious demands of its own organized social base (as with the case of agrarian reform and the MST), even creating important arms of social co-optation (as with the case of CUT).

In brief, Lulism was the unification of the main working class fraction without class politics, class forms of consciousness, organization or political struggle. Lulism was embodied by the election of an authentic working-class president devoid of working-class power, even though part of the left in Brazil pretended that this was the case (Oliveira, TV interview, '*Roda Viva*' Program, July 2012). This is exactly the uncritical treatment – or fetishization – of transformative politics, so emblematic of populism of the left. Lula did not reflect the ideology of the ruling class, but came to represent the notion that it was possible to succeed within the order.

The temporary success of his economic model was organically linked to a process that undermined long-term economic development and social cohesion, leaving two easy scapegoats – the left and the poor – increasingly exposed. Lula's populism was economically weak and politically vulnerable, allying a partial realization of the interest 'from below' to the reproduction and expansion of a pattern of accumulation 'from above'.

In 2011, with the global economy still in crisis, foreign investment stagnant and the commodity price boom at its end, the BoP, financial, fiscal, monetary and real crises started to swell, becoming critical after 2013. As they unfolded, they exposed the limits of the PT's political project and their deceptive representation of the working poor. The spell crumbled in Rousseff's hands. The next section sheds light into the political crisis and the recent authoritarian turn.

The 2013 crisis and the political turn

Eu não vou pagar o pato (Fiesp)
… e a multidão caiu feito um patinho.

Rousseff's administration reacted to the economic crisis by advancing the developmentalist agenda. She intended to stimulate investment by granting a tax-friendly agreement to targeted industries, making the exchange rate more competitive and reducing the interest rate to its lowest in years. This move, however, irritated the rentier coalition, who saw it as a threat to their economic privilege and political dominance. Rousseff also failed to facilitate the expected economic recovery, having underestimated the extent of the global crisis and taken a series of precipitated and clumsy measures. In 2014, she was reelected by a small margin of votes and, at the dawn of her second term, receded her developmentalist promises and redirected her policies to the priorities of the financial market – this time, irritating her supporters and being left politically on her own.

It is worth recalling that, in June 2013, the PT was taken by surprise when more than one million people angrily took to the streets to express widespread dissatisfaction with the lack of provision of public services across the country (Saad-Filho 2014). The initial protest against the rise of bus tariffs in São Paulo was catalyzed after ruthless political repression. Thereafter, demonstrations multiplied in size and diversified in terms of social composition and political demands throughout the month (Saad-Filho 2014, 1). Although originally ignited by leftist claims to services such as free transport, the protests were soon subsumed by the 'entry of a disparate mass of middle-class demonstrators supported by the mainstream media' (Saad-Filho 2014). The left withdrew from the streets, and subsequently, the 2013 events fermented into an anti-PT sentiment, ultimately boiling over with Rousseff's 2016 impeachment.

Operation Car Wash (*Operação Lava Jato*), an investigation of corruption and money laundering conducted by the Federal Police starting in April 2014, was an important catalyst. As it unfolded, the operation started to torment politicians, prominent entrepreneurs and former employees of state-owned companies (such as Petrobras). Under the radar of the investigation, they were threatened with the possibility of losing their political mandates and facing jail sentences, which mobilized them to seek the containment of the operation at all costs, including pushing for Rousseff's impeachment. In the public sphere, *Lava Jato* was not only demoralizing politicians, but also undermining the overall legitimacy of the state, the national congress and other political institutions. With the explicit use and support of the corporate media, this operation started to instrumentalize corruption and moralism to gain mass traction in favor of impeachment while keeping the interests of powerful financialized economic groups invisible and intact.[9]

The vote from the agribusiness caucus in congress was decisive for impeachment. The industrial and agrarian bourgeoisie abandoned the PT, voting against the developmentalist state – or against their interests – to form a single bourgeois coalition with the rentier class. Carvalho (2018) provides two possible explanations. First, taking state control from the PT, politicians could hold back *Lava Jato*, which could compromise the entire political system. Second, by supporting impeachment and securing tighter control of the state, economic sectors could save themselves from 'the cost of one of the greatest economic crises in recent history, imposing it on the rest of society' (Carvalho 2018, chapter 3, A panaceia do impeachment, author's translation). São Paulo's Industrial Federation (*Fiesp*), the main beneficiary of Rousseff's recovery plan, launched the pro-impeachment slogan, 'I will not pay the price' (*Eu não vou pagar o pato*), which was adopted by the people, unaware of the cynicism.

The vote of the agribusiness caucus, in particular, seems to reinforce one of the arguments put forward here: that the economic and political importance of the sector emerged and made sense in the context of neoliberalism and financialization.[10] Boito and Saad-Filho (2016, 194–5) also remark that the accumulation strategies of the domestic bourgeoisie (or the productive coalition) depended on imperialism and the international (rentier) bourgeoisie, sharing an ideology, culture, finance and other interests.

Singer (2015) suggests that the bourgeois political alignment that led to impeachment was motivated by the fear of growing state activism, particularly seen during Rousseff's first term, and of the PT's symbolic, moral and historical alliance with the working class. The bourgeoisie's relationship with Lula and the PT always carried the fear of radicalization. In a country with enormous social inequality such as Brazil, the ruling classes experienced Lulism as a first manifestation of the class struggle – even though it temporarily placated social tensions. Therefore, by giving up their immediate interests, the productive coalition could avoid the greater risk of a worker takeover of politics (Singer 2015).

Lulism possessed an organic transformative potential not usually found in other instances of populism. Considering the social profile of its supporters, Lulism had the potential to express demands deriving from, and thus compatible with, the material and political interests of the working class. It could also develop the latent possibility of mass mobilization and active intervention into the control of economic affairs. The development of such potential, however, was conditioned upon populism's very demise.

The PT's 13-year period of governance prompted certain transformations in that direction, for example, inciting an extensive and extended notion of citizenship and rights that could have unfolded into a new moral ethos to redefine social relations in the country.

---

[9] The rigged political role of *Lava Jato*, recently revealed (see the leaked material published by The Intercept-Brazil), reached a pinnacle with Lula's imprisonment, mentioned ahead.

[10] In 2005, the vote of the agribusiness caucus saved Lula from an impeachment process after the 'mensalão scandal'. In this context, commodity prices were high, and the sector was economically and politically more comfortable to support (and continuing to count on) Lula's government.

What could happen when the new mass of people with a formal education did not find employment opportunities compatible with their new material and cultural aspirations (Singer 2013)? The initial wave of protests in 2013 reflected the growing realization that good jobs were scarce, the quality of urban services had deteriorated, and the cost of such services had nevertheless increased. The situation evolved, however, in the least desired way up to the 2018 presidential election.

Safatle's (2018) remark is poignant: what was dramatic about the latest election was that those who rightly wanted a rupture with the establishment were captured by and radicalized to the extreme right, not the left. How did this occur? While this is not an easy question to answer, it is fundamental to Brazil's future. This new modality of populism of the left that aligns its progressive agenda to financial capital accumulation provides some insights into the recent shift to authoritarian, morally conservative and ultra-liberal economic politics.

The economic crisis the PT led the country into was a crisis of the neoliberal pattern of capital accumulation, externally dependent. Having done nothing to confront the power of the propertied and rentier bourgeoisie, or to organize and politicize its social base – having in fact concealed the antagonism in its class alliances and political representation – the party was left with no legitimate authority, no basis of defense, and no line of attack when the economic crisis and political accusations rebounded.

Lula and the PT, and, unfortunately, the left in general, were at the mercy of conservative forces and the media, who were left alone to frame the explanations for the crisis. A fictional 'radical left' (of 'Marxists' and 'communists') was forced to shoulder the burden of the economic, social and moral collapse of the country. The PT and the left were scorned and branded as irresponsible, incompetent, negligent and, above all, deeply corrupt.

The PT resorted to the only remaining option: reinforcing Lula's leadership. Avoiding explanations and self-critique, the party seemed to sustain the idea that the social successes of the 2000s were directly and solely attributable to Lula and that he alone could bring them back. Arguably, the party allowed for the political butchering of Rousseff – 'this inept woman' – in 2016, gambling that it could make its comeback under Lula in the 2018 election. It is important to note that Lulism is still alive and well; Lula was the favorite candidate in the presidential campaign and was likely to have been elected in 2018 if the Superior Electoral Court had not blocked his candidacy a month before the election was to take place.[11]

Lula's social base, having passively experienced a multitude of changes, particularly in purchasing power, but having not had a chance to understand why these changes were limited and short-lived, remained faithful. Almost as a corollary, that same social base was incapable of forming a political understanding to organize and oppose Rousseff's impeachment, which only reinforces the aspects and effects of populism discussed in this article. During the presidential campaign, Lula sought to unite the organized left – but around him – ultimately achieving the opposite.

The Brazilian people, resentful of the low quality of public services and other effects of the neoliberal order, indiscriminately voted for the absolute dismantling of the state and

---

[11] After a controversial and expedited trial in the context of Operation Car Wash, Lula received a 12-year prison sentence for corruption and money laundering in April 2018. His campaign continued even in prison until September 2018, when Brazil's top electoral court ruled that his candidacy should be barred. The PT's substitute candidate, Fernando Haddad, began his campaign a month before the election, adopting a strategy to make him a virtual image of Lula.

supreme neoliberal hegemony – a tragedy for which Lula bears responsibility. Bolsonaro was elected as the option to remoralize public life, to bring economic and social order, and to 'put things right'. But whose order?

Conclusion

The contrast between 'the sheer electoral weight of the poor, juxtaposed against the sheer scale of economic inequality' (Anderson 2011) makes Brazilian democracy latently explosive. The country's republican history expresses it well: it is permeated by dictatorships, coups d'etat and populism, all making it evident that 'political democracy was never meant to reach the economic realm' (Ayers and Saad-Filho 2015, 600). The political system itself is a historically entrenched structure against working class formation and organized struggle. Lula's populism is part of this history, as is the impeachment of Rousseff, Lula's imprisonment and the election of Bolsonaro.

Populism can be politically and economically transformative, but it is socially conservative, reproducing rather than transcending social hierarchies and inequalities. The PT captivated the support 'from below' by promoting marginal income redistribution, innocuous for a transformation – much less an inversion – in power relations in society and the political system. Lula's populism symbolically bent, but economically served the powers 'from above'. His political choices not only cast down the goal of development with social equity, but also launched Brazil into a long-term trajectory of instability and crisis (Gonçalves 2012).

Since the impeachment process, the MST became more openly supportive of the PT. Its overt participation in Lula's 2018 presidential campaign shed doubt on whether it represented a questionable electoral pragmatism or a regrettable Lulism. On the day of his imprisonment, Lula powerfully declared that he had become 'an idea', set loose to spread among the masses. This 'idea' must be disputed. In the face of growing authoritarianism and attacks on workers, Lulism risks being reinforced, instead of gaining a critical understanding of the political nature and related limits of the Workers' Party project. Without this understanding, no reliable counter-alliances and strategies can emerge, let alone a conceivable path to emancipation. '*A luta continua*', but class struggle (and class analysis) must resume its critical role.

Acknowledgments

I would like to express my appreciation to the ERPI team for creating this important platform for scholarship and movement-building. I am also grateful for the ERPI grant that contributed to this research. I would also like to thank my two anonymous peer reviewers for their constructive comments. Finally, I would like to extend a major thanks to professor Alfredo Saad-Filho for his encouragement and valuable insights in the early stages of writing this article.

Disclosure statement

No potential conflict of interest was reported by the author.

Funding

This work was supported by Emancipatory Rural Politics Initiative (ERPI): [ERPI Small Grant].

ORCID

Daniela Andrade http://orcid.org/0000-0002-0766-5545

References

Almeida, Lúcio Flávio Rodrigues de. 2012. "Entre o nacional e o neonacional-desenvolvimentismo: poder político e classes sociais no Brasil contemporâneo." *Serviço Social & Sociedade* 112: 689–710.
Amann, Edmund, and Werner Baer. 2012. "Brazil as an Emerging Economy: A New Economic Miracle?" *Brazilian Journal of Political Economy* 32 (3 (128)): 412–423.
Anderson, Perry. 2011. "Lula's Brazil." *London Review of Books* 33 (7): 3–12. Accessed 21 October 2017. https://www.lrb.co.uk/v33/n07/perry-anderson/lulas-brazil.
Andrade, Daniela. 2016. "'Export or Die': the Rise of Brazil as an Agribusiness Powerhouse." *Third World Thematics: A TWQ Journal* 1 (5): 653–672. doi:10.1080/23802014.2016.1353889.
Andreucci, Diego. 2017. "Populism, Hegemony, and the Politics of Natural Resource Extraction in Evo Morales's Bolivia." *Antipode* 00 (0): 1–21.
Arditi, Benjamin. 2005. "Populism as an Internal Periphery of Democratic Politics." In *Populism and the Mirror of Democracy*, edited by Francisco Panizza, 72–98. London: Verso.
Arruda, Roldão. 2011. "Incra infla números de reforma agrária." *O Estado de São Paulo*, Política. https://politica.estadao.com.br/noticias/geral,incra-infla-numeros-de-reforma-agraria,685346.
Ayers, A. J., and A. Saad-Filho. 2015. "Democracy Against Neoliberalism: Paradoxes, Limitations, Transcendence." *Critical Sociology* 41 (4-5): 597–618. doi:10.1177/0896920513507789.
Barbosa, Nelson, and José Antonio Pereira de Souza. 2010. "A inflexão do governo Lula: política econômica, crescimento e distribuição de renda." In *Brasil entre o passado e o futuro*, edited by Sader Emir and Marco Aurélio Garcia, 57–110. São Paulo: Boitempo.
Boito Jr., Armando. 2013. "O lulismo é um tipo de bonapartismo? Uma crítica às teses de André Singer." *Crítica Marxista* 37: 171–181.
Boito Jr., Armando, and Alfredo Saad-Filho. 2016. "State, State Institutions, and Political Power in Brazil." *Latin American Perspectives* 43 (2): 190–206.
Brass, T. 2000. *Peasants, populism and postmodernism: the return of the agrarian myth. Vol. 17*. London: Library of Peasant Studies.
Byres, T. J. 1979. "Of neo-populist pipe-dreams: Daedalus in the Third World and the myth of urban bias." *Journal of Peasant Studies* 6 (2): 210–244.
Carvalho, Laura. 2018. *Valsa brasileira: do boom ao caos econômico*. E-book. São Paulo: Todavia.
Castilho, Alceu. 2017. Frente Parlamentar da Agropecuária compôs 50% dos votos do impeachment e 51% dos votos para manter Temer. Accessed 14 January 2018. https://deolhonosruralistas.com.br/2017/09/25/frente-parlamentar-da-agropecuaria-compos-50-dos-votos-do-impeachment-e-51-dos-votos-para-manter-temer/.
CPT (Comissão Pastoral da Terra). 2017. *Conflitos no campo, Brasil, 2017*. Goiânia: CPT Nacional, Brasil.
de la Torre, Carlos. 2016. "Left-wing Populism: Inclusion and Authoritarianism in Venezuela, Bolivia, and Ecuador." *The Brown Journal of World Affairs* XXIII (I): 61–76.
de la Torre, Carlos. 2017. "Populism in Latin America." In *The Oxford Handbook of Populism*, edited by Cristóbal Rovira Kaltwasser, Paul Taggart, Paulina Ochoa Espejo, and Pierre Ostiguy, 1–22. Oxford: Oxford University Press.
DIEESE. 2011. "Estatísticas do meio rural 2010-2011." Departamento Intersindical de Estatística e Estudos Socioeconômicos; Núcleo de Estudos Agrários e Desenvolvimento Rural; Ministério do Desenvolvimento Agrário. São Paulo: DIEESE; NEAD; MDA.
Filgueiras, Luiz. 2013. A natureza do atual padrão de desenvolvimento brasileiro e o processo de desindustrialização. In *Novas interpretações desenvolvimentistas*, edited by Inez Silvia Batista Castro, E-papers, 532p. Rio de Janeiro: Centro Internacional Celso Furtado.
Filgueiras, Luiz, and Reinaldo Gonçalves. 2007. *A economia política do governo Lula*. Rio de Janeiro: Contraponto.
Fine, Ben, and Alfredo Saad-Filho. 2016. *Marx's Capital. Sixth ed.* London: Pluto Press.

Gonçalves, Reinaldo. 2012. "Governo Lula e o nacional- desenvolvimentismo às avessas." *Revista da Sociedade Brasileira de Economia Política* 31: 5–30.

Hunter, Wendy, and Timothy J. Power. 2007. "Rewarding Lula: Executive Power, Social Policy, and the Brazilian Elections of 2006." *Latin American Politics and Society* 49 (1): 1–30.

Kitching, Gavin. 1989. *Development and Underdevelopment in Historical Perspective: Populism, Nationalism, and Industrialization*. London: Routledge.

Laclau, E. 1977. *Politics and Ideology in Marxist Theory: Capitalism, Fascism, Populism*. London: NLB.

Laclau, E. 2005. Populism: What's in a name? In *Populism and the Mirror of Democracy*, edited by Francisco Panizza, 32–49. London: Verso.

Loureiro, Pedro Mendes. 2019. "Class Inequality and Capital Accumulation in Brazil, 1992-2013." *Cambridge Journal of Economics*, 1–26. Advance online publication. doi:10.1093/cje/bez030.

Mafort, Kelli Cristine de Oliveira. 2018. "Reestruturação produtiva no campo e os processos de trabalho nos assentamentos de reforma agrária do Estado de São Paulo." Doutorado, Programa de Pós- Graduação em Ciências Sociais, Faculdade de Ciências e Letras UNESP.

Marx, Karl. 1992 [1867]. *Capital: A Critique of Political Economy. Volume I: The Process of Capitalist Production*. Ernest Mandel (Introduction), transl. by Ben Fowkes. Harmondsworth: Penguin. 1990–1992, 1152p.

Mitidiero Junior, Marco Antonio, ed. 2018. "Dossiê Michel Temer e a Questão Agrária." *OKARA: Geografia em debate* 12 (2). http://www.periodicos.ufpb.br/ojs2/index.php/okara/issue/view/2129.

Morais, Lecio, and Alfredo Saad-Filho. 2011. "Da economia política à política econômica: o novo-desenvolvimentismo e o governo Lula." *Revista de Economia Política* 31 (4): 507–527.

Oliveira, Francisco de. 2006. "Lula in the Labyrinth." *New Left Review* 42: 5–22.

Oliveira, Francisco de. 2007. Hegemonia às avessas. *Piauí*. Accessed 22 November 2017. https://piaui.folha.uol.com.br/materia/hegemonia-as-avessas/.

Oliveira, Francisco de. 2009. Avesso do avesso. *Piauí*. Accessed 22 November 2017. https://piaui.folha.uol.com.br/materia/o-avesso-do-avesso/.

Pericás, Luiz Bernardo. 2017. "Monopólios, desnacionalização e violência: a questão agrária no Brasil hoje." *Margem Esquerda* 29: 59–71.

Pochmann, M. 2012. *Nova classe média? O trabalho na base da pirâmide social brasileira*. São Paulo: Boitempo.

Saad-Filho, Alfredo. 2010. "Neoliberalism, democracy, and development policy in Brazil." *Development and Society* 39 (1): 1–28.

Saad-Filho, Alfredo. 2014. "Brazil: Development Strategies and Social Change From Import-Substitution to the "Events of June"." *Studies in Political Economy: A Socialist Review* 94 (1): 3–29.

Saad-Filho, Alfredo, and Lecio Morais. 2018. *Brazil: Neoliberalism Versus Democracy*. London: Pluto Press.

Sabourin, Eric. 2007. "Que política pública para a agricultura familiar no segundo governo Lula?" *Sociedade e Estado* 22 (3): 715–751.

Sader, Emir, ed. 2013. *10 anos de governos pós-neoliberais no Brasil: Lula e Dilma*. São Paulo, Rio de Janeiro: Boitempo, Flacso.

Safatle, Vladimir. 2018. *Quando você não acerta suas contas com a história, a história te assombra*. interview by Andrea Dip. Publica: agência de jornalismo investigativo. Accessed 3 November 2018. https://apublica.org/2018/10/quando-voce-nao-acerta-suas-contas-com-a-historia-a-historia-te-assombra/.

Sampaio Jr., Plínio de Arruda. 2012. "Desenvolvimentismo e neodesenvolvimentismo: Tragédia e Farsa." *Serviço Social & Sociedade* 112: 672–688.

Scoones, Ian, Marc Edelman, Saturnino M. Borras Jr, Ruth Hall, Wendy Wolford, and Ben White. 2018. "Emancipatory rural Politics: Confronting Authoritarian Populism." *Journal of Peasant Studies* 45 (1): 1–20. doi:10.1080/03066150.2017.1339693.

Singer, André. 2009. "Raízes sociais e ideológicas do Lulismo." *Novos Estudos, CEBRAP* 85: 83–102.

Singer, André. 2013. "Os impasses do 'lulismo'." In *Brasil de Fato*, interview conducted by Antônio David, and Fernanda Becker. Accessed November 2017. https://www.brasildefato.com.br/node/11399/.

Singer, André. 2015. "Cutucando onças com varas curtas: O ensaio desenvolvimentista no primeiro mandato de Dilma rousseff (2011-2014)." *Novos Estudos, CEBRAP* 102: 43–71.

Sitcovsky, Marcelo. 2013. "Dez anos de governo do Partido dos Trabalhadores: pós-neoliberalismo, neodesenvolvimentismo, transferência de renda e hegemonia." *Revista Praia Vermelha* 23 (1): 117–139.

Teixeira, Gerson. 2011. Agravamento do quadro de concentração da terra no Brasil? In *Boletim DALUTA*. http://www2.fct.unesp.br/nera/artigodomes/7artigodomes_2011.pdf.

Vergara-Camus, Leandro, and Cristóbal Kay. 2017. "The Agrarian Political Economy of Left-Wing Governments in Latin America: Agribusiness, Peasants, and the Limits of Neo-Developmentalism." *Journal of Agrarian Change* 17: 415–437.

Weyland, Kurt. 2001. "Clarifying a Contested Concept: Populism in the Study of Latin American Politics." *Comparative Politics* 34 (1): 1–22.

Wood, Ellen Meiksins. 1995. *Democracy Against Capitalism: Reviewing Historical Materialism*. Cambridge: Cambridge University Press.

'They say they don't see color, but maybe they should!' Authoritarian populism and colorblind liberal political culture

Michael Carolan

ABSTRACT
While easy to empirically document the explicit bias underlying authoritarian populism, most of the individuals animating the movement are driven by sentiments harder to detect, such as implicit bias and what is known as the colorblind ideology. Drawing from semi-structured interviews of Colorado (USA) residents ($n = 71$), the paper makes the following three contributions: presenting populism as something more than a homogenous entity; its qualitative empirical material on the implicit biases held among Trump supporters even in the face of observed minority poverty; and, finally, its specific angle on race politics, building on prior accounts that unpack authoritarian populism through racialized imaginaries.

Introduction

There has been a resurgence of interest in the study of authoritarian populism – also identified as 'new rural populism' (Ulrich-Schad and Duncan 2018, 59) or 'anxiety-fueled nativism' (Wright and Levy 2019, 1) – among rural and agrifood scholars, owed to such events as Brexit, the emergence of Trumpism in the US, the Hindu nationalist BJP party's consolidation of power in India, and Bolsonaro's rise to dominance in Brazil (e.g. Anderson 2019; Borras 2020; Edelman 2019; Goldstein, Paprocki, and Osborne 2019; Mamonova 2019; Scoones et al. 2018; Vanaik 2017). As noted by Scoones et al. (2018), in their opening paper of the JPS Forum series on 'Authoritarian Populism and the Rural World,' it is important to understand the phenomenon not as something needing to be immediately explained by grand theorizing. Rather, the goal needs to be about first acquiring a more *situated* understanding of the process and practices:

> How are these aspects of the contemporary moment playing out in rural areas? How are they shaped by prior transformations in rural society and economy and how do they portend even more dramatic—and usually negative—changes for rural areas? (Scoones et al. 2018, 2)

DOI: 10.4324/9781003162353-16

Taking these questions to heart, this paper highlights and thinks through elements associated with authoritarian populism that could use additional empirical interrogation, looking specifically at the movement in the US. The study below puts a new spin on two key variables that have been widely identified for their roles in animating so much of today's bigotry, nativism, and economic nationalism, especially in the US and other democratic societies (e.g. Lopez 2017; Thiede, Lichter, and Slack 2018; Ulrich-Schad and Duncan 2018). The variables of which I speak are economic distress and racial resentment.

Scoones et al. (2018) note that 'not all populism is right-wing and authoritarian,' explaining that 'arguments in favour of "the people" can be a positive, mobilising force of solidarity and emancipation' (3). Statements like this could be taken as suggesting that while not all populism is right-wing, authoritarian populism must be, as it is neither positive nor emancipatory. Critical scholarship on the subject is incredibly nuanced and avoids casting populism as monolithic and as existing only in *either* right-wing *or* left-wing form – Borras (2020, 5) writes explicitly about the 'bookends' of right/left and the need to think in terms of a 'continuum.' Yet there is slippage, like when 'populism' and 'right-wing populism' are used interchangeably (e.g. Mamonova and Franquesa 2019, 2), when 'Trumpism' and 'right-wing populism' are presented as one-and-the-same (e.g. Wodak and Krzyżanowski 2017, 471), or when Trump's appeal is chalked up in large part to 'right-wing discontent' (Hochschild 2016, 685). Chances for misdiagnosis are increased when these conceptual missteps (and empirical inaccuracies) are made as they risk perpetuating the false narrative – especially acute in the mainstream media (e.g. Ford 2019; Slobodian 2018) – that this is solely a problem with right-wing political parties, partisans, and outlooks.

Somewhere between 6.7 and 9.2 million Americans voted for Obama in 2012, only to then cast their vote for Trump in 2016 (Beauchamp 2018). As the 2016 US Presidential Election was decided by 40,000 votes, based on Electoral College delegates, those Obama-turned-Trump supporters decided the outcome. There has been a strong correlation between support for Trump and a community's growing Latino population – many of those rural US counties that went for Obama in 2012 only to switch to Trump in 2016 had seen a large influx of non-whites in the interim (Enos 2017). This aligns with other research detecting a positive relationship between recent Hispanic immigration and state-level variation in anti-Hispanic hate crimes (Stacey, Carbone-López, and Rosenfeld 2011), even in historically Blue (rural) counties (Fahey and Wells n.d.). To lump all Trump supporters into the category 'right-wing' thus misreads the empirics of the case. A 2019 study published in *Socius* (a peer-reviewed journal published by the American Sociological Association), drawing upon data from two Internet-based survey experiments involving a total of 1,797 respondents, notes that a subset of liberals, not conservatives, are the group 'most responsive to the implicit – and sometimes explicit – racial appeals of Donald Trump's presidential campaign' (Wetts and Willer 2019, 15). To therefore cast authoritarian populists as a bunch of right-wing zealots with a long history of engaging in the ritualized demonization of 'the Other' (Berlet and Sunshine 2019, 480–1) misses the fact that this group includes millions of Independent- and Left-leaning citizens, even self-described *liberals*, if Wetts and Willer's (2019) findings are to be believed.

It is worth mentioning that I am talking about US politics. Given the country's two-party political system, moderate democrats and independents are better aligned with center-right parties in Europe. Alexadria Ocasio-Cortez, a rising star in the US for democratic-socialists – the self-described 'tea party of the Left' (Forgey 2020) – recently exclaimed when talking about Joe Biden, the former-Vice President and possible Presidential candidate for the Democratic Party: 'In any other country, Joe Biden and I would not be in the same party' (quoted in Forgey 2020).

Yet scholars looking at the rise of Trump in the US regularly frame their research as being about exploring 'the roots of right-wing populism in the United States' (Berlet and Sunshine 2019, 480; see also Berlet and Lyons 2018; de Wit et al. 2019). It is worth mentioning that many of those aforementioned Obama-turned-Trump supporters might be center-right in other parts of the world. But that should not come at the expense of denying their own identities as independents and Democrats. To label them as right-wing either denies their own standpoints or glosses over their role in the movement entirely, in which case authoritarian populism really does look like a right-wing activity as only individuals with those attributes are being paid attention to.

Drawing from research conducted for a larger project, this paper analyzes data from semi-structured, face-to-face interviews with two groups: (1) white Colorado (US) residents, from rural and urban counties, who voted for Obama in either 2012 or 2008 before voting for Trump in 2016 ($n = 43$); (2) Colorado residents of color, from rural and urban countries, who did not vote for Trump in 2016 ($n = 28$). This paper is principally about the former group – white individuals with Left-leaning inclinations ('Left' as defined in the US) who appear to find solace in the nativism and economic nationalism associated with authoritarian populism. Data from the latter group, people of color who did not vote for Trump, are included to ground truth claims about what minority groups are *actually* experiencing, in contrast to what those in the former group *think* is reality. Earlier, I mentioned that this paper places a new spin on the concepts of economic distress and racial resentment – two variables repeatedly mentioned in the literature when explaining support for authoritarian populism in the US. An element that could be interrogated with greater empirical rigor, however, is the implicit bias driving some of this activity. The paper contributes in three principle ways to the literature: presenting populism as something more than a homogenous entity (aligning with prior scholarship [e.g. Anderson 2019; Borras 2020; Walter 2019]); its empirical material on the implicit biases held among Trump supporters, which I hope feeds into the literature's already-strong theoretical tradition (e.g. Hall 1985, 2017; Laclau 2005; Rancière 2016); and, finally, its specific angle on race politics, building on prior accounts that unpack authoritarian populism through racialized imaginaries (e.g. Bhambra 2017; Walter 2019).

Those interviewed significantly underestimated the wealth gap between whites and non-whites. They therefore held considerable resentment toward non-whites when policies (e.g. affirmative action) and programs (e.g. welfare) were discussed that were viewed as disproportionately advantaging people of color. Rural white respondents were particularly resentful on this point. This was in large part because of the observed non-white poverty in their communities – observations that align with research describing that minorities face economic hardship at higher rates than whites, especially in non-metropolitan communities (e.g. Slack, Thiede, and Jensen 2019; Ulrich-Schad and

Duncan 2018). Curiously, rather than building empathy for minority households living in poverty, these observations were seen to be the result of personal weaknesses and not due to larger systemic inequalities.

As for how Left-leaning political ideology helped animate what some have diagnosed as a right-wing movement: the strong norms of colorblindness in liberal political cultures, at least in the US, discourages certain conversations about race and racial inequities among certain white populations – this is the idea that you are supposed to see *the person* and not *the color* of their skin (see also Kraus et al. 2019; Wetts and Willer 2019). These norms contributed to the white, Trump-supporting respondents not being sufficiently equipped to take observations of minority hardship as evidence of *systemic* racism.

The next section fills out the empirical and conceptual picture sketched above. This includes defining and further outlining some of the contours of authoritarian populism and the mutually reinforcing roles of economic distress and racial resentment that underlie it. I then review the literature pointing to the implicit bias held among Left-leaning US citizens that causes them to be 'responsive to the implicit – and sometimes explicit – racial appeals of Donald Trump's presidential campaign' (Wetts and Willer 2019, 15). This conversation also reviews the role that norms of colorblindness in liberal political cultures can play in exacerbating racial resentment. Attention then turns to the methods surrounding the paper's 71 semi-structured face-to-face interviews. The reminder of the paper reviews findings, where evidence is provided showing that elements of the Left and implicit colorblind biases also underlie authoritarian populism.

Contextualizing the debate

Authoritarian populism, as defined by Scoones et al. (2008, 2–3), 'typically depicts politics as a struggle between "the people" and some combination of malevolent, racialised and/ or unfairly advantaged "Others", at home or abroad or both.' A principle goal in harnessing this anxiety involves '"taking back control" in favour of "the people", returning the nation to "greatness" or "health" after real or imagined degeneration attributed to those Others' (Scoones et al. 2008, 3). Though composed in the US principally of historically privileged groups – white, Christian, heterosexual males – supporters (Serwer 2017), especially those in rural locales, feel strongly that *they* are at the receiving end of injustices (Carolan 2019b).

A lot of attention of late has been directed at rural grievances in the US, due largely to the economic and social restructuring taking place in these areas. Rural America at a Glance 2017 (USDA 2017), an annual report from the U.S. Department of Agriculture, highlights the economic stress felt by many rural communities since the Great Recession. While the recession impacted rural and urban areas with equal force (both recording average wage/salary employment declines of 2 percent per year during 2007–2010), recovery has looked very different to non-metro residents. Rural residents, on the whole, have not seen the same level of economic prosperity as those in urban areas (Drum 2017). The general consensus among social scientists looking into the subject is that there are 'strong feelings that economic restructuring had changed rural communities for the worse, and nearly everywhere we encountered nostalgia for the lost economy of the past' (Ulrich-Schad and Duncan 2018, 65; see also, Lichter and Ziliak 2017; Thiede, Lichter, and Slack 2018).

A deeper dive into the data also reveals ambivalence. A report drawing from a survey of 1,300 adults ages 18 or older living in the rural US, conducted for National Public Radio (NPR), the Robert Wood Johnson Foundation (RWJF), and the Harvard T.H. Chan School of Public Health, found that a majority of rural Americans rate their local economy as only fair or poor (NPR, RWJF, and Harvard 2018). And yet, almost paradoxically, rural Americans report being not only optimistic about the future but also personally content. For example, in the above-mentioned document, the majority of respondents claim that their lives have turned out either better than expected (41 percent) or about like they expected (42 percent), with only 15 percent saying their lives have turned out worse than expected. Fifty-five percent also felt they were better off financially than their parents were at their age, with 17 having reported being worse off (NPR, RWJF, and Harvard 2018, 5; see also Nebraska Rural Poll 2019).

This suggest that there is more to 'new rural populism' (Ulrich-Schad and Duncan 2018, 59) than objective economic grievances. Clearly these grievances exist and are, in certain contexts, perceived as being real. But we also know that material factors, like the economy, are filtered through a multitude of social lenses, which collectively give shape to a picture that is more than the sum of its financial parts (Sherman 2009).

This is where issues of race enter the picture. Cramer's (2016) research into the rural consciousness in Wisconsin shows that economic grievances are intertwined with cultural, geographical or community, and group identities. Her story, like that detailed by others (Fording and Schram 2017; Pied 2019; Sherman 2009), is one about the coming together of identity politics and economic decline. Take what happened during the 2016 Presidential Elections. Clinton defeated Trump among Americans making less than $50,000 a year. Yet if we look only at white voters, a different outcome emerges. Trump handily won over Clinton among white voters in every income category (Serwer 2017). Trump supporters are also more likely to be dissatisfied with their economic situation (Lopez 2017). This outlook is amplified by the fact that they are also likely to deny the existence of racism (Lopez 2017), suggesting that their stated economic dissatisfaction stems from a belief that their financial loss is the result of individuals of color receiving special treatment (Carolan 2020b).

The perception that 'others' receive special treatment has played an important role in assembling momentum behind authoritarian populism in the US. One way this gets expressed is in the belief that rural areas are being left behind – an all-too-common refrain repeated in ethnographic accounts of Trump supporters (e.g. Cramer 2016; Hochschild 2018; Wuthnow 2019). On the one hand, this criticism seems misplaced. Given rural areas' higher costs of healthcare (Wengle 2018), higher rates of disability (disability benefit rates are twice as high in rural as in urban areas [McCoy 2017]) and poverty (resulting in a large share of welfare-type support going to the countryside [Booker 2018]), and their aging and thus social-security-eligible citizens (Smith and Trevelyan 2019), it is hard to say that the federal government is not working for them given the subsidy flows to these people and places. And this says nothing about the *billions* in farm subsidies that help out this segment of rural economies annually (Charles 2019).

Yet, on the other hand, not all government funding is the same. Take the distinction between federal investments and government consumption, also known as consumption expenditures. 'Consumption' in this context refers to federal spending on things like social security payments and disability assistance; payments that make their way into the economy by way of recipients using them for purposes of consumption. Federal 'investments,' meanwhile, in addition to generating immediate jobs ultimately stimulate growth over the longer term – think how investments in broadband access attract future capital. With this distinction in mind, I examined data from the Economic Research Service (ERS) – a branch of the USDA that provides information related to agriculture and rural economies – capturing federal expenditures for each of Colorado's 64 counties. Attention was directed specifically at what the ERS codes as a 'community' expense – investments in transportation, telecommunications, environmental protections, business assistance, and the like. For this suite of federal investments, non-metro Colorado counties received, *on a per capita basis*, 46 percent of what metro counties did – $1,570 (non-metro) compared to $3,325 (metro). This provides important context to understand why these populations feel left behind and associate government tax flows with welfare and those who Morgen and Erickson (2017, 58) call 'tax others' – individuals unfairly benefiting from taxpayers' hard work.

According to the aforementioned collaborative survey between NPR, the RWJF, and Harvard University, the majority of rural Americans do not believe that non-whites face discrimination in their local communities, with the exception of recent immigrants. In contrast, respondents belonging to minority groups reported much higher rates of discrimination against members of their group (NPR, RWJF, and Harvard 2018, 2). This gap has also been reported in studies looking at perceptions of wealth/income between whites and non-whites. In one study, drawing on data from a nationally representative sample of adults ($n = 1,008$), white respondents thought that the minority wealth gap was smaller, by around 80 percentage points (Kraus et al. 2019). This translates into gross misperceptions among those white respondents when it comes to understanding where their non-white counterparts stand, economically speaking. In the authors words,

> The evidence indicates that the magnitude of these misperceptions is substantial, with respondents estimating that for every $100 in wealth held by a White family, a Black family has $90, when, in reality, that Black family has $10; misperceptions about the Latinx–White wealth gap are just as large. (Kraus et al. 2019, 917).

This misperception is both cause and consequence of individuals choosing not to see race as a sociologically relevant concept in a post-Civil Rights era, and post-Obama Presidency, America. According to what has come to be called colorblind theory, colorblind racial ideology generates outlooks and outcomes premised on the assertion that race no longer matters from the standpoint of realizing social, economic, and political success (i.e. the 'American dream') in the US (e.g. Bonilla-Silva 2001; Doane 2017; Hartmann et al. 2017; Lewis 2004). Colorblindness provides white Americans – and arguably segments of the non-white population too (Bonilla-Silva and Embrick 2001) – with cognitive and discursive devices that can be used to defend the status quo by denying that racism persists while presenting outcomes in ways that are themselves colorblind. Examples of this include justifying residential and school segregation patterns as matters of individual choice, explaining education, employment, and incarceration inequities between whites and non-whites as matters relating to differences in familial structure (e.g. single mothers vs. two-parent families) or culture, or opposing affirmative action on the grounds that is goes against the American principles of treating everyone the same.

Examples of this abound. Some can be subtle. Democrat 2020 Presidential candidate Pete Buttigieg recently made headlines after video emerged (from 2011) of him explaining educational underperformance in 'minority communities' by saying, 'There isn't somebody they know personally who testifies to the value of education' (Judd and Phillip 2018). He was quickly criticized for casting those education gaps as being about cultural deficits on the part of minority groups, versus systematic racism.

Other examples are more problematic but sufficiently ambivalent to give authoritarian populists cover. Trump, for example, regularly blames Democrats for decades of bad policy that have locked people of color into poverty. 'Our government has totally failed our African American friends, our Hispanic friends and the people of our country. Period,' Trump said in August 2016, adding, 'Democrats have failed completely in the inner-cities' (quoted in Scott 2017). I am not convinced that this language is so much directed at minority groups; after all, most non-whites are neither poor nor do they exclusively inhabit the urban core. By treating the black inner-city as a metonym for Black America, Trump risks turning off African American voters (Maskovsky 2017, 435), a reality expressed in a new poll showing that 8 in 10 black voters think Trump is racist (Stracqualursi 2020).

This language is clearly meant for his white supporters, to give them something to point to that 'proves' he is not a racist and therefore neither are they for supporting him. The colorblindness especially comes through when he talks about these inner-city communities, supposed inhabited mostly by people of color, as 'rat and rodent infested' (Rentz 2019), 'filthy,' and 'crime ridden' (Olorunnipa 2019). When cloaked in a broader narrative about wanting to help minority groups, it gives supporters just enough cover, in their minds, to deflect claims of racism. To quote Ainsley Earhardt, a co-host on Trump's favorite morning program *Fox and Friends*, after he called Baltimore, Maryland, rat-infested:

> The president is saying, look, I'm not a racist, I just want our country to stay safe. […] He says, look at the unemployment numbers for African Americans. He was in Baltimore talking about that very topic. (quoted in Media Matters 2019)

Taxpayer identity politics is another way for colorblindness-creep. Who, after all, are the so-called freeloading non-taxpayers being disparaged by those animating authoritarian populism, those Trump has claimed are 'going on welfare for 50 years, and that's what they want to be able to do – and it's no good' (quoted in Wegmann 2019). We *know* who those individuals are – people of color. 'Why would the US accept more immigrants from Haiti and Africa rather than places like Norway?' Trump once asked (quoted in Phillips 2018). Making the debate about those who do and do not pay taxes gives the discourse of authoritarian populism the appearance of race and ethnicity neutrality.

A notable historical example where government benefits had clear implications on racial politics in the US without ever explicitly being about race can be found in Ira Katznelson's (2005) book *When Affirmative Action Was White*. When the GI Bill was signed into law in 1944, veterans were entitled to governmental benefits ranging from college tuition subsidies and home mortgage assistance. Even though all soldiers returning from the war were supposed to receive these benefits black veterans were excluded in a variety of ways: they were mostly restricted to black colleges that were smaller and often under-funded; they were denied loans at higher rates by local (racist) loan officers; when they could qualify for a loan they were restricted by where to could safely own a house; etc. The GI Bill played an instrumental role in affording the upward mobility for millions of whites; opportunities that could not be realized by black veterans. And yet, the GI Bill has rarely, except for works like Katznelson's book, been presented as a case of affirmative action for whites because the story unfolds with the use of colorblind terms like 'veterans' (as if referencing some homogenous population) and phrases such as 'those with good credit.'

Finally, policies can be strategically promoted in colorblind terms so as to appeal to constituents holding to this ideology. This pragmatic move is done with the intent of moving policies forward that materially benefit people of color, even if not marketed as such. An example of this could include when Senator Cory Booker rolled out a bill designed to provide federal need-based savings accounts for newborns. The press release did not mention race until the ninth paragraph, even though the policy represented a carefully targeted approach to reduce the racial wealth gap (Kraus et al. 2019; Lane 2018). Such a strategy, however, also comes with risks. As Kraus et al. (2019, 915) point out, 'avoidance of the racial patterns of economic and other forms of inequality is in fact part of the reason there are such powerful, robust, yet inaccurate narratives regarding societal racial progress in the first place.'

It should be emphasized that scholars do not attribute a political affiliation to colorblindness. Western liberal philosophies emphasizing the progress of societies through the development of individualism, individual rights, equality, and democracy are values shared across the political spectrum (Deneen 2018). Thus, while those on the right are often targeted for standing in the way of racial equality, if not cited for activity making matters worse (e.g. Gonzales and Delgado 2016), blame can also be directed elsewhere. Research has identified colorblindness in politically Left–leaning environments. It has been documented, for example, in progressive Danish schools (e.g. Jaffe–Walter 2019). It has also been shown to be emblematic of progressive US Democratic principles more generally (Wetts and Willer 2019)–what Nancy Fraser (2019) has labeled progressive neoliberalism.

This overview provides the backdrop for the following study, where I interrogate data from seventy-one semi-structured interviews of rural and urban Coloradoans. These interviews – of white Obama-turned-Trump supporters and non-white Trump critics – are used to think through the contours and drivers of authoritarian populism in the US.

Methods

This paper draws from a larger research project, which in the aggregate involved close to three hundred face-to-face interviews with individuals from across the state of Colorado, spanning from 2012 to 2019 (Carolan 2019a, 2019b, 2020a). It started with me looking at local and regional value chains in Colorado and the food-related practices, attitudes and sentiments animating those activities. Interviews were semi-structured. This allowed some flexibility, whereby respondents were able to introduce topics if they wanted. In light of political and social realities during the project's life, this resulted in many participants wanting to talk about more than food. Specifically, this all happen during the contentious presidential primaries leading up to a vitriolic 2016 Presidential Election and after, meaning most respondents were eager to talk about Trump, immigration, politics, welfare, the rural-urban divide, etc. Not long into the project the decision was therefore made to extend its scope, which involved looking into not only the underlying moral economies of (rural) food production and (urban) food consumption (Carolan 2020a) but also issues related to authoritarian populism more broadly. While roughly two-thirds of the rural

Trump supporters reported on in this paper were farmers and ranchers, less than half had that occupation among the remainder of the sample population.

The data for this paper came from seventy-one face-to-face interviews conducted between July 2016, when Trump officially became the Republican nominee, and August 2019. Forty-three were of white Colorado residents, thirty of whom were located in rural counties, who voted for Trump in 2016 and for Obama in either 2012 or 2008. (I did not interview a single person of color who admitted to supporting Trump.) The other group consisted of twenty-eight – roughly evenly split between metropolitan ($n = 13$) and non-metropolitan ($n = 15$) counties – Colorado residents who identified as non-white who did not vote for Trump in 2016; all in fact expressed a strong dislike for the man and his policies. (Respondents were asked who they planned to vote for in interviews occurring before 8 November, 2016 – election night.) As noted earlier, those white Obama-turned-Trump supporters represent the paper's principle focus. So-called 'Trump Antagonists' are included to ground truth claims about what minority groups are *actually* experiencing, in contrast to what those in the former group *think* is reality.

For a breakdown of respondents according to various characteristics, see Table 1. Note especially respondents' political leanings/affiliations: more than a third ($n = 18$) were registered Democrats, slightly less than half ($n = 20$) were unaffiliated/independent, and five were registered Republican. (In Colorado, a little more than one million voters are registered active Democrats, slightly less than one million are registered active Republican, and more than 1.2 million are unaffiliated.) None of the respondents identified as being of the so-called right-wing of the Republican Party.

It would be useful at this point to say a little about Colorado's demographics and political leanings. Colorado is more than 83 percent white (U.S. Census 0000n.d.), though that is changing as approximately 40 percent of the under-24 population is non-white (Simpson 2017a). Clinton comfortably won the state by 5 percent of the overall vote in 2016. Trump, however, secured almost 40 percent more votes than Clinton in rural counties (Frank 2018). Obama not only handily won the state in 2008 and 2012, by roughly 9 and 5 percentage points, respectively, he also outperformed Clinton in rural communities (e.g. Berkes 2008; Dasgupta 2019).

Given the state-wide nature of the larger project this research was part of, the data presented below are not located in any one community or county. To situate these state-wide data, I present Figure 1. Note also that my designations of 'rural' and 'urban' follow broader government definitions and are county-level categorizations – a subset of the former is 'frontier,' defined by the federal government as counties with a population density of six or fewer persons per square mile category. Like any state, Colorado's counties are diverse in terms of their economies, histories, and racial biographies. Any perceived distress experienced by respondents is unquestionably rooted to place. This context matters. Yet just as thick descriptions (Geertz 2008) are important for research such as this, it is necessary also to understand that place-based distress resonates *across* space and time and to have data that speaks to how distress becomes *dis*-placed and animates the 'us' of populism. I do not, in other words, see the data's state-wide nature as being problematic *per se*. It simply brings something different to the argument compared to data rooted to a particular community. Colorblindness looks to be a mechanism to translate that distress across diverse white populations.

Table 1. Characteristics of respondents across sample populations (n = 71).

	Obama-Trump Supporters (n = 43)	Trump Antagonists (n = 28)
Location		
Rural	30	15
Urban	13	13
Self-described race/ethnicity		
White	43	0
Black/African American	0	15
Latinx/Hispanic	0	8
African	0	1
Native American	0	1
Asian American	0	1
Two or more	0	2
Household income		
Less than $20,000	0	0
$20,000–$39,999	4	3
$40,000–$59,999	4	5
$60,000–$79,999	12	5
$80,000–$99,999	2	4
$100,000–$119,999	10	5
$120,000–$139,999	4	2
$140,000 or more	3	2
Prefer not to answer	4	2
Age		
21–30	4	2
31–40	9	5
41–50	8	6
51–60	8	5
61–70	6	4
71–80	5	4
81–90	2	2
Prefer not to answer	1	0
Education		
Some High School	2	1
High School/Equivalent	19	12
Trade School/Associate's Degree	2	0
Bachelor's Degree	13	14
Master's Degree	2	1
M.D., J.D., or Ph.D.	3	0
Prefer not to say	2	0
Gender		
Male	32	8
Female	11	18
Political Party Registration		
Democrat	18	19
Unaffiliated/independent	20	8
Republican	5	0
Other, left-leaning	0	1
Other, right-leaning	0	0

Respondents were purposively selected, using snowball sampling methodologies, for their identities as Obama-turned-Trump voters. Those identified in Table 1 as 'Trump antagonists' were found with less intentionality on my part. For about half, their anti-authoritarian populist leanings were visible by participation in food and social justice-related activities and movements. Yet for others, their Trump opposition was more hidden (perhaps due to living a rural community where Trump support was widespread) and required purposive snowball techniques. The entire process was inspired by inductive (grounded) theorizing, as evidenced by the aforementioned expansion of scope as a result of listening to the data (Glaser and Strauss 1967).

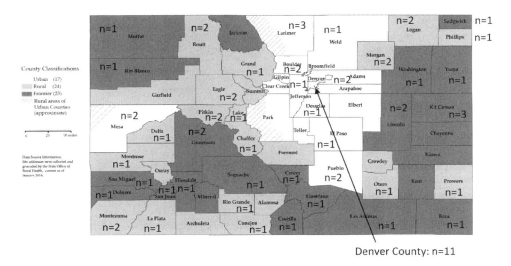

Figure 1. Colorado County Designations, 2019 (rural/frontier, $n = 45$; urban, $n = 26$).

Each interviewed lasted approximately two hours, was digitally recorded, and later transcribed and coded.

Findings: perceptions of wealth gaps and fairness

This section unfolds through three movements. In the first, evidence is provided indicating that the Obama-turned-Trump supporters held very different views about the racial wealth gap and the existence of racial prejudice more generally than interviewees of color. Next, I show that white respondents admitted to having witnessed significant levels of minority poverty in their own, and surrounding, communities. Finally, evidence is provided detailing how white respondents chose to view those observations of minority poverty as proof people of color are unfairly benefiting from government policies and programs. Moreover, when pushed to think about these disparities as evidence of systemic racism, respondents proved ill-equipped to tackle the subject.

What wealth gap?

Prior research looking at wealth gap perceptions surveyed individuals and asked them to assign a specific number to a group's average earning potential. For instance, one study asked about average black family wealth (on a $0 to $200 scale) for every $100 that a similar white family has with similar levels of education. The average guess was $90, when, in reality, that Black family had $10 (Kraus et al. 2019). Rather than gauging wealth perceptions with a number, I was interested in more qualitative descriptions. Attitudes between the two groups were stark. Obama-turned-Trump supporters often talked about the wealth gaps between people of color and whites as, for example, 'overblown' ($n = 16$), 'exaggerated' ($n = 5$), 'much ado about nothing' ($n = 1$), 'practically non-existent' ($n = 1$). Even among those who, often reluctantly, admitted to the existence of such gaps, the confession was usually qualified. Representative examples of this sentiment include the following.

> Do I think blacks or Hispanic have a harder time than whites? Maybe; sure. But we've come a long way, even in the last twenty years. (Julie, Urban, Nurse, 38 yrs. old)

> There are pockets of racism here and there. But come on, I don't believe for a second that employers discriminate against minorities anymore. Talk about inequalities between races are overblown. (Larry, Rural, Rancher, 58 yrs old)

This unwillingness to acknowledge a wealth gap paralleled views where white respondents greatly underestimated the amount of discrimination non-whites faced in their local communities, echoing the findings of the aforementioned NPR, RWJF, and Harvard (2018) survey. Above-mentioned terms like 'overblown' and 'exaggerated' could also be applied to how white respondents thought about claims that race-based discrimination is still a serious problem. The following exchange between myself and an owner of a rural grocery store illustrates some of the suspicion Obama-turned-Trump supporters had toward the idea that non-whites experienced prejudice, especially within their own community.

> This is a caring town. Good people. We couldn't care less about the color of your skin—that's not something I'd say we pay much attention to. If you're hard-working and law-abiding, that's all that really matters around here. (Bill, Rural, Grocery Store Owner, 61 yrs. old)

> 'What would you say to non-whites who say they feel otherwise,' I asked, adding, 'who say they don't feel like they are treated the same as people who look like long-timers, who say the color of their skin does matter, whether for finding employment or for making friends.'

> I'd say that's not how it is. Maybe from our standpoint we see people who don't want to be part of the community. It takes two to tango. If they want to be a part of the community they have to also be willing to put themselves out there.

Another respondent, Brian, an elementary school teacher from a rural school district, dismissed the idea that 'black and Hispanics experience any more discrimination than the rest of us' by arguing the following.

> We treat everyone the same here. That's part of the reason why I never left, that close sense of community. […] I think being a *rural* person is cause for more discrimination than having black or brown skin. […] It's not rural *black* people that are being discriminated against. It's *rural* white people, *rural* black people, *rural* Hispanics. The rural bit is the common denominator. Not their skin color or ethnicity. (Brian, Rural, Teacher, 28 yrs. old)

The attitude that a *rural* identity generates greater levels of discrimination than a racial one was volunteered by thirteen of the rural white respondents – I did not ask about this outright, thinking such a question might be leading. This reflects a sentiment documented by others who have studied non-metropolitan communities, the perception that societal norms make it acceptable to discriminate against, and make fun of, rural people, places, and practices (see also, Carolan 2019b; Vance 2016; Wuthnow 2019). This belief appeared to play a role in blinding rural Obama-turn-Trump supporters to prejudices and discriminatory practices toward people of color taking place right before their eyes.

Lois, a wheat farmer from the eastern plains, essentially admitted this much. The conversation had moved to the topic of her twelve-year-old son, when she said,

> He was teased on a band trip to Denver, teased about his bolo [string] tie [widely associated in the US with Western wear] 'by some city kids. […] I'm tired of talking about racism; we've just

had a black president for Christ's sake. Let's talk about the discrimination people like my son experience when they go to the city. (Lois, Rural, Wheat Farmer, 40 yrs. old)

The non-whites interviewed, however, told a very different story. Some came from the very same communities as those in the white population who claimed discrimination toward people of color was 'overblown' if not 'practically non-existent.'

Recall those earlier comments from Bill. He was the rural grocery store owner who talked about his town being colorblind (i.e. 'We couldn't care less about the color of your skin ... ') and who explained that white people should not be branded as racist. Rather, he suggests that it might be the non-white population's fault for not putting themselves 'out there', explaining how 'it takes two to tango.' Luis, a thirty-three-year-old immigrant from Mexico, lived in the same community as Bill. I had interviewed Bill the day prior and decided to share his anonymized quotes, which are reproduced above, with Luis, explaining simply that they 'came from another rural Colorado resident.'

With a look landing somewhere between incredulity and anger, he loudly proclaimed, 'They say they don't see color, but maybe they should!' He paused long enough to look at his hands as he rubbed them together. Staring back at me he added,

> My skin color is inescapable. It's my number one defining feature around here. That's why I get pulled over by police as much as I do, for no reason whatsoever, other than because I can't hide my darker skin. That's why I have people watching me at the gas station, the grocery store, the library. *You* [—pointing at me—] wouldn't be watched at those places. [...] People might not feel comfortable talking about skin color but they damn well need to admit that it matters. (Luis, Rural, Mechanic, 33 yrs. old)

All twenty-eight of the people of color interviewed talked about not only *thinking* non-whites experience discriminatory hurdles on an everyday basis but they shared with me examples of it *actually happening*, as Luis explained above. These examples ranged from outright illegal discriminatory practices – like when Robert, an African American living in the greater Denver metropolitan area, told about the time he went to apply for a job and was informed it was filled, only to later learn that a (white) friend applied for the same job two days later. More often, however, the stories of discrimination shared were of the sort that could be explained away by colorblind white residents as being less about racism and more about something else that had nothing to do with systematic racism.

Observed Poverty among non-whites

As discussed, Obama-turned-Trump supporters largely described race as a non-factor when explaining socio-economic outcomes – even though, for example, 2016 unemployment rates in Colorado varied significantly between whites and non-whites, from 2.8 percent to 4.5 percent and 4.8 percent for whites, blacks, and Latinos, respectively (Webster and Loayza 2017). And yet, members of this group admitted to having witnessed significant levels of minority poverty in their own, and surrounding, communities. When asked to identify 'what groups seem to be struggling the most in your communities,' not a single white respondent replied by isolating a racial or ethnic characteristic, which you would expect from a group believed to be animated in part by the racial colorblind ideology. Rather, when asked to identify locations or neighborhoods with high levels of poverty, a majority of white respondents pointed to places with unusually high concentrations of minority households – e.g. certain trailer parks, in the case of certain rural communities, or districts in metropolitan areas known to historically house people of color.

In some cases, I was familiar enough with the community to know that the places mentioned were minority hotspots – 'hotspots' being a relative term, as for some rural communities these areas might contain two or three non-white families. Regardless of whether I knew the location, respondents were pushed to say more about the people who lived there. While respondents seemed uncomfortable talking about skin color, noting a person's nationality or spoken language seemed entirely acceptable.

> That's where a lot of the Somalis live. (Ernest, Rural, Farmer, 71 yrs. old)

> There's a tienda there. That's actually what the sign says on the storefront. There's a lot of Spanish speakers in that area. (Beth, Rural, Delivery Driver, 57 yrs. old)

In some instances, when it seemed appropriate and unlikely to derail the rapport I had built, respondents were gently nudged to reflect more on what they were saying. An example of this occurred with Susanne (Urban, Farmer, 25 yrs. old) as she told me about a certain part of her community well-known for its poverty.

> 'Locals have a name for it, "Little Mexico."'

> 'I thought most of the families there are second or third generation residents,' I asked, adding, 'so why call it *that* if most of them are every bit as American as you or I? My ancestors immigrated to this country three or four generations ago too.'

> 'Oh, it's not like *that*!,' Susanne intoned, quick to distance herself from the suggestion that the label implied anything disparaging about another's race or ethnicity. She then added:

> 'It's like "Little Italy" in New York or "Chinatown" in San Francisco. It's a term that recognizes and embraces the diversity in our community.'

Emphasizing that she believes in respecting different cultures, she explained that 'this doesn't take away from the fact that that part of town is blighted and poor.'

Of the thirty white respondents located in rural counties, twenty-one volunteered a colorblind reference indicating that non-whites disproportionately struggled with poverty in or near their rural community, which is to say, nationality, immigration status, spoken language, or a food type (e.g. Susanne identified the aforementioned neighborhood as having a taco food truck) were mentioned as a substitute for having to talk explicitly about race. Six of the thirteen white respondents located in urban locales also did this.

Another example of colorblindness to come out of the interviews was introduced above in Susanne's final quoted sentence – her reference to minority spaces being *blighted*. It is a rhetorical technique used regularly by leaders of the movement. Trump, for instance, was quoted earlier using even more pejorative language. The importance of community aesthetics, as defined by its (white) leaders, has been a powerful way to police and protect the whiteness of place without ever having to talk about race or ethnicity (Kefalas 2003; Walter 2019). Calls to 'Make America Great Again' imply the need to recapture something lost. This is more than an economic call; though given the mid-twentieth century affirmative action for whites that existed post-war (Katznelson 2005), supporters' nostalgia has undeniable material components. This harkening to reclaim some past greatness also speaks to the movement's emphasis on aesthetics; on things and, importantly, people considered *out of place*. As Walter (2019, 7) explains, 'Nostalgia is used to stoke identity-based moral panics and in turn justify governmental overreach.'

In sum, minority poverty was not only observed among Obama-turned-Trump supporters. Some respondents were so 'concerned' about the issue that they talked about 'the steps being taken to clean those parts of the town up' (Jeff, Rural, Farmer, 44 yrs. old). The use of the term 'clean' in that sentence is certainly problematic, suggesting the need for not only aesthetic policing but interventions on *hygienic* grounds, which gives the argument additional weight – moral panics on medical principles are especially powerful (Wagner 2018). And again, these concerns were all expressed using language that others have described as postracial (Maskovsky 2017):

> We want to attract businesses [into the community]. When people [possible investors] come here they want to see a community with clear sense of who it is and where it's going. When you have some parts of the community not looking like the rest; well, that unevenness can turn away businesses. (Lori, Rural, Librarian, 66 yrs. old)

Resentful and ill-equipped

While thirty-six white respondents admitted that minorities in their community struggle economically at higher rates than white residents, none choose to see that as evidence of implicit and explicit bias against people of color. Rather, it was taken as validation of the belief that, to quote Jeff (Rural), 'the federal government isn't working for us anymore – hardworking Americans.'

This highlights an especially nefarious colorblind tactic: dog whistle-type language. 'Dog whistling' refers to rhetoric where race is not explicitly mentioned but instead is cued to play upon recipients' prejudices (e.g. 'welfare mothers') and/or fears about losing their privileged majority status (Haney-López 2014; Wetts and Willer 2019). It is the latter instance that I am referring to in this case. As Jeff's comment illustrates, respondents were not afraid to evoke 'us' language when creating contrasts with non-white community members. Yet they were extremely careful to make it clear that this 'us' had nothing to do with race or ethnicity. For instance, when Jeff was asked what he meant in evoking the term, he was quick to point out that he 'wasn't talking about race.' He then added, 'I'm talking about those of *us* that believe in the value of a hard day's work.' This aligns with what I earlier described as the widespread use of taxpayer identity politics among authoritarian populist participants; another example where colorblindness has crept into their political discourse: 'tax others' (Morgen and Erickson 2017, 58) are talked about to cloak biases in postracial language.

Another representative example of 'us' being used by respondents on account of its ability to cut both ways – as language that is simultaneously race baiting to enroll ingroup sympathy and race-neutral to evade criticism – comes from Lou, an organic wheat grower located in the sparsely populated eastern third of the state. During this exchange, we were discussing the recent influx of immigrants into the surrounding area over the last decade due to employment opportunities made available by a meat processing facility.

> My ancestors were immigrants too. We remain a nation of immigrants. But when my great-, great-, great-grandparents came here they had to do for themselves in basically every way

—teach themselves, feed themselves. Basically, it was a situation where you worked or you died. [...] Now you've got social services making house calls [to immigrant families], making sure they're doing okay. Their kids go to our public schools, paid for by the taxpayer. [...]. They're so well taken care of. [...] Well, what about us? (Lou, Rural, Farmer, 53 yrs. old)

'Who is this *they* and *us* that you're talking about?' I asked, 'Can you expand?'

Like I said, I have nothing against immigrants. This is about people paying their dues. For someone, regardless of the color of their skin, whatever county they come from, to come here and benefit from *others'* sweat and blood. [...] I guess by *us* I mean taxpayers, which can include immigrants, as long as they—well, yeah, like I said, pay their dues.

Twenty of the white respondents used the us/them language at some point in the interview when discussing *immigrants* of color, displaying evidence of some explicit biases toward this group. It could be said we live in a time where it is socially acceptable to target immigrants for verbal and physical harassment; after all, President Trump not only does this daily but arguably got elected in 2016 because of, rather than despite, those actions. Leaving the issue of immigration aside, how did white respondents talk about and explain racial disparities among people of color known to be US citizens?

As already noted, these disparities were less likely to be explained by this group with reference to phenomena like 'institutional racism,' 'systematic racism,' or 'bias, implicit and explicit, against people of color,' to take terms from interviews with the so-called Trump Antagonists when they spoke about the root causes of racial inequities. Instead, Obama-turned-Trump supporters talked about their observations of poor minority hotspots in their communities using classic colorblind discursive tactics. Examples of this include:

[It's evidence that] some groups are taught from a young age the importance of education and hard work. (Noel, Rural, Retail Worker, 32 yrs. old)

If you're not around adults who are successful, to see "success" patterned, it's no wonder younger generations struggle. [...] You see these kids coming to interviews not dressed appropriately or not having the tools—like how they talk—to successfully sell themselves. (Becky, Urban, Retired, 82 yrs. old)

Groups value things differently things. [...] Some people are brought up look to the government to help, others aren't—for them government's not a helping partner but a hindrance. If we want to change those behaviors [*–those* behaviors: a reference to those in the former group–] we'll have to change their culture. (Craig, Rural, Truck Driver, 25 yrs. old)

At one point in the interview, these same respondents we gently pushed to further explain their colorblind position. After being presented with evidence showing very real racial disparities – e.g. wealth gaps, incarceration gaps, healthcare/health disparities, credit inequities, hate crime data, etc. – they were asked to explain these statistics. 'Some would point to these statistics as evidence of deeply rooted, systemic racism,' I noted. Respondents were then asked, 'How would you respond to that?'

I pushed the interview in this direction to empirically explore a point made by Wetts and Willer (2019, 16; see also Wise 2010), specifically when they argue,

norms of colorblind-ness in liberal political culture impair the development of structural explanations of negative outcomes among black Americans, leaving liberals ill-equipped to rebuff messages linking outcomes such as welfare utilization or criminal justice involvement to negative racial stereotypes.

They further note that discussion about 'structural factors like concentrated poverty or lack of access to dominant institutions [...] is often self-censored' (Wetts and Willer 2019). I wanted to see how my group of participants responded to this type of probing.

Responses were interesting as much for what was *not* said as for what was said. In short, respondents struggled to talk about how racism might be at work even when presented with evidence that people of color are discriminated against and that white privilege is real. Representative quotes of this include the following:

> 'Well, hmmm—I'd say.' There was a seven-second pause before he continued. 'I can only tell you how things are like where I live. And that sort of thing'—racism—'doesn't factor into how folks around here operate.' (Marvin, Rural, Rancher, 49 yrs. old)

> I'm not going to disagree with your statistics. [...] I think in parts of this country blacks and Hispanics face a real uphill battle. But it seems more of a class issue to me. [...]. If they only lived in better neighborhoods they'd have access to better schools. If they had better jobs they'd have more opportunities. (Jonathan, Rural, Butcher, 45 yrs. old)

Both Marvin and Jonathan were registered Democrats, illustrating that even self-identified Democrats and those claiming to be politically liberal – e.g. 'I'm a full-on liberal with a long history voting Democrat, even volunteering for Ralph Nader back in 2000 because I didn't think Gore was *liberal enough*' (Jonathan, from above, intoned) – can be ill-equipped to cognitively and discursively tackle the subject of racial inequity. Note also Marvin's stumbling to find the words, before eventually taking that seven-second pause. He otherwise spoke with the precision of a newscaster or minister, making the rhetorical misstep all the more noticeable. Meanwhile, others simply made it clear with their body language and tone that the subject made them uncomfortable.

Tom (Urban, Restaurant Owner, 42 yrs. old), for example, said rather forcefully and defensively, 'I never said racism doesn't exist,' after being presented with those aforementioned data on racial disparities. Tom's retort was technically true. What he had said earlier in the interview was that racism was 'overblown by media.' Nevertheless, I abandoned this line of questioning at this point as was it was clear by his tone he did not wish to say anything more on the subject.

Discussion and conclusion

Before concluding, I want to further unpack the data. I begin by evoking the concept of motivated reasoning. This is the idea that we perceive data in ways that support existing values and beliefs, while discounting those data that cannot be contorted to fit our worldview (e.g. Druckman and McGrath 2019; Pasek 2018). The Obama-turned-Trump supporters were certainly viewing the world through particular cognitive filters. But what helped give shape to those selective perceptions? To answer this question, let us look briefly at the following two phenomena: community socio-economic restructuring, especially in previously homogenous communities now experiencing rapid demographic change and, second, the repeatedly-mentioned overture among rural white interviewees about how *they* were the ones facing discrimination.

Earlier, I noted research finding a strong correlation between support for Trump and a community's growing Latino population (Enos 2017), while other studies note a positive relationship between recent Hispanic immigration and state-level variation in anti-Hispanic hate crimes (Stacey, Carbone-López, and Rosenfeld 2011). A mix of conditional factors are driving these responses to local ethnic diversity. There is strong evidence correlating increasing economic deprivation among individuals with their expression of more negative attitudes toward ethnic groups not of their own (e.g. Ballard-Rosa, Jensen, and Scheve 2018). This link is especially pronounced when coupled with an out-group moving into a traditionally homogenous social space (Laurence and Bentley 2016; Recchi 2015), which describes the majority of the communities that respondents came from. While economic status might be beyond the control of these white, longer-term community members (due to economic and geopolitical realities beyond their control), norms dictating social status remain within the purview of a community's dominant group (Sherman 2009). This explains the emphasis signified by Obama-turned-Trump supporters on things like work ethic, 'proper' clothing attire and speech patterns, and the like – examples of cultural capital (Bourdieu 1984). These actions had the same stratifying effect as economic capital.

Of the forty-three Obama-turned-Trump supporters, thirty came from communities (rural = 26/urban = 4) that had seen a greater-than-five-percent increase in the non-white population since 2000. In some of these areas, non-whites accounted for as much as forty percent of the town's population growth during that period. This is a trend happening in a number of rural communities throughout the country (Johnson and Lichter 2019). A 2017 study of 278 rural counties in 11 (US) Western states, including Colorado, by Headwaters Economics (2017) out of Bozeman, Montana, reports that 'the vast majority [of these communities] have minorities increasing, in many cases either slowing or reversing overall population decline,' to quote a co-author of the study (quoted in Simpson 2017b; see also Walter 2019).

Tensions were further exacerbated by the age structure of some of the communities where respondents resided. Rural Colorado is experiencing a graying of its white population in many instances. On the one hand, there is metropolitan Denver with its fast growing, and relatively young, population – its median age is just under 35 years. On the other hand, the state's 10 counties with the highest median age are all located in rural areas and have a median age of at least 50 (Simpson 2017a). This is creating even starker contrasts in spaces where younger generations tend to concentrate, like schools, parks, and move theaters. In some of the communities that I visited while conducting interviews, classrooms were many times more diverse than the community as a whole – a sign of things to come, much to the chagrin of some residents. I interviewed one rural elementary school teacher who told me about a homeroom in her school that was more than 50 percent non-white. Twenty years ago, when she started teaching in the community, 'there were three or four non-whites in the entire school' (Mary, Rural, Teacher, 50 yrs. old).

There was also considerable uncertainty among the whites interviewed over whether race or ethnicity are relevant variables for thinking about discrimination in twenty-first century America. This was mentioned repeatedly among rural respondents. Rural white respondents' underestimation of prejudice toward people of color and their refusal to recognize the poverty they did see as an effect of racism appeared to be linked to a belief that *they* were the ones being discriminated against. Thus, while many witnessed minority groups living below the poverty line, these experiences were still not as immediate relative to the prejudice they claimed to experience regularly as rural denizens.

This brings us back the phenomenon of motivated reasoning. Motivated reasoning reminds us that facts never speak for themselves. We speak for them and, depending on our values and outlooks, do not always 'see' the same thing as a result of this filtering process. Take the example of climate change denial. When trying to communicate climate science to individuals holding what are known as hierarchical and individualist values, which are correlated with an acceptance of social and economic stratification and a valuing of individual freedoms over those of the collective, research into motivated reasoning warns us to not point to the enormous scientific consensus that exists on the subject. Why? Those underlying values mean this group is uncomfortable with communal institutions and signs of collectivistic thinking. Thus, for this group, scientific consensus might be viewed as groupthink or the product of some other nefarious, collectivistic influence (Douglas 2015; Solomon 2006).

For rural Obama-turned-Trump supporters, bombarding them with facts about minority wealth and wage gaps and with evidence demonstrating that racism remains alive-and-well may therefore have little effect on reducing their levels of racial resentment – it certainly did not change any minds when I presented them with evidence indicating the existance of systematic racism. As long as they believe, for example, that rural 'sacrifice zones' (Edelman 2019; Holifield and Day 2017) exist and are expanding in their number, feel that rural practices and symbols are dismissed for being backward, and believe practices they value are under existential threat (i.e. gun rights), then no amount of data will convince these individuals that racism exceeds the societal ill-will directed toward rural ways of life. To dismiss their claims as based on ignorance and hate – the result of a culture that 'embraces the past' and that 'wants to raise the drawbridge' (Longworth 2018) – misses an opportunity to tackle not only the racial resentment held by this group but also their own feelings and experiences of injustice.

In conclusion, this paper looks at the phenomenon of authoritarian populism in the US. Instead of viewing the movement as exclusively a 'right-wing' phenomenon, the data presented show things are a bit more complicated. In addition to focusing on Democrats and unaffiliated independents who voted for Obama before supporting Trump, data are also presented showing implicit and colorblind bias at work. It is easy to show the explicit bias and blatant racism that animates elements of this movement – swastikas and neo-Nazi symbols, white-pride chants and signs, and the like. Yet those vile displays arguably represent the beliefs of a small segment of this group. Scholars need to better understand what drives the rest of the movement. Given that somewhere between 6.7 and 9.2 million Americans voted for Obama in 2012, only to then cast their vote for Trump in 2016 (Beauchamp 2018), it seems a fair assumption that members of this population are neither open nor closet fascists, though they do harbor racially-based resentments. This research helps explain the animating elements of authoritarian populism driven by implicit biases and other factors that cause individuals to filter facts in ways that helps breathe life into the movement.

This paper follows in the tradition of wanting to advance projects that draw supporters away from authoritarian populist movements while growing and solidifying the united front of democratic challengers that look to afford alternatives to, or within, capitalism (Borras 2020; Holt-Giménez and Shattuck 2011; Wright 2016). To do this, we must understand the appeal of authoritarian populism so we can unsettle and have reimagined those political formations premised on postracial, colorblind outlooks and the biases they foster. This includes sustaining a critique of *both* Democratic neoliberalism and Republican neoconservatism, see each as playing a significant role in the nation's authoritarian turn (Fraser 2019; Maskovsky 2017; Streeck 2017).

Disclosure statement

No potential conflict of interest was reported by the author(s).

Funding

This research was supported in part by the Ministry of Education of the Republic of Korea and the National Research Foundation of Korea [grant number NRF-2016S1A3A2924243], the National Institute of Food and Agriculture [grant number NIFA-COL00725], and the Office for the Vice President for Research, College of Liberal Arts, and Office of Engagement at Colorado State University.

References

Anderson, P. 2019. *Brazil Apart: 1964-2019*. New York: Random House.
Ballard-Rosa, C., A. Jensen, and K. Scheve. 2018. *Economic Decline, Social Identity, and Authoritarian Values in the United States*. Boston: American Political Science Association.
Beauchamp, Z. 2018. "A New Study Reveals the Real Reason Obama Voters Switched to Trum." *Vox* October 16. https://www.vox.com/policy-and-politics/2018/10/16/17980820/trump-obama-2016-race-racism-class-economy-2018-midterm.
Berkes, H. 2008. "Poll: Rural Voters Not Reliably Republican in 2008." *Politico*, May 18. https://www.npr.org/templates/story/story.php?storyId=90555893.
Berlet, C., and M. Lyons. 2018. *Right-Wing Populism in America: Too Close for Comfort*. New York: Guilford Press.
Berlet, C., and S. Sunshine. 2019. "Rural Rage: The Roots of Right-Wing Populism in the United States." *The Journal of Peasant Studies* 46 (3): 480–513.
Bhambra, G. K. 2017. "Brexit, Trump, and 'Methodological Whiteness': On the Misrecognition of Race and Class." *The British Journal of Sociology* 68: S214–S232.
Bonilla-Silva, Eduardo. 2001. *White Supremacy & Racism in the Post-Civil Rights Era*. Boulder, CO: Lynne Rienner.
Bonilla-Silva, E., and D. G. Embrick. 2001. "Are Blacks Color Blind Too? An Interview-Based Analysis of Black Detroiters'." *racial Views. Race and Society* 4 (1): 47–67.
Booker, B. 2018. "Report: Rural Poverty In America Is 'An Emergency'." *NPR*, May 31. https://www.npr.org/2018/05/31/615578001/report-rural-poverty-in-america-is-an-emergency.
Borras Jr, S. M. 2020. "Agrarian Social Movements: The Absurdly Difficult but Not Impossible Agenda of Defeating Right-Wing Populism and Exploring a Socialist Future." *Journal of Agrarian Change* 20: 3–36. doi:10.1111/joac.12311.
Bourdieu, P. 1984. *Distinction*. Cambridge, MA: Harvard University Press.
Carolan, M. 2019a. "Filtering Perceptions of Climate Change and Biotechnology: Values and Views among Colorado Farmers and Ranchers." *Climatic Change*. doi:10.1007/s10584-019-02625-0.
Carolan, M. 2019b. "The Rural Problem: Justice in the Countryside." *Rural Sociology*. doi:10.1111/ruso.12278.
Carolan, M. 2020a. "Ethical Eating as Experienced by Consumers and Producers: When Good Food Meets Good Farmers." *Journal of Consumer Culture*. doi:10.1177/1469540519899967.
Carolan, M. 2020b. "Rural Sociology Revival: Engagements, Enactments and Affectments for Uncertain Times." *Sociologia Ruralis*. doi:10.1111/soru.12284.
Charles, D. 2019. "Farmers Got Billions From Taxpayers In 2019, And Hardly Anyone Objected." *NPR*, December 31. https://www.npr.org/sections/thesalt/2019/12/31/790261705/farmers-got-billions-from-taxpayers-in-2019-and-hardly-anyone-objected.
Cramer, K. J. 2016. *The Politics of Resentment: Rural Consciousness in Wisconsin and the Rise of Scott Walker*. Chicago: University of Chicago Press.
Dasgupta, S. 2019. "See How Rural Voters Have Shifted to the GOP Over the Last Three Presidential Elections." *McClathy*, November 5. https://www.mcclatchydc.com/news/politics-government/election/article237003749.html.

de Wit, M. M., A. Roman-Alcalá, A. Liebman, and S. Chrisman. 2019. "Agrarian Origins of Authoritarian Populism in the United States: What can We Learn from 20th-Century Struggles in California and the Midwest?" *Journal of Rural Studies*. doi:10.1016/j.jrurstud.2019.12.003.

Deneen, P. 2018. *Why Liberalism Failed*. New Haven: Yale University Press.

Doane, A. 2017. "Beyond Color-Blindness:(Re) Theorizing Racial Ideology." *Sociological Perspectives* 60 (5): 975–991.

Douglas, H. 2015. "Politics and Science: Untangling Values, Ideologies, and Reasons." *The ANNALS of the American Academy of Political and Social Science* 658 (1): 296–306.

Druckman, J. N., and M. C. McGrath. 2019. "The Evidence for Motivated Reasoning in Climate Change Preference Formation." *Nature Climate Change*. https://www.nature.com/articles/s41558-018-0360-1.

Drum, K. 2017. "Urban vs. Rural Recovery from the Great Recession: Another Look." *Mother Jones*, April 15. https://www.motherjones.com/kevin-drum/2017/04/urban-rural-recovery-great-recession/.

Edelman, M. 2019. "Hollowed Out Heartland, USA: How Capital Sacrificed Communities and Paved the Way for Authoritarian Populism." *Journal of Rural Studies*. doi:10.1016/j.jrurstud.2019.10.045.

Enos, R. 2017. "How Place Shapes Our Politics." *City Lab*, December 12. https://www.citylab.com/life/2017/12/how-place-shapes-our-politics/548147/

Fahey, M., and N. Wells. n.d. "The Places That Flipped and Gave the Country to TRUMP." *CNBC.com*. https://www.cnbc.com/heres-a-map-of-the-us-counties-that-flipped-to-trump-from-democrats/.

Ford, M. 2019. "The Great Lie of the Right-Wing Populists." *The New Republic*, August 30. https://newrepublic.com/article/154912/great-lie-right-wing-populists.

Fording, R. C., and S. F. Schram. 2017. "The Cognitive and Emotional Sources of Trump Support: The Case of Low-Information Voters." *New Political Science* 39 (4): 670–686.

Forgey, Q. 2020. "AOC: 'In any Other Country, Joe Biden and I Would Not be in the Same Party'." *Politico*, January 6. https://www.politico.com/news/2020/01/06/alexandria-ocasio-cortez-joe-biden-not-same-party-094642.

Frank, J. 2018. "Colorado's Growing Political Divide Leaves Rural Communities Feeling Forgotten and Voiceless." *The Denver Post*, January 26. https://www.denverpost.com/2017/12/24/colorado-politics-divide-rural-urban-communities-donald-trump/.

Fraser, N. 2019. *The Old is Dying and the New Cannot be Born: From Progressive Neoliberalism*. London: Verso.

Geertz, C. 2008. "Thick Description: Toward an Interpretive Theory of Culture." In *The Cultural Geography Reader*, edited by T. Oakes and P. Price, 41–51. New York: Routledge.

Glaser, B., and A. Strauss. 1967. *The Discovery of Grounded Theory: Strategies for Qualitative Research*. New York: Aldine.

Goldstein, J. E., K. Paprocki, and T. Osborne. 2019. "A Manifesto for a Progressive Land-Grant Mission in an Authoritarian Populist Era." *Annals of the American Association of Geographers* 109 (2): 673–684.

Gonzales, M., and R. Delgado. 2016. *Politics of Fear: How Republicans Use Money, Race and the Media to Win*. New York: Routledge.

Hall, S. 1985. "Authoritarian Populism: A Reply." In *New Left Review*, 115–124. London. https://newleftreview.org/issues/I151/articles/stuart-hall-authoritarian-populism-a-reply.

Hall, S. 2017. *Selected Political Writings: The Great Moving Right Show and Other Essays*. Durham: Duke University Press.

Haney-López, Ian. 2014. *Dog Whistle Politics: How Coded Racial Appeals Have Reinvented Racism and Wrecked the Middle Class*. New York: Oxford University Press.

Hartmann, D., P. R. Croll, R. Larson, J. Gerteis, and A. Manning. 2017. "Colorblindness as Identity: Key Determinants, Relations to Ideology, and Implications for Attitudes about Race and Policy." *Sociological Perspectives* 60 (5): 866–888.

Headwaters Economics. 2017. *Minority Populations Driving County Growth in the Rural West*, August. Bozeman, MT: Headwaters Economics. https://headwaterseconomics.org/economic-development/trends-performance/minority-populations-driving-county-growth/.

Hochschild, A. 2016. "The Ecstatic Edge of Politics: Sociology and Donald Trump." *Contemporary Sociology: A Journal of Reviews* 45 (6): 683–689.

Hochschild, A. 2018. *Strangers in Their Own Land: Anger and Mourning on the American Right*. New York: The New Press.

Holifield, Ryan, and Mick Day. 2017. "A Framework for a Critical Physical Geography of 'Sacrifice Zones': Physical Landscapes and Discursive Spaces of Frac Sand Mining in Western Wisconsin." *Geoforum; Journal of Physical, Human, and Regional Geosciences* 85 (October): 269–279. doi:10.1016/j.geoforum.2017.08.004.

Holt-Giménez, E., and A. Shattuck. 2011. "Food Crises, Food Regimes and Food Movements: Rumblings of Reform or Tides of Transformation?" *Journal of Peasant Studies* 38 (1): 109–144. doi:10.1080/03066150.2010.538578.

Jaffe-Walter, R. 2019. "Ideal Liberal Subjects and Muslim 'Others': Liberal Nationalism and the Racialization of Muslim Youth in a Progressive Danish School." *Race Ethnicity and Education* 22 (2): 285–300.

Johnson, K. M., and D. T. Lichter. 2019. "Rural Depopulation: Growth and Decline Processes Over the Past Century." *Rural Sociology* 84 (1): 3–27.

Judd, D., and A. Phillip. 2018. "Pete Buttigieg Says He Understands the Concern Over Past Remarks on Minorities and Education." *CNN*, November 26. https://www.cnn.com/2019/11/26/politics/pete-buttigieg-minorities-education/index.html.

Katznelson, I. 2005. *When Affirmative Action Was White: An Untold History of Racial Inequality in Twentieth Century America*. New York: W.W. Norton & Company.

Kefalas, M. 2003. *Working-Class Heroes: Protecting Home, Community, and Nation in a Chicago Neighborhood*. Berkeley: University of California Press.

Kraus, M. W., I. N. Onyeador, N. M. Daumeyer, J. M. Rucker, and J. A. Richeson. 2019. "The Misperception of Racial Economic Inequality." *Perspectives on Psychological Science*. doi:10.1177%2F1745691619863049.

Laclau, E. 2005. *On Populist Reason*. London: Verso.

Lane, S. 2018. "Booker Bill would Create Federally Funded Savings Account for Every Child." *The Hill*, October. https://thehill.com/policy/finance/412594-booker-bill-would-create-federally-funded-savings-account-for-every-child.

Laurence, J., and L. Bentley. 2016. "Does Ethnic Diversity Have a Negative Effect on Attitudes Towards the Community? A Longitudinal Analysis of the Causal Claims Within the Ethnic Diversity and Social Cohesion Debate." *European Sociological Review* 32 (1): 54–67.

Lewis, A. E. 2004. "What Group? Studying Whites and Whiteness in the Era of Color-Blindness." *Sociological Theory* 22 (4): 623–646.

Lichter, D. T., and J. P. Ziliak. 2017. "The Rural-Urban Interface: New Patterns of Spatial Interdependence and Inequality in America." *The ANNALS of the American Academy of Political and Social Science* 672 (1): 6–25.

Longworth, Richard C. 2018. *Blue Dot America*. Chicago, IL: The Chicago Council of Global Affairs. Accessed January 25, 2018. https://digit al.thech icago counc il.org/American-Urban-Rural-Divide/essay-1-9836-17232S.html.

Lopez, G. 2017. "The Past Year of Research has Made it Very Clear: Trump Won Because of Racial Resentment." *Vox*, December 15, https://www.vox.com/identities/2017/12/15/16781222/trump-racism-economic-anxiety-study.

Mamonova, N. 2019. "Understanding the Silent Majority in Authoritarian Populism: What can We Learn from Popular Support for Putin in Rural Russia?" *The Journal of Peasant Studies* 46 (3): 561–585.

Mamonova, N., and J. Franquesa. 2019. "Populism, Neoliberalism and Agrarian Movements in Europe. Understanding Rural Support for Right-Wing Politics and Looking for Progressive Solutions." *Sociologia Ruralis*. doi:10.1111/soru.12291.

Maskovsky, J. 2017. "Toward the Anthropology of White Nationalist Postracialism: Comments Inspired by Hall, Goldstein, and Ingram's "The Hands of Donald Trump"." *HAU: Journal of Ethnographic Theory* 7 (1): 433–440.

McCoy, T. 2017. "Did You Know in RURAL AMERICA, Disability Benefit Rates are Twice as High as in Urban Areas?" *Washington Post*, July 22. https://www.washingtonpost.com/local/social-issues/in-rural-america-disability-benefit-rates-are-twice-as-high-as-in-urban- areas/2017/07/22/3e600722-575c-11e7-a204-ad706461fa4f_story.html.

Media Matters. 2019. "Fox & Friends Hosts Outraged that Presidential Candidates Called Out Trump's Racism." *Media Matters*, September 13. https://www.mediamatters.org/fox-friends/fox-friends-hosts-were-furious-presidential-candidates-called-out-trumps-racism.

Morgen, S., and J. Erickson. 2017. "Incipient 'Commoning' in Defense of the Public?: Competing Varieties of Fiscal Citizenship in tax-and Spending-Related Direct Democracy." *Focaal* 2017 (79): 54–66.

Nebraska Rural Poll. 2019. *2019 Nebraska Rural Poll*. Lincoln, NE: University of Nebraska. https://ruralpoll.unl.edu/.

NPR, RWJF, and Harvard. 2018. Life in Rural America. Public Radio, the Robert Wood Johnson Foundation, and the Harvard T.H. Chan School of Public Health, October, https://cdn1.sph.harvard.edu/wp-content/uploads/sites/94/2019/06/NPR-RWJF-Harvard-Rural-Poll-Report_FINAL_10-15-18_-FINAL-updated1130.pdf.

Olorunnipa, T. 2019. "'This is What I'm Fighting': Trump Tries to Cast U.S. Cities as Filthy and Crime-Ridden in Attempt to Sway 2020 Voters." *The Washington Post*, July 2. https://www.washingtonpost.com/politics/this-is-what-im-fighting-trump-tries-to-cast-us-cities-as-filthy-and-crime-ridden-in-attempt-to-sway-2020-voters/2019/07/02/089463ca-9cda-11e9-b27f-ed2942f73d70_story.html.

Pasek, J. 2018. "It's Not My Consensus: Motivated Reasoning and the Sources of Scientific Illiteracy." *Public Understanding of Science* 27 (7): 787–806.

Phillips, K. 2018. "Freeloading Immigrants." *Kearney Hub*. Jan 20. https://www.kearneyhub.com/opinions/ltte/freeloading-immigrants/article_c1e3b04e-fda1-11e7-9e12-eb41ec54a131.html.

Pied, C. M. 2019. "Ethnography and the Making of 'The People': Uncovering Conservative Populist Politics in the United States." *American Journal of Economics and Sociology* 78 (3): 761–786.

Rancière, J. 2016. "The Populism That is not to be Found." In *What is a People*, edited by A. Badiou, et al, 100–106. New York: Columbia University Press.

Recchi, Ettore. 2015. *Mobile Europe: The Theory and Practices of Free Movement in the EU*. Basingstoke: Palgrave Macmillan.

Rentz, C. 2019. "Trump Called Baltimore 'Rat and Rodent Infested' 4 Months after He Tried Ending the Funding for its Rodent Control." *Baltimore Sun*, August 26. https://www.baltimoresun.com/maryland/baltimore-city/bs-md-ci-rat-budget-trump-k20190826-t6oay6qtqzexbefumapeyqp2hq-story.html.

Scoones, I., M. Edelman, S. M. Borras Jr, R. Hall, W. Wolford, and B. White. 2018. "Emancipatory Rural Politics: Confronting Authoritarian Populism." *The Journal of Peasant Studies* 45 (1): 1–20. doi:10.1080/03066150.2017.1339693.

Scott, E. 2017. "America is Divided on Whom to Blame for Black Americans' Challenges in Getting Ahead." *Washington Post*, October 5. https://www.washingtonpost.com/news/the-kfix/wp/2017/10/05/america-is-divided-on-whom-to-blame-for-black-americans-challenges-in-getting-ahead/.

Serwer, A. 2017. "The Nationalists' Delusion." *The Atlantic*, November 20. https://www.theatlantic.com/politics/archive/2017/11/the-nationalists-delusion/546356/.

Sherman, J. 2009. *Those Who Work, Those Who Don't: Poverty, Morality, and Family in Rural America*. Minneapolis, MN: University of Minnesota Press.

Simpson, Kevin. 2017a. "Colorado Divide: Seismic Shifts Create Rural-Urban Chasm in the Culture, Economy and Politics of the State." *The Denver Post*, July 21. https://www.denverpost.com/2017/07/21/colorado-divide-rural-urban-chasm/.

Simpson, K. 2017b. "Rural Colorado's White Population is Declining, and Minorities Are Transforming the REGION's Culture and Economy." *Denver Post*, November 9. https://www.denverpost.com/2017/11/09/colorado-rural-demographic-minority-increase/.

Slack, T., B. C. Thiede, and L. Jensen. 2019. "Race, Residence, and Underemployment: Fifty Years in Comparative Perspective, 1968–2017." *Rural Sociology*. doi:10.1111/ruso.12290.

Slobodian, Q. 2018. "Trump, Populists and the Rise of Right-Wing Globalization." *The New York Times*. October 22. https://www.nytimes.com/2018/10/22/opinion/trump-far-right-populists-globalization.html.

Smith, A., and E. Trevelyan. 2019. In Some States, More Than Half of Older Residents Live In Rural Areas, Oct 22, United States Census Bureau, Washington DC, https://www.census.gov/library/stories/2019/10/older-population-in-rural-america.html.

Solomon, M. 2006. "Groupthink Versus the Wisdom of Crowds: The Social Epistemology of Deliberation and Dissent." *The Southern Journal of Philosophy* 44: 28–42.

Stacey, M., K. Carbone-López, and R. Rosenfeld. 2011. "Demographic Change and Ethnically Motivated Crime: The Impact of Immigration on Anti-Hispanic Hate Crime in the United States." *Journal of Contemporary Criminal Justice* 27 (3): 278–298.

Stracqualursi, V. 2020. "8 in 10 Black Voters Say Trump is Racist, New Poll Shows." *CNN*, January 17. https://www.cnn.com/2020/01/17/politics/black-voters-trump-poll/index.html.

Streeck, W. 2017. *Buying Time: The Delayed Crisis of Democratic Capitalism*. 2nd ed. London and New York: Verso.

Thiede, B. C., D. T. Lichter, and T. Slack. 2018. "Working, but Poor: The Good Life in Rural America?" *Journal of Rural Studies* 59: 183–193.

Ulrich-Schad, J. D., and C. M. Duncan. 2018. "People and Places Left Behind: Work, Culture and Politics in the Rural United States." *The Journal of Peasant Studies* 45 (1): 59–79.

US Census. n.d. *Quick Facts: Colorado*. Washington, DC: US Census. https://www.census.gov/quickfacts/co.

USDA. 2017. *Rural America at a Glance 2017 Edition*. Washington, DC: United States Department of Agriculture. Accessed January 11, 2017. https://www.ers.usda.gov/webdocs/publications/85740/eib-182.pdf?v=43054.

Vanaik, A. 2017. *The Rise of Hindu Authoritarianism: Secular Claims, Communal Realities*. London: Verso.

Vance, J. D. 2016. *Hillbilly Elegy: A Memoir of a Family and Culture in Crisis*. London: William Collins.

Wagner, D. 2018. *The New Temperance: The American Obsession with Sin and Vice*. New York: Routledge.

Walter, B. M. 2019. "Nostalgia and Precarious Placemaking in Southern Poultry Worlds: Immigration, Race, and Community Building in Rural Northern Alabama." *Journal of Rural Studies*. doi:10.1016/j.jrurstud.2019.12.004.

Webster, M., and J. Loayza. 2017. *State of Working Colorado, 2017 Edition*. Denver, CO: Colorado Center on Law and Policy. https://cclponline.org/wp-content/uploads/2017/12/State-of-Working-CO-2017_FINAL.pdf.

Wegmann, P. 2019. "Trump to Bill Sponsors for Immigrants' Welfare Benefits." *Real Clear* Politics, May 23. https://www.realclearpolitics.com/articles/2019/05/23/trump_to_bill_sponsors_for_immigrants_welfare_benefits.html.

Wengle, E. 2018. *Are Marketplace Premiums Higher in Rural Than in Urban Areas?* November. New York: Robert Woods Johnson Foundation. file:///Users/mcarolan/Downloads/rwjf449986.pdf.

Wetts, R., and R. Willer. 2019. "Who Is Called by the Dog Whistle? Experimental Evidence That Racial Resentment and Political Ideology Condition Responses to Racially Encoded Messages." *Socius* 5: 17. doi:10.1177%2F2378023119866268.

Wise, T. 2010. *Colorblind: The Rise of Post-Racial Politics and the Retreat from Racial Equity*. New York: City Lights.

Wodak, R., and M. Krzyżanowski. 2017. "Right-wing Populism in Europe & USA: Contesting Politics & Discourse Beyond 'Orbanism'and 'Trumpism'." *Journal of Language and Politics* 16 (4): 471–484.

Wright, E. O. 2016. "Socialism and Real Utopias." In *Alternatives to Capitalism: Proposals for a Democratic Economy*, edited by R. Hahnel, and E. O. Wright, 25–40. New York: Verso.

Wright, M., and M. Levy. 2019. "American Public Opinion on Immigration: Nativist, Polarized, or Ambivalent?" *International Migration*. doi:10.1111/imig.12660.

Wuthnow, R. 2019. *The Left Behind: Decline and Rage in Small-Town America*. Princeton: Princeton University Press.

Agrarian anarchism and authoritarian populism: towards a more (state-)critical 'critical agrarian studies'

Antonio Roman-Alcalá

ABSTRACT
This paper applies an anarchist lens to agrarian politics, seeking to expand and enhance inquiry in critical agrarian studies. Anarchism's relevance to agrarian processes is found in three general areas: (1) explicitly anarchist movements, both historical and contemporary; (2) theories that emerge from and shape these movements; and (3) implicit anarchism found in values, ethics, everyday practices, and in forms of social organization – or 'anarchistic' elements of human social life. Insights from anarchism are then applied to the problematique of the contemporary rise of 'authoritarian populism' and its relation to rural people and agrarian processes, focusing on the United States. Looking via an anarchist lens at this case foregrounds the state powers and logics that underpin authoritarian populist political projects but are created and reproduced by varying political actors; emphasizes the complex political identities of non-elite people, and the ways these can be directed towards either emancipatory or authoritarian directions based on resentments towards state power and identifications with grassroots, lived moral economies; and indicates the strategic need to prioritize ideological development among diverse peoples, in ways that provide for material needs and bolster lived moral economies. The paper concludes with implications for the theory and practice of emancipatory politics.

Introduction

For the peasant, the state is a negative quantity, an evil, to be replaced in short shrift by their own "homemade" social order. That order, they believe, can run without the state, hence, peasants in rebellion are natural anarchists. – Eric Wolf in *Peasant Wars of the Twentieth Century* (1969, 295)

Throughout the rural world, capitalist 'economic-development' continues to exploit human and nonhuman resources, with the support of subnational, national, and international governments. Large-scale dams and 'green' infrastructures, plantation monocultures, urbanization, mining, and fossil fuel-seeking continue to reproduce the marginal status of rural people. Meanwhile, partially in reaction to this marginalization, electorates have turned to a variety of scapegoating nationalisms, bolstering the electoral success of certain neo-'authoritarian populists', like Trump, Modi, Erdogan, Bolsonaro and Duterte (see this journal's recent forum on authoritarian populism). Rightwing achievement of state power has emphasized the seemingly central role of state control in any emancipatory political project. Further emphasizing that salience is the surging threat of climate change to economic (re)production and societal stability. A standard assumption is that climate change could only be meaningfully addressed via a strong state (Wainwright and Mann 2013); indeed, that humanity's survival depends on the state – and who controls it.

In this paper, I make the claim that anarchism continues to be relevant to these issues, and to critical agrarian studies (CAS), even if both proponents and detractors of anarchism commonly understand anarchism as antithetical to any form of state. During the height of anarchist movement activity, it was most often self-described as 'libertarian socialism', distinguishing it from other socialisms of the time that believed it necessary to centralize coercive power in the course of making social change. When looked at in this way, anarchism seems ill suited to support sober assessment of current conditions in order to make positive change: how could anarchism aid emancipatory movements if those movements 'must' engage the state? Furthermore, what can anarchism offer those particularly interested in the *agrarian and rural* aspects of current conditions?

Regarding the latter question, in anarchism we see a parallel to the mistaken belief (found in some of the more determinist Marxist agrarian studies, committed to a 'historical materialist' science claimed to have predictive powers) that the peasantry would inevitably disappear: like the peasantry, anarchism has never died the death it was supposed to. It survives in existing social movements applying the label in action, in political theories that remain in circulation due to such movements, and (arguably) in social practices that reflect and produce anarchist ethos/ethics. Overtly anarchist movements continue to be disparaged, misunderstood, and attacked by almost every other political force in society – yet they continue to exist. Anarchism remains relevant in theory and practice to processes of human social organization, broadly, and to attempts to radically make make society. Anarchism's relevance, in short, is found at three levels: as *movements*, *theories*, and in *anarchistic behaviors*.

Few researchers commonly leverage the above lenses on questions of rural agrarian change, the politics of development, or (more specifically) the contemporary moment of regressive authoritarian populist politics. Some notable exceptions exist upon which this works seeks to build (Scott 2012; Wald 2015; Ashwood 2018a; Dunlap and Jakobsen 2020), but the anarchist lens is surely underutilized in CAS. This journal, for example, returns only 18 responses when searching for the keyword 'anarchism' (76 for 'anarchy'), compared with 263 for 'Marxism' (checked 25 February 2020). This is largely representative of Leftish critical social science as a whole, though some journals are expressly oriented to anarchist theory (e.g. Anarchist Studies) and others do exhibit greater inclusion (e.g. *ACME, Antipode* and *Journal of Political Ecology*). These trends may reflect the fact that anarchists reject the University-focused hierarchy of knowledge and have developed theory outside academia largely through (often anonymous) direct action; anarchist theory is less 'great thinker'-oriented and relies less on academic validation for its self-worth. In sum, anarchism remains relevant to political theory and practice, even if it appears marginal in academia and politics at large (Gordon 2008).

In the remainder of the introduction, I outline a few examples of the movements, theories/values, and anarchistic elements of anarchism, before detailing each in its own section in order to continue making the case for anarchist critical agrarian studies. After describing what these three lenses offer CAS, I apply them to the case of authoritarian populism in the United States (US). Though I pull in geographically diverse examples to make the case for anarchist CAS, I often return to my focus of the US, in order to provide continuity and focus in the application of the lens to a single case. I conclude with some reflections on what an anarchist lens offers a view of contemporary agrarian movement organizing in the US.

Movements, theories/values, and anarchistic elements

The hegemonic quantitative logic of political analysis – which anarchism rejects – makes it seem that overt anarchist movements have been weak, small, and ineffectual in comparison with right-wing and more mainstream left sectors (in parliamentary politics). Historically, as Carter (1971, 105) and others have reminded, anarchism can claim no definitive victories. Its 'near misses' are, however, quite important to world history: anarchism and anarchists played key roles in nineteenth-twentieth century development of socialism and socialist movements, e.g. in the Spanish Revolution (Gomez Casas 1986; Evans 2020); the Mexican Revolution (Wolf 1969); or in the contribution of Nestor Mahkno's anarcho-peasant militias to the Ukrainian and Russian Revolutions (Wolf 1969; Palij 1976). Perhaps most crucially, anarchist ideas have spread from overtly anarchist movements to other modern era movements.[1] Anarchism's influence has extended even to future non-anarchist state leadership, as in Dirlik's (1991, 294–297) study of early twentieth century Chinese anarchist revolutionaries whose 'work-study' programs were attended by future Chinese state leaders Mao Zedong and Deng Xiaoping.

Because common understanding is that anarchism has seen little success in formal politics, it is often a surprise to left activists and scholars that anarchism was a dominant, ascendant portion of revolutionary left movements at the turn of the twentieth century.[2] This prevalence was largely due to anarchism's ideas and social forms spreading via illegalist, insurrectionary networks and 'anarcho-syndicalist' unions, particularly the Industrial Workers of the World (IWW), founded in the US in 1905 (van der Walt 2016; Cole, Struthers, and Zimmer 2018). While anarchism and syndicalism do not completely or simply overlap, anarcho-syndicalism is more accurately traced to anarchist than other socialist sectors (McKay 2012). Eventually suppressed and largely dismantled by state and private forces, especially during the period leading up to and through World War I,

---

[1]See Epstein (1993), Cornell (2016) for studies referencing anarchist influence on US social movements.
[2]For historical references, see: Graham (2005, 2009, 2012), Hirsch and van der Walt (2010), Schmidt (2013), Marshall (2010), Cappelletti (2018), Maxwell and Craib (2015), Porter (2011), Zaragoza Rovira (1996), Ramos, Rodrigues, and Samis (2003), CILEP (2011), Páez (1986), Hart (1978), Hirsch (2010), Shaffer (2000, 2013), Quail (2019), Berry (2009), Pernicone (1993), de Góes (2017), Voline (2019), Mbah and Igariwey (2001), van der Walt (2011, 2016), Dirlik (1991), Hwang (2017), Crump (1993), Cornell (2016).

these movements spread over the globe including to Latin America, Europe, Asia, North America, and to a lesser degree Africa. Countries where nineteenth and twentieth century anarchist movements existed include: Algeria, Argentina, Bolivia, Brazil, Chile, Colombia, Cuba, Ecuador, Mexico, Peru, Puerto Rico, Uruguay, Venezuela, Jamaica, England, France, Germany, the Netherlands, Italy, Portugal, Russia, Spain, Switzerland, Ukraine, Algeria, Nigeria, South Africa, India, China, Korea, Japan, Malaysia, Vietnam, Australia, New Zealand, Canada, and the United States.

Ultimately, it is the ideas ('theories') developed through these struggles that have shaped and continue to shape social life and political change. These ideas most often were articulated by active movement organizers, who were also theorizers. Anarchist ideas have in different times and places resulted in different kinds of effects – impacts not always deep, or positive. But in general, CAS has ignored or forgotten canonical anarchist theory, and even less has it addressed recent anarchist theory. In the next section, I outline elements of anarchist theory, describing its relevance to contemporary rural politics and overlaps with other CAS traditions. Though overtly anarchist movements from the past have largely been forgotten, and in almost all cases the movements have reduced in numbers and influence, and overt anarchist movements today are less massive than in their heyday, anarchist movements still exist (including in less visible, underground and informal forms). Addressing historical and contemporary manifestations of overtly anarchist social organization is the focus of section three.

CAS is also better off taking a more decolonial approach to rural politics, and instead of seeking to find overt Anarchism outside of European and settler-colonial contexts, looking for its interconnections with freedom struggles elsewhere, as in James Scott's discussions (2009) of anarchistic rural peoples in Southeast Asia or Maia Ramnath's (2011) study of India in *Decolonizing Anarchism*. Ramnath (2011, 7) distinguishes between 'small a anarchism' and the Western (or 'Capital-A') Anarchist tradition:

> with a small a the word anarchism implies a set of assumptions and principles, a recurrent tendency or orientation–with the stress on movement in a direction, not a perfected condition–toward more dispersed and less concentrated power; less top-down hierarchy and more self-determination through bottom-up participation; liberty and equality seen as directly rather than inversely proportional; the nurturance of individuality and diversity within a matrix of interconnectivity, mutuality, and accountability; and an expansive recognition of the various forms that power relations can take, and correspondingly, the various dimensions of emancipation. This tendency, when it becomes conscious, motivates people to oppose or subvert the structures that generate or sustain inequity, unfreedom, and injustice, and to promote or prefigure these structures that generate and sustain equity, freedom, and justice.

Africa may of all continents lack substantial anarchist historical presence, but as African activists have argued (Mbah and Igariwey 2001) anarchist values are reflected in its many precolonial traditions (some of which survive today). If we take Wolf's (1969) analysis of anarchistic resonances in peasantries seriously, the result is that CAS must consider anarchism as part of the CAS tool set. Addressing these more anarchist*ic* elements of social organization in various contexts and their relation to agrarian change is the focus of section four.

Anarchist theory

> An anarchist objection to Marxism was that Marxism, with its preoccupation with the proletariat, had a blind spot towards the peasantry and ignored eighty percent of the world's

population. – Arif Dirlik (1991, 238, referring to the early twentieth century context, when peasantries formed the bulk of human populations)

I begin by focusing on anarchist theory, since theory forms the baseline for engaging with 'the literature' in CAS. Table 1 gives an overview of theoretical positions among five CAS lenses: orthodox and agrarian Marxism, agrarian populism, social and individualist anarchism. Anarchist theory was and is historically embedded in social movement experiences. Because of this, anarchism is weighted by its movement history – e.g. legacies of European ideologies and Eurocentric thinking – but it is also not static, being responsive to conditions and capacious in its internal diversity. Anarchist theory thus is best treated as open-ended and not quite fully definable. Yet in contrast to caricatures of it, anarchism is not bereft of theory. While male and European dominated (par for the nineteenth century course), its classical canon offers plenty to parse. The French philosophers Pierre Joseph Proudhon, Henri de Saint-Simon and Charles Fourier, and Welsh philanthropist Robert Owen formed the earlier proto-anarchists, while Errico Malatesta, Peter Kropotkin, Michael Bakunin, Élisée Reclus, Emma Goldman, Max Stirner, Ricardo Flores Magón, Lucy Parsons, Alexander Herzen, Leo Tolstoy, Nestor Mahkno and Rudolf Rocker are some of the more well-known from anarchism's heyday. Many less-known activist-agitators also have provided relevant theory in historical writings. Considering the breadth of anarchist thinking and positions, and these being diverse by nature, an essay like this can offer only a necessarily selective and truncated treatment of anarchist theory, in its barest of outlines. Accordingly, this essay introduces merely one of many potential perspectives on anarchist theory. Importantly, there exists a main division within anarchism between individualist and insurrectionary trends, and those sometimes described as 'social' anarchism. This essay focuses on the latter largely due to my own preferences and background; still, individualist anarchism should also be appreciated in CAS, especially given its particular influence on eco-anarchist and anti-civilizationist currents in environmentalist struggles worldwide (GA 2012; Seaweed 2013; Pellow 2014; Loadenthal 2017).

Anarchist theory flourished during the late nineteenth and early twentieth century, evolving and defining itself in dialogue and disagreement with other threads of revolutionary and left social thought, most notably Marxism (see Prichard et al. 2017). Anarchism shares with Marxism a fundamental concern for revolutionary change, though also like Marxism, it has developed more reformist aspects so as to fit with less revolutionary circumstances over time. Anarchism's theoretical relationship to Marxism is complex, both enmeshed and antagonistic. If the birth of CAS may be traced back to Marx's Capital, written under the influence of (and in debates with) Proudhon, and early Russian agrarian populists engaged with anarchist theories *and* sought counsel from Marx on the role of peasants in revolution (Gamblin 1999; Shanin 2018), we can see how drawing hard lines between lineages in CAS serves little but polemic value. Rather than continuing generations-long polemics, it seems preferable to start with a normative appreciation of both traditions and the importance of linking these in writing and action, as indicated in recent debates in geography and sociology (el-Ojeili 2014, 462; Harvey 2017; Springer 2017). Still, I touch upon some overlaps and divergences in CAS traditions, in order to better see what anarchism specifically has to offer.

Table 1. *Note that for simplicity internal variations in theory, between theorists, or between theory and practice, have been necessarily downplayed.

CAS tradition → issue ↓	Orthodox marxism	Heterodox/agrarian marxism	Radical agrarian populism (RAP)	Social anarchism	Individualist/insurrectionary anarchism
Unit of inquiry and intervention			Community, farm household	Class, community, and individual (depending on context)	Individual and its autonomously defined relations
Class and class differentiation	Economic class conflict (workers/capitalists) - class as key to politics - Peasants as petty bourgeois/commodity producers - capitalism causes inevitable differentiation into labor, middle peasants, and capitalist farmers	Economic class conflict, w/ intraclass nuances - Peasants as differentiated already, intersecting w race, gender, etc - Differentiation happens but not mechanistically	- alternative (non-capitalist) market logics of peasant class - Chayanovian/demographic differentiation - classes formed via political action & self-identification - In practice, RAP movements bring different classes together to claim common political project	- manifold kinds of 'class' based in various hierarchies - differences *within* classes are assumed (and also opposed) - no single class category given primacy but capitalism seen as structuring social relations, as in Marxism - Differentiation not a key analytical metric, more concerned with formation of class-in-opposition	- similar to social anarchism but more critical of Marxist reduction of individuals to members of economic classes
class politics (including revolutionary potential of varying classes)	- Peasants as 'sack of potatoes' – need for class leadership from vanguard - 'enemy' = capitalist class, including aspiring middle & upper peasant/land holders, bourgeois state - Lenin and others came to see peasants as part of rev. force in twentieth century	- Peasants as potential revolutionaries - recognition of semi-proletarian realities leading to more complex class identities - 'enemy' = capitalist class; (sometimes) state enablers	- 'People of the land' as progressive (if not revolutionary) unitary class - Anti-corporate, ostensibly anti-capitalist BUT - Its anti-capitalism is relatively quiet on issues of peasantry-based capitalism - 'enemy' = capitalist class (as outsider) and state enablers	- Enthusiasm for proletarians, but also peasants and 'lumpenproletariat' as revolutionaries - Not class-reductionist; does not identify class with political position (e.g. accepts 'class traitors' from upper class backgrounds; e.g. theorist/activists Kropotkin, Bakunin) - Opposes *any* vanguard: any worthwhile movement is endogenous and autonomous - 'enemy' = capitalist class AND political and other elites	- similar to social anarchism - individualist and insurrectionary tendencies also emphasize enemies 'within': critiquing both identification among activists with 'Left' social roles and the institutionalization of radical organizing as limiting prospects for revolutionary change
'Community' and the individual	- Individuals seen primarily as members of economic classes - community is a near-meaningless term, used by RAP to avoid (self) critique	- Allows for intersectional positionalities (more attention to gender, e.g.) - economic class still a key category for analysis	- moral economies tie communities together - identities as 'rural' or 'peasant' people define community, including shared values like autonomy	- The 'libertarian' side of anarchism foregrounds the individual as unit of inquiry and intervention (as in Marx's 'the free development of each is the condition of the free development of all'), but in social anarchism this is tempered with the	- similar to social anarchism BUT more so than social anarchist tendencies, foregrounds the individual as unit of inquiry and intervention

	- analyzes communities via political economy + insights from poststructural, ecological, feminist, anti-colonial traditions	- relative lack of attention to internal differentiation - shares with anarchism a preference for 'the grassroots' as space for politics	- understanding that people are only individuals-in-community, and politically collective action is prioritized - equality and liberty not opposed as assumed in liberal & Marxist traditions; 'the individual and the community are continually negotiated categories' (Springer 2017, 284) - differs from liberal individualism in emphasizing social solidarity and opposing market relations - collective action via mutual aid/solidarity *builds* community moral economies	- more so skeptical of 'community', even ostensibly 'radical' ones, as impositions on individuals
Capitalism/socialism and relation to the state	- Need capitalism to lead to socialism - forced agricultural collectivization / industrialization - state as essential vehicle for transition to socialism: 'dictatorship of the proletariat' (at least, before 'withering away') - strongly influenced by Lenin and Leninist revolutions	- capitalism not a necessary 'first step' - Gramscian influence: attention to 'political' and 'civil' society - some appreciation for non-party social movements - In practice, still assumes a state-based strategy for transition to socialism	- rhetorically in favor of transition to socialism, often via developmental state - socialism must not threaten (collective?) rights to land - in practice, state-focused (e.g. Pink Tide) politics to achieve socialism via party politics, even if rhetorically for autonomous 'communities'	- non-deterministic notions of 'progress' (not linked to, and often anti-, industrialization/productivity focus) - against wage labor, state sovereignty, unjust hierarchies no matter under what name - no need for the state (as it exists) for transition to socialism, little to no engagement in state politics - socialism as a classless, moneyless, stateless society of egalitarian and autonomous communities	- does not emphasize 'building new world in the shell of the old' so much as destroying the old world and refusing to feed it - 'communization' theory, oriented to here-and-now lived zones of autonomy - no need for the state (as it exists) for transition to socialism, no engagement in state politics - not interested in 'socialism', as it broadly rejects totalizing ideas imposed on anyone
Relation to poststructuralism's emphasis on discourses and dispersed forms of power	Antagonistic: materialism above discourses; power resides in production and the state and must be wielded to 'win'	Accommodating to / influenced by (esp. via developments in political ecology; see Dunlap and Jakobsen 2020)	RAP politics absorbed much of 'post-development' critique (Escobar) and definition of peasant *as* political project; RAP theorists not as overtly poststructural	Recognizes the key role of discourses in politics Poststructuralism as apt philosophy for anarchist politics (May 1994) Gives preference to direct/material over mediated politics (especially in insurrectionary trends) Power analysis: 'social' rather than political focus	Modern insurrectionary theory directly references poststructuralist authors

Positive and negative theory

Like Marxism, anarchism holds within its classical canon both theories about morally objectionable conditions in human society (what I call 'negative' theories) and what might be done to correct these (what I call 'positive' theories). The antagonistic elements of anarchist action, largely rooted in negative theory, have sometimes been divorced from its 'prefigurative' elements, rooted in positive theory, especially as proponents of the latter have sought to distance themselves from anarchism's violent history. Yet for many theorists and activists, negative and positive are linked.

Western Anarchism's negative theory starts with its anticapitalism, identifying capitalism as an evil to be eradicated from human existence. Marx is still the standard bearer regarding analyses of capitalism. Anarchists *have* offered economic theories, but these have more often proposed economic solutions and alternatives (e.g. Knowles 2004), than deepened or challenged Marx's critique of capitalism. Alongside their shared critique of capitalism, anarchism shares with Marxism an opposition to organized religion (which nineteenth century theorists identified as co-constituting oppressive social conditions with capitalists and states; see Bakunin 1970). Where anarchism's negative theory differs from Marxism (though perhaps not from Marx himself[3]), or moves beyond Marxism, is its deeper anti-authoritarianism. Positioning a liberated society against *all* coercive human social relations, anarchists considered states by definition built on coercion, and thus were inherently anti-state. Rather than the vaguely defined 'withering away of the state' foretold in a (Marxist) post-revolutionary period, anarchists have long argued against theories of change that involve taking state power at *any* point, and have thus struggled against liberal and Marxist tendencies to do so. They predict that entry into power will only serve to reproduce power (CrimethInc 2017; Anarchopac 2019), and have in some cases called for the end of 'the hegemony of hegemony' (Day 2005) – seeking no part in coercive political projects to construct totalizing power of any sort. They have insisted, instead, on a social revolution beginning here and now, whose goal is the elimination, not adoption, of political power. On the individualist-insurrectionary side, anarchists have even forgone any association with 'the Left', insisting that leftism reproduces a 'reification and mediation' of social revolt that undermines principles of self-organization (McQuinn 2009).

The rejection of political/hegemonic thinking resonates with poststructuralist understanding of power and leads in a direction that sees and seeks to combat domination in myriad forms. Poststructuralist analyses see power as 'diffuse rather than concentrated, embodied and enacted rather than possessed, discursive rather than purely coercive, and constitute[ing] agents rather than being deployed by them (Gaventa 2003, 3)'. Such perspectives are found in Escobar's (1995) pioneering work on (post)development, and influential CAS scholarship since, and have been argued as resonant with anarchism (May 1994; Antliff and Hutchens 2007). A similar analysis underpins the 'total liberation' framework

---

[3]Indeed, scholars including Marxists like Joel Wainwright (2017; drawing on Karatani 2005) and Terry Eagleton (1999, 55–56) have noted that Marx exhibited anarchist sensibilities: 'Marx's final vision would thus seem somewhat anarchistic: that of a cooperative commonwealth made up of what he calls "free associations" of workers, who would extend democracy to the economic sphere while making a reality of it in the political one'. While Marx's anarchism may be true theoretically (as Thomas points out in *Karl Marx and the Anarchists* [1990, 2, 13–14, 21], Marx's critiques of the state confuse readers into thinking his disagreements with anarchists were merely tactical), anarchists tend to emphasize praxis over abstract theory, and would likely dispute any argument placing Marx's words against statism over his repeated actions to undermine anti-statist sections of the global socialist movement (see Eckhardt 2016).

that Pellow (2014) describes based on his research with radical animal and earth liberation activists. According to Pellow (2014, 18–19), total liberation comprises 'an ethic of justice and anti-oppression inclusive of humans, nonhuman animals, and ecosystems; anarchism; anticapitalism; and an embrace of direct action tactics'. In practice, total liberation trends address power as not simply about the state, but as actionable outside it, towards an ever-enlarging circle of concern, by confronting for instance unequal dominance *within* movements, anthropocentric speciesism, and the personal internalization of coercive institutions and practices ('killing the cop in your head').

The central contribution of anarchist positive theory is the fusion of means and ends. All actions to bring about revolutionary change, by this theory, should prefigure ways of human organization desired in a post-revolutionary world. This is based on a view of human nature where human misbehaviors are at best the result of stifling structures of power, or at worst ineradicable but able to be attenuated through social revolution. Contrary to strawman critiques, anarchists do not assume a perfect human nature, just as contemporary radical agrarian populists do not, contra Brass (2015), assume peasants as bearing an inherent and positive nature. Consistency of means and ends contributes to anarchism's use and promotion of self-organization, mutual aid and solidarity between actors, and a commitment to flatten all existing hierarchies, thus liberating 'better' human natures to emerge and take root. The seeds of future social relations are to be planted in the imperfect soil of today's societies.

Anarchism's practical theory calls for linking personal, communal, economic, and societal transformation through collective and prefigurative direct action that cultivates cultural commitment to mutual aid among non-elite communities, and which fully developed into counter-institutions, can provide a 'dual power'[4] situation that would undermine existing structures of power. If the 'social revolution' was during revolutionary times a call for complete overthrow of the established order, it also came to represent for Malatesta (2019) and others a more 'gradualist' approach that slowly lays the groundwork for revolutionary change to take place. There is no 'waiting' for the revolution, as it happens here-and-now; there are no shortcuts to revolution by enforcing anarchist ideology through coercive means, only continuous agitation and organizing among the oppressed classes (worker, peasant, *and* lumpenproletariat). More recent theorists have also focused on the imperative of tackling inequalities *within* these groups, even if class rule and state power are major enemies (Dixon 2012), as seen in 'total liberation' and in anarchism's overlaps with ecological, decolonial, feminist, and anti-racist thought.

Some anarchists have put forward what could be called an 'agrarian theory of change'. Generally, such theories have been influenced by historical rural and agricultural communes (Dolgoff 1974), and ecological concerns, as in the 'social ecology' field popularized by Murray Bookchin (1982) and put into practice recently in the autonomous region of Rojava, a present-day experiment in overtly agrarian, revolutionary libertarian socialism (see Internationalist Commune 2018). Kropotkin's ideas of agrarian socialism via 'industrial-agricultural villages' developed in *Fields, Factories, and Workshops* (1899) and *The Conquest of Bread* (1892) may be most well-known. Anthropologist Brian Morris (2018, 89–102) distills

---

[4] Lenin, Trotsky, and other Marxist-Leninists originated and promoted the strategy of dual power based on working class counter-institutions, but as a means towards state power, not (as in anarchism) as a means to replace it. Later libertarian socialists also turned its use and applicability from revolutionary to non-revolutionary contexts (see DSA-LSC 2019).

Kropotkin's agrarian work into four themes: (1) intensive production, cooperatively managed to continually improve soil health, (2) decentralization of industry and its (3) integration at a small scale with smaller-scale agriculture, and (4) the democratized combination of manual and intellectual labor in all work. Kropotkin was inspired by the productivity of various peasant-driven intensive agricultural systems across Europe, believing they showed the possibilities of redirecting production towards satisfying the needs of all, without the underlying conditions of class, money, or a state. In a way, localized food sovereignty was seen by Kropotkin (though not in these terms) as a precondition for the kind of classless, moneyless, stateless society of sharing that he and his contemporaries promoted. There are reflections of Kropotkin's century old theories in later agrarian populist scholarship, exemplified by van der Ploeg (2008, 2013), whose research approach also considers agrarian possibilities through fieldwork among diverse global peasantries, and advocates ecological, cooperative intensification and the prioritization of producer autonomy from capital. Kropotkin's ideas remain helpful and relevant, for example in his advocacy of intensification and diversification of the countryside such that farmwork is integrated with artisan industrial production *and leisure*, farmwork therefore becoming more meaningful and less characterized by drudgery or overwork. In other ways, this classical theory is dated and would require updating to meaningfully engage contemporary conditions such as the strong integration of the global food economy, or the real demands of rural people for complex consumer goods.[5]

Although anarchism lacks a consistent and well-known 'agrarian theory of change', the elements of such a theory may be pieced together, and might involve: building autonomous rural counter-power on a material and social basis; craft and industrial producers allying with agrarian communes in mutual aid; federation across greater areas to integrate and socialize (means of) production; direct action against existing concentrations of power to expropriate the expropriators; all providing conditions for dual power sufficient to overthrow wage labor and state power. Consequentially, these elements sustain and advance emancipatory politics and social organization in anticipation of crisis moments and the eventual decline of business-as-usual (whether from climate change, pandemics, or war). While less 'social' anarchists would dispute the very idea of dual power as an aspiration, many adjacent Left traditions also endorse such elements. Situationists, autonomist Marxist, council communists, and 'communization' theorists like *The Invisible Committee* (2009) have shared affinities for non-vanguardist base building activities; most of these tendencies' modern manifestations also share a concern for subjectivity formation and the need for direct rather than mediated action (Clark 2019).[6]

We might consider anarchism as utopian not because such a theoretically-based agenda is provably unrealistic, but because anarchism maintains perennial skepticism and thus offers only an ever-unfinished project. Classical anarchist theorists understood and acknowledged this (Malatesta 2019, 167–170). As Martin Buber (1949, 43) paraphrased Kropotkin:

> when it comes to our real will for a "restructuring" of society, it is not a question of manipulating an abstract principle but only of the *direction* of realization willed; of the limits of realization possible in this direction in any given circumstances …

---

[5] These latter limitations are paralleled in contemporary critiques of agrarian populism (Bernstein 2014).
[6] What democratic self-determination actually looks like forms a central line of difference between these tendencies (CrimethInc 2017) – among differences too numerous to address here.

The idea of directionality rather than purity underlies the least dogmatic of anarchist theory, even as it maintains utopian aspirations. Monica White, whose 2018 book covers the cooperative agrarian traditions of African-Americans seeking liberation, emphasizes this dynamic as well, noting that

> autonomy is in fact an ideal and is always a matter of degree ... the economic autonomy that cooperatives seek is a process, a continuum that moves from complete dependence on an oppressive structure to independence. Arguably, in a global economy, independence is always partial and is extremely difficult to accomplish; however, progress toward it can be leveraged for power and self-determination. (11)

Anarchism may be attacked as unrealistically based on an untenable belief in a solidary human nature, but in practice anarchist theories can be and have been applied in very practical ways.

Movements

On this more concrete level, it is often underappreciated how wide and how significant anarchist movements were in the late nineteenth and early twentieth centuries. In Schmidt's (2013, 65) assessment of anarchism's 'second wave' (1895–1923), sometimes seen as its golden age, much was achieved, including

> the fostering of a deeply-entrenched tradition of rank-and-file labour militancy and a global proletarian counter-culture that eschewed bourgeois patronage, the establishment of near-universal labour protections, such as the eight-hour working day and worker's compensation, a substantial contribution to the virtual annihilation of absolute monarchism, and the mounting of the most serious challenge to clerical control of education across the world.

During this period, anarchism also engaged peasants and rural people, whose role in revolutionary politics was largely neglected by Marxist theorists and activists before the 1917 Russian Revolution, based on their interpretation of Marx's position as anti-peasant. This neglect underappreciated peasantries, even though Marx himself late in life took the position that peasants could be socialist revolutionaries and socialist revolutions could take place in agrarian societies like Russia (described well by his letter to Vera Zasulich in 1881; see Shanin 2018).[7] Anarchism, especially via syndicalism, engaged both industrial and agrarian workers and was important in anti-colonial struggles (Hirsch and van der Walt 2010), arguably forming the 'first and most extensive global transnational social movement' (Castañeda and Feu 2019, 2). Even the demonstrably anti-anarchist E.J. Hobsbawm (1973, 61) admitted that

> in 1905–14 the marxist left had in most countries been on the fringe of the revolutionary movement, the main body of marxists had been identified with a *de facto* non-revolutionary social democracy, while the bulk of the revolutionary left was anarcho-syndicalist, or at least much closer to the ideas and the mood of anarcho-syndicalism than to that of classical marxism.

Considering its wide social and geographic reach, it is difficult to establish anarchism's real political effects, partly because of the difficulty in tracing straightforwardly cause-and-

---

[7]In not seeking to strawman-critique Marxism from its history, we should recognize that peasant involvement in socialist revolutions through the twentieth century (among other developments) led Marxists by midcentury to less proletarian/industrial-class centric analyses and proposals (Levien, Watts, and Hairong 2018, 855).

effect in non-linear complex politics, but also because *diffuse* influence is not the same as *no* influence, as Carter (1971, 109–110) concludes in her study of *The Political Theory of Anarchism*. Indeed, studies have drawn attention to the relevance of anarchist organizing to future developments in politics with national significance, including Korea, China, Mexico, and the United States (respectively, Hwang 2017; Dirlik 1991; Hodges 1995, and Cornell 2016). The retrospective perception that organized anarchists accomplished little can be explained in part by the relative dominance of Marxist-nationalist movements within the Left since the early 1920s, and the fact that these movements established nation-states inspired by Marxist doctrine. Turn of the century anarchism also included its 'propaganda of the deed' adherents, who among other activities assassinated political and economic elites and robbed banks (e.g. Abidor 2019). The popular association of anarchism with these violent manifestations, combined with anti-anarchist action by capitalists and socialists with access to state power and widespread anti-communist propaganda, has also greatly obscured anarchist history and its varied and cumulative impacts.

The second half of the twentieth century saw a relative retreat of overtly anarchist organizing globally, compared with the many other kinds of social movements that gained traction. These included revolutionary nationalist types of movements, sometimes influenced by various forms of Marxism, and movements addressing discrete issues, or seeking reforms or redress for one or another oppressed sector of society. Still, that era did see anarchism continue as an overt label taken on by some social actors, as seen in notable figures from the US 'New Left' like Paul Goodman, Erich Fromm, and Noam Chomsky. Historical research shows that anarchists were influential on, and influenced by, pivotal midcentury US movements (Cornell 2016; see also Tanenbaum 2016 for the case of anarcho-feminism). Meanwhile, what Dana Williams (2017) calls 'anarchist franchise organizations' (most originating in the US) have spread anarchist theory and practice globally. Williams' 2017 book analyzes anarchist movements sociologically, showing how anarchist-initiated local projects like *Food Not Bombs*, *Needle Exchange*, and *Homes Not Jails* operate as 'franchises': organizing ideas that spread organically and translocally. Often, these efforts are linked to subcultures like punk music (Donaghey 2013), and in part due to this link have spread to locations as diverse as Burma, Indonesia, and Brazil.

Anarchism as transnational and cultural forces thus interact with local organizing in many contexts, including the US, touching people both rural and urban. One notable and recent US example of this is anarchism's influence on the Occupy Wall Street movement of 2011 (Bray 2013; Graeber 2013; Hammond 2015), which in turn more broadly influenced US politics (Stewart 2019). Those arrested protesting Donald Trump's inauguration in 2017 included many active anarchist organizers (Jaffe 2017). Recent class struggles, including teacher strikes in North Carolina and other typically 'rural' and 'conservative' states and the founding of the first fast food union at Burgerville in Portland, Oregon were organized in part by the IWW and members of the *Black Rose/Rosa Negra Federation*, a federation of anarchist groups that develops movement analysis and platforms for national action. There are also anarchist leanings to the Black Socialists of America, founded in 2017 (BSA 2019). With a growing following of 77,000 on Twitter, Black Socialists of America and its politics are not insignificant to the US political context, and not new: Black anarchism has a lineage of practice and theory from Lucy Parsons to Lorenzo Kom'Boa Ervin, Ashanti Alston and Kuwasi Balagoon. Also relevant is the active presence of indigenous anarchists among a broader resurgence in indigenous organizing and visibility, especially after 2016s Standing Rock oil pipeline protest. Such formations include both social and insurrectionary tendencies, such as community organizer and filmmaker Klee Benally and once-imprisoned earth liberation activist Rod Coronado (IAF-FAI, n.d.; Pellow 2014, 140–142; Táala Hooghan 2019). The anarchism-indigeneity overlap also has a lineage, as in Ward Churchill's (2003) 'indigenist' philosophy that opposed 'colonialist' Marxism and showed affinities with anarchist thinking. Indigenous anarchist activist-thinkers like Aragorn! (2005) have pointed to this overlap, though it is not a simple or conflict-free one (Barker and Pickerill 2012).

Overt anarchism can also be found in post-disaster solidarity work, such as the Common Ground Collective in New Orleans, which mobilized post-hurricane Katrina to provide recovery infrastructure while consciously building non-state political affinities among those involved (crow 2014), or Occupy Sandy, which emerged out of the decentralized networks developed during Occupy Wall Street. In other disaster responses, it is rather anarchistic behaviors that manifest without overtly political motivations. In her 2009 study on 'the extraordinary communities that arise in disaster', Rebecca Solnit describes the 'immediate aftermath of 9/11' in New York City, as a

> moment of mutual aid and altruism but also a moment of participatory democracy ... People decided to do something, banded together – usually with strangers – and made it happen. It was anarchy in Kropotkin's sense of self-determination rather than of chaos. It was also typical of what happens in disaster, when institutions fail and civil society succeeds. It demonstrated that both the will and the ability to make a vibrant society in the absence of authority can exist, at least briefly. (226)

Considering the ongoing dispossessions of non-elite people following 'natural' disasters, and the intensification of such processes with ever-increasing extreme climate events, the role of anarchism in responses to disaster should receive more attention than it does. Reflecting on the anarchist theory of change described earlier, and on histories of Rojava, Spain, and Ukraine wherein anarchist(ic) territorial control expanded in times of state crisis, we might posit that anarchism is instinctually 'crisis-ready'.

Anarchistic social organization

Human values and actions can overlap with anarchist ethics and principles of human organization – such as mutual aid, decentralized self-organization, direct democracy, horizontal noncoercive relations, critique of hierarchy, and freedom *with* equality – even when such values/actions are not directly traceable to overt anarchism.[8] Anarchism's principles and theories can be found in specifically rural and agrarian contexts, and in social contexts surrounding issues of food, land, and the politics of 'development'. Anarchistic elements to analyze could include those within interpersonal and community social relations, within forms of action to push back against unjust power, and as anarchist/ic critiques are absorbed into existing state/capitalist institutions. Because such incidences are arguably more common than overt anarchist movements globally, the *anarchistic* lens may be

---

[8]Likely some would object to an expansion of research on anarchism into anarchistic realms. Lucien van der Walt (2016, 86) argues that anarchism should *not* be seen as human impulses or as 'simple "anti-statism"', but should instead be seen as a specific political tradition of the struggling working classes since capitalism's rise (specifically, libertarian socialism and anarcho-syndicalism). I disagree that there should be one way to treat anarchism – for research that can take many tacks, at least. And we gain more by dissecting 'impure' forms of politics than by dismissing them as inadequately faithful to hard or historical definitions.

the most fruitful area of the three for CAS. It also offers much more theory to chew on, as in the widely taken up concept of 'moral economy' (Thompson 1971; Maghimbi, Kimambo, and Sugimura 2011; Galt 2013; Carlisle 2015), or James Scott's (1992) idea that below-the-radar grassroots 'infrapolitics' can be as impactful as overt political action. If anarchistic responses emerge anywhere where essential, universal human dignity faces impositions of oppressive authority (Holloway 2013), an attention to how anarchistic practices and values/ethics can emerge, and their impacts, can help CAS scholars understand the dynamics of rural continuity and change.

E.P. Thompson, James Scott, and other scholars have analyzed communities, often rural, and how they secure a subsistence and livelihood through 'moral economies' that do not abide by, and sometimes directly confront, hierarchical and capitalist logics. These include relations of solidarity in production and reproduction within villages and local communities, but also forms of collective action such as riots that challenge economic structures via moral claims (Thompson 1966; Randall and Charlesworth 2000). Scott's first book (1976) describes the resilient presence of a 'subsistence ethic' among Southeast Asian peasantries, which would not accept community member deprivation due to incursions of capitalist markets. Scott's works continued to elaborate the ways peasants manifest moral economies in negotiation with, but often pitted against, forces of state, capital, and local social hierarchies (1985). Along the research journey, Scott developed an appreciation for the resonances with anarchism in the region's people, resulting in his 2009 *The Art of Not Being Governed: An Anarchist History of Upland Southeast Asia* and 2012s *Two Cheers for Anarchism*. Like Graeber's (2005) *Fragments of an Anarchist Anthropology*, *Two Cheers* offers 'fragments' of theories and directions regarding the use of anarchist ideas in peasant studies. Scott (2012, xii) lays the groundwork for this paper's argument; namely that

> if you put on anarchist glasses and look at the history of popular movements, revolutions, ordinary politics, and the state from that angle, certain insights will appear that are obscured from almost any other angle. It will also become apparent that anarchist principles are active in the aspirations and political action of people who have never heard of anarchism or anarchist philosophy.

Scott describes the state as a consummate simplifier and destroyer of vernaculars – vernaculars being linked to the uniqueness of place-based cultures, and the rebellions generated by impositions against them (Scott 1998, 2012). Governmental and elite actions and non-elites' attitudes towards these action are key factors in the development of rural rebellions, and such attitudes towards the state can be seen as anarchistic, even if they are not overtly anarchist. In this way, and in echoes of Wolf (1969), Scott develops a theory of peasants as 'natural anarchists'. Importantly for CAS at large, Graeber (2005, 45–46) suggests anthropology has proven that there is no rupture between prehistoric and modern societies in terms of human nature and habits. Accordingly, it is nonsensical to approach peasants and indigenous people analytically any differently than modern, urbanized people. Peasants might be 'natural anarchists', but so might be other sectors of society. O'Hearn and Grubačic (2018) make this clear in the inclusion of solitary confinement prisoners alongside Mexico's Zapatistas and Russia's Cossacks in their study of 'exilic' spaces, or spaces of exit from the capital-state nexus, in which moral economies are foundational. Building on moral economy approaches, such studies can advance understanding of the possibilities and limits of both 'structural' and 'geographic' escape as means to emancipation.

While anarchism finds resonance in traditional and modern ways of rural and food-related life, and in critiques that rural people make of the state and capital, it is also important to recognize the internal contradiction in moral economy approaches. Anthropology has shown that there is no 'noble savage'; indigenous people, rural people, peasants are still people – contradictory, imperfect. In some cases, they gravitate towards the market, or enter the state. Graeber and Wengrow (2018) offer synthesized archaeological evidence showing hunter-gatherer societies shifted internal social relations between egalitarianism and hierarchy in yearly cycles, indicating the dynamism of non-agricultural societies (as opposed to conventional narratives that claim hunter-gatherers as inherently egalitarian and agricultural societies as inherently hierarchical). This non-fixedness of hierarchical social organization through history might provide comfort (for anarchists) in knowing that people have fought off state forms for eons (a point also made by Clastres 1989; Barclay 1996; Scott 2017), but equally it is discomforting in knowing that even 'prehistoric' hunter-gatherers have had forms of ritualized authority, indicating a likelihood that hierarchies will never disappear completely. Graeber and Wengrow also allude to but do not address the suggestion that generational and gender oppression are perhaps more fundamental and pernicious forms of human inequality. As such, the anarchist critique also provides a sobering reminder that family and community are likely the *oldest* sites in human social organization for hierarchies and unjust structures. This results in the contradiction that anarchism thus has something to say about *all* human societies, but it doesn't necessarily provide answers regarding what to *do* about this. Still, anarchistic readings of moral economy provide CAS valuable analytical tools – which, along with anarchist theory and movement lenses, I next apply to US authoritarian populism.

An anarchist reading of US authoritarian populism

In this section, I address 'populism' at large, and the particular relevance of 'authoritarian populism' (hereafter AP) to the US context, showing how an anarchist lens can help better understand contemporary rural and agrarian politics and the challenges of making emancipatory change. In the case of tackling US AP, the anarchist lens does this by foregrounding the ways that state powers and logics underpin AP political projects, even as these powers are created or reproduced under so-called 'liberal' and 'socialist' administrations; and by emphasizing the complex political identities of non-elite people, and the ways these can be directed towards either emancipatory or authoritarian directions based on resentments towards state power and identifications with grassroots, lived moral economies. Taken together with anarchism's positive theory and recent scholarship on the limitations of Left populist states, the section's analysis of existing agrarian and rural organizing indicates the strategic need to prioritize grassroots social-ideological development, in ways that counter forms of Othering while providing for material needs and bolstering lived moral economies.

Populism, US rightwing AP, and the inherently authoritarian state

Populism is well known as a slippery and capacious concept in scholarship (Panizza 2005, 1), and has been described variously by research as 'an ideology, strategy, discourse or political logic' (Moffitt 2016, 5). Laclau's influential theorizing (2005) contends that populist power builds through active identification against a common enemy, resulting in a new definition of 'the people'. This certainly overlaps with anarchism, which opposes various forms of elitist hierarchy and promotes collective action that constructs new identities and affinities in antagonism. 'Left' populism decries elite economic and political power and seeks expanded justice and democracy, but deviates from anarchism insofar as it abides Mouffe's (2018, 39–57) insistence that a Left populist strategy is inherently a state-focused project rooted in contesting and replacing hegemony (rather than one that entails a fundamental rupture with the existing liberal state). Grattan (2018) attempts to combine approaches, appreciating anarchistic, destabilizing, and disruptive forces in the US lineage of 'aspirational democratic populism', but also suggesting the eventual need to centralize and institutionalize such forces. While anarchism and contemporary Left populism overlap at times, they maintain fundamentally different orientations towards states, institutionalization, and hegemony.

Building on the Gramscian Marxist Stuart Hall (1985), we can propose that populism should be distinguished from movements that pursue 'popular' politics, and include anarchism only in the latter. As Hall (1985, 118) put it, we can 'distinguish the genuine mobilization of popular demands and discontents from a "populist" mobilization which, at a certain point in its trajectory, flips over or is recuperated into a statist-led political leadership'. Populism can be thought of as a political strategy appealing to real or imagined *voting citizen majorities*, in order to achieve political-institutional power. In contradistinction, anarchists prioritize direct forms of action and decision-making, and the primacy of individuals and communities as decision-makers, over politics of representation through voting and other means, and against representative institutions and ostensibly democratic nation-states as actors. From an agrarian anarchist perspective, populist politics undermine popular politics by leading non-elites toward a fundamentally dysfunctional state politics, which legitimizes an irreformable system that continues to prop up extractive agriculture, demobilizes movements during moments of state concessions, and reduces energy and emphasis towards grassroots alternative forms of organizing and institution building towards autonomy and dual power. And as discussed further below, (populist) legitimatization of *any* state power reproduces the foundation upon which more authoritarian future administrations can act. Anarchist theories easily predict the slide from Left populism to AP and the betrayal of agrarian movements by their leaders who gain state power – as seen in Ecuador and Bolivia (Tilzey 2019). Without claiming Left and Right forms as equivalent, across the spectrum of state politics we find populist ways of achieving and maintaining political power and authoritarian ways of wielding power. CAS has more so focused on the problematic of xenophobic, racist, and gender regressive (i.e. 'rightwing') forms of AP (Bello 2018; Scoones et al. 2018; Borras 2020). However, emancipatory politics should be informed by considering populism's inherent alienation of collective power into the state, and the state's inherently authoritarian nature, and thus approach rightwing AP as derivatives of this general pattern. Given these premises, and the constraints of state/capital capture, which reabsorbs subaltern agency into the existing hegemony, a Left populist emancipatory strategy (a la Mouffe 2018) constitutes a fool's errand. I return to these strategic considerations after discussing US rightwing AP.

The rise of Donald Trump has relied on authoritarian and populist rhetoric (Booth 2017; Campbell 2017), characterized by islamophobia, racial resentment, and nativism. Trump's words and acts thus continue a longstanding rightwing US tradition of Othering, which pits some non-elites against 'Othered' groups by dehumanizing the latter (Montenegro de Wit et al. 2019). The electoral success of Trump, via this Othering tradition, can be traced back to a decades-long rightwing ideological project, which utilized business-elite-funded think tanks, churches, universities, and media (particularly cable television news and talk radio), to successfully enroll large numbers of people in a shared ideological 'common sense' that involves elements of white supremacy, xenophobia, anticommunism, and free market idealism (Diamond 1995; Berlet and Lyons 2000; Phillips-Fein 2009; Berlet and Sunshine 2019). At a 2018 conference on AP and the rural world,[9] participants from the US noted how the Left had abandoned religion and its institutions (churches), leaving them to act as grassroots centers for rural rightwing ideological development. Similarly, it was noted that talk radio is so widely listened to by many non-elites, yet is overwhelmingly dominated by rightwing politics. Rightwing ideological projects have successfully enrolled rural whites who have negative experiences and perceptions of government, generating resentment at government and undeserving Others (notably, migrant workers and racialized urbanites) – resentments exacerbated by the 'hollowing out' of the rural economy and declining social cohesion over the last half century of neoliberal policy (Ulrich-Schad and Duncan 2018; Edelman 2019).

In addition to the demonization of Others, the US rightwing's ideological project also generated buy-in to a contradictory state power relation that characterizes rightwing AP, described originally by Hall (1985). Hall's original analysis of AP discussed the rightwing surge in British politics in the late 1970s and early 1980s. According to Hall (1985, 117–118), this surge took up 'strategic elements of popular opinion' concerned about the direction of the existing state, to craft an

> "anti-statist" strategy, [which] incidentally, is not one which refuses to operate through the state; it is one which conceives a more limited state role, and which advances through the attempt, ideologically, to represent itself as anti-statist, for the purposes of populist mobilization.

Furthermore, 'this highly contradictory strategy … [was] "anti-statist" in its ideological self-representation *and* highly state-centralist and dirigiste in many of its strategic operations' (ibid). We can see obvious reflections of this politics in Trump's anti-state rhetoric on the campaign trail, and his post-election mobilization of various state powers for the continuity of elite domination and interests. Notably for CAS, this 'contradictory' politics also imprints in decades-long US policy efforts to deregulate agrichemical corporations while passing 'Ag-Gag' laws to prevent organizing efforts against agribusiness harms, or to remove price floors for commodity crops, while subsidizing corn commodities through pro-ethanol policies.

Authoritarianism in politics is characterized by coercive force, whether threatened or used, the ideologies that justify such use of force, the insulation of elite power from non-elite influence (Bruff 2014, 115), and the active production of citizens 'indifferent to veracity and accountability in government and to political freedom and equality among the citizenry' (Brown 2006, 690). Insofar as states create, maintain, and enforce existing

---

[9]Part of the 'Emancipatory Rural Politics Initiative' (ERPI); see https://www.iss.nl/en/research/hosted-iss/emancipatory-rural-politics-initiative.

hierarchies with coercive force, they are built on and reproduce authoritarian premises and tactics (Malatesta 2019, 45). Even relatively 'free' social democracies rely on prisons, coercive taxation, physical borders and territorial control; and on power lorded over a state's denizens by politicians and police. State maintenance of hierarchy continues regardless of political party: for example, under Democratic US President Barack Obama more undocumented immigrants were deported from the country than under any prior president.[10] Under Obama, coercive state functions were exhibited in police violence deployed in 2016 against indigenous anti-fossil fuel pipeline 'water protectors' at Standing Rock. Obama also deepened the government's commitment to domestic surveillance (utilized against internal threats from eco-anarchists, indigenous water protectors, and other rural political actors) and avoided accountability by aggressively prosecuting whistleblowers. Just like every other US president, Obama continued military attacks on foreign soils, and promoted ecologically destructive economic growth.[11] Through the anarchist critique of authority and hierarchy we might better recognize how (authoritarian) populism is rooted in existing forms and structures of power, to understand the particular (Trump) *as continuity within a lineage* (of statist politics more broadly).

US AP relies (just like states in general) on legal structures as tools of coercion and to reproduce consent among the governed. It uses ostensibly democratic elections to achieve and justify its power, but undermines voting rights to consolidate power. It emphasizes 'law and order' when attacking political enemies, and ignores the law when convenient. AP's use of coercive violence cannot be seen as only a state enterprise, however. It also relies on collaboration between state and societal forces (including non-elite factions), as seen with law enforcement officials and grassroots white supremacists collaborating at Trump rallies and white supremacist gatherings (e.g. Wilson 2017). As the popular protest chant goes, 'Cops and Klan go hand-in-hand' (Anonymous 2018). Trump's argument that there were 'good people' involved in the violent white supremacist rally in Charlottesville that killed a counter-protestor, and his pardoning of Arizona Sherriff Joe Arpaio, who was indicted for racist corruption, remind us how law and discourse are wielded for statist political projects. The use of laws to enforce hegemony (including a *lack* of enforcement of laws against those promoting the hegemonic position) is not limited to AP, but forms a crucial tactic in the wielding of power when an AP political project is ascendant or hegemonic.

Rethinking rural positionalities, agrarian movements, and anarchism-informed emancipatory strategies

The anarchist lens complicates typical and simplified accounts of rural non-elite positionalities and their resulting (electoral) politics. Importantly, while a state- and election-focused politics emphasizes the voting habits of individuals and classes, focusing instead (as anarchism does) on moral economies of everyday life and ideologies

---

[10] As Brown and Getz (2008, 1186) note: 'Historically, immigration policy has served as a mechanism, not only for managing labor flow, but for actively producing an "other", in this case a labor force that can be viewed as undeserving of the rights and benefits afforded citizen workers and that can be scapegoated during periods of economic downturn'.

[11] Though Marxists have a long history of recognizing the state's incessant push for growth, this has not led to necessarily anti-state politics (e.g. Saed 2019). This puts eco-anarchist positions, often involving the decentralized solutions supported by climate resilience theorists, more closely in dialogue with the resonance of 'degrowth' thinking within CAS (Davidson 2009; Gerber 2020).

developed through relationship and lived experience encourages a more nuanced and hopeful reading of rural political possibilities (Gaventa 2019, 448). At times, so-called 'conservatives' harbor anti-state ideologies, which the mainstream Left ignores or disparages. In contrast, the movement 'Redneck Revolt' shows that anarchists are mobilizing such ideologies to oppose authoritarian populism in the rural US. Redneck Revolt evolved out of local chapters of the 'John Brown Gun Club', anarchist-organized anti-racist spaces for weapons training and mobilization for self-defense and to protect marginalized groups during demonstrations. Formed in 2016, Redneck Revolt purposefully reaches out to poor, rural whites, who are often the first recruits to authoritarian populist politics. Redneck Revolt tables at gun shows, purposefully seeking to counter-recruit from anti-'big government' paramilitary formations like the '3%ers' (who often display white nationalist leanings), while also supporting counter-protests against white supremacist rallies. Redneck Revolt's (n.d.) 'principles' indicate their anarchist perspective (emphasis original):

> WE STAND AGAINST THE NATION-STATE AND ITS FORCES WHICH PROTECT THE BOSSES AND THE RICH … we do not seek to merely replace one set of politicians for another. We know that our answers will always come from a community level, where every person should be allowed to participate in making the decisions that affect their lives. We believe in community power and community rights over the rights of any government body.

Redneck Revolt's very existence indicates CAS should pay attention to explicitly anarchist movements in the dialectic of AP and emancipatory alternatives, as it represents a struggle to undermine white supremacy and acceptance of capitalism among non-elite populations, and to develop a left rural politics in opposition to AP. Rural sociologist Loka Ashwood is one of the few scholars who has leveraged an anarchist lens on US rural politics. Ashwood's book length study (2018a) and article (2018b) look at rural communities in Georgia dealing with economic and environmental injustices relating to nearby nuclear power plants. In doing so, she finds that 'stateless' and 'anti-state' perspectives are widely held among the rural people she interviewed. One of her main informants,

> William, like his black and white Burke Country Neighbors, harbors a deep-seated distrust of the government. Scholars typically understand politics like Williams's as conservative, with complementary variants of social and fiscal. Some call such politics contradictory, resting on a moral code that violates rural economic interests. Others call such views dead set against progress, stymied in a culture of poverty that breeds complicity. I offer a counter explanation by taking at face value the state's historical and still persistent exploitation of rural people and places in order to centralize profit. (Ashwood 2018a, ix)

> Like William, Michel Foucault sees legal doctrines as a tool used by the elite to maintain control over those on the margins of society. For those excluded from the wealth of for-profit democracy, the deliverance of justice is not abstract. Rather, justice relies on, in Foucault's description, 'their own experience, that of the injuries they have suffered, that of the way in which they have been wronged, in which they have been oppressed.' For the rebel, the delivery of justice, rather than being entrusted to the state and its many apparatuses, is carried out directly by those avenging grievances. For William, retribution for wrongs came through what I call 'direct justice,' not the justice of the state, but the justice of a community responding outside of bureaucracy to personal oppression. In some senses similar to David Graeber's notion of direct democracy, direct justice is determined by the collective moral economy of the people and delivered accordingly. A justice of anarchy rendered against an oppressive, for-profit democratic state. (ibid, 151–152)

Ashwood's informants included the kind of rural whites who have been effectively enrolled in national AP politics, who Redneck Revolt has been actively recruiting to anarchist politics. Ashwood (2018b, 3–4) argues that there is a 'lack of genuine stateless representation on the political stage ... In the meantime, the opportunity grows for the exploitation of the stateless position by self-titled populists who have elite, pro-state agendas, but are well versed in stateless rhetoric'. By placing itself in defense of the state and its (corrupted) political project, Left populist responses may fail to meet people where they are, and fall on deaf ears.

Importantly, it is not only rural whites who hold negative perceptions of the state and its support for extractive, unequal relations. Many members of society, in particular those from groups who have historically been 'Othered', exhibit state skepticism. Indigenous, African-American, and Latinx/migrant histories of attempted genocide by the state, enslavement, and chronic exploitation may all hold relevance for questions of state-orientation and 'stateless' moral economies. According to environmental justice scholars Pellow (2016) and Pulido (2017), the state is almost always at the center of environmental injustices, and it behooves theorists of social change to take a more skeptical view of the prospects of emancipatory politics via the state. Similar skepticism of the state is found among 'afro-pessimist' (Samudzi and Anderson 2018), Black ecosocialist (Akuno 2018), 'Afrikan anarchist' (Meyer and Kersplebedeb 2019) and indigenous scholars and activists (Alfred 2005; Goodyear-Ka'ōpua 2011; Coulthard 2014).

Movements and their participants are to varying degrees 'faithful' to anarchist theories. Some social sectors and movements are directly inspired by anarchist thinking, while others are simply anarchistic in inclination. In my fieldwork, some US agrarian movement activists expressed strong doubt about prospects of transformation via state policy, influenced by experiences growing up in long-neglected farmworker communities. These same activists sometimes still engaged policy: people's ideas are dynamic; ideologies are not neatly bound. Anarchists at times participate in reformist labor organizing, in 'social enterprises' and businesses, and even in electoral and state-focused organizing. There are negative and positive aspects to this flexibility, but an important lesson for CAS is that attention to anarchist influence cannot be limited to visibly anarchist organizations, and must look additionally to anarchistic forms and individual anarchist participation in wider and diverse social movements. Anarchism can thus improve CAS's analysis of movements, seeing their internal functioning and external approach in relation to anarchist(ic) theory and movements. Rather than narrowing the field, anarchism can synergize with other CAS traditions, as indicated by recent convergence among Marxian and agrarian populist analysis with anarchist(ic) ideas (see below). In agrarian movement practice, similarly, we find influences from and resonances with all traditions. Rather than claiming anarchism as *necessarily strategically superior* or *theoretically thoroughly distinct (or consistent)*, I am suggesting simply that anarchism can bolster existing CAS. That said, I *do* conclude with anarchism-informed strategic suggestions, based on a short analysis of transnational and US agrarian movements and existing CAS strategizing vis-à-vis state power.

The transnational agrarian movement La Vía Campesina (LVC) came together in the early 1990s to horizontally deliberate on common causes, engage in direct action to counter spaces of political/economic power, and construct principled alternatives, like 'food sovereignty', while maintaining relative autonomy from states, funders, and political parties (Desmarais 2007). Not overtly anarchist, LVC resonates with many anarchist ideas and practices. Rather than claiming LVC for one tradition or another, we can simply note the many traditions at play in it. LVC largely reflects agrarian populist traditions intellectually[12] and in mobilization. Radical agrarian populist scholars similarly to anarchists favor socialism 'broadly defined' (Borras 2020, 4), grassroots ideological development – as in the farmer-to-farmer methods discussed by Val et al. (2019) – and community/farmer autonomy, central to van der Ploeg's (2008) argument on peasantries. Still, agrarian populism also considers how peasants might be inserted into existing markets, how states might support these economies, and how state revenues can support agroecological transitions. Prominent LVC members are associated with the rise of rhetorically pro-peasant, Left populist governments in Latin America. Anarchism's theories point in a similar direction to agrarian populism's emphasis on the grassroots and its 'solidarity from below' (Calvário, Desmarais, and Azkarraga 2019), but without the eventuality of state/policy intervention, and with a clearer rejection of state-reinforced commodity markets as anything emancipatory. With the notable exception of its anticivilizationist trends, anarchism generally lacks agrarian populism's anti-urban bias (as critiqued by Bernstein 2010, 122). Though LVC is rhetorically anti-capitalist, orthodox Marxists like Bernstein tend to see LVC as *too* agrarian populist and not Marxist enough.[13]

Progressive US agrarian movements contain examples that parallel LVC's organizing patterns and discourses, combining Marxian critiques of capitalism, agrarian populist ideologies and practices, and anarchistic elements.[14] These movements often align with anarchism's grassroots-prefigurative orientation, inspired by communalist visions of future localized regional food systems, but are diverse and even contradictory regarding its anti-state critique – sometimes engaging in reformist law-making and attempts to seek state power. Like LVC and other global agrarian movements, US movements are ambivalent towards the state, and additionally pressed to engage states in times of political regression.

The US Food Sovereignty Alliance (USFSA) attempts to be driven by its grassroots base, using internal direct democratic processes as its main form of political decision-making in 'assemblies' very similar to LVC's. USFSA is also explicitly anti-capitalist, and more focused on building movements through gatherings and direct actions than working to make change through policy. Also based largely in the US, the 'People's Agroecology Process' seeks to develop political analysis and technical skills among diverse communities via a grassroots-led democratic network which has not directly addressed policy. Though not explicitly anarchist, this effort matches many of the political leanings of agrarian populism, but without any governmental affiliations, or agrarian populism's associated politics of state developmentalism. National-level groups oriented more towards policy, like the HEAL Food Alliance, Family Farm Defenders, National Family Farm Coalition, and Rural

---

[12] See the work of Peter Rosset, Annette Desmarais, Jan Douwe van der Ploeg, and Phil McMichael as representations of this tradition.

[13] To his credit, Bernstein (2018, 1146) still insists Marxists engage rather than dismiss 'the most progressive' agrarian populism(s). In addition to Bernstein's perennial focus on differentiation within peasantries – pointing out (2010, 120–122) that 'any unity of "the people of the land" cannot be assumed' – he insists that movements should look at historically specific (class) conditions and build up from there, mirroring anarchism's attention to intracommunity hierarchy and its hallmark claim that any useful movement must be built endogenously.

[14] It should be noted that these movements are not comparable, in terms of massiveness, or political context. Information in this section comes mainly from participatory fieldwork among these movements. See usfoodsovereigntyalliance.org, whyhunger.org/category/blog/towards-a-peoples-agroecology/, healfoodalliance.org, familyfarmers.org, nffc.net and ruralco.org.

Coalition, all emphasize bottom-up processes of policy development and internal education to support grassroots work. Some leaders from these groups argue structural critiques that use agrarian populist and Marxist frames of analysis. Other leaders have proclaimed anarchist affinities in my fieldwork, but continue to address policy as a need to confront 'what is there': opportunities to gain greater state support and threats of even more regressive policies. That these movements focus on policy should come as no surprise, given the real threats of state-imposed harm, the mostly unquestioned hegemony of liberal-statist thinking, the legacy of environmental movements' reformist inclinations (Pellow 2014, 256), and the realities of nonprofit funding, where funders seek 'deliverables' over the kinds of grassroots, base building work prioritized in anarchism.

Considering the (burst) bubble of enthusiasm for Bernie Sanders' 2020 candidacy, US movements may want to heed lessons from CAS scholarship on failed efforts towards food sovereignty in Left populist states, and how failures of the Left-in-power can contribute to surges in AP (Giunta 2014; Andrade 2019; Tilzey 2019).[15] CAS scholars have come to conclusions that share affinities with anarchism, seemingly converging on a deeper pessimism about state-based change, and a valorization of social movement autonomy – longstanding tenets in theory *and* practice of anarchism.[16] Marxists Vergara-Camus and Kay (2017, 434) admit that social movements '[g]aining access to the state did not end up yielding more concrete results than building autonomy from below and outside the state'. Still, their anarchistic suggestions to prevent state political influence on movements remain focused on improving movements' relations *with political parties*, rather than how or why movements might avoid, subvert, or build alternatives to state politics. The assumption of state strategies remains. The lost potential of CAS scholarship, unfortunately, is that it mostly dismisses anarchism as purist (or ignores it), even when it is not in practice, and it assumes rather than investigates the effects of nonstate strategies on the state. For example, Tilzey (2019) belittles 'autonomism as a doctrine', [which] 'assumes that real change can occur "without taking power"' and concludes that (improved) future success relies on movements 'confronting' the state. Yet anarchist theory (like poststructuralism) denies that 'power' resides straightforwardly or only in state institutions. And autonomists/anarchists *do* confront (and thus affect) the state: directly, indirectly, and as participants in non-anarchist projects. US anarchists confront states through their substantial involvement in antifascist and prison abolition movements (Bray 2017), as lawyers defending direct action participants (Pellow 2014, 251), and via prefigurative direct actions that force state concessions, such as when an anarchist-inflected occupation of public land generated new food producing space and food sovereignty literacy and forced state agencies to co-manage land with local communities and activists (Roman-Alcalá 2018). More broadly, autonomy-oriented urban farms and cooperative food projects directly produce food and build bridges across various anti-oppressive struggles and rural/urban divides, strengthening intersectional analysis and action – which is sometimes later deployed in addressing state politics (Wilson 2013; Sbicca 2018).

---

[15]Especially considering the relative weakness and lack of autonomy among US agrarian movements compared with global counterparts, it is questionable how much a Sanders presidency could have accomplished.

[16]Admittedly, there remain orthodox Marxists who continue to favor attention to economic structure, class (de)composition, and class control over the state, over the ideological and grassroots concerns common to anarchism and agrarian populism (Bernstein 2014; Jessop 2015).

In emphasizing 'politics from below' to generate agroecological transitions, Giraldo and McCune (2019, 803) suggest movements should construct 'their own institutions and mak[e] use of the State when and only when such use concretely strengthens grassroots processes of emancipation, autonomy and self-determination'. The methods of 'dialogue, local struggles, and leadership building (Giraldo and McCune 2019, 805)' these authors endorse are the soil anarchists amend and till. Agrarian populism and Marxism also endorse grassroots-focused methods *in theory*. In practice, however, many movements inspired these frameworks end up concentrating effort on electoral processes and 'the long march through the institutions', and in doing so, experience redirection of energies, demobilization, absorption, and disillusionment (Oikonomakis 2020). Tilzey (2019) and Andrade (2019) demonstrate that active demobilization efforts and corruption of the Left-in-power can contribute to later resurgent authoritarianism and electoral turns to the right, indicating the strategic miscalculation of fighting AP with Left populism.

Conclusion

Considering the problems of state power (for ecological and justice-focused political projects) and the effective ways in which AP has enrolled some non-elites via a contradictory anti-state ideology, the anarchist lens suggests shifting strategy away from states and towards ideological development and grassroots capacity. Rather than reproducing the Right's successful strategy in total, which would be unrealistic for a less-resourced and structurally disadvantaged Left (and would involve concentrated effort on taking state power), an anarchist approach would parallel the Right only in emphasizing social-ideological development. Rather than an imposition from without, anarchist ideologies develop (and commitments deepen) through projects – like Redneck Revolt – that use direct action and mutual aid to provide for material needs, disrupt and oppose injustice, and bolster moral economies at the grassroots level. Differently from the ways that community spaces, ideological consent-building, and group identity are leveraged on the Right, such actions take place among diverse peoples, in ways that counter forms of Othering while building active solidarity. For example, in 2019, a group of anarchist transgender activists worked with coal miners in Kentucky, supporting the organization of a blockade of coal trains to demand withheld wages (Korman 2019).

Taking on anarchist insights does not entail a dogmatic refusal to engage the state; it means expecting disappointing results from leftist government, understanding disillusionment with states and its link to the rightward turn of electorates, and recognizing that any transition to AP is made possible by existing logics of capitalist state power. Anarchism, as an insurrectionary and revolution-oriented *philosophy*, provides few easy answers to *realpolitik* questions. The rejection of (state) hegemony as an organizing principle to mobilize social actors behind a political project is bound to leave some theorists and activists unsatisfied. Yet, anarchism challenges some conventional concerns in CAS theorizing and Left strategizing. For instance, it theoretically challenges agrarian populism's homogenization of 'community' *and* Marxism's overly-economistic analyses of it, while strategically it disputes seeking to 'solve' AP via parties or politicians. An anarchist lens recognizes the leadership of Othered groups in existing agrarian change efforts and *supports rather than criticizes* their occasionally state-critical perspective. Redneck Revolt's anarchist approach urges CAS to not ignore rural white non-elites in developing an emancipatory imagination in the rural US.

Anarchism makes imperative certain previously underappreciated inquiries, such as looking into the real anti-state motivations of non-elite people; or the impact of direct action, dual power institutions, and long-term ideological base-building efforts on state politics – even when such efforts are *not* state-oriented. These inquiries parallel political projects that anarchism promotes: building decentralized capacity (rural and urban, reproductive, productive, and discursive), towards subsistence or socialism, and in anticipation of societal breakdown; directly attacking infrastructures of oppressive, ecocidal capitalist extraction; linking communities through prefigurative efforts; and in the processes of horizontal self-organization, countering and undermining the Othering that is key to AP power. Arguably, the tendency towards Othering is inherent to capitalism (Patel and Moore 2017); anarchism's theoretical attention to *all* hierarchies keeps this tendency in view, while anarchism's preferred practices of rooted, place- and culture-based solidarity and mutual aid undermines it, far more than does majoritarian electoralism. Perhaps most importantly, what this paper has claimed about CAS – that it needs to recognize and appreciate anarchist(ic) positions – could be applied to the Left itself: state-focused reformers are not benefited by ignoring or throwing anarchism and anarchists aside.

Acknowledgements

The author would like to thank firstly Jun Borras and Julien-François Gerber for their suggestion to write this paper. Their comments, along with feedback from and conversations with Louis Thiemann, Gustavo de L.T. Oliveira, Adriana Requena, Shannon Malloy, Maywa Montengro, and four anonymous reviewers, were crucial to refining the paper. The typing (and intellectual) assistance of Nora Roman, Jean Yaste, Karina Utter, and Tanamá Varas was also invaluable. Any academic paper on anarchism is likely to be inadequately anarchist, so I preemptively apologize to anarchists for any deficiencies in that regard. Lastly, as someone who identifies as an active social movement participant, I would be remiss if I did not thank all the collaborators in collective action and thinking (too many to list) who have influenced who I am, why I think about these subjects, and what I think about them.

Disclosure statement

No potential conflict of interest was reported by the author(s).

ORCID

Antonio Roman-Alcalá http://orcid.org/0000-0001-9209-8786

References

Abidor, M. 2019. *Down with the Law: Anarchist Individualist Writings from Early Twentieth-Century France*. Chico/Edinburgh: AK Press.
Akuno, K. 2018. "Interview with Kali Akuno of Cooperation Jackson." https://cooperationjackson.org/blog/stirtoactioninterview.
Alfred, T. 2005. *Wasáse: Indigenous Pathways of Action and Freedom*. Toronto: University of Toronto Press.
Anarchopac. 2019. "Means and Ends: The Anarchist Critique of Seizing State Power." https://blackrosefed.org/anarchopac-critique-of-seizing-state-power.

Andrade, D. 2019. "Populism from Above and Below: The Path to Regression in Brazil." *Journal of Peasant Studies*. doi:10.1080/03066150.2019.1680542.

Anonymous. 2018. "Cops And Klan Go Hand In Hand: A Report From Berkeley." *It's Going Down*. https://itsgoingdown.org/cops-and-klan-go-hand-in-hand-a-report-from-berkeley/.

Antliff, A., and B. Hutchens. 2007. "Anarchy, Power, and Poststructuralism." *SubStance* 36 (2): 56–66.

Aragorn!. 2005. "Locating an Indigenous Anarchism." *Green Anarchy*, 19. https://theanarchistlibrary.org/library/aragorn-locating-an-indigenous-anarchism.

Ashwood, L. 2018a. *For-Profit Democracy: Why the Government Is Losing the Trust of Rural America*. New Haven, CT: Yale University Press.

Ashwood, L. 2018b. "Rural Conservatism or Anarchism? The Pro-state, Stateless, and Anti-state Positions." *Rural Sociology* 67: 120–129.

Bakunin, M. 1970. *God and the State*. New York: Dover Publications.

Barclay, H. 1996. *People Without Government: Anthropology of Anarchy*. London: Kahn and Averill Publishers.

Barker, A. J., and J. Pickerill. 2012. "Radicalizing Relationships to and through Shared Geographies: Why Anarchists Need to Understand Indigenous Connections to Land and Place." *Antipode* 44 (5): 1705–1725.

Bello, W. 2018. "Counterrevolution, the Countryside and the Middle Classes: Lessons from Five Countries." *The Journal of Peasant Studies* 45 (1): 21–58.

Berlet, C., and M. N. Lyons. 2000. *Rightwing Populism in America: Too Close for Comfort*. New York: Guilford Press.

Berlet, C., and S. Sunshine. 2019. "Rural Rage: The Roots of Right-Wing Populism in the United States." *Journal of Peasant Studies* 46 (3): 480–513.

Bernstein, H. 2010. *Class Dynamics of Agrarian Change*. Winnipeg, Canada: Fernwood Publishing.

Bernstein, H. 2014. "Food Sovereignty via the 'Peasant Way': A Sceptical View." *Journal of Peasant Studies* 41 (6): 1031–1063.

Bernstein, H. 2018. "The 'Peasant Problem' in the Russian Revolution(s), 1905–1929." *Journal of Peasant Studies* 45 (5–6): 1127–1150.

Berry, D. 2009. *A History of the French Anarchist Movement, 1917 to 1945*. Oakland: AK Press.

Bookchin, M. 1982. *The Ecology of Freedom: The Emergence and Dissolution of Hierarchy*. Andover, MA: Cheshire Books.

Booth, A. 2017. "The Rhetoric of Authoritarianism in the 2016 Presidential Campaign of Donald Trump." Texas State University Masters Thesis, English Department.

Borras Jr., S. M. 2020. "Agrarian Social Movements: The Absurdly Difficult But Not Impossible Agenda of Defeating Right-Wing Populism and Exploring a Socialist Future." *Journal of Agrarian Change* 20 (3): 3–36.

Brass, T. 2015. "Peasants, Academics, Populists: Forward to the Past?" *Critique of Anthropology* 35 (2): 187–204.

Bray, M. 2013. *Translating Anarchy: The Anarchism of Occupy Wall Street*. Winchester, UK: Zero Books.

Bray, M. 2017. *Antifa: The Anti-Fascist Handbook*. Brooklyn, NY: Melville House.

Brown, W. 2006. "American Nightmare: Neoliberalism, Neoconservatism, and De-democratization." *Political Theory* 34 (6): 690–714.

Brown, S., and C. Getz. 2008. "Privatizing Farm Worker Justice: Regulating Labor Through Voluntary Certification and Labeling." *Geoforum; Journal of Physical, Human, and Regional Geosciences* 39: 1184–1196.

Bruff, I. 2014. "The Rise of Authoritarian Neoliberalism." *Rethinking Marxism: A Journal of Economics, Culture & Society* 26 (1): 113–129.

BSA (Black Socialists of America). 2019. *Twitter Page*. Accessed September 19, 2019. https://twitter.com/BlackSocialists.

Buber, M. 1949. *Paths in Utopia*. New York: Macmillan.

Calvário, R., A. A. Desmarais, and J. Azkarraga. 2019. "Solidarities from Below in the Making of Emancipatory Rural Politics: Insights from Food Sovereignty Struggles in the Basque Country." *Sociologia Ruralis*. doi:10.1111/soru.12264.

Campbell, T. 2017. *Populism and Its Discontents: Populism on the American Left and Right During the 2016 Election Cycle*. Waco, TX: Baylor University.

Cappelletti, A. 2018. *Anarchism in Latin America*. Chico, CA: AK Press.

Carlisle, L. 2015. "Audits and Agrarianism: The Moral Economy of an Alternative Food Network." *Elementa: Science of the Anthropocene* 21: 1–16.

Carter, A. 1971. *The Political Theory of Anarchism*. New York: Harper Torchbooks.

Castañeda, C., and M. Feu. 2019. "Introduction: Hispanic Anarchist Print Culture." In *Writing Revolution: Hispanic Anarchism in the United States*, edited by Cristopher J. Castañeda and Montse Feu, 1–14. Springfield, IL: University of Illinois Press.

Churchill, W. 2003. *Acts of Rebellion: The Ward Churchill Reader*. New York & London: Routledge.

CILEP (Centro de Investigación Libertaria y Educación Popular) (editor). 2011. *Pasado y presente del anarquismo y del anarcosindicalismo en Colombia*. Buenos Aires: Libros de Anarres.

Clark, J. 2019. *Between Earth and Empire: From the Necrocene to the Beloved Community*. Oakland: PM Press.

Clastres, P. 1989. *Society Against the State: Essays in Political Anthropology*. Cambridge, MA: MIT Press.

Cole, P., D. Struthers, and K. Zimmer. 2018. *Wobblies of the World: A Global History of the IWW*. London: Pluto Press.

Cornell, A. 2016. *Unruly Equality: US Anarchism in the 20th Century*. Oakland, CA: University of California Press.

Coulthard, G. S. 2014. *Red Skin, White Masks: Rejecting the Colonial Politics of Recognition*. Minneapolis, MN: University of Minneapolis Press.

Crimethinc. 2017. *From Democracy to Freedom: The Difference Between Government and Self-Determination*. Salem, OR: Crimethinc. ex-Workers' Collective.

crow, s. 2014. *Black Flags and Windmills: Hope, Anarchy, and the Common Ground Collective*. 2nd ed. Oakland, CA: PM Press.

Crump, J. 1993. *Hatta Shūzō and Pure Anarchism in Interwar Japan*. New York: St. Martin's Press.

Davidson, S. 2009. "Ecoanarchism: A Critical Defence." *Journal of Political Ideologies* 14 (1): 47–67.

Day, R. F. 2005. *Gramsci Is Dead: Anarchist Currents in the Newest Social Movements*. London: Pluto Press.

Desmarais, A. 2007. *La Via Campesina: Globalization and the Power of Peasants*. Winnipeg, Canada: Fernwood Publishing.

Diamond, S. 1995. *Roads to Dominion: Rightwing Movements and Political Power in the United States*. New York: Guilford Press.

Dirlik, A. 1991. *Anarchism in the Chinese Revolution*. Berkeley and Los Angeles: University of California Press.

Dixon, C. 2012. "Building 'Another Politics': The Contemporary Anti-Authoritarian Current in the US and Canada." *Anarchist Studies* 20 (1): 32–60.

Dolgoff, S., ed. 1974. *The Anarchist Collectives Workers' Self-Management in the Spanish Revolution 1936–1939*. New York: Free Life Editions.

Donaghey, Jim. 2013. "Bakunin Brand Vodka: An Exploration into Anarchist-Punk and Punk-Anarchism." *Anarchist Developments in Cultural Studies* 1: 139–170.

DSA-LSC (Democratic Socialists of America-Libertarian Socialist Caucus). 2019. *Dual Power: A Strategy to Build Socialism in Our Time*. Accessed July 18, 2019. https://dsa-lsc.org/2018/12/31/dual-power-a-strategy-to-build-socialism-in-our-time/.

Dunlap, A., and J. Jakobsen. 2020. *The Violent Technologies of Extraction: Political Ecology, Critical Agrarian Studies and the Capitalist Worldeater*. Cham, Switzerland: Palgrave Macmillan.

Eagleton, T. 1999. *Marx (The Great Philosopher's Series)*. Abingdon, Oxfordshire, UK: Routledge.

Eckhardt, W. 2016. *The First Socialist Schism: Bakunin vs. Marx in the International Working Men's Association*. Oakland, CA: PM Press.

Edelman, M. 2019. "Hollowed Out Heartland, USA: How Capital Sacrificed Communities and Paved the Way for Authoritarian Populism." *Journal of Rural Studies*. doi:10.1016/j.jrurstud.2019.10.045.

el-Ojeili, C. 2014. "Anarchism as the Contemporary Spirit of Anti-Capitalism? A Critical Survey of Recent Debates." *Critical Sociology* 40 (3): 451–468.

Epstein, B. 1993. *Political Protest and Cultural Revolution: Nonviolent Direct Action in the 1970s and 1980s*. Oakland, CA: University of California Press.
Escobar, A. 1995. *Encountering Development: The Making and Unmaking of the Third World*. Princeton, NJ: Princeton University Press.
Evans, D. 2020. *Revolution and the State: Anarchism in the Spanish Civil War, 1936–1939*. Chico, CA: AK Press.
GA (Green Anarchy). 2012. *Uncivilized: The Best of Green Anarchy*. Green Anarchy Press. https://ia801909.us.archive.org/29/items/Uncivilized_201611/Uncivilized.pdf.
Galt, R. E. 2013. "The Moral Economy Is a Double-Edged Sword: Explaining Farmers' Earnings and Self-Exploitation in Community-Supported Agriculture." *Economic Geography* 89 (4): 341–365.
Gamblin, G. J. 1999. "Russian Populism and Its Relations with Anarchism 1870–1881." Thesis at The University of Birmingham Centre for Russian and East European Studies. Birmingham: University of Birmingham.
Gaventa, J. 2003. *Power after Lukes: An Overview of Theories of Power Since Lukes and Their Application to Development*. Brighton: Participation Group, Institute of Development Studies. https://www.powercube.net/wp-content/uploads/2009/11/power_after_lukes.pdf.
Gaventa, J. 2019. "Power and Powerlessness in an Appalachian Valley – Revisited." *Journal of Peasant Studies* 46 (3): 440–456.
Gerber, J.-F. 2020. "Degrowth and Critical Agrarian Studies." *Journal of Peasant Studies* 47 (2): 235–264.
de Góes, P., ed. 2017. *The Luso-Anarchist Reader: The Origins of Anarchism in Portugal and Brazil*. Charlotte, NC: Information Age Publishing.
Giraldo, O. F., and N. McCune. 2019. "Can the State Take Agroecology to Scale? Public Policy Experiences in Agroecological Territorialization from Latin America." *Agroecology and Sustainable Food Systems* 43 (7–8): 785–809.
Gomez Casas, J. 1986. *Anarchist Organisation: The History of the F.A.I*. Portland, OR: Black Rose Books.
Goodyear-Ka'ōpua, N. 2011. "Kuleana lāhui: Collective Responsibility for Hawaiian Nationhood in Activists' Praxis." *Affinities: A Journal of Radical Theory, Culture, and Action* 5: 130–163.
Gordon, U. 2008. *Anarchy Alive: Anti-Authoritarian Politics from Practice to Theory*. London: Pluto Press.
Graeber, D. 2005. *Fragments of an Anarchist Anthropology*. Chicago: Prickly Paradigm Press.
Graeber, D. 2013. *The Democracy Project*. New York: Spiegel and Grau.
Graeber, D., and D. Wengrow. 2018. "Are We City Dwellers or Hunter-Gatherers?" *New Humanist*. Accessed October 10, 2019. https://newhumanist.org.uk/articles/5409/are-we-city-dwellers-or-hunter-gatherers.
Graham, R., ed. 2005. *Anarchism: A Documentary History of Libertarian Ideas: From Anarchy to Anarchism (300 CE To 1939)*. Vol. 1. Montreal/New York/London: Black Rose Books.
Graham, R., ed. 2009. *The Emergence of the New Anarchism (1939–1977)*. Vol. 2. Montreal/New York/London: Black Rose Books.
Graham, R., ed. 2012. *The New Anarchism (1974–2012)*. Vol. 3. Montreal/New York/London: Black Rose Books.
Grattan, L. 2018. *Populism's Power: Radical Grassroots Democracy in America*. Oxford, England: Oxford University Press.
Giunta, I. 2014. "Food Sovereignty in Ecuador: Peasant Struggles and the Challenge of Institutionalization." *Journal of Peasant Studies* 41 (6): 1201–1224.
Hall, S. 1985. "Authoritarian Populism: A Reply to Jessop et al." *New Left Review* 151: 115–124.
Hammond, J. L. 2015. "The Anarchism of Occupy Wall Street." *Science & Society* 79 (2): 288–313.
Hart, J. 1978. *Anarchism & The Mexican Working Class, 1860–1931*. Austin, TX: University of Texas Press.
Harvey, D. 2017. "'Listen, Anarchist!' A Personal Response to Simon Springer's 'Why a Radical Geography Must Be Anarchist'." *Dialogues in Human Geography* 7 (3): 233–250.
Hirsch, S. 2010. "Peruvian Anarcho-Syndicalism: Adapting Transnational Influences and Forging Counter Hegemonic Practices, 1905–1930." In *Anarchism and Syndicalism in the Colonial and Postcolonial World, 1870–1940: The Praxis of National Liberation, Internationalism, and Social Revolution*, edited by S. Hirsch, and L. van der Walt, 227–272. Leiden, Netherlands: Brill.

Hirsch, S., and L. van der Walt, eds. 2010. *Anarchism and Syndicalism in the Colonial and Postcolonial World, 1870–1940: The Praxis of National Liberation, Internationalism, and Social Revolution*. Leiden, Netherlands: Brill.

Hobsbawm, E. 1973. *Revolutionaries. Contemporary Essays*. London: Weidenfeld and Nicolson.

Hodges, D. 1995. *Mexican Anarchism after the Revolution*. Austin, TX: University of Texas Press.

Holloway, J. 2013. *In, Against, and Beyond Capitalism: The San Francisco Lectures*. Oakland, CA: PM Press.

Hwang, D. 2017. *Anarchism in Korea. Independence, Transnationalism, and the Question of National Development 1919–1984*. Albany, NY: SUNY Press.

IAF (Indigenous Anarchist Federation). n.d. "What We Are About." https://iaf-fai.org/about/.

Internationalist Commune of Rojava. 2018. *Make Rojava Green Again: Building an Ecological Society*. London: Dog Section Press.

The Invisible Committee. 2009. *The Coming Insurrection*. Los Angeles: Semiotext(e).

Jaffe, S. 2017. "Trump Interruption: A Conversation with Legba Carrefour." *The Baffler*. https://thebaffler.com/latest/interviews-for-resistance-carrefour.

Jessop, B. 2015. "Margaret Thatcher and Thatcherism: Dead But Not Buried." *British Politics* 10 (1): 16–30.

Karatani, K. 2005. *Transcritique: On Kant and Marx*. Cambridge, MA: MIT Press.

Knowles, Rob. 2004. *Political Economy from Below: Economic Thought in Communitarian Anarchism, 1840–1914*. New York and London: Routledge.

Korman, C. 2019. "The Battle for a Paycheck in Kentucky Coal Country." *The New Yorker*. September 9.

Kropotkin, P. 1892. *The Conquest of Bread*. Paris, France: Le Révolté.

Kropotkin, P. 1899. *Fields, Factories and Workshops: Or, Industry Combined with Agriculture and Brain Work with Manual Labor*. London: Hutchison.

Laclau, E. 2005. "Populism: What's in a Name?" In *Populism and the Mirror of Democracy*, edited by Francisco Panizza, 32–49. London: Verso.

Levien, M., M. Watts, and Y. Hairong. 2018. "Agrarian Marxism." *Journal of Peasant Studies* 45 (5–6): 853–883.

Loadenthal, M. 2017. *The Politics of Attack: Communiqués and Insurrectionary Violence*. Manchester: Manchester University Press.

Maghimbi, S., I. N. Kimambo, and K. Sugimura. 2011. *Contemporary Perspectives on Moral Economy: Africa and Southeast Asia*. Dar es Salaam, Tanzania: Dar Es Salaam University Press.

Malatesta, E. 2019. *Malatesta in America 1899–1900*. Edited by D. Turcato. Oakland, CA: AK Press.

Marshall, P. 2010. *Demanding the Impossible: A History of Anarchism*. Oakland, CA: PM Press.

Maxwell, B., and R. Craib. 2015. *No Gods, No Masters, No Peripheries*. Oakland, CA: PM Press.

May, T. 1994. *The Political Philosophy of Poststructuralist Anarchism*. University Park, PA: Penn State University Press.

Mbah, S., and I. E. Igariwey. 2001. *African Anarchism: The History of a Movement*. Chicago, IL: See Sharp Press.

McKay, I. 2012. "Another View: Syndicalism, Anarchism and Marxism." *Anarchist Studies* 20 (1): 89.

McQuinn, J. 2009. "Post-Left Anarchy: Leaving the Left Behind." https://theanarchistlibrary.org/library/jason-mcquinn-post-left-anarchy-leaving-the-left-behind.

Meyer, M., and K. Kersplebedeb, eds. 2019. *Kuwasi Balagoon: A Soldier's Story: Revolutionary Writings by a New Afrikan Anarchist*. Oakland, CA: PM Press.

Moffitt, B. 2016. *The Global Rise of Populism: Performance, Political Style, and Representation*. Stanford, CA: Stanford University Press.

Montenegro de Wit, M., A. Roman-Alcalá, A. Liebman, and S. Chrisman. 2019. "Agrarian Origins of Authoritarian Populism in the United States: What Can We Learn from 20th-Century Struggles in California and the Midwest?" *Journal of Rural Studies*. doi:10.1016/j.jrurstud.2019.12.003.

Morris, B. 2018. *Kropotkin: The Politics of Community*. Amherst, NY: Humanity Books.

Mouffe, C. 2018. *For a Left Populism*. London: Verso.

Oikonomakis, L. 2020. "The Government of Hope, the Hope of Government, and the Role of Elections as Wave-Breakers of Radical Prefigurative Political Processes." In *Beyond Crisis: After the Collapse of*

Institutional Hope in Greece, What? edited by John Holloway, Katerina Nasioka, and Paagiotis Doulos, 40–61. Oakland, CA: PM Press.

O'Hearn, D., and A. Grubaçic. 2018. *Living at the Edges of Capitalism: Adventures in Exile and Mutual Aid*. Oakland, CA: University of California Press.

Páez, A. 1986. *El anarquismo en el Ecuador*. Quito: Corporación Editora Nacional.

Palij, M. 1976. *The Anarchism of Nestor Makhno, 1918–1921*. Seattle, WA: University of Washington Press.

Panizza, F., ed. 2005. *Populism and the Mirror of Democracy*. London: Verso.

Patel, R., and J. Moore. 2017. *A History of the World in Seven Cheap Things: A Guide to Capitalism, Nature, and the Future of the Planet*. Oakland, CA: University of California Press.

Pellow, D. N. 2014. *Total Liberation: The Power and Promise of Animal Rights and the Radical Earth Movement*. Minneapolis: University of Minnesota Press.

Pellow, D. N. 2016. "Environmental Justice and Rural Studies: A Critical Conversation and Invitation to Collaboration." *Journal of Rural Studies* 47: 381–386.

Pernicone, N. 1993. *Italian Anarchism, 1864–1892*. Princeton, NJ: Princeton University Press.

Phillips-Fein, K. 2009. *Invisible Hands: The Making of the Conservative Movement from the New Deal to Reagan*. New York: W.W. Norton.

Porter, D. 2011. *Eyes to the South: French Anarchists and Algeria*. Oakland, CA: AK Press.

Prichard, A., R. Kinna, S. Pinta, and D. Berry, eds. 2017. *Libertarian Socialism: Politics in Black and Red*. Oakland, CA: PM Press.

Pulido, L. 2017. "Geographies of Race and Ethnicity II: Environmental Racism, Racial Capitalism and State-Sanctioned Violence." *Progress in Human Geography* 41 (4): 524–533.

Quail, J. 2019. *The Slow Burning Fuse: The Lost History of the British Anarchists*. Oakland, CA: PM Press.

Ramnath, M. 2011. *Decolonizing Anarchism: An Anti-Authoritarian History of India's Liberation Struggle*. Oakland, CA: AK Press.

Ramos, R., E. Rodrigues, and A. Samis. 2003. *Against All Tyranny! Essays on Anarchism in Brazil*. Berkeley, CA and London, UK: Kate Sharpley Library.

Randall, A., and A. Charlesworth. 2000. "The Moral Economy: Riots, Markets and Social Conflict." In *Moral Economy and Popular Protest: Crowds, Conflict and Authority*, edited by A. Randall and A. Charlesworth, 1–33. London: MacMillan Press.

Redneck Revolt. n.d. "Redneck Revolt Organizing Principles." Accessed October 16, 2019. https://www.redneckrevolt.org/principles.

Roman-Alcalá, A. 2018. "(Relative) Autonomism, Policy Currents and the Politics of Mobilisation for Food Sovereignty in the United States: The Case of Occupy the Farm." *Local Environment: The International Journal of Justice and Sustainability* 23 (6): 619–634.

Saed. 2019. "James Richard O'Connor's Ecological Marxism." *Capitalism Nature Socialism* 30 (4): 1–12.

Samudzi, Z., and W. C. Anderson. 2018. *As Black as Resistance: Finding the Conditions for Liberation*. Oakland, CA: AK Press.

Sbicca, J. 2018. *Food Justice Now: Deepening the Roots of Social Struggle*. Minneapolis, MN: University of Minnesota Press.

Schmidt, M. 2013. *Cartography of Revolutionary Anarchism*. Oakland, CA: AK Press.

Scoones, I., M. Edelman, S. M. Borras, R. Hall, W. Wolford, and B. White. 2018. "Emancipatory Rural Politics: Confronting Authoritarian Populism." *The Journal of Peasant Studies* 45 (1): 1–20.

Scott, J. 1976. *The Moral Economy of the Peasant: Rebellion and Subsistence in Southeast Asia*. New Haven, CT: Yale University Press.

Scott, J. 1985. *Weapons of the Weak*. New Haven, CT: Yale University Press.

Scott, J. 1992. *Domination and the Arts of Resistance*. New Haven, CT: Yale University Press.

Scott, J. 1998. *Seeing Like a State: How Certain Schemes to Improve the Human Condition Have Failed*. New Haven, CT: Yale University Press.

Scott, J. 2009. *The Art of Not Being Governed: An Anarchist History of Upland Southeast Asia*. New Haven, CT: Yale University Press.

Scott, J. 2012. *Two Cheers for Anarchism: Six Easy Pieces on Autonomy, Dignity, Work and Meaningful Work and Play*. Princeton, NJ: Princeton University Press.

Scott, J. 2017. *Against the Grain: A Deep History of the Earliest States*. New Haven, CT: Yale University Books.
Seaweed. 2013. *Land and Freedom: An Open Invitation* (excerpt). https://theanarchistlibrary.org/library/seaweed-land-and-freedom.
Shaffer, K. 2000. "Cuba Para Todos: Anarchist Internationalism and the Cultural Politics of Cuban Independence, 1898–1925." *Cuban Studies* 31: 45–75.
Shaffer, K. 2013. *Black Flag Boricuas: Anarchism, Antiauthoritarianism, and the Left in in Puerto Rico, 1897–1921*. Chicago: University of Illinois Press.
Shanin, T. 2018. "1881 Letters of Vera Zasulich and Karl Marx." *Journal of Peasant Studies* 45 (7): 1183–1202.
Solnit, R. 2009. *A Paradise Built in Hell: The Extraordinary Communities that Arise in Disaster*. New York: Penguin Books.
Springer, S. 2017. "The Limits to Marx: David Harvey and the Condition of Postfraternity." *Dialogues in Human Geography* 7 (3): 280–294.
Stewart, E. 2019. "We Are (Still) the 99 Percent." *Vox*. https://www.vox.com/the-highlight/2019/4/23/18284303/occupy-wall-street-bernie-sanders-dsa-socialism.
Táala Hooghan Infoshop. 2019. Save the Date! Indigenous Anarchist Convergence. February 13. Accessed October 10, 2019. http://www.taalahooghan.org/save-the-date-indigenous-anarchist-convergence/.
Tanenbaum, J. 2016. "To Destroy Domination in All Its Forms: Anarcha-Feminist Theory, Organization and Action 1970–1978." *Perspectives on Anarchist Theory* 29. http://blackrosefed.org/anarcha-feminism-to-destroy-domination-in-all-forms/.
Thomas, P. 1990. *Karl Marx and the Anarchists*. London: Routledge.
Thompson, E. P. 1966. *The Making of the English Working Class*. New York: Vintage Books.
Thompson, E. P. 1971. "The Moral Economy of the English Crowd in the Eighteenth Century." *Past and Present* 50 (1): 76–136.
Tilzey, M. 2019. "Authoritarian Populism and Neo-extractivism in Bolivia and Ecuador: The Unresolved Agrarian Question and the Prospects for Food Sovereignty as Counter-Hegemony." *Journal of Peasant Studies* 46 (3): 626–652.
Ulrich-Schad, J., and C. Duncan. 2018. "People and Places Left Behind: Work, Culture and Politics in the Rural United States." *Journal of Peasant Studies* 45 (1): 59–79.
Val, V., P. M. Rosset, C. Zamora Lomelí, O. F. Giraldo, and D. Rocheleau. 2019. "Agroecology and La Via Campesina I. The Symbolic and Material Construction of Agroecology Through the Dispositive of 'Peasant-to-Peasant' Processes." *Agroecology and Sustainable Food Systems*. doi:10.1080/21683565.2019.1600099.
van der Ploeg, J. D. 2008. *The New Peasanties. Struggles for Autonomy and Sustainability in an Era of Empire and Globalization*. London and Sterling, VA: Earthscan.
van der Ploeg, J. D. 2013. *Peasants and the Art of Farming: A Chayanovian Manifesto*. Winnipeg, Canada: Fernwood Publishing.
van der Walt, L. 2011. "Anarchism and Syndicalism in an African Port City: The Revolutionary Traditions of Cape Town's Multiracial Working Class, 1904–1931." *Labor History* 52 (2): 137–171.
van der Walt, L. 2016. "Global Anarchism and Syndicalism: Theory, History, Resistance." *Anarchist Studies* 24 (1): 85.
Vergara-Camus, L., and C. Kay. 2017. "The Agrarian Political Economy of Left-wing Governments in Latin America: Agribusiness, Peasants, and the Limits of Neo-developmentalism." *Journal of Agrarian Change* 17 (2): 415–437. doi:10.1111/joac.12216.
Voline. 2019. *The Unknown Revolution 1917–1921*. Oakland, CA: PM Press.
Wainwright, J. 2017. "What if Marx Was an Anarchist?" *Dialogues in Human Geography* 7 (3): 257–262.
Wainwright, J., and G. Mann. 2013. "Climate Leviathan." *Antipode* 45 (1): 1–22.
Wald, N. 2015. "Anarchist Participatory Development: A Possible New Framework?" *Development and Change* 46 (4): 618–643.
White, M. 2018. *Freedom Farmers: Agricultural Resistance and the Black Freedom Movement*. Chapel Hill, NC: University of North Carolina Press.

Williams, D. 2017. *Black Flags and Social Movements: A Sociological Analysis of Movement Anarchism.* Manchester, UK: Manchester University Press.
Wilson, A. 2013. "Beyond Alternative: Exploring the Potential for Autonomous Food Spaces." *Antipode: A Radical Journal of Geography* 45 (3): 719–737.
Wilson, J. 2017. "Member of Portland Militia-Style Group Helps Police Arrest Anti-Fascist Protester." *The Guardian UK.* Accessed October 16, 2019. https://www.theguardian.com/us-news/2017/jun/08/portland-alt-right-rally-militia-member-police-arrest.
Wolf, E. 1969. *Peasant Revolutions of the 20th Century.* Norman, OK: University of Oklahoma Press.
Zaragoza Rovira, G. 1996. *Anarquismo Argentino, 1876–1902.* Madrid: Ediciones de la Torre.

'Actually existing' right-wing populism in rural Europe: insights from eastern Germany, Spain, the United Kingdom and Ukraine

Natalia Mamonova, Jaume Franquesa and Sally Brooks

ABSTRACT
This study depicts various manifestations of what we call 'actually existing' right-wing populism. Based on empirical insights from eastern Germany, Spain, the UK and Ukraine, we explored how nationalist tendencies unfold in different contexts and what role agriculture and rural imageries play in this process. We analyse contextual factors (rural 'emptiness', socio-economic inequality, particularities of electoral systems, politics of Europeanization) and citizens' perceptions of social reality (selective memory, subjective experiences of democracy, national redefinition, politics of emotions). We conclude that resistance and alternatives to right-wing populism should be context-specific, grounded in the social fabric and culture of the locale.

1. Introduction

Years of globalised capitalism, neoliberal restructuring and technocratic management have spawned an illiberal backlash manifesting itself in the rise of right-wing populist politics. Yet, this backlash has oftentimes come from the places 'where one should least expect it: the anger comes from rural idyll. Rural regions decide elections, surprise experts and change the course of entire nations[1]' (Müller 2017, 85). The European countryside is now often regarded as a bastion of populist, socially conservative, religiously dogmatic, and nationalist sentiments and politics (Hajdu and Mamonova 2020). The outbreak of Covid-19 has further intensified the authoritarian and protectionist sentiments in society, allowing many European populists to cement themselves onto the political landscape (Tisdall 2020).

---

[1]Translated from German by the authors.

DOI: 10.4324/9781003162353-18

To date, rural support for right-wing populism has been the subject of several research endeavours. Among the most notable are the 'Forum on authoritarian populism and the rural world' by the *Journal of Peasant Studies*, and several region-focused initiatives, such as the *Sociologia Ruralis*' special issue on right-wing populism in Europe, the *Journal of Rural Studies*' special issue on authoritarian populism in North America, and forthcoming collection of articles on rural populism in *Latin American Perspectives*.[2] These research initiatives were aimed at understanding the rise of regressive, authoritarian politics in rural areas, as well as the existing forms of resistance and the alternatives being built against them. The present authors contributed to some of these endeavours with analytical articles on several European countries: (Franquesa [2019] on Spain; Mamonova [2019] on Russia; Mamonova and Franquesa [2020a, 2020b] on Europe; Brooks [2019] on the UK; Hajdu and Mamonova [2020] on Romania). The studies demonstrated that 'populism does not come with uniform, clearly defined characteristics; it takes different forms depending on nationally specific factors such as political history, system and culture' (Mamonova and Franquesa 2020a, 8).

The current article aims to develop this argument further and examines the complexity of what we call 'actually existing'[3] right-wing populism. Instead of using the (often-contested) definition of right-wing populism as a starting point, we focus on the historically and culturally conditioned and context-specific manifestations of right-wing populism in rural Europe. This approach presents an opportunity for more effective analysis of the uneven and variegated realities of 'actually existing' right-wing populism, as it is guided by empirical manifestations of the phenomenon, not by its precise definition or conceptualisation. In other words, instead of moving analytically from the general and the ideal to the concrete – which would involve taking right-wing populism as a more or less coherent ideological position that takes hold of specific social realities – we approach it from the perspective of practice, focusing on how it emerges out of variegated forms of rural socio-economic livelihood change that are experienced from specific socially-situated positions in terms of class, gender and ethnicity.

Right-wing populism is analysed here from various angles: as a political movement, a discursive frame, and a mobilising strategy that 'depict politics as a struggle between "the people" and some combination of malevolent, racialised and/or unfairly advantaged "Others", at home or abroad or both' (Scoones et al. 2018, 2). In Europe, the term right-wing populism is commonly used to describe groups, politicians and political parties that combine an 'ethnic and chauvinistic definition of the people', authoritarianism, and nativism (Mudde and Kaltwasser 2017). Their authoritarianism manifests itself in the promise of a return to traditional values, a desire for law and order, nostalgia for past glories and strong leadership. Their nativism takes the form of an exclusive and xenophobic nationalism, framed in opposition to an immigration that allegedly threatens to 'distort or spoil' existing cultural values and strip prosperity, job opportunities, and public services from native people (Mudde and Kaltwasser 2017).

---

[2] Besides that, the Annals of the American Association of Geographers' special issue on 'Environmental Governance in a Populist/Authoritarian Era' included several contributions that addressed the link between populism and the rural (McCarthy 2020).

[3] The term 'actually existing' emerged in the critical studies of capitalism and neoliberalism but became widely used in other fields to emphasise discrepancies between theoretical conceptualisations of a phenomenon and its veritable manifestations (Konings 2012; Brenner and Theodore 2002).

We analyse right-wing politics and practices in four different contexts: eastern Germany, Spain, the UK and Ukraine. The first two countries were chosen to depict various nationalist tendencies triggered by what Dzenovska (2020) calls rural 'emptiness' – the real and imaginary abandonment of rural areas due to the concentration of capital flows and statecraft in 'global cities'.[4] The latter two countries were selected to discuss the role of the European Union in nationalist mobilisation: anti-EU sentiments as drivers behind Brexit and pro-EU sentiments in post-Euromaidan Ukraine. The discussion, however, goes beyond reviewing the primary characteristics of the selected cases, and addresses other issues such as the system of representative democracy, redistributive land reforms, the impact of historical legacies and the emotional roots of right-wing political populism.

The four countries do not serve as traditional case studies, but rather as illustrations of revealing trends. The authors have profound expertise and conducted extensive field research in the selected countries (except eastern Germany, which was studied based on secondary materials). Besides that, the authors consulted with national experts from the selected countries to receive their feedback and insights on the topic (see the acknowledgements). The recent publications on right-wing populism in rural Europe were employed here as secondary data and support material.

The article is structured as follows. The next section discusses agrarian transformation and the crisis of neoliberal capitalism in rural Europe that created a fertile ground for regressive nationalist politics. The subsequent section presents the insights from the four countries under study. It is followed by a discussion on distinctive and common features of right-wing populism in the analysed contexts and how our findings contribute to the critical agrarian studies debates. The final section provides some concluding remarks.

2. Agrarian transformation and multifaceted crisis of neoliberal capitalism in Europe

Borras (2020) argues that the recurring emergence of populist ideas and politics in different historical conjunctures can be explained by the cyclical nature of crises of capitalism and by extension of the crises of political rule. Indeed, populists appear when the capitalist system 'cracks' and requires reconfiguration of the existing order. These 'cracks' are not isolated events; they are elements of the 'creeping crisis' of capitalism – a slow-burning crisis that evolves over long periods of time before it explodes (see Boin et al. [2020] on 'creeping crises').

The economic uncertainties and rising inequalities in the 1970s demonstrated the inability of the post-war Keynesian model of the welfare state to remedy structural injustices. Then, the rising 'New Right' politicians[5] offered radical solutions in the form of neoliberal capitalism, characterised by a free market economy, increased deregulation, privatisation, and a reduction in spending on the welfare state (Harvey 2005). Since

---

[4]Dzenovska (2020) introduces the concept of 'emptiness' to study the abandonment of remote rural areas in post-socialist Eastern Europe, however, it may be applied to all areas that became abandoned by capital and the state. She understands the 'emptiness' as a discursive framework (used by its inhabitants to describe their lives), a complex historical formation (that has emerged in transition to capitalism) and an analytical lens (that captures the reconfiguration of relations between capital, the state, people, and place).
[5]Primarily, proponents of Thatcherism in the UK and Reaganism in the USA.

then, rapid globalisation and prevalent doctrines of neoliberal development gained hegemonic status (Shucksmith and Brown 2016). However, if previously neoliberal capitalism was seen as a market-based solution to socio-economic problems, now it is often criticised for exacerbating inequalities, degrading nature, eroding social capital, and limiting the power of democracies (see Mamonova and Franquesa [2020a]).

Neoliberal capitalism has fundamentally transformed rural Europe – in terms of both agricultural production and rural lifestyle. The modernisation paradigm – that prevailed in EU rural development policies – suggested that industrialisation and commercialisation of agriculture would not only increase food security, but would also constitute a powerful engine of overall economic development (see critique by Shucksmith and Brown [2016]). The EU's Common Agricultural Policy (CAP) has 'modernised' many family farmers in Western Europe by transforming them into capitalistic entrepreneurs that are oriented towards markets and dependent on credit, industrial inputs and technologies (van der Ploeg 2009). Many farmers have found themselves trapped in a vicious circle of scale enlargement, technologically driven intensification and increasing dependency on food industries, banks and retail chains. They either have to expand by getting further involved in financial markets, or go out of business (van der Ploeg 2010).

In Eastern Europe, former collective farm structures were dismantled, and land was distributed to the rural population. Yet, individual commercial farming emerged on a limited scale; most of the land became accumulated by industrial agribusiness, often with oligarchic or international capital involved (Visser and Spoor 2011; Gonda 2019). Only a few countries – such as Romania and Poland – are still characterised by large numbers of small farms, yet processes of land concentration also take place there (Hajdu and Visser 2017). The accession of post-socialist countries to the EU brought a number of positive effects to the rural economy, such as subsidies for farmers and increased income for poor households. However, the CAP was unable to address the specificities of post-socialist agrarian structures, thus deepening inequities between small and large farms (Swain 2013).

In both Eastern and Western Europe, scholars observe instances of land grabbing, agricultural intensification, 'hollowing out' of medium-sized farmers, and the rise of 'food empires[6]' that exert a monopolistic power over the entire agri-food chain (Kay 2016; van der Ploeg, Franco, and Borras 2015).

Although agriculture remains one of the largest employers within the EU and it is strongly associated with the CAP's rural development framework, most rural areas experience a process of economic and cultural deagrarianisation. Industrial farms use economies of scale and labour-saving technologies and, therefore, do not need a large workforce, except seasonal labourers. Meanwhile, family farms – the major agricultural employers – have been gradually disappearing. During the last decade, the number of full-time farmers across the EU fell by one third, representing five million jobs[7] (European Commission 2018). Today, only 4.3% of the EU's working-age population is employed

---

[6]'Food empires' have emerged through takeovers, facilitated by the unlimited availability of credit and the global corporate and government 'marriage'. Among the most powerful food empires are Nestlé, Unilever and Monsanto that continue expanding. Besides that, there are relatively new empires such as Ahold, Parmalat and Vion, the recently created north-west European meat empire. For further discussion read van der Ploeg (2010).

[7]The decline was especially severe in Romania (983,000 jobs lost), Poland (616,000), Bulgaria (387,000) and Greece (189,000).

in agriculture[8] (Eurostat 2020). This economic deagrarianisation entails a cultural deagrarianisation – i.e. the loss of interest in agriculture and rural lifestyle (Gallar and Vara 2010). The declining presence of agriculture in everyday life and disconnection with farmers have led to a decreased social understanding of farm processes and triggered various conflicts between farmers and society, especially in relation to climate change issues (Bunkus, Soliev, and Theesfeld 2020; van der Ploeg 2010, 2020a).

In addition to deagrarianisation, deindustrialisation has drastically transformed rural landscapes and their social make-up. The former industrial rural regions – those that were at the forefront of capitalist development at the beginning of the twentieth century – became the 'losers' in the globalisation process as factories and manufactures were shut down or moved to other countries (Hospers and Syssner 2018). Deindustrialisation reduced not only opportunities for employment but changed the nature of the work on offer. As a result, many low-wage, low-skilled workers – such as the Roma people in Eastern Europe[9] – became chronically unemployed and their housing and sanitary conditions deteriorated. This led to further stigmatisation and out-casting of the Roma, as discussed by Škobla and Filčák (2020) for the case of rural Slovakia.

Modernisation theory predicted that neoliberal capitalism would lead to the disappearance of socio-spatial polarisation (Williamson 1965). However, as Neil Smith (1990, 48) reminds us, 'the mobility of capital brings about the development of areas with a high rate of profit, and underdevelopment of those with a low rate of profit'. Although some areas and sectors benefited from the neoliberal turn in rural development (such as industrial agriculture and regional centres and peri-urban zones), others – mostly located in peripheral and economically weak rural regions – have lost (Shucksmith and Brown 2016). There is intense drain on the social, cultural and economic capitals in remote rural areas, creating the so-called spaces of 'emptiness' (see Dzenovska [2020]). Up to 60% of rural areas in the EU experience depopulation, which is especially severe in Eastern and Central Europe, where more than 80% of rural regions have shrunk since 2001 (ESPON 2020). Social welfare cuts and rural exodus cause deterioration of infrastructure and facilities (roads, schools and hospitals) that are critically important for the survival and wellbeing of rural communities. As young and active people leave economically weak rural areas, those who are 'left behind' experience declining living standards, the loss of social status, and high dependence on state transfers (Dzenovska 2020).

The function of a village, where agriculture has been traditionally organised and embedded into the social fabric, has been disappearing in Europe (Bunkus, Soliev, and Theesfeld 2020). The switch from productive land use to consumption-based demands has generated a consumerist ideology, which is especially pronounced in rural areas of Western and Northern Europe (Marsden 1999). In consumerist societies, economic capital is important for maintaining social identities, while personal success or failure are measured in employment and welfare benefits. When people are unable to live up to salient social identities and their constitutive values, they experience low self-esteem, shame and insecurity (Salmela and von Scheve 2017). Scholars observed

---

[8]This share is higher in post-socialist member states, where farming contributes up to 20% of total employment (Eurostat 2020).
[9]The communist governments were aimed at achieving full employment for all citizens, including the Roma population, who were commonly employed as unskilled industrial workers (Škobla and Filčák 2020).

increasing socio-economic tensions (Woods and McDonagh 2011) declining life-satisfaction (Bunkus, Soliev, and Theesfeld 2020), and widespread feelings of a loss of dignity (Franquesa 2018) in rural Europe during the recent years.

The rising discontent and resentment in rural society have triggered what Woods (2005) called 'rural reawakening' – an increase in rural mobilisation and activism in response to neoliberal policy reforms, globalisation, and extensive social change in the European countryside. However, rural protest groups remain mostly fragmented and only informally linked, which limits their ability to challenge the status quo (Woods 2015; Mamonova and Franquesa 2020a). Meanwhile, large-scale agribusiness and multinational corporations successfully lobby European governments. As a result, 'corporate policy is becoming more fully engaged in public policy to further its own interests, thus raising questions about accountability' (Lang and Heasman 2004, 127).

The creeping crisis of neoliberal capitalism entails a crisis in the system of representative democracy (Mamonova and Franquesa 2020a). Federal, supranational and international governance structures have become increasingly complex and non-transparent, while the dominant political parties often function like cartels – i.e. they focus on preventing their competitors from coming to power rather than solving actual problems (see Katz and Mair [2009] on 'cartel parties'). Consequently, many people have come to believe that their governments represent the interests of large corporations, political decisions are agreed on in back rooms, and the interests of 'the men and women on the street' are overlooked (Vorländer, Herold, and Schäller 2018, 183).

Political alienation is especially profound in the European countryside. Rural and farming issues are usually ignored and often misunderstood by mainstream political parties (Cramer 2016). The disconnection between politicians and rural areas is the result of the urban bias in politics, when urban-based politicians are 'unlikely ever to understand the true needs of rural people' (Cramer 2016, 17), and the parties' strategic focus on urban constituencies due to the declining numbers of rural voters and entrenched stereotypes about villagers' political apathy (Mamonova and Franquesa 2020a). Besides that, since the 2008 economic crisis, many rural municipalities have experienced a decrease in economic and political autonomy and a reduction in the number of units of local self-government (Ladner, Keuffer, and Baldersheim 2015). The political alienation and inability to influence local decision-making have further intensified rural discontent and fuelled public resentment against the 'market-compliant democracy' (Vorländer, Herold, and Schäller 2018).

The Covid-19 pandemic has exposed and exacerbated critical frailties, inequalities and the unsustainability of late capitalist economies. The biomedical crisis has quickly developed into a multi-facetted politico-economic crisis in, and of, the food-system (van der Ploeg 2020b). The 'badly balanced world market and the high degree of financialization of both primary agricultural production and food chains' have resulted in a situation where 'capital [was] acting as a de-activating instead of a productive force' (van der Ploeg 2020b, 2). The paralysing force of capital was especially visible in the beginning of the crisis, when supermarket shelves were empty, while farmers had to destroy tonnes of fresh food that they could no longer sell. The EU governments' attempts to guarantee food supply largely resulted in supporting global agribusiness and supermarket chains, while local farmers' markets were forced to close (Foote 2020). Lockdowns, movement restrictions, and reduced demand have resulted in widespread job losses and rising poverty across the EU. The pandemic has also highlighted structural inequalities and precarity generated by neoliberal regimes of labour market regulation. The agricultural workers – both seasonal (migrant) and processing factories' workers – occupied positions that made them extremely vulnerable to contracting the disease. The largest outbreaks of Covid-19 were reported in industrial meat processing factories, where social distancing is hard to enforce, and where low pay, illegal wage deductions and job insecurity forced many employees to go to work sick. Furthermore, the pandemic laid bare the persistent inequalities within the EU: health and safety of seasonal farmworkers, primarily from Eastern Europe, became largely overlooked in order to save the harvest in Western Europe. The governments' handling of the pandemic provoked discontent among certain social groups, especially those who are inclined to support right-wing ideas and policies (Youngs 2020).

3. Populism in rural Europe

Right-wing populist parties and nationalist movements are using societal resentment to gain support and spread their ideas in the countryside. They discursively portray themselves as acting on behalf of 'the people' against urban elites, the political establishment at home and 'unelected bureaucrats in Brussels'. They wholeheartedly criticise the neoliberal approach to the economy and the organisation of society, yet they are far from providing alternative solutions. Instead, as Mamonova and Franquesa (2020a) have demonstrated, European populists aim to 'defend and maintain capitalism "in the name of the people"':

> [W]hile right-wing populism is anti-liberal in terms of identity politics (e.g. multiculturalism, abortion rights, minority rights, religious freedom), it is very liberal in its economic policies. Populists become the protectors of a national identity with which the masses can identify, while simultaneously negotiating better global terms for the elite. They sell what [Jean-François] Bayart calls 'liberalism for the rich and nationalism for the poor'. (Mamonova and Franquesa 2020a, 7)

These characteristics are exceptionally useful to make sense of the populist rise in Europe and globally. Yet, as Scoones et al. (2018, 2) remind us, right-wing populist features 'are not evident everywhere, nor are they necessarily evident in their entirety anywhere'. We thus argue for the need to study 'actually existing' right-wing populism through specific case studies. Below, we contribute to this task by analysing the unfolding of regressive nativist politics in four different national settings, with a special focus on their rural dimensions.

3.1. The 'Dying' villages of eastern Germany as home to right-wing movements

Thirty years after the fall of the Berlin Wall, the river Elbe continues to mark the cultural, political and economic divide between Eastern and Western Europe. This divide became especially profound during the 2017 federal election, when the far-right party Alternative für Deutschland became the third-largest party in the Bundestag due to its success in the East, particularly in Mecklenburg-Vorpommern, Saxony and Thuringia (Oltermann 2017). The underpopulated and economically disadvantaged villages of Saxony became the 'synonymous for a xenophobic, anti-refugee "dark" side of Germany' – the image which now extends to the whole of eastern Germany (Vorländer, Herold, and Schäller 2018, 118).

Despite German reunification in 1990 and the development programme 'Aufbau-Ost', economic performance and living standards in the former communist eastern states remain lower than in the old federal states. Gross wages of eastern Germans are currently at 85% of the western German level, and unemployment is 20% higher in the East (BMWi 2019). The eastern German economy is still organised on a small scale, there are no headquarters of international corporations, and the region remains largely rural. The recent report on the 'status of German unity' revealed that 57% of eastern Germans feel that they are second-class citizens, and only 38% feel that reunification was successful (BMWi 2019).

The feelings of being 'disrespected' and 'disadvantaged' in relation to their western German compatriots are especially profound in rural areas of eastern Germany (Liebmann 2010). The transition from communism to capitalism resulted in rapid structural changes in agriculture and the rural economy. The former collective farm enterprises – which were the socio-economic backbones of rural regions – were dissolved and transformed into private agricultural firms. Such reform was aimed to mitigate the differences between western and eastern German agriculture and to create family farms. However, just a few families were able to reclaim their land and organise private farms. In most cases, collective lands were accumulated by former farm managers and, later, by non-local, non-agricultural investors. Bunkus and Theesfeld (2018) characterise this process as an instance of land grabbing with negative impacts on local rural communities.

Indeed, the majority (76%) of land investors come from West Germany or abroad and show little interest in investing in the economic and social development of the region (Tietz 2017). Land speculations drove land prices up, making access to farmland for new entrants limited and expensive (Bunkus and Theesfeld 2018). Young, well-educated, often female villagers left economically weak rural areas. Those 'left behind' experienced unemployment, a loss of social status, and 'the feeling of the devaluation of personal achievements in one's life during GDR times' (Vorländer, Herold, and Schäller 2018, 177). Local governments are often unable to provide public services and infrastructure maintenance in depopulated rural areas because the allocation of tax revenues to German municipalities depends on among other things – population figures. In result, many eastern German villages became zones of an economic and social vacuum (Chatalova and Wolz 2019).

This socio-economic vacuum became the breeding ground for right-wing populists and radical right groups. These groups exploit rural resentments against the 'domination' and 'arrogant presence' of 'import elites from the West' and more recent threats such as the refugee and Eurozone crises (Vorländer, Herold, and Schäller 2018). Contrary to common assumptions, the fear of Islamisation is not a major motivation for those taking part in far-right mobilisation in eastern Germany. Only 15.4% of participants in the Dresden demonstrations organised by PEGIDA (Patriotic Europeans against the Islamisation of the Occident) showed resentment towards Muslims. The majority joined the demonstrations not because of but despite the anti-Islam agenda of the movement.

In their analysis of political views of Dresden protesters, Vorländer, Herold, and Schäller (2018) reviewed that eastern Germans are more tolerant towards everyday expressions of xenophobic and nationalistic attitudes than the western German population. This is the result of the patriotic education in the GDR and the contemporary struggles with national redefinition due to transition from communism to capitalism. Furthermore, eastern Germans are more favourable to right-wing dictatorship than their western counterparts. Nearly 14% of respondents believed that under certain circumstances a dictatorship is a better form of government, and 12.8% wish for a strong leader for the benefit of all (4.8% and 9%, respectively, expressed the same views in West Germany).

Economic uncertainty and recession during the post-communist democratisation process contributed to the fact that, although democracy is viewed as a desired form of governance, its implementation is experienced by many as 'foreign', adopted from the West (Vorländer, Herold, and Schäller 2018). Population decline in eastern rural regions entailed the centralisation of some functions of local self-government, which limits public involvement in decision-making (Chatalova and Wolz 2019). Besides that, underpopulated rural councils are lacking enough candidates to fill seats, and right-wing populists are often elected as the only persons keen on the job (Nasr 2019).

The 'dying' villages of eastern Germany became attractive for Völkische Siedler (ethnic/folkish settlers). The settlers buy abandoned rural houses, set up organic farms, and get actively involved in revitalising village social, cultural and economic life. The self-definition of this group as settlers points to their colonising impetus (Röpke and Speit 2019). They largely follow the right-wing back-to-the-land ideas of Artamans – the former Nazi agrarian movement dedicated to the Blood and Soil-inspired ruralism. They aim to realise the dream of German 'Volksgemeinschaft' and to create 'racially pure', self-sufficient peasant communities. The settlers present themselves as helpful neighbours, hard-working craftspeople and committed parents and, therefore, are popular in villages. Rural resistance to right-wing incomers is uncommon. Social proximity in villages limits interpersonal confrontation, and those who stand up for democratic values are often labelled as 'troublemakers' and 'Nestbeschmutzer[10]' (Hellwig 2017). This allows these settlers to expand and spread their ethno-racial ideology almost unimpeded.

3.2. Vacía *or* vaciada: *rural Spain and the populist question*

Like in eastern Germany, depopulation is an acute problem in Spain's rural areas and plays an important role in right-wing populist mobilisation. Yet, in contrast to the German case, in Spain rural 'emptiness' triggers both right-wing and left-wing populist rhetoric and politics.

Up until very recently, Spain was heralded as the exception to the rise of right-wing populism in Europe (Franquesa 2019). This all changed in the 2018–19 electoral cycle. In December 2018, Vox (Latin for 'voice') obtained 10% of the vote in the Andalusian election, thus becoming the first far-right populist party to enter a Spanish regional parliament since the reestablishment of democracy in the late 1970s. This success was replicated in the national election held in April 2019. After this election, the unwillingness of the most voted candidate – Pedro Sánchez (the leader of centre-left PSOE) – to form a coalition with left-wing populist party Podemos led to an electoral repetition in November 2019, when Vox obtained 15% of the vote and became the third party in the parliament.

---

[10]German expression, which means 'those who foul their own nest' and used to describe a person who criticizes or abuses their own country or family.

Vox was formed in 2014 by disgruntled cadres of then ruling conservative party Partido Popular (PP), who wanted to move away from what they saw as the party's drift to moderate positions. From its creation, Vox's political discourse relied on extreme Spanish nationalism, anti-immigration and social conservatism, together with a tacit endorsement of neoliberal economic policy. However, up until 2018 the party harvested meagre electoral results. The recent rise of Vox is partly linked to conjunctural circumstances, but it also signals the success of the emotional conception of politics of Santiago Abascal – Vox's leader. As he argued in an interview: 'politics is not just urban planning, school schedules, street lighting [rather, it is about connecting] with feelings and convictions: honour, patriotism and things like that' (Sánchez Dragó 2019, 43). This appeal stems from Vox's call to 'Make Spain Great Again' – a project that is understood as a second Reconquista against separatists, communists, Islamists, foreigners and progressives.

Rural imagery plays a key role in Vox's politics of emotion. In a 2016 promotional video entitled 'A new beginning', Abascal was filmed wandering through rural landscapes.[11] The video visualises some ideas of the early decades of Franco's dictatorship: an organic view of the nation intertwining nation and nature where rural Spain comes to stand as the not-yet-corrupted origin of the Spanish nation, a pure and immortal Spain threatened by immoral, centrifugal forces (Del Arco 2005). Another example of using rural imagery is a tweet that Vox issued during the 2020 Covid-19 outbreak, which contrasted several well-known left-leaning movie stars (such as Pedro Almodóvar and Javier Bardem) to a tractor in a field, with the following words super-impressed: 'Maybe now Spaniards realize that we can live without puppeteers but not without our farmers'.

Vox ardently uses for its own interests the image of the so-called *España vacía* or 'empty Spain' (Del Molino 2016). Their 2016 promotional video depicts mountains, forests, cultivated fields and a group of horses, but no people, which is a metaphor for the acute depopulation affecting the Spanish countryside. Today, 70% of Spain's territory hosts only 10% of its total population (Recaño 2017). Yet, depopulated Spain holds a notable electoral sway due to existing electoral regulations (Jones 2019). Of Spain's 52 provinces, the 26 less populated ones (mostly in central, inland regions) contain 20% of the country's population but yield 29% of MPs in parliament (Gil Grande 2019).

Such an over-representation, combined with the little attention that Podemos paid to it, helps explain Vox's electoral focus on the 'empty' Spain. The party articulated a discourse in defence of 'the rural world and its traditions', which put emphasis on practices – such as hunting and bullfighting – that were allegedly under threat due to the attacks of urban progressives, animal-rights activists, separatists and 'radical environmentalists' (Fernández 2019a). Armed with this discourse, Vox initiated an organisational campaign aimed to tap into rural feelings of abandonment and to gain presence in the rural world. It reached out to well-established rural conservative organisations (among others, the agrarian union ASAJA and the Hunting Federation) and mobilised key personal connections (e.g. the president of the Hunting Federation successfully ran as an MP candidate for Vox in Guadalajara province).

Through these organisations Vox tried to infiltrate and hold sway of Alianza Rural (Rural Alliance) – a non-partisan umbrella platform that includes more than a hundred organisations aimed at environmental protection, sustainability and biodiversity. In March 2019,

---

[11] This video can be watched here: https://www.youtube.com/watch?v=RaSIX4-RPAI

Alianza Rural organised a large demonstration to demand governmental help for depopulated rural areas. Vox tried to turn this grassroots demonstration into a massive anti-government protest. Vox's intrusion was neutralised, and the demonstration was supported by all major parties (Fernández 2019b). A few weeks later, a larger demonstration under the slogan 'The Revolt of the Emptied Spain' was organised by a different array of organisations, with a stronger presence of progressive groups. Framed as a rallying cry against depopulation, the motto's use of the adjective 'emptied' (*vaciada*) instead of 'empty' signals a rather successful effort to articulate a different kind of response and multi-class alliance: Spain's countryside is not empty, rather, it became emptied after years of governmental neglect and cultural mainstream stigmatisation. The demonstrators argued that rural Spain did not need more hunting and more traditions, but better welfare services and realistic economic development plans. This reformulation counteracted Vox's emotional politics and made room for a centre-left articulation of populism in rural Spain.

Vox has gained notable popularity in the Spanish countryside – especially in Castilian-speaking regions, where right-wing populism tends to be strongest (Vampa 2020). This shows that the party has been able to capitalise on the feelings of abandonment and frustration produced by decades of depopulation, impoverishment and agricultural decline. Yet rural, emptied Spain is not Vox's stronghold: the monthly opinion polls published by the Centro de Investigaciones Sociológicas suggest no significant correlation between support for Vox and the size of respondent's settlement[12] (CIS 2020). Vox is most successful in two types of areas: upper and upper-middle class urban neighbourhoods, especially around Madrid, and historically right-leaning, poor rural areas with a strong presence of agri-business and agrarian labourers of migrant origin, such as in the peninsular Southeast (Reche 2019). Meanwhile, the party obtained rather modest results in rural areas dominated by family farming (Fernández 2019b), especially in non-Castilian-speaking rural Spain, where the party's extreme nationalism is the prime reason for its marginal electoral results in those regions (Balearic Islands, Basque Country, Catalonia, Galicia and Navarre, with the relative exception of the Valencian Country).

Although Vox has made important inroads both in urban and rural areas of central and southern Spain, it has largely failed to conquer *emptied* Spain. This failure is illustrated by the success of Teruel Existe (TE) in the November 2019 election in the small province of Teruel (Aragon region in eastern Spain). TE is a citizen platform created in 1999 to defend the interests of rural, depopulated Teruel. After playing a key role in orchestrating the shift from *empty* to *emptied* Spain, this platform decided to run in the November general election. TE won the election in Teruel with 26% of the vote, obtaining one MP. This victory shows that although authoritarian populist discourses have certainly gained strength, they have not become hegemonic in rural Spain, and that if progressive forces are able to create alternative left-leaning populist projects they are likely to succeed (Cortes-Vazquez 2020).

3.3. Brexit and politics of the rural

Although Brexit is not universally acknowledged to be a right-wing populist moment, public debate around it has been cast in recognisably populist terms that pit those

---

[12]Yet there is a higher-than-average support among those who work in the agrarian sector.

representing 'the will of the people' against an out of touch 'metropolitan elite' (Glaser 2016). Brexit was initially interpreted as a working-class revolt against the ravages of neo-liberal globalisation and post-industrial decline (Goodwin and Heath 2016). However, evidence shows that support for it came from a cross-class constituency of predominantly middle-aged and older white citizens (Dorling 2016). Slogans like 'take back control' and 'I want my country back' conveyed a desire of this constituency to return to an idealised past shaped by nostalgia for imperial power abroad and racial and cultural homogeneity at home (Virdee and McGeever 2018).

As in the case of Spain, images of rurality played an important role in the Brexit mobilisation, but in a way that cannot be reduced to geographical distribution of votes (Brooks 2019). Brexit support was significant among the English, and especially those identifying as English rather than British (Virdee and McGeever 2018). While the populations of England and Wales[13] voted for Brexit; Scotland and Northern Ireland delivered pro-remain majorities (Electoral Commission 2016). In a UK-wide referendum, however, these variations were ironed out by the votes of the 84% of the population residing in England. This reflected a characteristic of English nationalism, which, in contrast to other UK nationalisms, has historically aligned with Euroscepticism. This antipathy towards the EU merges with a nostalgia for Empire that conflates British with English identity: an identity anchored in rural landscapes as 'the ethnic homelands of the English' (Reed 2016, 228). The Eurosceptic UK Independence Party (UKIP) found a way to mobilise this Great Britain/Little England identity and, thereby, transformed the national political landscape.

The UK has a two party 'first-past-the-post'[14] system that has long been believed to mitigate against the rise of political extremes. Over the last century, power has alternated between the centre-right Conservative (Tory) Party and centre-left Labour Party within a relatively stable system. Divisions regarding EU membership surfaced, at times, within both parties, but these remained, for the most part, intra-party conflicts. This changed dramatically when UKIP transformed itself from a single-issue party formed to oppose the Maastricht treaty into a political force able to mobilise a broader set of 'feelings and experiences' of 'particular groups, especially older, white, English men' – who at the time felt alienated by a modernising Conservative Party's turn to social liberalism (Wellings and Baxendale 2015, 228).

UKIP reframed anti-EU politics in terms of ill-defined but emotive issues like immigration and 'political correctness', drawing on a seam of traditional conservatism that Stuart Hall has called 'organic patriotic Toryism' (Tournier-Sol 2015). In doing so, they made EU membership a wedge issue that opened divisions not only in the ruling Conservative Party, but also within the wider population. UKIP thus came to present an existential threat to the Conservative Party that its leader, David Cameron, concluded could only be neutralised by allowing the in/out referendum that was their *raison d'etre* (Tournier-Sol 2015).

UKIP's 'winning formula' blended Conservative traditions and dormant Euroscepticism with populism that tapped into contemporary political currents, particularly in the

---

[13]The referendum result in Wales was tipped towards support for Brexit by the votes of resident English retirees (Dorling 2016).
[14]'First-past-the-post' is the form of plurality/majority system which uses single member districts and candidate-centred voting.

countryside (Tournier-Sol 2015). UKIP's rural politics were more concerned with the rhetorical defence of traditional landscapes, punctuated by village pubs and hunting parties (and despoiled by wind turbines), than with tackling the material hardships faced by rural communities that had been exacerbated by austerity policies (Brooks 2019). This articulation of a 'politics of the rural' – focused less on substantive rural concerns than on contesting what constitutes 'the rural' (Woods 2005) – was prefigured by a rural protest movement that had occurred two decades earlier.

The 1990s were an uncertain time for rural areas, characterised by deagrarianisation, counter-urbanisation and gentrification. While elsewhere in Europe such conditions might have produced a left-wing agrarian populist response; in rural England a hegemonic 'conservative discourse of rurality' (Woods 2005) maintained its grip. This discourse emphasised the importance of maintaining the social order, and the countryside's historical role as repository of the 'national spirit and character' (Woods 2005).

In the 1997 election, the Labour Party (led by Tony Blair) won a landslide victory that extended, for the first time, into Tory rural heartlands, enabling it to enact its own distinct rural policy platform. The scale of their defeat was traumatic for the Conservative Party, which 'found itself with fewer MPs than at any time since 1906' (Ward 2002, 172). The loss was keenly felt by rural elites, who faced a 'crisis of representation' as the party vehicle through which their interests were traditionally secured entered the political wilderness (Ward 2002). The intention of the Labour government to introduce a hunting ban acted as a lightning rod for a very English protest. A rapidly assembled 'Countryside Alliance' framed the mobilisation as a defence of a rural 'way of life' under threat from an 'amorphous un-English, un-British urbanity' (Woods 2005, 114–115). A series of London protests culminated in a 'Liberty and Livelihood March' in 2002, attended by 400,000 people. However, livelihood issues raised by rural working-class participants (not all of whom were there voluntarily) were side-lined by a movement animated to defend a timeless 'natural order' that the traditional hunting party symbolised (Woods 2005).

The Countryside Alliance played an important role in the rehabilitation of the political right. For former Conservative Party officials and MPs, the Alliance provided a refuge from the post-1997 political wilderness in which they found themselves, and a platform from which to begin the long road to political recovery (Ward 2002). However, by 2005, and three lost elections later, the new party leader David Cameron followed calls to cast off the 'nasty party' image (White and Perkins 2002) and steer the Conservatives in a more socially liberal direction. This resulted in the party's electoral success in 2010, albeit in coalition with the Liberal Democrats. In the meantime, Cameron continued to make concessions to the party's Eurosceptic wing that did little to prevent them from becoming increasingly emboldened by – and fearful of – the rising popularity of UKIP (Bale 2016; Tournier-Sol 2015).

In January 2020, the UK exited the EU and began a one-year transition period during which new arrangements for cooperation with the EU would be negotiated. In 3.5 years since the referendum, the ruling Conservative Party had weathered two snap elections, two changes of leader, and a series of parliamentary and legal challenges, culminating in the wholesale capture of the pro-Brexit vote with the slogan 'Get Brexit Done' (Perrigo 2019). The Conservative Party had – again – transformed itself; this time into the voice of Anglo-British nationalism, marginalising smaller pro-Brexit parties like UKIP and the Brexit Party.

The rural economy now faces new challenges with the loss of migrant labour in the horticulture industry, particularly in Lincolnshire constituencies where the highest Leave votes were polled (Kaufmann 2016). Meanwhile, concerns are rising among farmers' representatives and some rural Conservative MPs that agriculture, especially family farms, will be sacrificed in trade negotiations that prioritise continuity for the prized financial sector above all else (Lang 2020). These challenges have intensified in the context of the Covid-19 pandemic. Labour shortages have been exacerbated by the lockdown as a yet more severe brake on freedom of movement, for which attempts to mobilise wartime spirit with a call for a 'land army' have failed to compensate, leading producers to charter planes to fly in workers from Romania at the risk of accelerating the spread of the pandemic (Pencheva 2020).

3.4. The role of land sales in populist mobilisation in Ukraine

Land issues have long been of critical concern in Ukrainian society. Historically, the fertile arable land – known as *cheronozem* – played an important role in the Ukrainian national identity and nationalist mobilisation against foreign colonisation (Shulman 1999). Today, the land question is the key political and ideological question in Ukraine, as the country has been struggling to forge an independent path, torn between Europe and Russia (Mamonova 2018). The current government's plan to lift the moratorium on farmland sales – which has been in place for 16 years – has brought into play various populist and nationalist forces and triggered societal unrest across the country.

Since Ukraine gained independence from the Soviet Union in 1991, its government launched a land reform aimed to distribute the former collective lands to the rural population for private farming. The land reform was never completed and the moratorium on farmland sales was implemented to prevent land concentration. Nevertheless, large multinational corporations and domestic oligarchs were able to accumulate vast areas of land, primarily by leasing land parcels from impoverished rural populations (Mamonova 2015). Thereby, Ukraine followed the path of other post-Soviet countries, such as Russia and Kazakhstan, where large agribusiness controls the most land, while rural populations conduct subsistence (peasant-like) farming on their tiny household plots (Visser and Spoor 2011).

The 2014 Euromaidan revolution aimed to break up with the Soviet past and step on the way of a 'bright' European future (Ryabchuk 2014). Most rural Ukrainians believed that the Association Agreement with the EU and consequent Eurointegration of Ukraine would bring prosperity and justice to the countryside. Mamonova (2018) observed transformation in popular attitudes towards small-scale farming as a result of the pro-European shift in the country's politics. Previously, subsistence farming was seen as a backward relic of the socialist past that is doomed to disappear in the nearest future. After Euromaidan, it became viewed as sustainable food production similar to organic and eco-farming in Europe (Mamonova 2018).

While striving for European norms and values, Ukrainians did not foresee that the Association Agreement would imply the abolition of the moratorium on land sales. The upcoming opening of the land market has triggered various fears in the Ukrainian society. According to the USAID public opinion poll, people were afraid that the open land market would lead to massive land purchases by foreigners (51%), excessive concentration of land (39%), and destruction of the Ukrainian villages (33%) (Yaremko, Lukomska, and Nizalov 2017). Consequently, most people (68.9%) believe that the land reform should be submitted to a nationwide referendum and 72.0% of those would vote in favour of extending the moratorium (Razumkov Centre 2020).

The societal resentment against the abolition of the moratorium gave a wide base of support for farmers' protests, organised by agrarian and farmers' unions in 2019. Farmers condemned the land market opening conditions and prophesied massive land grabs. Protests intensified in November 2019, when the Verkhovna Rada (Ukrainian Parliament) was discussing the land reform. Populist political parties wholeheartedly joined the protests and tried to exploit the discontent for electoral gains. The variety of politicians who supported the protests depict the diversity of Ukrainian opposition. There were representatives of the far-right 'National Corps' (Natscorpus) party, the pro-European conservative-nationalist party 'Fatherland' (Batkivshchina), the pro-Russian Eurosceptic 'Opposition Platform – For Life' (OP Za zhyttya), the extreme nationalist party 'Freedom' (Svoboda), and even the outlawed Communist Party of Ukraine (KPU).

However, while criticising the land reform, Ukrainian populists do not clearly formulate their own agrarian reform programmes (see the analysis of AgroPolit [2019]). Instead, they stir up fears and make use of societal misunderstanding of the moratorium. In their political campaigns, populists use highly emotional slogans such as 'don't sell the fatherhood' or 'halt the theft of land!' warning for 'a huge civil war by the agrarian mafia against farmers' (see Kuzio's [2018] analysis of the party Batkivshchina's discourse). Some activists even brought a coffin with a pig corpse and funeral wreath flowers in front of the Verkhovna Rada to symbolise the approaching collapse of Ukrainian agriculture (Balachuk 2019).

Yaremko et al. (2016) studied paradoxes concerning the land market in Ukraine. They revealed that 'although almost 2/3 of the citizens protest against the abolition of the moratorium on the sale of agricultural land, almost half of them would like to have a possibility to sell their land'. This societal misunderstanding of the moratorium is the result of the fact that only 6% of respondents study legislation on their own or read analytical reviews. The overwhelming majority of the population form their opinion based on contradictory information received from politically-biased mass media (Yaremko, Lukomska, and Nizalov 2017).

Ukrainian oligarchs play an important role in sponsoring political parties and influencing political decisions, and their influence is particularly evident in land matters (Pleines 2016). How Ukraine solves its land question will largely determine the country's development path and, therefore, the future of the Ukrainian oligarchy. For example, oligarch Igor Kolomoisky supported the current president Vladimir Zelensky in his presidential campaign. Later, Kolomoisky changed his position, when Zelensky reconsidered returning PrivatBank to Kolomoisky following the pressures from the IMF and the EU (PrivatBank was nationalised in 2016 due to banking fraud and corruption). Currently, Kolomoisky has switched to pro-Russian rhetoric and tries to sabotage Ukraine's cooperation with the IMF, particularly regarding the land reform (Troianovski 2019). He became an informal sponsor of the All-Ukrainian Agrarian Council that organised the mass farmers' protests in November 2019 (Pirozhok and Denkov 2019).

The conditions of the moratorium abolition were also criticised by left-wing progressive rural movements – such as Ukrainian Rural Development Network. Yet, they are concerned about peasant rights and the future of small-scale farming, which could be jeopardised by the land market liberalisation. While not inherently opposing the moratorium abolition, these groups aim to reformulate the moratorium-related discourse by substituting the 'accent on the peasants' right to sell their land plots, [with] the accent on the peasants' land ownership as the means to provide decent existence for themselves and their families' (URDN 2019).

On 31 March 2020, when gatherings were forbidden amid the Covid-19 lockdown, the Verkhovna Rada adopted amendments to the Land Code that would lift the moratorium on farmland sales from 1 July 2021. To prevent land concentration, the amount of land in one's hands is limited to 100 hectares during the transition period until 2024, and after – to 10 000 hectares. Land ownership for foreigners will be allowed only after a referendum (gov.ua 2020). However, not everyone is satisfied with these amendments and protests will most likely resume when the quarantine restrictions are lifted.

4. Discussion

The four cases presented above provide insights into multifaceted, historically conditioned and context-specific manifestations of nationalist politics. Below, we discuss several distinctive and common features that could help to elaborate an account of 'actually existing' right-wing populism. As we briefly point out throughout our discussion, all of these features connect with classic and contemporary themes of critical agrarian studies and its effort to understand how 'agrarian life and livelihoods shape and are shaped by the politics, economics and social worlds of modernity' (Edelman and Wolford 2017, 960).

4.1. Territorial dimension of right-wing selective memory

Our study confirms that orientation towards an idealised past is one of the defining features of far-right populism (Mamonova and Franquesa 2020a). The four analysed cases reveal that the right-wing memory of the past has a selective nature: populists tend to highlight some facts while forgetting inconvenient others. Indeed, if nations are imagined communities (Anderson 1991), the images that are selected to build this imagination must be critically analysed. In Spain and the UK, populists have reached for imagery that links rurality with ideas of the true nation 'not yet corrupted' by 'foreign' influences. In both cases, the images interweaving rurality and nationhood conjure nostalgia for an imperial past, which in Spain becomes most obvious through reference to the Reconquista. In the UK, they recall the ties that once bound colonial era administrators, settlers and servicemen alike to idealised images of 'home' where timeless rural traditions were upheld by a 'natural' social order.

In Ukraine, the relationship with the past is just as pertinent but the formulation is a very different one. In contrast with the UK, in which a break with the EU is seen as a way to reconnect with the past, for most Ukrainians their country's accession to Europe is a means to break with the Soviet past and 'return to normality' – the metaphor which captures the transformation embarked on in Central and Eastern Europe, including the Baltic states (Wolczuk 2001). However, far from a clear break, the Ukrainian 'return to normality' has opened up the Pandora's Box of land politics which has lain at the heart of the country's politics since 1991. In eastern Germany, the socialist past experiences and the post-1990 transformation carved nationalist manifestations in another way. There, the 'return to normality' through German reunification has resulted in socio-spatial polarisation and persistent inequalities between eastern and western states, which triggered the feelings of being 'second class citizens' among many eastern Germans. The image of 'dying villages' of eastern Germany is being used by right-wing nationalists as an ideological symbol and as target areas for infiltration. Again, there is a historical precedent for Völkische Siedler settlers who style themselves according to the 'blood and soil' ruralism of the Artemans movement in the Nazi era.

In the four cases analysed we observe that the memories being selected and idealised are part of the changing articulation between country and city. As Raymond Williams (1973) argued, this articulation has as much to do with material transformations as with the ways in which the relationship between country and city is constantly reimagined to serve political agendas, often structured around allegedly neutral definitions of 'modernity', 'development' or the 'nation' (Baka 2017). Because of its historical and constructed character, selective memory is bound to be the object of contention and competing forms of manipulation. This can be appreciated by observing that in all our cases rightwing selective memory has a territorial dimension. In the UK and Spain, we see a story of multiple nationalisms: from the secessionist movements of Catalonia and Scotland that gravitate towards progressive politics, to nationalisms attached to imperial identities that identify with the political right. Popular mobilisation for Brexit tapped into a suppressed English nationalism that mourned its loss of power and status, globally, through decolonisation, and internally, with the creation of devolved assemblies in other UK nations. This nationalism draws on a sense of Englishness rooted in an imagery of pastoral landscapes characteristic of more wealthy rural areas of southern counties of England, an association consciously cultivated by government propaganda in the early twentieth century (Matless 2016). Similarly, the 'immortal nation' called forth by Vox is quintessentially Castilian, identified with the political right at least since the Francoist dictatorship. This helps explain why the nostalgic allure of España vacía has worked its magic at a distance, with populations in affluent districts close to Madrid, and in rural areas dominated by agribusiness that employ migrant labour. What these areas of Vox support have in common is a history of support for right-wing politics in which this kind of imagery has proved resonant in the past. Displacements such as this show how nostalgic rural imagery anchored in specific locations can have as much, or in this case even more salience among populations located far from the region that has animated this type of populist politics.

The territorial dimension of Ukraine's selective memory manifests itself in two kinds of nationalism: 'liberationist and pro-European patriotism' in western Ukraine and the separatist mobilisation in eastern Ukraine that is nationalistically inclined toward Russia (Mamonova 2018). The ongoing land reform is highly important in highlighting this division: the country's development path will largely depend on how Ukraine answers its land question. Ukrainian populists, both 'pro-Western' and 'pro-Russian', exploit societal fears of a resurgence of land grabbing following the anticipated lifting of the land moratorium. Yet, our analysis shows that the parties themselves are instrumentalised by oligarchs more interested in jostling for power than resolving the land question. In Germany, the east–west divide defines the character and intensity of nationalist mobilisation (eastern German society is more tolerant towards everyday expressions of authoritarian and nationalistic attitudes than the western German population). Besides that, the territorial division highlights the longstanding politico-cultural lines of conflict in Germany: between the cosmopolitan Western regions and conservative areas in the interior of the country, between the industrial North and the agricultural South, and, generally, between urban and rural regions (Vorländer, Herold, and Schäller 2018).

4.2. The problem with democracy

Our four cases highlighted several shortcomings in the system of representative democracy, both in terms of specific characteristics of electoral systems and societal perceptions of the ideas of liberal (market-oriented) democracy. In Spain, the electoral system is key to understanding some paradoxical features pervading the political institutional representation of the countryside. Thus, whereas the electoral law privileges lowly populated (i.e. rural) provinces, the high percentage of vote (around 20%) required to obtain representation promotes the 'useful vote' to established parties, thus discouraging electoral competition and new entrants. This helps explain why rural and agrarian concerns are underrepresented in political and electoral debates even when the rural vote is overrepresented. On the other hand, the phenomenon of the useful vote places limits on the capacity of the electoral system to represent rural politics, for whereas political representation tends to be very stable, underlying political currents are much more volatile. Thus, if at some point there is a switch in political representation, with Vox or another right-wing populist party obtaining high voting percentages, this situation is likely to perpetuate in time. This underlying volatility can also be observed in the case of eastern Germany, where philo-Nazi settlers have taken advantage of the emptying of the countryside to achieve positions of municipal power, a circumstance that suggests the importance of considering local-level electoral politics to understand the (quiet) rise of right-wing populism.

The paradox of political representation discussed for the Spanish case is clearly at play in the UK case. The UK's two-party system has traditionally been regarded as inherently discouraging of political extremes as it rewards parties able to build broad national appeal. 'No party, it was argued, could simply give up on half the electorate' (Drutman 2018). These assurances have unravelled in recent years with the rise of 'wedge politics', that is the use of emotional (wedge) issues to divide the electorate into two opposing sides. However, the electoral power of these divisive, emotional issues could only come into full force once they were played in electoral contests, such as referendums, that circumvent the established system of representation. This is perfectly illustrated in the redrawing of the country's political map in terms of 'Remain' and 'Leave' areas, a shift all the more remarkable given that the question of EU membership was previously a niche concern (Wellings and Baxendale 2015). The unexpected surge in popularity of the 'Leave' cause, sufficient to tip the result towards a narrow Leave majority, came particularly from citizens holding socially conservative and/or authoritarian values (Norris and Inglehart 2019). As such, this reflected a previously unremarked geographical redistribution of political power from urban centres to rural areas and small towns whose voters were distributed across the electoral system 'more efficiently' (Beckett 2016).

In post-socialist European countries, systemic transformations were associated with the democratisation process, including the establishment and consolidation of democratic political institutions. As shown in the eastern Germany case, democracy is recognised by many as a desired form of governance, yet it is still experienced as 'foreign', 'borrowed from the West'. This (mis)impression grounded the societal support for national variations of democracies 'with adjectives', such as illiberal democracy in Hungary or sovereign democracy in Russia (see Mamonova [2019]). The illiberal turn in Eastern European political development is not surprising. According to Humphrey (2002, 12), the ongoing capitalist development in post-socialist countries is not unidirectional: 'there is rather an unpredictable propensity to "turn back", or at least resolute refusal to abandon values and expectations associated with socialism'.

The Eastern European 'reverse wave' of democratic breakdowns is also related to the ways of how democracy is operationalised within the European Union. Klumbyte (2011) argued that rising nationalism in Central and Eastern Europe is embedded in the power politics of Europeanization. The post-socialist European countries are typically portrayed as 'less advanced […] and imaginary provinces of the EU' and that their political and economic interests are often sacrificed in favour of Western Europe (Klumbyte 2011, 869). The unequal distribution of power, authority, and privilege within the EU results in societal reassertions of national superiority and its newly rediscovered 'Easternness'. In Ukraine, however, the politics of national redefinition are related to the country's association with the EU. Yet, the recently ratified EU-Ukraine Association Agreement requires liberalisation of the Ukrainian land market, which, in turn, triggered societal fears about foreigners buying up the 'fertile arable land' that is an intrinsic part of Ukrainian national identity.

The problem of the political representation of rural dwellers – codified in Marx's infamous reference to the 'sack of potatoes' – is one of the central concerns of some of the foundational references of critical agrarian studies, such as Wolf (1969) and Moore (1966). The distance towards the capitalist, state and seigneurial powers to which the peasantry has been historically subordinated is experienced both as a curse and an aspiration: 'The peasant utopia is the free village, untrammelled by tax collectors, labour recruiters, large landowners, officials. Ruled over, but never ruling, they also lack acquaintance with the operation of the state as a complex machinery, experiencing it only as a "cold monster"' (Wolf 1969, 294). Our cases suggest that rural areas and groups have historically developed particular political dynamics and cultures that democratic mechanisms of representation are seldom able and often unwilling to acknowledge, and in so doing they open the door for the siren songs of right-wing populists promising direct representation and the righting of historical wrongs through a strong leadership.

4.3. Inequalities and politics of emotion

European rural dwellers tend to suffer from three interconnected forms of inequality, which we may call economic, social, and cultural. Cultural inequality is expressed in the mainstream rejection of some of the practices and values that rural populations hold (local traditions, hunting, etc.), but also with the stigma of backwardness (often coupled with that of apoliticism) associated with rural living, peasant identities, and farming livelihoods. These stereotypes have a material base in the other two forms of inequality: economic inequality (i.e. the progressive impoverishment of the European countryside) and social inequality (the fact that basic social infrastructure – such as hospitals, schools, communications and transport – is crumbling or simply lacking). These inequalities are inseparable of the growing feeling among the rural population of being abandoned and disrespected, leading to resentment and shame. Right-wing politicians have shrewdly oriented this powerful emotional reservoir towards their own exclusionary agenda, as indicated in the cases of eastern Germany and, to a lesser extent, Spain.

The highlighted inequalities intertwine with anxieties over how the future may unfold. Fear of the future is most acutely felt by groups that anticipate precarisation. It is the threat, more than the actuality, of declassement, or loss of social and material status, that induces feelings of shame and resentment. In this regard, nostalgia is rather a restorative discourse, through which an individual reclaims one's own dignity and respect (Klumbytė 2009). As noted in the UK example, this is often gendered. Even though men are at a greater advantage overall in the labour market, they feel more threatened as their advantages are linked to the currently receding jobs, while new jobs have been in service industries where they do not enjoy the same advantage relative to women (Salmela and von Scheve 2017).

As evident from our study, right-wing politicians capitalise on the nostalgia for the past. They often utilise false notions of a common European – or in the case of the UK, exceptionalist Anglo-British – history and Christian heritage to justify their xenophobic, anti-immigration, anti-globalisation, and monoculturalist political attitudes. Such politics of emotion manifest themselves in Vox's motto to 'Make Spain Great Again' and the Brexit slogan 'Take back control'. Right-wing politicians often blame Muslim minorities and refugees for stripping prosperity, job opportunities, and public services from local people. However, as the case study of eastern Germany demonstrates, resentments towards Islam and Islamisation are not central motivations for right-wing supporters. On the contrary, Dresden protesters joined the far-right PEGIDA movement not because but despite its anti-Islam agenda. Thus, we argue that socio-economic inequalities are the fundamental driving force in defining political cleavages and conflicts in rural Europe today.

The emotional appeals drawing on rural imagery can have a broader appeal where such imagery is evocative of a national identity. Particularly where this identity is based on a notion of nationhood that is somehow under threat. This is evident in Ukraine, where populists use emotional appeals like 'don't sell the fatherhood' and forecast a decay of Ukrainian villages and, by extension, the Ukrainian nation if the moratorium on land sales is lifted. In the UK case, UKIP's politicisation of traditional rural landscapes perceived as under threat from 'politically-correct' environmentalists was prefigured by the reactionary rural movement spearheaded by the Countryside Alliance in the late 1990s and early 2000s, which saw itself as an emotional response to a left of centre government claiming legitimacy to legislate on matters affecting ways of life in the countryside (Woods 2010).

The connection between inequality and emotion allows many classical themes of agrarian studies to be reconsidered. How rural residents cope with and make sense of the changes within their communities influence their self-definitions, perspectives on rural life, and previously taken-for-granted notions of gender, racial-ethnic, and class relations (Naples 1994). Although the themes of gender, class and ethnicity have only been briefly touched upon in this paper, our research highlights the need to understand how inequality and politics of emotions translate into distinct political affects that can be mobilised in multiple and contradictory directions.

4.4. The role of 'Emptiness'

The phenomenon of 'emptiness' found across rural Europe is a concrete historical formation that has arisen as a result of neoliberal policies that draw capital away from regions with a low rate of profit. It has been particularly severe in countries where socialist modernity has been replaced by a capitalist modernity that has failed to live up to its promises (Dzenovska 2020). In the eastern Germany case, for example, initial speculative activity soon waned and regions like rural Saxony came to resemble a 'socio-economic vacuum'. Its inhabitants' sense of relative disadvantage in an otherwise wealthy country made them receptive to incoming settlers whose right-wing ideology is embedded in a homely conservatism that coheres with rural traditions and promises to bring 'dying villages' back to life. Through this rural activism that appears apolitical – embodying principles of hard work, neighbourliness, and family values – the neo-Nazi settlers are able to stifle support for progressive politics that, in contrast, appears to threaten the rehabilitation of rural traditions of which the settlers are now the defenders.

The case of Spain provides an interesting contrast with eastern Germany. Right-wing populists attempted to mobilise the apparently neutral idea of 'empty Spain', but left of centre parties were able to reframe this discourse to one that centred on a rural Spain 'emptied' by failed neoliberal policies. For Fernández (2019b) this achievement signalled that 'a new political subject entered the scene, one that situated the territorial debate in broader terms.' Furthermore, the name with which this demonstration was branded – 'The Revolt of the Emptied Spain' – makes evident that emotional politics are not the exclusive patrimony of the populist right, and that multi-class, left-leaning alliances can (perhaps should) also aim to mobilise feelings of indignation that have long been brewing in a politically-neglected countryside ravaged by depopulation and decades of neoliberal restructuring.

In the UK, the Brexit mobilisation drew on an idealised image of rurality anchored in rural areas that represent the winning side of neoliberal globalisation: gentrified landscapes within commuting distance of thriving urban centres in the South of England. While the term emptiness may not have acquired the same salience here as in Spain, these areas have increasingly been emptied of viable employment and affordable housing for the rural working class in this 'consumption countryside' (Marsden 1999). Nevertheless, as in the case of Spain, the strongest support for Brexit came from a very different rural region; one that has been transformed by an intensification of agricultural production driven by the demands of supermarket chains (Rogaly 2008). Indeed, while the rural vote for Brexit was higher than for the country as a whole (55% as opposed to 52%), the highest polls for exiting the EU (between 70 and 75%) were in constituencies in Lincolnshire (Electoral Commission 2016). With some of the best agricultural land in the country, much of the farming in this county is highly mechanised, with the exception of horticulture producers to the south of the county that rely heavily on seasonal migrant labour from other EU countries (Kaufmann 2016).

Ukrainian and eastern Germany's rural emptiness is part of the larger process of post-socialist reconfiguration of political and economic power under neoliberal capitalism. The emergence of stagnant 'dying villages' used to be discussed as a temporary side-effect – an unavoidable 'correction' on the way of 'a return to normality' and 'catching-up with the West'. Yet, as Dzenovska (2020, 11) rightly pointed out, post-socialist emptiness cannot be fixed via reintegration or catching up, it is rather a path towards a 'radically different future' in which those who live the present will have no part. The societal disappointment with the liberal politics of post-socialist transition and the elites responsible for implementing these reforms is ardently manipulated by populist political parties and nationalist movements for their political gains.

The theme of emptiness connects with processes of capitalist domination and appropriation of rural landscapes, which has been a central topic of recent research in critical agrarian studies (see, e.g. Borras et al. 2011). The production of emptiness needs to be analysed as part of capital's tendency to produce uneven development (Walker 1978; Harvey 1999): Spatial differentiation and capital mobility result in concentration of capital flows and statecraft in 'global cities', while places of low use-value for capital become the zones of 'emptiness' (Dzenovska 2020; Harvey 2014). The tendency to view rural emptiness in Eastern Europe as a by-product of 'catching up' obscures a more likely explanation; that the post-socialist transition has in fact 'propelled Eastern Europe from Europe's past to Europe's future'. Today, the region is 'ahead [of] rather than behind' the rest of Europe 'with regard to implementing radical neoliberal reforms' (Dzenovska 2018, 24).

The 'lumpen geography of capital' (Walker 1978) produces at the same time an uneven development of the surplus population – a new 'class' of 'three nothings' – no land, no work, no social security (Walker 2008; Li 2017). According to Li (2017; see also Smith 2011), these are people who find themselves 'surplus' to the needs of capital, hence highly vulnerable in a global economy organised on capitalist lines. In this context, the rise of regressive populism may be interpreted as a form of revolt of some sections of the 'surplus population' against the existing capitalist order. Thus, our cases suggest the need to analyse how processes of capitalist development and appropriation generate specific forms of political subjectivity that can either support or challenge the existing status quo.

5. Conclusion

This study depicts various manifestations of what we call 'actually existing' right-wing populism. Based on empirical insights from eastern Germany, Spain, the United Kingdom and Ukraine, we explored how xenophobic nationalist tendencies unfold in different contexts and what role agriculture and rural imageries play in this process. We demonstrate that rural communities are severely affected by the crisis of globalised neoliberal capitalism and the related crisis of representative democracies, which triggered rural resentment against the existing order. This resentment manifests itself in rural support for right-wing populist parties and in grassroots nationalist movements. We analysed various drivers of populist success, including some contextual factors (rural 'emptiness', socio-economic inequality, particularities of electoral systems, outcomes of post-socialist 'return to normality', politics of Europeanization) and citizens' perceptions of social reality (selective memory, subjective experiences of democracy, national redefinition, politics of emotions).

We conclude that the forms that right-wing populism takes vary widely, therefore, solutions to these dangerous trends should be context-specific, grounded in the social fabric and culture of the locale. We believe that top-down 'one size fits all' strategy would not be effective. The resistance and alternatives should come from below. In the examples of Spain and Ukraine, we demonstrate how progressive left-leaning rural social movements were able to contest the right-wing narratives and stream them in more progressive directions.

Acknowledgements

The authors would like to thank Dr. Olena Borodina and Dr. Andrii Martyn for their valuable insights on the contemporary developments in Ukraine. We thank Dr. Ramona Bunkus, Prof. Dr. Insa Theesfeld and Dr Bernhard Forchtner for sharing their opinions and recent literature on the far-right movements in eastern Germany. We would also like to thank Fernando Fernández, Paul Nicholson, Pep Riera and the team of Soberanía Alimentaria for sharing their views on political developments in Spain. We are also grateful to the Journal's chief editor Prof. Jun Borras and other colleagues from the Emancipatory Rural Politics Initiative (ERPI) for initiating the Forum on 'Authoritarian populism and the rural world', of which this paper is a part.

Data availability statement

Data sharing is not applicable to this article as no new data were created or analysed in this study.

Disclosure statement

No potential conflict of interest was reported by the author(s).

ORCID

Natalia Mamonova http://orcid.org/0000-0001-6618-877X
Jaume Franquesa http://orcid.org/0000-0001-8416-2792
Sally Brooks http://orcid.org/0000-0002-1005-1245

References

AgroPolit. 2019. "The 2019 Parliamentary Election: An Analysis of the Agrarian Programmes of 22 Political Parties." https://agropolit.com/spetsproekty/580-parlamentski-vibori-2019-analiz-agrarnoyi-chastini-politichnih-program-22-partiy.
Anderson, B. 1991. *Imagined Communities: Reflections on the Origin and Spread of Nationalism*. London: Verso.
Baka, J. 2017. "Making Space for Energy: Wasteland Development, Enclosures, and Energy Dispossessions." *Antipode* 49 (4): 977–996.
Balachuk, I. 2019. "They Brought a Coffin with a Corpse of a Pig and Wreaths in front of the Verkhovna Rada." https://www.pravda.com.ua/news/2019/11/13/7231819/.
Bale, T. 2016. "'Banging on About Europe': How the Eurosceptics Got their Referendum." https://blogs.lse.ac.uk/politicsandpolicy/banging-on-about-europe-how-the-eurosceptics-got-their-referendum/.
Beckett, A. 2016. "From Trump to Brexit, Power Has Leaked from Cities to the Countryside." https://www.theguardian.com/commentisfree/2016/dec/12/trump-brexit-cities-countryside-rural-voters.

BMWi (Bundesministerium für Wirtschaft und Energie). 2019. "Annual Report of the Federal Government on the Status of German Unity." https://www.bmwi.de/Redaktion/EN/Publikationen/annual-report-of-the-federal-government-on-the-status-of-german-unity.pdf?__blob=publicationFile&v=4.

Boin, A., M. Ekengren, and M. Rhinard. 2020. "Hiding in Plain Sight: Conceptualizing the Creeping Crisis." *Risk. Hazards and Crisis in Public Policy.* doi:10.1002/rhc3.12193.

Borras Jr, S. M. 2020. "Agrarian Social Movements: The Absurdly Difficult but not Impossible Agenda of Defeating Right-Wing Populism and Exploring a Socialist Future." *Journal of Agrarian Change* 20 (3): 3–36.

Borras Jr, Saturnino M., R. Hall, I. Scoones, B. White, and W. Wolford. 2011. "Towards a Better Understanding of Global Land Grabbing: an Editorial Introduction." *The Journal of Peasant Studies* 38 (2): 209–216.

Brenner, N., and N. Theodore. 2002. "Cities and the Geographies of 'Actually Existing Neoliberalism'." *Antipode* 34 (3): 349–379.

Brooks, S. 2019. "Brexit and the Politics of the Rural." *Sociologia Ruralis.* doi:10.1111/soru.12281.

Bunkus, R., I. Soliev, and I. Theesfeld. 2020. "Density of Resident Farmers and Rural Inhabitants' Relationship to Agriculture: Operationalizing Complex Social Interactions with a Structural Equation Model." *Agriculture and Human Values* 37 (1): 47–63.

Bunkus, R., and I. Theesfeld. 2018. "Land Grabbing in Europe? Socio-Cultural Externalities of Large-Scale Land Acquisitions in East Germany." *Land* 7 (3): 98. doi:10.3390/land7030098.

Chatalova, L. and A. Wolz. 2019. Die Probleme der Anderen: Sind Landwirte für den ländlichen Raum zuständig? Berichte über Landwirtschaft-Zeitschrift für Agrarpolitik und Landwirtschaft. doi:10.12767/buel.v97i2.227.

CIS (Centro de Investigaciones Sociológicas). 2020. Barómetro Resultados. http://www.cis.es/cis/opencm/CA/11_barometros/depositados.js.

Cortes-Vazquez, J. A. 2020. "In the Name of the People: The Populist Redefinition of Nature Conservation in Post-Crisis Spain." *Geoforum; Journal of Physical, Human, and Regional Geosciences* 108: 110–118.

Cramer, K. J. 2016. *The Politics of Resentment: Rural Consciousness in Wisconsin and the Rise of Scott Walker.* Chicago, IL: University of Chicago Press.

Del Arco, M. Á. 2005. *Las Alas del Ave Fénix: La Política Agraria del Primer Franquismo (1936-1959).* Granada: Comares.

Del Molino, S. 2016. *La España Vacía. Viaje por un País que Nunca Fue.* Madrid: Turner.

Dorling, D. 2016. "Brexit: The Decision of a Divided Country." *British Medical Journal* 354. doi:http://doi.org/10.1136/bmj.i3697.

Drutman, L. 2018. "Why America's 2-Party System is on a Collision Course with our Constitutional Democracy." https://www.vox.com/polyarchy/2018/3/26/17163960/america-two-party-system-constitutional-democracy.

Dzenovska, D. 2018. "Emptiness and its Futures." *Focaal* 2018 (80): 16–29.

Dzenovska, D. 2020. "Emptiness: Capitalism Without People in the Latvian Countryside." *America Ethnologist* 47 (1): 10–26.

Edelman, M., and W. Wolford. 2017. "Introduction: Critical Agrarian Studies in Theory and Practice." *Antipode* 49 (4): 959–976.

Electoral Commission. 2016. "Results and Turnout at the EU Referendum." https://www.electoralcommission.org.uk/who-we-are-and-what-we-do/elections-and-referendums/past-elections-and-referendums/eu-referendum/results-and-turnout-eu-referendum.

ESPON (European Spatial Planning Observation Network). 2020. "Shrinking Rural Regions in Europe. Towards Smart and Innovative Approaches to Regional Development Challenges in Depopulating Rural Regions." https://www.espon.eu/sites/default/files/attachments/ESPON%20Policy%20Brief%20on%20Shrinking%20Rural%20Regions.pdf.

European Commission for Agriculture and Rural Development. 2018. "Annual Activity Report 2018 - Agriculture and Rural Development." https://ec.europa.eu/info/publications/annual-activity-report-2018-agriculture-and-rural-development_en.

Eurostat. 2020. "Farmers and the Agricultural Labour Force. Statistics." https://ec.europa.eu/eurostat/statistics-explained/index.php/Farmers_and_the_agricultural_labour_force_-_statistics#Fewer_farms.2C_fewer_farmers.

Fernández, F. 2019a. Cómo Frenar el Avance de la Ultraderecha en el Medio Rural. http://eldiariorural.es/como-frenar-el-avance-de-la-ultraderecha-en-el-medio-rural/.

Fernández, F. 2019b. La Ultraderecha Penetró en el Mundo Rural, Pero Hemos Logrado Frenar su Avance. https://fernandofernandezsuch.wordpress.com/2019/06/09/la-ultraderecha-penetro-en-el-mundo-rural-pero-hemos-logrado-frenar-su-avance/.

Foote, N. 2020. "Open-air markets ban: Another blow to struggling small farmers." https://www.euractiv.com/section/agriculture-food/news/open-air-markets-ban-another-blow-to-struggling-small-farmers/.

Franquesa, J. 2018. *Power Struggles: Dignity, Value, and the Renewable Energy Frontier in Spain*. Bloomington: Indiana University Press.

Franquesa, J. 2019. "The Vanishing Exception: Republican and Reactionary Specters of Populism in Rural Spain." *Journal of Peasant Studies* 46 (3): 537–560.

Gallar, D., and I. Vara. 2010. "Desagrarización Cultural, Agricultura Urbana y Resistencias Para la Sustentabilidad." *PH Cuadernos* 26: 236–257.

Gil Grande, R. 2019. Los Políticos Luchan por el Voto de una España Vaciada que Clama por Subsistir. https://www.rtve.es/noticias/20190330/politicos-luchan-voto-espana-vaciada-clama-subsistir/1910540.shtml.

Glaser, E. 2016. "In Defence of the Metropolitan Elite." https://www.newstatesman.com/politics/staggers/2016/10/defence-metropolitan-elite.

Gonda, N. 2019. "Land Grabbing and the Making of an Authoritarian Populist Regime in Hungary." *Journal of Peasant Studies* 46 (3): 606–625.

Goodwin, M., and O. Heath. 2016. "The 2016 Referendum, Brexit and the Left Behind: An Aggregate-Level Analysis of the Result." *The Political Quarterly* 87 (3): 323–332.

Gov.ua. 2020. "Comment of the Mission of Ukraine to the EU: Ukraine Launches Land Market Reform." https://ukraine-eu.mfa.gov.ua/en/news/comment-mission-ukraine-eu-ukraine-launches-land-market-reform.

Hajdu, A., and N. Mamonova. 2020. "Prospects of Agrarian Populism and Food Sovereignty Movement in Post-Socialist Romania." *Sociologia Ruralis*. doi:10.1111/soru.12301.

Hajdu, A., and O. Visser. 2017. "A Genealogy of the 'Land Rush'. Waves of Farmland Acquisition and Diverse Investor Strategies in Romania." Paper #96, Conference on The future of food and challenges for agriculture in the 21st century, April 24-26, Vitoria Gasteiz, the Basque Country http://elikadura21.eus/wpcontent/uploads/2017/05/96-Hajdu-and-Visser.pdf.

Harvey, D. 1999 [1982]. *The Limits to Capital*. London: Verso.

Harvey, D. 2005. *A Brief History of Neoliberalism*. Oxford: Oxford University Press.

Harvey, D. 2014. *Seventeen Contradictions and the End of Capitalism*. London: Profile Books.

Hellwig, M. 2017. Völkischer Rechtsextremismus im Ländlichen Raum https://www.schwalbach-saar.de/images/generation_integration/newsletter-14-hellwig.pdf.

Hospers, G. J., and J. Syssner. 2018. *Dealing with Urban and Rural Shrinkage: Formal and Informal Strategies*. Zurich: LIT Verlag.

Humphrey, C. 2002. "Does the Category 'Postsocialist' Still Make Sense?" In *Postsocialism: Ideals, Ideologies and Practices in Eurasia*, edited by C. M. Hann, 12–15. London: Routledge.

Jones, S. 2019. "'Empty Spain': Country Grapples with Towns Fading from the Map." https://www.theguardian.com/world/2019/apr/22/empty-spain-government-urged-to-act-as-towns-fade-from-map.

Katz, R. S., and P. Mair. 2009. "The Cartel Party Thesis: A Restatement." *Perspectives on Politics* 7 (4): 753–766.

Kaufmann, E. 2016. "It's NOT the Economy, Stupid: Brexit as a Story of Personal Values." *British Politics and Policy at LSE* https://blogs.lse.ac.uk/politicsandpolicy/personal-values-brexit-vote/.

Kay, S. 2016. *Land Grabbing and Land Concentration in Europe*. Amsterdam: Transnational Institute.

Klumbytė, N. 2009. "Post-Socialist Sensations: Nostalgia, the Self, and Alterity in Lithuania." *Lietuvos Etnologija: Etnologija ir Socialinė Antropologija* 9 (18): 93–116.

Klumbyte, N. 2011. "Europe and its Fragments: Europeanization, Nationalism, and the Geopolitics of Provinciality in Lithuania." *Slavic Review* 70 (4): 844–872.

Konings, M. 2012. "Neoliberalism and the State." In *Neoliberalism: Beyond the Free Market*, edited by D. Cahill, L. Edwards, and F. Stilwell, 54–66. Cheltenham, UK: Edward Elgar.

Kuzio, T. 2018. "Populism in Ukraine and Europe: Similar but Also Different." In *Populism in Europe: An Overview*, edited by K. Segbers, 16–28. Berlin: Centre for Global Politics.

Ladner, A., N. Keuffer, and H. Baldersheim. 2015. "Self-Rule Index for Local Authorities. European Commission Directorate-General for Regional and Urban Policy." https://ec.europa.eu/regional_policy/sources/docgener/studies/pdf/self_rule_index_en.pdf.

Lang, T. 2020. Food and Agriculture, Post-Brexit https://ukandeu.ac.uk/food-and-agriculture-post-brexit/#.

Lang, T., and M. Heasman. 2004. *Food Wars: The Global Battle for Mouths, Minds and Markets*. London: Routledge.

Li, T. M. 2017. "After Development: Surplus Population and the Politics of Entitlement." *Development and Change* 48: 1247–1261.

Liebmann, H. 2010. "Zivilgesellschaft Unter Schrumpfungsbedingungen." In *Stadtentwicklung, Zivilgesellschaft und Bürgerschaftliches Engagement*, edited by Elke Becker, Enrico Gualini, Carolin Runkel, and Rupert Graf Strachwitz, 71–85. Reihe: Maecenata Schriften.

Mamonova, N. 2015. "Resistance or Adaptation? Ukrainian Peasants' Responses to Large-Scale Land Acquisitions." *Journal of Peasant Studies* 42 (3-4): 607–634.

Mamonova, N. 2018. "Patriotism and Food Sovereignty: Changes in the Social Imaginary of Small-Scale Farming in Post-Euromaidan Ukraine." *Sociologia Ruralis* 58 (1): 190–212.

Mamonova, N. 2019. "Understanding the Silent Majority in Authoritarian Populism: What can we Learn From Popular Support for Putin in Rural Russia?" *Journal of Peasant Studies* 46 (3): 561–585.

Mamonova, N., and J. Franquesa. 2020a. "Populism, Neoliberalism and Agrarian Movements in Europe. Understanding Rural Support for Right-Wing Politics and Looking for Progressive Solutions." *Sociologia Ruralis*. doi:10.1111/soru.12291.

Mamonova, N., and J. Franquesa. 2020b. "Right-Wing Populism in Rural Europe. Introduction to the Special Issue." *Sociologia Ruralis*. doi:10.1111/soru.12306.

Marsden, T. 1999. "Rural Futures: The Consumption Countryside and its Regulation." *Sociologia Ruralis* 39 (4): 501–526.

Matless, D. 2016. *Landscape and Englishness*. London: Reaktion Books.

McCarthy, J., ed. 2020. *Environmental Governance in an Authoritarian/Populist era*. London: Routledge [This book was originally published as a special issue of Annals of the American Association of Geographers 110(2)].

Moore, B. 1966. *Social Origins of Dictatorship and Democracy: Lord and Peasant in the Making of the Modern World*. Boston, MA: Beacon Press.

Mudde, C., and C. R. Kaltwasser. 2017. *Populism: A Very Short Introduction*. Oxford: Oxford University Press.

Müller, H. 2017. *Nationaltheater: Wie Falsche Patrioten Unseren Wohlstand Bedrohen*. Frankfurt: Campus Verlag.

Naples, N. A. 1994. "Contradictions in Agrarian Ideology: Restructuring Gender, Race-Ethnicity, and Class." *Rural Sociology* 59 (1): 110–135.

Nasr, J. 2019. "German Village Elects Neo-Nazi, Sole Candidate, as Council Head." https://www.reuters.com/article/us-germany-neonazis/german-village-elects-neo-nazi-sole-candidate-as-council-head-idUSKCN1VU1PY.

Norris, P., and R. Inglehart. 2019. *Cultural Backlash: Trump, Brexit, and Authoritarian Populism*. Cambridge: Cambridge University Press.

Oltermann, P. 2017. "How a German River Marks Cultural Divide Between East and West." https://www.theguardian.com/world/2017/sep/02/germany-elbe-river-cultural-divide-east-west-federal-elections.

Pencheva, D. 2020. "Coronavirus: Flying in Fruit Pickers from Countries in Lockdown is Dangerous for Everyone." https://theconversation.com/coronavirus-flying-in-fruit-pickers-from-countries-in-lockdown-is-dangerous-for-everyone-136551.

Perrigo, B. 2019. "'Get Brexit Done.' The 3 Words That Helped Boris Johnson Win Britain's 2019 Election." https://time.com/5749478/get-brexit-done-slogan-uk-election/.

Pirozhok, O., and D. Denkov. 2019. "Rada Votes on the Land Market: Zelensky Managed to Persuade His Allies." https://www.epravda.com.ua/rus/publications/2019/11/13/653650/.

Pleines, H. 2016. "Oligarchs and Politics in Ukraine." *Journal of Post-Soviet Democratization* 24 (1): 105–127.

Razumkov Centre. 2020. "Attitudes of citizens towards democratisation of the land market and abolition of the moratorium on farmland sales." http://razumkov.org.ua/napriamky/sotsiologichni-doslidzhennia/stavlennia-gromadian-do-zaprovadzhennia-rynku-zemli-ta-skasuvannia-moratoriiu-na-kupivliuprodazh-zemli-silskogospodarskogo-pryznachennia-liutyi-2020r.

Recaño, J. 2017. "La Sostenibilidad Demográca de la España Vacía." *Perspectives Demograques* 7: 1–4.

Reche, E. 2019. El Bastión Murciano de Vox: Empresarios del Campo, 'Kikos' y Miedo al Migrante. https://www.eldiario.es/murcia/politica/murciano-Vox-empresarios-Kikos-migrante_0_894161064.html.

Reed, M. 2016. "'This Loopy Idea' an Analysis of UKIP's Social Media Discourse in Relation to Rurality and Climate Change." *Space and Polity* 20 (2): 226–241.

Rogaly, B. 2008. "Intensification of Workplace Regimes in British Horticulture: the Role of mi- Grant Workers." *Population, Space and Place* 14 (6): 497–510.

Röpke, A., and A. Speit. 2019. *Völkische Landnahme: Alte Sippen, Junge Siedler, Rechte Ökos*. Berlin: Links Christoph Verlag.

Ryabchuk, A. 2014. "Right Revolution? Hopes and Perils of the Euromaidan Protest in Ukraine." *Journal of Contemporary Central and Eastern Europe* 22 (1): 127–134.

Salmela, M., and C. von Scheve. 2017. "Emotional Roots of Right-Wing Political Populism." *Social Science Information* 56 (4): 567–595.

Sánchez Dragó, F. 2019. *Santiago Abascal. España Vertebrada*. Barcelona: Planeta.

Scoones, I., M. Edelman, S. M. Jr Borras, R. Hall, W. Wolford, and B. White. 2018. "Emancipatory Rural Politics: Confronting Authoritarian Populism." *Journal of Peasant Studies* 45 (1): 1–20.

Shucksmith M., and D. Brown. 2016. "Framing Rural Studies in the Global North." In *Routledge International Handbook of Rural Studies*, edited by M. Shucksmith and D. Brown, 31–56. London: Routledge.

Shulman, S. 1999. "The Cultural Foundations of Ukrainian National Identity." *Ethnic and Racial Studies* 22 (6): 1011–1036.

Smith, N. 1990. *Uneven Development*. Cambridge, MA: Blackwell.

Smith, G. 2011. Selective Hegemony and Beyond-Populations with 'no Productive Function': a Framework for Enquiry." *Identities* 18 (1): 2–38.

Swain, N. 2013. "Agriculture 'East of the Elbe' and the Common Agricultural Policy." *Sociologia Ruralis* 53 (3): 369–389.

Škobla, D., and R. Filčák. 2020. "Mundane Populism: Politics, Practices and Discourses of Roma Oppression in Rural Slovakia." *Sociologia Ruralis*. doi:10.1111/soru.12286.

Tietz, A. 2017. *Überregional Aktive Kapitaleigentümer in Ostdeutschen Agrarunternehmen: Entwicklungen bis 2017*. Bundesallee: Johann Heinrich von Thünen-Institut.

Tisdall, S. 2020. "Power, equality, nationalism: how the pandemic will reshape the world." https://www.theguardian.com/world/2020/mar/28/power-equality-nationalism-how-the-pandemic-will-reshape-the-world.

Tournier-Sol, K. 2015. "Reworking the Eurosceptic and Conservative Traditions Into a Populist Narrative: UKIP's Winning Formula?" *Journal of Common Market Studies* 53 (1): 140–156.

Troianovski, A. 2019. "A Ukrainian Billionaire Fought Russia. Now He's Ready to Embrace It." https://www.nytimes.com/2019/11/13/world/europe/ukraine-ihor-kolomoisky-russia.html.

URDN (Ukrainian Rural Development Network). 2019. "Ukrainians Reject the Forced 'Free Sale' of Their Land." http://urdn.org/wp-content/uploads/2019/12/Open-Letter-from-Ukraine.pdf.

Vampa, D. 2020. "Competing Forms of Populism and Territorial Politics: the Cases of Vox and Podemos in Spain." *Journal of Contemporary European Studies*. doi:10.1080/14782804.2020.1727866.

van der Ploeg, J. D. 2009. *The New Peasantries: Struggles for Autonomy and Sustainability in an Era of Empire and Globalization*. London: Routledge.
van der Ploeg, J. D. 2010. "The Food Crisis, Industrialized Farming and the Imperial Regime." *Journal of Agrarian Change* 10 (1): 98–106.
van der Ploeg, J. D. 2020a. "Farmers' Upheaval, Climate Crisis and Populism." *Journal of Peasant Studies* 47 (3): 589–605.
van der Ploeg, J. D. 2020b. "From Biomedical to Politico-Economic Crisis: the Food System in Times of Covid-19." *Journal of Peasant Studies*. doi:10.1080/03066150.2020.1794843.
van der Ploeg, J. D., J. C. Franco, and S. M. Borras Jr. 2015. "Land Concentration and Land Grabbing in Europe: a Preliminary Analysis." *Canadian Journal of Development Studies* 36 (2): 147–162.
Virdee, S., and B. McGeever. 2018. "Racism, Crisis, Brexit." *Ethnic and Racial Studies* 41 (10): 1802–1819.
Visser, O., and M. Spoor. 2011. "Land Grabbing in Post-Soviet Eurasia: The World's Largest Agricultural Land Reserves at Stake." *Journal of Peasant Studies* 38 (2): 299–323.
Vorländer, H., M. Herold, and S. Schäller. 2018. *PEGIDA and new Right-Wing Populism in Germany*. Basingstoke: Palgrave Macmillan.
Walker, R. A. 1978. "Two Sources of Uneven Development Under Advanced Capitalism: Spatial Differentiation and Capital Mobility." *Review of Radical Political Economics* 10 (3): 28–38.
Walker, K. L. M. 2008. "From Covert to Overt: Everyday Peasant Politics in China and the Implications for Transnational Agrarian Movements." *Journal of Agrarian Change* 8 (2-3): 462–488.
Ward, N. 2002. "Representing Rurality? New Labour and the Electoral Geography of Rural Britain." *Area* 34 (2): 171–181.
Wellings, B., and H. Baxendale. 2015. "Euroscepticism and the Anglosphere: Traditions and Dilemmas in Contemporary English Nationalism." *Journal of Common Market Studies* 53 (1): 123–139.
White, M., and A. Perkins. 2002. "'Nasty party' warning to Tories." https://www.theguardian.com/politics/2002/oct/08/uk.conservatives2002.
Williams, R. 1973. *The Country and the City*. London: Chatto and Windus.
Williamson, J. 1965. "Regional Inequality and the Process of National Development: A Description of Patterns." *Economic Development and Cultural Change* 13: 3–45.
Wolczuk, K. 2001. *The Moulding of Ukraine: The Constitutional Politics of State Formation*. Budapest: Central European University Press.
Wolf, E. 1969. *Peasant Wars of the Twentieth Century*. New York: Harper and Row.
Woods, M. 2005. *Contesting Rurality: Politics in the British Countryside*. Aldershot: Ashgate.
Woods, M. 2010. "Performing Rurality and Practising Rural Geography." *Progress in Human Geography* 34 (6): 835–846.
Woods, M. 2015. "Explaining Rural Protest: A Comparative Analysis." In *Rural Protest Groups and Populist Political Parties*, edited by D. Strijker, G. Voerman, and I. J. Terluin, 27–41. Wageningen: Wageningen Academic Publishers.
Woods, M., and J. McDonagh. 2011. "Rural Europe and the World: Globalization and Rural Development." *European Countryside* 3 (3): 153–163.
Yaremko, V., I. Lukomska, and D. Nizalov. 2017. "What Political Parties Say About the Land Reform and What the Voters Hear." https://voxukraine.org/en/what-political-parties-say-about-the-land-reform-and-what-the-voters-hear/.
Yaremko, V., O. Nivievskyi, O. Kaliberda, and M. Zarytska. 2016. "'I Support the Moratorium, but Want to be Able to Sell Land': The Paradoxes of Ukrainians' Attitudes to Lifting the Moratorium on Sale of Agricultural Land." http://www.kse.org.ua/en/research-policy/land/analytical/?newsid=1865.
Youngs, R. 2020. "Coronavirus and Europe's New Political Fissures." https://carnegieendowment.org/files/Youngs_Coronavirus_and_fissures.pdf.

Unpacking 'authoritarian populism' and rural politics: some comments on ERPI

Henry Bernstein

ABSTRACT
This paper provides an overview of work published under the auspices of ERPI, which remains somewhat elusive as a coherent intellectual and political project. I comment on several matters including lack of distinction between the 'agrarian' and the 'rural', issues of (spatial) scale and temporality and of identifying agrarian and rural classes, the costs as well as possible benefits of embracing the ambiguities of populism, and instances of 'resistance' to 'authoritarian populism' that are reported and proposed. The overall conclusion is that ERPI requires a more consistent, sharper and fuller class-based approach.

Introduction: the ERPI project

Issues of rural politics, both reactionary and oppositional/progressive, were proposed by the Emancipatory Rural Politics Initiative (ERPI) in 2017 following the US presidential election, and then launched at the ERPI conference on 'Authoritarian Populism and the Rural World' in The Hague in 2018.[1] First published were a 'framing paper' by Scoones et al (online in 2017 and in print in 2018), Bello (2018, 2019) on whom more below, and Ulrich-Schad and Duncan on the USA (2018), followed by nine articles in a subsequent forum in the *Journal of Peasant Studies* 46 (3–4), of which two are on the USA (Gaventa 2019; Berlet and Sunshine 2019), and two on Turkey (Adaman, Arsel, and Akbulut 2019; Gürel, Küçük, and Tas 2019), with one each on Russia (Mamonova 2019), Belarus, (Ivanou 2019), Hungary (Gonda 2019), Spain (Franquesa 2019), and Bolivia/Ecuador (Tilzey 2019). At the time of writing there are further articles by Andrade on Brazil (2019), Monjane and Bruna on Mozambique (2020), Beban et al. on Cambodia (2020), Carolan (2020) on the USA, and Roman-Alcalá's argument for injecting 'Critical Agrarian Studies' with anarchist conceptions of emancipatory politics,

---

[1] The conference papers can be found at https://www.tni.org/en/search/language/en?search=ERPI.

(forthcoming)[2], all in the *Journal of Peasant Studies*, with the addition of Mamonova and Franquesa's overview of rural populism in Europe in *Sociologica Ruralis* (2019). Also linked with ERPI are Sandwell et al. (2019) and its most ambitious political statement by Borras (2020), as well as a series of short pieces posted on Open Democracy.[3]

The article by Bello (2018) provides a larger and comparative frame on 'Counterrevolution, the countryside and the middle classes'.[4] 'Counterrevolution' here features as a generic if historically differentiated notion, illustrated through five case studies: Italian fascism in the early 1920s; the Indonesian massacres of 1965–6; Chile in the 1960s to the overthrow of the Allende government in 1973; Thailand since the 1970s and its several 'counterrevolutions'; and Duterte as a 'fascist original' in today's Philippines. The rationale for considering Italy, where initial fascist activity in the countryside was a response to successful 'reformism' rather than revolution, is that it marked contradictions in transitions to capitalism subsequently replayed in the South after 1945. Bello's case studies and their key moments of violent intervention (Italy, Indonesia, Chile, Thailand) leave him only the Philippines to exemplify a current authoritarian regime with majority electoral support which is the main focus of ERPI (below). His subsequent short book added chapters on Modi's India and 'The North: The Far Right Breaks Through', and a 'prescript' on the crisis of the Workers' Party in Brazil, written in 2015 with Cecilia Lero, prior to Bolsanaro's election victory (Bello 2019). In the book (2019, 142) he distinguishes between 'classical class-driven counterrevolution' against 'an insurgent underclass' (e.g. Italy, Indonesia, Chile, Thailand, as above) and reactionary movements directed against 'a liberal democratic regime' (e.g. Modi in India, Duterte in the Philippines, the extreme right in the North).

It is striking that ERPI's use of the term 'authoritarian populism' is taken up from its 'revival' by Stuart Hall in the 1980s on Thatcherism in the UK. Hall defined it as:

> … a movement towards a dominative and 'authoritarian' form of democratic class politics – paradoxically, apparently rooted in the 'transformism' (Gramsci's term) of populist discourses …. Essentially, it refers to changes in the 'balance of forces' … to the modalities of political and ideological relationships between the ruling bloc, the state and the dominated classes. (Scoones et al. 2018, 2; quoting Hall 1985)

The UK, which Hall addressed, is commonly regarded as a long established and durable liberal democracy (thus his designation '*democratic* class politics'), while other cases of widely recognised and more recent 'authoritarian populism' cited by ERPI authors include Russia, Hungary, Poland, Belarus, Turkey, Bolsanaro's Brazil, Duterte's Philippines, Modi's India: all with hardly 'mature' (or continuous) liberal democracies albeit with current more-or-less parliamentary governments installed by more-or-less electoral means.[5] The ERPI papers suggest various synonyms for 'authoritarian populism', e.g.

---

[2]How 'an anarchist lens can help better understand contemporary rural and agrarian politics and the challenges of making emancipatory change.' (17).
[3]See https://www.tni.org/en/page/erpi-opendemocracy
[4]Franquesa (2019, 541) also applies a 'dialectic between revolution and counterrevolution' in the *longue durée* of Spain's modern political history.
[5]An implicit reference to the major issues contained in notions and experiences of liberal democracy comes in Monjane and Bruna on the PROSAVANA programme in Mozambique, a joint undertaking between the Mozambican, Brazilian and Japanese governments. Assessing the campaigns of resistance to PROSAVANA by 'civil society' in the three countries, they suggest that 'Despite its controversies, the democratic system in Japan is operating at a much higher degree than in Brazil or Mozambique' (2020, 89). Also illustrative is Beban et al's report of the crackdown on any independent journalism in Cambodia given that 'freedom of the press' is so often asserted as one of the pillars of liberal democracy, and was mandated in the 'liberal peace' of the 1991 Paris Peace Agreement and the new Cambodian Constitution; that

'right wing' and 'reactionary' populism(s), and for its other, thus 'left wing', 'democratic', 'class conscious', 'counter-hegemonic' and 'republican' populism(s). The instances cited illustrate a global wave of 'authoritarian populism' at this stage of an era of neoliberal capitalism (Bello 2019), with regimes mostly established, as noted, by *electoral* wins, and to which we might add Trump's USA, Brexit Britain, and the votes gained by a number of far-right parties in Europe and elsewhere.

A key question posed by ERPI – hence also departing from Bello's original focus on moments of violent intervention that establish counterrevolutionary regimes, and following the lead of Hall on Thatcherism – is 'how regressive practice so often becomes hegemonic "common sense"' (Scoones et al. 2018, 9). Or as Gaventa (2019, 441) puts it, citing his earlier work (Gaventa 1980): 'Why in a situation of glaring inequality where one may intuitively expect upheaval, does one instead find, or appear to find, acquiescence? Under what conditions and against what obstacles does rebellion begin to appear?'

Another question that immediately follows, appropriately taken up by some ERPI papers, concerns the *rural* 'roots' of, or inclinations towards, 'authoritarian populism' although, again strikingly, with little apparent interest in its urban counterparts to provide a comparative perspective. While some ERPI papers consider voting in the countryside for 'authoritarian populist' parties and leaders, it is evident that a focus on election results (perhaps a legacy of taking up Hall's ideas on Thatcherism?) leaves out too much of the social and ideological dynamics of rural politics, and at best can tell us only part (sometimes a very small part) of stories of rural support for – and contestations of – 'authoritarian populism', a point emphasised particularly by Gaventa (2019).[6]

In what follows, I make some selective observations on several of the main themes, and connections, of the ERPI to raise several issues. Some of those issues are noted, if not pursued in depth, in ERPI papers which range greatly in type, from (mini-)case studies to reports of surveys and other overviews to theoretical reflection. One should also acknowledge, as indicated, the limits of the papers cited in terms of geographical range, and their empirical and analytical quality.

However wide the net cast by ERPI (intentionally so?), some articles published under its aegis bypass the key questions of its original 'framing paper'.[7] My reflections cannot substitute a more coherent object of analysis for ERPI than it has itself been able (or wished?) to construct.[8] Nor can they anticipate future papers sponsored, or inspired, by ERPI although one can hope that such studies will try to take into account some of the issues raised here.

'freedom' included the broadcasts of the US government funded *Radio Free Asia* (Beban, Schoenberger, and Lamb 2020, 99–100).

[6]Which is not to deny that analyses of election results can be productive. A positive example is Carolan's follow-up survey of former Obama voters in Colorado who switched to Trump in 2016 (Carolan 2020), and his explanation in terms of the 'colour blindness' of liberal political culture in the USA.

[7]And concerning terminology: 'authoritarian populism' or 'populist authoritarianism' (e.g. Beban, Schoenberger, and Lamb 2020): is there a difference? If so, does it matter? It should as struggles, actual or prospective, between 'authoritarian' and non- or anti-authoritarian (progressive) populism are at the core of ERPI's 'framing statement' and explored most fully by Borras (2020), on which more below. Differences between 'populist' or non- or anti-populist authoritarianism do not provide the same space for analytical and political exploration.

[8]Many ERPI papers begin with various characterisations of 'authoritarian populism' which do not need to be listed for the purposes of this commentary. Carolan (2020) prefaces his article with useful observations about the dangers of conflating some of the traits identified as 'authoritarian populism'.

The rural and the agrarian

A first observation concerns the problematic relationship of the 'rural' and the 'agrarian' and the dangers of reducing the former to the latter. This is acknowledged, if not followed through, to varying degrees in the ERPI papers, by Borras (2020, 7); Edelman (2018), Berlet and Sunshine (2019, 502) and Ulrich-Schad and Duncan (2018) on the USA; and Mamonova (2019, 568) on Russia. The 'Southern Revolt' in Catalonia that peaked from 2000–2004 was above all a mobilisation against energy and water extractivism in the area concerned where the Revolt shifted from 'strictly agrarian to rural concerns' (Franquesa 2019, 555 note 13), while the case study by Adaman, Arsel, and Akbulut (2019) is on coal mining in Soma, Turkey, and its terrible disaster of 2014. That the rural is not reducible to the agrarian is otherwise perhaps most evident in papers on the USA with its rural 'sacrifice zones' (Edelman 2018) or 'hollowed out heartland' (Edelman 2019) of economic decline in mining, timber, and some processing (poultry plants) and manufacturing (textiles) as well as (some) farming, with attendant decline in employment as well as public services such as education and health care. Indeed, the 'non-agricultural' looms large in Ulrich-Schad and Duncan's (2018) typology of American rural areas as 'amenity rich', 'transitioning' and 'chronically poor'. It is no doubt fitting that their vignettes of an 'amenity rich' area and a 'transitioning' area suggest how important the 'service economy' of prisons is to both.[9]

Borras (2020, 4) proposes an expansive conception of '"working people" in the countryside – peasants, landless labourers, indigenous communities, fishers, pastoralists, lower middle class, and the vast number of people in the informal sector including those who live and work in nearby small towns.' It remains the case, however, that his political focus, both historical and contemporary, is exclusively on agrarian populism and its progressive expressions (as the title of his article suggests). His conception of 'working people in the countryside' clearly points to class relations, contradictions and ambiguities in rural politics, which is its purpose. For that reason, his and other ERPI papers advise us to (re-)consider class categories and their applications to agrarian and more broadly rural social structures and dynamics. I return to all this but can note here the distinction in several of the ERPI papers between 'peasants' and (family) commercial farmers, for example, in Russia (Mamonova 2019), and in Bolivia/Ecuador where the distinction, formulated in various ways, plays a central part in Tilzey's account of 'pink tide' governments and their contradictions (2019).[10]

A final brief observation concerns demography. The declining, and ageing, populations of so many rural areas, not least in farming, are noted for Russia, Spain, and the USA in the ERPI papers considered here, together with some passing references to labour migration and its effects.[11] More generally, Bello (2018, 55) notes the 'reduced role and significance

---

[9]Andrade provides a cogent analysis of the compromised macroeconomic policies of the Workers' Party presidencies in Brazil from 2003 to 2016, the fetishism of 'Lulism' as 'progressive' (or 'pro-poor') populism, and the (re)formations and manipulations of Brazilian capital, including its powerful agribusiness, during that period. There is, however, nothing on rural (class) constituencies of support of 'Lulism', and indeed her principal explanation of Bolsanaro's victory is the 'conservatism' of the 'informal working class', manifested again once its gains from welfarist redistribution under Workers' Party governments were eroded (2020, 9–12, 24). Among ERPI authors published to date Andrade is probably the most sceptical of the claims for 'progressive' ('pro-poor') populism, both for theoretical reasons and drawing on the experience of 'Lulism' in Brazil.
[10]See also the strategic contrast between 'family' farmers in Western Europe and 'peasant' farmers in Central and Eastern Europe sketched by Mamonova and Franquesa (2019).
[11]On these themes see the important text by White (in press).

of the countryside' in the national politics of most countries, the 'declining proportion of agricultural workers and peasants in the labour force', and the 'ageing of farmers', as well as 'even greater differentiation of the peasantry': social trends which are not considered further in his subsequent book.[12]

'Economistic' and 'culturalist' approaches

Several ERPI papers recognise a tension between 'economistic' and 'culturalist' approaches – and their adequacy – in inquiring whether rural populations are especially prone to the seductions of 'authoritarian populist' ideologies, movements and ostensibly charismatic leaders.[13] Gürel, Küçük, and Tas (2019) who consider 'the rural roots of the rise of the Justice and Development Party (AKP) in Turkey' with reference to farming on the Black Sea coast, explicitly state their intention to examine economic factors that explain the success of the AKP *contra* 'culturalist' approaches that can be as common on the left as the right, of course. Mamonova rejects 'culturalist' explanations of support for Putin(ism) in rural Russia in favour of explanation from 'agrarian property regimes and power relations in the countryside' (2019, 561) yet observes that '… even though rural Russians are not traditional peasants, a number of conservative peasant values are still preserved in the countryside, which make villagers more responsive to the traditionalist authoritarian appeals of Putin's regime' (580). She further suggests that most 'individual smallholders' (commodity producers) are pro-democratic as they require 'free competition' (570), a somewhat startling borrowing from liberal ideology.

A potent example of the centrality of culture is Tilzey (2019) on Bolivia, where indigenous ideologies/identities are central to explaining the initial social base of the Morales governments. He also makes a familiar claim, albeit lacking any evidence, that 'Both peasants and workers seek refuge in the peasant situation' seeking to resist full proletarianisation (2019, 645, and further below).

Of course, class analysis should embrace and connect both 'the economic' and 'the cultural' as many scholars note (e.g. Mamonova and Franquesa 2019, 4–5) – and indeed the more encompassingly 'social' (practices of reproduction, health and ill-health, ecology, migration, residence and housing, and so on) – even though this is typically easier to prescribe than to satisfy. However, thorough investigation of material conditions of existence, and social relations, remains a *sine qua non* from the necessary abstractions of the capitalist mode production to any specific or concrete class analysis (see note 14 following). For the latter 'cultural politics' is no less real in class terms, which should not evaporate in discourses of 'identity politics. 'Culture' is no less subject to complex class determinations and contradictions; the challenge is always to grasp the intricate dynamics and connections between class structures and ideologies in capitalist social formations, and their effects (see further below).

---

[12]'The decline of the peasantry as a political factor' is briefly noted in Bello's account of the Philippines but mostly concerns serious conflicts within and between the country's communist parties which undermined their capacities for rural organisation/mobilisation (Bello 2019, 113).

[13]Indeed dispute between materialist and discursive interpretations of Thatcherism marked the debate around Stuart Hall's formulation of 'authoritarian populism'; see, for example, the critique by Jessop et al. (1984).

Scales

Dispossession – by various means, with varying intensities – is the widespread experience of classes of labour within contemporary capitalism. I prefer the term 'classes of labour' to most inherited usages of 'peasants', 'proletarians' and the like; recognising continuing or intensified dispossession does not signal agreement with David Harvey's thesis of 'accumulation by dispossession' as the means for capital to 'fix' its crises of over-accumulation in the period of neoliberal globalisation (Harvey 2003).[14]

The ravages of neoliberal globalisation provide, as one might expect, an indispensable context to most ERPI papers, some of which highlight the financial crash of 2008 and its fallout, especially in the USA. It is not their object to explore recent and current mechanisms of imperialist accumulation and its contradictions. A partial and limited exception is Tilzey (2019) on 'pink tide' governments in Ecuador and especially Bolivia, able to fund social programmes using rents from multinational companies investing in the commodity boom associated with China's growth and its demand for imports.

More attention is paid to the national level, and there are several cases of extractivist policies justified in the name of ('national' or 'endogenous') development: in export driven mineral, fossil fuel and agri-fuel production in Bolivia and Ecuador (Tilzey 2019); in the 'New Culture of Water' and 'New Culture of Energy' in Spain's 'second miracle' that sparked the 'Southern Revolt' in Catalonia (Franquesa 2019); and in Turkey where the Erdogan government pursues a policy of 'self-sufficiency' in energy supplies, marked in the expansion of coal mining (Adaman, Arsel, and Akbulut 2019). Such instances also feature some of the emblematic types of capital in this period of neoliberal globalisation: multinational extractive companies in Bolivia and Ecuador; the 'incessant extension of the frontier of ground rent valorization' driven by banks, electric utilities, construction and real estate corporations in Spain (Franquesa 2019, 546, 552); privatised companies in mining in Turkey (privatised in Soma in 2005), supported by the Erdogan governments; and above all finance capital and its characteristic modes of operation, illustrated in Edelman's account of the 'hollowing out' of local economic services and circuits in the rural USA (2019).

Otherwise, as is evident by now, a key focus of ERPI studies is on national governments and politics (not least electoral politics, as noted). Among the papers cited, Bello (2018) makes some useful suggestions about determinations of the balance of forces and their political consequences at the national level and in the countryside, and of their interconnections.

Concerning the (rural) local, most of the ERPI papers cited describe some specificities – socioeconomic, ethnic and cultural, political – of different rural localities they consider, if not in much detail or depth. This is often motivated by the desire to find examples of 'resistance' and opposition, emancipatory politics in effect, considered further below.

Ideally, of course, a full analysis from political economy would aim to link the various scales of the global, the national, and the 'local' without any *a priori* commitment to determinations that move in either direction between these scales: a problem manifested in 'world system determinism' on one hand, celebrations of localism on the other. Indeed,

---

[14]Kalb (2011) provides a sophisticated theoretical review of material and ideological/cultural dispossession, its dynamics, forms, varieties of experience, and effects.

problematising these scales, and not least the 'local', is necessary to avoiding such *a priorism*.

Temporalities

A pervasive issue underlying the ERPI papers is that of time frames, of the longer-term tendencies that different time frames may reveal (or obscure), and of conjunctural features among which the political balance of forces and its fluidity is to the fore (Bello 2019). For example, Mamonova (2019, 568) suggests that Putin did not win the Russian election in 2000 on a populist platform, which was adopted only from 2012 onwards. In Hungary, Gonda (2019, 615–6) reports shifting election results for the authoritarian populist right (Orban's Fidesz and its Jobbik allies) in 2014 and 2018, when it maintained a majority of seats due to 'extreme disproportionality of the new electoral system', while their vote held up in the poorest rural areas 'receptive to simplistic and racialized explanations for their economic hardships'. Another somewhat different, and interesting, example comes from Tilzey's (2019, 630) suggestion of a shift from (counter-hegemonic) populism to authoritarian populism in Bolivia and Ecuador in face of the contradictions of extractivist policies and opposition to them. In this instance, the move towards authoritarianism marks not so much a change of ideology but suppression of opposition coming from original social bases of the 'pink tide' governments in the poor 'peasantry' and 'semi-proletariat'. Monjane and Bruna (2020) suggest the growing authoritarianism of FRELIMO governments in Mozambique, exemplified by the adoption and implementation of PROSAVANA. Roman-Alcalá's anarchist lens proposes that '(populist) legitimatization of *any* state power reproduces the foundation upon which more authoritarian future administrations can act', and that 'Through the anarchist critique of authority and hierarchy we might better recognise how (authoritarian) populism is rooted in existing forms and structures of power, to understand the particular (Trump) *as continuity within a lineage* (of statist politics more broadly)' (forthcoming, 18, 20, emphases in original). Such statements point towards a kind of anarchist 'philosophical anthropology', hence in an apparently ahistorical (or trans-historical) fashion: all forms of hierarchy oppress all 'non-elites' at all times?

In an analysis of the shift from Congress to BJP hegemony in India, Vanaik (2018) traces the dynamics of a 'long interregnum' from the late 1960s to the 2014 BJP victory led by Modi. This is integrated with an account of India's economy over those decades, and its effects for different classes. A decisive moment in that trajectory was the adoption of neoliberal policy 'reforms' from the mid-1980s by Congress governments, later central to Modi's BJP too. The transition from Congress to BJP hegemony in India is, of course, marked by many specific political determinations, both conjunctural and institutional; important among the latter are the effects of India's (British modelled) 'first past the post' system of electing Members of Parliament. However, Vanaik also discusses broader and longer-term socioeconomic drivers and effects of the career of neoliberalism in Modi's India, above all the failure of Congress's (originally Nehruvian) 'developmentalism' to deliver improved living standards to the vast majority of the country's classes of labour. Indeed, Modi's government in India has a particular claim to characterisation as a fascist form of 'counterrevolution' due to the country's long history of extreme Hindu political formations and their virulent ideology of *Hindutava*, combined with their cadre base, discipline and organisational capacities, as well as strategic uses of street violence (see further Vanaik 2018; and Ahmad 2000, 2016).

Just as Vanaik proposes that the record of Congress over the first three decades of Independence, including its 'soft' Hindu nationalism and 'Hinduized state apparatus', helped pave the way for the subsequent success of the BJP and Modi, so Bello (2019, 110) considers that the way for Duterte's election victories in the Philippines was paved by 'the deep disenchantment with the liberal democratic regime' of EDSA that followed the end of the Marcos regime in 1986, and 'the deadly combination of elite monopoly of the electoral system, uncontrolled corruption, continuing concentration of wealth, and neoliberal economic policies' of the EDSA period.

These brief examples suggest that political, as well as socioeconomic, dynamics can also unfold over decades as well as in key conjunctural moments.[15] How this, and such widespread processes of the rise of authoritarian populism, are best considered in the frame of neoliberal globalisation – including the demise of social democracy, and indeed crises of liberal democracy – is something I return to at the end.

Which are the 'rural classes?

Answers to this question always entail well-known difficulties. One reason, I suggest, is the impulse to find the most appropriate 'labels' for different rural class formations, and to attach such labels to (almost inevitably) heterogeneous groups. It is then expected that the groups so labelled will behave in more or less predictable ways, including their susceptibility towards 'progressive' or 'reactionary' (authoritarian) populism, whether in general (thereby running the danger of essentialism) or in different circumstances at different times. It is more useful, in my view, to begin with exploring how the class dynamics of capitalism play out in various countrysides, and then investigating whether, how and how much, those dynamics generate (relatively) clear class categories manifested in distinct forms of ideology, identity, and collective political practice. Passages from the former to the latter, of course, entail many further determinations which bring their own challenges. One arises from the many interconnections of agrarian with other (non-farming) sources of livelihood/reproduction, both rural and urban.[16] Another is that this leads to a great deal of fluidity in the reproductive activities and locations of rurally based 'classes of labour' (Bernstein 2010).

The ERPI papers do not do much to clarify which are the rural classes they focus on, reflecting rather than resolving the kinds of difficulties indicated; Borras's view of populism as intrinsically comprising 'disparate and even competing and contradictory class and group interests' (2020, 5; see further below) requires, of course, specification of what those classes are, their relations with others, and their interests.

Gürel, Küçük, and Tas (2019) suggest two principal axes of 'class struggle' in the hazelnut and tea farming areas they studied on Turkey's Black Sea coast: between farmers and capital over producer prices, and between farmers and Kurdish migrant farm workers.

---

[15]A useful warning against the common temptation to 'foreshorten' analyses of politics – perhaps encouraged by a focus on elections? For an interesting discussion in relation to the British Labour Party's strategy in 2019, see the third of Jeremy Gilbert's commentaries on the general election of that year (2020).

[16]As Ferguson and Li (2018, 3) rightly observe, many in the countryside pursue 'mixed livelihoods which may have little to do with agriculture'.

These are hardly equivalent forms of 'class struggle'. Indeed, the first – between more or less specialised petty commodity producers and the agribusiness capitals that integrate them into produce (and also 'factor') markets – is often an important motif of various agrarian populisms historically and comprehensively so today. The second is vastly different – one manifestation of the capital-labour relations at the core of capitalism. Here too, that seasonal migrant farm workers are ethnically distinct, as so often, makes its own contribution to 'authoritarian populist' ideology, in this case that of the AKP. Gürel et al point this out (2019, 469) but it is strange then that they conclude with observations about 'the rural masses' who seem to comprise only the farmers (2019, 475): what about the workers then ('former Kurdish peasants displaced in the early 1990s')? This is indeed a very far stretch for any populist 'emancipatory rural politics'.

Also on Turkey, Adaman et al note the 'destruction of the viability of peasant farming' (centred on tobacco) in the area of Soma, a process of 'de-peasantisation' and 'semi-proletarianisation', of 'peasant-turned-miners' in substantially informalised patterns of employment (2019, 515–6, 523). A distinctive feature of the Soma case, unlike many instances of 'extractivist' appropriations of rural land, appears to be that mining capital has an interest in the surplus labour made available for labour-intensive forms of coal mining.

Does the term 'semi-proletarianisation' often conceal more than it reveals? The notion is also widely deployed in Tilzey's account of Bolivia and Ecuador (2019), claiming the gains *contra* 'orthodox Marxism' of innovative styles of Marxian analysis, such as the Gramscian and neo-Gramscian, Poulantzian, and 'Political Marxism' (2019, 644) as well as a number of agrarian and other class categories and their 'hegemonic', 'sub-hegemonic' and 'anti-hegemonic' political projects and practices. These are deployed in an account of 'indigenous' peasants and 'semi-proletarians' with class differentiation in the countryside to the fore: 'expropriation of lowland indigenous peoples and progressive proletarianization of the lower peasantry' (631) while 'semi-proletarian peasants' predominate in the highlands or *altiplano* (640). At the same time, the 'lower peasantry' are 'dependent' on wage labour for their reproduction (639) which suggests a working class (or at least 'class of labour'), often engaged in cyclical migration, rather than a 'peasantry'.

On the other hand, there is a strong emphasis on a class variously named as 'rich' or 'upper peasants', 'commercial upper peasantry', 'small commercial farmers', 'stratum of commercial peasantry' (636–7), and so on. Presumably most of those are 'indigenous', including some migrant Quechua and Aymara peasants from the *altiplano* who have become 'small-scale, but capitalist, producers of such export crops as coca, soy, and quinoa' (637). Once more, if they are 'capitalist producers' why term them 'peasants'? In fact, in Tilzey's account, they played a central role in the decline of left hopes for the Bolivian 'pink tide' of which they were 'a key' (636) or 'core' (637) constituency for Morales which grew under his governments (635), benefitting from 'productivist' policies of food sovereignty and from the limited land reform that occurred (636), as well as from an 'infiltration of upper peasant fractions into the state apparatus' (637).[17]

---

[17]Webber (2017a) provides an overview of Bolivia's agrarian structure from 1952 to 2005, and a fuller account of the limited land reforms and their politics after 2005 (336–345). Tilzey's analysis largely parallels (or follows) that of Webber (2017a) and Webber (2017b). There is a number of recent articles in the *Journal of Agrarian Change* and *Journal of Peasant Studies* on the peasantries of Ecuador and their responses to the agrarian policies of the Correa governments between 2006 and 2017, notably that of 'food sovereignty'; see, *inter alia*, the illuminating article by Soper (2020) and the references therein.

In sum, analysis of the countryside requires closer and more precise attention to the specific contours of its class formations, their determinations and effects. Two examples given here are, first, class (and often ethnic) difference between petty commodity producers and the wage labour they typically employ; and, second, processes of class differentiation among so-called 'family farmers'.

Class ambiguities of populism: virtue and vice?

Borras (2020) is the most ambitious theoretico-political statement of ERPI to date. He uses the term 'populism' to mean

> the deliberate political act of aggregating disparate and even competing and contradictory class and group interests and demands into a relatively homogenized voice, that is, 'we, the people', against an 'adversarial them' for tactical or strategic political purposes. As such, populism is inherently relational. It tends to be a means towards an end rather than an end itself, giving it a very generic character that is open-ended and flexible, facilitating easy adaptation by various ideological camps, even competing ones. (2020, 5)

He further proposes that right/reactionary and progressive/left populism represent 'a *dynamic continuum* rather than fixed categories in between' (2020, 5) and that 'The boundaries between right-wing populist currents and their social base in the countryside on the one hand, and the populism of agrarian movements on the other, are porous, blurred, and malleable' (2020, 7). While 'there is nothing inherently progressive in agrarian populist movements' (11), Borras suggests that

> the opposite worldviews of right-wing populism and progressive agrarian movements is their *competing notions of property or claims to fruits of labour*. ... *social relations around property and labour* will remain among the most important defining elements that differentiate or create cleavages between progressive agrarian populism and right-wing populism. (21–2, emphases added)

In an important sense, what Borras means here is that although populist movements are multi-class by his own definition, the more progressive, in effect, have a high(er) degree of 'classness' (to borrow a term of the late Teodor Shanin 1966) centred on 'social relations around property and labour'.

Borras's recognition of the ambiguities of populism is shared by other ERPI contributors, for example, Berlet and Sunshine (2019, 481) who quote Catherine Stock that 'the roots of violence, racism and hatred can be and have been nourished in the same soil and *from the same experiences* ... that generate movements for democracy and equality.' Franquesa (2019, 538), similarly notes 'the thin but all-important line that separates republican (or "left wing" or "popular democratic") from reactionary (or "right wing" or "authoritarian") populism', and that the 'demand for dignity and the experience of indignation', an important discursive trope in Catalonia's 'Southern Revolt', are not an exclusive 'patrimony of the left'. They can be mobilised by either democratic or authoritarian populism: 'dignity is a largely empty concept, which simply asserts the presence and value of a group that

---

One wonders where her three examples from the Ecuadorean highlands of specialised (indigenous) petty commodity producers of broccoli, milk and quinoa would fit in Tilzey's schematic of agrarian classes. Surprisingly Roman-Alcalá (forthcoming) uses the residual term 'non-elite' to refer to all exploited and subordinated groups, perhaps to avoid what he might see as a straitjacket of class terminology?

feels disenfranchised' (556). He also points to popular anger generated by 'slow dispossession' with its 'unspectacular, gradual and mundane character' (Franquesa 2019, 547).

A final point here concerns what has been called 'social neoliberalism' in an essay on Turkey by Dorlach, who defines it as 'a development model ... combining relatively orthodox neoliberal economic policies and retrenchment of the protective welfare state (e.g. labour market institutions) with a significant expansion ... of the productive welfare state (e.g. public health care)', and suggests its relevance to some other middle income countries (2015, 519) although, more generally, it is of limited range and impact on the lives of classes of labour. This is taken up in the ERPI Turkish case study by Gürel, Küçük, and Tas 2019, to refer to agricultural support policies, as well as 'ummediated/individual incorporation' (quoting Dorlach), in the expansion of consumer credit and some social assistance. A different kind of example is provided by Tilzey (2019) on Bolivia and Ecuador where, as already noted, a primary rationale was to generate export revenues to be used for welfarist redistribution (like similar moments in Brazil under Workers' Party governments and in Venezuela), which did not prevent popular opposition as the fragility of extractivist 'developmentalism', not least in declining export earnings, started to be manifest.

If a number of ERPI authors are well aware of the ambiguities of populism, some also rightly point to the failures of the left in its analyses, programmes and practices, thereby contributing to those political spaces which authoritarian populism (and 'counter-revolution') have been able to occupy. They include Andrade on Brazil (2019); Gürel, Küçük, and Tas (2019, 469, 474) and Adaman, Arsel, and Akbulut (2019, 528) on Turkey; Franquesa (2019, 545) on Spain; Bello (2018, 35) on Chile in the Popular Unity period; and the entire thrust of Tilzey (2019) on Bolivia and Ecuador. More generally, Bello (2019, 8) aspires to analysis that is not 'class reductionist or class determinist', that can take 'into account the indeterminacy ... [of] complex dynamics of concrete political struggles', and recognises that 'in some cases or at least certain junctures, class interest can play second fiddle to culture and ideology in driving a counterrevolutionary process' - the last, in effect, highlighting the key questions of ERPI noted at the start of this paper. While Bello's criticism of class reductionism is well taken, his last observation –instances of class as 'second fiddle', key to 'counterrevolution' – resonates a 'factorialist' (which is to say, empiricist) notion of how class and other dimensions of social difference and their divisions (gender, ethnicity, religion and other 'culture'/ideology) can (or should) be *'counted'* or *weighted*.

This indicates only the tip of a familiar iceberg, composed of the many complexities of class and its connections with other social differences, whether and how they become actual or potential social divisions, and the struggles they can feed into: over gender, race, generation, and 'nation'.[18] The constructions and exploitations of patriarchy, ethnic and/or religious supremacism, and 'national'(ism) by 'authoritarian populism' and other reactionary ideologies of 'identity', achieve many successes that have to be confronted. Indeed, the fight against them can take the form of 'popular' or 'democratic' struggles involving class alliances albeit with a clear class rationale. A 'guiding thread' (Marx) in confronting these complexities is the *ubiquity* of class relations and dynamics in capitalism,

---

[18]A tension central to the Marxist tradition and that provides much grist to the mill of its critics. Political practice is rarely informed by any 'pure' forms of class consciousness and interest on the part of exploited and oppressed classes.

rather than assuming their 'primacy' in all political processes and moments, as suggested by Balibar's formulation that 'in a capitalist world, class relations are "*one determining* structure, covering *all* social practices, without being the *only* one" (quoted by Therborn 2007, 88, emphasis in original). From there one can move forward to investigating and explaining the myriad and complex ways in which gender, generation, caste, ethnicity, religion and the like, shape *experiences* of class divisions, how they *express* those experiences, and with what *effects*.

Bello (2019) is also clear that the rise of 'authoritarian populism' has key roots in a period marked by globalisation (as a new phase of imperialism), by the collapse of any 'alternative' promised (for some on the left) by the USSR, and by the implosion of social democratic parties (in Europe) and (ostensibly) 'developmentalist' parties (India, Philippines) and their electoral support as they fatally embraced neoliberalism. In some cases the discourses of authoritarian populism can include explicit attacks on the norms of liberal democracy, and indeed liberalism more broadly including its claims to cosmopolitanism and universalism. Bello (2019) gives examples of such attacks in Hindutava ideology in India (79–80) and some of Duterte's inflammatory statements in the Philippines (116), to which could be added the rhetorical excesses of Bolsanaro in Brazil, Orban in Hungary, and Trump in the USA, a society marked by the colour, or racial, 'blindness' of its liberalism, as Carolan (2020) points out.

Alternatives

What then are some of the 'alternatives' of 'emancipatory rural politics' – the central concern of the ERPI project – proposed by its authors. Here again we are on (intrinsically?) ambiguous terrain. The more class-oriented ERPI authors point to radical oppositional movements or organisations that they favour: for Borras (2020, 15) Brazil's MST, the Philippine Peasant Movement (*Kilusang Magbubukid ng Pilipinas*) 'which is within the close orbit of a Marxist-Leninist-Maoist left', and Andalucía's *Sindicato Obrero del Campo* 'which comes from a broad left-wing tradition with significant anarcho-syndicalist influences'; while Tilzey (2019, 645–7) selects the Bolivian MST among the country's agrarian movements best exemplifying counter-hegemony vs reformism. These instances then represent one end of Borras's spectrum of (agrarian) populist politics, those with the highest degree of (oppositional) 'classness' (above) – and perhaps to the extent that they fall off that end of the spectrum (albeit member organisations of *La Via Campesina*)?

This points to an unresolved tension in Borras's construction of a continuum or 'sliding scale' approach to the 'classness' of populisms, deploying a conception of the core of progressive left populism: its commitment to 'five goals of deep social reforms' – 'redistribution, recognition, restitution, regeneration and, resistance – or in short, revolution' (2020, 22–23). Furthermore, these goals 'are not to be treated like a checklist from which one can cherry pick' (23–24). Unless populist movements take seriously all the five interlinked goals, they are not progressive for the 'absurdly difficult but not impossible' task of contributing to a socialist future. This seems at least to restrict severely the scope of 'ambiguity' in the approach of Borras and others, and, as noted, would surely exclude many of the member organisations of *La Via Campesina* (itself not clearly committed to all 'five goals'), from which Borras 'cherry picks' political formations that he likes best for their radicalism (and 'classness')? Borras, in effect, slips between the more demanding criteria of his 'five Rs' and adopting the late Erik Olin Wright's much looser notion of 'real utopias' (Borras 2020, 4, 22).[19] Perhaps it would serve his purpose better to construct a scale, however schematic, of the class coordinates of different populisms: both the class interests they support (see below) and the class constituencies they attract?

For some ERPI authors 'food sovereignty' *qua* (small) farmer agroecology seems to serve as a kind of default position for 'resistance', for example Tilzey (2019), Mamonova and Franquesa (2019) and Borras (2020) [20], while Roman-Alcalá invokes 'anarchism's preferred practices of rooted, place- and culture-based solidarity and mutual aid' (forthcoming, 23) which he elaborates with sometimes startling examples from the USA.

More specific examples of 'alternatives' in the ERPI papers considered include Gaventa's discovery (2019) of 'a more radical and potentially transformative local place-based politics' in a part of the Appalachians that voted for Trump (448), while noting that 'Not all such grassroots efforts are of course progressive' (449), and recognising the need for 'scaling-up': 'how do small-scale actions for change and resistance come together for larger-scale transformations of the political landscape? ... how do national and global politics fuel or diminish local place-based action?' (453; see also Scoones et al. 2018; Bello 2019; Borras 2020). Less robust is the (faint) echo of this in the conclusion of Gürel, Küçük, and Tas (2019, 474) that 'the rural masses' in their study areas have 'used both protests and the ballot box as mechanisms of negotiation with the government'. The term 'rural masses' notwithstanding (above) what they point to is a form of politics common among petty commodity producers and small capitalist farmers, widespread in Europe, for example, and also in India's 'new farmers' movements'. In Hungary the 'alternative' is in the hands of 'neo-rural' people of urban origin or 'bobos' (bourgeois-bohemians), well-educated dissidents who move to the countryside with the intent of small-scale (agroecological) farming (Gonda 2019, 618–9). The other side of this particular coin, as Fernando Fernandez (quoted by Franquesa 2019, 548), rightly noted are those who take up positions 'that have nothing to do with the defense of the rural world'.[21]

Some tentative conclusions

Why the project of ERPI? Something of a clue is provided, once more, by Borras (2020, 15): 'agrarian populism is, in reality, far more differentiated than its homogenised and caricaturized depiction by some sections of the Marxist intellectual community (academics or party cadres)'. To illustrate this he provides several examples of movements within the broad umbrella of *La Via Campesina* with strong emancipatory class ideologies and identities (above), by contrast with other member organisations of *La Via Campesina* (14–5). In effect, this exemplifies the point about 'classness' as a riposte to Marxist criticism of *La Via Campesina*. At the same time, this riposte must be read as an implicit defence of *La Via Campesina* as an encompassing international configuration of agrarian 'movements'

---

[19]Wright's legacy is considered by Burawoy (2020) who designates Wright's 'two Marxisms' 'class without utopia' and 'utopia without class', and Riley (2020) who criticizes both Wright's and Burawoy's versions of a 'Marxist sociology'.
[20]The *Journal of Peasant Studies* publishes many articles on 'alternative' experiments in (small) farmer production and marketing, for example, van der Ploeg, Ye, and Schneider 2012.
[21]See van der Ploeg's illuminating analysis (2020) of the Dutch 'farmers' protests' of 2019 deploying a reactionary populist discourse and spearheaded by 'entrepreneurial' (i.e. capitalist) farmers and their agribusiness allies, who were nonetheless able to generate some support from 'peasant'-type farmers committed to agroecology and 'the defense of the rural world'.

with quite different class bases and projects. Presumably herein lies the virtuous inclusiveness ('plurality') of its agrarian populism, even though some of its member organisations are known for pro-'small farmer' (and not so small farmer) stances that include the suppression of farm workers.

The wide range of instances of rural support for authoritarian populism and the search for potentially 'emancipatory' alternatives to it in the ERPI papers considered here raise some key questions about their framing and its limits. One that has been signalled is the problem of the 'rural' and the 'agrarian' and the irreducibility of the former to the latter, marked by the importance of rural working classes/classes of labour and the many ramified interconnections between the rural and the urban, together with the attendant need for investigation and explanation of the roots of authoritarian populism among urban classes, and indeed those that straddle city/town and countryside in pursuit of their reproduction (and accumulation). A small and incidental indication of this is given by Bello's observations about the support of the newly urbanised for authoritarian populism in Thailand and India (Bello 2019, 58, 97), as part of his broader reflections on the places of substantial and 'volatile', albeit typically amorphous, 'middle classes' in the cases of counterrevolution he considers.

What should be clear enough is that authoritarian populism, for all its diverse manifestations, should always be interrogated first through the questions: what class interests does it serve? By what means? And with what effects? Such questions serve to safeguard against analysing authoritarian populism in a solely discursive manner. For example, Bello (2019, 129) suggests that 'the extreme right' tends to detach itself from the neoliberal agenda it otherwise shared with the 'centre right', as part of its constitutive nationalism. While it is true, as he says, that 'the right [often, HB] eats the left's lunch' (2019, 127–131; also Mamonova and Franquesa 2019) – especially when the message of the left is expressed in populist and nationalist terms – when the right is in government this is almost never at the expense of core neoliberal policies of market liberalisation and the suppression of classes of labour, organised or otherwise.

The first two questions are (too) often taken for granted given the principal (or exclusive) focus on why exploited and oppressed classes support authoritarian populisms. Here there is a need for more fine-grained analysis of the class bases of support for reaction, not least in the countryside given the complexities, and often novelties, of the social forms of contemporary capitalism in agriculture. As Mike Davis suggested: 'Although it is heresy to say so, we need *more* economic interpretation, not less' (2018, 178, emphasis in original).[22] And, one can add, more 'cultural' investigation to synthesise with the 'economic': what explains the breadth and depth of apparent support for 'authoritarian populism' among exploited and oppressed classes, or sections of classes? And what do answers to such questions disclose of its contradictions and (indeed) ambiguities, hence opportunities to overturn its ideological projects?

A useful starting point here is Borras's proposal (above) that '*social relations around property and labour* will remain among the most important defining elements that differentiate or create cleavages between progressive agrarian populism and right-wing populism'. It was not surprising, if not inevitable, that in Chile in the UP (Popular Unity) period,

---

[22] Exemplified in the class-based (but not 'economistic') ethnographies, mostly from Central and Eastern Europe, in Kalb and Halmai, eds (2011).

'the small and medium' farmers (that is, the rural 'middle class'), driven by the propaganda of landed property/agrarian capital, 'scurried to the right' in the face of extended land reform measures of the Allende government (Bello 2019, 40). Nor that in Bolivia and Ecuador the governments' 'productivist' version of 'food sovereignty' (in effect, national food self-sufficiency vs *Via Campesina* style agroecological food sovereignty) generated the support of small and medium capitalist farmers, and indeed 'family farmers' (Soper 2020), to whom it provided subsidies and other incentives (Tilzey 2019). Questions of labour and farm labour regimes provide, if anything, an even more sure guide to agrarian class relations given how widely petty commodity (as well as capitalist) production in agriculture depends on wage labour, as Gürel, Küçük, and Tas (2019) indicate, and which underlies the observation by Indian activist and farmer Uma Shankari: 'It is much easier to work on issues [of caste] that do not involve conflicting class interests' (Shankari 2018, 60).

I leave the last word to Walden Bello (2018, 55): 'the politics of class continues to be capable of springing big surprises'. We can only hope that it will do so in positive ways and that, while resisting the seductions of voluntarism and triumphalism, we are able to contribute to and to recognise such surprises when they occur.

Acknowledgements

Thanks to Ben Cousins and Jens Lerche, as ever, for useful discussions and comments, also to two thoughtful anonymous referees for the Journal, all of whom are absolved from the failings of the final product.

Disclosure statement

No potential conflict of interest was reported by the author(s).

References

Adaman, F., M. Arsel, and B. Akbulut. 2019. "Neoliberal Developmentalism, Authoritarian Populism and Extractivism in the Countryside: the Soma Mining Disaster in Turkey." *Journal of Peasant Studies* 46 (3-4): 514–536.

Ahmad, A. 2000. *Lineages of the Present. Ideology and Politics in Contemporary South Asia*. London: Verso.

Ahmad, A. 2016. "India: Liberal Democracy and the Extreme Right." Indian Cultural Forum. https://indianculturalforum.in/2016/09/07/india-liberal-democracy-and-the-extreme-right/.

Andrade, D. 2019. "Populism from Above and Below: The Path to Regression in Brazil." *Journal of Peasant Studies*, 1–27. doi:10.1080/03066150.2019.1680542.

Beban, A., L. Schoenberger, and V. Lamb. 2020. "Pockets of Liberal Media in Authoritarian Regimes: What the Crackdown on Emancipatory Spaces Means for Rural Social Movements in Cambodia'." *Journal of Peasant Studies* 47 (1-2): 95–115.

Bello, W. 2018. "Counterrevolution, the Countryside and the Middle Classes: Lessons from Five Countries." *Journal of Peasant Studies* 45 (1-2): 21–58.

Bello, W. 2019. *Counterrevolution. The Global Rise of the Far Right*. Halifax, NS: Fernwood.

Berlet, C., and S. Sunshine. 2019. "Rural Rage: The Roots of Right-wing Populism in the United States." *Journal of Peasant Studies* 46 (3-4): 480–513.

Bernstein, H. 2010. *Class Dynamics of Agrarian Change*. Halifax, NS: Fernwood.

Borras Jr, S. M. 2020. "Agrarian Social Movements: The Absurdly Difficult but not Impossible Agenda of Defeating Right-wing Populism and Exploring a Socialist Future." *Journal of Agrarian Change* 20 (3): 3–36.
Burawoy, M. 2020. "A Tale of Two Marxisms." *New Left Review NS* 121: 67–98.
Carolan, M. 2020. ""They Say They Don't See Color, But Maybe They Should!" Authoritarian Populism and Colorblind Liberal Political Culture." *Journal of Peasant Studies*, 1–25. doi:10.1080/03066150.2020.1739654.
Davis, M. 2018. *Old Gods, New Enigmas. Marx's Lost Theory*. London: Verso.
Dorlach, T. 2015. "The Prospects of Egalitarian Capitalism in the Global South: Turkish Social Neoliberalism in Comparative Perspective." *Economy and Society* 44 (4): 519–544.
Edelman, M. 2018. "Sacrifice Zones in Rural and Non-Metro USA: Fertile Soil for Authoritarian Populism." TNI. https://www.tni.org/en/publication/sacrifice-zones-in-rural-and-non-metro-usa-fertile-soil-for-authoritarian-populism.
Edelman, M. 2019. "Hollowed out Heartland, USA: How Capital Sacrificed Communities and Paved the Way for Authoritarian Populism." *Journal of Rural Studies*. doi:10.1016/j.jrurstud.2019.10.045.
Ferguson, J., and T. M. Li. 2018. *Beyond the 'Proper Job:' Political-economic Analysis after the Century of Labouring Man*. Working Paper 51. Cape Town: PLAAS, UWC.
Franquesa, J. 2019. "The Vanishing Exception: Republican and Reactionary Specters of Populism in Rural Spain." *Journal of Peasant Studies* 46 (3-4): 537–560.
Gaventa, J. 1980. *Power and Powerlessness: Quiescence and Rebellion in an Appalachian Valley*. Urbana: University of Illinois Press.
Gaventa, J. 2019. "Power and Powerlessness in an Appalachian Valley." *Journal of Peasant Studies* 46 (3-4): 440–456.
Gilbert, J. 2020. "Labour Should Have Argued Against the Last 40 Years, Not Just the Last Ten." Open Democracy. https://www.opendemocracy.net/en/opendemocracyuk/labour-should-have-argued-against-last-40-years-not-just-last-ten/.
Gonda, N. 2019. "Land Grabbing and the Making of an Authoritarian Populist Regime in Hungary." *Journal of Peasant Studies* 46 (3-4): 606–625.
Gürel, B., B. Küçük, and S. Tas. 2019. "The Rural Roots of the Rise of the Justice and Development Party in Turkey." *Journal of Peasant Studies* 46 (3-4): 457–479.
Hall, S. 1985. "Authoritarian Populism: A Reply to Jessop et al." *New Left Review* 151: 115–124.
Harvey, D. 2003. *The New Imperialism*. Oxford: Oxford University Press.
Ivanou, A. 2019. "Authoritarian Populism in Rural Belarus: Distinction, Commonalities, and Projected Finale." *Journal of Peasant Studies* 46 (3-4): 586–605.
Jessop, B., K. Bonnett, S. Bromley, and T. Ling. 1984. "Authoritarian Populism, Two Nations, and Thatcherism." *New Left Review* 147: 32–60.
Kalb, D. 2011. "Introduction" in Kalb and Halmai, eds, Headlines of Nation, Sub-Texts of Class: Working-Class Populism and the Return of the Repressed in Neoliberal Europe. New York: Berghahn: 1–36.
Kalb, D., and G. Halmai eds. 2011. *Headlines of Nation, Sub-Texts of Class: Working-Class Populism and the Return of the Repressed in Neoliberal Europe*. New York: Berghahn.
Mamonova, N. 2019. "Understanding the Silent Majority in Authoritarian Populism: What Can We Learn from Popular Support for Putin in Rural Russia?" *Journal of Peasant Studies* 46 (3-4): 561–585.
Mamonova, N., and J. Franquesa. 2019. "Populism, Neoliberalism and Agrarian Movements in Europe. Understanding Rural Support for Right-wing Politics and Looking for Progressive Solutions." *Sociologica Ruralis*. doi:10.1111/soru.12291.
Monjane, B., and N. Bruna. 2020. "Confronting Agrarian Authoritarianism: Dynamics of Resistance to PROSAVANA in Mozambique." *Journal of Peasant Studies* 47 (1-2): 69–94.
Riley, D. 2020. "'Real Utopia or Abstracted Empiricism?'" *New Left Review NS* 121: 99–107.
Roman-Alcalá, A. forthcoming. "Agrarian Anarchism and Authoritarian Populism: Towards a More (State-) Critical 'Critical Agrarian Studies'." *Journal of Peasant Studies*.
Sandwell, K., A. Castaneda Flores, L. Fernanda Forero, J. Franco, S. Monsalve Suarez, A. Nuila, and P. Seufert. 2019. *A View from the Countryside: Contesting and Constructing Human Rights in an Age of Converging Crises*. Amsterdam: TNI.

Scoones, I., M. Edelman, S. M. Borras Jr, R. Hall, W. Wolford, and B. White. 2018. "Emancipatory Rural Politics: Confronting Authoritarian Populism." *Journal of Peasant Studies* 45 (1-2): 1–20.

Shanin, T. 1966. "The Peasantry as a Political Factor." *Sociological Review* 14 (1): 5–27.

Shankari, U. 2018. "Agrarian Crisis. A Ringside View - II." *Economic and Political Weekly* 53 (8): 56–61.

Soper, R. 2020. "From Protecting Peasant Livelihoods to Essentializing Peasant Agriculture: Problematic Trends in Food Sovereignty Discourse." *Journal of Peasant Studies* 47 (1-2): 265–285.

Therborn, G. 2007. "After Dialectics. Radical Social Theory in a Post-Communist World." *New Left Review NS* 43: 63–114.

Tilzey, M. 2019. "Authoritarian Populism and Neo-extractivism in Bolivia and Ecuador: The Unresolved Agrarian Question and the Prospects for Food Sovereignty as Counter-Hegemony." *Journal of Peasant Studies* 46 (3-4): 626–652.

Ulrich-Schad, J. D., and C. M. Duncan. 2018. "People and Places Left Behind: Work, Culture and Politics in the Rural United States." *Journal of Peasant Studies* 45 (1-2): 59–79.

van der Ploeg, J. D. 2020. "Farmers' Upheaval, Climate Crisis and Populism." *Journal of Peasant Studies*, doi:10.1080/03066150.2020.1725490.

van der Ploeg, J. D., J. Ye, and S. Schneider. 2012. "Rural Development through the Construction of New, Nested, Markets: Comparative Perspectives from China, Brazil and the European Union." *Journal of Peasant Studies* 39 (1): 133–173.

Vanaik, A. 2018. "India's Two Hegemonies." *New Left Review NS* 112: 29–59.

Webber, J. R. 2017a. "Evo Morales, *Transformismo*, and the Consolidation of Agrarian Capitalism in Bolivia." *Journal of Agrarian Change* 17 (2): 330–347.

Webber, J. R. 2017b. *The Last Day of Oppression and the First Day of the Same: The Politics and Economics of the New Latin American Left*. Chicago: Haymarket Books.

White, B. in press. *Agriculture and the Generation Problem*. Halifax, NS: Fernwood.

From 'populist moment' to authoritarian era: challenges, dangers, possibilities

Marc Edelman

ABSTRACT
This essay, inspired by the huge outpouring of research generated in and around the Emancipatory Rural Politics Initiative, reflects on the challenges of analysing authoritarian populism and particularly its rural expressions. The paper first examines key features of authoritarian populism and early populist movements in the Americas and Russia. Then it turns to 'illiberal' neoliberalism and the origins of neoliberalism under brutal dictatorial regimes in Indonesia and Chile. The paper scrutinizes the scepticism about populism in the work of prominent liberal and neoliberal media pundits and scholars. The affinities and tensions between different authoritarian populist rulers, the worrisome transnational linkages of their support bases and the massive flows of right-wing donor money between white supremacist and nationalist movements in different countries suggest the emergence of a fractious axis, not as consolidated as the fascist axis of the 1930s and 1940s, but a rising threat to democracy nonetheless. The paper considers the degeneration of progressive populisms, such as Venezuelan *chavismo*, and the problem of resorting to 'automatic' or 'unconditional' solidarities as a factor in the delegitimizing of left alternative voices. The last sections discuss emancipatory politics, the recent phenomenon of pandemic authoritarianism and the rising protest movements that constitute a possible opportunity for progressive forces.

Introduction

The 'populist moment' is turning into a nightmarish authoritarian populist era with no end in sight.[1] A few examples should suffice to drive home both the severity of the unfolding horror show and the central role of rural populations in its spread. In 2019 Indian voters re-elected Prime Minister Narendra Modi of the Hindu fundamentalist Bharatiya Janata Party; the BJP swept most rural districts, confounding predictions that depressed crop prices and rising costs would curtail farmers' support (Koyanagi 2019). Brazilians chose Jair Bolsonaro as President in an election process marred by the jailing on dubious corruption charges of Lula da Silva, the popular ex-President and Workers Party leader; nicknamed 'the Trump of the Tropics', Bolsonaro won with strong support from agribusiness sectors eager to

---

[1]For Chantal Mouffe (2018, 11), 'the populist moment' occurs when political or socioeconomic transformations destabilize the dominant hegemony and 'a new subject of collective action [emerges] – "the people" – capable of reconfiguring a social order experienced as unjust'.

jettison environmental regulations and burn the Amazon (Matias 2019). In Mozambique's 2019 elections the FRELIMO Party, an historical anticolonial liberation movement increasingly committed to imposing commercial farming on a recalcitrant peasantry, made a surprisingly strong showing (Monjane and Bruna 2020). In Spain the neofascist Vox Party, a breakaway group from the already pro-Franco Popular Party, aligned with ultranationalist parties elsewhere in Europe and made strong gains in 2019, particularly in the significantly rural and impoverished regions of Andalusia and Extremadura (Franquesa 2019). In Bolivia a right-wing coup – fomented in part by large landowners with links to separatist and fascist movements in the heavily agricultural lowland Departments of Beni and Santa Cruz – ousted President Evo Morales, perhaps the last remaining head-of-state with a credible claim to be part of Latin America's (largely) progressive populist 'pink tide'. At the same time, rural people were prominent in some efforts to resist the authoritarian onslaught, perhaps most notably in Ecuador, where indigenous protests intensified after an erstwhile 'pink tide' government sought to impose harsh austerity measures.

This essay – inspired by the immense outpouring of research generated since 2018 in the Emancipatory Rural Politics Initiative – highlights aspects of the current and future research agenda that deserve more sustained attention.[2] After a brief discussion of the central features of authoritarian populism, the paper calls for a longer view, both as regards the early populist experiences in the Americas and Russia and as regards the origins of neoliberalism under brutal dictatorial regimes in Indonesia and Chile. It then analyses the curious denial about populism found in the work of prominent liberal and neoliberal media pundits. The affinities and tensions between different authoritarian populist rulers, the worrisome transnational linkages of their support bases and the massive flows of right-wing donor money between white supremacist and nationalist movements in different countries suggest the emergence of a fractious axis, not as consolidated as the fascist axis of the 1930s and 1940s, but a rising threat to democracy nonetheless. The paper goes on to consider the degeneration of progressive populisms, notably Venezuela's *chavista* experiment, and the problem of resorting to 'automatic solidarities' as a factor in the delegitimizing and silencing of left alternative voices. Finally, I briefly discuss some of the ERPI analyses of emancipatory politics and the more recent phenomenon of pandemic authoritarianism, as both a major threat and a possible opportunity for progressive forces.

The authoritarian populist nightmare

'Authoritarian populism' almost always has the following characteristics: (1) a claim to represent or advocate on behalf of 'the people', with the latter typically defined in exclusionary terms; (2) a multi-class political base; (3) disdain for traditional political and economic elites and their cultural cosmopolitanism; (4) hatred and repressive policies directed at stigmatized Others at home; and (5) suspicion of 'threatening' adversaries abroad, whether unscrupulous trading partners, potential terrorists, criminal networks or

---

[2]Among notable ERPI outputs are an extensive series of short videos and articles – some condensed versions of longer scholarly papers – on OpenDemocracy.net (2018); a special issue of *Sociologia Ruralis* on European cases (Brooks 2019; Calvário, Desmarais, and Azkarraga 2019; Lubarda 2019; Mamonova and Franquesa 2019), a special issue of *Annals of the American Association of Geographers* (McCarthy 2019), a forthcoming special issue of *Latin American Perspectives*, a cluster of U.S.-focused papers in the *Journal of Rural Studies* (Edelman 2019; Montenegro de Wit et al. 2019; Walter 2019; Watson and Wilson 2020), and a number of other articles in leading journals (Borras 2020; Cortes-Vásquez 2020).

immigrant caravans (Scoones et al. 2018). Writing on the environmental dimensions, James McCarthy adds that such

> regimes often arise directly from tensions between rural and urban areas; assert "blood and soil" claims of indissoluble links between the nation and the biological and physical environment; deploy resurgent tropes of territorialized bodies politic, contagion, and disease; exploit national natural resources to buy political support and underwrite their political agenda; attack environmental protections and activists to give extractive capital free reign; eliminate or attack environmental data and science in a "posttruth" era; and are especially dysfunctional political responses to the security threats, fears, and divisions associated with climate change. (2019, 302)

Often authoritarian populist movements and regimes are personalist and revolve around the figure of a single charismatic or messianic leader who claims to be the incarnation of the people and its will. Frequently, the leader spawns a 'vulgarization' of political discourse intended to shore up his – apart from Margaret Thatcher and Marine Le Pen, they are almost always men – anti-elitist and anti-cosmopolitan credentials, with invocations of xenophobic, racist, misogynist, homophobic and anti-immigrant sentiments (Brubaker 2017; Mazzarella 2019; Robotham 2020). Spectacular politics – mass rallies, TV and radio harangues, belligerent tweets, endorsements of conspiracy theories – may come to replace the staid procedures of parliaments, ministries and state agencies. In India, for example, Modi's 2014 election campaign deployed holograms of the candidate throughout the country, making him magically ubiquitous. As M. Madhava Prasad observed, in a comment with obvious relevance to the Philippines, the United States, Turkey and elsewhere, Modi's use of 'the aggressive lingo of the street fighter, produces in audiences the experience of vicarious self-expression', something that decades of 'moderate' Congress Party rule largely denied to all but the minority of highly educated English speakers. The active 'development of undereducation' is a key enabling condition for authoritarian populism, in India and elsewhere (Prasad 2020).

Once in power, authoritarian populists seek to undermine, capture and instrumentalize institutions of democratic governance and oversight. Often they attempt, with considerable success, to extend their terms of office by forcing through constitutional or other legal changes (Versteeg et al. 2019). Sometimes they harness territorial ambitions to their programs of domestic incitement and repression. Authoritarian populist regimes often have roots in and connections to historical fascism and today's neofascist movements, since they usually define 'the nation' or 'the people' in ethnically or religiously exclusionary ways. Several have enacted policies that mimic historical fascist practices, such as Italy's registration of Roma and Sinti people (and the Jobbik Party's calls in Hungary for registering Jews) or the US government's ongoing practice of holding asylum seekers and refugees in squalid concentration camps (Paterson and McDonald-Gibson 2013; Kirchgaessner 2018; Serwer 2019). Reliance on 'big lie' propaganda techniques, such as those pioneered in Nazi Germany, is another feature that today's authoritarian populists share with the fascism of the 1930s and '40s (Washington Post 2020). Like historical fascism, twenty-first-century authoritarian populism is frequently 'an alliance of convenience' between sectors of big capital and 'reactionary elements of the petty bourgeoisie or lower-middle class' (Yates and Foster 2020). Authoritarian populist regimes differ from historical fascism, however, in their efforts to preserve at least a façade of electoral competition and to claim legitimacy on the basis of electoral outcomes, however much these may be corrupted or manipulated (Finchelstein 2017).

If neoliberalism was in part an elite response to the exhaustion of earlier state-led models of development, the initial 'populist moment' was possible because neoliberal policies exacerbated economic inequality and concentrated wealth and income, brought stagnating or declining wages, eroded labour rights, undermined small businesses and farms, eviscerated public sector institutions, and severely cut social provisioning of all kinds. Importantly, these impacts frequently had a disproportionately negative impact on already disadvantaged rural zones, especially after the 2008 economic crisis, and this in turn exacerbated rural resentment of both affluent, cosmopolitan and low-income minority urbanites (Cramer 2016; Foa and Wilmot 2019). At the same time, social democratic parties (and the Democratic Party in the United States) increasingly embraced 'Third Way' neoliberalism and largely abandoned their earlier commitments to the welfare state and the working classes (Giddens 2000; Fraser 2017). This political shift opened a space for right-wing politicians and movements to exploit 'cultural' and identity-related anxieties, especially festering bitterness against various 'Others' at home and abroad.

Populist responses to the neoliberal onslaught and social democratic abandonment were often exclusionary and authoritarian, though sometimes – as with the 'pink tide' governments in Latin America – they deepened social inclusion, implemented heterodox economic policies, created regional institutions that countered imperial hegemony (e.g. the now moribund UNASUR [Unión de Naciones Suramericanas]), and took impressive strides in reducing poverty and asserting sovereignty over natural resources. Indeed, as Don Robotham (2020) observed (echoing Mouffe [2018, 23]), 'who "the people" are understood to be … will often determine whether this is a "left" or a "right" populism' (or a 'progressive' or 'reactionary' one, in Nancy Fraser's [2019, 23] terms). Right-wing populisms characteristically define 'the people' in ethno-national or religious terms; left-wing populisms, on the other hand, typically view 'the people' as a series of social classes or interest groups. Left-wing populisms thus have to be justified in political terms, which makes them contestable and may give them progressive and democratic potential. Right-wing populism, in contrast, usually minimizes or denies class distinctions and rests on mystical justifications linked to 'blood', 'soil' and 'nation'. To complicate matters further, 'there are right-wing and left-wing authoritarian populisms' with 'a diversity of possible combinations' (Borras 2020, 9). Nonetheless, as I discuss in more detail below, most of the progressive populisms relied on environmentally and economically unsustainable models of natural resource extraction and were relatively short-lived. In some cases this had to do with falling commodity prices and in others with reverses at the hands of revanchist elites, but in several instances inclusionary and progressive populisms evolved in increasingly authoritarian directions largely as a result of their internal dynamics and policies (and sometimes with assists from external imperial pressure campaigns). As I will indicate, the political left has often ignored, downplayed or rationalized this evolution, which contributes to weakening its credibility and legitimacy as a force that can defend the working classes in the face of illiberal neoliberalism and associated authoritarian populist demagoguery.

Illiberal neoliberalism comes full circle

Conventional histories often suggest that the first implementation of neoliberal economic policies occurred in developed-country liberal democracies, with the elections of Margaret

Thatcher in the U.K. (1979), Ronald Reagan in the U.S. (1980) and Brian Mulroney in Canada (1984). This periodization – apart from analytically privileging Global North, developed-country cases – makes it easier to posit an isomorphism or at least an association between free-market economics and political democracy. Like Fukuyama's 'end of history' (1992), these are blatantly ideological claims. It is important to recall that the first experiments with neoliberal policies occurred not in Thatcher's U.K. but under vicious authoritarian regimes in the Global South, notably Suharto's Indonesia and Pinochet's Chile (Ffrench-Davis 2003; Simpson 2008; Sánchez-Ancochea 2017). Both the Indonesian and Chilean variants of neoliberalism were selective in their application of free-market doctrine and maintained significant public sectors intended to steer development in directions that the regimes and their allies favored. In Indonesia, Suharto's policies had all the draconian hallmarks of what later came to be called 'stabilization' and 'structural adjustment' programs, albeit while preserving a major role in the economy for the military and its officers. Despite the privatization zeal characteristic of most neoliberal projects, in Chile the Pinochet dictatorship maintained the copper industry in the public sector in order to capture the foreign exchange it generated and used new and existing government agencies to promote agricultural and other 'non-traditional' exports. These early experience with illiberal neoliberalism also had a pronounced agrarian dimension. In both the Indonesian and Chilean cases a major part of the coup regimes' agenda was to roll back agrarian reforms implemented under previous democratic governments and to repress or physically liquidate both beneficiaries and advocates of those reforms. Chile and Indonesia were, moreover, both places where, even as the working classes and peasantry suffered intensified repression, new middle classes emerged with neoliberalism and became bulwarks of political support for the conservative regimes.

A growing chorus of scholars and activists indicates – rightly, in my opinion – that neoliberalism has now entered an 'illiberal' or authoritarian stage. Some view this as a reason to eschew the term 'populism' (though usually for different reasons than the media pundits discussed below) (Bruff 2014; Fine and Saad-Filho 2017; Hendrikse 2018; Bruff and Tansel 2019). Prominent figures in the current cohort of authoritarian populist despots embrace the language of 'illiberalism', which they see as a positive form of self-ascription. Hungary's Viktor Orbán, for example, proudly asserts that 'the new state that we are building is an illiberal state' and suggests that it is not impossible to build such a state within the European Union.[3] Orbán, however, is also a quintessential populist, including some and excluding others, and placing great stress on building a 'community' of Hungarians, including those 'living outside the borders of Hungary' (Orbán 2014).

If we take more fully into account that the origins of the neoliberal experiment involved brutal dictatorships that murdered thousands of their citizens, we can more fully grasp the savagery of neoliberalism in its contemporary authoritarian stage. In effect, today's neoliberalism in its 'illiberal' phase has just come full circle. The 'democratic' phase of neoliberalism may have been an historical anomaly, much as the vaunted prosperity of capitalism's 'thirty glorious years' – the rising living standards and narrowing inequality that characterized the period 1945–1975 in many developed and developing countries – is now understood to have been an aberration. But to recognize the illiberal phase of neoliberalism

---

[3]Orbán is likely quite pleased to be in the E.U., since he has managed to channel large amounts of E.U. Common Agricultural Policy subsidies to his relatives and cronies (Gebrekidan, Apuzzo, and Novak 2019; Gonda 2019).

need not and should not mean dispensing with an analysis of how authoritarian populist leaders discursively construct and politically implement their exclusionary visions of the 'nation' or 'community'.

Genealogies of authoritarian populism

In our earlier analysis, we sketched a genealogy of authoritarian populism that essentially began with Stuart Hall's discussion of Margaret Thatcher's election and its aftermath (Scoones et al. 2018). There are several reasons for pushing the analysis further back and widening its geographical scope. First, a historically deeper and geographically wider analysis of populism points to tensions and contradictions that persist in contemporary populist projects of both democratic-inclusionary and authoritarian-exclusionary stripes. Second, the rootedness of many (though not all) populist movements in agrarian and rural crises is amply evident if we take a longer view. And third, the ideological ambivalence and cross-class alliances that have characterized so many populist projects go a long way toward explaining the frequent transformation of populisms with strong emancipatory platforms and programs into more regressive and repressive ones.

The People's Party in the United States was probably the first party labeled 'populist' in anything like the contemporary meaning of the term. Founded in 1892, the U.S. Populists were mainly an alliance between labour reformers and small farmers, both proprietors and tenants, and a response to the consolidation of a powerful bourgeoisie centered in finance, railroads and industry. But their broader coalition also included temperance crusaders,

> salon utopians of Edward Bellamy's Nationalist Clubs, … the mostly working-class advocates of Henry George's single tax on land, … and … Christian Socialists in seminaries and evangelical churches across the land. (Kazin 1995, 28)

Their 'Omaha Platform' foreshadowed rhetorical and programmatic features of other historical and contemporary populist movements and regimes. 'Corruption dominates the ballot-box, the Legislatures, the Congress, and touches even the ermine of the bench', they declared.

> The people are demoralized … The newspapers are largely subsidized or muzzled, public opinion silenced, business prostrated, homes covered with mortgages, labor impoverished, and the land concentrating in the hands of capitalists. The urban workmen are denied the right to organize for self-protection, imported pauperized labor beats down their wages … The fruits of the toil of millions are boldly stolen to build up colossal fortunes for a few, unprecedented in the history of mankind … From the same prolific womb of governmental injustice we breed the two great classes—tramps and millionaires. (People's Party 1892)

Notwithstanding their appeals to 'urban workmen', the U.S. Populists were mainly an agrarian party. They proposed a system of commodity reserves to stabilize prices and a ban on foreign ownership of land. They demanded an end to the gold standard and called for inflationary policies that would both benefit indebted farmers and provide them higher prices for their production. 'In effect', according to Harvey Wasserman, 'the farmers were demanding a currency based on food rather than gold' (1972, 73). The Populists sought the nationalization of railroads and telegraphs, but mainly to protect small producers from the depredations of monopolists rather than from any kind of socialist vision.

In the South, burgeoning African American agrarian movements, with tenuous ties to the Populists and occasional cross-race alliances, crumbled in the face of white supremacist violence (Ali 2012). Ultimately the U.S. Populists won many governorships, state legislatures, and congressional seats, mainly in the South and west of the Mississippi. But their strength rapidly waned in the face of implacable opposition from mining, railroad and industrial interests and as they tied themselves to the unsuccessful 1896 presidential campaign of the Democratic Party, which eventually adopted and enacted into legislation some elements of their program (Judis 2016).

Along with the U.S. People's Party, the Russian *Narodniki* were the other 'classical' populist movement and 'Russia's main indigenous revolutionary tradition', dating to the 1870s (Shanin 1983, 8; Mamonova and Franquesa 2019). In contrast to the U.S. populists, who arose in a dynamic capitalist economy, the Russian *narodniki* were part of a society only recently emerging from feudalism, where capitalism was, if anything, embryonic. The broad term '*narodnik*' ('of the people [*narod*]') was typically glossed as 'populist', although it encompassed a range of movements and political positions the adherents of which almost always eschewed the label. Even in the late nineteenth century observers recognized the category 'populist' or '*narodnik*' as overly capacious and imprecise (Pipes 1964). With a political base among the 'working intelligentsia' and certain sectors of peasantry, some *Narodniki* believed that intellectuals should 'go to the peasants' *to lead them*, others that intellectuals should go to the peasants *to learn from them*; some favored insurrection and organized the 1881 assassination of Tsar Alexander II, while others opposed revolutionary violence. Indeed, as Teodor Shanin remarked, 'In Russian speech a populist (*narodnik*) could have meant anything from a revolutionary terrorist to a philanthropic squire' (Shanin 1983, 8).

From our perspective, the legacy of the Russian *Narodniki* is significant for two main reasons. First, *Narodniki* often believed that the rural peasant commune or *mir* was part of a longstanding collectivist tradition of the Russian people and would permit bypassing the capitalist stage of development and leaping directly to a socialist society. While Marx signaled tentative openness to this view in his correspondence with key figures in the Russian movement, his letters were only discovered in 1911 and were long consigned to oblivion by the Bolshevik keepers of his legacy, who maintained that full-blown capitalist development was a necessary precursor of socialism (Shanin 1983). This transition debate has many echoes later in the Global South and in academic discussions of development and underdevelopment and the agrarian question. The second important legacy of the Russian *Narodniki* has to do with this confrontation with orthodox Marxism, especially as it became institutionalized in the Russian Social Democratic (later Communist) Party and eventually in the Soviet Union and the world Communist movement. For Communist Parties everywhere, 'populist' became a term of opprobrium, in large part because Lenin, in *The Development of Capitalism in Russia* (1964 [1899]), criticized 'a couple of writers who stood … on the extreme right wing of the populists'. According to Shanin, 'This made Lenin's anti-populist argument of 1898 easier, while increasing the obscurity of the populist creed to his readers of today' (1983, 8). Until the mid-1930s, this fundamental misunderstanding and the Leninist imprimatur on anti-populism meant that Communists throughout the world manifested unremitting hostility to non-Communist progressive movements. This division between the non-Communist and the Communist left had well-known consequences in Germany. It also had tragic impacts in

Latin America, where Communist Parties adamantly opposed 'populist' parties, movements and leaders, even when these were profoundly anti-imperialist and had genuine programs of broad social reform.

Latin American intellectuals have tended to see the region's populisms as representing varied and sometimes tortured routes to development and modernity (Di Tella 1965; Germani 1978). Torcuato di Tella, for example, argued that a defining feature of populism is that it 'enjoys the support of the mass of the urban working class and/or peasantry but ... does not result from the autonomous organizational power of either of these two sectors' (1965, 47). Gino Germani, similarly, noted that 'populism often becomes a mass movement only in societies where typical Western European leftist ideologies of the working class fail to develop into mass parties' (1978, 88). If the first populist leaders that came to power in Latin America in the early to mid-twentieth century were broadly progressive and enacted significant top-down social reforms, by the 1930s some also flirted with European fascist ideas, symbols and practices.

José Batlle y Ordóñez, president of Uruguay in 1904–1907 and 1911–1915, laid the groundwork for a modern welfare state and greatly expanded fundamental democratic rights. Similarly, Hipólito Yrigoyen, of Argentina's Radical Civic Union, won the presidency in 1916 and 1928 and tried to enact social legislation like that next door in Uruguay. But Yrigoyen faced a more intransigent and powerful oligarchy in Argentina and the military toppled him in 1930. After the rise of fascism in Europe, Brazilian dictator Getulio Vargas decreed higher wages for formal-sector workers and enacted health and housing reforms, but all under the aegis a 'New State' modeled on Mussolini's Corporate State in Italy. In the Dominican Republic Rafael Trujillo's thirty-year dictatorship created the country's first modern state institutions and held populist-style rallies in remote rural areas. The regime brutally persecuted opponents at home and abroad, but it had broad support from the peasantry, which benefited from agrarian reform and heightened social recognition and from its incorporation into a tightly regulated national economy (Turits 2003).

Juan Domingo Perón, president of Argentina in 1946–1955, established the most durable populist project in the region, raising living standards for the urban working class, massively increasing membership in corporatist-type unions, and expanding diverse aspects of the social welfare apparatus, including education, health and retirement systems. When he briefly returned to power in 1973–1974, just before the 'dirty war', his political coalition ran the gamut from Maoists to latter-day fascists. Peronism continues to have deep roots among the Argentine working class, as evidenced in the 2019 election when a Peronist candidate ousted a discredited president who had implemented harsh neoliberal 'reforms'. Importantly, while Perón lamented the loss of 'poor Mussolini', he saw fascism as an ideology of the past and, like today's authoritarian populists, sought legitimation in electoral democracy, albeit an illiberal, hollowed out one (Finchelstein 2017, 22, 165).

Liberal and neoliberal denial about populism

One curious feature of the current debate is liberal elites' resistance to using the term 'populism' to describe today's crop of demagogic rulers. *New York Times* columnist and Nobel Prize-winning economist Paul Krugman, for example, insists that Trump 'isn't a populist' since his policies benefit only the rich and not the "little guy[s]" of his non-college-educated white "base"' (2019). In another column he argues that

> there's overwhelming evidence against the 'economic anxiety' hypothesis — the notion that people voted for Donald Trump because they had been hurt by globalization. In fact, people who were doing well financially were just as likely to support Trump as people who were doing badly. What distinguished Trump voters was, instead, racial resentment. Furthermore, this resentment was and is driven not by actual economic losses at the hands of minority groups, but by fear of losing status in a changing country, one in which the privilege of being a white man isn't what it used to be. (Krugman 2018)

That well-off white voters were just as likely to support Trump of course says nothing about that substantial sector of the white electorate that *was* experiencing severe economic stress and that voted for Trump. Claims like Krugman's do not analyse sufficiently the synergetic, mutually-constituting character of economic stress, status anxiety and racist attitudes. They also fail to acknowledge the extent to which mainstream political parties and elites, as well as their preferred Democratic candidate, appeared tone deaf and out-of-touch to working-class and rural voters. While one sector of the liberal intelligentsia insistently denied that economic distress was a factor in the 2016 U.S. presidential election, in part because of their own commitment to or complicity with the neoliberal project, another sector energetically promoted economics-based explanations for the rise of Trump because of their blindness to or reluctance to recognize the centrality of racial inequality to U.S. capitalism. In both cases, they failed to grasp the different ways in which economic suffering, racism, and community decline have interacted to prepare the ground for authoritarian populism (Edelman 2019).

Some analysts who reject the 'populist' label have gone as far as to insist that

> "Populism" has been spreading partly because some did not find the right word, but also because some others deliberately chose a euphemistic expression to cut the edges of a debate and avoid arriving to antagonising conclusions (Andor 2019).

Others, such as Thomas Piketty, find the term imprecise because it is used to refer to completely different things. Some people would like to use it to refer to both Trump and Sanders in the US, or to Bolsonaro and Lula in Brazil, or to Le Pen and Mélenchon in France (Steinmetz-Jenkins 2020).

The idea that 'populism' is not a suitable category because its meanings shift and it has a wide range of referents expresses a desire for a unitary, ahistorical essence and amounts to a denial of the extent of today's authoritarian nightmare. I am less interested in debating 'the right word' or in engaging in an undisciplined use of the term, than in specifying common features of the various authoritarian populist movements and regimes that are on the rise worldwide, as I have attempted to do in the introduction to this paper. To characterize these as 'authoritarian populist' does not mean abandoning other apt characterizations, such as 'ethno-nationalist', 'illiberal' or 'demagogic'. But because these related features are not always present to the same degree in today's authoritarian populist movements and regimes, to rely on them alone could obscure broader trends and connections. Moreover, the apparent capaciousness to which Piketty (and others) object, when adequately specified, actually facilitates analysis of a key phenomenon discussed below, the degeneration of progressive populations into regressive authoritarian ones.

The authoritarian axis

To what extent are the world's 'ogres galore', as Perry Anderson (2019) termed them – Trump, Duterte, Erdoğan, Modi, Orbán, Putin, Bolsonaro, among others – simply a mutually reinforcing collection of erratic rulers? Or are they taking shape as a global authoritarian populist axis?

I posed this question two years ago (Edelman 2018) and now, with additional hindsight, I would argue that the current cohort of authoritarians has constituted a loose, though frequently fractious axis. This must be analyzed along three interrelated dimensions: (1) the alliances and the contradictions and frictions between heads-of-state and governments; (2) the transnationalization of nationalist and white supremacist movements, ideologies and media infrastructure; and (3) national and international flows of ultra-right-wing donors' money and know-how.

The objectives and ideologies of contemporary authoritarian populist rulers overlap to a significant degree, but not completely. Most are extreme nationalists and thus wary of strong transnational alliances and collaboration. Their loyalties to each other are shifting and sometimes fragile. Trump, for example, closed Russian consulates in the United States but acquiesced in Russia's illegal annexation of Crimea from Ukraine. Modi, who was banned from entering the United States for more than a decade because of his role in the 2002 anti-Muslim riots in Gujarat, invited Trump to a 2019 mass rally in Houston with Indian American supporters and in 2020 staged another joint mass rally in Ahmedabad. While Modi and Trump are united in their Islamophobia and exclusionary rhetoric, and Trump turned a blind eye to the Indian crackdown in Kashmir, the United States is also involved in a delicate balancing act that requires it to maintain good relations with Pakistan.

Paradoxically, frictions between authoritarian populists in different countries can serve each party because these ultimately burnish their respective nationalist credentials by claiming that they are standing up to foreign aggression, insults or impositions. When Trump writes a scathing and undiplomatic letter to Erdoğan, for example, the latter can take umbrage and gain credibility at home by denouncing the U.S. president, even as Turkey purchases Russian missile defenses and Trump facilitates the long-sought Turkish invasion of Rojava, the utopian enclave that Kurdish fighters defended in northern Syria.

Some of today's authoritarians are explicit about seeking an 'axis', as in 2018 when Austrian Chancellor Sebastian Kurz shut down seven mosques and days later called for the creation of an ominously titled 'Axis of the Willing' to halt 'illegal immigration' (Bleifuss 2018).[4] Proto-axis formations, moreover, already exist. The Visegrád Group – linking governments in Hungary, Poland, the Czech Republic and Slovakia – formed to oppose immigration quotas for E.U. member states. These coalitions are less coherent than the historical fascist-Nazi axis of the 1930s and 1940s. But the shared anti-immigrant discourses and policies of their members point to the way in which authoritarian populist regimes seek to maintain some superficial trappings of democracy in order to placate their own intelligentsias and international public opinion, while at the same time enacting

---

[4] Kurz's term combines the terms 'Axis Powers' and the 'Coalition of the Willing' that George W. Bush called for in the lead-up to the US invasion of Iraq.

cruel, fascist-like measures – internment camps, deportations, raids on residences and workplaces – for members of their stigmatized out-groups, undocumented migrants in particular.

The more prominent figures in the authoritarian populist group play an important role in enabling and legitimizing their counterparts in other countries and in normalizing views long considered unacceptable in democratic societies. Trump's hostility to empirical evidence and cries of 'fake news', and his repeated racist, Islamophobic and anti-immigrant diatribes and personal insults, have not only corroded U.S. political discourse and fueled the American 'alt-right' but have also served as models and inspiration for other authoritarians, notably Bolsonaro, Modi, Duterte, Orbán and Erdoğan.

Authoritarian populist regimes sometimes link nationalism, territorial expansion and extra-territorial aggression of various kinds. Putin seized Crimea from Ukraine. Modi revoked Kashmir's autonomy to bring it under more direct central state control. Erdoğan attacked the Kurds' Rojava in northern Syria and aspires to set up a buffer zone along the border. In 2017 his bodyguards attacked anti-Erdoğan protestors in Washington and the U.S. government dropped all charges against them on the eve of a visit to Ankara by the U.S. Secretary of State. Netanyahu threatened to annex the occupied Jordan Valley as part of his 2020 re-election campaign and continued piecemeal annexations of areas in and around Jerusalem. Trump launched a farcical and abortive yet typically aggressive attempt to bully Denmark into selling Greenland to the United States. In these cases and others, actual or aspirational territorial expansion shores up the authoritarian populists' political bases and keeps nationalist passions at a boil.

The transnationalization of white supremacist and nationalist movements is especially worrisome. These groups aim to strengthen the authoritarian axis between states from the bottom up by seizing political power and implementing racist and anti-immigrant programs. Many have significant roots in rural zones. White supremacist and Islamophobic ideas circulate between Europe, the United States, Australia and New Zealand, as both the 'manifestos' left by mass killers and scholarly analyses indicate (Bangstad 2014; Feffer 2019). Key motifs – the 'replacement' of white Christians by Muslims, Jews, immigrants and people of color, for example – recycle among a small group of canonical extremist authors, such as French conspiracy theorist Renaud Camus, and recur in viral memes and internet posts. Some groups, such as the neo-Nazi Atomwaffen, have branches in the United States, Canada, the United Kingdom, Germany, and the Baltic States (Bertrand, Toosi, and Lippman 2020; Jones, Doxsee, and Harrington 2020). Similar groups, such as 'the Base' stretch across North America, Europe and Australia. U.S. anti-terrorism experts Max Rose and Ali Soufan indicate that

> White supremacists today are organizing in a similar fashion to jihadist terrorist organizations, like Al Qaeda, in the 1980s and 1990s. They transcend national barriers with recruitment and dissemination of propaganda. And just as jihadists exploited conflicts in Afghanistan, the Balkans and Syria, so too are white supremacists using the conflict in Ukraine as a laboratory and training ground. (Rose and Soufan 2020)

That 'the Base' is English for 'Al Qaeda' is hardly coincidental. Today, white supremacists not only study violent Islamists' online videos about homemade explosives and their processes for vetting new recruits, but also hail their 'culture of martyrdom [as] something to admire and reproduce in the neo-Nazi terror movement' (NJOHSP 2020, 18). Just as hundreds of U.S. and European white supremacists joined Croatian paramilitaries fighting for 'ethnic cleansing' in the 1990s Balkan wars, the current training of foreign white nationalists in Ukrainian military units, such as the neo-Nazi Azov Battalion, points to the historical ties that connect today's violent ethno-nationalists to historical fascism and to the transnational anti-Communist networks that emerged in the early years of the Cold War (Burke 2018, 20–22, 217; Jones, Doxsee, and Harrington 2020).

This ideological 'work' and military preparation are part of the broader push to unite ethno-nationalist and white supremacist movements across borders. Paralleling the efforts of white supremacist terrorist groups such as Atomwaffen and the Base, Trump acolyte Steve Bannon, together with like-minded allies in Europe, has laboured full-time on consolidating an extreme right-wing 'Movement' since his departure from the White House, with a particular emphasis on electing nationalist extremists to the European Parliament. The emergence of an ultra-right-wing International has generated alarm among progressives, but little concrete action, apart from a tepid and ephemeral effort by Yanis Varoufakis and Bernie Sanders to launch a Progressive International with an 'ecological, feminist, humanist, rational program' (Corbett 2018; Sanders 2018).

Ideological and organizational affinities are just part of what binds together authoritarian populist and right-wing extremist movements in different countries. Massive flows of resources are increasingly important. An extensive network of far-right Christian fundamentalist organizations in the United States, including the World Congress of Families and the Alliance Defending Freedom International, has channeled at least US$50 million to counterpart groups and to lobbying efforts in Europe over the last decade. This has fueled campaigns in the name of 'family values' against LGBT+ and reproductive rights. These U.S. groups have also contributed to the spread of white supremacist ideas and neo-fascist parties, such as Italy's Forza Nuova, Spain's Vox and France's Rassemblement national (National Rally, until recently National Front). If Germany's ultra-right Alternative für Deutschland (AfD) party wins representation in the 2021 federal elections, it will receive funds from Berlin like the foundations of the other large German parties, possibly as much as €70 million per year to fund global activities (Feffer 2019; Provost and Fitzgerald 2019; Ramsay and Provost 2019).

The intensifying efforts of ultra-right parties and movements to unite across borders are not only the result of Bannon's and others' grassroots campaigns. Meetings between authoritarian populist heads-of-state have now become occasions for inviting representatives of nationalist movements, as occurred when Bolsonaro visited Trump in Washington in 2019 and right-wingers from both countries, including Bannon and his Brazilian counterpart Olavo de Carvalho, mingled in the Brazilian ambassador's residence (Casarões and Flemes 2019; Schreckinger 2019). This blurring of boundaries between ethno-nationalist movements and governments was also apparent in Trump's and Modi's twin rallies in Texas and Gujarat, where BJP militants and MAGA Indian Americans mingled. Trump's professed love for Indian Americans and Hindus – terms which, despite India's diversity, he uses interchangeably – allows him to affirm that he is not a racist at the same time that Hindu nationalists stake a claim to being the original 'Aryan race', an assertion that some U.S. white supremacists find congenial (Thangaraj 2017).

The degeneration of progressive populisms and the danger of 'automatic solidarities'

One of the most vexing problems for scholars and activists on the left has been the reversal or degeneration of progressive populist experiments that claimed to constitute alternatives after decades of neoliberal shocks and restructuring. In Latin America especially dramatic turnarounds included the 2019 ousting of Evo Morales in Bolivia after a disputed election, the 2017 about-face of Lenín Moreno that called into question the continuity of Ecuador's 'Citizens' Revolution', the 2016 impeachment of Dilma Rousseff in Brazil, the 2012 coup that toppled Fernando Lugo in Paraguay, the 2009 coup against Mel Zelaya in Honduras, and the long 'de-democratization' of Nicaragua that accelerated after 2007 under the increasingly personalist, unaccountable and repressive regime of Daniel Ortega (Martí i Puig and Serra 2020). These reversals and processes of degeneration – such as that in Venezuela, analyzed below – must be acknowledged and understood in all their complexity (and alongside the positive achievements of some of these experiments), since they potentially offer lessons for progressive researchers and social movements.

The 1998 election of Hugo Chávez in Venezuela marked an abrupt break with an ossified two-party system which, despite the country's immense oil wealth, had failed to deliver adequate living standards to the majority of the population. Elected with the enthusiastic backing of the working classes, the charismatic Chávez's Bolivarian Revolution initiated new forms of grassroots political participation and social services delivery that endeared him to the poor and some progressive sectors of the middles classes and intelligentsia and that contributed, at least initially, to significant reductions in poverty. For more than a decade Chávez's government enjoyed a high level of legitimacy, winning successive elections and empowering the popular sectors as political subjects (Lander 2018). Wielding oil revenues as collateral for a massive expansion of its foreign debt and as a tool of geopolitical influence, Venezuela became the leading force in a regional alliance, the Bolivarian Alternative for the Peoples of Our America (ALBA), which at its height included Bolivia, Cuba, Ecuador, Honduras, Nicaragua, and several smaller Caribbean countries. Together with other left-leaning governments – some longer-lived than others – in Brazil, Uruguay, Chile and Argentina, the ALBA countries were part of Latin America's 'pink tide'.

Following Chávez's death in 2013, the less magnetic Nicolás Maduro assumed the presidency in a society and economy that were already manifesting signs of crisis. When commodities prices plummeted in 2014, the 'pink tide' governments in South America began to crumble. In Venezuela the Maduro government took an increasingly authoritarian approach to crisis management, the oil, health and food sectors began collapsing, and growing numbers of migrants fled to neighboring countries. GDP dropped 22.5 percent in 2017 and inflation reached 130,000 percent in 2018, the last years for which data are available (Webber 2020). In addition, in moves that exacerbated the unraveling of the economy, the United States, the European Union, Canada and several Latin American countries backed a self-declared parallel president with a dubious claim to constitutional legitimacy, National Assembly Deputy Juan Guaidó, seized Venezuelan assets abroad, and blocked access to credit and to diverse other kinds of transactions. By 2019, Michelle Bachelet – United Nations High Commissioner for Human Rights, former President of

Chile, Socialist Party leader, and political prisoner during the Pinochet dictatorship – issued a damning report detailing massive violations of economic, social and political rights and a severe humanitarian crisis in which many Venezuelans did not earn a living wage and could not afford basic foods (Bachelet 2019).

There is no single explanation for the degeneration of Venezuela's *chavista* experiment, though part of the crisis was clearly rooted in some of the specific features of authoritarian populism outlined above. First, the cross-class character of all populisms has been abundantly evident, though infrequently acknowledged, in the alliance that Chávez and then Maduro forged with high-ranking military leaders and some sectors of the business elites – the '*boliburguesía*', as Fernando Coronil (2011, 39) called them, 'a nouveau riche sector of parasitical capitalists dressed in revolutionary costume'.[5] A grossly overvalued exchange rate devastated industry and agriculture, since it became vastly cheaper to import than to produce. The overvalued *bolívar* also became a key mechanism that Chávez and Maduro employed to cement ties with a new bureaucratic-military caste of importers who acquired dollars at preferential rates in order to purchase abroad essential goods not produced in the country's oil-dominated economy. Fraudulent invoicing schemes for fake, 'paper' imports proliferated, while those who obtained cut-rate dollars changed their excess hard currency on the parallel market, reaping massive profits and exacerbating shortages of the food and medicine that they weren't really importing (Di Stasio 2019; Webber 2020). Between 2003 and 2012 – before the death of Chávez and while the oil boom reached its zenith – some 70 billion U.S. dollars were likely transferred from the Venezuelan treasury to fraudulent 'importers' (Sutherland 2018, 148). Speculation in dollar-denominated bonds, many owned by rich Venezuelans and among the best performing financial instruments in the world, further worsened hyperinflation and shortages of food and medicine but also constituted a significant pay-off to the elites (Nelson 2016). PDVSA, the state oil company, has been rife with corrupt contracting schemes that led to arrests of dozens of its top officials. The speculative purchase for resale in Colombia of subsidized gasoline – 250 liters of which cost the same as a cup of coffee – now represents a significant, if unrecorded, portion of the Venezuelan economy (Lander 2018, 144–45, 2019). Since 2016 the Maduro government's efforts to expand metallic mining in the Orinoco basin, an area of extraordinary biodiversity and home to numerous indigenous groups, further highlighted both the model's dependence on environmentally destructive extractivism and the opportunities available to high-ranking military and state officials to grease the wheels for Canadian, Chinese and other foreign concessionaires (Nahon-Serfaty 2018).

The instrumentalization of institutions of democratic governance, especially the courts and electoral system, another key feature of authoritarian populist rule, led traditional elite sectors to stage anti-government street protests, joined in some cases by working-class

---

[5]For detailed analyses of the material and political foundations of Venezuela's 'Bolivarian bourgeoisie', see Sutherland (2018) and Webber (2020). In Brazil, similarly, Svampa maintains that the Workers Party (PT) was 'co-opted by the economic elite' (2018). Andrade echoes this assessment, arguing that Lula's Workers Party government 'emerged as representative of interests "from below" while advancing a political project that protected and nurtured interests "from above" — a populist ambiguity' (2019). In Nicaragua, according to Martí i Puig and Serra (2020, 125), the consolidation of a 'Sandinista bourgeoisie' dates at least to the 1990 '*piñata*', when FSLN leaders, defeated at the ballot box, seized state resources for their individual benefit or for their party. After 2007, the 'cooptation of the [traditional] elites was possible because Ortega had maintained the [neoliberal] economic production and commercialization model promoted since 1990 and had boosted it with privileged access to the Venezuelan market'.

erstwhile *chavistas* desperate for food, water, medicine, a living wage, and the right to collective bargaining, as well as for physical security in poor neighborhoods where crime had spiked. These demonstrations and spiraling crime triggered increasingly ruthless government responses (Lander 2019, 143–44). The Bachelet UN report documents 5287 homicides at the hands of the security forces in 2018, mostly racialized poor youths and fully one-third of all homicides in the country that year (Bachelet 2019).

Venezuelan critics *on the left* have been scathing in their criticism. 'In spite of these data', as Keymar Ávila observes,

> some sectors of the orthodox left — who haven't overcome Cold War logic — appeal to automatic solidarities. Their arguments rest on denial, justification and very harmful propagandizing, which delegitimizes them. Ever fewer in number, when they don't justify, legitimise or relativize what is happening in Venezuela, they simply remain silent or look the other way. (2019)

Edgardo Lander further argues that the 'unconditional solidarities' of

> the orthodox left prioritize geopolitical dimensions and Manichean frameworks constructed around the anti-imperialist/imperialist binary, according secondary importance to other essential aspects of the reality of the contemporary world, such as anthropocentrism, patriarchy, racism, colonialism [and] Eurocentrism. (2019, 12)

For Manuel Sutherland,

> The global left does not have to silence its criticisms or engage in outlandish and atavistic defences for the sake of 'not cozying up to the right'. Rather, it needs a rigorous analysis of the national process of capital accumulation in Venezuela. (2018, 151)

The Venezuelan experience also illustrates the role that a charismatic leader – Chávez – played in constructing a vision of 'the people' rooted in historically excluded sectors of the population. This was a radical departure from previous Venezuelan politics and irksome to many in the largely European-descended elite, who weren't included in this broader conception of 'the nation'. When Maduro took over, just as petroleum prices were about to plummet, his decided lack of charisma and declining oil revenues complicated efforts to sustain the high levels of mobilization and enthusiasm that marked the earlier period of *chavismo*. The overreliance on the extraction of oil and other minerals also proved to be the Achilles heel of the other pink tide governments, creating new varieties of dependency, heightening social tensions and eroding livelihoods of the working classes and poor (Hidalgo Pallares and Hurtado Pérez 2016; Tilzey 2019). As Andrés Malamud remarked about Ecuador, since the end of the commodities boom, 'with oil at US$50 per barrel, it's all bitterness and there's no *petroprogresismo* that can survive' (2017).

Emancipatory politics

Various papers produced in the framework of the ERPI observed that progressive social movements, especially though not only in rural areas, face daunting challenges under authoritarian populist governments. Beban, Schoenberger, and Lamb (2020) show how the nearly half million Cambodians involved in violent land struggles have experienced an intensifying intimidation campaign and are increasingly cut off from the independent media that used to provide sympathetic coverage to their struggles. McCarthy (2019, 301) asserts that 'environmental issues, movements, and politics can and must be central to resistance against authoritarian and reactionary populist politics and to visions of progressive alternatives to them', but provides little evidence of actual on-the-ground environmental resistance. In Spain, as Franquesa (2019, 537) points out, left populist movements emerged after 2008 that managed to keep authoritarian populism largely at bay. In several cases, notably Turkey, authoritarian populist regimes bolster their support in the countryside through social compensation, agricultural subsidy and infrastructure construction programs that serve as palliatives for smallholding agriculturalists and rural workers negatively impacted by otherwise urban-biased and oligarchical policies (Adaman, Arsel, and Akbulut 2019; Gürel, Küçük, and Taş 2019; Adaman and Akbulut 2020). In Bolivia and Ecuador, similarly, populist but increasingly authoritarian 'pink tide' governments relied on extractivism to fund the 'compensatory state' that supported small commercial farmers and too often side-lined poorer sectors of the peasantry and rural working class (Tilzey 2019).

Experiences of rural resistance to authoritarian populist regimes are many and varied, though everywhere struggling in unfavorable circumstances and shrinking political space. Tilzey (2019) documents how indigenous and food sovereignty movements in Bolivia and Ecuador have pushed back against extractivist and pro-free market projects of 'pink tide' governments, especially as these lurched to the right. Levi Van Sant (2018), in an important contribution to the ERPI's series of short articles on OpenDemocracy.net, describes how the Redneck Revolt movement attempts to steer supporters of U.S. white supremacist militias in a more progressive direction and excoriates the left for abandoning the countryside to regressive forces. Several analyses of the various 'compensatory' authoritarian populisms point to how regimes work hard to channel rural grassroots politics into conventional corporatist frameworks that mire popular movements in endless negotiations and typically demobilize them. Another significant contribution of some ERPI researchers is simply to insist on a more complex view of rural societies as diverse in class, occupational and ethnic terms and not solely agrarian (Bernstein 2020). Some describe how on-the-ground social relations defy the polarizing stereotypes propagated by urban media pundits as, for example, when Brian Walter (2019) documents the grudging appreciation white rural Alabamans express for the entrepreneurial energy and work ethic of their newer Latin American immigrant neighbors. John Gaventa, similarly, shows how Appalachia has 'long been the source of strong grassroots-led organizations and mobilizations which challenge the status quo' and among these are community empowerment, anti-corporate, environmental justice, immigrant defence, LGBTQ+ and labour movements (2019, 448–50).

Conclusion: class analysis, pandemic authoritarianism and envisioning what comes next

Even critical scholars sometimes tacitly accept populists' claims to embrace the entire 'people' and fail to analyse sufficiently the social class and interest group bases of the right- and left-wing regimes and movements that embrace populism. Paul Krugman, for example, quoted above, refuses in the face of abundant evidence to acknowledge the severe economic distress of much of the U.S. white rural population and working class by conflating them with that other sector of Trump backers that consists of well-off small and large business interests. The refusal of international supporters of *chavismo* to engage in the 'rigorous analysis of the national process of capital accumulation in Venezuela' (Sutherland 2018, 151), also discussed above, is yet another example of how forsaking class analysis produces misleading and impoverished understandings of actually existing social crises. A deeper class analysis of rural areas – and not just agrarian social classes but of the countryside more generally – may also shed light on the peculiar relationship that binds so many authoritarian regimes and movements to populations in zones that have suffered disproportionate economic devastation under neoliberalism and that at the same time embody, in many exclusionary national imaginaries, the racial, religious or occupational essence of 'the people'.

In early 2020 a novel coronavirus pandemic swept the planet and sharpened already worsening contradictions in one society after another. In the world's three largest and increasingly fragile democracies – India, the United States and Brazil – Modi, Trump and Bolsonaro used the coronavirus crisis to inflame hatred, deepen attacks on immigrants and minorities and incite their respective 'bases' to violence. By July 2020, not coincidentally, these three countries also led the world in COVID-19 cases. Denial, bluster, quackery, incoherent policies, incompetent leadership and efforts to foster division resulted in the deaths of thousands.

The pandemic and ensuing economic crisis also upended a globalized, market-driven world system. If neoliberalism had moved rapidly in an illiberal direction, as indicated above, its proponents also had to confront its own dysfunctionality. The nationalist strain of neoliberalism is on the ascent (Mirowski 2020), with policymakers and leaders increasingly insisting that overly long global value chains – especially for food, pharmaceuticals, and medical supplies and equipment – must be reined in and reconfigured in smaller spaces, with greater redundancies as backup. Agile, just-in-time supply and inventory systems have given way to stockpiling and hoarding. Excess industrial capacity now looks like a wise precaution rather than a troubling inefficiency. Expensive stimulus packages with massive bailouts for giant corporations and crumbs for formal-sector workers and the unemployed call into question neoliberals' historic aversion to deficit spending and the big state (Brenner 2020). The grotesque juxtaposition of farmers destroying vegetables and milk and euthanizing millions of animals while consumers suffer ever greater levels of hunger threw into sharp relief the pretense of a productivist agricultural system that claims to be 'feeding the world' but increasingly demonstrates its inability to do so.

The social tensions and economic crisis unleashed with the pandemic and physical distancing required – from the standpoint of the dominant groups – intensified social control. Authoritarian populist leaders have used the pandemic as a pretext for seizing additional powers and instituting draconian forms of surveillance and repression. By mid-April 2020, some 84 countries had declared states of emergency and many had granted heads-of-state the power to rule by decree (Economist 2020a; 2020b). Authoritarian governments have banned street protests and postponed elections, allegedly because they could spread infection, even as some high-profile demagogic leaders also encourage mass rallies of their supporters. Some are selectively enforcing quarantine rules and threatening to send dissidents to overcrowded, infected jails in order to isolate and derail political opposition. As of early April 2020, two billion people worldwide lived in countries where parliaments had shut down or partially adjourned their activities as a result of the pandemic, dramatically diminishing oversight and accountability of executive branches, security forces and rapacious corporations (Provost, Archer, and Namubiru 2020).

COVID-19 is a tailor-made opportunity for authoritarian populist rulers and movements to spread bogus medical information and conspiracy theories and to keep citizenries off balance (Gusterson 2020). Alexander Lukashenko of Belarus declared that the best way to fight the virus was to drink vodka and drive a tractor. Trump did him one better by suggesting that injecting household disinfectant might provide a cure. Bolsonaro asserted that Brazil, unlike Italy with its large elderly population, was not especially vulnerable to the virus, which he ridiculed as 'a little flu'. Alongside these campaigns of denial and official mis- and disinformation, the pretext of controlling 'fake news' had led some governments to shutter media, prosecute critics and fire scientists who were attempting to provide accurate information about the pandemic. To make matters worse, the economic shutdown brought steep declines in advertising revenue, which put many media outlets on an even more precarious footing, further limiting access to reliable reporting, oversight of official corruption and scrutiny of rampant misinformation. As quarantined and now unemployed young people spend more and more time online, extremist groups target them for recruitment, preying on their isolation and loneliness and propagating 'explanations' for their plight that blame scapegoats and distract attention from the incompetence, dishonesty and abuses of those in power.

The pandemic has also been an occasion for reinforcing clientelist politics. Trump insisted on placing his signature on the paltry stimulus checks his government mailed to taxpayers, which makes them appear as if they were a personal gift. Modi has pressured wealthy Indians and obligated some government employees to donate to a "PM-CARES" relief fund, which will not be subject to state auditing and which rolled out despite the pre-existing National Relief Fund that ostensibly serves the same purposes. In many countries, however, the costs of the pandemic and economic shutdown have led cash-strapped governments to slash patronage spending and to rely more heavily on force for social control.

Accompanying and facilitating these power grabs is a slippage from the monitoring necessary for contact tracing and isolation of infected individuals to broader surveillance. Many countries now require cell phone users to install monitoring apps and some, such as India, punish any refusal to do so with fines, job loss or even jail (O'Neill 2020; O'Neill, Ryan-Mosley, and Johnson 2020). In most countries few protections are in place for the information gathered and in some cases data collected includes purchase and web browsing histories that governments want to be able to access for social control purposes. Like the broader emergency powers, heightened surveillance measures frequently lack a sunset clause or expiration date.

Authoritarian populist leaders, such as Trump and Bolsonaro, have made reopening shattered economies a top priority, putting on full display the cross-class alliances characteristic of such regimes that I discussed briefly above. This push responds to electoral imperatives as well as to the demands of their corporate allies, who are eager to restart production and revive consumption, whatever the cost to frontline workers' health, and to pressures emanating from their small business sector and working-class base. The 'reopen' rallies that occurred across the United States (and their counterparts in other countries) became crucibles for a toxic 'crossover' of far-right conspiracy theory enthusiasts, armed militia members, white supremacists and neo-Nazis, along with libertarian anti-vaccine activists, into more mainstream pro-corporate conservative politics (Goldenberg and Finkelstein 2020; Mondon and Winter 2020; Ohlheiser 2020). The push to reopen, propelled by corporate 'astroturf' money and social media manipulation, involves a cynical ranking of human life based on race, caste, class and citizenship status that again echoes historical fascist ideology. Not only are those workers forced to sacrifice their health and lives on the front lines of the reopened economy disproportionately people of color and immigrants, but the 'Others' who were always central to authoritarian populism's exclusionary definition of the nation now face intensified stigmatization and violence as supposed vectors of disease.

As the coronavirus and economic shutdown ravaged the United States, a video of the 25 May 2020 police murder of George Floyd, a black man in Minneapolis, sparked the largest street protests in U.S. history (Buchanan, Bui, and Patel 2020). The overwhelmingly nonviolent, youthful and multiracial Black Lives Matter demonstrations against police brutality took place in major cities and in hundreds of conservative small towns in all 50 states. Protestors were often on the receiving end of violence from the police and right-wing vigilantes, which confirmed their claims about police brutality and systemic racism. On dozens of occasions, vehicles ploughed into crowds of protestors; right-wing social media made videos of the attacks into celebratory memes (Hauck 2020). The breadth and the intensity of the protests were such that eminent elite institutions rushed to establish their anti-racist bona fides, stripping buildings of the names of pro-slavery benefactors and issuing contrite statements about their problematical pasts. Enraged demonstrators toppled statues of Confederate soldiers and Spanish conquistadores that had long sullied public spaces. Mass mobilizations took place despite fears of COVID-19 contagion and of violence from the police and right-wing gangs. Demonstrators expressed deepening anger, not just at systemic racism and police brutality, but at widespread unemployment, economic devastation and the denialism, incompetence and corruption that characterized the Trump administration's response to the pandemic. Demands and concepts that were distant from the mainstream for years – defund the police, cancel rent, reparations for slavery, a Green New Deal – suddenly found a central place in conventional mass media and policy discussions. In some 60 other countries, people poured into the streets in solidarity with U.S. Black Lives Matter protestors, often raising their own local and national grievances over racism and policing. In the intensity and commitment of the protestors, it was possible to imagine an end of the long authoritarian nightmare.

Even before the advent of the coronavirus pandemic, Saturnino Borras acknowledged that it would be 'absurdly difficult … but not impossible' to defeat right-wing populism. Part of the problem is that 'right-wing populist agitations are anchored in a rhetoric in which salvation, ironically, is thought to depend on capitalism – the very cause of the crisis', a contradiction that 'is not always obvious' (2020, 20). In the pre-pandemic era crisis, agrarian populists and other progressives fought to make obvious the systemic forces contributing to impoverishment, extreme inequality and racial, gender and class oppression. This was always an uphill fight and in some respects this is even more the case since the onset of the pandemic. In other ways, however, the pandemic and its associated crises present unprecedented opportunities for pushing back against authoritarian populism and advancing progressive alternatives. To cite just one example, government economic intervention in favor of the masses of the population is now vital and apparently feasible, even if inadequate in most parts of the world. The crisis has exposed the speciousness of the neoliberal mantra 'there's no money for that', because – at least in the more developed countries – the reality is that money can be found for meeting at least some human needs. Under crisis conditions, people have also become reacquainted with their own sense of agency and their desire and need for solidarity. Mutual aid efforts have proliferated, including neighborhood provisioning networks and self-organized production of scarce protective equipment. Many invoke an ethic of 'solidarity, not charity' and aim at maintaining and strengthening this consciousness and these experiences in any post-quarantine period (CJA 2020; PReP 2020; Solnit 2020). The Black Lives Matter protests in the United States and elsewhere suggest that multiracial solidarity, so elusive in 'normal' times, is both possible and powerful.

Rural regions are key sites where these opportunities and alternatives may emerge and become visible. In the United States, for example, warehouse, transport, delivery, food and agricultural workers have some of the worst working conditions and pay, yet all of a sudden they have become 'essential'. These workers also labour in high-density contexts which – like prisons and elder housing, both often sited in rural zones and staffed with poorly paid labour – have become key foci of infection. COVID-19 penetrated rural areas along nodes of the extended food and transport chains that these workers populate. Meat and poultry plants, in particular, have emerged as especially perilous, leading many workers to realize 'what they've suspected all along: that employers see them as dispensable, caring only about their labor power, not their health and wellbeing' (Longazel 2020). This has sparked a wave of walkouts and wildcat strikes – in fields, packinghouses and warehouses – to demand everything from better health and safety conditions to hazard pay, sick leave, union representation, and slower line speeds in the plants. The workers' very 'essentialness', which they share with nurses and other hospital and eldercare employees, potentially gives them unprecedented bargaining power.

While many rural zones in the United States remain strongholds of authoritarian populism – and many rural people express scepticism about COVID-19 – the impact of the pandemic in some rural zones will be devastating, especially given the inadequate or non-existent healthcare infrastructure. Governors of largely rural states often imposed physical distancing late or not at all, and have lifted restrictions early, imperiling their constituents. Those most in denial will be worst hit and many may come to question not only their own living and working conditions, but also the decades-long drumbeat of ideological indoctrination and lies that both neoliberal and authoritarian populist politicians and media fed them. As Michael Pollan asks,

> Are we willing to address the many vulnerabilities that the novel coronavirus has so dramatically exposed? It's not hard to imagine a coherent and powerful new politics organized around precisely that principle. (2020)

These vulnerabilities are myriad. They include everything from the industrial agriculture system to healthcare, education, housing, environmental justice, public transit and the extreme wealth and income inequality evident in the accelerated rollback of environmental and regulatory protections and the extraordinary gains accruing to a tiny handful of billionaires and 'pandemic profiteers' at a moment when mass unemployment and food insecurity are spiking to levels not seen since the 1930s depression (Collins,

Ocampo, and Paslaski 2020; GRAIN 2020). At the same time that the pandemic exposes systemic vulnerabilities and generates new practices and consciousness of solidarity, however, dominant groups are 'striking while the iron is hot', rapidly enacting a longstanding agenda that includes reengineering education and healthcare delivery towards greater reliance on distance learning and telemedicine and pushing for other regressive 'reforms' at a moment when much of the population is demobilized and scrambling to survive (Mirowski 2020). The growing convergence between traditional or mainstream conservatives and violent ultra-right movements – with its potential embrace of more extreme fascist practices – is one of the most troubling aspects of an emerging, reconfigured system of domination.

Peasant and farmer movements, food sovereignty advocates and environmentalists have for years campaigned for rural and agrarian justice and proposed viable alternatives, as have advocates of a Green New Deal more recently (Patel and Goodman 2020). These alternatives may achieve greater salience in a world where the nostrums of neoliberals and advocates of industrial agriculture clash with realities of mounting deaths and weakening food supply chains. The pandemic has provided brutal lessons about human interdependence – at the level of communities and nations and in scientific and medical research. The market-driven policies that exalted individualism and sought to corral the public sector and defund healthcare, science and education, among other public goods, have collided with a worldwide pandemic, a profound economic crisis and a mass movement against systemic racism that appears willing to brave contagion and violence to stay in the streets. These realities inevitably will become obvious to many and the forces of reaction may find it increasingly difficult to spin a persuasive counter-narrative. But the weakening of persuasion and hegemonic domination always raises the possibility of coercion-based rule. The 'absurdly difficult agenda' of defeating right-wing populism may have become even more challenging in a pandemic moment when millions are protesting in the streets. The heightened uncertainties of the current moment are suggestive of the kind of 'interregnum' or 'crisis of authority' of which Gramsci spoke, in which things could go either way, 'the great masses have become detached from their traditional ideologies, and no longer believe what they used to believe previously', and in which 'a great variety of morbid symptoms appear' (1972, 276).

Acknowledgements

I gratefully acknowledge Lesley Gill, Don Robotham, Julie Skurski and *JPS*'s anonymous peer reviewers for their suggestions and their challenging and constructive critiques of an earlier version of this paper. The essay's shortcomings are of course entirely my own.

Disclosure statement

No potential conflict of interest was reported by the author(s).

ORCID

Marc Edelman http://orcid.org/0000-0001-7359-1858

References

Adaman, Fikret, and Bengi Akbulut. 2020. "Erdoğan's Three-Pillared Neoliberalism: Authoritarianism, Populism and Developmentalism." *Geoforum*. doi:10.1016/j.geoforum.2019.12.013.

Adaman, Fikret, Murat Arsel, and Bengi Akbulut. 2019. "Neoliberal Developmentalism, Authoritarian Populism, and Extractivism in the Countryside: The Soma Mining Disaster in Turkey." *Journal of Peasant Studies* 46 (3): 514–536. doi:10.1080/03066150.2018.1515737.

Ali, Omar H. 2012. "Black Populism: Agrarian Politics from the Colored Alliance to the People's Party." In *Beyond Forty Acres and a Mule: African American Landowning Families since Reconstruction*, edited by Debra Ann Reid and Evan P. Bennett, 109–131. Gainesville: University Press of Florida.

Anderson, Perry. 2019. "Bolsonaro's Brazil." *London Review of Books*, February 7. https://www.lrb.co.uk/v41/n03/perry-anderson/bolsonaros-brazil

Andor, László. 2019. "The Poverty of Anti-Populism." *International Politics and Society*. https://www.ips-journal.eu/regions/europe/go/98/article/show/the-poverty-of-anti-populism-3648/.

Andrade, Daniela. 2019. "Populism from Above and Below: The Path to Regression in Brazil." *Journal of Peasant Studies*, 1–27. doi:10.1080/03066150.2019.1680542.

Ávila, Keymer. 2019. "Una masacre por goteo: Venezuela y la violencia institucional." *Nueva Sociedad*. http://nuso.org/articulo/venezuela-maduro-represion-izquierda/.

Bachelet, Michelle. 2019. "Human Rights in the Bolivarian Republic of Venezuela." A/HRC/41/18. Annual Report of the United Nations High Commissioner for Human Rights. Geneva: United Nations Human Rights Council. https://www.ohchr.org/EN/HRBodies/HRC/RegularSessions/Session41/Documents/A_HRC_41_18.docx.

Bangstad, Sindre. 2014. *Anders Breivik and the Rise of Islamophobia*. London: Zed Books.

Beban, Alice, Laura Schoenberger, and Vanessa Lamb. 2020. "Pockets of Liberal Media in Authoritarian Regimes: What the Crackdown on Emancipatory Spaces Means for Rural Social Movements in Cambodia." *Journal of Peasant Studies* 47 (1): 95–115. doi:10.1080/03066150.2019.1672664.

Bernstein, Henry. 2020. "Unpacking 'Authoritarian Populism' and Rural Politics: Some Comments on ERPI." *Journal of Peasant Studies*, 1–17. doi:10.1080/03066150.2020.1786063.

Bertrand, Natasha, Nahal Toosi, and Daniel Lippman. 2020. "State Pushes to List White Supremacist Group as Terrorist Org." POLITICO. March 9. https://www.politico.com/news/2020/03/09/state-department-white-supremacist-group-124500.

Bleifuss, Joel. 2018. "From Italy to Hungary, the Trumps of Europe Are Rising to Power." *In These Times*, July 23. https://inthesetimes.com/article/21269/from-italy-to-hungary-the-trumps-of-europe-are-rising-to-power.

Borras, Saturnino M. 2020. "Agrarian Social Movements: The Absurdly Difficult but Not Impossible Agenda of Defeating Right-Wing Populism and Exploring a Socialist Future." *Journal of Agrarian Change* 20 (1): 3–36. doi:10.1111/joac.12311.

Brenner, Robert. 2020. "Escalating Plunder." *New Left Review* 123 (June): 5–22.

Brooks, Sally. 2019. "Brexit and the Politics of the Rural." *Sociologia Ruralis*. doi:10.1111/soru.12281.

Brubaker, Rogers. 2017. "Why Populism?" *Theory and Society* 46 (5): 357–385. doi:10.1007/s11186-017-9301-7.

Bruff, Ian. 2014. "The Rise of Authoritarian Neoliberalism." *Rethinking Marxism* 26 (1): 113–129. doi:10.1080/08935696.2013.843250.

Bruff, Ian, and Cemal Burak Tansel. 2019. "Authoritarian Neoliberalism: Trajectories of Knowledge Production and Praxis." *Globalizations* 16 (3): 233–244. doi:10.1080/14747731.2018.1502497.

Buchanan, Larry, Quoctrung Bui, and Jugal K. Patel. 2020. "Black Lives Matter May Be the Largest Movement in U.S. History." *The New York Times*, July 3. https://www.nytimes.com/interactive/2020/07/03/us/george-floyd-protests-crowd-size.html.

Burke, Kyle. 2018. *Revolutionaries for the Right: Anticommunist Internationalism and Paramilitary Warfare in the Cold War*. Chapel Hill: University of North Carolina Press. www.jstor.org/stable/10.5149/9781469640754_burke.

Calvário, Rita, Annette Aurélie Desmarais, and Joseba Azkarraga. 2019. "Solidarities from Below in the Making of Emancipatory Rural Politics: Insights from Food Sovereignty Struggles in the Basque Country." *Sociologia Ruralis*. doi:10.1111/soru.12264.

Casarões, Guilherme, and Daniel Flemes. 2019. "Brazil First, Climate Last: Bolsonaro's Foreign Policy." *GIGA Focus*, no. 5 (September). https://www.giga-hamburg.de/en/system/files/publications/gf_lateinamerik_1905_en.pdf.

CJA. 2020. "What Is Mutual Aid? A Primer." *Climate Justice Alliance*, May 13. https://climatejusticealliance.org/what-is-mutual-aid-a-primer-by-the-climate-justice-alliance/.

Collins, Chuck, Omar Ocampo, and Sophia Paslaski. 2020. "Billionaire Bonanza 2020: Wealth Windfalls, Tumbling Taxes, and Pandemic Profiteers." Washington, DC: Institute for Policy Studies. https://ips-dc.org/wp-content/uploads/2020/04/Billionaire-Bonanza-2020.pdf.

Corbett, Jessica. 2018. "Sanders and Varoufakis Announce Alliance to Craft 'Common Blueprint for an International New Deal'." *Common Dreams*, October 26. https://www.commondreams.org/news/2018/10/26/sanders-and-varoufakis-announce-alliance-craft-common-blueprint-international-new.

Coronil, Fernando. 2011. "Venezuela's Wounded Bodies: Nation and Imagination During the 2002 Coup." *NACLA Report on the Americas* 44 (1): 33–39. doi:10.1080/10714839.2011.11725529.

Cortes-Vásquez, José A. 2020. "In the Name of the People: The Populist Redefinition of Nature Conservation in Post-Crisis Spain." *Geoforum* 108 (January): 110–118. doi:10.1016/j.geoforum.2019.12.004.

Cramer, Katherine J. 2016. *The Politics of Resentment: Rural Consciousness in Wisconsin and the Rise of Scott Walker*. Chicago: University of Chicago Press.

Di Stasio, Alessandro. 2019. "¿Qué ha llevado al fracaso de los sistemas cambiarios en Venezuela?" *Efecto Cocuyo*, May 17. https://efectococuyo.com/economia/que-ha-llevado-al-fracaso-de-los-sistemas-cambiarios-en-venezuela/.

Di Tella, Torcuato S. 1965. "Populism and Reform in Latin America." In *Obstacles to Change in Latin America*, edited by Claudio Veliz, 47–74. London: Oxford University Press.

Economist. 2020a. "A Pandemic of Power Grabs: Autocrats See Opportunity in Disaster." *The Economist*, April 23. https://www.economist.com/leaders/2020/04/23/autocrats-see-opportunity-in-disaster.

Economist. 2020b. "Protection Racket: Would-Be Autocrats Are Using Covid-19 as an Excuse to Grab More Power." *The Economist*, April 23. https://www.economist.com/international/2020/04/23/would-be-autocrats-are-using-covid-19-as-an-excuse-to-grab-more-power.

Edelman, Marc. 2018. "Sacrifice Zones in Rural and Non-Metro USA: Fertile Soil for Authoritarian Populism." *OpenDemocracy*, February 9. https://www.opendemocracy.net/en/sacrifice-zones-in-rural-and-non-metro-usa-fertile-soil-for-authoritarian-populism/.

Edelman, Marc. 2019. "Hollowed out Heartland, USA: How Capital Sacrificed Communities and Paved the Way for Authoritarian Populism." *Journal of Rural Studies*. doi:10.1016/j.jrurstud.2019.10.045.

Feffer, John. 2019. "Nationalism Is Global. The Left Is on the Defensive." *The Nation*, November 6. https://www.thenation.com/article/far-right-nationalist-climate-crisis/.

Ffrench-Davis, Ricardo. 2003. *Entre el neoliberalismo y el crecimiento con equidad: tres décadas de política económica en Chile*. Santiago: J.C. Sáez.

Finchelstein, Federico. 2017. *From Fascism to Populism in History*. Oakland: University of California Press.

Fine, Ben, and Alfredo Saad-Filho. 2017. "Thirteen Things You Need to Know About Neoliberalism." *Critical Sociology* 43 (4–5): 685–706. doi:10.1177/0896920516655387.

Foa, Roberto Stefan, and Jonathan Wilmot. 2019. "The West Has a Resentment Epidemic." *Foreign Policy*. https://foreignpolicy.com/2019/09/18/the-west-has-a-resentment-epidemic-populism/.

Franquesa, Jaume. 2019. "The Vanishing Exception: Republican and Reactionary Specters of Populism in Rural Spain." *Journal of Peasant Studies* 46 (3): 537–560. doi:10.1080/03066150.2019.1578751.

Fraser, Nancy. 2017. "The End of Progressive Neoliberalism." *Dissent*. https://www.dissentmagazine.org/online_articles/progressive-neoliberalism-reactionary-populism-nancy-fraser.

Fraser, Nancy. 2019. *The Old Is Dying and the New Cannot Be Born: From Progressive Neoliberalism to Trump and Beyond*. London: Verso.

Fukuyama, Francis. 1992. *The End of History and the Last Man*. New York: Free Press.

Gaventa, John. 2019. "Power and Powerlessness in an Appalachian Valley – Revisited." *Journal of Peasant Studies* 46 (3): 440–456. doi:10.1080/03066150.2019.1584192.

Gebrekidan, Selam, Matt Apuzzo, and Benjamin Novak. 2019. "The Money Farmers: How Oligarchs and Populists Milk the E.U. for Millions." *The New York Times*, November 3. https://www.nytimes.com/2019/11/03/world/europe/eu-farm-subsidy-hungary.html.

Germani, Gino. 1978. *Authoritarianism, Fascism, and National Populism*. New Brunswick, NJ: Transaction Books.

Giddens, Anthony. 2000. *The Third Way and Its Critics*. Cambridge: Polity Press.

Goldenberg, Alex, and Joel Finkelstein. 2020. "Cyber Swarming, Memetic Warfare and Viral Insurgency: How Domestic Militants Organize on Memes to Incite Violent Insurrection and Terror Against Government and Law Enforcement." New Brunswick: Network Contagion Research Institute & Rutgers Miller Center for Community Protection and Resilience. https://ncri.io/wp-content/uploads/NCRI-White-Paper-Memetic-Warfare.pdf.

Gonda, Noémi. 2019. "Land Grabbing and the Making of an Authoritarian Populist Regime in Hungary." *Journal of Peasant Studies* 46 (3): 606–625. doi:10.1080/03066150.2019.1584190.

GRAIN. 2020. "Agro-Imperialism in the Time of Covid-19." July 14. https://grain.org/e/6502.

Gramsci, Antonio. 1972. *Selections from the Prison Notebooks*. New York: International Publishers.

Gürel, Burak, Bermal Küçük, and Sercan Taş. 2019. "The Rural Roots of the Rise of the Justice and Development Party in Turkey." *Journal of Peasant Studies* 46 (3): 457–479. doi:10.1080/03066150.2018.1552264.

Gusterson, Hugh. 2020. "COVID-19 and the Turn to Magical Thinking." SAPIENS. May 12. https://www.sapiens.org/column/conflicted/covid-19-magic/.

Hauck, Grace. 2020. "'I Would Be Very Careful in the Middle of the Street': Drivers Have Hit Protesters 66 Times since May 27." *USA Today*, July 9. https://www.usatoday.com/story/news/nation/2020/07/08/vehicle-ramming-attacks-66-us-since-may-27/5397700002/.

Hendrikse, Reijer. 2018. "Neo-Illiberalism." *Geoforum* 95 (October): 169–172. doi:10.1016/j.geoforum.2018.07.002.

Hidalgo Pallares, José, and Felipe Hurtado Pérez, eds. 2016. *El socialismo del siglo XXI tras el boom de los commodities*. Quito: Corporación de Estudios para el Desarrollo & Konrad Adenaueer Stiftung SOPLA.

Jones, Seth G., Catrina Doxsee, and Nicholas Harrington. 2020. "The Escalating Terrorism Problem in the United States." Center for Strategic & International Studies. June 17. https://csis-website-prod.s3.amazonaws.com/s3fs-public/publication/200612_Jones_DomesticTerrorism_v6.pdf.

Judis, John B. 2016. *The Populist Explosion: How the Great Recession Transformed American and European Politics*. New York: Columbia Global Reports.

Kazin, Michael. 1995. *The Populist Persuasion: An American History*. New York: Basic Books.

Kirchgaessner, Stephanie. 2018. "Far-Right Italy Minister Vows 'action' to Expel Thousands of Roma." *The Guardian*, June 19, sec. World news. https://www.theguardian.com/world/2018/jun/19/italy-coalition-rift-roma-register-matteo-salvini.

Koyanagi, Ken. 2019. "For Clues to BJP's Landslide Win, Look to Modi's Rural Support." Nikkei Asian Review. May 28. https://asia.nikkei.com/Politics/India-election/For-clues-to-BJP-s-landslide-win-look-to-Modi-s-rural-support2.

Krugman, Paul. 2018. "The Angry White Male Caucus." *The New York Times*, October 1. https://www.nytimes.com/2018/10/01/opinion/kavanaugh-white-male-privilege.html.

Krugman, Paul. 2019. "Why Isn't Trump a Real Populist?" *The New York Times*, June 17. https://www.nytimes.com/2019/06/17/opinion/trump-populist.html.

Lander, Edgardo. 2018. "Venezuela: el fracaso del proceso bolivariano." Aporrea. August 16. https://www.aporrea.org/ideologia/a267859.html.

Lander, Edgardo. 2019. *Crisis civilizatoria: Experiencias de los gobiernos progresistas y debates en la izquierda latinoamericana*. Guadalajara: Universidad de Guadalajara & Centro Maria Sibylla Merian de Estudios Latinoamericanos Avanzados en Humanidades y Ciencias Sociales. http://editorial.ucr.ac.cr/ciencias-sociales/item/download/192_9030537ba661a50bb26ed9642c9df2aa.html.

Lenin, Vladimir Ilyich. 1964. *The Development of Capitalism in Russia*. 4th ed. Vol. 3. Collected Works. Moscow: Progress Publishers.

Longazel, Jamie. 2020. "How Reaganomics and Nativism Made This Meatpacking Plant a COVID-19 Hotspot." Strikewave. April 29. https://www.thestrikewave.com/original-content/reaganomics-made-this-meatpacking-plant-a-covid-19-hotspot.

Lubarda, Balsa. 2019. "'Homeland Farming' or 'Rural Emancipation'? The Discursive Overlap between Populist and Green Parties in Hungary." *Sociologia Ruralis*. doi:10.1111/soru.12289.

Malamud, Andrés. 2017. "Qué cosa fuera la patria sin Correa." *Nueva Sociedad*, March. http://nuso.org/articulo/que-cosa-fuera-la-patria-sin-correa/.

Mamonova, Natalia, and Jaume Franquesa. 2019. "Populism, Neoliberalism and Agrarian Movements in Europe. Understanding Rural Support for Right-Wing Politics and Looking for Progressive Solutions." *Sociologia Ruralis*. doi:10.1111/soru.12291.

Martí i Puig, Salvador, and Macià Serra. 2020. "Nicaragua: De-Democratization and Regime Crisis." *Latin American Politics and Society* 62 (2): 117–136. doi:10.1017/lap.2019.64.

Matias, Ivaci. 2019. "Grupo usou whatsapp para convocar 'dia do fogo' no Pará." *Revista Globo Rural*, August 25. https://revistagloborural.globo.com/Noticias/noticia/2019/08/grupo-usou-whatsapp-para-convocar-dia-do-fogo-no-para.html.

Mazzarella, William. 2019. "The Anthropology of Populism: Beyond the Liberal Settlement." *Annual Review of Anthropology* 48 (1): 45–60. doi:10.1146/annurev-anthro-102218-011412.

McCarthy, James. 2019. "Authoritarianism, Populism, and the Environment: Comparative Experiences, Insights, and Perspectives." *Annals of the American Association of Geographers* 109 (2): 301–313. doi:10.1080/24694452.2018.1554393.

Mirowski, Philip. 2020. "Why the Neoliberals Won't Let This Crisis Go to Waste." *Jacobin*, May 16. https://jacobinmag.com/2020/05/neoliberals-response-pandemic-crisis.

Mondon, Aurelien, and Aaron Winter. 2020. *Reactionary Democracy: How Racism and the Populist Far Right Became Mainstream*. New York: Verso Books.

Monjane, Boaventura, and Natacha Bruna. 2020. "Confronting Agrarian Authoritarianism: Dynamics of Resistance to PROSAVANA in Mozambique." *Journal of Peasant Studies* 47 (1): 69–94. doi:10.1080/03066150.2019.1671357.

Montenegro de Wit, Maywa, Antonio Roman-Alcalá, Alex Liebman, and Siena Chrisman. 2019. "Agrarian Origins of Authoritarian Populism in the United States: What Can We Learn from 20th-Century Struggles in California and the Midwest?" *Journal of Rural Studies*. doi:10.1016/j.jrurstud.2019.12.003.

Mouffe, Chantal. 2018. *For a Left Populism*. London: Verso.

Nahon-Serfaty, Isaac. 2018. "La devastación minera en Venezuela y el silencio del ecologismo global." Letras Libres. June 20. https://www.letraslibres.com/espana-mexico/politica/la-devastacion-minera-en-venezuela-y-el-silencio-del-ecologismo-global.

Nelson, Eshe. 2016. "Venezuela Is Too Poor to Import Food. So Why Is the Country Still Paying off Its Debt?" *Quartz*, December 20. https://qz.com/866593/venezuela-is-too-poor-to-import-food-and-medicine-so-why-is-the-government-still-paying-off-its-debt/.

NJOHSP. 2020. "2020 Terrorism Threat Assessment." Trenton: New Jersey Office of Homeland Security and Preparedness. https://static1.squarespace.com/static/54d79f88e4b0db3478a04405/t/5e9f332ff92d080928b942f9/1587491645834/2020+Terrorism+Threat+Assessment.pdf.

Ohlheiser, Abby. 2020. "How Covid-19 Conspiracy Theorists Are Exploiting YouTube Culture." *MIT Technology Review*, May 7. https://www.technologyreview.com/2020/05/07/1001252/youtube-covid-conspiracy-theories/.

O'Neill, Patrick Howell. 2020. "India Is Forcing People to Use Its Covid App, Unlike Any Other Democracy." *MIT Technology Review*, May 7. https://www.technologyreview.com/2020/05/07/1001360/india-aarogya-setu-covid-app-mandatory/.

O'Neill, Patrick Howell, Tate Ryan-Mosley, and Bobbie Johnson. 2020. "A Flood of Coronavirus Apps Are Tracking Us. Now It's Time to Keep Track of Them." *MIT Technology Review*, May 7. https://www.technologyreview.com/2020/05/07/1000961/launching-mittr-covid-tracing-tracker/.

openDemocracy. 2018. "Authoritarian Populism and the Rural World." OpenDemocracy. https://www.opendemocracy.net/en/authoritarian-populism-and-rural-world/.

Orbán, Viktor. 2014. "Full Text of Viktor Orbán's Speech at Băile Tuşnad (Tusnádfürdő) of 26 July 2014." *The Budapest Beacon*, July 29. https://budapestbeacon.com/full-text-of-viktor-orbans-speech-at-baile-tusnad-tusnadfurdo-of-26-july-2014/.

Patel, Raj, and Jim Goodman. 2020. "The Long New Deal." *Journal of Peasant Studies* 47 (3): 431–463. doi:10.1080/03066150.2020.1741551.

Paterson, Tony, and Charlotte McDonald-Gibson. 2013. "The shadow of anti-semitism falls on Europe once more as Hungary's far-fight Jobbik party protests against World Jewish Congress meeting in Budapest." *The Independent*, May 5. http://www.independent.co.uk/news/world/europe/the-shadow-of-anti-semitism-falls-on-europe-once-more-as-hungarys-far-fight-jobbik-party-protests-8604656.html.

People's Party. 1892. "The Omaha Platform: Launching the Populist Party." History Matters. 1892. http://historymatters.gmu.edu/d/5361/.

Pipes, Richard. 1964. "Narodnichestvo: A Semantic Inquiry." *Slavic Review* 23 (3): 441–458.

Pollan, Michael. 2020. "The Sickness in Our Food Supply." *New York Review of Books*, June 11. https://www.nybooks.com/articles/2020/06/11/covid-19-sickness-food-supply/.

Prasad, M. Madhava. 2020. "Virtual Populist Regimes." Social Science Research Council - The Immanent Frame. March 11. http://tif.ssrc.org/2020/03/11/virtual-populist-regimes/.

PReP. 2020. "What Is Mutual Aid? A COVID-19 Primer." Pandemic Research for the People. https://www.prepthepeople.net/dispatches.

Provost, Claire, Nandini Archer, and Lydia Namubiru. 2020. "Alarm as 2 Billion People Have Parliaments Shut or Limited by COVID-19." OpenDemocracy. April 8. https://www.opendemocracy.net/en/5050/alarm-two-billion-people-have-parliaments-suspended-or-limited-covid-19/.

Provost, Claire, and Mary Fitzgerald. 2019. "Revealed: Trump-Linked US Christian "Fundamentalists" Pour Millions of 'Dark Money' into Europe, Boosting the Far Right." OpenDemocracy. March 27. https://www.opendemocracy.net/en/5050/revealed-trump-linked-us-christian-fundamentalists-pour-millions-of-dark-money-into-europe-boosting-the-far-right/.

Ramsay, Adam, and Claire Provost. 2019. "Revealed: The Trump-Linked 'Super PAC' Working behind the Scenes to Drive Europe's Voters to the Far Right." OpenDemocracy. April 25. https://www.opendemocracy.net/en/5050/revealed-the-trump-linked-super-pac-working-behind-the-scenes-to-drive-europes-voters-to-the-far-right/.

Robotham, Don. 2020. "Populism and Its Others: After Neoliberalism." In *Beyond Populism: Angry Politics and the Twilight of Neoliberalism*, edited by Jeff Maskovsky, and Sophie Bjork-James, 23–41. Morgantown: West Virginia University Press.

Rose, Max, and Ali H. Soufan. 2020. "The White Supremacist Threat Is Real." *The New York Times*, February 13.

Sánchez-Ancochea, Diego. 2017. "The Political Economy of Inequality at the Top in Contemporary Chile." In *Has Latin American Inequality Changed Direction?*, edited by Luis Bértola, and Jeffrey Williamson, 339–363. Cham: Springer International Publishing. doi:10.1007/978-3-319-44621-9_14.

Sanders, Bernie. 2018. "A New Authoritarian Axis Demands an International Progressive Front." *The Guardian*, September 13. https://www.theguardian.com/commentisfree/ng-interactive/2018/sep/13/bernie-sanders-international-progressive-front.

Schreckinger, Ben. 2019. "Right-Wing Movements Merge as Bolsonaro Visits Trump." POLITICO. March 19. https://politi.co/2TJ3GLc.

Scoones, Ian, Marc Edelman, Saturnino M. Borras, Ruth Hall, Wendy Wolford, and Ben White. 2018. "Emancipatory Rural Politics: Confronting Authoritarian Populism." *Journal of Peasant Studies* 45 (1): 1–20. doi:10.1080/03066150.2017.1339693.

Serwer, Adam. 2019. "A Crime by Any Name." *The Atlantic*, July 3. https://www.theatlantic.com/ideas/archive/2019/07/border-facilities/593239/.

Shanin, Teodor, ed. 1983. *Late Marx and the Russian Road: Marx and 'the Peripheries of Capitalism': A Case*. New York: Monthly Review Press.

Simpson, Bradley. 2008. *Economists with Guns: Authoritarian Development and U.S.-Indonesian Relations, 1960-1968*. Stanford: Stanford University Press.

Solnit, Rebecca. 2020. "'The Way We Get through This Is Together': Mutual Aid under Coronavirus." *The Guardian*, May 14, sec. World news. https://www.theguardian.com/world/2020/may/14/mutual-aid-coronavirus-pandemic-rebecca-solnit.

Steinmetz-Jenkins, Daniel. 2020. "Thomas Piketty: Confronting Our Long History of Massive Inequality." *The Nation*, March 26. https://www.thenation.com/article/culture/thomas-piketty-interview-inequality-book-covid/.

Sutherland, Manuel. 2018. "La ruina de Venezuela no se debe al 'socialismo' ni a la 'revolución'." *Nueva Sociedad*, no. 274 (April): 142–51.

Svampa, Maristella. 2018. "Del cambio de época al fin de ciclo (I Parte)." Aporrea - Centro de Estudios de la Realidad Latinoamericana. September 7. https://www.aporrea.org/actualidad/n331057.html.

Thangaraj, Stanley. 2017. "Many Hindus Saw Themselves as Aryans and Backed Nazis. Does That Explain Hindutva's Support for Donald Trump?" *Quartz India*, February 2. https://qz.com/india/901244/many-hindus-saw-themselves-as-aryans-and-backed-nazis-does-that-explain-hindutvas-support-for-donald-trump/.

Tilzey, Mark. 2019. "Authoritarian Populism and Neo-Extractivism in Bolivia and Ecuador: The Unresolved Agrarian Question and the Prospects for Food Sovereignty as Counter-Hegemony." *Journal of Peasant Studies* 46 (3): 626–652. doi:10.1080/03066150.2019.1584191.

Turits, Richard Lee. 2003. *Foundations of Despotism: Peasants, the Trujillo Regime, and Modernity in Dominican History*. Stanford: Stanford University Press.

Van Sant, Levi. 2018. "A Redneck Revolt? Radical Responses to Trumpism in the Rural US." OpenDemocracy. April 16. https://www.opendemocracy.net/en/redneck-revolt-radical-responses-to-trumpism-in-rural-us/.

Versteeg, Mila, Timothy Horley, Anne Meng, Mauricio Guim, and Marilyn Guirguis. 2019. "The Law and Politics of Presidential Term Limit Evasion." 14. Public Law and Legal Theory Paper Series. Charlottesville: University of Virginia School of Law. https://papers.ssrn.com/sol3/papers.cfm?abstract_id=3359960.

Walter, Brian Murray. 2019. "Nostalgia and Precarious Placemaking in Southern Poultry Worlds: Immigration, Race, and Community Building in Rural Northern Alabama." *Journal of Rural Studies*. doi:10.1016/j.jrurstud.2019.12.004.

Washington Post. 2020. "Tracking All of President Trump's False or Misleading Claims." *The Washington Post*, July 9. https://www.washingtonpost.com/graphics/politics/trump-claims-database/.

Wasserman, Harvey. 1972. *Harvey Wasserman's History of the United States*. New York: Harper Colophon.

Watson, Tracy, and Brad Wilson. 2020. "Two Hidden Histories of Rural Racial Solidarity Movements." *Journal of Rural Studies*. doi:10.1016/j.jrurstud.2020.06.022.

Webber, Jeffery R. 2020. "State, Bureaucracy, and Rentier Capital." *Dissent*, February 7. https://www.dissentmagazine.org/online_articles/state-bureaucracy-rentier-capital-maduro-venezuela-crisis.

Yates, Michael D., and John Bellamy Foster. 2020. "Trump, Neo-Fascism, and the COVID-19 Pandemic." *MR Online*, April 11. https://mronline.org/2020/04/11/trump-neo-fascism-and-the-covid-19-pandemic/.

Index

Note: Page numbers in **bold** refer to tables and those in *italic* refer to figures.

Abrahamic religions 127
Acção Académica para o Desenvolvimento das Comunidades Rurais (Academic Action for the Development of Rural Communities) 324
actually existing right-wing populism: analysis 421; brexit and politics of the rural 430–3; crisis of representative democracies 441; definition 421; different contexts 422; dying villages of eastern Germany 426–8; European countryside 420; inequalities and politics of emotion 438–40; neoliberal capitalism 422–6; populist mobilisation in Ukraine 433–5; problem with democracy 437–8; role of emptiness 440–1; rural support 421; Spain and Ukraine 442; territorial dimension 435–7; traditional case studies 422; unelected bureaucrats in Brussels 426; *vacía* or vaciada 428–30
Adalet ve Kalkinma Partisi (AKP): agricultural policies 103–5; anti-capitalist coalition 115; arguments 99–100; comparative-historical perspective 100–3; DSP-MHP-ANAP coalition period 114; economic factors 98–9; *enfants bien-aimés* of 155; environmental and social costs of 161; fieldwork, archival research and quantitative analysis 100; hazelnut producers 107–10; Kurdish movement 115; political power 98; rural politics, contemporary Turkey 114; rural politics, context of construction, mining and energy booms 112–14; sections 100; series of political liberalization 160; social neoliberalism 114; social neoliberalism in rural Turkey 105–7; in Soma 168–71; tea producers 110–12; Turkish Islamism 97–8; vote share, 2007–2015 98, **98**
Adaman, F. 451, 456, 458
Afghanistan 123, 132
African American community 61
African National Congress 4
agrarian anarchism: anarchistic social organization 401–3; anarchist movements 390; anarchist theory 392–3, **394–5**; anti-state motivations of non-elite people 412; critical agrarian studies 390–1; movements 399–401; neo-authoritarian populists 390; *Peasant Wars of the Twentieth Century* (Wolf) 389–90; populism, US rightwing AP and authoritarian state 403–6; positive and negative theory 396–9; Redneck Revolt 411–12; rural positionalities, agrarian movements and anarchism-informed emancipatory strategies 406–11; theories/values, anarchistic elements and movements 391–2; US authoritarian populism 403
Agrarian Revolution 276
agrarian theory of change 397, 398
agribusiness 4, 9, 105, 107, 110, 131, 132, 211, 303, 320, 322, 323, 339, 350–2, 355, 359, 405, 425, 433, 436, 456, 465
Agribusiness Parliamentary Front 339
Agricultural Reform Implementation Project (ARIP) 162
agroecology 10
Aho, James 130
Akbulut, B. 451, 458
Akins, John Keith 134
aksi sepihak (forcible land seizures) 27
aldeamentos comunais (villagization) 317
Alfredo Nhamitete Agricultural Association 331
Algeria 392
Allende, Salvador 32, 462
All-Ukrainian Agrarian Council 434
Al Qaeda 475
Alternative für Deutschland (AfD) party 476
Alternative Right 141
altiplano (highlands) 456
A luta continua 361
Amann, Edmund 354
ambiguous politics 342–4
amenity-rich areas 60, 61–3, **62**, 65–6, **66**, **67**, **69**, 69–72, **70**, 451
American Community Survey 60
America's urban–rural divides 68
Analgesic subculture of the Southern Appalachias (Ball) 90
anarchism: agrarian theory of change 398; anarchistic elements of 391; anarchists 391, 412;

Christian evangelicals and fundamentalists, communism 127; critical agrarian studies 390, 392; *Decolonizing Anarchism* (Ramnath) 392; emancipatory movements 390, 406–11; indigeneity 401; individualist and insurrectionary trends 393, **394–5**; Marxism 396; Occupy Wall Street movement of 2011 400; *The Political Theory of Anarchism* (Carter) 400; popular politics 404; practical theory 397; principles and theories 401; second wave 399; social **394–5**; and syndicalism 391; *Two Cheers for Anarchism* (Scott) 402
anarchistic social organization 401–3
anarchist movements 390
anarchist theory 392–3, **394–5**
Anavatan Partisi (ANAP) 104
Anderson, Benedict 27–8
Anderson, Perry 345, 347, 474
Andrade, Daniela 411, 458
Antentas, Josep M. 183
anti-austerity movement 185
anti-capitalist coalition 115
anti-Catholic movement 130
anti-communism 30, 42, 126, 129, 405
anti-EU politics 431
anti-globalisation 439
anti-immigrant xenophobia 123
anti-immigration 139–41, 439
anti-Muslim riots in Gujarat 474
Antipode and Journal of Political Ecology (ACME) 390
anti-refugee activism 139–41
antisemitism 126
anti-state motivations of non-elite people 412
anti-Thaksin 'Yellow Shirt' movement 45
Apocalypse: The Coming Judgment of the Nations (Grant) 128
apocalypticism 127
apocalyptic millennialism 126–8
apocalyptic survivalists 121
Appalachian Land Ownership Task Force, 1983 91, 92
Appalachian Regional Commission 83
Appalachian Studies Association (ASA) 91
Appalachian Valley: Appalachia High Intensity Drug Trafficking Area Map 83; Central Appalachia 82; consent, quiescence or resistance 87–90; inequality of land ownership 92; natural resources or manufacturing 64; and Northeast 71; *Power and Powerlessness: Quiescence and Rebellion in an Appalachian Valley* (Gaventa) 80–2; re-visit 82–4, 93; and rural South 62; scholar-activism in region 90–3; Trump support 84–7; *What You Are Getting Wrong about Appalachia* (Cat) 89
Appalshop 89
Approaching Hoofbeats: The Four Horsemen of the Apocalypse (Graham) 128
Ara (newspaper) 195

Arendt, H. 3
Argentina 392, 472
Armed Citizens Militias 121
Arora, S. 241
Arsel, M. 451, 458
The Art of Not Being Governed: An Anarchist History of Upland Southeast Asia and 2012s Two Cheers for Anarchism (Scott) 402
Ashwood, L. 407, 408
Asian Financial Crisis 42
The Atlantic 85
Aufbau-Ost 427
Aung San Suu Kyi 4
austerity economics 4
Australia 392, 475
authoritarianism 295–9; in Cambodia 295–9; confronting agrarian authoritarianism (*see* Triangular Co-operation Programme for Agricultural Development of the Tropical Savannah in Mozambique Project (ProSAVANA)); contemporary Turkey 101; economic-cum-political crisis 183; elite dirigisme and clientelism 181; Erdoğan's presidency 169; neoliberal developmentalism and extractivism 158–61; New Authoritarianism 22, 47; normalisation of 8; Partido Popular's government 184; populism, AKP 169–71; rabid Islamophobia and bellicose ultra-nationalism 141; splice nationalism 53; violence 282
authoritarian populism 2–4, 275–9, 283–5, 294, 449, 461
Azar, R. 237

Badiou, Alain 3, 8
Baer, Werner 354
Bakunin, Michael 393
Balagoon, Kuwasi 400
balance of payments (BoP) 344–5, 352
Baltic States 475
Barma, N. H. 308
Barnes, A. 207
Batlle y Ordóñez, José 472
Beban, A. 448, 479
Beck, Glenn 126
Belarus 226–32, 235, 239, 241, 242, 448, 449, 482
bellicose ultra-nationalism 141
Bello, W. 177, 181, 448, 449, 451, 453, 458, 459, 461, 462
Benigno Aquino III 51
Berlet, C. 451, 457
Bernstein, H. 230
Bharatiya Janata Party (BJP) 365, 454, 455, 465, 476
biadab (savage) 30
biennio rosso (two red years) 25
Big Capital 22
Blackwell 74
Bloch, Ernst 182

Blood Moon, 1996 128
bobos (bourgeois-bohemians) 460
Boito, A. Jr. 349, 359
boliburguesía 478
Bolivarian Alternative for the Peoples of Our America (ALBA) 477
Bolivia 267–70, 273–9, 340, 356, 392, 404, 448, 452–4, 458, 459, 462, 466, 477, 480; authoritarian populism and neo-extractivism 275–9; MST and emancipatory rural politics 285–7
Bologna 24, 25
Bolsa Família 9, 347, 355
Bolsonaro, Jair 339, 361, 365, 390, 465–6, 474–6, 481, 482
BONAFARM 253, 258
Bookchin, Murray 397
Boonmee, Thirayut 45
Borras, J. 316, 334
Borras, S. M. Jr. 186, 228, 328, 366, 422, 451, 457, 459, 460, 483
bourgeois-bohemians (Hungarian *bobos*) 258–9
Brashear, Ivy 91
Brass, T. 397
Brazil 4, 7, 9, 267, 286, 321–4, 330–2, 348, 357, 365, 392, 400, 448, 449, 458, 459, 473, 477, 481, 482; agribusiness 350–2; agricultural production and exports 340; '*A luta continua*' 361; Chamber of Deputies 339; 2013 crisis and political turn 358–61; democratic representation 341–2; development pattern and social relations 352–4; economic and political tide 339; ERPI 338; family farm sector 339; fetishism and ambiguous politics 342–4; leader of the poor 344–5; left-wing populism 355–8; Lulism 346–9; Lulism and PT's politics 340; political instability 333; political tensions and appeasements 354–5; populism 340–1, 348–9, 361; PT's political project 349–50; resistance and mobilization 339
Brazil Agrarian Movements 325
Brazilian Agricultural Research Corporation 321
Brazilian Cooperation Agency (ABC) 314, 320, 333
Brexit Party 432
BRICS 267–71
Brooks, Sally 421
Brown, David 142
Bruna, N. 321, 323, 448, 454
Buber, Martin 398
Buchanan, Pat 125
buen vivir 270, 283, 286
Bunkus, R. 427
Burawoy, M. 81, 227
Bureau of Economic Analysis data 60
Burlein, Ann 135
Burma 3, 400
Bush, George W. 122, 134

Cambodia 42, 47, 295–9, 448; authoritarianism 295–9; authoritarian peace 308; authoritarian populism 294; Cambodian People's Party 293–4; co-opting social media 307; a dark space for rural people 304–5; democracy 302–4; Fresh News 307, 309; government 307; illiberal power 295; journalists 294; liberalism and democratic norms 293; media, authoritarianism, and emancipation 299–302; methods 295–6; political communication theory 308–9; populist authoritarianism and (un)free press 296–9; *Radio Free Asia* (RFA) 294; social media and news online 305–7
The Cambodia Daily (newspaper) 294, 295, 298, 304
Cambodian National Rescue Party (CNRP) 293–4
Cambodian People's Party (CPP) 293–4, 297
Campanha não ao ProSAVANA (No to ProSAVANA Campaign) 314, 324
Campanha Terra (Land Campaign) 329
Canada 392, 469, 475, 477
capital's transcendence 288
Cardoza, Anthony 24
Cargill 132
carino brutal 48
Carlson, C. C. 128
Carolan, M. 448, 459
Carr, P. J. 67
Carter, A. 391, 400
Carvalho, Laura 351
Catalan 195, 196
Catalonia 178, 182, 183, 185, 187–9, 192, 193, 195, 196, 430, 436, 451, 453, 457
Catte, Elizabeth 85, 89
caudillismo 278, 288
Çay Kurumu (ÇAYKUR) 110–11
Central Appalachia 64, 82
Central Intelligence Agency (CIA) 30
Central Valley 35
Chachapongpun, Pavin 44
The Chamber of Agriculture 108
Chamber of Deputies 339
Chávez, Hugo 477
chavismo 479–81
Chayanov, A. V. 228
cheronozem 433
Chile 22, 36, 40, 41, 55, 392, 458, 466
China 5, 392, 400
Chomsky, Noam 400
Christian Democratic Party 32–3
Christian evangelicals 127
Christians, Godly 126, 127
Chronically Poor Areas 62–3
Chronicle of a Death Foretold (Márquez) 155
Chulalongkorn University Social Research Institute (CUSRI) 42
Churchill, Ward 401
Çiftçi-Sen (The Farmers' Union) 108
civic culture 61, 62, 72–4, 76

civilian paramilitary 41–2
Civil Society Coordination Mechanism for the Development of the Nacala Corridor (MCSC-CN) 326
class-conscious left-wing populism 194
clientelism 181
climate justice movements 10
Clinton, Hillary 70, 87
closed contexts 299–300
coal mining 74–5, 155, 156, 165, 167, 171, 411, 451, 453, 456
collective action 10, 89, 207, 209, 211, 212, 220, 240, 294, 301, 402, 404
Colombia 392, 478
Colonialism in Modern America: The Appalachian Case (Lewis) 90
colorblindness 368, 372, 373, 378, 379
colorblind theory 370
Comissão Arquidiocesana de Justiça e Paz de Nampula (Archdiocesan Commission for Justice and Peace of Nampula) 324
Common Agricultural Policy (CAP) 248, 423
communism 27, 127, 250, 427–8
Communist Party 31, 42, 109, 471–2
Community and Environment in Rural America (CERA) survey 60–1, 65, **66, 67, 69, 70**
Comunidad Andina de Naciones (CAN) 277
Confederación Sindical Única de Trabajadores Campesinas de Bolivia (CSUTCB) 277
Confederation of Indigenous Peoples of Bolivia (CIDOB) 278
The Conquest of Bread (Kropotkin) 397
Conservative (Tory) Party 431, 432
Constitutional Sheriffs and Peace Officers Association (CSPOA) 137, 138
contemporary populist politics 3
contemporary Turkey 101
co-opting social media 307
Coronado, Rod 401
coronavirus 481, 483, 484
Coronil, Fernando 478
counter-hegemony 172, 267–70, 273, 274, 277, 279, 281, 285–7, 450, 454, 459; authoritarian populism 283–5; in Bolivia 285–7
counterrevolution 21, 22, 25, 26, 449
COVID-19 420, 425–6, 429, 433, 435, 481–4
Cramer, K. J. 59, 64, 67, 71, 369
critical agrarian studies (CAS) 390, 391, 393, 422, 435, 441
Cuba 392
Cumhuriyet Halk Partisi (CHP) 99, 105

Dahlia 75–6
The Daily 298, 305
Davis, Dee 68
dayıbaşı system 167
Decennial Census 60
Decolonizing Anarchism (Ramnath) 392

deindustrialisation 6
De la Torre, C. 272
de Lozada, Sánchez 268
democracy 302–4
Democratic Party 32–3, 36, 72, 99, 134, 367, 459, 468, 471
demográfiai földprogram (demographic land program) 255
Demokratik Sol Parti (Democratic Left Party) 104
Denver Post 68
Derviş, Kemal 104
Despair of Poor White Americans 85
Deutsche Welle 330
Deutschland, Neues 330
Development of Agribusiness 322
The Development of Capitalism in Russia (Lenin) 471
Dirlik, A. 391
disciplined corporate organization 24
dispossession 4, 177–9, 187–8, 195, 204, 227, 228, 241, 248, 401, 453, 458
Distressed Communities Index (DCI) 83
Doğru Yol Partisi (DYP) 104
Domination and the Arts of Resistance: Hidden Transcripts (Scott) 87
double movement 8
DSP-MHP-ANAP coalition period 105, 114
Duke, David 125
Duncan, C. M. 451
Durham, Martin 133
Duterte, Rodrigo 22, 47–9, 390, 474, 475; counterrevolution 54; EDSA project 51–2; fascist category 50–1; fascist character 54; fascist original 54; leaders 54; middle classes 49–50; nationalism and geopolitics 53–4; political project 50, 54; populist rhetoric 54; role of the countryside 54; *sozialepolitik* 52–3
Dzenovska, D. 422, 441

Eastern Black Sea region 100
Ebner, Michael 25
economic crisis 23, 104, 108, 114, 179, 182, 184, 217, 331, 332, 355, 358–60, 425, 481, 485
economic-cum-political crisis 183
Economic Innovation Group 83
Economic Land Concessions (ELCs) 297
Economic Research Service (ERS) 370
economic restructuring 59, 62, 368, 381; rural US 63–5
economic shutdown 482, 483
The Economist (newspaper) 68
Ecuador 267–70, 276, 279–82, 287–8, 392, 404, 453, 454, 458, 462, 466, 477, 479
Edelman, Marc 451
Eighteenth Brumaire (Marx) 7
eliminationism 26, 48–9
elite dirigisme 181

El que no salta es momio (He who does not jump is a reactionary) 35
El Siglo (newspaper) 35
emancipation 3, 7–10, 240–1, 247–9, 254, 257, 299–302, 343–4, 356, 361, 366, 392, 402, 411; alliances 258–9; emotions 260; Hungarian rural politics 260; Kishantos Rural Development Centre 259–60; State Secretary for Agriculture 260
emancipatory movements 390, 406–11
emancipatory politics 6–7, 9–12, 92, 93, 185, 258, 259, 285, 293, 295, 340, 390, 398, 404, 408, 448–9, 453, 466, 479–80
Emancipatory Rural Politics Initiative (ERPI) 13, 81–2, 100–1, 114, 178, 247, 248, 259–61, 285–7, 305–7, 338, 339, 341, 456, 459; Allende government 462; alternatives of 459–60; authoritarian populism 2–3, 449, 461; authoritarian populist parties and leaders 450; in Brazil 4; contemporary populist politics 3; counter-hegemony in Bolivia 285–7; counterrevolution 449; deindustrialisation 6; dispossession 453; double movement 8; economic growth 4; economistic and culturalist approaches 452; global economy 6; industrial economies 5; international agreements 1; Laclau, Ernesto 8; libertarian socialist-anarchist tradition 7; Marxist intellectual community 460; Marxist scholars 7; National Rural Youth Service Corps in South Africa 5; the people 3–4; political-economic dynamics 1–2; political-religious movements 3; populism 457–9; radical equality 8; resisting, organising and building alternatives 10–12; rural and agrarian 451–2; rural classes 455–7; rural democratization 8; rural livelihoods 6; scholar-activists 12–13; in South Africa 4; temporalities 454–5; UK 449; youth 5
Emanuel African Methodist Episcopal Church 123
employment-guarantee schemes 9
emptiness 186, 234, 422, 424, 428, 440–1
endogenous economic development 190
enfants bien-aimés 155
England 392
environmental justice 10
Erdoğan, Recep Tayyip 97, 154, 155, 164, **168**, 169, 202, 390, 474, 475
Ervin, Lorenzo Kom'Boa 400
Escobar, A. 396
España vacía (empty Spain) 429, 430
Ethiopia 3
Europe 3, 6, 421, 422, 428, 472, 475
Euroscepticism 431
Eurosceptic UK Independence Party (UKIP) 431–2
EU-Ukraine Association Agreement 438
extractivism 3, 6, 156–61, 168, 267, 268, 272, 275, 278, 279, 282, 341

Fabricant, N. 286
Fairhead, J. 191
Family Farm Defenders 409
family farmers 457, 462
Farmers' Federation of Thailand (FFT) 39–41
fascism's mass base 23–4
fascist *squadristi* 24
Federación Nacional de Organizaciones Campesinas, Indígenas y Negras (FENOCIN) 282
federal Appalachia High Intensity Drug Trafficking Area Map 83
Fernández, F. 440
fetishism 342–4
feudalism 7, 471
Fields, Factories, and Workshops (Kropotkin) 397
Filčák, R. 424
Filgueiras, Luiz 348, 355
Fındık Tarım Satış Kooperatifleri Birliği (Fiskobirlik) 107
Fındık Üreticileri Sendikası (Fındık-Sen) 109
First World War 23, 272
Fiskobirlik 107–10
Food Acquisition Program (PAA) 339
Food Not Bombs 400
food sovereignty 10, 267, 268, 271, 272, 279, 280, 282, 283–5, 287–8, 331, 398, 408, 410, 456, 462, 485
forajidos 279
Fórum Mulher 324
Fox, J. 8
Fragments of an Anarchist Anthropology, Two Cheers (Scott) 402
France 392
Franco, Jennifer 186, 328
Franks, J. 299
Franquesa, J. 421, 457, 458, 460, 480
Fraser, N. 9, 372
Frei Montalva, Eduardo 31
Frente de Libertação de Moçambique (Mozambique Liberation Front (FRELIMO)) 313, 314, 317, 327, 332, 454
Fresh News 307–9
Fromm, Erich 400
Frykholm, Amy Johnson 128
Fukuyama, Francis 469
Fuller, Robert C. 126, 127
Funada-Classen, S. 321
Fundação Getulio Vargas (FVG) 323
fundamentalists 127

Garcia Linera, Álvaro 268
García Márquez, Gabriel 155
Gaventa, J. 171, 204, 450, 460
Germany 21, 392, 422, 436, 441, 475
Gidwani, Vinay K 194
Giraldo, O. F. 411
Global Rally for Humanity 140
Goldhagen, Daniel 26

Goldman, Emma 393
Gonçalves, E. 321
Gonçalves, Reinaldo 355
Goodman, Paul 400
Gorenberg, Gershom 128
Graeber, D. 402, 403
Gramsci, A. 193, 273
Grattan, L. 404
Gray Mountain 72–3
Greece 8
Growth Acceleration Program (PAC) 351
Grubaçic, A. 402
grupos de choque (paramilitary groups) 33
Guillaumin, Colette 125
Gürel, B. 204, 221, 452, 455, 458, 460, 462

Haitian Revolution 70
Hajdu, A. 421
Halk Bank 170
Halkevleri (People's Houses) 109
Halklarin Demokratik Partisi (HDP) 99
Hall, S. 2, 204, 206, 228, 405, 470
Hamilton, C. 60
HEAL Food Alliance 409
Hemşin 112
Henderson, T. 280
Henly, Megan 60
Herold, M. 427
Herzen, Alexander 393
Hillbilly Elegy: A Memoir of a Family and Culture in Crisis (Vance) 85, 91
Hindutava 454–5, 459
Hipólito Yrigoyen 472
Hobsbawm, E. J. 399
Hochschild, Arlie Russell 135
Holy Men Rebellions 39
Homes Not Jails 400
Honneth, A. 9
How the Irish Became White (Ignatiev) 124
Humphrey, C. 227, 438
Hungarian Association for Environmental Protection 258
Hungarian authoritarian populist government 246
Hungarian Forints (HUF) 253
Hungarian rural politics 260
Hungary 158, 221, 438, 448, 449, 454, 459, 460, 467, 469; domestic land-grabbing and conflicts 261; EU's land policy and CAP 261; Hungarian authoritarian populist government 246; land grabbing 247 (*see also* land grabbing); land rights 246

Ignatiev, Noel 124
illiberal neoliberalism 468–70
Import Substitution Industrialization (ISI) policies 344
India 3, 9, 11, 392, 454
indigeneity 401
indignados movement 183
indignation 194–5

Indonesia 3, 22, 28, 29, 31, 36, 37, 40, 41, 55, 466
Indonesian National Party (PNI) 36
Indonesia Peasants Union (BTI) 27
Industrial Workers of the World (IWW) 391
Inglehart, R. 206
inquilinos (tenant-farmers) 32
Institute of Agrarian Reform (INCRA) 354
Instituto Nacional de Reforma Agraria (INRA) 277
International Criminal Court (ICC) 54
International Institute of Social Studies (ISS) 248
International Labour Organisation's (ILO) 170
International Monetary Fund (IMF) 42
The Invisible Committee 398
Iraq 123
Islamophobia 123, 135–7, 140–1, 404–5, 474
Italy 21, 26, 29, 392

Jamaica 392
Japan 324, 330, 332, 392
Japan International Cooperation Agency (JICA) 314, 320, 325, 333
Jaroś horapašnyj (working without letup) 237
Jessop, B. 204–6
Jews 127
Jobbik Party 467
John Birch Society 121, 126
Johnson, Kenneth M. 63
Joint Coordination Committee (JCC) 322
Jones, Alex 126
The Journal of Peasant Studies 448–9
Journal of Rural Studies 421
Juraviçy: cultural barriers 236–9; empirical setting 232–3; local economy's rationale 234–6; political settlement 239–41; villagers 233–4
Justiça Ambiental (Environmental Justice) 324
Justice and Development Party (Erdogan) 97, 452; *see also* Adalet ve Kalkinma Partisi (AKP)

Katznelson, Ira 371
Kautsky, K. 231, 242
Kay, C. 353, 410
Kazakhstan 227
Kefalas, M. J. 67
Kennedy, John 84
Kilusang Magbubukid ng Pilipinas (Philippine Peasant Movement) 459
Kishantos Rural Development Centre 259–60
Klein, Naomi 22
Klumbyte, N. 438
Kneen, Brewster 132
Know Nothing movement 130
Korea 392, 400
Kovács, Zoltán 255
Krasznai Kovács, Eszter 257
Kraus, M. W. 372
Kropotkin, Peter 393
Krugman, Paul 480
Küçük, B. 221, 252, 255, 260, 462
Ku Klux Klan (KKK) 122, 124, 131, 141

Kurdish movement 106, 115
Kurtz, M. 207

Labour Party 431, 432
Laclau, Ernesto 8, 403
LaHaye, Tim 128
Lamb, V. 479
Land Campaign 329–30
Land Deals Politics Initiative 13
land grabbing: emancipation (*see* emancipation); Hungarian authoritarian populism 257–8; land speculation and consolidation of privileges 253; Orbán's rural support 253–7; state-owned land and European subsidies 250–3; theoretical and methodological approaches 247–50
Land Reform Act, 1975 40
land registration 277
Land Rent Control Act (LRCA) 40
Land Reserve for Investment 322
land rights 246
Lane, Max 26–7
Laothamatas, Anek 45
LaRouche, Lyndon H. Jr. 132
The Late, Great Planet Earth (Lindsey) 128
latifundistas (landlords) 34
Latin American Perspectives 421
Lava Jato 359
La Vía Campesina (LVC) 408–9, 459, 460
Leach, M. 191
Lefebvre, Henri 193
left-wing populism 181, 194, 355–8, 468
Lenin, Vladimir Ilyich 7, 227
Levada-Center 203, 219
LGBTQ rights 123, 125, 134, 142–3
libertarian socialism 390
Lincolnshire constituencies 433
Lindsey, Hal 128
Li, T. M. 441
Livaningo 324
lockdowns 425–6
Looming Crisis on American Farms 142
Lopez, Gina 52
Lugo, Fernando 477
lukascism 228–30, 233, 234, 238, 242
Lukes, Stephen 81
Lulism 340, 346–9, 352, 357, 359–61

MacKinnon, R. 305
Mack, Richard 136
Maduro, Nicolás 477
Magón, Ricardo Flores 393
Magyar Természetvédők Szövetsége 258
Mahkno, Nestor 393
Make Spain Great Again 429, 439
Malatesta, Errico 393, 397
Malaysia 392
Mamonova, N. 229, 231, 241, 421, 426, 433, 451, 454, 460

Mapuche 36
Marcos, Ferdinand 47–8
Martínez Alier, Joan 189
Marxism 6, 396
Marxist intellectual community 460
Marxist scholars 7
Marx, K. 227
Maryland 371
Master Plan Zero of 2015 322–4
Matanza Masiva (indiscriminate killings) 35–7, 40, 49
Mattelart, Armand 37
Matveyev, I. 208
Mayer, Arno 21
McCargo, Duncan 43
McCarthy, James 479
McCoy, Terrence 69
McCune, N. 411
McDowell County 89
Mecanismo de Coordenação da Sociedade Civil para o Desenvolvimento do Corredor de Nacala (Civil Society Coordination Mechanism for the Development of the Nacala Corridor) 326
Mecklenburg-Vorpommern 426
Mesa Agraria (a coalition of four peasant/indigenous organizations) 268
metropolitan elite 430–1
Mexico 5, 392, 400
Mezőgazdasági es Vidékfejlesztési Hivatal (Agricultural and Rural Development Agency) 252
middle class 22, 23, 25, 30, 32–5, 37, 38, 43–6, 54, 62, 72–4, 76, 123, 181, 193, 353
Middle East 3
Midnight Call (television series) 128
militia movement 122
Militias 29, 30, 121, 122, 130–4, 137, 391, 480
Millennialism and Antichrist (Mooney) 127
Milli Görüs Hareketi 103
Milliyetçi Hareket Partisi (MHP) 104
Mincyte, D. 237
Mind Siege: The Battle for Truth in the New Millennium (LaHaye and Noebel) 128
Ministerio de Desarrollo Rural y Tierra (MDRyT) 277
modernism 127
Modi, Narendra 158, 390, 449, 454–5, 465, 467, 474–6, 481, 482
Modi's India and 'The North: The Far Right Breaks Through 449
Monjane, B. 448, 454
Monnat, Shannon 142
monoculturalist political attitudes 439
Monopoly Capital 22, 25
Mooney, Michael Eugene 127
Moore, Barrington 8, 21, 24, 25, 206, 438
moral economy 6, 11, 226, 228–30, 232–4, 236–7, 239, 241, 242, 372, 402, 403, 406–8, 411

Morales, Evo 466, 477
Morris, Brian 397
Mosca, J. 318, 321, 323
Motherland Party 104
Mouffe, C. 404
Mountain Justice 88
Movement of the Revolutionary Left (MIR) 32
Movimento dos Trabalhadores Sem Terra (Landless Workers' Movement) 339
Movimiento al Socialismo (MAS) 267–8
Movimiento de los Trabajadores Rurales sin Tierra (MST) 285–6
Mozambican Human Right League 324
Mozambican Institute of Agricultural Research (IIAM) 321
Mozambican Ministry of Agriculture and Food Security (MASA) 314
Mozambique 313–15, 321–30, 333–4, 448, 454, 466; authoritarianism, populism and coercive rural policies 316–18
Mudde, Cas 129, 143
Mulroney, Brian 469
Multiple Use Strategy Conference, 1988 129
Murrah, Alfred P. 133
Muslim Defenders' Front 5
Muslim Perpetrators 136
Mussolini 22–3, 25, 49, 50, 53, 55, 101, 472
Myanmar 4, 309

načalstva 229–31, 235–6, 240, 241
Nahdatul Ulama 30
Narodniki 471
Narotzky, Susana 194
National Corps (Natscorpus) party 434
National Council of *Allyus and Markas of Qullasuyu* (CONAMAQ) 278
National Democratic Front (NDF) 50
National Development Bank (BNDES) 351
National Family Farm Coalition 409
Nationalist Action Party 104
National Party 31, 33
National Peasant Union (UNAC) 315; NPC 329–33; and ProSAVANA 327–8; roots and constituency 326–7
National Public Radio (NPR) 369
National Relief Fund 482
National Rural Youth Service Corps in South Africa 5
National Vision Movement 103
Nation-Religion King 41
Natural Farming movement 11
Needle Exchange 400
Nehring, R. 321
Nemzeti Földalap Kezelő szervezet (NFA) 258
nemzeti vidékstratégia (national rural strategy) 254
neo-authoritarian populists 390
neo-developmentalism 269–71, 341, 353, 357, 382

neo-extractivism 275–9; authoritarian populism 283–5; Bolivia 275–9; BRICS and Latin American 'pink tide' 267–71; capital's transcendence 288; conceptual framework 271–5; Ecuador 279–82; Morales and Correa/Moreno 287–8; MST and emancipatory rural politics 285–7; radical food sovereignty 288
neo-Gramscian International Political Economy 271
neoliberal capitalism 4, 156, 204, 227, 268, 422–6, 440, 441, 450; agrarian transformation and multifaceted crisis of 422–6
neoliberal developmentalism 156, 158–61, 168
neoliberal globalisation 7
neoliberalism 4, 9, 99, 114, 159, 160, 267, 269, 272–4, 281, 285, 344, 348, 349, 357, 359, 372, 383, 454, 459, 466, 468, 481
neo-Nazi terror movement 124, 475–6
Nestbeschmutzer 428
Netherlands 248, 253, 392
New Alliance for Food Security and Nutrition in Africa 4
New Authoritarianism 22, 47
New Culture of Energy 191, 453
New Culture of Water 191, 453
new emancipatory politics 9
newly industrializing countries (NICs) 42
The New Republic 89
New Right politicians 422
New York Times (newspaper) 84–5, 472
New Zealand 392, 475
Nigeria 392
Nixon, Rob 187
non-aligned movement 27
non-emancipatory 9
Norman, L. 208
Norris, P. 206
North Africa 3
Not In My Back Yard (NIMBY) organizations 191
nullification 130
Nunca Máis 193, 196

Oath Keepers 137, 139, 140
Obama, Barack 70, 74, 87, 123, 125, 126, 128–9, 135, 366, 367, 406
Öcalan, Abdullah 7
Occupy Wall Street movement of 2011 400
offensive resistentialism 183
O'Hearn, D. 402
O'Laughlin, B. 317, 318
oligopsony 167
Oliveira, Francisco de 348
Oltan Gida 110
Operação Lava Jato (Operation Car Wash) 358
Orbán, Viktor 204, 247, 249–52, 254–7, 261, 469, 474, 475
Ordem dos Advogados de Moçambique (Mozambique Bar Association) 324
Orejel, Keith 64

Organized White Supremacist Groups 124, 125
The Origins of Totalitarianism (Arendt) 3
Orlove, B. 236
The Other America (Harrington) 82
Otten, Justin 252
Özgürlük ve Dayanişma Partisi (Freedom and Solidarity Party) 109

Pablo Rodriguez Grez 36
Packer, George 59
Pacto de Unidad (Unity Pact) 268
Paige, J. M. 7, 229
Pambazuka News 330
Paraguay 477
paramilitaries 131
Parsons, Lucy 393, 400
Partido dos Trabalhadores (Workers' Party) 339–41, 344–6, 349–52, 354, 356, 359–61
Partido Popular (PP) 184, 429
Party of Indonesia (PKI) 26–7, 30
passive revolution 182
Patria y Libertad (Fatherland and Liberty) 36
Patriotic Europeans against the Islamisation of the Occident (PEGIDA) 427, 439
Patriot movement 121–3, 134–7; anarchists 130; colorblind approach 139; Islamophobia 140; nullification 130; paramilitaries 131; right-wing oppositional movements 129–30; Sovereign Citizens 131; Three Percenters 130; 2008 to present 136–7; Trump's presidency 142; United States 130, 131; white nationalism 139
Patriots 121
patrones (landlords) 32
Paxton, Robert 101
Peasant Wars of the Twentieth Century (Wolf) 389–90
Pellow, D. N. 397, 408
Pemuda Pancasila 5
penghianat (traitor) 30
People's Agroecology Process 409
People's Party 470, 471
Pericás, Luiz Bernardo 355
Perón, Juan Domingo 472
Peru 392
Peters, M. A. 205
pharmaceutical colonization 83
Philippines 3, 5, 22, 47, 158, 449, 459, 467
The Phnom Penh Post (newspaper) 298, 307
Piketty, Thomas 473
Pinckney, Reverend Clementa 125
pink tide 3, 267–71, 340–2, 451, 453, 454, 456, 466, 468, 477, 479–80
Plano Director (Master Plan) 322
Plano Estratégico para o Desenvolvimento do Sector Agrário (PEDSA) 314
Plataforma de Afectados por la Hipoteca (Platform for Mortgage Victims) 180
Platform in Defense of the Ebro (PDE) 190
"PM-CARES" relief fund 482

pocket contracts 254
Podemos 8, 180, 183, 184, 195, 428, 429
Polanyi, K. 8
political liberalization, series of 160
political-religious movements 3
The Political Theory of Anarchism (Carter) 400
Politico 68
politics of resentment 122
The Politics of Resentment: Rural Consciousness in Wisconsin (Cramer) 67
Popular Unity (UP) government 31–3
populism 340–1, 348–9, 361, 457–9
populist mobilisation 433–5
Portugal 392
Poulantzas, Nicos 21, 271, 284
Poulantzian state theory 271
Po Valley 24, 25, 40
Power and Powerlessness: Quiescence and Rebellion in an Appalachian Valley (Gaventa) 80–2, 87; see also Appalachian Valley
Pramoj, Kukrit 41
Prasad, M. Madhava 467
Pratt, Larry 136
Prayuth Chan-ocha 46
press freedom 158, 294, 297, 302
pro-European conservative-nationalist party 'Fatherland' (Batkivshchina) 434
pro-Franco Popular Party 466
progressive neoliberalism 4
Projecto de Investigação (Research Project) 322
pro-Kurdish People's Democratic Party 99
pro-Russian Eurosceptic 'Opposition Platform–For Life' (OP Za zhyttya) 434
Protestant Far Right: William Dudley Pelley, Gerald B. Winrod, and Gerald L. K. Smith (Ribuffo) 127
pro-Thaksin movement 45, 46
Puerto Rico 392
Pulido, L. 408
Putin, Vladimir 202, 209, **209**, 211, 212, 214, 216, 218, 220, 452, 474

Qin, Hua 60
Queer Appalachians 89

radical democracy 8
radical equality 8
radical food sovereignty 288
Radical Party 31
Radio Free Asia Cambodia 294, 295, 298
Ramnath, Maia 392
Ramos, Tarso 129
Rancière, Jacques 2, 8
Reaganomics 122
Reagan, Ronald 121, 469
reassentamentos (resettlement zones) 318
Recep Tayyip Erdoğan's Justice and Development Party see *Adalet ve Kalkinma Partisi* (AKP)
Recession Catches Rural America 134

Reclus, Élisée 393
Redneck Revolt 407, 411–12, 480
Red Shirt Movement 44, 46, 47
Red Tide, in Southeast Asia 30
Refah Partisi (RP) 103–4
reformism 274–5
Regime of 78 182
Regulation Theory 271
Reicher, S. 205
representative democracy 221, 272, 341, 342, 344, 422, 425, 437, 441
Republican Party 71, 373
Republican People's Party 99
Resistência Nacional de Moçambique (RENAMO) 317–18, 332
retoma 32
Revelation Unveiled (LaHaye) 128
The Revolt of the Emptied Spain 430, 440
Richmond, O. 299
RightWing America (Kintz) 135
right-wing movements 54, 123, 143, 368, 426–8
right-wing populism: Alternative Right 141; anti-immigrant and anti-refugee activism 139–41; apocalyptic millennialism 126–8; apocalyptic survivalists 121; basic Patriot movement beliefs 130–1; economic stratification of society 121; extractive resource industries and 'wise use' 129; guns and armed land use conflicts 138–9; Islamophobia 135–7; land conflicts in rural West 128–9; LGBTQ rights 123, 142–3; Looming Crisis on American Farms 142; Midwest and Rocky Mountain states 121; organizational clusters 137–8; Patriot movement 122, 123, 136–7; Patriot movement oppositional movements 129–30; Republican Presidential Candidate Mitt Romney 123; *The Road to Serfdom* (Hayek) 121–2; 'rural consciousness' 122; rural economic crises 131–5; Trump, Donald 141; United States 120–2, 142; white nationalism 123–6
The rise of Italian fascism 23
River Town 71–2
The Road to Serfdom (Hayek) 121–2
Robert Wood Johnson Foundation (RWJF) 369
Robotham, Don 468
Rocker, Rudolf 393
Roda Viva Program 357
Roman-Alcalá's argument 448
Roman Catholicism 127
Romania 421
Rome 25
Romney, Mitt 123
Roof, Dylann 123
Roosevelt, Franklin D. 84, 136
Roszík, Péter 254
Rueschemeyer, D. 207, 209
rural Appalachia 6
Rural Association for Mutual Aid (ORAM) 324
rural Belarus 227, 232, 242

rural classes 9, 207, 209, 275, 455–7
Rural Coalition 409–10
rural consciousness 122
rural democratization 8
rural economic crises, Patriot movement: armed citizens militias, 1990s 132–4; banking collapse, 2008 134–5; Islamophobia, role of 135–6; 1970s and 1980s 131–2
rural emptiness 440–1
rural Europe: brexit and politics of 430–3; dying villages of eastern Germany 426–8; neoliberal capitalism 422–6; populism 426; populist mobilisation in Ukraine 433–5; rural Spain and the populist question 428–30
ruralization of distress 83
rural livelihoods 6
rural politics 86, 93, 100, 112–14, 216, 231, 295, 392, 407, 437, 448, 451; *see also* emancipatory rural politics
rural reawakening 425
rural resistance 216, 227, 231, 294, 428, 480
rural sacrifice zones 86
rural social movements 9, 300, 301, 309, 442
rural support 68, 99, 101–2, 105, 111, 203, 205, 220, 221, 253–7, 421, 441, 450, 461
rural US 6, 60, 366, 369, 407, 412, 453; amenity-rich areas 61–2; Chronically Poor Areas 62–3; demographic composition 63–7; economic changes 63–7; transitioning areas 62
Russia 6, 227, 392, 421, 448

Saad-Filho, Alfredo 344, 359
Safford, Thomas G. 60
Sagebrush rebellion 128–9
Sánchez, Pedro 428
Sandwell, Katie 449
Satan Is Alive and Well on Planet Earth (Lindsey and Carlson) 128
Saxony 426–7, 440
Schäller, S. 427
Schmidt, M. 399
Schoenberger, L. 479
scholar-activism 90–3
Scoones, I. 188–9, 191, 228, 236, 258, 316, 318, 338, 340, 365, 366, 368, 426, 448
Scott, J. 87, 90, 91, 228, 233, 333, 392, 402
The 1980s Countdown to Armageddon (Lindsey) 128
Second Miracle: and ecological regime 191–3; land grab 186–7
second wave 399
Second World War 38, 39, 237, 239, 272
Shanin, T. 230
Shankland, A. 321
Sherman, J. 68
silent majority 202, 204–6, 220, 221
Sindicato Obrero del Campo 459
Singer, André 346, 359
Škobla, D. 424

Skousen, W. Cleon 138
slow dispossession 178, 187–8, 457–8
Smith, Barbara Ellen 92
Smith, Neil 424
Snyder, T. 239
social democracy 4
social ecology 7
social grants 9
socialism 127
Socialist Democracy Party (SDP) 109
Socialist Party 23–6, 31
social movements 9, 10, 12, 107, 122, 126, 127, 129, 135, 211, 228, 267, 268, 297, 300, 301, 309, 326, 329–31, 390, 393, 399, 400, 408, 410, 477, 479
social neoliberalism 102–3, 105–7, 114, 458
Sociologia Ruralis 421
Sociologica Ruralis 449
Soil Products Office 110
Solnit, Rebecca 401
Soma 163, *164*, 166, *166*, **168**, 168–72, 456
South Africa 3–5, 9, 392
Southern Poverty Law Center 134
Southern Revolt 195, 196, 451, 453
Sovereign Citizens 131
sovereign democracy 214
Soviet Union 127
spaces of emptiness 424
Spain 8, 392, 421, 422, 435, 437, 441, 442, 448, 458, 480
The Spanish Exception', argues: 'One country seems immune to it all: Spain (Encarnación) 177
Spanish Revolution 391
splice nationalism 53
Spoor, M. 227
squadristi 26, 33
Sri Lanka 3
stabilization 469
stateled programmes 4
State Secretary for Agriculture 260
Statewide Organizing for Community eMpowerment 88
Stephens, E. H. 207, 209
Stephens, J. D. 207, 209
Stirner, Max 393
Stochastic Terrorism 142
Strategic Plan for the Development of the Agrarian Sector (PEDSA) 314, 321
Strijker, D. 189
strip-mining technologies 83
structural adjustment programs 469
Stuart Hall, Gramscian Marxist 404
subjectivities 178, 180, 193, 248, 249, 257–60
sub-proletariat 346–7
sumak kawsay 286
Sunshine, S. 451, 457
Sustainable Development Goals (SDGs) 246
Swidler, Ann 68

Switzerland 392
syndicalism 391

Tasca, Angelo 23, 24
Tas, S. 221, 252, 255, 260, 462
Taylor, C. 203
Tayyip Erdoğan 104
T.C. Gümrük ve Ticaret Bakanligi Kooperatifçilik Genel Müdürlügü, 2017 107
Tea Party activists 135
Tea Party movement 134, 137
Teixeira, Gerson 354
Tennessee and Kentuckians for the Commonwealth 88
The Tenth Development Plan 164, 165
Terluin, I. 189
The Terminal Generation (Lindsey and Carlson) 128
Teruel Existe (TE) 430
Thabchumpon, Naruemon 43
Thailand 6, 22, 55; revolution and counterrevolution 38
Thai Rak Thai ('Thai Love Thai') Party 43
Thaksin ascendant 43–4
Thaksin Shinawatra 38
Thanom-Praphat military dictatorship 38, 39
Thatcher, Margaret 468–9
Thaugsuban, Suthep 45
Theesfeld, I. 427
Thompson, E. P. 228, 402
Three Percenters 130, 137
Thuringia 426
Tierras Comunitarios de Origen (TCOs) 276
Tilzey, Mark 410, 411, 451, 454, 456, 458–60, 480
The Tobacco Law of 2001 104
Tolstoy, Leo 393
tomas de fundos 32
Toprak Mahsulleri Ofisi (TMO) 110
"transformism" 2
transitioning areas 60–2, 65–7, 69–73, 294, 451
Transnational Institute (TNI) 13
trasformismo 273, 277, 282, 285
Triangular Co-operation Programme for Agricultural Development of the Tropical Savannah in Mozambique Project (ProSAVANA) 313, 327–8; actions, strategies and fragmentation 325–6; agrarian policies 334; authoritarianism, populism and coercive rural policies 316–18; components of 322–3; deficiencies, contradictions and the Nacala fund 323–4; FRELIMO's regime 314; imposition of 319–21; Joint Coordination Committee 322; methods 315; Mozambican civil society 321–2; National Peasant Union (*see* National Peasant Union (UNAC)); NPC 334; PEDSA 314; questions and structure of 314–15; rise of the 'no to ProSAVANA campaign': an agrarian 'populist' confrontation 324–5
Tribulations 133
True Path Party 104

Trump Antagonists 373, 380
Trump, Donald 9, 59, 67, 68, 70–1, 73, 75, 81, 82, 84–9, 92, 93, 120, 135, 136, 140–3, 158, 159, 184, 202, 204, 205, 221, 365–9, 371–82, 390, 400, 404–6, 454, 459–60, 472–6, 480–3
Turkey 3, 98–102, 108–11, 114, 115, 155, 156, 160, 162, *164*, 165, 167, 168, 171, 172, 202, 204, 221, 448, 449, 451, 453, 456, 458, 467, 474, 480; AKP's social neoliberalism 105–7; urban workers in 115
Turkish Islamism 97–8
Türkiye Komünist Partisi (TKP) 109
Two Cheers for Anarchism (Scott) 402
Two Colorados 68

Ukraine 227, 392, 422, 433, 434, 441, 442
Ukrainian Rural Development Network 434
Ulrich-Schad, J. D. 60, 451
unapologetic utilization 92
União Nacional de Camponeses (National Peasant's Union) 324
Unión de Naciones Suramericanas (UNASUR) 468
The Union of Hazelnut Producers 109
The Union of Hazelnut Sales Cooperatives 107
United Kingdom 421, 422, 435, 440, 441, 469, 475
United Mountain Defense 88
United States (US) 3, 5, 6, 28, 36, 37, 54, 59, 82, 84, 90–2, 120–31, 134–6, 138, 140–2, 158, 218, 221, 367, 391–2, 400, 467–70, 474–7, 481–4
UN Transitional Authority in Cambodia (UNTAC) 297
Uruguay 392, 472
US Food Sovereignty Alliance (USFSA) 409

vacía (vaciada) 428–30
vaciada (emptied) 430
Val, V. 409
Vanaik, A. 454, 455
Vance, J. D. 69, 85, 91
van der Ploeg, Jan Douwe 186, 195, 398
Van Dyck, B. 241
Van Sant, Levi 480
Venezuela 238, 340, 392, 458, 466, 477–81
Verdery, K. 237
Vergara-Camus, L. 353, 410
Vergonya i Dignitat (Shame and Dignity) 195
Vida, György 255
Vidékfejlesztési Minisztérium (Ministry of Rural Development) 254
Vietnam 28, 392
violence 282
Visser, O. 227, 241
vivir bien 278

Voerman, G. 189
Volksgemeinschaft 428
Vorländer, H. 427
Vox Party 429, 430, 436, 466

Walter, B. M. 379, 480
Washington, DC 131
Washington Post (newspaper) 69, 84
Waylen, K. 211
Weapons of the Weak (Scott) 87
wedge politics 437
Wegren, S. K. 210, 230
The Welfare Party 103
Wengrow, D. 403
Western frontier 128
Wetts, R. 366, 380
What You Are Getting Wrong about Appalachia (Catte) 89
When Affirmative Action Was White (Katznelson) 371
White Anglo-Saxon Protestants (WASPS) 124
white nationalism 120, 123–6, 139
White Nationalist Perpetrators 136
White Supremacist System 124
White Supremacy 123
Widodo, Joko 31
Wierenga, Saskia 28
Willer, R. 193, 366, 380, 436
Williams, Dana 400
Winn, Peter 36
Wise Use movement 129
Wolf, E. R. 7, 392, 402, 438
Wolford, W. 321
Women's March in Washington, DC 10
Woodland Community Land Trust 88
Woods, Michael 425
Workers' Party 339–41, 344–6, 349–52, 354, 356, 359–61
World March of Women 324
Worlds apart: poverty and politics in rural America (Duncan) 61

xenophobia 123, 142, 204, 405, 439

Yaremko, V. 434
Yesterday's People (Weller) 90
Yingluck government 46
Yudin, G. 208
Yusufeli Dam project 113

Zelensky, Vladimir 434
Ziraat Odasi 108

9780367753948